A HISTORY OF
ENGLISH DRAMATIC LITERATURE

A HISTORY OF ENGLISH DRAMATIC LITERATURE

to the Death of Queen Anne

ADOLPHUS WILLIAM WARD

Volume I

FREDERICK UNGAR PUBLISHING CO.
NEW YORK

Republished 1970
from the second edition of 1899

Printed in the United States of America

Library of Congress Catalog Card Number 70-118868

ISBN (3-volume set) 0-8044-2962-6
Volume I 0-8044-2963-4
Volume II 0-8044-2965-0
Volume III 0-8044-2969-3

PREFACE

THE theoretical Introduction with which the First Edition of this book opened has been omitted in the Second, certainly not from any disregard of a most important branch of dramatic studies, but in order to make room for a more ample treatment of various passages in the body of the work. This has been revised throughout, and in parts rewritten. It has, however, seemed well to leave the plan of the whole unaltered, and to abstain from re-casting either general or particular conclusions, except when they have been modified by maturer consideration.

My sincere thanks are due to the numerous friends who have given me voluntary help towards this new Edition by information, criticism, and encouragement—three forms of literary liberality and goodwill which, as my experience during the last quarter of the century has proved to me, are very commonly associated with one another. The shortcomings, avoidable or unavoidable, in such a book as this, rarely remain a secret to its author,—even in his younger days ; but (if I may venture to mention one name in the place of many) the stimulus to effort conveyed by such criticisms as those which the late

Professor F. T. PALGRAVE found time to bestow, both publicly and privately, upon the First Edition of this *History*, remains invaluable to a student, however imperfectly he may have succeeded in turning the criticisms themselves to account.

I have endeavoured to make use of such of the publications on English dramatic literature as have appeared since the issue of the First Edition of this work, and among these I have freely availed myself of the treasures of that great store-house of English literary as well as historical lore, the *Dictionary of National Biography*. I desire to repeat here the expression of my regret that my Fourth Chapter should have passed through the press before vol. li of the *Dictionary* had appeared, containing its present editor Mr. Sidney Lee's masterly monograph on Shakspere.

A. W. WARD.

MANCHESTER,
July, 1898.

CONTENTS OF VOL. I

CHAPTER I.

THE ORIGIN OF THE ENGLISH DRAMA.

CHAPTER II.

THE BEGINNINGS OF THE ENGLISH REGULAR DRAMA.

CHAPTER III.

SHAKSPERE'S PREDECESSORS.

ENGLISH
DRAMATIC LITERATURE

CHAPTER I.

THE ORIGIN OF THE ENGLISH DRAMA.

THE purpose of these volumes is to sketch the history of *Scope and* English Dramatic Literature from its beginnings to the *limits of this work.* close of the reign of our last Stuart sovereign. It has at no time entered into my design to rewrite what for different sections of this period has been already written by more competent hands—the *Annals of the English Stage* [1].

But with reference both to the times before the Stuart Restoration, and to so much of those ensuing upon that transaction as falls within my limits, I shall seek to bear in mind the organic connexion between our dramatic literature and its proper vehicle of presentment—the national theatre. Such contributions to our drama as seem unworthy of

---

[1] The late Mr. J. Payne Collier lived to publish, in 1875, a second edition of his *History of Dramatic Poetry and Annals of the English Stage* (3 vols.), first put forth in 1831. The proved fictitiousness of some of the statements contained in this book cannot deprive it of its general value for students of our drama ; and I am bound once more to acknowledge my own numerous obligations, more especially in the earlier passages of the present work, to a writer whose name, for better and for worse, must remain inseparably connected with the records of this branch of English literature. Of Mr. F. G. Fleay's *Chronicle History of the English Stage*, 1559-1642 (1890), on the other hand, as of companion books by the same author, time may be trusted to digest some of the conclusions, without in any way impairing the credit due to single-minded candour and indefatigable research. Among other chronicles of the English theatre, Genest's latter-day dramatic *Fasti* (*Some Account of the English Stage from* 1660-1830, 10 vols., 1832) stand unrivalled as the consistent execution of a comprehensive scheme.

a place in our literary history will accordingly be noticed only where they obviously illustrate particular tendencies, styles or fashions in the art to which it was their pretension to belong. The period of the English drama which preceded its coalescence with the general progress of our literature will be treated as summarily as possible; while (not without regret) the attempt will be foregone to present even an outline of those later periods in which, taken as a whole, the efforts of our dramatic poets continued estranged from their legitimate means of exposition. Thus the question whether an estrangement which has been anything but uninterrupted is likely to prove permanent, cannot here be so much as discussed. Within the limits indicated, however, there lies a field wide and varied, as it seems to me, beyond parallel. This field I shall attempt to survey, so far as possible, in the order of chronological sequence, though with a certain allowance of freedom in the arrangement demanded by the mass of material. Instead of seeking to lay down critical laws, I shall hope to make the founda-tions on which any laws of the kind must rest more plain and palpable to the students of the particular dramatic literature of which it is my purpose to treat. Ben Jonson, rare among artists if only because he is almost as well worth listening to when he discusses the theory of his art as when he illustrates it in practice, observes with truth that ' before the grammarians or philosophers found out their laws, there were many excellent poets that fulfilled them[1].' Code and actions stand in an inseparable relation to one another. The continuous summary attempted in these pages will, it is hoped, help to show how the practice of our English dramatic writers evolved itself out of the relations between their individualities and the rational canons or conditions of the particular literary form within which their creations moved and had their being. Neither, however, will my sketch pretend to ignore the successive relations of the dramatic to other contemporary branches or species of our national literature; and I should be false to the experience of a lifetime, were I to shrink from marking where it seems

[1] *Discoveries* (Sophocles).

to call for notice the influence exercised upon our dramatic
literature by the general progress of our national life and
history, of which in its turn that literature has formed so
memorable a part.

The main source of the modern drama, of which the *Main and*
English is a branch laden with fruit, lies outside the domain *subsidiary*
elements in
of literature.   It springs, as indeed does that of the drama *the sources*
at large in so far as we are acquainted with its beginnings, *of the Eng-*
lish drama.
from popular religious worship ; and to trace this process of
derivation in the instance of the English drama and of the
Christian worship of our forefathers, must be the main task
of the present chapter.   But the mistake of pushing a truth
— or a theory founded on truth—too far may be avoided at
the outset by remembering that other elements prepared
the way for our English drama, or had a share in its early
history.   These were in part purely literary, in part at all
events connected with literary pursuits or with the profession
of literary accomplishments.

Nothing that has had a real life in literature wholly dies. *Early*
Although it was not until a relatively advanced period of *Christian*
dramas
the history of the modern, including the English, drama *based*
that the dramatic writings of classical antiquity came to *directly*
upon
exercise a direct influence upon it, a few stepping-stones *classical*
lead across from the lingering reminiscences of the one to *models.*
the unconscious beginnings of the other.   The early religious
dramas based immediately upon classical examples are
essentially literary efforts—things of the school, not of life.
There seems no necessity for reckoning among these the
pre-Christian Ἐξαγωγή (*Exodus*) of the Jewish poet Ezechiel
(probably between 200 and 100 B. C.) ; for this dramatic
version of the scriptural narrative of Moses leading the
Chosen People out of Egypt, although written in Greek,
is apparently not a direct imitation of any classical model [1].
Coming to Christian times, we are met, from the fourth or
fifth century onwards, by instances of dramatic compositions

---

[1] The fragments preserved by Eusebius and St. Clement of Alexandria
have been edited by Gaisford and Dübner ; and the accepted critical view
of the piece is that of J. M. Philippson's essay on *Ezechiel and Philo* (Berlin,
1830). See Du Méril, *Origines Latines du Théâtre Moderne* (1849), i. 2 note.

by Christian writers following classical examples. An
Apollinaris, who has been rightly or otherwise identified
with the heretical bishop of Laodicea (370 c.), wrote
tragedies and comedies modelled on Euripides and
Menander—in all probability for scholastic use [1].

They
must have been of much the same cast as a celebrated
extant work, the Χριστὸς πάσχων; and, indeed, Apollinaris
was variously credited with the authorship of an earlier
tragedy on the Passion of Christ, and with that of the
work which has been actually preserved under that title.
But this latter has been more persistently attributed to
St. Gregory the Nazianzene, who died about 390. No more
venerable and no more attractive figure is to be found among
the Fathers of the Church than

> ‘ Blest Gregory, whose patriarchal height
> Shed o'er the eastern sphere celestial light [2] ’;

but the supposition seems untenable that he was the author
of this well-known piece. It has also been assigned to
another Gregory, called of Antioch ; while John Tzetzes,
who was active as a writer at Constantinople in the first
quarter of the twelfth century, has been thought to have
composed the epilogue, and further to have been author of
the entire play. Its language and metrification are no
doubt held to point unmistakeably to the period of the
twelfth century as the time of its composition. But conjecture seems now to have settled preferentially upon
Theodore Prodromos, a prolific Byzantine *littérateur* of the
earlier part of the century, known in religion as Hilarion, as
the author of the Χριστὸς πάσχων, which first became known
to the Western world through its *editio princeps*, printed in
Rome in 1542 [3]. The introductory lines, which profess to

---

[1] Welcker, *Die griechischen Tragödien*, &c. (Bonn, 1841), iii. 1330 ; Du
Méril, *u. s.*, 9 and note.

[2] See Bishop Ken's Dedication of his *Hymns*. It is noticeable that
Ken, who loved to trace analogies between his own experiences and
writings and those of the Father, makes no reference to the tragedy.

[3] The edition of J. G. Brambs (Leipzig, 1885) contains, together with
other useful matter, a long list of the passages and phrases borrowed by
the author of the tragedy from Lycophron and Aeschylus, and above all
from Euripides.

be written by ' Gregory the Divine,' state the object of the work to be to narrate, 'after the manner of Euripides,' the Passion which redeemed the world.   The action of the play itself revolves round the figure, constant through the changes of surrounding scene, of the Virgin Mother of God. A *Chorus* and Messengers take part in the Greek manner in the dialogue of this tragedy; but, apart from the fact that it lacks the lyrical element, the expositions of the Divine (Θεολόγος) in the latter part of the piece show its aims to have been essentially didactic.   In short, it is a rhetorical exercise in Euripidean diction, animated by religious enthusiasm, but intended for the closet and not for the stage [1].

These are the only Greek plays preserved to us in whole or in part, or remembered by name, as connecting the ancient classical with the modern religious drama.   To what extent Greek classical tragedy continued to be performed in the public theatre even after the Christianisation of the Empire, is a question which may be left aside here [2].   By the side of the masterpieces of the Greek tragic drama Latin comedy, which was itself derived from the only species of Greek comedy admitting of transplantation from Greek soil [3], was thought capable of adaptation by early Christian writers. To the fourth century of our era (as the best authorities

---

[1] The Χριστὸς πάσχων must have suggested to Hugo Grotius something more than the title of his *Christus Patiens* (1617) ; but this tragedy, in which the Redeemer Himself is the starting-point as well as the central figure, is executed on independent lines.   As to George Sandys' English version of the *Christus Patiens*, published in 1640, and as to Milton's idea of a drama on the same subject, see *infra*, vol. ii.

[2] A *Clytaemnestra* is mentioned as dating from about the sixth century of our era, to which likewise belongs a curious early instance of a play with a political purpose—a ' tragedy ' addressed to the Emperor Anastasius by the grammarian Timotheus of Gaza on the subject of a tax on industries called χρυσάργυρον.   Welcker, *u. s.*, 1331 ; Du Méril, *u. s.*, 10 note.

[3] The *Ludus septem Sapientium*, attributed, apparently on unsatisfactory grounds, to the celebrated descriptive poet of the fourth century, D. Magnus Ausonius, is passed by, as being, according to Teuffel, *Geschichte der römischen Literatur* (1870), p. 872, ' a sort of a puppet-play, in which, after a Prologus and Ludius (actor), the Seven Wise Men in succession come on the stage and repeat their proverbs (Solon being the most long-winded), and in conclusion demand a *Plaudite.*'   As to the *Delirus* (the *Idiot*) of Accius Paulus nothing seems to be known.

Querolus. seem to agree) belongs the *Querolus*, which, although in its
Prologue distinctly announced as an adaptation of the
Aulularia of Plautus, was pertinaciously fathered upon
Plautus himself from the days of John of Salisbury to
those of Salmasius. This comedy, of course, conveys the
familiar lesson of 'the biter bit' through an ingenious plot;
but, whether or not the influence of Christian sentiment be
traceable in the merciful conception of the close of the
action, there seems every indication that the work was
composed for the closet only[1].

Comedies of But of the Christian scholastic drama leaning (though in
Hrotsvitha. this instance ostensibly far more than in substance) upon
classical Latin models, the most notable early examples are
furnished by the ' comedies' of Hrotsvitha, the Benedictine
nun of Gandersheim in Eastphalian Saxony. The ancient
religious foundation to which she belonged had been renewed
in the middle of the ninth century by the ancestor of the
great Saxon house to which the German kingdom owed its
solid establishment and the Roman Empire its pretended
restoration. She lived herself in the latter part of the tenth
century, and had a share of her own in the spiritual revival
associated with this most memorable epoch of German
history. She sang the praises of Otto the Great, and commemorated the *origines* of the foundation over which several
princesses of his house presided, although there is no proof
of her own connexion with Ludolf's line. The avowed
object of her dramatic compositions, which as a matter of
course were written in Latin, was to impart a fresh vitality
to the traditions of the Christian Church by presenting them
in the framework, with occasional reminiscences of the
phraseology, of a classical author whose fame was still
fresh. The endeavour to serve the ends of religion by
the means of art was characteristic of the Order to which
the pious Hrotsvitha belonged[2]; nor is it surprising that
she should have had recourse to the particular writer whom

---

[1] See the analysis in Klein, *Geschichte des Dramas* (Leipzig, 1865–1876),
iii. 638–643; cf. Teuffel, 118–9.

[2] The church-music of the Church of Rome is said by Southey (*Life of
Wesley*, ii. 117) to be due to the Benedictines.

she professed to imitate. It was the good fortune of Terence to lead a charmed life in the darkest ages of learning, through the course of which his works survived under the safe guardianship of monastic libraries [1]. Hrotsvitha, however, borrowed from Terence merely the general form of his plays, without adopting even his metre ; while she both distinctly and of avowed purpose reversed the tendency of his plots. Such an incident, e.g., as the conversion of Thais in her *Paphnutius*, would have been purely unintelligible to the Roman writer. The six plays of Hrotsvitha are dramatised legends of Christian martyrdoms and miraculous conversions ; nor can she be supposed to have pursued any design beyond that of conveying strong religious impressions by means of examples shining as brightly as the illuminations in her Breviary. Where, as in her drama of *Fides, Spes et Charitas*, her characters bear abstract names, it is simply that the sentiments uttered by them specially illustrate their designations. Deficient neither in literary ability nor in occasional pathetic power—and even, as in *Dulcitius*, condescending to an approach to farce—she displays an intuitive knowledge of dramatic effect which is under the circumstances singularly remarkable. Whether she ever consciously or unconsciously thought of the possibility of her plays being acted, it is idle to conjecture [2] ; as a matter of fact they were doubtless read aloud or recited by the nuns of her convent, very likely on occasions appropriate to their particular themes, but most assuredly without any anticipatory design of educational Terentian or quasi-Terentian performances [3].

---

[1] This fact was noted by Joseph Hunter in his treatise on *English Monastic Libraries* (1831). Hrotsvitha herself says :—
   ' Sunt etiam . . .
   Qui, licet alia gentilium spernant,
   Terentii tamen fragmenta frequentius lectitant.'
It was remarked of the famous Archbishop Bruno, the brother of Otto the Great, that when as a youth he read the comedies of Terence, he never smiled at the laughable passages, his attention being wholly absorbed by the beauty of the form. Cf. Giesebrecht, *Geschichte der deutschen Kaiserzeit*, i. 322.

[2] As du Méril points out, p. 19, Hrotsvitha accumulates the most difficult problems of stage-business as well as the most revolting situations to such a degree as to render any such supposition highly improbable.

[3] Hrotsvitha's comedies, after being edited with most of her other works

The monastic literary drama of the tenth and eleventh centuries.

Such convents as Gandersheim were anything but isolated from contact with the outer world, and the example of Hrotsvitha could hardly fail to become known and to be followed. Apart from unauthenticated rumour as to the existence of Old-Frisian monastic comedies at an even earlier date (ninth century), there is every reason for concluding that the comedies of Hrotsvitha by no means remained a solitary phenomenon. Insufficient attention has perhaps been paid, in broader surveys of the history of European civilization, to the simultaneous revival of classical study and religious life in the middle of the tenth century. The centre of this movement was the school at the Emperor's Court, an institution of Charles the Great restored by Archbishop Bruno of Cologne, Duke of Lotharingia, under the protection of his brother Otto the Great; and hence it spread through the monastic schools of the Empire on either side of the Rhine[1]. It was the age when German kings once more dreamt of a world-empire consecrated by the Church ; and the tendencies encouraged by both powers rapidly communicated themselves to neighbouring lands. Thus the Benedictine monk Notker Labeo (who died in 1022), the most celebrated teacher of the school belonging to the monastery of St. Gallen, enumerates among the works 'expounded' or edited by him, apparently in a mixture of the original and the vernacular tongues, the *Andria* of Terence[2]. He can hardly have failed to impart a Christian

by the celebrated humanist Conrad Celtes in 1501, and by H. L. Schurzfleisch in 1707, have been translated into French by A. Magnin in 1845 (with Introduction and Notes), and into German by Bendixen in 1858. An ample analysis of her comedies will be found in Klein, iii. 648–754. Her works were published in a complete edition by K. A. Barack (Nürnberg, 1858). As to J. Aschbach's attempt to prove her works forgeries, refuted by R. Koepke, cf. Wattenbach, *Deutschland's Geschichtsquellen im Mittelalter*, fifth edition 1885, i. 314 note. As to her connexion with the general activity in the ecclesiastical world of Saxony to which she belonged, see O. V. Heinemann, *Geschichte von Braunschweig und Hannover*, i. 152 seqq. Hallam directed the attention of English readers to her in the first chapter of his *Literature of Europe*. At the beginning of A. Cohn's *Shakespeare in Germany* (1865) the inevitable Shakesperean parallels are suggested to certain passages in her comedies. A *Terentius Christianus, utpote Comoediis Sacris transformatus*, was published at Cologne 1592.

[1] See Giesebrecht, *Geschichte der deutschen Kaiserzeit*, i. 329.

[2] See Meyer von Knonau's notice of this Notker (to be distinguished

colouring to his ' exposition '; although there may have been other ecclesiastics who, anticipating the spirit of the Renascence rather than following that of their own age, made no attempt to utilize their adaptations or imitations of classical examples for a religious end [1].

With the Norman Conquest the literary tendencies and impulses to which I have adverted very possibly found their way across the sea; and as the English monasteries soon began to be filled with French, it would be no violent assumption to suppose that Latin religious dramas treating of the legends of saints and martyrs, after the fashion of Hrotsvitha's comedies, should likewise have found their way there.   The recitation of these plays, from which to their performance the step, whenever it was first taken, was easy enough, would in the first instance find its natural place, as it had at Gandersheim or at St. Gallen, in the educational life of the children committed to the care of the religious foundations.   Thus the legends of the patron-saints of boys and girls, St. Nicholas and St. Catharine, might *a priori* be expected to have met with the predilection which in the case of the former they are known to have commanded [2].   A possible genesis, to say the least,

Possible migration of the monastic drama to England.

from the earlier Balbulus Notker, the author of the 'Sequences,' who taught at the same school) in *Allgemeine deutsche Biographie*, vol. xxiv.

[1] Thus, in the twelfth century, Vitalis Blesensis (of Blois) reproduced in elegiac verse the substance of the *Querolus*, already mentioned, and of the *Amphitruo* of Plautus. Teuffel, *u. s.*, 118-9. The same writer was probably the author of the *Comoedia Bubionis*, a purely literary effort in Latin distichs, but dramatic in form. This, together with his comic narrative poem of the *Geta*, is printed in Wright's *Early Mysteries and other Latin Poems of the Twelfth and Thirteenth Centuries*.

[2] Geoffrey's contemporary and compatriot Hilarius, to whose liturgical mysteries reference will be made below, wrote a *Ludus super Iconia S. Nicolai*, which ten Brink, ii. 247, describes as exhibiting altogether the character of a scholastic drama. Though in certain respects resembling the more elaborate productions of its author, it is in fact little more than a dramatic anecdote, and certainly less inspiring than any of those expounded by Hrotsvitha. Not less than four of the religious plays, in the Orléans MS. occupy themselves with the miracles of St. Nicholas ; but although the MS. belongs to the thirteenth century, the plays which are of monastic origin and display a smattering of scholastic learning, were probably written in the twelfth. See A. W. Pollard, *English Miracle Plays, Moralities and Interludes* (1890), Introd. xvii. All of these plays, together with Hilarius' version of the story treated by one of them, are printed *ap.* du Méril, 254 seqq.

accordingly suggests itself for the *Ludus de S. Katharina*, to be again mentioned below, which the Norman Geoffrey, afterwards Abbot of St. Albans, caused to be represented at Dunstable some time before the year 1110, and which is the earliest play of any kind known by name to have been acted in England. This play is indeed usually held to have been written in French; but I must confess myself still unconvinced by the arguments that have been advanced in favour of this supposition. It is of course conceivable that vernacular refrains were mixed with a Latin text[1]. As to the general character of this play of St. Catharine, it is true that Matthew Paris, writing about the middle of the thirteenth century, classes it with the miracle-plays 'commonly so called' of his own day; but he is unlikely to have intended any precise definition. That 'choral copes' were borrowed for the purposes of the performance, is hardly decisive of its character; more to the purpose, if a seventeenth-century statement could be considered authoritative, would be the *dictum* of Bulaeus, the historian of the University of Paris, that the production was in accordance with University custom. The circumstance that Geoffrey was at the time only expectant of clerical office, adds to the uncertainty of the nature of the play which he put forth or brought out. In any case, we do not possess this crucial *Ludus de S. Katharina*, and are therefore unable to determine whether it was a belated specimen of the literary monastic drama, or whether is was already cast in the broader mould of the popular miracle-plays, of which several Latin examples are extant from the same century[2].

[1] As in some of the plays of Hilarius, and in an early German religious play of about the same period on the subject of St. Mary Magdalene. Wülcker has suggested (in a review of the first edition of this book) yet another possibility; viz. that 'the play' was merely a pantomime, intended as an accompaniment to the reading aloud of the legend.

[2] See Collier, ii. 56, *note*. There appears to have been an old French *Mistère de Sainte Cathérine*, of quite uncertain date. As to the legend of St. Catharine and its popularity in the Middle Ages see Jusserand, *Histoire Littéraire du Peuple Anglais, des Origines à la Renaissance* (Paris, 1894), 477 and note. Among the aftergrowths of what I have called the literary monastic drama to be found in Anglo-Norman literature may perhaps

While it would be useless to speculate further on the probable character of an extinct effort, and wholly futile to dogmatise on a merely alternative solution of the problem which the mention of it suggests, one inference may safely be drawn from the preceding data. The religious drama may have been to some extent cultivated in our English monasteries during the period succeeding upon the Norman Conquest as a growth directly traceable to the influence of Greek and Roman literature. That influence, as exerted in the present connexion, cannot at the most be regarded as other than altogether subsidiary; but even so the fact is not to be overlooked, that it was precisely the class to whose fostering care the actual beginnings of our popular drama will hereafter be shown to have been due,—viz. the ecclesiastics—which had not altogether lost sight of the examples of dramatic compositions handed down to them from the literatures of ancient Greece and Rome.

It would be misleading to suggest that in our English literature before the Norman Conquest there existed any dramatic impulses or tendencies which might have met half-way such isolated influences of the study of classical models as have been described above. The dialogue often forms the first step towards the drama [1]; but no application of this proposition is possible with regard to the dialogue-literature which has come down to us from the so-called Anglo-Saxon times, whether the works comprised in it are translated or (more or less) original. When King Alfred interpreted for his people the lofty wisdom of the *Consolation of Philosophy* of Boëthius, his object was purely didactic, in the highest sense of the term. This famous book is an argumentative colloquy, interspersed, after a fashion which peculiarly commended it to our English ancestors, with quasi-lyrical passages ; the personages carrying on the

No English dramatic literature before the Norman Conquest.

---

be included the two allegorical dramas of ' Guillaume ' Herman and 'Étienne' Langton, referred to below in another connexion. For other Latin plays of the same description see Wright, *u. s.*

[1] See below, on the growth of comedy, more especially in Italy and in England. As to more primitive times, M. Jusserand, *u.s.*, p. 13, has well brought out the dramatic element in early Irish poetry, while showing, p. 77, the absence of it from the Anglo-Saxon dialogues.

dialogue are, with the exception of the author himself,
abstractions—Wisdom, the Reason and the Mind. In the
Dialogues of Gregory the Great, which at the wise king's
behest Bishop Werfrith of Worcester abridged in a vernacular version, the recital of the legends of Italian saints
finally tapered off into an elaboration of the doctrine of
Purgatory. Nor is there any dramatic element in either
of the two fragments of a poem on *Christ and Satan* which
used to be regarded as forming an integral part of Cædmon's
Paraphrase. The earlier of these, indeed, I only mention,
because a special treatment of its theme (the descent of
Christ into hell), taken from the apocryphal *Gospel of
Nicodemus,* played so important a part in the mystery-
drama [1]. The much briefer fragment attached to it adds
a species of anecdote to the dialectical episode of the
temptation of Christ by Satan. Again, the very curious
series of dialogues between *Salomon and Saturnus,* of which
the origin seems traceable to ancient Scandinavian usage,
proceed no further than a contention—an alternation of
question and answer, or assertion and counter-assertion,
between the representative of biblical wisdom and the
mouthpiece of old-world love or mother-wit [2]. So, too, in
the Anglo-Saxon version of the theme which in Middle-
English literature appears under the well-known designation
of *The Debate of the Body and the Soul* there is really no
debate at all, but rather a mixture of simple narrative and
apostrophe [3]. Even the Anglo-Saxon *Passion of St. George,*

---

[1] This fragment is not in dialogue. Even a much later poem on the same
subject, belonging to the reign of Edward II and probably written some time
after the theme had been dramatically treated as a mystery, is described, as
'not a dramatic piece, but a mere poem in dialogue.' (Wright, *Introduction to
Chester Plays,* Shakesp. Soc. Publ., 1843, p. xiv. See also *Reliquiae Antiquae,*
i. 253; and cf. ten Brinck, *u. s.*; i. 111; ii. 251).

[2] Saturn here takes the place of Marculf, the usual Teutonic champion
in these wit-combats, who also appears as Malcon or Marcol in Old
French popular literature, and is cited by Rabelais. See Jusserand, *u. s.,*
77 note.

[3] See *The Departed Soul's Address to the Body* in J. M. Kemble's *Poetry
of the Codex Vercellensis, with an English Translation* (printed for the Ælfric
Society, 1843). In Part I (*The Condemned Soul*) the Soul addresses the
Body, which can return to it no answer, consolation, or comfort; in Part II
(*The Blessed Soul*) the vessel of clay, which long ago bore the now
emancipated spirit, remains likewise mute.

lively as is the combination of relation and dialogue presented in it, can at the most be regarded as having fostered traditions afterwards utilised for a popular miracle-play, without really containing any dramatic elements of its own [1]. These instances must suffice in illustration of the futility of straying into any attempt at searching for dramatic beginnings where they are not to be found.

Retracing our steps once more, we may think it worth while to enquire whether any other influences survived from the ancient world which, though not in themselves constituting the origin of the modern drama, or of the English branch of it, were yet of a nature sensibly to affect them in the beginnings of their growth. Now, it is well known that in the history of the Roman stage we have to distinguish between two lines of developement—the one native, the other largely foreign and artificial. The latter, which to all intents and purposes is alone represented in the Latin dramatic literature handed down to us, was, like the body of that literature at large, borrowed from the Greeks. It is doubtful whether at any time the reproductions or imitations of Greek tragedy among the Romans secured the favour of more than a small cultivated minority; it is, for instance, still an open question whether the tragedies of Seneca were represented at all; if they were, it can only have been fashion which gave them a passing vogue. On the other hand, the *praetextae*, which treated themes of national historical interest, seem in all other respects to have followed the Greek model, and not to be really distinguishable as a separate literary species. As a matter of fact, already in the latter days of the Republic the multitude (including, according to Horace, even the knights in the stalls) could only be reconciled to tragedy by the introduction of that species of accessories which in our own times have established themselves as an integral part of any important theatrical 'production.' At Rome there was no tragic drama capable of sustaining itself enduringly with or

The relics of the Roman stage.

---

[1] It was edited for the Percy Society (vol. xxviii.) by the late Archdeacon Hardwick.

without such adjuncts[1]. In the early days of the Empire
tragedy was easily dissolved into the two elements of choral
music and pantomimic action ; and on its fragile ruins the
pantomime, a species of ballet of action to the elaboration of
which 'every art and science' contributed their refinements[2],
established itself as a class of entertainment favoured by both
the masses and their masters.   Greek comedy, i. e. the New
Comedy of Menander and his school, with which we are
acquainted in the versions of Plautus and Terence, survived
more honourably both in Rome and in the provinces ; it is
praised by faint blame in a work of St. Augustine at the
beginning of the fifth century; and it thus, as has been
already seen, furnished some sort of literary link between the
ancient and the mediaeval world.   But both tragedy and
comedy are to be regarded as essentially the diversions of
cultivated Romans.   The popular dramatic appetite of the
Italian capital had long fed with greater relish upon dramatic
entertainments of native, or at least neighbouring origin.
Probably those farces which combined pantomime, dance,
and music with humorous dialogue, and were termed
Saturae or mixtures, were of Etruscan origin.   With them
were united the *Fabulae Atellanae*, which came from Campania, and, originally improvisations, were introduced into
literature in the early part of the first century B. C.   These
were distinguished by their four established character-
figures, which have survived to this day in the popular
Italian comedy[3].   Another species, apparently more peculiar
to the town, was the *Mimus*, which, like the *Atellana*,
took its figures from common life, but had no established
characters.   These popular farces were at all times the
favourite dramatic entertainment of the Romans, whom
they delighted by their vigour, vulgarity, and obscenity,
while constant opportunity was found in them for that

---

[1] Its extinction was, however, more gradual than is perhaps sometimes
supposed.   Cf. Welcker, *Die griechischen Tragödien,* iii. 1466 *seqq.*

[2] See Gibbon's *Decline and Fall*, ch. xxxi.

[3] The Italian *farsa* is the origin of the *commedia dell' arte* of the sixteenth
century, as to the influence of which on our English comedy I shall have
something to say below.   The quays of Naples remain to the present time
a favourite summer-evening haunt of Arlecchino.

licence of speech which, in spite of law and government, tempered the despotism of nearly all the Caesars.

In the days of the close of the Republic, and of the early Empire, the vastness of the Roman theatres, as well as the diversity of nationality which was beginning to characterise the Roman population, made it necessary to devise entertainments suitable for large masses of spectators, and at the same time adapted to the craving for mere enjoyments of the eye.   The circus had at all times, and the amphitheatre had since its establishment, outvied the theatre in popularity : as they exhibited a constantly increasing variety of spectacles, processions, and contests by land and water, their attractions more and more superseded those of the theatre proper, which in its turn came to supplement its waning attractions by every species of illegitimate intermezzo. The ribald jests of Atellanes and mimes, and the lascivious charms of the pantomimes, were not enough to feed an endless appetite for amusement ; and it had to be gratified, in addition, by ' crowds of rope-dancers, conjurors, boxers, clowns, and posture-makers, men who walked on their heads, or let themselves be whirled aloft by machinery, or suspended upon wires, or who danced on stilts, or exhibited feats of skill with cups and balls[1].'   Nor was the degradation of tastes inevitably produced by such entertainments confined to the public theatre ; Roman supper-tables were enlivened by similar exhibitions, as a relief to the recitations by which the guests had to allow themselves to be fatigued, or to the conversation which they must not unfrequently have found it difficult to maintain at a high level of interest, when politics were dangerous, and when philosophy and wit had alike taken flight from the couches round the overladen board.

In short, the decay of the Roman theatre, and the degraded character of the body of the dramatic or quasi-dramatic amusements which survived this decay, are

Mimes and strollers.

---

[1] Quoted from Merivale's *History of the Romans under the Empire*, v. 67 ; where see a curious passage from Bulenger, *De Theatro*.   Further details, together with a general review of the Roman entertainments of the days of the Empire, and of the decay of the Roman drama, will be found in Friedländer's *Sittengeschichte Roms* (1864), ii. 125-396.

abundantly attested for the whole period of the Empire. The history of Roman pantomime connects itself both glaringly and grotesquely with that of the Imperial Court from Nero to Theodora ; while from among the subjects of the Caesars luxury, lust, and licence attracted to the panto-mimic stage generations of votaries, and were stigmatised as its shame by the Fathers of the Christian Church [1]. But though pantomime gradually ceased to flourish as a diver-sion of State, its traditions as well as those of the humbler mimes were carried on by a class of performers which is of its nature indestructible. The strolling mimes conveyed the last, and probably some of the worst, reminiscences of the Roman acting drama across the period of those Great Migrations which changed the face of the Western world. In the fifth century we meet with a condemnation of *histriones*, *mimi*, and *joculatores* by an ecclesiastical council. Even before this, not only actors of all kinds, but also persons addicted to 'theatromania,' had been excluded by the Church from her benefits. The judicial system of the Frankish empire analogously refused the exercise of public rights to *histriones* and *nugatores* among other classes of persons whom it branded as *viles* and *infames* [2]. Yet the craving for theatrical entertainments of a popular descrip-tion continued to evoke a supply in the face of Church canons and national laws, and in defiance even of that occasional apathy in high places which professional art may be excused for regarding as 'the most unkindest cut of all [3].'

Here and there, remnants of ancient heathen religious rites may have survived among both Celtic and Teutonic nations, which partook of the nature of what were after-wards known as pageants or masques, and which accordingly

[1] For an anthology of such anathemas see du Méril, *u. s.*, 7–8, and notes. The keynote of invective was struck by Tertullian, whose treatise *De Spectaculis* (second century) set the example, followed by many subsequent assistants of the stage, of ignoring all distinctions of either time or kind.

[2] See R. Sohm, *Die Fränkische Reichs- und Gerichtsverfassung*, (1871), 354 *note*.

[3] It is related of Lewis the Pious. that he never raised his voice in laughter, not even when at festivals there appeared for the enjoyment of the people, '*thymelici, scurrae et mimi.*' Klein, iii. 635. Cf. ib. iv. 104 ; ii. 665.

contained possibilities of dramatic developement. But these
phenomena either belong to the boundless field of comparative mythology, or are too isolated to bear any solid
superstructure. The activity of the strolling mimes, on *Mimes.*
the other hand, which more especially concerns us here,
must inevitably have been so multitudinously varied in
character as to defy either classification or record. It is
the pride of the true popular entertainer to be all things to
all men ; to intensify and enhance every element of excitement or diversion which the efforts of voice, face, or limbs can
furnish by means of any adventitious aid which ingenuity can
suggest or to which experience can impart an additional
screw. The *joculatores,* the successors of the mimes, whose *Joculatores.*
name they occasionally bore and whose custom of shaving
the head they perpetuated, were therefore in nature and
purpose Protean. The designation may be understood as
including reciters, singers, musicians, dancers, posture-makers,
buffoons, and actors of every description ; and doubtless
several or all of these characters were frequently united
in a single person. According to the nature of their accomplishments, or to the frequency of their appearance, these
entertainers would be welcome among high and low, at the
court and in the castle, in the market-place and on the
village-green.

But as these perennial purveyors of amusement came to
associate themselves with particular countries, and in the
course of time, prompted by occasion or genius, sought to
gratify higher as well as lower recreative demands, their
efforts gradually fell into more distinctive forms, and the
appellations bestowed upon them began to assume more
specific meanings [1]. In Rome itself *histriones* and *thymelici*
appear to have survived into a period—the twelfth century
—in which no mention yet occurs of any beginnings of the

---

[1] Du Méril, *u. s.,* pp. 26 *seqq.,* has some interesting observations on the
literary elements traceable in some of the performances of these popular
entertainers. The general nature of the process whereby the art of acting
was transmitted to the early Middle Ages from the Roman Empire is well
indicated in the *Mémoire sur les jeux scéniques des Romains* in vol. i. of
Œuvres Complètes de Duclos (Paris, 1806), which also furnishes a graphic
account of the decay of the Roman stage.

The jong-
leurs in
France
before the
Norman
Conquest of
England;

Christian religious drama in the Eternal City [1]. In France, to which for our purpose it will now suffice to confine our attention, the literary tastes of the higher classes had by the eleventh century taken two principal directions—in the North that of epical, in the South that of lyrical song. The age was an age of wars. Its social system everywhere asserted the personal tie, in default of what was in time to become the bond of the nation or the state. Furthermore, the ideas of chivalry had established an artificial code, consciously devised for imposing self-restraint during the pursuit of the two passions which animated the lives of men—love and fighting. Under these influences flourished the poetry of the *troubadours* and the *trouvères*. The home of the former was Provence, where the chief business of the *jongleurs* (another form of the term *joculatores*) was to accompany with music and song the expressions of sentiment habitual to the masters who had taken them into their employ. In Normandy, on the other hand, and in the North of France generally, the *trouvères* found themselves called upon to sing their *chansons de geste*, commemorative primarily of deeds of war. Successful skill in this direction required a special and in time an elaborate training; and the names of *trouvères, gestours* [2], and *jongleurs* became interchangeable as more or less professional designations. And both here and afterwards in England the custom arose of great personages employing such craftsmen or artists of their own, who, being chosen from or enrolled among the members of their own households, were called by the general name implying this relation, though not necessarily indicating a *status* of unfreedom [3]. The name of *menestrels (ministeriales)* was however, it would seem, only occasionally applied to this class of skilled performers in France. At times they evidently enjoyed considerable regard and a

---

[1] See F. Gregorovius, *Das römische Passionsspiel*, &c., in *Kleine Schriften zur Geschichte und Cultur*, iii. (1892), 177.

[2] 'Of all manner of minstrales
   And jestours, that tellen tales
   Both of weeping and of game.' *House of Fame*, iii. 571-3.
Cf. *The Rime of Sir Thopas.*

[3] See Waitz, *Deutsche Verfassungsgeschichte*, ii. 152.

recognized position ; indeed, it is quite possible that the intimate relation between the Norman dukes and barons and their *jongleurs* may be traceable to an ancient Scandinavian origin ; for the duty of the *skald* had been to sing the warlike deeds of his chief [1].

It is easy to understand how of these *jongleurs* considerable numbers came to seek and to enjoy a licensed liberty, which may be supposed to have not unfrequently grown into a liberty without the license, of wandering from castle to castle, and of occasionally displaying their skill to less exclusive audiences outside the gates or at the foot of the hill.   Here they must at times have, in more senses than one, fallen into the ways of those humbler kinds of entertainers who had survived as remnants of an earlier age, and who are nowhere likely to have been more numerous and more tenacious of their habits than in countries which had been so long and so thoroughly romanised.   The itinerants in their turn had, no doubt, occasionally gained admission to the castles, where *more ribaldorum* they had furnished facile opportunities of amusement.   The two classes of entertainers had characteristics in common ; and although the distance was wide between the favoured dependant who sat at his lord's board and accompanied him into the field, to share with him the danger and the honour of his warlike exploits, and the stroller who amused high and low in their hours of relaxation, yet it was a distinction bridged over by many intermediates.   The best illustration of the sort of confusion which prevailed is to be found in the intermixture of names which certainly ensued.   The renowned Taillefer, who furnished a treble prelude to the fight at Senlac—of songs, of a juggling trick, and of self-sacrificing intrepidity,—is by one of the chroniclers who recount his heroic death

---

[1] I have not thought it worth while to enquire into the possibilities as to some notion of this relation having been imported from the same source into England before the Norman Conquest.   In *Beowulf* the gleeman who narrates the great actions of the past in a solemn and religious strain is the associate of the warriors whom he addresses ; afterwards we find the *scop* ranking at the court of his king or at other courts, where he appears on his wanderings as an honoured guest.   The songs of the Anglo-Saxon gleeman are epical, stabile sections of the existing body of national legend sung by him to an epical instrument (the *glee-beam*).

mentioned under designations which in the mouths of churchmen were traditional terms of opprobrium[1].

and in England after the Conquest.

The Norman Conquest brought into England a wide and heterogeneous variety of novel visitors; and they all came to stay. The Norman chivalry were accompanied by their poets—the *jongleurs* or *trouvères*—by whom not only new forms but a new spirit of composition was introduced into this land, and through whom and whose imitators among English-born singers the character of our epical and lyrical literature was largely changed, although its native features were neither wholly destroyed nor in some instances even obscured. The process was a very gradual one; it occupied over three centuries, and even then remained only partial in its effects[2]. But the conquering expedition likewise included a motley crew of adventurers from all parts of what is now France, and from adjacent territories[3]; and stragglers of this description no doubt continued to follow in the wake of the immigrations which ensued after the victory. The mental diversions of Messires Boutevilain and Trussebot cannot have ordinarily lain in the direction of the 'chansons de Karlemaine è de Rollant,' which Taillefer had sung 'before the dukes.' Thus, if the simple strains of the gleeman that had formerly been heard in the house where the English lord sat with his thegns gathered round him were now succeeded by the songs of the minstrel in the castle of the Norman baron—neither need we doubt but that vagrant entertainers of a less select class likewise found their way into the hall on the hill, after affably pausing at its foot to furnish a taste of their quality to less discriminating audiences. And not unfrequently in England, as in France,

---

[1] ' *Histrio,* cor audax nimium quem nobilitabat'; and again,
    ' Incisor-ferri *mimus* cognomine dictus.'
(Guy of Amiens.) See Freeman's *Norman Conquest,* iii. 478, *note.*

[2] This is not the place in which to enquire whether some of the conclusions on this head advanced in the brilliant volume by M. Jusserand already cited require modification. I rather direct attention to the passages in which he speaks of the continued treatment of their accustomed subjects by the French *jongleurs* in England, and of the imitation of them by English minstrels, even when treating native themes. See pp. 146, 244 *seqq.*

[3] In Thierry's picturesque phrase, 'tous les enfans perdus de l'Europe occidentale.'

it may have from the eleventh century onwards been frequently a matter of difficulty, or of indifference, to pronounce
to which of the two classes any particular minstrel belonged.

As a matter of course, during the reigns of our Norman
and Angevin kings at all events, the connexion between
the two countries and their baronages was too close for the
minstrelsy, high or low, of the one to diverge altogether in
its developement from that of the other. Neither, however,
was there anything like parallelism between the two growths;
and the difference between them reflects itself very notably
in the history of the beginnings of the French and of the
English drama respectively. In France the literary activity *Their influ-*
of the *jongleurs* induced them, as early at least as the twelfth *ence upon*
and thirteenth centuries, to follow the example of the monks *the begin-*
nings of
in composing plays on sacred themes, such as had already *the drama*
in the eleventh been produced by clerical authors. Of this *in France.*
kind, for instance, was the activity of Rutebeuf, who from
the life of a wandering *jongleur* or miscellaneous entertainer
rose to secure to himself a place among the poets and
moralists of his country. The numerous works of this
versatile genius include a typical example of the satirical
' debate ' of the period—a species verging under such treatment as his upon the vivacity of a dramatic scene, although
not admitting of being called a drama in miniature[1]. But
they also comprise *Le Miracle de Théophile*, a dramatic
attempt on a religious subject familiar to Hrotsvitha and other
early mediaeval writers, and ending with an orthodox ' *Te
Deum laudamus*[2].' But while the literary ambition of the
French *jongleurs* early addressed itself to the dramatic treatment of such a theme as this, the popular performances of their
strolling brethren had likewise never ceased to be carried on
with a vigorous persistence and, attaching themselves to the
comic usages of popular festivals, in their turn gave rise to
early attempts of an unmistakeably dramatic nature. From
the popular *jeux*[3] which heightened the fun of the *fêtes de*

---

[1] The famous *Desputizon du Croisié et du Descroisié*, in which the rather
cynical common-sense of the Non-Crusader is intended to come off best.

[2] *Histoire Littéraire de la France*, xx. 775-7. I shall have occasion for
returning to this 'play' below.

[3] These *jeux* must be distinguished from the *jeux-partis* or *partures* of the

l'âne and similar jollifications, were derived the first *farces*
of the Basoche and the *sotties* of the *enfans sans souci*, whence
French comedy in its turn derived some of its constituent
elements[1]. Thus from an early date religious and profane
plays, as it were, kept pace with one another in the history of
the French drama; and two further facts explain themselves,
which it is beyond my purpose to seek further to elucidate
in this place. First, the early and active cultivation of the
religious drama in France was by no means wholly owing to
clerical hands; and, again, the French stage as early as the
thirteenth century almost entirely emancipated itself from
dependence on the Church. The absence of a common
national consciousness capable of exciting a commanding
interest in secular actions and heroes may help to explain
the monopoly long enjoyed by the sacred drama of themes
such as could engage the nobler sympathies of the people at
large. But the contemporary dramatic performances which
pursued a less elevated aim were from an early date equally
successful after their kind; and thus the history of the

North (of which Rutebeuf's *Crusader and Non-Crusader* may serve as an
example), called *tensons* in Provence, which are merely satirical poems in
dialogue-form. *Histoire Littéraire*, &c., xx. 657.

[1] See Ebert, *Entwicklungsgeschichte der französ. Tragödie*, 20; Klein, iv. 24;
Hagenbach, *Kirchengeschichte*, iii. 414. The lay Brotherhood of the Passion
performed mysteries. The moralities of the *clercs de la Basoche* (i. e.
Basilica) were their serious, the *farces* their humorous plays. From the
latter are to be distinguished the *sotties*, which were entirely satirical, and
in form largely allegorical. (See for abundant examples of the last three
species vols. i.–iii. of Viollet le Duc's *Ancien Théâtre Français*.) The species
were often interchanged between the several associations (Arnd, *Geschichte
der französ. Nationalliteratur*, i. 221). The burlesquing of religious rites,
which was so popular in France, and which seems traceable to a Byzantine
origin, was also carried on occasionally in England. See Jusserand, *u. s.*,
466 seqq., where is quoted the letter of Bishop Robert Grosteste, prohibiting
the celebration of the 'Feast of Fools' on the Feast of the Circumcision in his
cathedral—a prohibition afterwards extended to his whole diocese. Of this
mock-feast traces are said to be discoverable as late as the reign of Henry IV,
about which time it is supposed to have been abolished. The well-known
ceremony of the election of a Boy-Bishop, whose reign lasted from
St. Nicholas' to Innocents' Day (December 6 to 28), was practised in
schools as well as in parishes, and in the former survived to the Reformation
period. See Hone, *Ancient Mysteries Described*. 'The Mass of the
Drunkards' (Wright's *Reliquiae Antiquae*, ii. 208) was probably a mere
literary squib. The ribaldry of mock-litanies will never cease to find
a grateful public, so long as there remains a religious sentiment to deride.

French drama became, and long continued to be, a record of a competition or struggle between associations of players severally representing its serious and its comic side [1].

On the English side of the Channel, different conditions led to different results. It has been already said that the Norman Conquest brought into this country the *minstrels*, as the *jongleurs* from Normandy and Northern France were here more usually called ; and that this designation included, together with the authors and singers of romantic verse, the miscellaneous entertainers with whom even at home they were largely intermixed and in consequence freely confounded. In the eyes and to the ears of the English population the two classes gradually came to be regarded as a single class or profession [2]. To what extent and by what processes some sort of relation established itself between the Norman singers and the remaining representatives of native English song, is wholly unknown ; very probably before long, and more especially after English University life had begun, the wandering clerks, with their sufficient Latin and ready ear, proved the most effective intermediaries of literary as well as of social communication [3]. Musicians, dancers, and fortune-makers stood less in

The minstrels in England.

---

[1] Cf. P. Albert, *La Littérature Française des Origines au XVIIme Siècle*, p. 69 ; where an effective contrast is drawn with the intimate relations between the national epos and the national tragedy of ancient Greece. One or two French mysteries on subjects taken from secular literature are, however, mentioned by Ebert, *u. s.*, p. 33. From the closing period of the Middle Ages dates a *Mistère du siège d'Orléans*, on which a monograph has been published by F. Guescard.

[2] In *Piers Plowman* (*Passus*), *Activa Vita*, to prove himself *not* a true minstrel, says :

'Ich can not tabre ne trompe · ne telle faire gestes
. . . ne fithelen · at festes ne harpen,
Japen ne Jogelen · ne gentilliche pipe,
Nother sailen [dance] ne sautrien · ne singe with the giterne.'

This is a very similar list of accomplishments to that cited by Jusserand, 160 note, from the tale *Des deux bordeors rivaux* :

'Je sais contes, je sais fabliaux,
Je sais conter beaux dits nouveaux . . .
Je sais [bien] jouer des couteaux
Et de la corde et de la fronde,
Et de tous les beaux jeux du monde
Je sais bien chanter à devis,
Du roi Pepin de Saint-Denis . . .
De Charlemagne et de Roland,' &c., &c.

[3] Ten Brinck, i. 242 ; 379–80.

need of go-betweens to secure the applause of any kind of public, and in time they must have without effort absorbed fragments of the native population into their elastic fraternity.

Whatever influence was exercised upon the beginnings of the English drama by the minstrels, must have been more or less in proportion to their rate of progress in becoming part of the life—literary and social—of the English people. It seems to follow that for some time after the Conquest— and it was within this period that the beginnings of our drama fell—this influence could not be exerted at the same rate by the two classes of minstrels which at the time of their first introduction into the country it is still possible to distinguish. It might indeed be supposed, that when in the middle of the twelfth century John of Salisbury, discoursing on the idle pursuits of courtiers, condemned *totam istam joculatorum scenam,* and declared that the Holy Sacrament should be refused to *histriones* and *mimi,* he meant to include both the higher and the lower description of minstrels in the same anathema as actors on some sort of stage. But it is extremely doubtful whether this very learned clerk intended any reference whatever to dramatic performances or performers of his own day and country [1].

The begin-nings of the English drama un-connected with the higher class of minstrels;

It would accordingly be futile to search in the remains of Anglo-Norman literature, whether composed in French or in Latin, for any links connecting it with the beginnings of the English drama properly so called. As a matter of course, those productions cannot be here taken into account which themselves formed part of the early efforts of the liturgical drama in France, and may thus have indirectly affected the growth of the same species in England. Among these the remarkable compositions, belonging to the earlier half of the twelfth century, of Hilarius, a monk of English descent, who though resident in France kept up, as some of his lighter poems show, a correspondence with Englishmen, will be

---

[1] See Wright, *Introduction to Chester Plays,* p. vi, and cf. Henry Morley, *English Writers,* i. 599 : ' The world of his own day did not concern John of Salisbury, when he sat pen in hand. . . . When he talks of writers and plays, it soon appears that his mind is upon Plautus and Terence.' Indeed, he asserts that tragic and comic actors came to an end with tragic and comic poets. (Cf. the passage cited by Du Méril, p. 24, *note.*)

described in their proper place a little further on. And I may similarly postpone a notice of the two religious plays written respectively by the Anglo-Norman *trouvère* Guillaume Herman, and by the Paris doctor Étienne (Stephen) Langton, afterwards renowned as Archbishop of Canterbury. They date from the latter part of the same century; but while on the one hand, like one of the plays of Hilarius already mentioned, they share some of the features of the literary religious drama which I have already discussed, on the other their general conception and treatment recall the moralities of which the genesis will be traced below. In the general current of Anglo-Norman literature we can at the most discern a not unfrequent dramatic ripple upon the wave; in accordance with the undying tendency of French song, it abounds in those satirical tendencies which in Anglo-Saxon literature had only here and there manifested themselves [1]. Gradually the dialogues, disputations, or *estrifs* which found so much favour in the Norman castles came to be from

[1] Ten Brinck, ii. 307.—In Wright's *Anglo-Latin Lyrical Poets of the Twelfth Century* (1872) I perceive no reference to dramatic representations, and (with the exception perhaps of the allegorical figures in the *Liber Alani de Planctu Naturae*) nothing that calls up any reminiscences of the early drama. There is no dramatic element in any of the writings of the witty Walter Map. In the slight dialogue between Norman barons (printed in *Reliquiae Antiquae*, i. 134, from a MS. dating from about 1300) there is nothing which can fairly be called dramatic. I am not acquainted with all the literature mentioned by Klein, iv. 105, and Jusserand, 459 seqq., but so far as my knowledge extends, the same remark holds true of it. Thus, although in its versions from the thirteenth century onwards the *Debate between the Body and Soul* passes from the form of address into that of dialogue, it is not on that account any more of a drama. (In the French *Débat du Corps et de l'Âme* (*Ancien Théâtre Français*, iii. 325-336) an 'Acteur' narrates the action springing from the dialogue.) Nor can I conceive of its having been, in accordance with Klein's conjecture as to these dialogues, acted by Norman *jongleurs* in the castles before lords or ladies. So also with a *Disputatio inter Mariam et Crucem* imitated by an English writer of this period (Ten Brinck, i. 390-1); nor can such *estrifs* as *The Owl and the Nightingale* or *The Thrush and the Nightingale*, or the rather later humorous *Debate of the Carpenter's Tools*, have been composed with any dramatic intention. A solitary link between these disputations and the early religious drama is to be found in the *Harrowing of Hell*, which will be noticed below as our earliest extant religious drama, but which its author announces as a 'strif' (disputation), and which was not intended for representation. See Jusserand, 459, *note*. But the date of this piece, which is preserved in a MS. of the reign of Edward III, is not supposed to be earlier than the reign of Henry III.

time to time imitated by English wits for the delectation
of native ears ; but this was after the English drama
had already taken root as a popular growth not directly
affected by these compositions.   During the century and a
half following upon the Norman Conquest our English literature seemed to sleep the sleep of death ; what survived of it
(witness the English Chronicle) clung in form as in language
to an obsolete world ; and the Norman minstrels of the
higher class, or the Englishmen who under the stress of
circumstances or from interested motives adopted the tongue
of the conquerors, were not the poets of the people.

*and con-
nected only
in ways not
easily ascer-
tainable
with the
lower.*

On the other hand, it is difficult to persuade oneself but
that some elements of dramatic action survived in the multitudinous efforts of that lower or more popular species of
minstrels whose first representatives in this country have
been described above as a kind of camp-followers of the
Norman Conquest ; and that these seeds, though scattered
by the roadside, failed to spring up here and there into
some kind of ear.   Proof must in this case be out of the
question ; but it is hard to suppress the notion that in
England too something like a thread of continuity attaches
the undistinguishable remnants of the ancient to the vague
beginnings of the modern stage.   It was the activity of
the stage which, as we shall see below, towards the close
of the fifteenth century, in all but the remote regions of
their activity, cut the last sods of ground from under the
feet of the ' last minstrels' of this class ; yet this very stage
owed to their predecessors a debt not to be altogether
repudiated, although never likely to be accurately apprised.
For, while they may not have been direct contributors to
the beginnings of our drama, they helped to urge these
beginnings onwards in the direction in which they were to
ensure vitality to themselves, viz. in that of popularity. This
could hardly have been otherwise ; for in the nomad life of
the Middle Age, as it has been so graphically depicted
by a distinguished French writer, in whose pages Old England seems to have come to life again [1], these minstrel-strollers

[1] Jusserand, *La Vie nomade et les routes en Angleterre* (1884). See also
his *Histoire Littéraire du Peuple Anglais*, pp. 455 *seqq.*

had a signally important share. Doubtless, even of the
Norman minstrels of the higher class who crossed the
Channel in the eleventh and twelfth centuries some, instead
of having been domesticated in particular castles of the
baronage, may have been welcome guests both there and in
the monasteries as keeping alive by their narrative songs the
traditions of the nationality *d'outre mer*; and in time,
though only very gradually, some of their *gestes* began to
be translated into the English vernacular [1].   But where
their songs were unintelligible other *joculatores*—whom the
monks in their Latin called also *lusores, mimi, citharistae,*
but whom barons and people knew indifferently as *jongleurs*
or *jugglers, jestours* or *jesters*—sought to gratify either the
ear by music without words, or the eye by pantomime and
other exhibitions.   No very great or subtle display of art
was needed to make them popular.   For they were the
story-tellers and newsbearers upon whom depended in no
small measure what brightness and variety enlivened the
homes, high or low, of the land.   Gradually, as the literary
remains of the latter half of the thirteenth century and of the
ensuing period instruct us, the English-born or English-
speaking minstrels became the interpreters of the popular
sentiments which in course of time were to assume the
importance of public opinion.   But long before this had
been brought about they had fulfilled the function primarily
incumbent upon them—to make life from one point of view
at least liveable. While the working-day seemed dull in their
absence, no festival could be complete without them ; mirth
and minstrelsy became interchangeable terms ; and the
rewards showered upon these servants of the public absorbed
the kindly and even the charitable feelings of no slight
a proportion of the population [2].

    When, as will be seen in the course of the following pages,

---

[1] Probably not much before the close of the thirteenth century.   Robert
de Brunne (1260–1340) complains of the strange and quaint English of such
translations.   Warton, *History of English Poetry*, sec. iii.

[2] The decay of minstrelsy, both accredited and vagrant, is a subject
which cannot be pursued here.   As late a writer as Alexander Barklay
bears witness to the popularity both of minstrels and singers, and of jugglers
and pipers.   (See his *Eclogues*, ii. and iv.)

the religious drama suggested to these minstrels subjects of wide popularity for their entertainments, it was not *a priori* likely that they would be slow in seeking to make use of some of the opportunities before them. But they had to reckon with jealous and powerful monopolists, and it is long before we meet with any English dramatic attempts of a popular character traceable to any other than a clerical, or quasi-clerical, origin. By this time of course the *histriones* had become to all intents and purposes Englishmen. In earlier days their efforts had to be carried on in the teeth of peculiar difficulties ; but it seems clear that such efforts were made. In the thirteenth century we shall find the representation of religious plays by *histriones* reprobated as improper ; so that they had evidently thrust themselves in as the imitators, although at the same time as the rivals, of the clergy and their attendants or pupils [1]. Even so, and before as well as after the monopoly of the clergy had been broken by the more respectable and systematic local competition of the trade-guilds, the strolling minstrels must have helped to enliven and strengthen a growth from any contribution to which they were anxiously warned off; and the share which they took in the early efforts of our drama is not to be altogether overlooked, because it was by interested exclusiveness pronounced illegitimate and intrusive.

It is thus that I would venture in general terms to answer the question as to the relation of the minstrels to the origin of the English drama. The higher class remained as a whole unconnected with it; the lower may be held to have facilitated its popular beginnings, but is not in any essential sense to be reckoned among its originators.

We have thus briefly traced to their historical source two contributory streams ; the current which was to absorb them descended from a more august height than either.

---

[1] Warton, sec. vi., shows how the monks invited the minstrels (no doubt of the higher class) to their festivals, and through their guests became acquainted with romantic stories. In return, minstrels of another sort may be supposed to have carried away with them tempting reminiscences of religious plays of which they had witnessed the performance.

The meaning attached by the Greeks to the word *liturgy*, and illustrated by historical associations which would have made it memorable even had it never come to form part of Christian life, was that of a service performed by an individual or by an association of individuals on behalf of the community to which they belonged. This expression was appropriated by the Christian Church, and applied by her to the public performance of a religious rite of paramount significance. The celebration of the Eucharist constitutes the portion of the religious worship of the early Christians to which none but duly instructed or initiated believers were admitted, while both the unbelieving and mere catechumens were excluded from it. Of this part of the worship the highest conceptions of the Christian faith—culminating in the *mysterium tremendum* of the Real Presence—formed the very essence, so that, apparently in the Eastern Church in the first instance, there was attached to it the designation of the 'divine' or the 'mystical' liturgy[1]. But in course of time the term 'mystery' was in the Western Church applied to the religious service of any of the great festivals of the Calendar, and even to the services of the Church in general[2]. As visibly representing the work of Redemption and renewing it as a *mystery*, i. e. in its inner and moral significance, the office of the Eucharist must however at all times have been considered of unequalled importance. In the West it received and generally retained the name of *missa* or mass, the use of which may conceivably have owed something to similarity of sound with the Greek designation. From the time of Gregory the Great, at all events (590–604)— although the particular Roman office may possibly be of even earlier origin—the Mass formed the central act of public worship in the Western Church. 'In the wide dimensions,' writes an eminent Protestant ecclesiastical historian, 'which in course of time the Mass assumed, there

[1] See Palmer, *Origines Liturgicae*, i. 3, 31.
[2] See du Méril, *u.s.*, 57 and *notes*. The expression '*Resurrectionis mysterium*' was used at the Synod of Worms in 1316. In a German glossary of the fifteenth century '*misterium*' is translated 'divine revelation.'

lies a grand, we are almost inclined to say an *artistic,*
idea. A dramatic progression is perceptible in all the
symbolic processes, from the appearance of the celebrant
priest at the altar (*Introitus*) and the confession of sins,
to the *Kyrie Eleison,* and from this to the grand doxology
(*Gloria in Excelsis*), after which the priest turns with the
Dominus vobiscum to the congregation, calling upon it to
pray (*Oremus*). Next, we listen to the reading of the
Epistle and the Gospel. Between the two actions or acts
intervenes the *Graduale* (a chant), during which the deacon
ascends the ambon (*lectorium*). With the *Halleluia* concludes the first act (*Missa catechumenorum*); and then
ensues the Mass in a more special sense (*Missa fidelium*),
which begins with the recitation of the Creed (*Credo*). Then
again a *Dominus vobiscum* and a prayer, followed by the
Offertorium (*Offertory*) and, accompanied by further ceremonies, the *Consecration.* The change of substance—the
mystery of mysteries—takes place amidst the adoration of
the congregation and the prayer for the quick and the
dead; then, after the touching chant of the *Agnus Dei,*
ensues the *Communion* itself, which is succeeded by prayer
and thanksgiving, the salutation of peace, and the benediction [1].'

*Readiness
of the
times for
liturgical
symbolism.*

Now, without any need of refining too much—a danger
which may frankly be allowed to beset any discussion
of this subject—it is obvious that in this Liturgy of the
Mass we have a dramatic action, in part pantomimically
presented, in part furnished forth by both epical and
lyrical elements. As a matter of course, there is not the
faintest likelihood that it entered into the head of any priest,
or into the heads of any congregation, of the earlier Middle
Ages to regard the service of the Mass in any such light;
and it would accordingly be going too far to attribute to
the dramatic features of the service *per se* the *attempts*
actually made to bring this feature into stronger relief.
The objectors to the pomp and circumstance surrounding

---

[1] Hagenbach, *Kirchengeschichte*, ii. 65–6. It is worth remembering that in
the execution of the *Ordo Romanus* the several Churches preserved certain
national peculiarities. See Ebert, p. 18.

ecclesiastical worship, although by no means altogether
absent, were still comparatively few; and their censures
seemed futile against the manifest twofold purpose of the
Church to make her services on the one hand symbolically
complete, and on the other generally attractive. The historian
just cited has pointed out with much force, how the fact
that the services of the Roman branch of the Church were
conducted in the same Latin tongue illustrates her plan of
placing their chief effect in the *symbols* rather than in the
words employed [1]. The scepticism which questioned any
part of the dogma symbolised was rare and isolated, and still
more exceptional—however noteworthy in itself—was the
philosophy which turned away from what seemed to it an
excess of form and sound and colouring. Thus whatsoever
enriched, expanded or diversified the services was assured
a widespread and unstinting welcome; and no fear existed
of the intrusion of that sense of ridicule which, since it
was reawakened by the severer taste of the Renascence,
has in later times cavilled at some ornamentations of
religious worship as redundant and at others as incongruous.

Nor shall we forget what the Church services and Church
festivals—what the Churches themselves, with their peace
and security, their brightness and their grandeur, illustrated
and enhanced by all the arts in combination with one another
—were to the period of which we are speaking. Not only were
they, as in a measure they remain to this day, associated
with the cardinal events of private and of public life; but to
large masses of the population the sacred edifice was the
centre of their social as well as of their religious life. To
no age do these hints at a description, which has furnished
an almost inexhaustible theme to so many eloquent pens,
apply more strikingly than to that extending from the
ninth to the eleventh centuries, when the Papacy was
gradually establishing its claims, at first under the protection, and then in face of the illwill, of the Empire.
But already at much earlier dates the service of the Mass

---

[1] Hagenbach, *Kirchengeschichte*, ii. 397.

had, in accordance with its most characteristic features, begun its progressive developement.

The dramatic elements of the liturgy:

This service has a beginning, which is at the same time an explanation or exposition of its cause, a central action (the Immolation and Consecration), and a close or completion. The remark seems therefore strictly correct, that from the mystery of the liturgy to the liturgical mystery-drama no step is needed but that of a dramatic *intention* [1]. So long as the reality of the central action (and such the immolation actually possesses for the believing worshipper or spectator) causes everything else to be regarded as merely an adjunct to it, so long the mystery will preponderate over the drama. No sooner will the adjuncts begin in any degree to emancipate themselves from their original character as such, than the play will prevail over the mystery.

The *pantomimical* element in the Mass lies in the first instance in the action of the officiating priest. It seems sufficient to suggest, without attempting to define too closely, the typical significance of the several things acted or done by the priest in the liturgical process—the cruciform gestures of his arms, the breaking of the bread, the dipping of the bread in the cup, the delivery of it to the people [2].

The *epical* element is to be found in the portions of Scripture read to the congregation. Of these there are two kinds —the Apostle or Prophet (*Epistle*), and the *Gospel*. Originally it seems to have been customary to read aloud portions of the Law, the Prophets, the Psalms, the Epistles, and the Gospels ; but in the Western Church the Lessons from the Old Testament were often omitted, the Psalm being in compensation placed between the Epistle and the Gospel. Even at the present day, the Roman liturgy occasionally prefixes Lessons from the Old Testament to the Epistle and Gospel, following these Lessons up with a Psalm [3].

Finally, the *lyrical* element presents itself in those portions

[1] Klein, iv. 2.

[2] Cf., as a curiosity where it is cited, a passage in Honorius Augustodunensis (Honorius of Autun, who died sometime after 1130), *de Antiquo Ritu Missarum*, which explains in detail the dramatic action of the Mass, quoted in Prynne's *Histrio-Mastix*, 1632, p. 113.

[3] Palmer, *u.s.*, ii. 48.

of the service which are prescribed by the *Antiphonary*, just as the portions of Scripture to be read aloud are prescribed by the *Lectionary*. The Antiphonies were originally chants or psalms sung in alternate verses by different choirs or parts of the choir; they afterwards came to include introductory verses, often Scripture texts, prefacing the Offertory and other salient passages of the service (*Introits*[1]). The congregation being expected to return certain *Responses*, the element of dialogue was, as it were, unconsciously introduced into the liturgy. The practice was further fostered by its being largely introduced into the supplementary service of prayer termed the *Litany*. These litanies, which either preceded or followed the ordinary service, were very generally accompanied by *Processions*[2]. In various ways the litanies were the most flexible and varied forms of prayer; and into them was introduced, in the Western Church from about the seventh or eighth century, the invocation of saints, lyric addresses to whom accordingly constituted from a comparatively early period a part of religious worship[3].

Thus, there were three main directions in which it was possible for the liturgy to develope itself dramatically, while at the same time meeting popular tastes and sympathies. The language of the service being in Latin, *their developement;*

[1] Palmer, *u. s.*, ii. 308; cf. Mone, *Schauspiele des Mittelalters* (1846), i. 6 and *note*.

[2] In the reigns of Edward VI and Elizabeth, all processions were prohibited except the perambulation on Rogation days. Palmer, *u. s.*, ii. 97 (*Supplement*). As to the technical use of the term *processus* for religious plays see below.

[3] Palmer, *u. s.*, i. 279. Concerning the Italian *laude* of the thirteenth century, and the transition from these to the dramatic mystery, see E. Gebhardt, *L'Italie Mystique* (*Histoire de la Renaissance Religieuse au Moyen Age*), Paris, 1890, pp. 267-275. A peculiar developement of these *laude* was that of the hymns and short quasi-dramatic pieces recited in the lay confraternities of the Flagellants in the later stages of their activity in Italy (where they were then known as the *Laudesi* or *Disciplinati*) and possibly elsewhere, under the titles of *Praises* and *Complaints of Mary*, together with other short pieces in commemoration of the Passion. This clue, well deserving of being followed out, was suggested to me by Captain Ivan J. A. Herford of Salisbury, who also drew my attention to the ordinance of the Council of Constantinople, A.D. 692, which, in order that the humanity of our Lord should not be obscured by the excess of Eastern symbolism, enjoined that when certain episodes of this life were treated in church, He should be represented in human form.

there was an additional reason why it should seek to
secure new attractions for the eye as well as for the ear.   At
a very early period, certainly already in the fifth century, it
became usual to animate public worship on special occasions
by living pictures of scenes from the Gospel, such as the
Adoration of the Magi, the Marriage of Cana, the Death of
the Saviour [1].   Still earlier, great attention seems to have
been paid to the antiphonary songs ; and when the *tableaux*
were introduced, such songs doubtless accompanied their
presentation.   That into these *tableaux* a certain degree of
action should have gradually introduced itself, was of its
nature inevitable.   The living pictures, however, together
with the songs appertaining to them, were in the first instance
interpolations introduced into the service for the purpose of
prolonging and sustaining an interest in it.   The mystery
proper was still the liturgy itself.

and com-
bination.
The litur-
gical
mystery.

It remains uncertain when the important step was first
taken of connecting the epical portions of the liturgy
with the spectacular, and in some measure pantomimical,
portions, as well as with the lyrical adjuncts already admitted into it.   The process seems to have been completed
by the eleventh century, when in a treatise on the Offices
of the Church, by John of Bayeux, bishop of Avranches,
we find these performances within the sacred edifice viewed
as a component part of the service at large [2].   But it must
necessarily have been gradual.   A very famous French
ecclesiastic of the tenth century refers to the custom of performing on Christmas Day after the *Te Deum* the Office of
the Shepherds, while others of a similar description, such as
that of the Infants (the Innocents of Bethlehem), the Star, the
Sepulchre, were celebrated each in its season [3].   The earliest
of these offices may without hesitation be concluded to have
been connected with the events of which the commemoration
leads up to and culminates in the festival of Easter.   So
cherished was the usage of reproducing the events of the
first Easter morning in association with the service appropriated to it, that in many English churches structures of

---

[1] Klein, iv. 11 ; Ebert, p. 18.   [2] Klein, iv. 3.
[3] See the quotation from Gerbert, *ap.* Wilken, *u. s.,* 5, *note* 4.

stone were built in lieu of the wooden erections that had originally served to represent the Sepulchre. Hither, after the office had stereotyped itself, the clergy went in procession to an altar erected in the so-called Chapel of the Sepulchre, where the Sacrament had been kept since Holy Thursday. Three of the clerics, robed in white, represented the Three Maries of the scene, and replied to the enquiries addressed to them by two of the choristers in the character of the angels ; while the whole of the clergy joined in the concluding acclamation. The Apostles St. Peter and St. John were at a subsequent date likewise introduced into the action [1]. Similarly, on Palm Sunday and on Holy Thursday, the services of the day readily furnished dramatic moments—such as the procession to the gates, and the Last Supper. It is conceivable that the first suggestion of the kind may have arisen out of the early usage of chanting the words uttered by the Suffering Christ in the narrative of the Passion itself in a different tone from that in which the remainder of the text was read [2]. Perhaps, on the other hand, the measure of independence belonging to the interpolations in the services may seem greatest in the case of those which illustrated, not portions of the actual narrative of the New Testament, but certain of the parables of our Lord reproduced in it, such as the striking Christmas office of the Foolish Virgins, to which reference will again be made immediately [3].

[1] See Furnivall's note to *Digby Mysteries* (*New Shakspere Society's Publications*, 1882, pp. 227–8) ; and cf. Parker's *Glossary of Architecture*, cited by Pollard, *u. s.*, *Introduction* xiv–xv. The office is reproduced in *Mary Magdalene* in the *Digby Mysteries*, and in the *Mysterium Resurrectionis*, printed by Wright from a thirteenth century MS. in the Orleans Library and reprinted by Pollard in his *Appendix*. According to du Méril, *u. s.* 43–4, missals were used in the diocese of Paris as late as the fifteenth century, continuing the same kind of Easter office.

[2] See *ib.*, 47 *note*.

[3] M. Sepet, from whose *Drame Chrétien au Moyen Age* (1878, pp. 24 *seqq.*) I reproduce in a briefer form the following abstract of this famous composition, applies to it, apparently following the teaching of Léon Gautier, the designation *tropes*; but I do not understand him to confine this name to representations of parables.—We may, if we will, imagine to ourselves the performance of this liturgical mystery as taking place in the Abbey of St. Martial at Limoges. The Foolish Virgins are ranged on the one side of the entry to the choir, the Wise on the other. The

Thus these offices, in a more or less developed form, sprang directly from the portions of Scripture recited in church on particular days, and in fact constituted a visible repetition of these recitals[1]. The church formed their given scene; the clergy and their acolytes were the actors; and the function of the congregation consisted of lyrical responses to particular passages evoking them. The text was from first to last as brief as possible, comprising only so many words as sufficed to connect the successive stages of the action, and being largely made up of questions and answers.

Examples of the liturgical mystery.

The earliest *liturgical mysteries* (to describe them by a convenient technical name) of this description which have been preserved date from the twelfth, or perhaps in part from the eleventh century[2]. Although of French or Anglo-Norman origin, they are as a matter of course composed in the Latin tongue, French being only admitted in the case of certain refrains. An exception is the *Sponsus* (the Heavenly Bridegroom) or *Play of the Wise and Foolish Virgins*, to which reference has just been made; it is written partly in Latin, partly in a Poitevin or half Provençal dialect, and, although an earlier date has been assigned to it, probably

precentor and clergy chant an invocation by way of prologue; from the lectionary the Angel Gabriel bids the Virgins await the Heavenly Bridegroom; whereupon there begins the simple action of the piece. The Foolish Virgins have fallen asleep and their oil is wasted; when they awake they in vain entreat the Wise Virgins to share with them their store. They are met by a refusal and bidden buy oil from the merchants sitting behind their stalls at the other end of the nave. Along its entire length the Foolish Virgins pass to buy them oil; but the merchants have none to sell them, so that with loud lamentations they have to make their way back to their original station at the entrance to the choir. Here they kneel down in terror; for since their departure the Wise Virgins have entered in, and from beyond the screen a Voice makes answer to their cry of despair—or a Mighty Presence advances to warn them against entering in their turn—'Verily, I say unto you, I know you not'; and they are consigned to everlasting torments. Black figures, gruesome to behold, bear them away; and down in the nave the congregation, half believing in the reality of what it has seen and heard in the dim light and amidst the sound of many voices, returns to its accustomed exercises of prayer and praise.

[1] For examples see du Méril, p. 89 *seqq.* Cf. the pictorial relic of a Suabian pantomimical Easter office of the twelfth century, and an Alemannic office of the thirteenth (at Zürich), *ap.* Mone, *u. s.*, 8-9.

[2] They are printed in Wright's *Early Mysteries*.

belongs to the middle of the twelfth century [1]. The subjects of these *liturgical mysteries*, as it seems convenient to designate them, are as a rule taken from the New Testament [2]. From the same period survive divers dramatic versions of legends concerning the popular Saint Nicholas, which savour rather of the early monastic literary drama [3], and thus bear witness to the fluidity of a growth of which it is easier to detach the successive stages from one another in accordance with *a priori* theory than to arrange the sequence in proved chronological order.

To this group of compositions, which still maintain an organic connexion with the religious services in the Church and are introduced into it, if at Matins before the *Te Deum*, if at Vespers before the *Magnificat*, belong the productions of Hilarius. They seem to call for a brief notice, since he is usually supposed to be the earliest known English author of plays ; although, being written in Latin, with occasional French refrains, they cannot claim a place in our national dramatic literature. *The plays of Hilarius.*

There is no real proof that Hilarius was an Englishman ; but the conjecture which has been adopted from Mabillon by subsequent writers is a probable one [4]. He celebrates at great length the virtues of an English lady named Eva, who became a recluse and ended her saintly life in Anjou ; and four of his epistles in verse are addressed to persons of English origin. If he was a native of England, he must have been born there some time in the earlier part of Henry I's reign, *i. e.* about the beginning of the twelfth century [5]. For while still very young, he became a student

---

[1] Ten Brinck, ii. 246 *note*.

[2] A good example is the Easter mystery published at Tours by Luzarche, and described by Moland, *Origines Littér. de la France*, p. 132 *seqq*. Its performance took place in various parts of the church, and the congregation joined in the concluding *Te Deum*.

[3] Cf. *ante*, p. 9, *note* 2.

[4] *Hilarii Versus et Ludi* have been edited from a MS. known to André Duchesne (1616) and Mabillon (1713), but unknown to the authors of the *Historie Littéraire de la France* (1763), by J. J. Champollion-Figeac (Paris, 1838), with a brief critical Introduction. For a more easily accessible account of Hilarius and his plays see Henry Morley, *English Writers*, vol. i. pt. 2 (*From the Conquest to Chaucer*), 1866, pp. 542 *seqq*. Cf. Sepet, *u. s.*, 33 *seqq*.

[5] Champollion-Figeac, vii.

under Abelard at Paraclete, the monastery which had
grown out of the hermitage near the Seine, south of Paris,
whither the great teacher had retreated after his condemnation at Soissons a few years earlier. Hilarius had
chanced upon a patron saint congenial in name to a disposition little in sympathy with the drier or duller aspects
of scholasticism. During his course of study he underwent, with the rest of his fellow-students, a process of
rustication, commemorated by him in a humorous Latin
poem which mentions his own stoutness of body (*gravitas*),
and of which each stanza ends with a French refrain to
the effect that 'the Master has something against us[1].'
He seems to have cherished a warm personal attachment
towards his eloquent teacher ; for when the latter removed
from Paraclete to a Breton abbacy, Hilary likewise took
his departure, and recommenced his studies at the school
of Angers. Here (to judge from the specimens preserved
to us) we may conclude that he continued to versify as the
humour suited him. Neither his metre nor his morality
was exacting ; he was in point of fact an ecclesiastic
distinguished from his fellows by nothing but an irrepressible literary turn. This, however, would be quite sufficient
to account for his eyes having been open to the possibilities
to be found in the liturgical, or semi-liturgical, mystery.

The most interesting of the plays of Hilarius is, notwithstanding its brevity, the *Suscitatio Lazari*. To perform it,
says a rubric, there are necessary ' Lazarus, his two sisters,
four Jews, our Lord and His twelve Apostles, or six of
them at all events.' Very manifestly, the action proceeds
under the simplest external conditions, and the dialogue is
restricted to the narrowest, or absolutely necessary, dimensions. The first scene or ' movement ' discovers Lazarus sick
in bed amidst the lamentations of his sisters, who despatch
the four Jews sitting by his side to seek the counsel of
' the Supreme Physician, the King of Kings.' They betake
themselves to the Saviour, Who promises that the sickness
of His brother shall not be a cause of death to him. But on
their return the messengers find Lazarus dead, and Mary

---

[1] ' *Tort a vers nos li mestre.*'

and Martha lamenting him.   Each sister chants a series
of four stanzas with a French refrain[1].   Before the sounds
of these wailings have wholly ceased, voices are heard
from a group assembled in another part of the scene: 'The
Jews of late sought to stone Thee, and goest Thou into
Judæa again?'   'Lazarus sleepeth; I go that I may awake
him out of sleep.'   So, though the disciples are full of fear,
they proceed on their way; and as they are in the midst
of the path, the Master is heard explaining to them the
difference between the sleep which is, and the sleep which is
not, death.   Arriving at the house at Bethany, they are met
by the heartbroken Martha, who, in stanzas of which the
verses alternate between Latin and French, expresses both
her grief and the hope inspired by the Saviour's presence[2],
whom Martha beseeches to intercede.   In Mary, hope
has become belief; and to this belief He responds without
hesitation.   They pass together to the sepulchre where
Lazarus had been laid, and without delay the action reaches
its climax in the loosing of Lazarus.   Whereupon, turning
to his deliverer, the man who has been raised from the dead
exclaims: 'Thou art our Master, our King, our God!
Thou shalt blot out the guilt of Thy people ; what Thou
orderest is straightway accomplished ; Thy kingdom shall
have no end.'   Thus, the play being over, the transition
is natural and easy to the *Te Deum* or the *Magnificat*,
intoned, as is directed by Lazarus, i. e. by the priest who
has assumed the part, according as the play may have been
introduced in the service at matins or at evensong.

Hilarius' second scriptural play, the *History of Daniel*,

---

[1] Mary's runs thus:
> ' *Hor ai dolor;*
> *Hor est mis frere morz ;*
> *Por que gei plor* [this is why I weep].'

Martha's (with more penetrating feminine pathos):
> ' *Lase, chative !*
> *Dès que mis frere est morz,*
> *Porque sue vive?* '

[2] ' Si venisses primitus,—   Quod in vivum poteras,—
 Dol en ai,—   *Dol en ai,—*
Non esset hic gemitus ;—   Hoc defuncto conferas !
 Bais frere, perdu vos ai.   *Bais frere, perdu vos ai.'*

  &c., &c.

exhibits a similar willingness to lean upon the narrative
of Holy Writ, but as was perhaps inevitable in the present
instance, a far less close dependence upon it. Doubtless,
however, this play, in which no French refrains relieve the
Latin text, depended considerably upon arrangements partaking of the character of spectacular or scenic effects in such
passages as Belshazzar's feast and the lions' den. Of these
however we know nothing. In the composition of *Daniel*
Hilarius seems to have been assisted by two other writers,
'Jordanus' and 'Simon.' There is a very notable amount of
life in this composition, which in its general character bears
a certain resemblance to the libretto of a modern oratorio.
To the third play of Hilarius, a dramatised anecdote concerning a miracle wrought by an image of St. Nicholas
with the Saint's own co-operation, it seems unnecessary to
return[1], except by way of noting that this play contains
French refrains, which are partly cadences identical with
those to be found in *The Raising of Lazarus*. The piece is
a trifle in both theme and tone[2].

Transition
from the
liturgical
to the
popular
mystery.

Thus, in the gradual developement of the Mystery-
drama from its beginnings certain tendencies make themselves manifest from an early date, which as they continue their course may almost be said to make up the
entire history of the subject. Of these, the first is the
substitution of the vernacular for the Latin tongue[3]. This
substitution, at first restricted to the choral responses of
the congregation, was, as has been seen, extended to the
lyrical passages in general, and thence found its way into

---

[1] Cf. *ante*, p. 9, *note 2*.

[2] *Barbarus*, who has committed his possessions to the care of the image
of St. Nicholas, finds that they have been stolen :

> 'Hic res plus quam centum
> Misi et argentum ;
> Sed non est inventum.'

He flogs the image, and the Saint quickly brings up the robbers with the
goods. *Barbarus* exclaims :

> 'Nisi visus fallitur
> *Jo en ai*
> Tesaurus hic cernitur
> *De si grant merveile en ai*'—

and becomes a Christian.

[3] As to the encouragement given to this tendency by the practice of the
Church see du Méril, *u. s.*, 73-4.

the speeches of certain of the characters (as we may call them) of the Mystery-drama. The French mystery of *La Resurrection* (dating from the twelfth century), which is described as still entirely recitative in character, i. e. performed by persons standing still, is regarded as the earliest extant religious drama in the vulgar tongue [1].

The second step is to be sought in the detachment of the mystery- or miracle-drama from the office of which it had at first formed a dependent, and then a more or less independent, part, and of which it now came to form merely an interesting adjunct.

The third advance was not like' the other two logically unavoidable; nor indeed was it at all invariably entered upon. It consisted in the joining together of a whole series of mysteries on different incidents from the Scripture (more especially the Gospel) history into a single work or production. This joining together, although it seems to have been attempted already at an early date, was at first only roughly effected [2]. Its final result is the so-called *Collective Mystery*,—the form in which the principal English contributions to the mystery-drama were composed [3].

Before noticing this species, however, one or two further general remarks may be in place. A distinction legitimate in itself, although as will be seen by no means observed with precision or uniformity, is usually drawn between *Mysteries*, *Miracle-plays*, and *Moral-plays* or *Moralities*. Properly speaking, *Mysteries* deal with Gospel events only, their object being primarily to set forth, by illustrating the

Mysteries, miracles, and morals distinguished.

---

[1] See Klein, iv. 14. Ebert, *u. s.* 19, points out how since the eleventh century the vernacular had by means of the so-called *Epistolae farcitae* been introduced into the liturgy itself. These were songs generally referring to the martyrdom of St. Stephen. Cf. *Ancien Théâtre Français*, vol. i. *Introd.* p. vii.

[2] See the description of the earliest German mysteries, *ap.* Wright, p. viii, and Wilken, pp. 5 *seqq.*, who thinks the eleventh century the earliest date that can be assumed for them, but a later date more probable. They are partly in Latin and partly in German.

[3] In England the *Collective Mystery* may be concluded to have been the result of an expansion of the Easter and of the Christmas mysteries, and of the combination between the two groups after the celebration of the festival of Corpus Christi had become generally prevalent. Ten Brinck, ii. 257; and cf. *infra*.

prophetic history of the Old Testament, and more particularly the fulfilling history of the New, the central mystery of the Redemption of the world, as accomplished by the Nativity, the Passion, and the Resurrection. *Miracle-plays*, on the other hand, are more especially concerned with incidents derived from the legends of the Saints of the Church. Lastly, *Morals* teach and illustrate the same religious truths, not by direct representation of scriptural or legendary events and personages, but by allegorical means, abstract figures of virtues or qualities being personified in the characters appearing in this species of plays.

Nature of the combinations between these species in England.

Of these three species there are frequent combinations; and in England, at all events, no accurate distinction was drawn between mysteries and miracle-plays; indeed, the former name was not in use in this country [1]. When the religious drama reached England, the two species had already to some extent combined; and, in fact, the earliest French religious plays which we possess are partly of one kind, partly of the other. But the origin of the miracle-play was to a great degree literary, as has been previously shown; and in England the first miracle-plays proper of which we know accordingly precede the first mysteries proper of which traces are preserved to us. On the other hand the miracle-plays were the earliest to fall into desuetude, their significance having been to a large extent of a local nature [2]. The moralities, in their turn, occur in early specimens, such as the literary dramas of Herman and Langton, already mentioned; but it was not till a comparatively late date (probably the earlier half of the fifteenth century) that, under the influence of the epical allegories which were then popular in English as well as French literature, they were popularly cultivated. Their origin was therefore proper to themselves, and will be briefly discussed as such below; but at the time when they began to flourish in England, the form of the mysteries

---

[1] See Collier, ii. 53, *note* 2. In France, the term *mystère* was applied to all religious plays indiscriminately from the fifteenth century. Ebert, *u. s.*

[2] Cf. du Méril, 65. These plays seem in some measure to have replaced the legends of saints, of which towards the end of the eighth century Pope Adrian I. had prohibited the reading aloud in churches.

and miracles was already so far advanced and fixed, that it was inevitably borrowed by the moralities. Elements of the moralities, in the shape of abstract figures, will however frequently be found to occur in the mysteries and miracle-plays.

The main elements contributory to the progress of the popular drama which had arisen out of the liturgy have thus been established, and there is no need to pursue in detail their co-operative processes. In the natural order of things, consequently upon the growing length of the plays, the elaboration of their paraphernalia, and the increasing number of their spectators, they began to be represented outside the church as well as inside[1], and to be composed in the vulgar tongue in preference to the Latin. Plays treating of the legends of saints were less dependent on their connexion with the service of the Church than mysteries proper; and as lay associations, gilds and schools in particular, possessed each its saintly patron, they soon began to act plays in his honour in their own halls or the vicinity of them. In these performances the services of professional mimes could hardly fail to be occasionally employed. Lastly, when the clergy allowed the introduction into the religious dramas acted or superintended by them of scenes and characters of a more or less trivial description; when to certain personages were attached conventional peculiarities of voice or speech[2]; when devils and their chief advanced to prominence, and had to be made hideous or contemptible in order to inspire instantaneous antipathy,—the comic element could not fail to assert itself. Here the traditions of popular entertainments would, in France at all events, be at hand with their influence, and contribute to give a profane character to what could no longer be regarded as essentially a part of religious worship.

Such—without going into further particulars—were some

The drama begins to emancipate itself from the Church.

---

[1] This was ordered by Pope Innocent III in 1210. Hagenbach, ii. 414.

[2] These became proverbial. See e.g. in *The Milleres Prologue* in the *Canterbury Tales* how the unmannerly Miller,—

'in Pilates vois he gan to crie,
And swore by armes and by blood and bones.'

of the causes contributing to the inevitable result, that the clergy began to lose their control over the performances which their order had originated, and to become seriously

Attempted reaction. divided as to their expediency. A memorable attempt was however made in the middle of the thirteenth century to sanctify more emphatically to a religious use a popular taste that was fast outgrowing the purposes for which it

Origin of Corpus Christi plays. had been at first encouraged. This attempt connects itself with the endeavour to bring home to popular consciousness the central doctrine of the Church of Rome. I refer of course to the institution by Pope Urban IV, in the year

1264. 1264, of the festival (hitherto only local in its celebration) of Corpus Christi, when he granted a pardon of a certain number of days to all attending various parts of the divine service held on the occasion[1]. The office in question was composed by the Angelic Doctor, St. Thomas Aquinas, of whose teaching it has been said that he ' sought to make the supernatural significance of the doctrine of the Church accessible to the natural intelligence, without at the same time in any way analysing that doctrine into something natural or comprehensible[2].' But Pope Urban having died in the same year, his bull remained unexecuted, and the disturbed times into which the Church had fallen pre-vented the carrying out of his design for nearly half

1311. a century[3]. At last, in 1311, by which time the Papacy was securely if not gloriously housed at Avignon, the bull of institution was confirmed under Pope Clement V by a decree of the Council of Vienne, so memorable in political as well as in ecclesiastical history[4]. The special features of the festival of Corpus Christi were the distinct proclamation of the Creed of the Church, and the exhibition at four altars, after procession through the streets, of the Host,— the symbol of the mystery of the Incarnation. With this latter feature the plays which it became usual to exhibit on

---

[1] Collier, i. 19, *note.*

[2] Hagenbach, ii. 425.

[3] It was the troublous time of the *Interregnum* in the Empire (1254–1271) and of the commencement of the struggles between the Papacy and France, which ended with the transfer of the Holy See to Avignon (1309).

[4] It abolished the Order of the Templars.

this festival seem to have been closely connected ; hence the term *processus* is frequently applied to the plays them-selves. But on the developement of the drama the fact that the mystery to which the festival was sacred was not in itself immediately adapted for representation or calcu-lated to concentrate the thoughts of the spectator upon any particular events in the sacred narrative, would appear to have had the effect of extending the range and suggesting a wider choice of dramatic subjects. Thus especially towards the close of the Middle Ages, Old Testament subjects were treated with great frequency at Corpus Christi[1].

This festival seems to have exercised a very marked *General progress of the early religious drama,* influence upon the progress of the drama, though Pope Urban IV appears in the 'pardon' accompanying its institution to have made no reference to religious plays. (The 'pardon' mentioned in the *Proclamation for Whitsun Plays* at Chester (of which immediately), and then attributed to 'Clement y'en bishop of Rome,' is supposed to have been granted by Pope Clement VI (1342–52).) I cannot, however, here further pursue the progress of the beginnings of the modern drama in the case of any country besides our own[2]. It must suffice to note here that, for reasons already indicated, the drama in France already in the *in France,* thirteenth century largely[3] emancipated itself from the Church. The French theatrical associations, whose ten-dencies were not only rival but conflicting, continued in activity down to the period of the Renascence,—when under literary influences a new era began to open, endea-vouring, as is usual with new eras in France, to make

[1] Cf. Pollard, *Introd.* xxv, where it is also pointed out that this result was further favoured by the fact that Corpus Christi is celebrated on the Thursday (sometimes on the Sunday) after Trinity Sunday, i. e. as a rule not far away from the longest days of the year.

[2] A most useful bibliographical survey of the productions of the religious drama among the several European nations will be found in Mr. F. M. Stoddard's *References for Students of Miracle-plays and Mysteries, University of California Library Bulletin,* no. 8, Berkely, 1888.

[3] Largely, not entirely. The emancipation had not altogether accom-plished itself even in the fifteenth century, when ecclesiastics still appear as chief actors in the Passion-plays, and performances are still arranged under episcopal sanction. Du Méril, *u. s.,* 61 *seqq.* As to the extraordinary fertility of the religious drama in France see Pollard, *Introd.* xli, *note.*

tabula rasa of what had gone before,—and in isolated instances to an even later date.   The early religious dramas of both Italy and Spain are considerably later in date, so far as we are acquainted with them, than either the French or our own.   No Italian mystery has been preserved from an earlier date than 1243 ; no Spanish from either the thirteenth or the fourteenth century, though it is clear that such existed in a variety of forms[1].   On the other hand, in Germany there seems no doubt that both the plays which it was usual to perform at Christmas and those which were generally exhibited at Easter belong in their origin to about the twelfth century.   In the Middle Ages Easter was by far the more popular as a season for dramatic performances,— a circumstance to be attributed not only to obvious con- siderations of temperature, but also to the fact that Easter is by far the more ancient festival in the Christian Church, and that in dramatic significance the subject of the Passion far surpasses that of the Nativity[2].   Corpus Christi plays

Italy,

Spain,

and Ger- many.

---

[1] The *origines* as well as the developement of both the Italian and the Spanish drama have been traced with extreme fulness by Klein in the fourth and succeeding volumes of his work, to which I have already repeatedly referred.   The labour which its unfortunate author bestowed on it was so enormous, that he may well be pardoned occasional eccen- tricities both of expression and combination.   That his general view of the origin of the drama is just, I venture at the same time to believe; and I have not scrupled to adopt some of his theories.—For a brief account of the origin of the Spanish drama, as springing from religious sources and wholly unconnected with the ancient Roman theatre, see also Ticknor's *History of Spanish Literature*, chap. xiii.—It is, by the bye, well known that in Spain mysteries are by no means things of the past; I remember comparing with the Oberammergau Play the *Sacrado Passio y Mort de Nostre Senyor Jesu-Crist*, which professed to be prepared for representation in the principal theatres of the kingdom, being published (at Barcelona) by a dignified ecclesiastic.   The Spanish play seemed to me much inferior to the more recent versions of the German.

[2] See Mone, *Schauspiele des Mittelalters*, vol. i. (1846), for a series of religious plays dating from the thirteenth and fourteenth centuries, with a list of others reaching to the end of the sixteenth, in which the Easter plays hold the most prominent position.—'The Seven Joys of the Blessed Virgin' seem to have been arranged for the stage by Flemish writers; at least this is known to have been the case with two of them, *de Eerste Bliscap van Maria*, which dates from 1444 and was performed at the court of Charles the Bold, and *de Sevenste*, which was discovered in our own day in a MS. purchased by the Royal Library at Brussels.   A decree of the city of Brussels orders the annual production of one of these *Joys*.—

are likewise noted ; while the Ascension, Assumption, and Whitsuntide plays are to be regarded as extensions of the Easter plays. It is curious, by the way, that the advent of the Reformation (which by no means extinguished the favour shown to the religious drama as such[1]) reversed the relative popularity of the Easter and Christmas plays, partly perhaps in consequence of the importance attached in the former to the laments of the Blessed Virgin. With the revival of Catholic feeling in the seventeenth century, and the continued cultus of the Blessed Virgin in this and the eighteenth, the Easter plays recovered their preferential position, being now tinged with a sentimental character, which found its vent in allegories and in external effects, while the incident of the Resurrection itself was treated with relative slightness. The first edition of the Oberammergau Play, the peculiar origin of which is well known, though due to Benedictine monks, seems to have borne unmistakable traces of the influence of the Jesuit school of theology, paramount in Bavaria and in Catholic Germany at large in the latter half of the Thirty Years' War. By the side of the mysteries proper the Germans in the fourteenth century became familiar with plays celebrating the legends of saints—such as St. Catharine and St. Dorothy —*miracles* in the stricter sense of the term ; and in the fifteenth and sixteenth centuries it became usual to select from legendary lore subjects of historical importance, whether general or local, so that the transition to the historical drama became easy. While the *moral* element finds a place in the history of the early German drama, it only exceptionally connects itself with the lyrical and epical poetry of the minstrels ; and its growth is in this respect analogous in its earlier stages to our own. But the progress of the German drama from the ecclesiastical

I have preserved an account in a newspaper of our own times of a representation in a small people's theatre at Madrid of a Passion-play called *Los siete dolores de Maria*.

[1] Cf. the curious quarrel in April 1523 between the clergy and the citizens of Strassburg, on the occasion of a competition between the religious plays of the latter and the Indulgences' processions organised by the former, *ap*. Baum, *Capito und Butzer* (Elberfeld, 1860), p. 194.

basis, where like ours it had its beginnings, was less fortunate.
The attempts made in those parts of the nation which were
seized by the spirit of the Reformation to pour new wine
into the old bottles, and to create a national drama,
though interesting and as will be seen connecting themselves with the English drama in its greatest period,
remained practically abortive as a literary movement [1].

The re-
ligious
drama in
England.

 The peculiar political and social condition of our own
country, in the period succeeding upon the Norman Conquest, could not but considerably affect the development in
England of the religious drama, which had come to our
English ancestors as a Norman gift. Before the Conquest,
as I have already shown, they had neither possessed a
drama, nor displayed any disposition towards it; and it
would have been little in accordance with the national
character had the tendency to expand and diversify the
dramatic elements in religious worship met with a speedy
and general welcome here [2]. At the time, therefore, when
the drama came among us, there is every reason to conclude
that mysteries and miracle-plays alike at first remained in
the hands of the clergy by whom they had been introduced;
while miracle-plays were also occasionally composed by
ecclesiastical hands as literary works. But the Conquest
had also brought across the Channel a professional class of
performers, who must naturally have been prompt to seize
upon an attractive form of entertainment, and bring home to
secular audiences the facilities at their command for enjoying
it. Ecclesiastics, then, or persons connected with the Church,
introduced the drama into England; they composed the
first dramas produced in this country, and performed them
in person, or caused them to be performed by their pupils;
but the *histriones* soon followed in their footsteps, and in the
end certain sections of the unprofessional laity followed in
the footsteps of the *histriones*.

 The first play of which we have nominal mention as acted

---

[1] Of the early German religious plays an account will be found in
Dr. C. Wilken's *Geschichte der geistlichen Spiele in Deutschland* (Göttingen,
1872).

[2] Ten Brinck, ii. 246.

in England has already been stated to be the *Ludus de*
St. Katharina, which the Norman Geoffrey, who afterwards
became Abbot of St. Albans, caused to be performed at
Dunstable about the year 1110. Of this ' play ' we know
nothing, except that the writer who mentions it (Matthew
Paris in his *Lives of the Abbots of St. Albans*) says that it
was a play of the kind ' quem *miracula* vulgariter appella-
mus.' Matthew Paris wrote about 1240 ; and since there is
no reason to suppose that in the interval any progress had
taken place in the miracle-plays, this dramatic treatment of
a favourite theme of ecclesiastical poetry cannot have differed
widely from that adopted in the other Latin or French
religious plays that have come down to us from the same
century. There remains, as observed above [1], no evidence
to enable us to determine the character of this piece more
precisely; while the twofold fact that no French plays acted
in England are preserved from this period, and that no Latin
miracle-play can be proved to have been performed here [2],
makes any conclusion hazardous as to the language in which
the *Play of St. Katharina* was written. What seems clear
is that whether or not this particular example was among
the earliest of its kind known to this country, such plays
were not unfrequently performed in English monasteries in
the course of the century following upon the Conquest.

William Fitz-Stephen, who wrote about half a century
before Matthew Paris, states in reference to the period
1170–1182 *c.*, that London, instead of theatrical spectacles
and scenic plays (such, for example, as those of Rome),
has plays of a more sacred character,—' *repraesentationes*
miraculorum quae sancti confessores operati sunt, seu
repraesentationes passionum quibus claruit constantia mar-
tyrum [3].' Here, again, it is impossible to pronounce in
what language the plays referred to were composed [4]. As
in France, so in England, the legends of the saints appear

---

[1] *Ante,* p. 10.

[2] Pollard, *Introd.,* xxi.

[3] First published by Stow from the *Vita S. Thomae Archiep. et Mart.*
(Becket), and quoted by Collier, i. 11.

[4] Ten Brink (ii. 248) thinks it may be assumed to have been Anglo-
Norman.

to have met with dramatic treatment before the more arduous and more important experiment was made of applying it to scriptural subjects; among which Old Testament seem to have been essayed earlier than New Testament themes. Unfortunately not a single complete miracle-play, in the more restricted sense of the word, that was performed in England, has been preserved to us ; and those of which the names remain are mentioned at comparatively late dates[1]. Everything points to the performers of these miracle-plays, or of their prototypes, in the twelfth century, and in the earlier part of the thirteenth, having been exclusively ecclesiastics.

Profes-sional players, 1258. In the year 1258, however, we suddenly come across a statement that *histrionum ludi* must not be seen, heard, or allowed to be performed before abbot or monks. It may remain open to doubt whether the interpretation to be given in the passage in question to the terms *histriones* and *ludi* is to be restricted to dramatic performers and performances[2]. But even were this inadmissible, such performances may fairly be supposed to have been included among the exhibitions which the itinerant performers produced where they were likely to find most favour. Actors of this kind cannot as yet have been very common ; indeed, a century and a half later Lydgate in a famous enumeration of social types passes by the professional player, while he finds room for the minstrel and the juggler (*tragitour*)[3]. That these actors, when they

[1] The *Pageants of St. Fabyan, St. Sebastian* and *St. Botolf* mentioned by Pollard, *Introd.* xx., are noticed in company with the *Pageant of the Trinity* in an early Chartulary of the Brethren of the Holy Trinity of St. Botolph without Aldersgate, whose fraternity was founded in 1373. See Hone's *Ancient Mysteries described* (1823), 77 *seqq.* The plays of *St. George of Cappadocia* at Windsor and of *St. George* at Bassingbourne in Cambridge-shire are mentioned under the dates 1416 and 1511 respectively (Collier, i. 29; Warton (ed. 1871), ii. 233). The *Ludi Beatae Christinae* at Bethers-den, Kent, appear in the Churchwardens' Accounts of the year 1522 (Miss Toulmin Smith, *York Mystery Plays, Introd.* lxv). In Dublin, at Christmas 1528, the shoemakers presented *Crispin and Crispianus* as part of an elaborate entertainment composed of biblical and classical elements (Sharp, p. 142). Cf. ten Brink, ii. 303.

[2] This is the opinion of Collier, by whom the passage in the *Annales Burtonenses* is cited (from Gale), i. 14. The passage cited by Warton, iii. 161, from Matthew Paris, *ad ann.* 1236, shows that the term *histrio* was also used in a wider and more varied sense; and I cannot find that Warton considers its use to require restriction in the particular case in question.

[3] In the *Daunce of Macabre,* a version of the famous and long-lived

performed their plays, made use of the native English tongue, is again merely a matter of conjecture ; but 1258, as will be remembered, was the very year in which this tongue received a public acknowledgment of unparalleled significance[1].

The two centuries ensuing upon the Conquest, together with a further span of time of which the limits cannot be defined with precision, may therefore be regarded as the age in which the drama in England was still mainly under the control and management of the clergy. The miracle-plays performed by them, whether written in Latin or in French, were unmistakeably of French origin, and differed in no important point from their exemplars *d'outre mer*. The plays already mentioned, composed by Guillaume Herman and Étienne (Stephen) Langton in the middle and latter part of the twelfth century, were the earliest examples produced on English ground, though in the French language, of the theological morality ; but although they present few features indicating the prospect of a new dramatic or literary species, and although in point of fact the English moralities of later date start in a large measure from a fresh basis, it seems preferable to treat in its entirety the growth to which they belong.

The direct connexion between the clergy and the miracle-plays continued, if not quite to the last, at all events till the period when those plays were on the eve of being super-seded by the beginnings of the regular drama[2]. Even when the clergy did not perform in plays, they wrote them,

The clergy and the miracle-plays.

mediaeval device of the Dance of Death and of its lesson as to what awaits us all, from Pope and Emperor to handicraftsman and hind.—On the other hand, according to Collier, i. 30, in a later work of Lydgate's, *The Interpretacyon of the names of Goddys and Goddesses*, it is said of Sensuality that he ought to change his character, and that
> 'well shall he be taught,
> As a player sholde.'
As to Lydgate's own productions containing dramatic elements see below.

[1] The English Proclamation made in the name of Henry III.

[2] According to Bale, cited *ap.* Warton, ii. 214, Robert Baston, a Carmelite friar of Scarborough, who accompanied Edward II on his Scottish expedition and wrote a Latin poem on the siege of Stirling Castle, wrote *Tragoediae et Comoediae vulgares* ; but nothing in English remains from the hand of this versatile but unlucky author. He was taken prisoner by the Scots and compelled to write a Latin panegyric (to match his *Siege of Stirling*) on Robert Bruce.

or at least paid their performers. Bishop Bale, the author of our first Chronicle history, was likewise the author of our last miracle-play, or at least of the last preserved to us (1538); and the *lusores, minstrells*, and *jocatores* enjoyed the 'adjutorium' of the Priory of Thetford in several hundreds of instances between the years 1461 and 1547[1]. Yet very different opinions were held at different times among the clergy, both as to the propriety of the performances of these plays in themselves, and as to the permissibility or participation in them by ecclesiastics. The objecting voices became louder and angrier, as those waves passed over the face of society which by their recurrence remind us that Puritanism is of no single age, and again as the dramatic performances themselves began to lose their specially religious character when lay hands came to engage in the same pursuit. Early in the thirteenth century the high-minded Pope Gregory IX prohibited in indignant terms the exhibition of dramatic spectacles in consecrated places, 'lest the honour of the Church should be defiled by these shameful practices.' In 1227, the first year of his papacy, the Council of Treves had decreed the same prohibition. He passed away, however, in 1241, and before long the attitude of the Papacy towards the practice of religious plays was to undergo the memorable change already noticed, marked by the institution of the festival of Corpus Christi. About halfway between these two dates falls the publication of the celebrated *Manuel des Pechiez*, of which the original was erroneously attributed to Bishop Grosseteste of Lincoln, the unsparing assailant of the shortcomings of the Church. Both the French original of this work, by William of Wadington, and the English version composed by Robert Mannyng of Brunne in 1303, under the title *Handlyng Synne*, enter at length into the question of miracle-plays, and lay it down that the clergy, though forbidden to 'make or se' miracles, may 'play the Resurreccyun' in church, and the Nativity[2]. I am inclined to conclude this to mean

---

[1] Collier, ii. 69-70. As to Bishop Bale, and as to the possible monastic authorship of some of the collective mysteries, see below.

[2] Collier, i. 15 *seqq.*; cf. Pollard, *Introd.* xxiv-xxv.

that an illustration of the service—a liturgical mystery in short—was held tolerable, while a miracle-play emancipated in scene, and more or less in treatment, from the control of authority was condemned as worldly foolishness. Nor did the actual establishment of Corpus Christi, although marking a *redintegratio amoris* between Church and stage, by any means put a complete stop to even more sweeping censures.

From the fourteenth century we have a sermon, by no means devoid of power, against 'miraclis playinge' in general[1], and in *Piers Plowman's Crede*, which was written shortly before the close of the same century, a friar minor piously exults :—

> 'We haunten no tavernes, ne hobelen abouten ;
> At marketes and Miracles we meddley us never.'

Yet, as has been pointed out, less than a generation afterwards we find a friar minor at York interfering to bring about the annual representation of Corpus Christi plays, and called ' a professor of holy pageantry[2].' Wiclif, when reprobating the gross amusements by which the 'great solemnity' of Christmas is supposed to be honoured, speaks with scorn of him ' that can best play a pageant of the devil[3],' but he does not recur to the subject when discussing the various ' heresies and errors of friars.' To the fifteenth century (in which, however, the Benedictine Lydgate composed a series of pageants ' from the Creation '), belongs a satirical poem against the ' free mynours ' and their miracle-plays, in which the author expresses a pious hope that the friars will in due season burn in reality, as they now occasionally burn in character, in a ' cart made al of fyre ' on the stage[4]. Early in the reign of Henry VIII Dean Colet, when delivering an *oratio ad clerum* at St. Paul's, quoted an old ordinance against a clergyman's being ' a public player,' and complained that in despite of it the clergy gave themselves up '*ludis et jocis*[5].' Not long afterwards Cardinal Wolsey included among ordihances framed by him for the Canons

---

[1] *Reliquiae Antiquae*, ii. 42 *seqq.*
[2] Appendix to Drake's *History of York, ap.* Collier, i. 20.
[3] See *The Ave Maria*, in *The English Works of Wyclif*, &c., ed. by F. D. Matthew for the Early English Text Society (1880), p. 206.
[4] *Reliquiae Antiquae*, i. 322.   [5] Collier, i. 64.

Regular of St. Austin a provision against their being players. Finally, in 1542, Bishop Bonner forbade all performances of plays in his diocese ; but the practice was not altogether extinguished, and from a tract of 1572 it appears that even at so late a date ' interludes' were occasionally played inside churches [1]. Indeed, in Queen Mary's reign, when an attempt was made to revive the religious, while suppressing the secular, drama, we hear of the performance ' on St. Olave's day at night' in the church dedicated to that saint in Silver Street, London, of a stage-play treating of his miraculous life [2].

Perform-ances by members of gilds and other lay actors.   As has been already stated, an impulse of a quite unprecedented kind was given to the performance of religious plays by the Church herself, through the confirmation of the Papal Bull instituting the festival of Corpus Christi. Indeed the actual institution of that festival might be concluded to have been immediately followed by the performance of such plays by the members of the gilds in at least one important English city, were it possible to credit the tradition dating the origin of the Chester plays as falling within the years 1268–1276.   Whether or not (as we have no right to assume) Chester set the example, and in whatever order of time and place that example was followed, or in part anticipated, the custom in question certainly flourished in a considerable number of English cities and towns during a period extending from the latter years of the thirteenth, through the course of the fourteenth and fifteenth, down to near the end of the sixteenth centuries. As will be seen immediately, the actors in these representations were usually the members of the gilds or companies of tradesmen or handicraftsmen ; but these worthies were not possessed of anything in the nature of an exclusive privilege.   Thus in London, when after a lapse of nearly two centuries from the date mentioned above [3], we come in the year 1378 upon a mention of plays, the choristers of St. Paul's are found intent upon shutting the door on inexpert performers ; and in 1391, as on subsequent occasions, the parish-clerks of the

---

[1] Collier, ii. 72-3.   [2] *Ib.* i. 165.   [3] *Ante*, p. 49.

city are in possession of the field [1]. At Winchester, it was
the almsboys who as late as 1487 performed some version
of the theme of *The Harrowing of Hell*; and the circumstance
that at several localities (not only at smaller places like
Bassingbourne in Cambridgeshire, Bethersden in Kent, and
Heybridge in Essex, but also at Reading and Tewkesbury)
the churchwardens' accounts are charged with the expenses
of the performances, points to the probability that they
were carried on by mixed companies of laymen, organised
under more or less clerical direction [2].

External evidence of an inevitably uncertain kind, sup- *Their geo-*
ported by suggestive analogies in other branches of early *graphical*
English literature of relatively ample productivity inspired *distribution.*
by the study of Scripture, points to the Anglian regions
of the kingdom as the regions which most readily favoured
these beginnings of our national drama [3]. Adopting this
clue, we may give prerogative mention in this connexion to
Wymondham near Norwich [4], and to Norwich itself. We
may thence trace the movement through Eastern Mercia by
Sleaford and Lincoln into Northumbria, where at Leeds, at
Woodkirk near Wakefield, at Beverley, at York itself from
about the middle of the fourteenth century, and at Newcastle-
on-Tyne, the religious drama was assiduously cultivated by
the citizens. Leaving aside its devious migration to
Edinburgh and as far north as Aberdeen, we find it
prevalent in a series of towns in our English North-West,
in Kendal, Lancaster, Preston, and nearing the Welsh

[1] Stow records that in this year the parish-clerks of London enacted
a play at Skinner's Well, near Smithfield, in the presence of king, queen,
and nobility, which lasted for three days. Another play, which began with
the Creation and lasted eight days, was performed at the same place in 1409.
Collier, i. 27–8. Everybody remembers in Chaucer's *Miller's Tale* the parish-
clerk, the 'joly Absolon':
> 'Sometime to shew his lightnesse and maistrie
> He plaieth Herode on a skaffold hie.'

[2] See the data *ap.* Miss L. Toulmin Smith, *York Plays, Introduction,*
lxiv–lxviii.

[3] See ten Brinck, ii. 262–3. For the data on which the list in the text is
based see Miss L. Toulmin Smith, *u. s.*, and Stoddard, 51–66, where will also
be found a list of editions of English Mysteries.

[4] It was at the annual festival at Wymondham that in 1549 Ket's rebellion
first broke out. See Froude's *History of England,* chap. xxvi.

border, firmly rooted at Chester. Thence it spread across the sea into the English Pale at Dublin, and along the Welsh boundary to Shrewsbury, Worcester and Tewkesbury, reappearing beyond that boundary under altogether distinct conditions in Cornwall [1]. In the heart of the Midlands, Coventry, where the first notice of plays exhibited by the companies is not earlier than 1416, was a well-known home of the religious drama, which was likewise familiar to Leicester in both the fifteenth and sixteenth centuries; while to the East in Cambridgeshire it was cherished both at Cambridge itself and at Bassingbourne. In Saxon England proper a taste for dramatic performances seems to have exerted itself more fitfully. Their occurrence is mentioned, as has been seen, in London; in Essex, Heybridge and Manningtree [2] are noted for per-

---

[1] In Cornwall miracle-plays were at an early date performed in the native Cymric dialect. Three of these have been edited and translated by Mr. Edwin Norris, under the title of *The Ancient Cornish Drama* (2 vols., Oxford, 1859). He states that the earliest MS. of these dramas is apparently of the fifteenth century, but that their language shows their origin to belong to a period earlier than the fourteenth. The three plays ostensibly constitute a connected trilogy of which the several plays are to be performed on successive days; but they are really four in number, viz. (1) the *Origo Mundi*, which in three divisions carries on the Old Testament story through some of its principal incidents from the Creation to the building of the Temple by Solomon, who consecrates a bishop to take care of it; there is added the episode of the martyrdom of Maximilla on refusing to abjure her belief in Christ. (2) The History of Christ from the Temptation to the Crucifixion; here there is no break in the action. (3) The Resurrection and the Ascension; but the action of this play is interrupted by that of (4) the Death of Pilate, which is quite detached from the rest. The whole ends with an antiphony of angels on the reception of the Son into Heaven by the Father, and an epilogue by 'the Emperor.' There is not much in these Cymric plays to distinguish them from the many plays on Scriptural themes in Latin, French, and English, and, indeed, occasional French words occur.—It may be added that we possess no notice of the actual performance of plays in Cornwall earlier than that occurring in Richard Carew's *Survey*, first printed in 1602. He mentions the Guary miracles, for the representation of which amphitheatres are, he says, raised in some open field. Two of these, of larger dimensions than those referred to by Carew, and popularly called *Rounds*, were described by Borlase in the middle of the eighteenth century; and one of these situate close to the principal inn in St. Just Church-town, not far from the Land's End, I remember visiting some sixteen years since.

[2] I am aware that the plays acted at Manningtree were morals, but as in his reference to them in his *Seven Deadly Sinnes of London* (1606, Arber's edition, p. 45) Dekker expressly states that they were acted by tradesmen,

formances, as also are Reading in Berkshire, Winchester in Hampshire and Canterbury and Bethersden in Kent[1].

Before calling attention to the most interesting features in such of the above-mentioned plays as have been preserved to us, I may premise one or two remarks as to the nomenclatures by which it has been sought to distinguish between them.

Their usual contemporary designation was *plays, miracle-plays* or *miracles*; the term *mysteries* not being employed in England[2]. Yet their character is essentially the same as that of the *mysteries* in France; nor is there any obvious distinction as to method of treatment to be drawn between the popular mysteries and the popular miracles in England, even if we choose to accord to them respectively the designations actually appropriate to their several subjects[3]. I perceive no proof of the theory that in England, as in France, the popular dramatic treatment of legendary preceded that of biblical subjects; nor am I struck by the suggestion of the *a priori* probability of such an order of sequence[4]. As the well-known example of the play of *Mary Magdalene*[5] shows, the species were

Names given to the religious plays.

they have been included in the above list. On the other hand, I have omitted performances at royal palaces. I have also omitted the production of the *Shipwright's Play* (which probably related to Noah's Flood) before Henry VII at Bristol, because it was in dumbshow.—Collier, ii. 67-8. According to a review of C. Penley, *The Bath Stage*, in the *Athenaeum*, November 19, 1892, miracle-plays were acted at Bath as early as the reign of Edward III in the church of St. Michael without the walls.

[1] The *Resurrection* at Witney in Oxfordshire seems to have been a puppet-play presented by priests. It contained the phrase 'Jack Snacker of Witney,' as applied to the watchman who, seeing our Lord rise from the grave, made a continual noise 'like to the sound that is made by the meeting of two sticks.' See Lambarde, *ap.* Warton, ii. 221.

[2] Chaucer's *Wife of Bath,* we may be sure, intended no nice distinction when mentioning 'playes of *miracles*' among the other social diversions or excitements which were open to her.

[3] In the *Household Book of Henry VII* they are on one occasion entered as '*marvels*,' evidently a synonym of *miracles*. Collier, ii. 53 *note.*— Although the term *mysteries* was not in popular use in England, it may be well to guard against any possible confusion (since these plays were performed by members of particular gilds or trades) by observing that the word has no connexion with its homonym *mystery* or mistery (Lat. *ministerium*, Fr. *métier*), signifying an art or trade.

[4] See ten Brinck, ii. 248-9.

[5] *Digby Mysteries.* Cf. Pollard, *Introduction*, xx.

freely intermingled within the framework of a single composition. These plays also contain elements of the *moralities*, and in one instance at least we meet among them with a morality proper, in accordance with the definition given above. But since the moralities, although their form was moulded by the example of the miracles, have an origin of their own, it will be preferable to treat of them separately.

The individual plays were usually called *pageants*,— a word spelt in every conceivable way, but indisputably derived from the Latin *pango* and Greek πήγνυμι (whence *pagina*, pegma = πῆγμα). It was no doubt originally applied to these plays in reference to the vehicles on which they were exhibited, but was afterwards used of stage-plays in general, even when regarded as books or literary compositions rather than as pieces actually put upon the stage [1].

Collective character of the chief English series.

In their origin many of the individual plays are doubtless founded on French models; others are taken directly from the text of Scripture, from the Apocryphal Gospels, and to some extent from the legends of the saints. But one of the most remarkable characteristics of the English religious plays, although by no means common to the whole body of them, is their combination into *collective series*, exhibiting the entire course of Bible history, from the Creation to the Day of Judgment. These collective series as such are essentially original national creations, not translations or even indirect copies of French or any other foreign works [2]. These were the series performed by the gilds, crafts, or trade-companies of most of the towns mentioned above at Corpus Christi, though some of them were likewise, or even exclusively, performed at other great Church festivals, such as Whitsuntide and Candlemas.

Method of their performance.

The method of performing these plays has been frequently described; nor is it part of my purpose to attempt another detailed exposition of it. The following brief statement, based chiefly, but not altogether, upon late accounts of

[1] Cf. as to the *Pageant of the Holy Trinity* (a bound and illuminated MS., *temp*. Hen. VI), Collier, i. 35; and see *ib*. 56.

[2] As to the relation between the French *Mystère du Vieil Testament* and the Chester plays see below; but this can in no case be held to contradict the general statement in the text.

the Chester series[1], must therefore suffice in the present place. It seems to have been usual in some towns for public proclamation to be made beforehand of the performance of these plays, and a document of this kind has been preserved dating from the early part of the fifteenth century, in which the Mayor of York impresses upon the crafts the duty of bringing forth 'ther pagantez in order and course by good players, well arayed and openly spekyng, vpon payn of lesyng of C.*s.* to be paide to the chambre without any pardon.' In the same proclamation he bids 'euery player that shall play be redy in his pagiaunt at convenyant tyme, that is to say, at the mydhowre betwix iiij[th] and v[th] of the cloke in the mornynge'; whereupon all the pageants are to follow on one another without delay, under a penalty of 6*s.* 8*d.* (an angel)[2]. Elsewhere, a special messenger made the round of the city some time before the actual date of the performances; at Chester, where the Whitsun performances were thus proclaimed as early as St. George's Day (April 23), this proceeding was called 'the readinge of the banes' (bans). It seems to have been distinct from a species of general prologue, spoken by a herald of one kind or another immediately before the performances themselves. Each series was divided into a number of 'pageants,' plays, or actions, according to the number of the companies between whom the performance as a whole had been distributed. At Woodkirk there were thirty-two, at York forty-eight, at Chester twenty-four, at Coventry forty-three. Thus the performance of the series occupied from three days (at Chester) to double that number, unless (as at Coventry) it was broken off in the middle and played in two parts in two successive years. The distribution of the individual plays among the companies seems in the first instance to have depended upon the 'properties' and 'business' required for the several plays. Who but the goldsmiths could furnish the Three

---

[1] By Archdeacon Rogers, who died in 1595, and who saw the Whitsun plays performed at Chester in the preceding year. See Wright, *Introd.* to *Chester Plays* (*Shakespeare Society's Publications*, xix–xx), and Sharp, *Dissertation on Coventry Mysteries*, 17–18.

[2] See Miss Toulmin Smith, *York Plays*, *Introd.* xxxiv.

Kings with the golden crowns marking their royal dignity ;
who but the shipwrights could build up Noah's ark[1]? Thus
then 'euery company brought forthe their pagiente, which
was the carriage or place which the played in' (i. e. on).
'And they first beganne at the Abbaye gates ; and when
the firste pagiente was played at the Abbaye gates, then it
was wheeled from thence to the pentice' (penthouse) 'at
the highe crosse before the Mayor; and before that was
donne, the seconde came, and the firste wente into the
Watergate streete, and from thence vnto the Bridge-streete,
and soe all, one after an other, till all the pagientes were
played appoynted for the firste daye, and so likewise for
the seconde and the thirde daye[2].' Thus in the course of
each day, as moveable scaffold after moveable scaffold
passed from station to station, the crowd gathered in the
different parts of the town had an opportunity of witnessing
the whole sequence of the series presented, and of critically
comparing the efforts of the tanners with those of the
plasterers, those of the hosiers with those of the spicers, and
so forth.   As for the actual arrangement of these moveable
stages, 'these pagientes or cariage was a highe place made
like a howse with ij rowmes, beinge open on the tope: in
the lower rowme they apparelled and dressed them selues;
and in the higher rowme they played : and they stoode
vpon 6 wheeles.' To this description it may be worth
adding, first, that the moveable stage at times was insufficient to meet the demands of the action, and at times the
street itself had to serve as a sort of supplementary scene.
Balaam, for instance, and the Three Magi, and Saul on his
journey to Damascus, had to appear mounted[3]; and as for
Herod, he 'ragis in the pagond and in the streete also[4].'
Again, when the action was of a more complicated nature,
two or more scaffolds seem to have been ranged side by
side of one another, the actors moving from scaffold to

---

[1] Ten Brinck, ii. 257-9.

[2] See a similar programme at York, *York Plays, Introd.* xxxii-iii.

[3] Thus we have the following stage-direction in the Conversion of Saul
(*Digby Mysteries*, Abbotsford Club ed., p. 37: 'Here Sale rydyth forth with
his seruant about the place owt of the pagond.'

[4] *The Shearmen and Taylors Pageant* at Coventry, *ap.* Sharp, p. 107.

scaffold as might be necessary.   This device, together with the simple expedient of writing the name of each locality over whatever rude pretence of scenery may have been painted or set up at the back of the stage, made it possible to execute dramatic movements of some complexity without their becoming unintelligible [1], and to carry on the double action necessitated by the plan of some of the plays [2]. Much, as a matter of course, was left to the imagination, and there is no proof that the English mystery-stage was, like that in France, regularly divided into three platforms with a dark cavern at the side of the lowest, appropriated respectively to the Heavenly Father and his angels, to saints and glorified men, to mere men, and to souls in hell. Hell-mouth, however, was an English as well as a French institution ; and much care seems to have been bestowed upon representing it with sufficient elaboration [3].   Demons with hideous heads issued from it [4], or flames burst forth in token of the fire within [5] ; but the introduction of 'yerthe-quakes' seems to belong to the degeneracy of the religious drama.   The costumes, as to which we have an abundance of details in the accounts of the gilds, no doubt varied according to the liberality as well as according to the tastes of the several trades, and we may be sure there was no lack of glitter or colour.   In part the dress or attributes were con-ventional.   Divine and saintly personages were distinguished by gilt hair and beards [6].   Herod, as he swore ' by Mahownde.' was also dressed as a Saracen ; Judas had a red hair and beard ; the demons wore hideous heads and long tails [7] ; the

---

[1] E. g. in the Coventry *Trial of Christ* (*Ludus Coventriae*, p. 303) : ' Here thei take Jhesu and lede hym in gret hast to Herowde ; and then Herowdys scafald xal unclose, shewing Herowde in a stat [on a throne], alle the Jewys knelyng, except Annas and Cayaphas.'

[2] E. g. of the York play of *The Dream of Pilate's Wife and Jesus before Pilate*.   Cf. *Introduction* to *York Plays*, liv.

[3] See the startling illustrations *ap*. Sharp, pp. 61 *seqq*.

[4] In the *Transfiguration* in the *York Plays* Elias is brought from paradise and Moses from hell.

[5] ' It^m,' says an entry relating to the *Drapers' Pageant* at Coventry, ' payd for kepying of fyer at hell mothe . . . iiij*d*.'   Sharp, p. 73.

[6] See the Coventry *banes* mentioned above, where gilt is described as a sufficient ' disfigurement,' i. e. disguise, for the purpose.

[7] Hodge, in *Gammer Gurton's Needle*, gives a very distinct description of

souls were clad in white or black coats according to their kind, and the angels shone in gold skins and wings. Customary tricks of manner added their aid; the devil never entered upon the stage without bustle, fuss, and violent language ; while alliteration more impartially emphasised the fury of Herod, the enthusiasm of the Magi, and the solemnity of the Saviour on His liberating descent into hell.

The spectators of the miracle-plays.

Many further details of this description have been collected by Mr. Sharp and other authorities, together with much interesting matter as to the system by which provision was made for the considerable expenditure involved in the production of these plays. But it may perhaps be advisable, where no enquiry of a specialistic kind is in question, to refrain from dwelling too much upon these external points, and thereby indulging the sense of the grotesque at the risk of overlooking more important features common to all these compositions. No doubt the surroundings amidst which they were produced cannot, and should not, be dissociated from them. For these surroundings go some way to account for what has struck other generations as incongruous or odd. The visible symbols of their religious creed, the personalities or the supposed personalities of its most sacred figures, marked with every detail of attribute as long conventionally established,—all this was as familiar to the eyes of the mediaeval population as the diction and cadence of the Bible text afterwards became to their puritanised successors. When at the corner of every street men were accustomed to see a sculpture in stone or wood representing the Passion, or the Mourning Mother of the Saviour, or the Saint of the Keys, or the Saint of the Wheel,—when in every church coloured frescoes brought before them the familiar figures and scenes,—when in every procession banners waved with dazzling reproductions of the same types,—men interlarded their common speech with reminiscences of the sights to

the devil, as he appeared in these plays. Cf. Sharp, p. 58. One of the stage-directions in Skelton's *Nigromansir* (1515 c.) is, 'Enter Balsebub with a berde,' appendages of this kind being attached, conveniently for stage-use, to a vizard.

which their eyes were habituated, and appealed without a thought of irreverence to Mary and Paul, and to the bones and the wounds, and the instruments of the Passion, of the Saviour Himself. Thus the attitude of the spectators towards the miracle-plays, of the action, moved entirely round these figures and conceptions, was in a word the *naïf*, which is the direct opposite of that which many modern witnesses have (in their case quite as naturally) assumed towards them [1].

Their literary features. The writers of these plays (whether or not, as may usually have been the case, their training as clerks raised them above their public) could not for a moment mistake the audiences for whom they wrote. This by no means implies an utter absence from this body of literary remains of the graces and charms of composition; as a whole their literary talent may be said to surpass their dramaturgic skill, although even of this evidence is by no means wanting. But these graces and charms—except perhaps in some of the lyrical passages, where we cannot be wrong in perceiving something like an attempt at elaboration [2]—may fairly be described as the result of accident. Frequently, no doubt, the simple and direct handling of such themes, and the use of language always clear and vigorous, and thus often recalling or resembling that of our own Authorised Version, creates efforts which in their way nothing could surpass; at times (especially, I think, in the earlier collections) we seem to recognise the unmistakeable ease of priests and monks dealing with religious subjects which have become part of their daily life as well as of their highest thoughts; and yet at other times, as is the case even with the dullest writers into whose hands such materials fall, the cry of nature reaches

[1] 'It is very difficult for me,' wrote the late Mr. Charles Lowder from Oberammergau, 'to write just after coming from the Passion Play; for it is like coming out of a Retreat, with one's feelings worked up to the very highest pitch, and so very difficult to return to one's ordinary state.'

[2] I refer to the text only, not to what has been preserved or discovered of the music. The songs belonging to the *Shearmen's and Taylors' Pageant* (*The Shepherds and the Three Kings*) are printed with their music *ap*. Sharp, 113 *seqq*. One has the burden 'lully lullay.' As to the reminiscences of old church music preserved in connexion with the York plays, see the notes of Mr. W. H. Cummings and Miss L. Toulmin Smith, *York Plays*, pp. 523-7.

from heart to heart.   On the other hand the familiarity of treatment, springing from the *naviete* of sentiment already referred to, expresses itself most strikingly in the considerable comic element which these plays contain.   It certainly would not have occurred either to authors or audience that the former were dishonouring the sacred narrative by patching it with rude lappets of their own invention; or that a bit of buffoonery introduced into a religious play implied irreverence towards its holy theme, any more than a grotesque head disfigured the column in a church of which it diversified the ornamentation.   Of course the historic sense—the sense of what is correct—was as completely wanting in these plays as a sense of what was fitting; but the anachronisms of the Middle Ages do not puzzle us as much as their improprieties, more especially as the jester in these plays as elsewhere thrusts himself forward with loud laugh or protruded tongue, often at the most critical points in the action.   So far as there is herein anything incomprehensible, it may be worth remembering that Greek, and more especially Roman, paganism seems to have shared this way of feeling with mediaeval Christendom; for it was often on the greatest festivals of the greatest among the deities of classical heathendom that vulgar licence was allowed to run riot.   To sum up the chief interest of these plays, as has been well said, was in England, as it was in Germany, tragic [1].   This was in accordance with the temperament of our nation, and with the general character of its literature, while untouched by other national influence. But although the gaiety of France, which is the gaiety of Chaucer, had not yet permeated the population of England as a whole, the grossness of many passages in these plays is manifestly of indigenous origin, and points to the slow progress of aesthetic culture rather than to an absence of moral sentiment.

Collective Mysteries.   It seems most convenient to treat of the extant cycles of English *Collective Mysteries*, as they have been appropriately termed, before speaking of a few isolated plays, some of which may in date possibly be anterior to any of the series preserved to us.   In the form in which these cycles—four in

---

[1] By Henry Morley, *English Writers, &c.,* i. 355.

number—have actually come into our hands two of them appear to belong to the fourteenth, and the other two to the fifteenth and the sixteenth century, respectively. I proceed to say a few words concerning each, in their probable chronological order.

The *York Plays*[1] are not actually mentioned before the   *York Plays.* year 1378, but the references to them in this and subsequent years imply that they had been in progress for some considerable time before, and there cannot be much doubt but that they were written about 1340–50, if not even rather earlier. They exhibit a closer parallel than any of the other cycles to a very notable poem, which in epic form had not more than a generation earlier set an example which was of unmistakeable influence upon the Collective Mysteries, and the phase of the English religious drama to which they belong. The *Cursor Mundi* (*Cursur o Werld*) survives in many MSS., for it was a very popular work in various parts of the country—

'The best book of all,'

according to a rubric in one of the MSS.—but its origin was in Northumbria, and its conception of treating the sacred history of the world in its entire course was congenial to the soil from which it sprang. Although undertaken with the definite purpose of rendering honour to the Virgin Mary, with a glorification of whose miraculous conception it ends, its plan is as comprehensive as that of the Collective Mysteries which followed in its wake, and like them it is built up not from the Scriptural narrative alone, but also from the Apocryphal Gospels and a number of legends of later growth. Its treatment of its subjects distinctly points in the direction of the drama, being full of terse and lively dialogue[2].

---

[1] *York Plays, &c.*, edited with Introduction and Glossary by Lucy Toulmin Smith, 1885—a contribution of the highest value to the study of the English religious drama.

[2] See e. g. the legend of Seth and Adam (which is reprinted in Morris' well-known *Specimens of Early English*, and which seems to have been reproduced in one of the Beverley plays (non-extant), which were doubtless connected with the York cycle. As to the relations between the *Cursor Mundi* and the Mysteries see ten Brinck, i. 360.

To the *Cursor Mundi* the *York Plays*, as observed, are more closely parallel than any other of the extant collections ; and the York cycle is comparatively free from the tendency to jocularity and vulgarity which becomes already very perceptible in the *Towneley Plays*, beyond all reasonable doubt the next oldest of our cycles.   In any case it is certain that either the *Towneley Plays* were indebted to the *York* for the substance of five of each series, or *vice versâ* ; and since, though both series are written in the Northumbrian dialect, the *Towneley* collection appears in part at least to have been put together from other sources, whereas the *York* plays as a whole exhibit a nearer approach to unity of manner, there can be little hesitation as to crediting them with the higher antiquity.

York, says Miss Toulmin Smith, 'was from the fourteenth to the sixteenth century a play-loving city,'—and indeed it has enjoyed the same reputation in times nearer to our own.   To the *Paternoster* and *Creed* plays, which were performed at the cost of gilds established in the city for the purpose, some reference will be made below ; moreover, York, like other towns, had at Midsummer a play of *St. George*, with a procession appertaining to it.   But its chief dramatic glory is to be found in the Corpus Christi plays, performed by the crafts under conditions carefully supervised by Mayor and Corporation, and after about half a century of popularity famous enough to be honoured (in 1394) by the presence of King Richard II.   The distribution of the plays among the several crafts must have varied according to the fluctuations of trade ; hence the statements on this head of the extant MS. of the plays, which seems to belong to the period from 1430 to 1440, do not altogether tally with a list of plays performed and crafts performing drawn up by a town-clerk of York in the year 1415.

The author of the plays, the bulk of which may, as already observed, be fairly concluded to have been the work of a single hand, was in all probability a monk of Northern training, if not of Northern birth.   He may be supposed to have been familiar with the religious poetry of his own part of England, and likewise, as the variety and grace of his metrification seems to show, with French verse or native verse of a Southern origin. He had, however, a genuine Northern love of alliteration, which he uses copiously, and even in combination with a tolerably complicated stanza-form [1]. His sources were in the first instance the Old and the New Testament, but the former in a very much smaller proportion than the latter. Of the very first of the Old Testament plays, *The Creation, and the Fall of Lucifer*, the portion indicated in the latter half of the title is taken from legend, not from Scripture [2]; while in the New Testament plays, which are linked to their predecessors by a series of prophecies recited by a Prologue as introductory to the play of the *Annunciation*, use is made of the *Apocryphal Gospels of James* and of *Nicodemus*, and of legendary sources which still await complete identification [3]. What the author adds of his own consists in the main of homely figures, names and illustrations, together with a tendency, creditable to his dramatic instinct, to draw out to some length scenes and episodes such as naturally lend themselves to effective treatment. Yet he rarely becomes tedious, and is as a rule free from inclination towards the rough fun which becomes so prominent in some of the later cycles [4].

The story of the *Creation* with which the series of the *York Plays* opens, is divided into two plays—of which the first brings the audience face to face with the majesty of the Creator, and exhibits the angels singing their ' Holy, Holy, Holy!' before His throne. But among them appear the

---

[1] See the ornate stanzas sung by eight burgesses in welcome of the Lord on His *Entry into Jerusalem on an Ass*; pp. 216-8.

[2] Whether the legend belongs in its origin to the fourth or to the fifth century must here be left an open question.

[3] Such is the case, as Miss Toulmin Smith points out, with the incident, alike poetically beautiful and dramatically effective, of the brilliant light shining round Jesus which amazes the soldiers seeking Him in the garden of Gethsemane (*The Agony and the Betrayal*, p. 251), which by the way has its counterpart in the light perceived by Joseph in the stable at Bethlehem at the moment of the Saviour's birth (p. 114) ; and again with the blossoming of Joseph's rod in the Temple, whereby as by a sign he was led to take Mary to wife (*Joseph's Trouble about Mary*, p. 103). It would not be difficult to supply analogies to the notion of the light from secular poetry and legend.

[4] See, for instance, *The Angels and the Shepherds.*

' *angeli deficientes*,' whose spokesman, Lucifer, after exulting
in his pride [1], falls down into hell, whence he speedily sends
forth his complaints, beginning with the familiar ' Owte
owte! harrowe!' The story of Adam and Eve, and of
their Fall, occupies the next four plays, of which the last,
with Adam's fluent and not unmusical lamentation over his
doom [2], may be specially noticed. Neither the *Sacrificium
Cayme and Abell* nor *Noah and his Wife* has the force or
the raciness which respectively characterise later versions of
these themes; but in the former there unluckily occurs a gap
at the height of the action [3]. Noah's wife already presents
herself as the popular type of the burden which, when on the
eve of action, a man is apt to find in a wife with a will of
her own [4]; but what is farcical in the situation—her determination not to be saved, because she had no due notice,
and her refusal to let Noah ' go qwitte' by an appeal to
God's declaration of His will—is not overdone, and the
' incident' itself is not unduly protracted. The latter part
of the play (which, by the way, was performed by the
Mariners and Fishers)—the life in the ark, as the waters
wane, and the skies clear, and after the visit of the dove
the patriarch sees

> ' here certaynely
> The hillis of hermonye [5],'—

strikes me as picturesquely conceived; it ends with a cheerful summons to work such as a pilgrim father might have

---

[1]   ' O! what I am fetys and fayre and figured full fytt,' &c.

[2]   ' *Eve.* Be stille, Adam, and nemen it na mare;
>   It may not mende.'

[3] Brewbarret, Cain's servant, who brings corn for the altar, is a later
addition; but his arrival seems out of place as the text stands, unless Cain's
behaviour to him is intended to illustrate the devil-me-care mood which
may follow upon crime.

> ' *Cayme.* Come vp! sir knaue! . . .
> *Brewb.* O! maister Cayme, I haue broken my to!
> *Cayme.* Come vp, syr, for by my thryst,
>   Ye shall drynke or ye goo.'

[4] The episode was an inexhaustible source of fun to the Middle Ages.
Chaucer alludes in *The Milleres Tale* to

> ' The sorwe of Noe with his felawship,
> Or that he might get his wif to ship.'

[5] Armenia.

addressed to his family on the shores of the New World[1]. In the *Sacrifice of Abraham and Isaac* the tragic effects seem subjected to a certain restraint like the comic in the instances referred to ; and it may need something of an effort to picture to ourselves an Isaac of thirty years ' and a good bit more.' But the notion lends force to the central idea of the play, when the strong man is found urging his aged father to bind him for the sacrifice[2].

Of the plays concerned with the New Testament narrative and early Christian narrative several, as already observed, are in substance common to the York and to the Towneley cycles. Although in these instances the *York Plays* may have been the originals, yet of the cycle in general in its relation to its successors, we may fairly assume that in its progress from edition to edition—or from performance to performance—it frequently borrowed enlargements and improvements in its turn. But the author remains true to his own peculiarities of treatment or interest. Joseph is a character for whom he exhibits a special tenderness, and whom he treats, although from a wholly human point of view, with a degree of respect not always vouchsafed to this saint in the religious drama. The Shepherds' worship of the Babe, and their primitive gifts,—

> ' A baren broche by a belle of tynne
> At youre bosome to be,'

two cob-nuts on a ribbon, and a horn spoon that will harbour forty pease—furnish an innocent little idyll. In some of the

---

[1]   ' Sones, with youre wiffes ye salle be stedde,
And multyplye your seede salle ye.
Youre barnes sall ilkon othir wedde,
And worshippe god in gud degre ;
Beestes and foules sall forthe be bredde,
And so a world be-gynne to bee.
Nowe travaylle sall ye taste
    To wynne you bred and wyne,
For alle this worlde is waste ;
These beestes muste be unbraste,
And wende we hense in haste
    In goddis blyssing and myne.'

[2]   ' For ye are alde and all vnwelde,
And I am wighte and wilde of thoghte.'

later plays the author shows a more vigorous vein of dramatic inventiveness. In the *Woman taken in Adultery*, which forms a kind of proemium to the *Raising of Lazarus*, the clamorousness of the lawyers contrasts effectively with the calm of the Saviour; and the effect of His triumphant ride into Jerusalem is effectively enhanced by the introduction of the Blind Man and the Lame Man, following as suppliants in the track of His progress. In the treatment of the episode of Pilate's wife and her dream the author gives more rein than usual to his fancy; his notion of 'Dame Percula' seems to have been that of a fashionable beauty, without whom the grandeur of Pilate, the son of 'Sesar' and of Pila the daughter of Atus, would have lacked completeness. After drinking together, both Pilate and Percula go to sleep, and (this is a curious touch) the Devil whispers into her ear the dream which moves her to try to arrest the doom of Jesus whereby the world is to be redeemed. The incidents of the Passion are represented at considerable length; and in the actual process of the crucifixion or nailing to the cross there is a calculated realism of which it is easy enough to picture to oneself the effectiveness. In the latter part of the series are included three plays, the *Death of Mary*, the *Appearance of our Lady to Thomas*, and the *Assumption and Coronation of the Virgin*, alike taken from the apocryphal legend known under the name of *Transitus Mariae*; but the last play of all, *The Judgment Day*, rounds off the cycle, as in the *Towneley Plays*, by bringing back the whole of the action, as it were, into the hollow of the hand of God [1].

Of the *Beverley* Corpus Christi plays, the notices of which cover a period of nearly two centuries from the year 1407 onwards, no texts remain to us; there can, however, be no doubt as to their intimate connexion with the York cycle. Of the *Newcastle-on-Tyne* Corpus Christi plays, first men-

---

[1] *The Coronation of our Lady* is a fragment added to the MS. in another hand, conjectured by Miss Toulmin Smith to be of the end of the fifteenth century. The Son's apostrophe of the Father as
'fulgent Phœbus and fader eternall'
apprises us that we are here in the Renascence age. Cf. ten Brinck, ii. 300.

tioned in 1426, on the other hand, a single one has been
preserved of which some account will be given below.
We pass at once to the second collective series which has   *Towneley*
been preserved to us—the *Towneley Plays*, or *Mysteries*,   *Plays.*
as it has been usual to designate them [1]. Although the
MS. in which they are preserved is not held to have an
earlier date than the beginning of the fifteenth century, they
were in all likelihood of earlier origin. But the considerations advanced above [2] render it very unlikely that they
were put together before the middle of the fourteenth century; nor can a passing allusion to costume [3], which has
been thought to warrant dating them from an even earlier
age than the fourteenth century, be looked upon in the light
of serious evidence. The supposition of Douce, that these
plays were composed so late as the reign of Henry VI
or Edward IV, seems to have been formed on general
grounds. I have already referred to the probability that
their sources were composite, and that they were largely
indebted to the *York Plays* in especial. The curious circumstance, that in the *Magnus Herodes* King Herod ends
by saying that he ' can no more Franche ' (he has previously
used a French phrase : ' *Yei ditizance doutance,*' i. e. *j'ai dit
sans doutance*), might be supposed to point to a French origin
of this particular play ; it is more likely, however, that
Herod, like Octavian in one of the *Chester Plays (vide infra)*,
talks French in order to indicate his royal station, in which
case the origin of this particular play can hardly be dated
later than the fourteenth century [4].

The *Towneley Plays* take their name from the circumstance that the MS. in which they have been preserved
formed part of the library of Towneley Hall in Lancashire.
According to what appears to have been a tradition in the

---

[1] *The Towneley Mysteries*, printed for the Surtees Society, 1836. The
editors are not named, but are understood to have been Dr. James Raine
and Mr. James Gordon. A good Glossary, attributed to the latter, accompanies the plays, which are preceded by a brief Introduction, but unfortunately unaccompanied by notes.

[2] *Ante*, p. 66.

[3] The 'hornyd headdress' of the lady referred to in the *Juditium.*

[4] See also below as to the French of the Nuncius in the Coventry
Shearmen and Taylors' Pageant.

Towneley family, the volume had formerly belonged to the
'Abbey of Wildkirk near Wakefield.' Although no such
Abbey, nor so far as is known any place of the name ever
existed near Wakefield, there is in that neighbourhood
a place called Widkirk or Woodkirk [1], where the Austin
Friars had a cell, in dependence on the great house of
St. Oswald at Nostel. Fairs were kept up at Widkirk
from an early date to the time of the Reformation; and
as the local allusions in the plays are plentiful, they may be
presumed to have been performed at the fairs in question.
'Merry' Wakefield, four miles from Widkirk, must have
been a town very conservative of old customs [2]; and that
these plays were acted by the Wakefield gilds is clear
from the words 'Wakefelde Barkers,' 'Glover Pageant,'
'Fysher Pageant,' inserted at the commencement of three
among their number. The last two of the plays, which
out of the chronological order of the series form part of
the MS. in which it is preserved [3], seem later in origin
than the rest; and in the *Johannes Baptista* a passage in
honour of the Seven Sacraments is crossed through and
marked, doubtless by a hand belonging to the times of the
Reformation, as 'correctyd and not played.'

In general, there is no reason to doubt that the composition or compilation of the *Towneley Plays* is due to the
friars of Widkirk or Nostel. The ecclesiastical learning
shown is, however, by no means ostentatiously introduced;
the plays have an essentially popular character, and were
unmistakeably written for the delectation of the multitude.
Hence they are written in the dialect of the district where
they were acted, and contain so endless a number of dialect
words and forms—many of them undoubtedly of Scandinavian origin—so that, like the *York Plays*, they are by
no means easy reading. This is matter for regret; for it
seems to me that, while less self-restrained than the *York*

---

[1] 'Widkirk' is the older and more correct spelling. See Prof. Skeat's
letter to the *Athenaeum*, December 2, 1893.

[2] Cf., as to one of these, Greene's *George-a-Greene, the Pinner of Wakefield*
(*infra*).

[3] *Lazarus* and *Suspentio Judae*. The former is largely, and the latter
altogether, in monologue.

series, they are far superior to the *Coventry*, and even more enjoyable than the *Chester*, plays. Their dramatic vivacity, and in many parts their original humour, are to my mind very striking.

They are thirty-two in number, beginning with the *Creatio* and ending (apart from the two later additions) with the *Juditium*, i. e. Doomsday. Of the play of the *Shepherds*, which by reason of its homely characters and action and local allusions could not fail to be a favourite, there are two independent versions. But the object of the writers of these plays was manifestly to amuse and interest as well as to edify; and the literary composition, though of course rude, is at times anything but contemptible. How effectively clear and concise e. g. is the narrative of St. Joseph in the *Annunciacio*; how conversationally easy, yet dignified, is the beginning of the dialogue between the Blessed Virgin and St. Elisabeth in the *Salutacio Elisabeth*; and how adequate in diction are the opening reflexions on the uncertainty of human life in the *Prima Pastorum*: 'Lord, what thay ar weylle that hens ar past,' &c.! At the same time, a striking feature in these plays is undoubtedly the familiar and frequently comic treatment of sacred story with which they abound. Thus in the *Mactacio Abel* much farcical entertainment is furnished by Cain's boy or *garcio*, whom we have already met with in the *York Plays*, and whom here his master, in order to shut his mouth, after addressing him by the name of *Pike-harnes* (i. e. one who cannot keep his hands from picking and stealing the implements of labour[1]), in vain proposes to manumit from serfdom. Cain's dispute with Abel, his defiance of God, and his mock proclamation of peace after his deed of blood, are, I regret to say, likewise in a vein calculated to move the laughter of the spectators.

In the *Processus Noe cum Filiis*[2], which follows, Noah begins with a kind of summary of the previous history of the world, and is then bidden by *Deus* to build the ark. He sets to work with great lamentations over the stiffness

---

[1] I am told, however, that in Scotland '*pike-harnes*' signifies a kind of crow that picks out the brains of sheep.

[2] As to the significance of the term *processus* vide *ante*, p. 44.

of his 'bak' and the starkness of his 'bonys'; and when
the ark is built he has the greatest possible difficulty in
inducing his wife to enter.   In their quarrel, both Noah and
his wife appeal to the sympathy of husbands or wives in the
audience, and finally she is only brought to reason by being
'bet blo.' The *Abraham* represents with effective vivacity, and
some genuine feeling, the sacrifice of Isaac, who here clings
desperately to life.   The two plays which follow under the
respective titles of *Isaac* and *Jacob* have been thought to
admit of being separated from the rest of the cycle as an
independent Northumbrian play *Jacob and Esau* of earlier
origin [1].   It is not till the *Processus Prophetarum* that action
is exchanged for recitation ; Moses recites the commandments (ending with—

> 'My name is callyd Moyses,
> And have now alle good day') ;

he is followed by David, and *Sibilla propheta*.   The
figure of the Sibyl is familiar to the mysteries [2] ; but
here, after two Latin hexameters (not from Vergil), she
merely recites a general Messianic prophecy.   The *Pharao*,
again, is full of action ; the Egyptian king swearing by
'Mahowne,' like Caesar Augustus in the   next pageant,
where he is found instituting the universal payment of a
poll-tax in order to discover the Child, Whose approaching birth and royal destiny have been announced to him.
With the *Annunciacio* commences the series of New Testament plays.   Of these, the two *Shepherds' Plays* are in
the main comic pieces, especially the former of the pair,
where the supper and drinking-bout of the shepherds are
represented at great length.   In the latter, a 'play within
the play'—a 'merry tale' of the sheep-stealer Mak—is

---

[1] See ten Brinck, ii. 253-4, and *Appendix*, p. 626.

[2] The Christian Apologists took over from their pagan contemporaries
the habit of appealing to the so-called 'oracles of the Sibyl'; and the *Missa
pro Fidelibus Defunctis* cited her testimony with that of David, whence the
well-known line in the *Dies Irae*:

> '*Teste David cum Sibyllâ.*'

See *Edinburgh Review*, July, 1877. A representation of her may be seen at
this day on the walls of the *Salle du Consistoire* in the Papal Palace at
Avignon, alongside of the other 'Prophets.'

introduced. Historians will find in these passages interesting illustrations of the contemporary manners and customs, the food, and the language of the labouring classes, which lie beyond my subject ; and will condone the odd anachronism of the invocation addressed by one of the shepherds, as he falls asleep before the appearance of the Angel, to

> ' Jesus o' Nazorus,
> Crucyefixus,
> Marcus, Andreas.'

The low humour—and it is very low—of these two plays doubtless constituted their special attraction for their audience [1]; the charming *naïveté* of the shepherds' worship of the Divine Babe, to whom they offer simple gifts—a ball, a bird, a ' bob of cherrys '—and whom they address in touchingly tender terms of endearment, may have been suggested by the corresponding *York* play.   The remaining *Towneley* plays, in particular those concerned with the incidents of the Passion, are of course serious in tone ; but a strong desire is manifest throughout to diversify the action by the introduction of minor characters—see e. g. the *Tortores* in the *Coliphizatio* (i. e. Buffeting), in the *Crucifixio*, and in the curious *Processus Talentorum*, which treats of Pilate's decision as to the garments of the Saviour.   This play is opened by Pilate with a macaronic speech, half in Latin rimes, and closes with a moral reflexion on the part of one of the *Tortores* on the vanity of ' dysyng,' and with their dismissal by Pilate with ' Mahowne's ' blessing.   The next play is the *Extractio Animarum ab Inferno*, or the saving of the souls of the just (Adam and Eve, Isaias, John the Baptist, &c.) from limbo,—the familiar topic of so much mediaeval poetry [2]. ' Belzabub ' and ' Rybald ' appear in this play as the counsellors of ' Sir Sathanas ' ; on the whole, however, the Devil appears unfrequently in the *Towneley*

---

[1] The following ' advice to people about to marry ' occurs in the *Secunda Pastorum* :—

> ' Bot yong men of wowyng, for God that you boght,
> Be welle war of wedyng, and thynk in youre thought
> " Had I wyst " is a thing it servys of noght.'

[2] See below as to *The Harrowing of Hell.*

Plays. The *Resurrectio,* the *Peregrini* (the journey to
Emmaus), the *Thomas Indiae* (the unbelief of Thomas),
the *Ascencio Domini,* and the *Juditium*[1], close the series
proper of this Collective Mystery.

Of the *Chester Plays*[2], preserved to us in four MSS.
varying in date between the years 1597 and 1607, it seems
unsafe to carry the origin further back than the earlier part
of the fifteenth or the end of the fourteenth century, though
tradition has assigned to them a much earlier date, attributing their composition to the period of the mayoralty of
John Arneway (1268–1276), and to the authorship of ' one
done Randle' (Randall Higgenett), a monk of Chester
Abbey. To what extent some of them were indebted to
French originals remains doubtful; not only, however,
have several remarkable coincidences been pointed out
by both Collier and Wright between the Chester Plays
and French Mysteries, in particular the *Mystère du Vieil
Testament*[3]; but a more systematic enquiry seems to make

---

[1] In the *Juditium* the most loquacious of the devils, *Tutivillus,* says that
he is now ' master Lollar.' Collier, ii. 146, points out that this establishes
'that the writer was an enemy of Wickliffe's heresy, and probably an ecclesiastic,' but the date of the composition of this play is not determinable by
the passage.

[2] *The Chester Plays,* edited by Thomas Wright (2 vols. *Shaksp. Soc.*
1843 and 1847). The first thirteen of the plays were re-edited from the 1607
text, which both he and Mr. Pollard consider the best, by the late Dr. H.
Deimling for the *Early English Text Society,* (*Extra Series, LXII,* 1892).

[3] See Dr. H. Ungemach's exhaustive research, *Die Quellen der fünf ersten
Chester Plays* (Erlangen und Leipzig, 1890).—The curious circumstance
that the Emperor Octavian (in the play of *The Salutation and Nativity*)
makes a French speech, is regarded by Mr. Wright as ' only a picture of the
age when French was the language of courtiers in the English Court.'
(Pilate, too, introduces himself with a few lines of French both in *The
Passion* and in *The Resurrection.*) Now, French had ceased to be the
language of the English Court by the reign of Richard II, to whom
Gower dedicated the first edition of his English poem, and to whose queen
Chaucer contingently offered his *Legende of Good Women.* Under the Lan-
casters (Chaucer certainly wrote for John of Gaunt, although the *Assemblie
of Foules* may not have referred to his wedding) French had beyond a doubt
vanished from the English Court; and Shakspere was quite justified in
assuming the victorious Henry V to have been the reverse of well-seen in it.
The transition period, marked by the works of Gower, was the reign of
Edward III, in which therefore this particular play might hence be concluded to have been, at the latest, composed.—In the dramatic literature
of India, Sanscrit is the language of gods and holy personages; Pràcrit of

it probable that the author or authors of the *Chester Plays*
on Old Testament subjects were likewise acquainted with
earlier, non-collective French mysteries. In the main the
plays follow the narrative of Scripture ; but there are
passages and episodes taken from legend, and at least one
from an apocryphal Gospel. In this series also many
resemblances have been found to the *Cursor Mundi*[1].

These plays were acted at Whitsuntide, and, consisting of
twenty-five, occupied three days in the performance. It
was preceded by banes (i. e. bans or proclamations), forming
a species of prologue. In the banes preserved to us from
the year 1600, an apology is made for the rudeness of the
plays, as dating from ' the tyme of ignorance, wherein we
did straye' ; and the subjects of the several plays, with the
names of the gilds or companies of tradesmen and handicraftsmen to whom they were severally allotted, are enumerated. Among these the Drapers as a ' wealthy Com-
panye' are bidden, ' according to their wealth,' to ' set out
wealthilye' the Creation of the World, while ' the good
symple' ' water-leaders and drawers of Deey' are charged
with the performance of the story of ' Noy.'

The *Chester Plays* are unequal in merit, but in very few
instances is there to be traced in them any attempt to supplement by pathos or humour in the language the force of
the situations represented. They are altogether less popular
in character than those of the two cycles previously described,
and in several of the plays an ' Expositor' or ' Doctor'
deliberately ' moralises' the action. *The Fall of Lucifer*,
which commences the series, although very simple and
straightforward in its exposition—no mistake is allowed to
remain as to the fact that pride and pride alone is the cause
of Lucifer's fall—is by no means ineffective, and connects
itself in a natural way with its successor. *The Creation and
Fall, and Death of Abel* consists of two plays in one ; first,
the Creation is very dryly narrated by the Creator ; where-

women and genii ; but this distinction is more analogous to that familiar to
the modern drama, where elevated persons so often use blank verse, while
their inferiors talk in prose.
   [1] Cf. *ante*, p. 65.

upon Lucifer appears and assumes the form of the serpent
or 'edder' in order to tempt Eve. He chooses a method
of temptation to which he thinks she must succumb, for, as
he states with singular prescience—

> ' — wemen the be full licoris,
> That will she not forsake.'

After the fall, the action is rapidly carried on over thirty
years ; and the sacrifice of the brothers Cain and Abel and
the murder of Abel are represented.   Cain, after being
reproved by Deus, wanders forth, taking leave of his 'mame
and dadd.'   The lament of Eve pathetically closes the play.
In *Noah's Flood* there is more originality of execution.
God orders Noah to build the ark ; and ' Sem,' ' Cam,' and
' Jaffette,' with their wives, set to work in tradesmanlike
fashion with axe, 'hacchatt,' and 'hamer,' till the ark is
built, and caulked and 'pyched' to boot.   Then ensues, as in
the corresponding Towneley play, the difficulty of inducing
Noah's wife to enter the ark.   Though adjured in the name
of 'Sante John,' and subsequently admonished in less civil
fashion, she long bides outside, even after the ark has been
filled with birds and beasts (they are, according to the stage-
direction, to be ' painted on the borde,' and are enumerated
at length in the text [1]), among her 'gossippes,' who recklessly drink a ' pottill full of Malmsine good and stronge,'
and sing a song before they take their departure.   At last,
however, her sons induce her to enter ; and the saving of
Noah and his household is accomplished.

  The Histories of Lot and Abraham is a far more didactic
piece ; and the ' Expositor ' (who seems to have attended on
horseback) explains the application of the events to the New
Testament.   Abraham's sacrifice of Isaac is, with the aid it
cannot be doubted of both a native and a French predecessor,
carefully elaborated, and, to my mind, the language here rises

---

[1] Such enumerations of animals seem to have pleased the Middle Ages. The
' Bestiaries' were favourite vehicles of moral teaching. (See below.)   Readers
of Chaucer will remember his list of birds in the *Assemblie of Foules*. Spenser
imitated this enumerative tendency of Chaucer ; see his list of trees in Bk. i.
of the *Faëry Queene*.   Chaucer's observation of birds calls to mind Dante (see
Church's *Essay on Dante*).

to pathos [1]. *Balaam and his Ass*, in which a ' Doctor ' helps the action on by narrative, must have been a favourite play ; the speaker of the banes evidently looked forward to it with particular relish. King Balacke, who appears *equitando*, calls on ' mightie Marse ' against Israel ; and then orders a soldier to summon Balaam. Permitted to make the journey, Balaam sets forth—but, ' what the devill ! my asse will not goe '; he beats her (' *et nota quod hic oportet aliquis trans-formari in speciem asine* '), and ' she speaketh.' After Balaam has blessed Israel and converted the king, the ' Doctor ' concludes with more narrative, supplying a transition to the next play, which opens the series of New Testament subjects.

In the *Salutation and Nativity* it is only necessary to note the introduction of the characters of the Emperor Octavian and the Sibyl, and of her prophecy of the birth of Christ. This play contains a large admixture of legends, including the two midwives called in by Joseph ' for usage here of this cittie,' but only to behold a Birth without pain [2], that of Salome's incredulity and punishment, and that of the falling down of idols at Rome in the hour of the Nativity, which latter legend is narrated by an expositor. The *Play of the Shepherds*, which succeeds, is in its earlier and longer portion purely comic and exceedingly coarse. The drinking-bout and quarrels of the shepherds are seasoned with homely English allusions ; and even the appearance of the star and the song of the Angels fail to subdue the animal spirits of Trowle. But the latter portion, the visit of the shepherds to Bethlehem, and the offerings made by themselves and their boys to the Divine Babe, is managed with much simple effectiveness ; and Trowle in the end has recourse to an *ancker* (anchorite), while one of the shepherds becomes a pilgrim for the rest of his days.

---

[1] See the instructive parallel *ap.* Ungemach, *u. s.*, pp. 135 *seqq.* The relation between the Chester and the East-Anglian (Browne MS.) play (as to which see below) of *Abraham and Isaac* is not certain, but the probability is in favour of the supposition that an earlier Chester play on the subject was revised with the aid of the East-Anglian treatment of it. Both were clearly indebted to the *Mystère du V. T.*

[2] This notion is from the *Protevangelium Jacobi.*

The Three Kings connects itself with the play of *Balaam*, to whose prophecy reference is made at the outset. When the star appears, and the *Magi* are summoned by the angel, they follow him on ' drombodaries.' A very drastic scene ensues between the Kings and Herod, who in a speech of extreme vigour warns them, and expresses his perturbation at the birth of a royal babe. A ' Doctor' expounds prophecy to him, but Herod declares it false ' by Mahownde full of mighte,' and sends the Kings on their way, with ominous oaths as to his future proceedings. *The Offering and Return of the Three Kings* and the *Slaughter of the Innocents* form a necessary sequel. The latter play is infinitely the coarsest of the series ; but a sense of effective dramatic construction is shown at its end, where the scene in which Herod is carried away by a demon, after bewailing the torments of his last hours, is followed by the tranquil return from Egypt. In *The Purification* and *The Temptation* Scripture is more closely adhered to ; in the latter, however (with which *The Woman taken in Adultery* is rather ingeniously combined into a single piece), a ' Doctor' expounds the significance of the events represented from ' Gregorye' and from ' Austyne.' The solemn prologue to the *Lazarus* is spoken by the Saviour Himself, after which the healing of the blind man is represented at great length, and followed by the raising of Lazarus, treated with much moderation of tone and appropriateness of manner.

Christ's Entry into Jerusalem is full of life, containing incidents elsewhere distributed among two or three plays. The sitting at meat in the house of Simon the Leper (' messille' he is here called), the offering of Mary Magdalene, and the discontent of Judas Iscariot, then the expectancy of the citizens and the entry of the Saviour into Jerusalem, with the expulsion of the merchants from the Temple, and the preparation of the arrest in the Sanhedrim, are all crowded into a single pageant. It will be noticed that the discontent of Judas at the permitted waste of the precious ointment is put forward as a dramatically sufficient motive for his treason. In *Christ Betrayed*, the action progresses through the Last Supper and the night at Gethsemane to

the arrest of the Saviour ; the washing of the disciples' feet
is introduced, and the dialogue accompanying it is at once
simple and touching [1]. The *Passion* and the *Crucifixion*
follow.   In the former, much vivacity is added by a judicious
change of metre, from that used by the ' bushoppes ' to that
employed by the common Jews who torture and mock the
Saviour.   The *Harrowing of Hell* is another elaborate treatment of the well-known legend, introducing the curious fancy
that Enoch and Elias inhabited Paradise alone during the
interval between their ' vanishing ' from earth and the descent
of Christ into hell, and that on the coming of Antichrist, as
is fully shown in the subsequent play of that name, they
suffered death as martyrs, and rose again ' in daies three and
an halfe.'   After the souls of the Just have been saved by the
Harrowing, a personage appears as remaining behind in the
hands of the devils—a woman who describes herself and her
sins at length.   She was ' some tyme '

> ' a tavernere
> A gentill gossipe and a tapstere,
> Of wyne and ale a trustie brewer,'

and in the exercise of her profession was guilty of ' marring
good maulte.'   She impresses the warning of her irrevocable
doom upon

> ' All tipling tapsters that are cuninge,
> Mysspendinge moche maulte, brewinge so theyne,
> Selling small cuppes moneye to wyn,
> Againste all truth to deale.
> Therfore this place ordeyned is
> For such ylle doeres so moche amisse ;
> Here shall the have ther joye and blesse,
> Exsaulted by the necke,
> With my mayster, mightye Mahownde,
> For castinge moulte besyddes the combe,
> Moche watter takinge for to componde,
> And littill of the secke ;

---

[1] Nothing at Oberammergau (1871) better illustrated the powerful effect
of a faithful and simple following of the Gospel narrative than the incident
of the feet-washing.   But the grace and dignity displayed in this scene by
the representative of Christ were beyond praise, and on the level of really
high art.

> With all mashers minglers of wyne in the nighte,
> Brewinge so blendinge againste daye lighte,
> Suche newe made clarrytte is cause full righte
> Of sicknes and desease.
> This I betake you, more and lesse,
> To my sweete mayster, Sir Sathanas,
> To dwell with hym in his place,
> When it shall you please;'

—so that to this solemn play a homely lesson is attached, which doubtless came home to the bosoms of many virtuous tradesmen.

In the *Resurrection*, Pilate (oddly using the affirmation ' as I am a trewe Jewe') sets the watch over the sepulchre ; and there is an unusually clever touch of sarcasm in the remark of *Secundus Miles* that

> ' Our prince hath sworne that we shall dye
> Without anye propheseye.'

Indeed this play is very effectively written; and the speech of the risen Saviour is not without a genuine poetic afflatus[1]. But I must pass over this play and its next successors, the *Pilgrims of Emaus* and the *Ascension*[2], in order to point out the special attention which appears to have been devoted, as was indeed natural in the case of a Whitsuntide perform-ance, to that entitled the *Emission of the Holy Ghost*. Its elaborate and at the same time didactic character (the speech of *Deus* should be especially noted) constitutes it in a manner the central play of this collective mystery. The effect of the miraculous acquisition of the gift of tongues by the Apostles is ingeniously indicated by the appearance of two *alienigenae*, who marvel at their 'jongling' the languages of ' Mesopotamye, Capodorye, and Jurye,' ' the yle of Ponthus

---

[1] ' Eirthlye mon that I have wroughte,
    Awake out of thy slepe;
    Eirthlye man that I have bought
    Of me thou have no kepe,' &c.

[2] In the *Ascension* may be observed a striking instance of the translation of Latin versicles into a free vernacular paraphrase (' Quis est iste venit de Edom,' &c.). Such passages serve from time to time to remind the reader even of those later Mysteries of the liturgical origin of the Mystery-drama. See also the *Credo* and its paraphrase in the *Emission of the Holy Ghost*.

and Asye, Friceland and Pamphani, Egipte righte into Billi[1],'
and others. The next play, *Ezekiel*, is purely didactic, containing a recital by Ezekiel of several of the prophecies of
the Old Testament, and a ' morolizing ' upon them by an
Expositor. The play of *Antichrist* is exceedingly remarkable. No play besides this exists on the subject, except the
very remarkable Latin drama of the twelfth century on the
End of the Roman Empire and the Advent of Antichrist,
exhibited during the reign of the Emperor Frederick
Barbarossa (1152–1190), and pervaded very strikingly by
the spirit of Teutonic self-consciousness[2]. The two plays
are based on the same legend, but the German possesses a
distinctly political significance, and its conclusion is abrupt
and in some measure mysterious. The English cannot be
said to attempt any application whatever of the legend of
Antichrist, whose triumph and slaying of Enoch and Elias
are followed by his own overthrow by the sword of the
Archangel Michael. He then reveals his true character,
appealing for help to

> ' Sathanas and Lucifier,
> Bellsabube, bolde Balacher,
> Ragnell, Ragnell, thou arte my deare,
> Nowe fare I wounder evill '—

but he is carried off to hell ; Enoch and Elias rise again,
and are conducted to heaven by the Archangel. The last
play of the series is of course *Doomsday*, the action of which
is arranged with tolerable symmetry, a *Papa, Imperator, Rex*
and *Regina salvati* being contrasted in speech with their coun-
terparts, and a *Justiciarius* and *Mercator* into the bargain,
damnati. In spite of the free treatment of the Popes, this

---

[1] One of the later MSS. reads ' Pamphily ' and ' Lybby,' doubtless
rightly. ' Friceland ' seems a confusion between Frisia and Phrygia.

[2] It was printed by Wright in the second volume of his *Chester Plays*, but
was re-edited from the Tegernsee MS., and furnished with a most interesting
commentary by Prof. G. von Zezschwitz (*Vom Römischen Kaisertum
deutscher Nation*, Leipzig, 1877), who subsequently published a German
translation (*Das Drama vom Ende des Römischen Kaisertums und von der
Erscheinung des Antichrists*, 1878). Another German translation had been
previously published in the same year by J. Wedde.—According to
Zezschwitz, the probable occasion of the play was the diet of Mainz, at
which, the Crusade being under debate, the Emperor declined to preside.

play breathes a distinctly ecclesiastical spirit ; one of the lawyer's sins was 'payering holye churches possession'; one of the merchant's 'never hying to holye churche'; and no trace occurs of the ideas of the Reformation. Significantly enough, this play, and together with it the entire collective mystery, terminates with the appearance of the four Evangelists, who bear witness to the words of Christ which have received their fulfilment, and thus appropriately conclude a series of representations in the main based upon the Sacred Narrative itself. A living Bible has thus in a sense been unrolled before the people; or, if the expression be preferred, a sermon has been preached of which the whole Scripture Narrative is the text[1].

Coventry Plays.

Finally, the principal part of the MS. containing the *Coventry Plays* was written in 1468; but the title which it now bears was only added by an authority of much later date, though there is no reason to suppose any error in it. This title terms the collection *Ludus Coveniriae* s. *Ludus Corpus Christi*[2]; and that Corpus Christi plays were performed at Coventry in the fifteenth and sixteenth centuries is beyond all doubt. There is a well-known allusion to them in one of Heywood's *Interludes*[3]; and the authentic information regarding this exhibition is stated to cover the years from 1416 to 1591[4]. Of the plays as they have reached us, one (the *Assumption of the Virgin*) is said to be written in a more recent hand than the rest, from which it certainly differs to some extent in manner.

As to the performance of these plays, it is known that they began on Sunday, at six in the morning; and that

---

[1] It will not be forgotten that about the close of the thirteenth century—a period to which the origin of these mysteries is at least traditionally carried back—sermons had ceased to be generally preached in English churches. See Palmer, *Origines Liturgicae*, vol. ii. p. 65.

[2] *Ludus Coventriae. A Collection of Mysteries, formerly represented at Coventry on the Feast of Corpus Christi.* Edited by J. O. Halliwell, F.R.S. (*Shaksp. Soc. Publ.* 1841).

[3] *The Four P's :*—

> 'For as good happe wolde have it of chaunce,
> Thys devyll and I were of olde acqueyntaunce;
> For oft, in the play of Corpus Christi,
> He hath played the devyll at Coventry.'

[4] See the notices *ap.* Sharp, pp. 8-12.

they were acted at other towns besides Coventry[1]. We gather
from a passage in the twenty-ninth of these plays (they are
altogether forty-two in number), that they were not always
all acted in one year[2]. In the copy preserved they are
preceded by a prologue, spoken by *vexillatores* (banner-
bearers), and composed in a rather elaborate stanza. It
is addressed to ' bothe more and less, gentyllys and yemanry
of godly lyff lad '; and on several occasions in the plays
the audience is addressed as ' sovereynes.' This last seems,
however, a term of address frequently employed in the
English mediaeval drama.

Though it has been remarked[3] that ' during the whole of
the period from 1416 to 1591 there is not the slightest indication that the clergy in any way co-operated,' I cannot but
think that in their composition the Coventry Plays show
signs, not perhaps of an ecclesiastical origin, but of the
distinct influence of ecclesiastical minds[4]. Inasmuch as
the Grey Friars of Coventry are known to have performed
a cycle of Corpus Christi plays, it has been usually supposed that the MS. preserved to us is that of the series now
in question ; but it is rather of internal evidence that I am
speaking. In the first place these plays show a remarkable

---

[1] Collier, ii. 82.

[2] ' Be the leve and soferauns of allemyhthy God,
      We intendyn to procede the mater *that we lefte the last yere.*

          .   .   .   .

  The last yere we shewyd here how oure Lorde for love of man
      Cam to the cety of Jherusalem mekely his deth to take ;

          .   .   .   .

  Now wold we procede, how he was browth than
      Beforn Annas and Cayphas,' &c.

At Oberammergau, it was formerly usual to alternate between the Old
Testament and New Testament portions of the play now condensed into
a collective whole. E. Devrient, *Das Passions-Schauspiel in O.,* p. 8.

[3] By Collier, ii. 74.

[4] It does not follow that they were performed by monks domesticated at
Coventry ; so that ten Brinck, ii. 295-6, who inclines to conclude from the
Prologue and from the language of the plays, which points to the North-
East Midlands rather than to the neighbourhood of Coventry, as well as
from the mixed character of the series in general, that these plays were performed by strolling actors, may conceivably be so far in the right. I notice
that Mr. Pollard, *Introduction,* p. xxxviii, without undertaking to dogmatise,
expresses his own belief ' that further investigation will lead to the decisive
connexion of this cycle, not with Coventry, but with the Eastern Counties.'

familiarity with ecclesiastical literature. The promise of the prologue—

> 'Of holy writ this game shall bene
> And of no fablys be no way'—

is in so far kept that the plays are uniformly based either on the canonical books of Scripture, or on apocryphal Gospels[1]. But the Latin quotations from Vulgate or Liturgy are very numerous; hymns and psalms are frequently referred to or paraphrased[2]; and the Commandments are likewise paraphrased at great length (in *Moses and the Two Tables*). Even the shepherds refer in a very learned way to the Prophets, while in the play devoted to the latter we appear to have before us an intentional display of biblical learning. The *Disputation in the Temple*, again, would hardly have been written by a layman; and the Institution of the Eucharist is very elaborately treated. The emphasis with which the character and history of the Virgin are dwelt on, is very striking; all the incidents of her life, as presented by canonical or apocryphal Scripture, and as forming the occasions of Church festivals, are treated at length; her Birth, her Presentation and Betrothal, the Salutation and Conception, the *Trial of Joseph and Mary*, her visit with the two other Maries to the sepulchre, finally her Assumption[3]. This may be regarded as a characteristic of the age in which the plays were written; but it may also be noted how constant a reference there is in them to the episcopal office, and how we are introduced in the *Trial* to an ecclesiastical court. There seems no irony in the advice to those summoned:

> 'loke ye rynge wele in your purs,
> ffor ellys your cawse may spede the wurs;'—

---

[1] According to Halliwell, five on the *Apocryphal Gospel of the Birth of Mary*, three on the *Protevangelion* of St. James, one on the *Gospel* of Nicodemus. The story of Lamech the blind archer is a legendary amplification of *Gen.* iv. 23. Cf. Smith's *Dict. of the Bible*, ii. 57.

[2] Mary's devotion to her 'sawtere' is very pleasingly expressed:—
> 'O holy Psalmys! holy book!
> Swetter to say than any ony!'

[3] Observe in the *Visit to Elisabeth* the passage:—
> 'Thus the Chirch addyd Maria and Jhesus her:
> Who syth our ladyes sawtere dayly for a yer thus,
> He hath pardon ten thousand and eyte hundred yer.'

a passage which, so far as I can see, has no bearing, such as has been attributed to it, upon the question of payment for the performances of the plays[1].

But the chief reason for suspecting clerical hands to have been concerned in the composition of these plays, is the difference which as literary efforts, if the term be permissible, they exhibit when compared with the Chester Plays in particular. The Coventry Plays, especially those taken from the Old Testament, are far more regular in form, and considerably in advance as to versification and diction. There is usually a species of expository prologue to each play, spoken by its principal character (Deus, Adam, Noah, Abraham, Jesus, Lazarus, Daemon); and the action itself seems to be managed with a view rather to close adherence to authority than to the production of immediate drastic effect. The action, at least in the Old Testament plays, is decidedly less lively than in the Chester series (compare e. g. the treatment of the subject of *Abraham and Isaac*); and if there is in general much less humour than in the Chester or Towneley Plays, there is also upon the whole less coarseness. (Some half-comic touches were apparently inevitable in connexion with St. Joseph as a husband advanced in years; the *Trial of Joseph and Mary* begins with a comic introduction, the people being called upon by English Christian and surnames; and Lucifer's description of fine dress is in a vein of popular satire on *le luxe effréné* practised by both sexes in that age.) Yet what indecency there is—although it is but little—strikes me as not altogether of the *naïf* kind. The shepherds, as already stated, address themselves to very different topics from those which they discuss in the earlier part of the corresponding Towneley and Chester Plays ; and Herod, though his discourse is boastful and extravagant enough,—though, as does Satan in *Pilate's Wife's Dream*, he alliterates freely,—and though he swears a good deal by ' Mahownde[2],' cannot be

---

[1] See Halliwell's note, p. 413.

[2] The soldiers at the sepulchre use the same oath. It is well known that in consequence of the Crusades the name of Mahomet had become typical of all false religious worships.

said to rave, or to approach the border-line of the comic, except perhaps when, in ordering a banquet after the Massacre, he shows an ultra-royal disregard of expense—

> 'Thow that a lytel pint cost a m¹ pownde.'

Into a detailed examination of the Coventry Plays I must refrain from entering; but I may point out, as calling for commendation, the verse at the close of the *Adoration of the Shepherds*; the forcible speech of *Mors* in the *Slaughter of the Innocents*; the exceptional dramatic vigour in parts of the *Trial of Christ*; and the simple effectiveness of the scene in which the Saviour after the Resurrection appears to Mary Magdalene¹. And in one speech of the Blessed Virgin (in the *Betraying of Christ*) there is a gleam of tragic passion beyond what is usual in these early productions—

> 'A! Jhesu! Jhesu! Jhesu! Jhesu!
> Why xuld ye sofere this tribulacyon and advercyté?
> How may thei fynd in here hertys yow to pursewe,
> That nevyr trespacyd in no maner degré?
> For nevyr thyng but that was good thowth ye,
> Wherfore than xuld ye sofer this gret peyn?
> *I suppoce veryly it is for the tresspace of me,*
> *And I wyst that myn hert xuld cleve on tweyn.'*

On the other hand, these plays, as a matter of course, abound in evidence of the rudely material conceptions of the age in

---

¹ The authors here could not go wrong, if they followed the Sacred Text. There was perhaps nothing in the Oberammergau Play more wonderfully effective than the utterance by the Christ of the solitary word MARIA. In the Coventry Play, however, He subsequently briefly addresses her. In the corresponding Towneley Play the supreme effectiveness of the single word is missed: it is seized in the Digby MS. play of *Mary Magdalene*. I hardly venture to refer to the mysterious meaning which is suggested by the rapturous self-devotion of Mary Magdalene, though surely the suggestion is not incompatible with a reverential reading of the text of Holy Scripture itself. But the gentle reticence of the Gospel, which is followed by the mysteries, is more eloquent than the expansive rhetoric of such a poet as the author (said to be Gervase Markham) of *Marie Magdalen's Lamentations for the Losse of her Master* (see Grosart's *Miscellanies of the Fuller Worthies' Library*, vol. ii), beautiful as the latter is in at least one passage. These poems are written in the spirit of Crashaw, from whom they are not very far distant in their date (1601). The confusion of the *Phariseus* and *Accusator* (in the *Woman taken in Adultery*) by the words, and by the writing in the sand, of the Saviour is also dramatically very effective.

which they were produced. Such is above all to be found
in the repulsive reproduction in action of an extraordinary
legend in the *Salutation*, and in the *Resurrection*. Compared with such instances of a tendency to reduce every
mystery of the faith to a realised actuality, all mere
anachronisms or oddities of ignorance[1] are insignificant.

It should in conclusion be noticed, that though the characters represented in the *Coventry Plays* are in the main
actual personages, they already contain an element of
abstract figures. *Contemplacio* appears in several plays to
introduce the action as a kind of Prologus (so in the eighth,
and again in the eleventh, where she announces the advent
of the Redemption after ' ffowre thowsand sex undryd foure
yere' of unexpiated sin) or to accompany it as a kind of
Chorus. But other allegorical personages are also occasionally introduced; the Virtues of *Justicia, Misericordia,
Veritas,* and *Pax,* who (in the eleventh play) hold conference
with the Three Persons of the Trinity; and in the eighteenth
Mors, who, after casting down Herod's pride, and delivering
his dead body, and those of the two soldiers who form his
executive, into the hands of *Diabolus,* moralises for the
benefit of the audience on the suddenness and omnipotence
of his agency. In the *Assumption* we meet with the figure
of *Sapientia*; but this play may be of a later date than the
rest. (The concluding play, *Doomsday*, in which there was
room for other abstract figures, though none appear, is merely
a fragment.) Thus we notice in these plays, though they
essentially are to be classed among the *mysteries*, an element
of the *moralities*, to be treated of below. On the other hand,
there is here no evidence of any intention to treat the Devil
as a comic character, though under various names—Lucifer,
Belial, Satan, or Daemon—he largely participates in the
several actions, into which inferior angels of darkness are
likewise occasionally introduced.

Besides these collective series, we possess isolated plays
of the same type, which I do not propose to examine at
length. The oldest of these, and in all probability the

*Other
miracle-
plays.*

---

[1] See for instance the strange geography of the prospect opened by
Sathanas in the *Temptation.*

earliest dramatic work of any kind in the English tongue
preserved to us, is the *Harrowing of Hell*, a version of a
theme with which we have repeatedly met in the collective
mysteries [1].   For a dramatic work this primitive piece
deserves to be called, although (to use ten Brinck's expres-
sive phrase) it has not yet entirely cast off the epico-liturgical
egg-shell, and although it seems to have been intended for
recitation rather than for performance.   The introductory
exposition announces to the listeners

> ' A *strif* will I tellen ou '—

this being the technical name for one of those debates or
wrangles, in which English as well as French literature in
the thirteenth century took pleasure [2].   And the action
itself begins with the approach of our Lord to the gates
of hell and His contention with Satan, instead of any
scene being prefixed between those who are awaiting their
deliverance from hell, as in the versions of the legend
which were derived directly from the Apocryphal Gospel
of Nicodemus [3].   This contention, in which Satan claims the
fealty of Adam as having taken his apple, while our Lord
retorts that the apple itself was His, is broken off by
His bursting open the gates, whose warden flies in terror,
and receiving in succession the salutations of Adam and
Eve, Abraham, David, St. John the Baptist and Moses,
whom He is about to set free.   After He has pronounced
their liberation, ' *Auctor* ' concludes with a prayer, commencing :

> ' God, for his moder loue
> Let ous neuer thider come ! '

But though the action is simple, it is complete ; and the

---

[1] It is printed in his Appendix by Mr. Pollard, who calls it ' a poem in
dialogue.'   The earlier English editions by Collier and Halliwell-Phillipps are
privately printed, but there is a German edition by Dr. E. Mall (Breslau,
1871).—Collier, ii. 136, gives some extracts.

[2] Cf. *ante*, p. 25.

[3] In the York *Harrowing of Hell*, e. g. (*York Plays*, 372 *seqq*.), and in the
corresponding Towneley Play, Jesus introduces the action and sends a light
before Him as a sign that He is at hand ; but a striking scene follows in
which the patriarchs and prophets in Limbo rejoice at the light, and the
devils in their turn give voice to their alarm.

severe dignity of the diction (which is held to show an East-
Midland origin) cannot be said to fall short of the striking
solemnity of the theme.

Among other isolated plays not already incidentally
noticed may be mentioned *The Story of the Creation of*   *Adam and*
Eve, with the Expelling of Adam and Eve out of Paradyce—   *Eve.*
the Grocers' Play (and thus presumably part of a cycle)
at Norwich[1].   The Shipwrights' Play of *Noah's Ark* is   *Noah's*
the only play remaining from the   Corpus Christi cycle   *Ark.*
performed   at Newcastle-on-Tyne[2].   It is composed in no
very elevated vein, though the action is introduced by *Deus*,
who sends forth his Angel to bid Noah build the ark.

> 'What art thou for heaven's King
> That wakens Noah off his sleeping?
> Away I would thou went.'

But the Angel insists, and after receiving the necessary
instructions, Noah sets to work.   *Diabolus* then intervenes
to induce 'his friend,' Noah's wife, to stop the building
by persuading her husband to drink a potion prepared for
the purpose, and Noah nearly 'loses his wits' in consequence.
But he recovers, 'cowls' (cows?) his wife, builds the ship,
and leaves *Diabolus* to utter impotent curses in the name of
'Dolphin prince of dead.'

A play on a still more favourite theme of a different   *Abraham*
character (of which not less than six versions are altogether   *and Isaac.*
extant from different series) is the East-Midland *Abraham
and Isaac*, discovered by the late Dr. G. H. Kingsley in
a MS. book seemingly compiled for the owners of the
manor of Brome (in Suffolk), near Diss[3].   It treats the

---

[1] Privately printed by its editor, Mr. Robert Fitch (Norwich, 1856).
Stoddard, p. 63.

[2] Reprinted from Brand's *History of Newcastle-on-Tyne* (1789), by Sharp,
u.s., 221–5. Three other plays of the series are mentioned, viz. *The Deliverance of the Children of Israel out of the Thraldome, Bondage and Servitude of
King Pharo; The Buriall of Christ;* and *The Buriall of our Lady Saint Mary
the Virgin.* An order for the performance of the last-named play is dated as
late as 1581.

[3] Edited by Miss L. Toulmin Smith in *Anglia* (vol. vii. pp. 16–337), Halle,
1884. Mr. Pollard, pp. 173–6, prints an extract containing the *dénouement.*
—As already stated (*ante*, p. 78, *note* 1), ten Brinck's view that use was made

subject with much tenderness of feeling; the Isaac here is a young boy, whose laments direct themselves largely to his apprehensions of his mother's grief, while his joy on discovering the ram, apostrophised by him :

'A! scheppe, scheppe, blyssyd mot thou be !'

is mingled with the same motive. The versification is mostly in stanza-form. Another, and not dissimilar, treatment of the same subject, the Weavers' Play on the *Sacrifice of Abraham*, has been discovered at Dublin [1]. A *Ludus Filiorum Israel* was acted at Cambridge by the gild of Corpus Christi at that festival in 1355 [2]. Of plays on New Testament subjects we have the series known as the *Digby Mysteries*, from the quarto volume among the Digby MSS. in the Bodleian Library which contains them [3]. The date of part of the MS. is 1512, but it is written in three if not more different hands, some of which seem rather earlier than that which inserts the above date, nor has any mutual connexion been established between the several plays included among its miscellaneous contents. The first of these plays is usually spoken of as *Parfre's Candlemas Day*, the copyist having signed to it his name 'John Parfre'; but its full title adds '*and the Kyllynge of the Children of Israel.*' This subject, together with the flight into Egypt, makes up the earlier part of the play, upon which follow the Purification and other Scriptural incidents in the Temple. The play explicitly states that the performance of it corresponds to 'last year's' of *The Shepherds, and the Three Kings*, while no mention is made

Digby Mysteries.

Parfre's Candlemas Day, &c.

of this play for the extant edition of the corresponding Chester play has much in its favour, and has been elaborated by Dr. H. Ungemach.

[1] Privately printed by Collier, 1836. See an account of it by Miss L. Toulmin Smith in *Anglia, u.s.*, 321-2.

[2] Warton, ii. 219.

[3] The first of these plays was printed in vol. i. of Hawkins' *Origin of the English Drama* (Oxford, 1873); the series of four was first edited by Mr. T. Sharp for the Abbotsford Club (1835), and has been more recently re-edited for the New Shakspere Society (1882) by Dr. Furnivall, who has included in it *Christ's Burial and Resurrection*, as in his opinion belonging to it, though found in another Bodleian MS.—The 'morality' printed in Sharp's quarto without a title, but designated by Collier, *Mind, Will and Understanding*, and by Furnivall, *A Morality of Wisdom, Who is Christ*, forms part of the Digby MS., but will more appropriately be noticed a little further on.

of any gild or trade as concerned in its production. Thus the conclusion seems warranted, that it formed one of a cycle of plays acted in annual succession in small towns or villages—probably in the Midlands, to which region the language is thought to point—that could not afford themselves a more extensive dramatic entertainment. The performance began and ended with singing and dancing by 'minstrels' and 'virgins[1].' The earlier part of this play has nothing to differentiate it very specially from the *Coventry Plays*, and we once more meet here with Herod's pompous and inflated speeches, and with his alliteration. A larger admixture is however observable of the purely farcical element, represented by 'Watkyn,' who is anxious to join in the expedition against the Innocents of Bethlehem, but is afraid of their mothers' distaffs. This character already displays features of the typical poltroon of comedy, while the timorous adventurer's anxiety to be dubbed a knight points to a Tudor period of civilisation. The contrast between the tumult of the earlier and the peaceful triumph of the second part of the play, however, is of its kind effective. The second of these plays (which stands first in the MS. volume), the *Conversion of St. Paul*, seems *The Conversion of St. Paul.* to have been designed for performance in a larger town, as is shown by its being acted at three stations and by the more ambitious nature of some of its stage requirements[2]. The *Poëta* who introduces the action, and whom a later hand in the MS. names 'Myles Blomefylde,' though possibly this worthy was only the author of 'additions' to the first part of the play, appeals to the *Acts of the Apostles* as his authority. But the first part of the play is not taken from

[1] They are bidden show 'summe sport and plesure these people to solas.' The 'virgins' were doubtless maidens of the locality. In the play, Anna bids them worship the Divine Child; and the stage-direction adds: 'her virgynes, as many as a man wyll, shall holde tapers in ther handes &c.' The stage arrangements too must have been very simple; in Sc. 1 the knights receive from Herod their instruction as to the massacre which they are to execute in Sc. 3; the intervening scene is occupied with the Flight from Bethlehem, and the stage-direction at the end of Sc. 1 instructs the knights to 'walke a-bought the place tyll Mary and Joseph be conveid in-to Egipt.'

[2] Furnivall, *Introd.*, p. ix.

a Scriptural source[1]; for Saulus is here introduced as a knight-adventurer arrayed in character[2], with other knights in his service and of underlings, one of whom carries on an unsavoury comic altercation with the 'stabularius' (ostler). The miraculous Conversion occupies the second part; the third, which represents St. Paul's escape from the toils of Caiaphas and Annas, is enlivened by an ingenious later interpolation. The Infernals hold a council, in which Belial and his messenger Mercury appear, in order to avert the dangers to their cause apprehended from the Conversion of Saul. After the devils have vanished in fire and tempest, 'Saulus' appears 'in a disciplis wede' (dress) and delivers a sermon on the Seven Deadly Sins. The action closes with St. Paul in prison, from which however *Poëta* in the Epilogue announces the saint's approaching deliverance. The play, which ends with an apology for its lack of 'lytturall scyens' (literary aptitude), and which certainly has no special merit to distinguish it, is thought to be likewise of Midland origin.

Mary Magdalene.

The remaining miracle in this collection, *Mary Magdalene*, is by far the most remarkable, as it is also by far the most elaborate, of the three. Its dialect is East Midland and it largely employs alliteration, but it is of a different dramatic type from that represented by the two other Digby plays ; or rather, it combines with matter derived from the Scriptural narrative, which fills the body of the first part of the play, a larger number of scenes though a smaller amount of text taken from legend ; while the whole is pervaded by an element of originality, so far as arrangement if not actual invention is concerned, and there is a free introduction of allegorical figures after the manner of the moralities, to be described below. Thus this piece is in substance as well as in name a miracle-play rather than a mystery; but the astounding complexity and romantic imaginativeness of the action remove it into a literary as well as a dramatic sphere foreign to that of the plays previously described.

---

[1] There seems no connexion between this play and the *Jeux du Martire S. Estienne et de la Conversion de S. Pol*, printed *ap.* Fournier, *Le Théâtre Français avant la Renaissance*, pp. 2 *seqq.*

[2] 'Goodly besene in the best wyse lyke an aunterous knyth.'

Unfortunately, I cannot accompany the heroine on her journey through life and through more then two thousand lines of text. It begins in the home of her infancy—the castle of Maudleyn where her father Cyrus 'glystering in gold' rejoiced in a son Lazarus, to whom he bequeathed his lordship of Jerusalem, and two daughters, Mary, who respectively inherited the castle from which she derived her second name, and Martha, whose share was Bethany; and after an Iliad of sins and woes and of redeeming martyrdom it ends with her reception into bliss. I print in a note the full title or bill in which the latest editor of this extra-ordinary composition has summarised the main points of the action; but to convey a notion of its variety, his list of the successive scenes and the previous editor's analysis of the action at large would need to be added [1]. In Part I no less a personage than 'Imperator,' who identifies himself as the 'incomparable tyberyus sesar,' opens the play; and this opening prepares us for the strange commingling as the action proceeds of the familiar Bible episodes with a fantastic allegory of the heroine's downfall. Her castle is besieged by the Seven Sins, and Lechery penetrating into it seduces her out of its protection into the paths of sin. In Part II, which is introduced by a colloquy between the King and Queen of Marcylle, shipwrecked on an island in the sea, where the Queen gives birth to a child, we are launched into the midst of romance, through which, not without re-currences to Scriptural episodes, the action steers more or less rapidly to its end. There is a certain charm, however, about the central figure, and a certain harmony diffuses itself through the various stages of her pilgrimage [2].

---

[1] See Furnivall, *Introd.*, p. 53: '*PART I, in 20 scenes. (In Rome, Bethany, Hell, Jerusalem, and beyond Jordan.)—Mary's Father Cyrus, and his death.—Her seduction by Lechery, and a Gallant.—Her repentance, and wiping Jesus's feet with her hair.—Her brother Lazarus's death, and again-rising.—PART II, in 31 scenes. (In Marcylle, Hell, Jerusalem, the Wilderness and Heaven.)—Christ's appearance to Mary at His sepulchre.—Her conversion of the King and Queen of Marcylle.—Her feeding by angels from heaven in the wilderness.—Her death.*'—For an analysis of the action, see the *Introduction* to Sharp's Abbotsford Club edition, pp. vi–xxxii.

[2] '*Das Ewigweibliche in Maria's Gestalt ist dem Dichter nicht entgangen.*' Ten Brinck, ii. 322.—As to Lewis Wager's *Life and Repentance of Mary Magdalen* (1574), see Collier, ii. 167–170. This is an Elisabethan morality

Christ's Burial and Resurrection.

Of a far earlier type, so far as the limits of the action are concerned, is the *Burial and Resurrection of Christ*, to which reference has already been made as exhibiting in certain passages the religious drama in its organic connexion with the liturgy of the Church [1]. But the text of this bipartite mystery, as it has come down to us, and which is authoritatively pronounced [2] to be a West-Midland modernisation of a Northumbrian original, appears to date from the middle of the fifteenth century, or somewhere between the years 1430 and 1460 [3]. This supposition is borne out by the general evidence of style, of versification, and more especially of skill in the handling of the rimes (largely in the case of words with double-endings). Manifestly the edition which we possess was designed for readers in the first instance. Although it repeats the original direction that the first part of the play (the *Burial*) is ' to be played on Good Friday afternoon,' and the second (the *Resurrection*) 'upon Easter-day after the Resurrection' (i. e. I suppose after the reading of the Gospel of the day), the 'Prologue' is ordered 'not to be said' when the play is actually performed. And indeed, while the Prologue itself appeals to feelings which lie deeper than those of the ordinary spectator of any kind of play [4], the entire treatment of the theme is meditative or lyrical rather than dramatic. In the laments of Mary Magdalene and of the Virgin Mary, long, elaborate, and occasionally touched with a surprising delicacy of pathos [5], will be found the most distinctive features of this interesting composition.

of the anti-papal kind, which 'ends with a short dialogue between Mary, Justification and Love, the two last triumphing in the salvation of such a sinner.' It has no connexion with the Digby MS. play.

[1] Cf. *ante*, p. 35, *note* 1.—See p. 91, *note* 3.

[2] By the late Dr. Richard Morris. See Furnivall, 170.

[3] Ten Brinck, ii. 299.

[4] 'A soule that list to singe of loue
　　Of Crist . . . .
　　Rede this treyte [treatise, poem], it may hymm moue,
　　And may hym teche lightly with awe,
　　Of the sorow of Mary sumwhat to knawe.'

[5] (*Of Calvary*):
　'Thy greyn color is turnyd to rede
　　By a blessit lamm's blode which now is dede.' (*ll.* 29–30.)

The above list has no pretension to being exhaustive ; but no further English miracle-plays of the kinds treated above are known to me as extant which may not (as in the case of the sacred plays of Bishop Bale, to be noticed below) be fairly included among the beginnings of our regular drama. A particular species of miracle-plays belonging to the same period seemed however worth reserving for separate notice. These are plays of which the action turned on the sacrosanct attributes and miraculous powers belonging to certain portions of the actual services of the Church. The earliest of these which we find mentioned is 'a play setting forth the goodness of the *Lord's Prayer*,' performed in the city of York by a gild of men and women that had been founded for the purpose[1]. Inasmuch as Wiclif, who died in 1384, refers to 'the *paternoster* in englissch tunge, as men seyen in the pley of York[2],' and inasmuch as there is evidence to show that the gild was in a flourishing condition fifteen years later, we may conclude that its origin is to be dated at no great distance of time from that of the York Corpus Christi plays. In the last year of Queen Mary's reign (1558), though the gild had been previously dissolved, the play was performed on Corpus Christi in lieu of the regular cycle, and it was repeated in 1572 ; but it was soon afterwards suppressed by that vigilant shepherd, Archbishop Grindal. We are told that in this play, which accordingly may have partaken of the nature of a morality, 'all manner of vices and sins' (the vice of gluttony is specially mentioned) 'were held up to scorn, and the virtues were held up to praise'; and we cannot but suppose that the lessons thus conveyed were connected with the seven supplications, in token of which

Paternoster, Creed and Sacrament Plays.

(*Of the Redeemer's Body on the Cross*) :
' How many bludy letters beyn writen in this buke ;
    Small margente her is.'
(*The Mother of Jesus gazing on the face of Jesus in death*) :
' Till Egipte in myne Armes softly I did you lede;
    But your smylinge countenaunce I askit non other mede.'

[1] See Miss L. Toulmin Smith, *Introduction* to *York Plays*, xxviii–xxx.
[2] *De Officio Pastorali*, cap. 15, in the *English Works of Wyclif*, edited by F. D. Matthew for the Early English Text Society, 1880, p. 429, and see Mr. Matthew's note, pp. 530–1.

the gild maintained in the Minster 'a candle-bearer of seven lights,' together with 'a table showing the whole meaning and use' of the Prayer confessed of them.

We are less fully informed as to the nature of *The Creed Play*, which in 1446 was bequeathed to the Corpus Christi gild at York by a member of the gild, a chantry priest named William Revetor, together with the books and banners belonging to the play [1]. It seems to have been no novelty at this date, but it was regularly performed about Lammastide, once in every tenth year, between 1483 and 1535. It was finally suppressed about a generation later. It was a composition of considerable length, and not the mere syllabus of a processional pageant, although a series of pageants, perhaps corresponding to the several articles of the Apostles' Creed, may have formed an integral part of it.

Distinct in character from the above, and approaching more nearly to the miracle-plays derived from the legends of favourite saints [2], is the curious piece with a purpose preserved in a MS. at Trinity College, Dublin, and known under the more generic than specific title of *The Play of the Sacrament* [3]. The handwriting of the MS. belongs to the latter half of the fifteenth century; nor is there any evidence of language to point decisively to a much earlier date. The Prologue states that 'this little processe' is designed for performance at Croxton; and among the various places of that name the East Midland dialect of the play is thought to indicate one of the Croxtons in Cambridgeshire or Norfolk. *Vexillatores* introduce the action in alternating stanzas, stating that the facts represented occurred at Heraclea in Aragon, and furnishing an argument of what is to follow. The story is that of the wondrous triumph of the Holy Wafer over the wicked

---

[1] See Miss Toulmin Smith, *u.s.*, p. xxx. Cf. ten Brinck, ii. 303.

[2] Cf. *ante*, pp. 9, 37. Others were Christina (honoured by *Beatae Christinae Ludi* at Bethersden in Kent), Crispin and Crispian (whom the Dublin shoemakers celebrated in part of a play acted in 1528), &c.

[3] *The Play of the Sacrament*. A Middle-English Drama, edited from a MS. in the Library of Trinity College, Dublin, with a Preface and Glossary, by Whitley Stokes, *Philological Society's Transactions*, 1880-1, Appendix, pp. 101-152. Cf. Collier, ii. 267-8; ten Brinck, ii. 303.

designs of the Jew Jonathas and his vile crew—infidels who freely appeal to 'Almighty Machomet,' and who shrink from no extreme of impiety. By way of a crowning insult they cast the Host into an oven, which thereupon bursts asunder, bleeding from its crannies, and revealing an image of the wounded Saviour, Who speaks in His own personality to the awe-struck offenders. In the end they are all christened 'with great solemnity,' and (as if to illustrate the comparative mildness of the treatment experienced by their race in this country) are allowed to seek atonement for their crimes by a pilgrimage 'by contre and cost.' Apart from its gentle ending, this sort of legend was familiar enough to the thirteenth and fourteenth century (when the story of Hugh of Lincoln was its best-known type in England), and doubtless in the fifteenth also. A comic element is supplied by the doings of 'Colle the leech's man,' who before the arrival of his master 'Breadryche of Braban' proclaims him as a doctor who

> ' Seeth as well at none as at nyght,
> And sumtyme by candel-leyt
> Can gyff a Judgyment aryght,'—

or, in other words, is never to be caught napping. On the physician's appearance Colle proceeds to trumpet his merits with all the energy of the professed cheap-jack. ' Nine men,' it is stated, ' can play this at ease.'

Before referring to those essentially spectacular entertainments which from a very early period, but in an increasing measure as time progressed, absorbed into themselves a large proportion of the interest attaching to the miracle-plays, I proceed to discuss another dramatic growth which, although exposed to the same chances as these, indisputably displayed a superior literary vitality and flexibility.

In tracing the origin and course of unconscious growths, *Moralities.* it is well to abstain from any endeavour to draw hard and fast, and therefore more or less arbitrary, lines of demarcation. The origin of the *moralities*, or *moral-plays*, has been much disputed; and in their English developement they have been diversely described as springing from the miracle-plays, and again as wholly unconnected with these.

As it seems to me, the *moralities* cannot be simply described as the direct offspring of the religious drama; but
they were nowhere wholly independent of it, and in England
they both adopted its external form, and were anything but
rigorously distinguished from it in the popular mind.

A *morality* may be defined as a play enforcing a moral
truth or lesson by means of the speech and action of
characters which are personified abstractions—figures representing virtues and vices, qualities of the human mind, or
abstract conceptions in general [1].

*Their
origin;*   Now, in the first instance, it was impossible that the
Christian religious drama, whether appearing as an essentially literary growth, or primarily designed as a species of
popular entertainment, should refrain from at least occasionally introducing the essential elements of the species
which I have just defined. And this, because the very basis
of Christian religious teaching—the Bible—so largely employs this very method of enforcing the truths and lessons
which it is its object to convey. Both the Old and the
New Testament, besides containing entire books which
the Church has at all times accepted as allegorical in
design—such as the *Song of Solomon* and the *Revelation*—
are, as primarily addressing themselves to Eastern readers
or hearers, full of figurative passages introducing personified
abstractions. The prophetical character of a great part
of the Old Testament depends on an interpretation proceeding on the same assumption.

In any attempt to paraphrase or reproduce, whether
dramatically or otherwise, portions of the Bible, or of
Church traditions connecting themselves with its narrative,
it was therefore inevitable that the use of personified abstractions should be introduced. Wisdom (in the *Book of
Proverbs*), the Bride and her companions (in the *Song of
Solomon*), had already been clothed with personality in the
Sacred Text itself. But more than this. It has at all times
been impossible for the ordinary human mind to regard

---

[1] The ordinary scheme of a morality is accordingly very like that of the
game ' wherin vices fyghte with vertues ' described in Book II of More's
Utopia.   Cf. the description of the *Paternoster* play at York, *ante*, p. 97.

unpersonified conceptions emotionally. Neither Athenians nor Romans nor Englishmen have at any time, either in oratory or in poetry, found it easy to think or speak of Athens or Rome or England without clothing them with the attributes of personal beings, or at least unconsciously treating them as such. Thus, too, the early Christians, so soon as the figure of the Founder of their community had ceased to be a personal reminiscence among them, began to regard that community itself as a personal being, under the name of the Church. On this analogy it was possible to people the world of ideas with an endless number of personal forms.

On these germs of the distinctive characteristic of the moralities—which in their dramatic method, as will be seen, at first differed in no essential respect from the religious plays—already noticed, there seems no necessity of enlarging further. Perhaps, however, it may be worth while in connexion with this part of the subject, to suggest the probability that the custom of using as the proper names especially of women the designations of abstract qualities, and of virtues in particular (*Sophia*, &c.), became much more common after the introduction of Christianity[1]. We have seen[2] how some of the characters in the plays of Hrotsvitha are accordingly called by names corresponding to the qualities which the behaviour of these characters illustrates ; and the device was one which might easily be borrowed by the popular from the monastic religious drama. A peculiar product of the same allegorical taste connecting itself with religious associations, was the attempt, of which germs are to be traced in the earliest patristic literature, to invest natural objects and phenomena with a symbolical meaning ; hence those *bestiaries, herbaries* and *lapidaries*, of which a notable example is preserved in the English

---

[1] I should have been inclined to go further, but for some notes with which my friend Dr. Wilkins has furnished me. The earliest *Pietas* is the cognomen of L. Antonius cos. B.C. 41. The earliest *Felicitas* seems to be the martyr of 202 A.D., but there are two instances of the same name in inscriptions undated, but with no traces of Christianity in them. The earliest dated *Irene* and a *Victoria* (the mother of Victorinus) are not Christian.   [2] Cf. *ante,* p. 7.

thirteenth-century version of the Latin *Physiologus*. It treats its subject with no small measure of poetic fancy and feeling, while its machinery possesses a popular element of picturesqueness [1].

In England, the soil was peculiarly favourable for the cultivation of moral allegory in the dramatic as in other literary forms. It would lead me too far to speculate in this place on the causes of the ancient and enduring national predilection for this species of imaginative composition. But it seems probable that, inasmuch as our literature had more distinctly than that of almost any other modern nation a specifically Christian origin, so it was the Bible itself which implanted in the English mind its ineradicable love for allegory, and for religious or moral allegory in especial. Already the *Paraphrase* ascribed to Caedmon and Cynewulf's *Christ* have allegorical elements, although it may not always be easy to distinguish between these and reminiscences of native mythology. Then, while in accordance with the general tendencies of the age, fostered by the teaching of its wholly clerical learning, the allegorical interpretation of Scripture and of traditions associated with Scriptural themes, spread more and more among the people, another influence lent its co-operation. This was the growth, contemporaneous with the building-up of the system of chivalry on the social basis of feudalism, of the allegorical treatment of the conception of Love. At probably no very different periods in the fourteenth century the *Vision concerning Piers Plowman* and *The Pearl* signally illustrated these co-operating tendencies. The former is a work of genuinely native origin; but while its design, which is one of striking directness, still moves within the lines of the religious teaching of the Church, depth of individual feeling and a homely boldness in applications suggested by an observant study of contemporary life invest it with a force hitherto unknown to allegorical composition. *The Pearl* is an attractive but rather long drawn-out endeavour to treat a theme of a kind familiar to French love-allegory in native

---

[1] See *Reliquiae Antiquae,* vol. i, and cf. the very instructive *Introduction* to Mätzner's *Altenglische Sprachproben,* i. 1 (Berlin, 1867).

forms of language and to some extent of verse. Not more
than a generation afterwards Chaucer and Gower opened
the first period in which our poetic literature appealed to
the height of contemporary literary culture; and while the
Confessio Amantis of the latter is wholly allegorical in its
framework, Chaucer began his poetical career by a version
of the *Roman de la Rose*. Although, as it stands, this poem,
in accordance with Chaucer's own demure confession, marks
a revolt against the moral pretensions of the orthodox love-
allegory, yet it had adhered, and gave a new vogue, to the
allegorical literary form. Down to the middle of the sixteenth
century, in the words of an eminent French critic[1], it exercised
over French poetry the supreme authority of an *Iliad* or a
Divine Comedy. As is well known, the machinery of the
Dream of Scipio suggested a whole series of Chaucerian
poems, but even in these he vindicated to himself a certain
freedom of treatment, until, partly under Italian influence,
partly inspired by his own genius, he passed from the reproduction or invention of allegorical figures and situations
to the creation of types of human nature and life. His successors, however, both in England and afterwards in Scotland,
were unable to emancipate themselves with similar completeness; the conventional machinery recurs even where lyrical
pathos or satirical humour give individuality to the general
treatment or realistic effect to particular figures. When,
after the half-century's silence which poetic literature had
kept in England amidst the clash of arms, we once more
take up the tale of allegorical compositions, we find indeed
the old spirit gone, but the old form toughly surviving.
Stephen Hawes' *Pastime of Pleasure* may be described as
the last work of the older schools of allegory in the pre-
Elizabethan age of literature, though of course influenced by
later models. The infinitely more interesting *Ship of
Fooles*, adapted by Alexander Barclay from the German of
Sebastian Brant, is already occupied with human types
rather than with personified abstractions. But Skelton's
Bowge of Courte, although modern both in the learning of its
matter and in the looseness of its tone, still employs the old

[1] Ste-Beuve, *Tableau de la Poésie Française au* 16ᵐᵉ *Siecle*, p. 2.

abstractions; and in form even this 'lytell' product of the later Renascence spirit still mainly follows the traditions of the species to which it claims to belong.

These considerations, which it belongs to a *History of English Poetry* rather than to a *History of English Dramatic Literature* systematically to develope[1], may suffice to indicate the fallacy of the supposition that the moralities, of which I am about to discuss the chief examples, were either nothing but an outgrowth of the mysteries and miracles already described, or a mere literary expansion of the allegorical figures exhibited in those 'pageants' (in the narrower sense of the term) which constituted the chief popular attraction of the religious and other 'processions' of the Middle Ages. In their general method of treatment, indeed, the moralities followed closely in the footsteps of the religious drama, which they could hardly have avoided doing, inasmuch as their stage and its appliances, and their audience and its tastes, were virtually the same as those of the mystery-plays. But although these had occasionally anticipated some of the favourite personifications of the moralities, and although the latter as a matter of course fell back upon some of the dominating figures of the mysteries, a vast variety of new opportunities was opened by a face-to-face treatment of moral and consequently of social problems, which had hitherto been only suggested or implied by a reproduction of Scriptural and legendary narrative. Furthermore, the moralities connected themselves directly with the prevalent tendencies of the literature of the age which produced them; while the mysteries had been

[1] As these sheets were passing through the press, I had the satisfaction of ascertaining, by a necessarily hasty perusal of vol. i. of Mr. W. J. Courthope's *History of English Poetry*, and more especially of its admirable chapter (ix) on *The Progress of Allegory*, that the suggestion conveyed in my text has become an accomplished fact. Mr. Courthope's volume contains so much both in this chapter and in that which follows on *The Rise of the Drama in England*, that I would gladly, had circumstances permitted, have revised the whole of my own first chapter with the aid of his masterly treatment of a subject which I have approached only on a single side. As it is, I have only here and there felt myself able to make use of a guidance which would have been a godsend to me at any time within my last twenty years of broken literary studies.

out of touch, unless incidentally, with the learning of the
schools, and with the ways and habits of those privileged
classes which have at most times delighted in following to
the death a prevailing fashion in the literary as in other
forms of art.

Reference has already been made to two productions, of *and early developement.* which one had for its author the Anglo-Norman poet
Guillaume Herman (1127–1170), and the other has been
(on perhaps not altogether conclusive evidence [1]) attributed
to Étienne Langton, who after graduating as doctor of
theology at Paris became, as everybody knows, Cardinal
(1206) and Archbishop of Canterbury. These compositions,
while in so far to be regarded as belonging to the Christian
religious drama, that in each the promised or actual intervention of the Saviour solves the complication of the action,
in general conception and method of treatment resemble
the moralities of later date.   Herman's composition, written
in Langue d'Oil, or Northern French, at the request of the
Prior of Kenilworth, is a dramatic version of the Bible text
(*Psalm* lxxxv. 10): ' Mercy and Truth are met together ;
Righteousness and Peace have kissed each other.'   These
four virtues appear personified as four sisters, who meet
together after the Fall of Man before the throne of God to
conduct one of those disputations which were so much in
accordance with the literary taste of the age [2] ; Truth and
Righteousness speak against the guilty Adam, while Mercy
and Peace plead in his favour.   Concord is restored among
the four sisters by the promise of a Saviour, who shall
atone to Divine Justice on behalf of man.   The composition
attributed to Stephen Langton treats the same theme with
a relative intensity which, could either of these works be
credited with a dramatic purpose, might be termed superior
force of action.   After a contention has been carried on
between the four sisters, and Mercy and Peace are about to
withdraw unsatisfied, the Divine Father summons the Son,

---

[1] It was found, together with the sermon on a text taken from the song on
' la bele Alix ' and a canticle on the Passion, in a MS. in the Duke of
Norfolk's library, now in that of the Royal Society. Cf. *Dictionary of National
Biography*, xxxii. 127–8.   [2] *Ante*, p. 25.

and with Him, in order to meet the demands of the case as
it presents itself to His own judgment, concerts the saving
remedy of the Incarnation of the Word ; whereupon a
reconciliation takes place between the sisters [1].

It will be remembered that in one of the *Coventry Plays*,
the four virtues *Veritas, Justitia, Misericordia, Pax* are
introduced into the action ; while in another *Mors*—the
awful abstraction of the power against which all men are
impotent—lays hands upon the murderous Herod and his
myrmidons, and delivers them over to the Devil [2]. Without
however attempting an enquiry, which could hardly be made
conclusive, into the dates of these particular plays, or of
others in which abstract figures may be found among the
subsidiary *dramatis personæ*, we may assert that there is no
proof that the moralities became a form of popular stage-
entertainment in England before the second quarter of the
fifteenth century, which was covered by the reign of Henry VI.
The continuous spread, through a wider area, of the literary
tastes represented by the successors of Chaucer, and the
enduring receptivity of the English public for the distinctive
element of this new kind of plays, combined to secure to
them gradually a share of favour by the side of the miracles.
As a matter of course, the new species, which addressed
itself to no new public and was occupied with no new
problems of life or thought, accommodated itself to the
manner and method of the old.   Between the performance
of a morality and that of a miracle no external difference is
noticeable ; the pageants used for the one were used for the
other ; *vexillatores* proclaimed the intended performance,
and the performers in some cases went from place to place,
whether they were representing the misdeeds of Herod and
Pilate, or the struggle of the Soul with the Seven Deadly
Sins [3]. But although in this sense there was no break in the
progress of our drama from its beginnings, the sense of
there being something not altogether indigenous in the new
dramatic growth which was establishing itself by the side of
the old, was never entirely lost, or at all events seems only

---

[1] Klein, iv. 107–9.   [2] *Ante*, p. 89.
                [3] Collier, ii. 193, 200-1.

gradually to have succumbed to an appreciation of its usefulness in those conflicts that absorbed the interests of the people at large. For it may be broadly stated that the moralities never became domesticated in this country, or at least never acquired any influence here comparable to that of the miracle-plays, until they had been made to connect themselves with the political and religious questions which were so inextricably intermingled in the Reformation age [1]. This was in the changeful reign of Henry VIII, and during the pressure in the direction now of advance now of reaction which followed under his successors ; but the fitful and uncertain character of these movements in their earlier phases, and the unwillingness of Henry, Somerset, Mary, and Elisabeth to leave the direction of these movements to the people itself, caused the English moralities as vehicles for the expression of public opinion to lead a troubled and chequered course. Finally, before they had as a species reached the full vigour of maturity, they found the process already in operation which was to supersede them by more advanced dramatic growths.

If this be borne in mind, we shall not expect to find the *French moralities.* history of the English moralities either as interesting or as entertaining as that of the French. In France, as has been already observed, a popular drama of secular origin, and concerning itself mainly with secular topics, had throughout maintained itself by the side of the religious plays, although the two species were frequently intermixed. To the French taste for allegorical and satirical poetry the drama had no doubt in its turn contributed ; and in the fourteenth and fifteenth centuries the religious drama of the *Confrèrie de la Passion* found it no easy task to contend against the moralities of the *Basoche*, the *sotties* of the *Enfans sans souci*, and the *sotties* or *farces* after a time represented by the older as well as the younger of these brotherhoods. In these congenial productions public opinion long continued to find an outlet for itself as to both political and social topics ; and the gay and outspoken genius of mediaeval

---

[1] Cf. Henry Morley, *First Sketch of English Literature*, p. 246.

France contrived to temper distress and despotism alike by
the sallies of an untrammelled wit. The pressure of the
English invasion and the radical despotism of Lewis XI are
alike reflected by the contemporary French popular stage ;
here Lewis XI's system of ' new men ' found its critics, and
Lewis XII's struggle against the Papacy its supporters.
But these French plays, even when called *moralities*, have
rather the character of interludes with typical personages
(such as the immortal *Maître Pathelin*) than of allegorical
moralities, though personified abstractions are frequently,
and even Scriptural personages occasionally, introduced
into them. They bear a certain resemblance to the Athenian
comedy of the second period, the period represented by the
Plutus of Aristophanes[1].

English moralities. In the English moralities it is not easy to draw a distinction between particular groups ; the signs of advance
which they successively exhibit would best be gathered
from an attempt, such as it would be here inconvenient to
make, to survey the whole of them in their actual or
probable chronological order. Moreover, only part of the
series is as yet accessible without difficulty ; and as to
several of these plays I am still obliged to fall back upon
the analyses furnished by Collier[2]. A misapprehension
may be avoided by noticing at the outset that the name
of *Interludes* is from a very early date applied to these
plays, as indeed it seems to have been applied to plays
performed by professional actors from the time of Edward
IV onwards. Its origin is doubtless to be found in the fact
that such plays were occasionally performed in the intervals
of banquets and entertainments[3], which of course would

---

[1] As Ebert (*Entwicklungsgesch.*, p. 25) says, the French moralities were
developed, not *invented*, in this period. For examples see the collections of
Viollet le Duc and Fournier, already cited. Cf. also an excellent sketch of
the famous Pierre Gringore, the *Mère Sotte* of his famous company, in
L. Moland's *Origines, &c.*, p. 345 *seqq.* The sprightliness of diction in these
French plays makes them delightful reading. Molière's indebtedness to
them is well known.

[2] Vol. ii. pp. 200-323.

[3] It is curious in the above connexion to find that in France they were
occasionally acted in the intervals of the mysteries. Hence they were sometimes called *Pauses.* Cf. Fournier, *Introd.*, p. iv.

have been out of the question in the case of religious plays proper. As will be seen below, the name *Interludes* is, as a technical term, of literary history, usually restricted to a special dramatic form.

In the English moralities, and in the plays immediately derived from this species, it is impossible to ignore the two closely associated figures of the *Devil* and the *Vice*. The treatment of the *Devil*—a long-lived impersonation of a conception to which dogma and legend have been joint contributories—has signally varied at different times and in the hands of different writers ; but it has rarely altogether excluded those humorous elements which the complexity of the principle of negation involves. They assert themselves already in an early period of English literature [1] ; and they pervade the part played by the Devil in the religious drama as it has been surveyed in the preceding sketch, and taken over, beard and all, from the miracles into the moralities and their derivatives [2]. In the English moralities proper, as in their French originals or analogues, the Devil is consistently charged on his own account with the conduct of the opposition to the moral purpose or lesson which the action of these compositions is designed to enforce. In some of the later English plays, on the other hand, which grew out of the moralities and which more or less partook of their nature, the Devil is accompanied by a personage whose relation to him is primarily that of a foil, but whose functions are so peculiar that in the end he is frequently left to stand on his own legs, and to appear without the master-spirit of whom he was at first the faithful attendant [3]. Ingenious etymologies have been suggested for the name of the *Vice*, as this character, which must be concluded to have

The Devil and the Vice.

---

[1] Cf. ten Brinck, i. 337, as to the legend of St. Dunstan.

[2] In Skelton's lost *Nigromansir* one of the stage directions is stated to have run, 'Enter Balsebub with a berde'—no doubt the vizard with an immense beard familiar to the old religious drama.   Cf. Warton *ap.* Collier, i. 57, *note.*

[3] Collier, ii. 289.   His original secondary position is illustrated by the amusing passage in Ben Jonson's *Staple of News*, Act i. Sc. 2, which attests the enduring popularity of his chief: 'My husband, Timothy Tuttle, God rest his poor soul ! was wont to say, there was no play without a fool and a devil in 't ; he was for the devil still, God bless him ! The devil for his money, would he say, I would fain see the devil.'

been of native English origin, was usually called; but the
most natural explanation is probably the correct one. The
Vice has numerous *aliases*—such as *Shift, Ambidexter, Sin,
Fraud, Iniquity,* which are but variations of his ordinary
name. At times, however, he wears the more specific
designation of some particular vice or failing; while elsewhere again, in accordance with the growing tendency to
supersede abstractions by types, he appears under some
typical designation of an onomatopœic kind [1]. Of these
various appellations that of *Iniquity* acquired a special
vogue on the stage, where we find the species of *Vice*
differentiated under that name for a long time established
as a favourite [2]. As to the origin of the Vice, no reasonable
doubt remains. Inasmuch as he was ordinarily dressed in
a fool's habit [3], and occasionally assumes the part of a jester
pure and simple [4], it is obvious that the invention of this
popular character was first suggested by the familiar custom
of keeping an attendant fool. Hence, while the Vice is in
some sort an attendant or serving-man of the Devil's, his

[1] See Douce, *Illustrations of Shakespeare*, vol. i. p. 469. Cf. Pug's
enumeration of the Vice's names in *The Devil is an Ass*, Act ii. Sc. 1:

> 'Fraud,
> Or Covetousness, or Lady Vanity,
> Or Old Iniquity.'

Other names are *Hypocrisy, Inclination, Ambition, Desire, Haphazard,
Nichol Newfangle.* In Lewis Wager's *Repentance of Mary Magdalene*
he appears as *Infidelity.* See Collier, ii. 189–90. In George Wapull's
Tide tarrieth no man, a personage called *Courage* is introduced after the
manner of the *Vice*, but without his ordinary characteristics. *Ib.* p. 296.

[2] *Iniquity* appears in *King Darius* (printed 1565), and is summoned to give
an account of himself and his functions in the passage already cited from
The Devil is an Ass.

[3] See the Clown's song in *Twelfth Night*, Act iv. Sc. 2:

> 'I 'll be with you again,
> In a trice,
> Like the old vice,
> Your need to sustain;
> Who, with dagger of lath,
> In his rage and his wrath
> Cries, ah, ah! to the devil.'

[4] In John Heywood's *Play of the Wether* (1553) the Vice appears as a jester
called *Mery Report*; in *Jack Juggler* (before 1560) *Jack* himself is called the
Vice, and in *Godly Queene Hester* (1561) the latter is personified as a jester
called Handy-Dandy. Cf. Pollard, liii, *note.*

function is to twit, teaze and torment the fiend for the edification of the audience. The latter very commonly takes his revenge for having been ridden and beaten by the Vice by carrying him off on his back to hell at the end of the play [1]. Gradually the character was lost in, or reverted to, that of the domestic Fool, who, as is well known, survived as a standing figure of no small significance in the Elisabethan drama [2].

The Devil and the Vice, the latter in particular, are of much importance to the moralities as a popular dramatic species, both because these characters went some way to counterbalance the dead weight of the abstractions constituting the main agents of these plays, and because the aid of these elements largely contributed to the gradual growth of comedy. It would, however, be an error to suppose that (leaving the Devil out of the question) the Vice constituted the solitary concrete element in the moralities, where no doubt he formed the most salient one. *Other concrete elements in the moralities.* The personified abstractions will be found from time to time fitted with names appropriate to concrete individuals, and thus brought, so to speak, within view of the point at which they will be transmuted into human characters pure and simple. At first, it is only occasionally that an abstraction like scorn is translated into a concrete Hycke-Scorner ; but the tendency towards this kind of change proves stronger as we proceed, and is assisted by the alliterative nomenclature in which English popular humour has at all times delighted, and of which there are instances already in the mysteries [3]. Such personal names as Cuthbert Cutpurse and Tom Tosspot, when taking the place of abstract designations of the sins of Robbery and Inebriety, unmistakeably imply a step forwards into the atmosphere of real life. Again, as at least one writer [4] has pointed out before me, even where the characters of

---

[1] Collier, ii. 192–3. Cf. the character of Miles, and his doom, in Greene's *Friar Bacon and Friar Bungay.*
[2] Douce, *u.s.,* ii. 304–5.
[3] Conscious of this tendency, Pilate in the Processus Talentorum in the *Towneley Plays,* says that he is '*nomine vulgari* Pownce Pilate.'
[4] M. Jusserand.

these plays still remain abstractions, frequent allusions to the actual world around the audience give a colouring of reality to the action. *Folly* glories in his adventures in Holborn, at Westminster, and in disreputable Southwark ; *Youth* (probably Cambridge-bred) demands from *Humility* whether she was not born at Trumpington—as if this were just beyond the limit set to pride ; *Mind,* in a state of corruption, expresses his intention of putting in an appearance between two and three of the clock in the afternoon under the Parvis at St. Paul's—the lawyers' hour and place.

Passing by a small number of religious plays which display a mixture of miracle and morality, which it would hardly be worth while to subject to a minute analysis— more especially as these plays belong to so comparatively late a period as the beginning of the reign of Elisabeth [1]—

[1] These plays which are described by Collier, ii. 167–182, include Lewis Wager's *Life and Repentance of Mary Magdalene* (printed 1567), the ' Interlude' of *King Darius* (printed 1565), of which the main interest lies in a disputation on the question, ' What is strongest ? ' propounded by Darius in a portion of *Esdras* (Bk. iii), ' not applied by the Church to establish any doctrine ; ' and *Godly Queene Hester* (printed 1561), in which Hester after her elevation to the throne is provided with a chapel royal, whose members are brought in to sing before her like the *jeunes filles* who sang before Madame de Maintenon, and in which Haman   ' plays the first pagente '

on the gallows erected by himself. Arthur Golding's translation of Beza's *Tragedie of Abraham's Sacrifice* (printed in 1577, about a quarter of a century after the appearance of the original) furnishes one more version of the favourite Old Testament theme, the single more or less novel feature being the part played by *Satan,* who, attired as a monk (a favourite combination of the Reformation age), soliloquises on the mischief done by him to the world in that character and comments aside on the progress of the action. *The Comedie or Enterlude, treating upon the Historie of Jacob and Esau* (which has been printed in vol. ii. of Hazlitt's edition of Dodsley, 1874), is even more absolutely free from any admixture of elements proper to the morality. Beyond all doubt this play is, as Collier has already pointed out, one of the freshest and most effective productions of the dramatic period to which it belongs ; although not printed till 1568, it may have been written as early as 1557, when a piece of the same name was entered in the Stationers' Registers. The characters in this play are real characters ; and although the author takes most delight in the comic aspect of the story, he has contrived with a certain skill to supply some sort of dramatic justification of the success of Rebecca's ingenuity. The moral of the story is turned to account for the doctrine of predestination and election ; so that no doubt can exist as to the religious creed of the author, who winds up with a brief sermon and a prayer for Church, Queen, nobility and ' the Queen's subjects universal.'

I proceed to a brief survey, in the natural order of the groups into which they fall, of the chief moralities proper preserved to us. For the York play on *The Lord's Prayer*, of which mention has been previously made as to all intents and purposes a morality, was acted in or before the year 1399, and thus preceded by at least a generation, and possibly by a considerably longer period, the extant plays of the reign of Henry VI [1]. Of these three plays two still remain in MS., and can therefore here only be described at second-hand [2]. Their theme is the struggle between the principles of Good and Evil in and for the soul of man—an inexhaustible subject to be sure, and the same in essence as that which occupied the mysteries, only that in these it was robed in the historical folds of sacred tradition. It must at the same time be remembered that the age in which these moralities were produced was one of which the circumstances were altogether unfavourable to any freedom of literary movement, and when a rigidly orthodox Church, favoured by a pious prince with no will of his own, controlled the spiritual forces at work in the minds of men. The earliest of the plays in this group is the *Castell of Perseverance* [3], which allegorises the theme of the conflict between the Powers of Good and Evil for the Soul of Man in the form of a warfare carried on against *Humanum Genus* and his defenders, the Seven Cardinal Virtues, by the Seven Deadly Sins [4] and their commanders, *Mundus, Belyal* and *Caro*. The struggle is preceded by a contest for the

Moralities of the reign of Henry VI.

The Castle of Perseverance.

---

[1] Cf. *ante*, p. 97.   [2] See Collier, ii. 200–216. Cf. ten Brinck, ii. 311 *seqq.*

[3] This is one of the three plays usually called the *Macro Moralities*, from the circumstance that the MSS. once belonged to Mr. Cox Macro.—Of the *Castell of Perseverance* a considerable extract is printed by Mr. Pollard, who proposes to edit the play for the Early English Text Society. See his *Introduction*, xlv–xlviii.

[4] The Seven Deadly Sins, with whom we have already met in one of the mysteries, reappear in Medwell's morality *Nature* (*infra*); but there is no need for following these abstractions through their long and varied career in English imaginative literature from Langland onwards. The date of Dunbar's famous *Dance of the Sevin Deidly Synnis* seems to be about the second decade of the sixteenth century. The procession of the Sins in the *Faerie Queene* (Bk. I. Canto 4) is noteworthy, as suggesting the popular effectiveness of a 'moral' pageant of this description:

> 'Huge routs of people did about them band,
>   Showting for joy.'

naked and helpless *Humanum Genus* between *Bonus* and
Malus Angelus—figures familiar to several of our later
plays as well as to the early religious drama [1]. In this
contention the Good Angel is temporarily defeated, and he
has to summon to his side *Confessio* or *Schryfte*, with whose
aid and that of *Penitencia, Humanum Genus* is lodged in
the Castle of Perseverance. To this castle his enemies,
after mustering their forces, lay siege [2], the defending
Virtues beating back their assault with roses, the emblem
of the Passion of our Lord. As old age overtakes him, he
is at last lured away from the castle by *Avaritia*, the failing
proper to declining years. But the money received by him,
hid away in the ground, avails him naught against Death;
and his spirit is arraigned by *Pater sedens in judicio*, where
the appeal of *Misericordia* to Christ's Passion prevails at
last. Thus here too, as in so many of the mysteries, the
Day of Judgment concludes the action. This earliest extant
English morality, which is of great length, already furnishes
an adequate example of the species to which it belongs;
and there seems no reason for concluding that it was
derived from a French original [3].

Wisdom who is Christ.

The morality, of which the chief characters are *Mind,
Will* and *Understanding*, and to which in his description of
it Collier accordingly gave this title, has been renamed by
Dr. Furnivall, who has recently edited part of it [4], *A Morality*

[1] See especially Marlowe's *Doctor Faustus.*—In his very interesting analysis of the passion-play seen by him at Thiersee in the Bavarian Tyrol, F. Gregorovius (*Kleine Schriften,* iii. (1890) 190) mentions the appearance of a 'good spirit' who in vain attempts to dissuade Judas from suicide.

[2] The machinery of the siege of a castle is common in English allegory, both dramatic and non-dramatic. See above, p. 95, as to the curious use made of it in the mixed play *Mary Magdalene* (*Digby Mysteries*). The favour enjoyed by the story of the Trojan War during a great part of the Middle Ages may have contributed to the popularity of this device; but the experience of real sieges had much to do with it, just as the same kind of experience no doubt led Bunyan, who had been a soldier in the great Civil War, to imagine the siege of the city of Mansoul in his *Holy War.*

[3] The besieged Castle of Perseverance is described as 'strenger thanne any in France,' and *Voluptas* uses the phrase '*Je vous pry.*'—But the resemblance to the French *Moralité de Mundus, Caro, Demonia,* &c., printed *ap.* Fournier, u.s. pp. 200 *seqq.*, of which the date is 1506, appears to be at the most superficial.

[4] From the Digby MS., for the New Shakspere Society, 1882, pp. 137–168.

of Wisdom who is Christ. The nature of the conflict is here
the same as in *The Castell of Perseverance*, but the treatment is of a kind which comes more directly home to the
modern reader than the artificial allegory of the earlier
piece [1]. The first personage who enters upon the scene is
Wisdom, robed in 'a ryche purpyll cloth of gold,' and
wearing 'a ryche Imperiall crowne, set with ryche stonys
and perlys.' To this Divine Embodiment of Wisdom, Who
soon reveals Himself as the Second Person of the Trinity,
enters *Anima*—the human soul—'as a mayde in a whight
cloth of gold, gyntely purfyled with menyver' and 'a mantyll
of blak.' She kneels to Wisdom, confessing how from her
youth up she has loved Him ; in return He reveals to her
that He is gracious to all pure souls and withholds His
love from none that are steadfast in their devotion to Him.
Then ensues a dialogue, in which allegorical phraseology is
combined with direct homiletic exposition. Wisdom's explanation to the Soul of the compound nature of her being
is illustrated by the actual introduction on the stage of the
Five Wits or Senses, the servants of the Soul, maidens
arrayed 'in white kertelys and mantelys, with chevelers
and chapellyttes,' and of the three Powers or 'Myghtes'
belonging to her—*Mind, Will* and *Understanding*, from
whom *Wisdom* explains that Faith, Hope and Charity
severally proceed in order to contend against the World, the
Flesh and the Devil. He leaves her, thus fortified, to fight
the good fight to a glorious issue, and her lyrical outburst
of gratitude brings the introductory, and in this instance
most attractive, portion of the play to a close. With the
next scene enters Lucyfer announcing himself in accustomed
fashion with 'Out herowe I rore [2],' wearing his 'devil's

---

[1] To my mind it recalls some of the mystic imaginings of Jacob Böhme.
See for instance his *Way from Darkness to True Illumination.*

[2] ' Ho, ho, ho ' and ' Oute haro out out ' are the exclamations by which
the Devil is wont to announce himself in the miracles. See Sharp's
Dissertation, p. 85 *sqq.* In *Mary Magdalene* the seducer announces himself
at his entry as ' Hof, hof, hof! a frysh new galaunt.' Even in Ben Jonson's
The Devil is an Ass Satan appears on the scene with the usual ' Hoh, hoh,
hoh,'—an evident reminiscence from the old mysteries and moralities, as
Whalley observes, although Gifford dictatorially pronounces the reference
' out of place.'

array' over the habit of 'a prowde galaunt,' and reciting
in short and lively lines his own hateful past and his hostile
intentions against the soul. In the following scene he carries
on a long disputation with *Mind* and, arguing in a pleasant
and as one might say gentlemanlike fashion, beguiles both
her associates and herself into accepting with a light heart
his gay philosophy of life. The passages which hereupon
exhibit the corruption of the three powers have considerable interest as illustrations of contemporary manners.
Mind in the service of a great lord makes money by
working the practice of maintenance, which was widely seen
to be immoral long before it was made illegal; *Understanding* flourishes by turning informer, by simony and by
perjury in the law-courts; while *Will* surrenders himself to
recklessness and loose companionship. So they call in their
retainers, and the minstrels play a hornpipe to their dance.

In the remainder of this play, not contained in the
Digby MS., there ensues a quarrel between the three
perverts and their crews; and the defiled *Anima*, now
the parent of 'six small boys in the lyknes of devyllys,'
is, together with her dependants, brought face to face with
her degradation by the admonition of *Wisdom*. They are
restored to their pristine purity, and a brief epilogue brings
to an end both the play and its lesson. The former never
loses sight of the latter; but pre-eminently didactic as this
morality is, I will not deny that to me it seems to possess
a certain charm of its own.

Mankind.   A third piece[1], called by Collier *Mankind*, introduces
Mercy as the protecting power of the central personage,
who is assailed by three adversaries, felicitously distinguished as *Naught*, *New-Gyse* (Guise) and *Nowadays*. By
the advice of *Myscheff* they summon to their aid a fiend
called *Tytivillus*, a name known to us already from the
Towneley Mysteries[2]. Having taken away from the sleeping *Mankind* his spade, the symbol of work, this impersonation of the lust of the flesh corrupts the soul of

---

[1] Like the preceding, one of the so-called 'Macro moralities.'
[2] Cf. *ante*, p. 76, note 1. Cf. as to Tutivillus, Dyce's note to Skelton's
Poetical Works, ii. 284-5.

the sleeper by an evil dream, from which he wakes as
a thorough scoundrel. Not until the pangs of remorse
have overtaken him, and until he longs for death, does
Mercy take pity on him and save him from the toils of his
tempters, who rapidly descend to the place whence they
came. In this morality the comic element, and with it that
of coarseness, are already very notable .

The above form the earliest group of our extant English   *Early
moralities; of the next the majority belong to the early   Tudor mo-
Tudor period, while in all the influences of Renascence   ralities.*
and Reformation already made themselves felt, though in
the earlier instances only like the breath of the coming
wind as it lightly stirs the quiet of the waters. The date   *Nature.*
of the 'goodly interlude of *Nature*,' by Henry Medwell,
chaplain to the famous Cardinal Morton (the enemy and
as some have thought the biographer of Richard III), seems
fixed by the fact that the first of its two parts was in all
probability performed before the Cardinal, during his tenure
of the Archbishopric of Canterbury, 1486–1500 [2]. It has
nothing in subject or treatment to differentiate it from the
earlier moralities. Nature, by God's appointment, allows
Reason and Sensuality to contend for the guidance of Man
through life ; and the Seven Deadly Sins have their part in
the struggle. One direct stroke of satire, however, seems
to call for notice in a play of ecclesiastical authorship, as
reflecting upon the clergy at large [3]. The same author
wrote another interlude which was played by the king's
players and which 'was of the fyndyng of Truth, who was
caryed away by ygnoraunce and ypocresy.' This, it appears,
was so long that it was not liked ; and the fool's part, of
which one might wish to have heard more, was considered
the best [4].

---

[1] Cf. ten Brinck, ii. 314.
[2] See the account of this play *ap.* Collier, ii. 217–224.
[3] 'Covetise' is said to have
  'dwelled wyth a prest, as I herd say,
  For he loveth well
  Men of the church, and they him also,
  And lawyers eke.'
Other sallies occur against monks and nuns, but these are delivered by
wicked characters.   [4] Collier, i. 69.

The World and the Child.

To the reign of Henry VII, and possibly to an early part of it, may also be ascribed *The World and the Child* (printed in 1522 [1]). In this play, of which the action is simple, but effective, man is represented as passing through the several stages of his life; first he appears as *Infans*, and then receives from *Mundus* the name of *Wanton* [2]. He describes the 'quaynte games' of childhood, as reckoned from the age of seven to that of fourteen years; and then becomes for seven years more *Love-Lust and Lykynge*, the representative of adolescence. *Mundus* once more re-christens him as *Manhode*, and commends to him the service of seven kings, i. e. the seven deadly sins [3]. Hereupon *Conscyence* appears, 'a techer of the spyrytualete' ('spyrytualete! what the deuyll may that be?' is *Manhode's* irreverent enquiry), and in a long dialogue converts *Manhode*. But he is led astray by *Folye*, whose 'chefe dwellynge' is in London and who was 'broughte forthe in holborne.' *Conscyence* calls to his aid *Perseueraunce*, who meets man now in *Age*, and bearing the name (which he owes to *Folye*) of *Shame*. *Perseueraunce* preaches 'contrycyon,' and teaches *Age*, whom he has re-named *Repentaunce*, the creed of Christianity, with the acceptance of which by the hero the morality closes.

Hycke-Scorner.

The concrete element, already perceptible in the above moralities, together with the evidence of that knowledge of the ways of the world and its wickedness which has always been of service to the moralist, present themselves with increased strength in a very curious play, printed probably a few years after *The World and the Child*. This is the morality called *Hycke-Scorner* [4]—a name personifying

---

[1] Reprinted for the Roxburghe Club in 1817; in vol. xii. of Dodsley's *Old Plays*, and in vol. i. of Hazlitt's Dodsley.

[2] See the passage cited *ap.* Pollard, *Introd.* li.

[3] Collier, ii. 225, has directed attention to the alliterative description of himself by *Mundus*, which is quite in the style of the Herod of the miracle-plays. The historical allusion to 'kynge robert of cysell' (Robert of Naples, who died in 1343) belongs indeed to the fourteenth century, but romance had kept his memory alive. (A play called *Robert Cicil* was acted at Chester in 1529; Collier, i. 111.)

[4] Printed in Hawkins' *Origin of the English Drama*, vol. i, and in vol. i. of Hazlitt's Dodsley.

a species of folly very forcibly reprobated in Barclay's *Ship of Fools*, the popular satirical allegory of the age, but branded long before by the Psalmist : ' The fool has said in his heart, there is no God.' The type, in other words, is that of the man who in the emptiness of his heart, puffed up by a pretence of experience and knowledge of the world, exults in scoffing at religion [1]. The date of this play is fixed as belonging to the reign of Henry VII by an incidental allusion to the *Regent*, a ship of war fitted out under that sovereign. The action introduces us to *Pity* as the chief representative of a virtuous resistance against the iniquity of the age, upheld in its turn by *Free-will* and *Imagination*. The last-named calls in to his support the personage who gives his name to the play although he acts only a secondary part in it,—a travelled libertine who, after enumerating his voyages all over the world and ' in the londe of Rumbelowe, thre myl out of hell,' favours the audience with a variety of personal reminiscences which need not here be republished. With his aid the enemies of *Pity* contrive to put him into the stocks, where (the situation reminds us of Kent's in *King Lear*) he delivers a long diatribe, with a species of lyric refrain, on the sins of the age. In the end *Free-will* and *Imagination* are without any great effort successively converted by *Perseverance* and *Contemplation*, *Free-will* taking part in the rescue of his belated comrade ; and *Perseverance* draws a concluding lesson from what has gone before. This morality might seem to show that the ordinary resources of the species would have quickly run dry but for the admission of an element of interest which, although subordinate, notably adds to the freshness of the general effect. Yet the play to be next noticed, which by general consent stands at the head of this class of compositions in our literature, adheres in the main to the old lines.

It has indeed been supposed that the morality of *Every-man* [2], of which the first impression is traceable to about

Every-man (pr. 1529 c.).

---

[1] ' Hycke ' or ' Hick ' seems to be a sort of cant masculine prefix (= *hic*). Cf. the word ' Hykman,' used = man or husband, in a vulgarly colloquial passage in *The Nature of the Four Elements*.

[2] Printed in Hawkins' *Origin of the English Drama*, vol. i, and in vol. i.

the year 1529, was written at a considerably earlier date ; but Collier has not substantiated his conjecture that this date should be placed as far back as the reign of Edward IV. A Dutch poet, Peter van Diest (Petrus Diesthemius), soon after the appearance of *Every-man* composed a version of the play in Dutch, which was performed before a *civitatum brabanticarum conventus*, probably to be interpreted as a representative meeting of the *rederyk*-chambers of these towns. This Dutch version again was reproduced in Latin, with what measure of fidelity we do not know, under the title of *Homulus*[1] by 'Christian Ischyrius,' who dates his preface Mæstricht, 1536. This Latin version again became the basis of a German, and the latter was in its turn translated into Dutch. Without pursuing the history of the theme further, I merely note that the publisher of the Latin *Homulus* sought to add to its attraction by prefixing to it a series of scenes, taken in part from the contemporary Latin comedy of *Hekastus* by Macropedius, which was independently derived from the same sources as *Every-man*, and which was itself followed by a long series of reproductions and imitations in Germany[2].

The immediate sources of *Every-man* are not ascertainable ; very probably the author may have taken the story of his morality from the *Legenda Aurea* of Jacobus Voragine (d. 1298), to which it was appended as a later addition in a brief form derived from the *Speculum Historiale*, a compilation of the thirteenth century by Vincentius of Beauvais. But there can be no doubt that the

---

of Hazlitt's Dodsley. The edition by Goedeke (published under the title *Every-man, Homulus and Hekastus*, Hannover, 1865) justly calls itself 'a contribution to international literature ' ; for its *Introduction* traces with masterly completeness the origin and developement of the theme, while the notes furnish a full survey of its later treatments. A large part of this morality is printed by Mr. Pollard in his *English Miracle-Plays*, &c., pp. 77–96.

[1]   ' QUILIBET, *ante fui, mutato nomine dicor*
              Nunc HOMULUS ; *per me nam resipiscet homo.*'

[2] The *Hekastus* of George Lankveld (Macropedius) appeared in 1538. Its author, a Dutch scholar and member of the Fraternity of the Common Life, was led by the example of Reuchlin to compose a long series of Latin comedies. He died at Utrecht.—The most famous of the imitators of Macropedius was Hans Sachs in his *Comedie von dem reichen sterbenden Menschen, der Hecastus genannt* (1549).

story itself is a parable narrated in the religious romance of
Barlaam and Jehoshaphat, which has been ascribed to the
John of Damascus who died in 780, but is now held to be
more probably the work of his younger namesake, afterwards
Patriarch of Antioch, who died in 1090. It is impossible to
mistake the singular force and profundity of this parable of
the man and his three friends. When he was called before
the king to answer for a heavy debt, two of these friends,
although he had dearly loved them and held them in the
highest honour, deserted him in his hour of trial, while the
third, for whom he had done little or nothing, went with him
to the judgment-seat and pleaded on his behalf before the
king. The first friend, we learn, is the superfluity of wealth
and the love of gain, and the second is wife and child and
the rest of man's kith and kin ; but the name of the third is
the sum of his own best works and deeds, to wit faith, hope,
charity, pity, human-kindness, and the rest of all the
virtues. This parable, which was probably not invented by
John of Damascus but (although there is no direct evidence
in the case) derived by him, like the framework and the
leading features of his romance, from a Buddhist source,
became known to the Middle Ages in various forms
through various collections of legends ; but into these
there is no reason for entering here.

In our English morality, after a brief prologue spoken by
a *Messenger*, the action opens with a scene in heaven,
where God looking down upon the sinful earth perceives
how *Every-man* 'lyveth after his owne pleasure,' as if
ignoring the utter uncertainty of the tenure of human life.
He therefore calls upon *Death*, His ' mighty messengere,' to
proceed to *Every-man*, and summon him to undertake a
pilgrimage which he in no wise may escape, and bid him
bring with him without delay a sure reckoning. *Death*
delivers his message to *Every-man*, who at once appears
upon the scene [1], and who tries in vain by pleas and bribes
to turn the summoner away [2]. Then, having received a hint

---

[1] We may suppose it, in so popular a play, to have changed from scaffold
to scaffold, or even from storey to storey.

[2] The passage furnishes a good example of the impressive simplicity of

that he should 'prove his friends if he can,' to see whether
any of them is so hardy as to accompany him on the journey
which he must take, *Every-man* left alone in his terror,
bethinks him of appealing to his old friend, '*Felawship*,'
his comrade in many a day of sport and play, to go with
him. *Fellowship*, accosted as he passes over the stage, is
full of assurances, for which he will not be thanked :

> 'Shewe me your grefe, and say no more.'

But a mention of the service required soon brings a change
over his professions :

> 'For no man that is lyvnge to daye
> I wyll not go that lothe journaye,
> Not for the fader that begate me—'

though he is quite at *Every-man's* service for a dinner or
a murder, or anything of that sort. When he has departed,
and *Every-man* has made a similarly futile appeal to two
associates called *Kynrede* and *Cosin*, he calls to mind one
other friend whom he has loved all his life and who will
surely prove true to him in his distress. '*Goodes*,' as this
abstraction is called—'Property' would be the modern
equivalent—was doubtless represented on the stage by
some grotesque allegorical figure :

> 'Who calleth me? Every-man? what hast thou to haste?
> I lye in corners trussed and pyled so hye,
> And in chestes I am locked so faste,
> Also sacked in bagges, thou mayst se with thyn eye,
> I can not styre; in packes lowe I lye.
> What wolde ye have, lightly me saye.'

But although, with the self-confidence of capital, *Goods*
avers that there is no difficulty in the world which he

the style of this morality (the allusion to the Dance of Death will not be
overlooked) :
'*Every-man.* O Dethe, thou comest whan I had the leest in mynde,
            In thy power it lycth me to save.
            Yet of my good wyll I gyve the, if thou wil be kynde.
            Ye a thousande pounde shalte thou have,
            And dyffere this mater tyl another daye.
    Deihe. Every-man, it may not be by no waye.
            I set not by gold, sylver, nor rychesse,
            Nor by pope, emperour, kynge, duke, ne prynces,' &c.

cannot set straight, *Every-man's* difficulty is unfortunately
not one this world can settle.   He has therefore in despair
to fall back upon the very last of the friends of whom he
can think, his *Good-Dedes.   Good-Deeds* answers that she
is so weak that she can barely rise from the ground, where
she lies cold and bound in *Every-man's* sins.   Yet not only
will she respond to his entreaty, but she will bring with
her *Knowledge,* her sister, to help him in making 'that
dredeful rekenynge.'   *Knowledge,* by whom we may
suppose to be meant the discreet and learned advice which
religion has at her service, declares her willingness to stand
by *Every-man* at the judgment-seat, and meanwhile by
her advice he addresses himself to *Confession,* who bestows
on him a precious jewel,

> ' Called penaunce, voyder of adversyte.'

His passionate prayer for mercy to God and to Mary for
her intercession has the effect of restoring *Good-Deeds* to
health and strength, so that she can accompany him before
the judgment-seat.   The allegory hereupon becomes more
directly didactic, showing how *Every-man* disposes of half
his possessions in charity by his last will and receives
extreme unction, while his *Five Wits* or senses discourse
on the dignity of the priesthood and on the Seven Sacraments of which it is the guardian.   On the return of the
shriven *Every-man* the action recovers its human interest.
As he begins his last journey, a mortal weakness comes
over him [1]; one after one his companions—*Beauty, Strength,
Discretion,* the *Five Wits*—take their leave, *Good-Deeds*
and *Knowledge* alone holding out by him in accordance
with their promise.   And so he dies, and *Knowledge*
announces that he has suffered what we shall all suffer ; that
Good-Deeds shall make all sure ; and that the voices of

---

[1] ' Alas ! I am so faynt I may not stande,
My lymmes under me doth folde ;
Frendes, let us not tourne agayne to this lande,
Not for all the worldes golde ;
For in to this cave must I crepe,
And tourne to erthe and there to slepe.'

angels are even now welcoming the ransomed soul. And as an angel descends to carry it heavenward, a personage called *Doctor* epitomises the lesson which the action of the play has illustrated.

There can of course be no pretence that the effect of this action is otherwise than impaired by its repetitions, its lengthiness, and its purely didactic passages. But the work calls itself a 'treatyse' in the very MS. in which it is preserved to us ; and though it may not have been written with a controversial intention, it was manifestly intended to uphold much of the specific teaching of the Church of Rome on the efficiency of works for salvation, on the mediating influence of the Blessed Virgin, on the Seven Sacraments, on the use of Confession and Penance, and on the authority and dignity of the priesthood—as to which last the language of the author is ecstatic[1]. But this tendency and its effects seem incidental only in contrast with the sustained force of the general action and the simple solemnity with which it is carried through from first to last, unmarred by a trace of frivolity or vulgarity, and yet coming straight home from *Every-man* to every man. The whole pitiful pathos of human life and death is here, and with it the solution of the problem which—theological controversies apart—has most enduringly commended itself to mankind. What wonder that a morality which is successful in bringing these things before hearers and readers should, by a *consensus* of opinion to which I know of no exception, be regarded as the flower and crown of the literary species to which it belongs?

R. Wever's Lusty Juventus (1550 circ.).
If *Every-man* is the production of Catholic piety, the teachings of the Reformation are reflected with the utmost distinctness in *Lusty Juventus*[2]. This morality was written in the reign of Edward VI, and breathes the spirit of the dogmatic reformation of the Protector Somerset[3]. Nothing

---

'Thus be they [priests] above aungells in degree.'

[2] Printed in the new edition of Dodsley, vol. i, and in Hawkins, vol. i. Ben Jonson refers to this morality in *The Devil is an Ass*, Act i. Sc. 1.

[3] See the concluding lines, where a prayer is offered for the king and those of the nobility

is known of its author except the name—R. Wever. Yet
in spite of its abundant theology, including an exposition
of the doctrine of justification by faith, it is neither ill
written, nor ill constructed [1]. *Lusty Juventus* is the representative of that younger generation to which the author
hopefully looks, for he makes the Devil say,

> 'Oh, oh, ful well I know the cause
> That my estimacion doth thus decay;
> The olde people would beleve stil in my lawes,
> But the younger sort lead them a contrary way;
> They wyll not beleve, they playnly say,
> In old traditions and made by men,
> But they wyll lyve as the scripture teacheth them.'

Thus *Lusty Juventus*, who opens the play with a pretty
lyric to the refrain, 'In youth is pleasure, in youth is pleasure,' is speedily converted by the teachings and preachings
of *Good Councel;* and to bring him back from these the
Devil has to call in *Hipocrisye* to his aid. *Hipocrisye* encourages the faltering fiend by a long and vigorous speech,
in which he praises his stock-in-trade of

> 'Holy fyre, holy palme,
> Holy oyle, holy creame,
> And holy ashes also;
> Holy bronches, holy rynges,
> Holy knelinge, holy sensynges,
> And a hundred trim trams mo.'

We have here the full Puritan hatred of those paraphernalia of Roman Catholic worship and ritual upon which
Somerset and his Commission made merciless war—the
feeling which made Spenser introduce Superstition as an
old woman mumbling over her beads, Idleness as a monk
with his useless breviary, and the Evil One himself now as
a monk and then as a pilgrim. With the aid of a frail
female called *Abhominable Living*, *Hipocrisye* succeeds in

> 'whom his grace hath authorised
> To maynteyne the publike wealthe over us and them,'—

i. e. the Council of State.

[1] Perhaps it may be regarded as evidence of its enduring popularity that
in as late a play as Thomas Heywood's *Wise Woman of Hogsdon* (pr. 1638)
a gallant is apostrophised as 'Lusty Juventus' (Act iv).

leading *Juventus* astray. The lyric which the tempters
sing is very pleasing, especially the stanza,—

> ' Do not the flowers sprynge freshe and gaye,
> Plesaunt and swete in the month of Maye?
> And when their time cometh, they fayde awaye.
> Report me to you, reporte me to you.'

The hero is, however, finally recovered by *Good Councel*,
the exhortations of the latter being supported by a personage who is called *God's Mercyfull Promises*[1] and, discoursing in accordance with his name, expounds the
Lutheran doctrine of Justification by Faith.

Interlude of Youth (1555 circ.).
    The *Interlude of Youth*[2], though resembling *Lusty
Juventus* in subject as well as in title, is less elaborate,
and manifestly the work of a Catholic author[3]. The contention for the guidance of Youth here lies between *Charity*
and *Humility* on the one hand, and *Pride, Riot* and *Lechery*
on the other. There is little or nothing of a controversial
tone in this piece ; and altogether this morality may be
said to be distinguished by unusual gracefulness and ease
of manner. It was doubtless composed in Queen Mary's
reign.

Renascence moralities.
    Besides these moralities of a religious tendency may be
noticed two others—probably belonging to the early part of
the Reformation period—which remind us of the wideness
and variety of the range of ideas opened to the literary
mind by the Renascence movement. The interlude of *The
Nature of the Four Elements*[4] is a genuine *curiosum*. It
was printed in 1519 by Rastell, and possibly written by him ;
the date of its composition, if a passage referring to the
discovery of ' newe londs ' as having occurred ' within this
xx yere ' is to be taken quite literally, may be ascribed to the
year 1517[5]. The lesson which it is designed to teach is the

Rastell's(?) *Nature of the Four Elements* (1517-9).

---

[1] See below as to Bale's play bearing a similar name.
[2] Printed in vol. ii. of Mr. Hazlitt's Dodsley.
[3] See, besides *Charity's* opening speech, the allusions to the Virgin, and
Humility's gift of a rosary to *Youth*.
[4] Printed in vol. i. of Mr. Hazlitt's Dodsley.
[5] ' Americus,' to whom the author ascribes the discovery, sailed from Cadiz
in 1497 (cf. Collier, ii. 321, *note*).

advantage of the pursuit of science, which is urged upon *Humanity* by *Natura Naturata* (i. e. Created Nature), *Studious Desire*, and his friend *Experience*, while he is tempted astray by *Sensual Appetite*, assisted by the concrete presence of a Taverner, and *Ignorance* (with a song[1]). First, *Humanity* goes through a course of astronomy, and after an interval of relaxation resumes his studies on the subject of the rotundity of the earth under the guidance of *Experience*, a travelled cosmographer. But *Ignorance* intervenes with his medley; and in the end (which is imperfect) *Nature* is left giving counsel to *Humanity* to continue his studies, although he may now and then ' for his comfort' have to satisfy his sensual appetite. Thus the close of this well-meant endeavour seems to have been as flat as its exordium is sobering[2].

John Redford's morality of *Wyt and Science*[3] was likewise composed in the reign of Henry VIII, but in its later part. This morality resembles the preceding in its endeavour to enforce the value of well-digested and well-applied learning; the principal characters are *Wit, Science* and '*father Reson*,' without whom *Wit* is impotent, and, on the other side, *Idlenes, Ignorance* and *Tediousnes.* There is an amusing scene, in which *Ignorance* is put through a spelling-lesson by *Idlenes*, the word which he is set to spell

Redford's Wyt and Science (temp. Hen. VIII, later part).

---

[1] Consisting of a series of quotations from popular ditties. *Ignorance* is an upholder of plain-song *versus* prick-song (melody *versus* counterpoint); and observes that it is
> 'as good to say plainly
> Give me a spade,
> As give me a spa, ve, va, ve, va, ve, vade.'

[2] We have to deplore the loss of eight pages in the middle of this morality (in the course of *Experience's* scientific demonstration); but the author—or printer—expressly observes that when the piece is played ' ye may leave out much of the sad matter,' without spoiling the consistency of the construction. He clearly (see also the close of the Messenger's prologue) did not feel quite sure of his public, and took care, like other preachers of popular science after him, to put a little alloy into his silver. Criticism is disarmed by the excellence of his intentions, which announce themselves already in a kind of syllabus, notifying the principal scientific truths to be found in the play side by side with the *dramatis personae.* The description of the regions of the New World, which had been recently discovered, Labrador (1497), and Virginia (1502), the former in particular, are not without interest.

[3] Edited by Halliwell for the *Shakespeare Society's Publications*, 1848.

being *Ingland*. The density of *Ignorance*, and his rustic speech, are extremely diverting [1].

To the reign of Henry VIII also belongs the solitary extant dramatic work of a writer who, notwithstanding the admirable edition of his works which we possess [2], has hardly as yet received the degree of attention to which his merits entitle him. Skelton, as was inevitable in such a career as his, brought down upon himself the ill-will of literary as well as political contemporaries; he was sneered at by Barclay, and persecuted by Wolsey. But his reputation [3] has suffered from the defective sympathy of Warton, the orthodox indignation of Johnson, and the epigrammatic unfairness of Pope. Skelton is extremely and ostentatiously coarse; but it cannot be said of him that he panders to vice or prostitutes himself to the service of immorality. The ends of his satire were in the main moral; and its tendency was in full sympathy with the great movement of his age. His rime, as he says himself, 'hath in it some pith'; and there is life in his 'tumbling' verse. His political note is the hatred of ecclesiastical domination which was one of the motive forces of the Reformation; his literary note is the return to natural sense and vivacity which was one of the mainsprings of the Renascence [4].

Skelton's 'goodly interlude and mery' of *Magnyfycence* was certainly written after the year 1515 [5]. In construction

---

[1] The costume of Ignorance, who is 'deckt lyke a very asse,' resembles that of *Anerie* in the French farce *Science et Anerie*. See Fournier, p. 334; but I do not know what authority there is for the details of the admirable illustrations to this volume.

[2] *The Poetical Works of John Skelton : with notes and some account of the author and his writings*, by the Rev. Alexander Dyce. 2 vols., 1843.

[3] Puttenham (1589) simply speaks of him as 'I wot not for what great worthines surnamed the Poet *Laureat*.'

[4] Ben Jonson, who seems to have been thoroughly familiar with Skelton's works, introduces him in person into his Antimasque of *The Fortunate Isles*. He had already appeared as presenter, manager, and actor in Munday's *Downfall of Robert Earl of Huntingdon*, where the Skeltonical verse is imitated (cf. *infra*).—In later times, justice was already done to Skelton by the author of the *Curiosities of Literature*. Miss Strickland discerned in the early intimacy between Henry (VIII) and Skelton the probable foundation of the grossest crimes of the royal pupil.

[5] This appears from an allusion to a dead 'Kynge Lewes of Fraunce' as famed for largesse, who must be Lewis XII.

and purpose it has nothing to distinguish it from earlier
moralities.   Its object is, as one of the characters states at
the close, to offer

> 'A playne example of worldly vaynglory,
> Howe in this world there is no sekernesse,
> But fallyble flatery enmyxyd with bytternesse.'

Magnyfycence, the hero of the allegory, is seduced by
a company of false friends, among whom are *Counterfeit-
countenance, Crafty-conveyance, Cloked-collusion,* and *Courtly-
abusion,* into a life without measure, such a life as the
introduction to the main action has, on the authority of
'Oracius,' stigmatised as leading to ruin.   He accordingly
becomes associated with *Adversity* and *Poverty*, and then
with *Despair* and *Mischief*, the latter of whom advises him
to commit suicide; but he is recovered by *Good-hope*, and
with the aid of *Redress, Circumspection,* and *Perseverance*,
brought to recognise the error of his ways, and to follow
above all the exhortation, 'to knowe him selfe mortall, for
all his dygnyte,' 'not to set all his affyance in Fortune full
of gyle,' and to 'remember this lyfe lastyth but a whyle.'
The teaching of this morality was singularly appropriate to
the extravagant and arrogant age to which it was addressed;
but contrary to his practice in his Satires, Skelton abstains
from any personal applications.   The merit of the play
consists in the vigour and vivacity of its diction.   The
author gives free utterance to the wealth of his vocabulary;
the rhymes are, as in his Satires, frequently happy and
ingenious, and he freely permits himself to lapse into the
short irregular lines which he loved.   Upon the whole, the
dignity of the morality is well sustained, but there are
occasional passages of a lighter character, and a lyric song
by *Lyberte* is introduced, further to relieve the monotony of
the piece.   In one speech (that in which *Magnyfycence*
exults at the height of his prosperity) we are reminded by
the general manner and by the alliteration of the tirades of
the Herods and Pilates in the Mysteries [1].   The learning
with which Skelton was stuffed full is not always lightly

---

[1] 'I drede no daunger, I dawnce all in delyte.
My name is Magnyfycence, man most of might,

Other
dramatic
works by
Skelton.

applied, and in truth, had the scholarship of the Renascence been able to master the beginnings of our drama, they would have run some risk of being smothered in the process.

Besides this morality, Skelton, as he tells us in his *Garlande of Laurell*, produced 'of *Vertu* the souerayne enterlude,' and a 'commedy, *Achademios* callyd by name.' Both of these are lost ; and the loss of the latter is perhaps to be especially regretted, since it probably contained satirical remarks on the education of the age, resembling those which Skelton introduces in his odd satire of *Speke, Parrot*[1]. A fourth play by the same author, *Nigromansir* (i. e. Necromancer), now also lost, had been seen by Warton. From his account[2], it seems to have been an attack, in a dramatic form, on some abuses in the Church, 'yet not without a due regard to decency, and an apparent respect for the dignity of the audience.' The story or plot, Warton further informs us, is the trial of *Simony* and *Avarice*; the Devil is the judge, and to his jurisdiction the culprits are consigned. The chief use of the personage giving his name to the play is really to speak the prologue, in which he summons the Devil—who kicks him for his pains, objecting to being called so early in the morning[3]. Latin and French are stated to have been freely introduced into this piece, in the *Rococo*-Renascence manner so typically represented by its author.

It would not have suited the temper of King Henry VIII at any time in his reign to allow so direct a dramatic lesson to be read to his lieges as that which a con-

---

       Hercules the hardy, with his stobburne clobbyd mase,
       That made Cerberus to cache, the cur dogge of hell,
       And Thesius, that prowde was Pluto to face,
       It wolde not become them with me for to mell,' &c.

[1] Skelton, who 'lernyd to spelle' Henry VIII himself, and whom Erasmus described as 'unum Britannicarum literarum lumen ac decus,' was laureate of both the English Universities, as well as of Louvain.

[2] *History of English Poetry*, sec. xxxiii. *Il Negromante* is the title of a comedy by Ariosto.

[3] I cannot perceive in this a proof that plays were acted in the morning. At all events they were not acted before the hours when gentlemen were in the habit of rising.

temporary Scottish poet was allowed to put into this form in order to attract the public ear with the aid of the public eye. I leave aside any attempt to put together what data remain as to early dramatic performances in Scotland [1], inasmuch as they seem as a whole to be without claims upon the attention of any but specialist students. The earliest Scottish religious play of which we have any information, the *Haliblude*, was acted at Aberdeen in 1445, and may from its name be conjectured to have been of a kind which specially provoked the Scottish Reformation, about a century later, to put a stop upon all dramatic growths whatever within the range of its censure. It is all the more interesting to observe that Sir David Lyndsay's morality, entitled *Ane Satyre of the thrie Estaits*, which in vigour and variety far outstrips any contemporary or analogous English effort, was distinctly designed to commend and encourage the Reformation movement. It was acted at Cupar in 1535, and performed on more than one subsequent occasion ; an eye-witness, who saw it acted at Edinburgh in 1554, before the Queen-Mother (Mary of Guise, who for a time winked at the new doctrines), states that the performance lasted from 'nyne houris afoir none till sex houris at evin.' I add some account of this remarkable work in a note rather than in my text, because, although the 'Lowland Scotch' in which it is written is of course nothing but an English dialect [2], the particular

Lyndsay's Satire of the Three Estates.

---

[1] For an account of the beginnings of the drama in Scotland see Dr. D. Irving, *The History of Scottish Poetry*, ed. Dr. J. A. Carlyle, 1861, chaps. xvi. and xxi. The latter chapter mentions, as more nearly approaching to the modern drama, Lyndsay's morality, a play called *Philotus*, printed at Edinburgh in 1603, and absurdly attributed to John Heywood. See Halliwell, *Dictionary of Old English Plays*, 194. See also Dr. Irving's *Dissertation on the Early Scottish Drama in the Lives of the Scottish Poets*, i. 197-222. Mr. Lecky, *History of England in the Eighteenth Century*, ii. 88, asserts that no theatre was opened in Scotland before 1726.

[2] See the passage in Part II, where Lyndsay adds to a quotation from St. Paul, '*Qui non laborat non manducet*' (2 *Thessalonians*, iii. 10), the explanation :

'This is, in Inglische toung, or leit :
QUHA LABOURIS NOCHT HE SALL NOT EIT.'

The same Scriptural quotation is made in the French *Moralité Nouvelle des Enfans de Maintenant*, *Anc. Th. Fr.* iii. 14.

literature of which it forms part continued for many a generation afterwards to run its course apart from, and without
influence upon, the main stream of English literature[1].

With certain exceptions, to be noted below, the pre-

[1] Sir David Lyndsay's *Satyre of the thrie Estaits in commendation of Vertew
and Vitvperation of Vyce* (printed at Edinburgh in 1602) is reprinted in
Chalmers' edition of Lyndsay's *Poetical Works*, and was edited for the *Early
English Text Society* in 1869 by Dr. Fitzedward Hall. Lyndsay was the
faithful servant and intimate counsellor of his sovereign, James V, whom he
had anxiously tended as a child, and whom his sympathy and advice consistently supported as a man.   This intimacy accounts for the extraordinary
outspokenness which the author of this morality permitted himself. It exposes
with the utmost ardour and freedom the existing abuses in the State, and
more particularly in the Church.   The play (for a more complete analysis of
which see H. Morley, *First Sketch of English Literature*, pp. 171–6) is divided
into two Parts, of which · the best pairt,' as the author says, or at all events
the most explicit, is the Second. The earlier Part resembles many of the English moralities, although it is written with greater spirit and force than any of
these with which I am acquainted. *King Humanitie*, the hero of the action, is
seduced by *Sensualite* and her helpmates. *Gude-Counsell* and his companions
are resisted by *Dissait, Flatterie*, and *Falset*, who appear as the Vices, and
who assume disguises (*Flattery* that of a friar).   They put *Verity* in the
stocks, after exclaiming against the New Testament 'in English toung,' which
she holds in her hands ; but *Divine Correction* at last brings the king to a
better mind, and *Sensuality* takes her departure to the lords of the Spirituality,
who have previously refused to have anything to do with *Chastity*.

Already in the first part, some characters of a popular kind are introduced,
whose fooling is carried on with the utmost licence (Lyndsay's muse is at
times very unmannerly).   The second part commences with the complaints
of *Pauper*, who is seeking a remedy by law against the exactions imposed
upon him by clerical hands, for he is, as *Diligence* informs him,
          'The daftest fuill, that ever I saw;
      Trows thou, man, be the law to get remeid
      Of men of kirk? Na, nocht till thou be deid.'
So he lies down in despair ; and a Pardoner appears, by name 'schir Robert
Rome-raker,' who gives
          'To the devill, with good intent,
      This unsell wickit New-testament
        With thame that it translaitit';
prays 'to the rude,' that
          'Martin Luther, that fals loun,
      Black Bullinger, and Melanchthoun
      Had been smorde in their cude';
and cries his own 'geir,' administering a penance to a 'sowtar' (shoemaker)
and his wife, and selling a thousand years' pardon to *Pauper* for his last
groat. But *Pauper* repents him of his bargain, and a free-fight ensues, in
which the relics are thrown into the water.

After this horse-play the more serious part of the morality commences.
The Three Estates appear before the king; and the representative of the
suffering people, *Johne the Common-weill*, comes forward with his complaints.

dominant purpose of the English moralities produced
during the Tudor reigns remains, in accordance with the
broad meaning of the term, moral teaching.   Thus *The*
Triall of Treasure (first printed, apparently in two editions,
in 1567 [1]) furnishes no evidence as to whether it was written
by a Catholic or a Protestant.   It is however interesting
in more than one respect.   Its most distinctive feature
is the learning of its author, who displays an equal
familiarity with biblical and with classical lore.   The
prologue illustrates the doctrine of the vanity of human
self-indulgence from the philosophy of Diogenes and from
the Epistle of St. James.   Classical allusions and quotations
are frequent, and we are evidently here confronted by
a genuine scholar of the Renascence.   But he is also fond
of lyrical efforts, which abound in the piece, and are chiefly,
though not uniformly, of a merry description.   *The Triall
of Treasure* signifies the testing by experience of the vanity
of confiding in earthly prosperity ; the hero of the morality,
Luste, being misled by evil counsellors, *Inclination* the
Vice among the number (upon whom a bridle is literally
placed by *Sapience* and *Juste*), gives himself up to the
love of *Treasure* and the friendship of *Pleasure*, but *God's
Visitation* comes upon him, and finally *Time* reduces him
and his paramour to naught [2].

The result is that the Vices are put in the stocks, and *Good-Counsel* is
called in as adviser.   A long debate ensues, witnesses are examined, and
summary measures of punishment adopted against the adversaries of social
and religious reform.   Not fewer than two sermons are preached, one by
the *Doctour* and another by *Folly*; but previously to the latter, Acts have
been passed and proclaimed comprehending the necessary changes in the
state of the commonwealth.   Undoubtedly, the great length of the second
division of this morality renders it, as *Diligence* avows in his short epilogue,
' sum part, tedious ' ; but the distinctness and earnestness of its serious
passages are its most striking characteristics, the fun and grossness of the
comic passages having evidently been introduced as a foil.   Altogether, this
dramatic satire is one of the most noteworthy of Lyndsay's works, and by far
the most elaborate as well as in its way the most powerful of all our
mediaeval moralities.

   [1] Edited for the Percy Society (*Publications*, vol. xxviii) by Mr. J. O. Halliwell (1850), and printed in Mr. Hazlitt's Dodsley, vol. iii.

   [2] It may be noted that *Greedy-Gutte*, one of the companions of *Luste* in this
morality, uses the rustic dialect which reappears in so many of our old plays,
and is employed by both Peele and Shakspere.

Ulpian Fulwel's *Like wil to Like quod the Devel to the Colier* [1] (printed in 1568) exhibits with a very robust realism the pernicious results of riotous living. The Collier, who is introduced to the tune of 'Tom Collier of Croydon,' plays merely an incidental part in the piece, emblematical of the irresistible force of natural affinities [2]. As he is attracted by the Devil, so Nichol Newfangle, the Vice of the play, who was 'bound prentice before his nativity to Lucifer himself,' draws into his company a congenial crew, consisting of Ralph Roister (the name will be noted), Tom Tosspot, Hankin Hangman, and so forth. After an abundance of boisterous fun [3] ensue moralisings by *Virtuous Living*, *Good Fame*, *God's Promise*, and *Honour*, and the punishment of the offenders by *Severity* as judge. Hangman leads off Cuthbert Cutpurse and Pierce Pickpurse; and Nichol Newfangle rides off for 'a journey to Spain' on his master's back.

The Marriage of Witte and Science [4] (licensed 1569-70), though its plot and chief characters are borrowed from Redford's earlier morality already noted, deserves attention as in execution altogether one of the most advanced specimens of its class. The excellence of the diction and versification of *Nature's* opening speech prepare the reader for a production of well-sustained literary merit; and no better example could be given of a well-constructed and well-executed morality than this piece, which is regularly divided into acts and scenes. Of the lesson which it enforces I will venture to say that it is thoroughly sound

---

[1] Printed in Mr. Hazlitt's Dodsley, vol. iii.

[2] 'Tom Collier of Croydon hath sold his coals,
    And made his market today;
    And now he danceth with the Devil,
    For like will to like alway.'
The character of Grim, the Collier of Croydon, appears in Edwards' *Damon and Pithias*, and gives its name to another old play noticed below. According to Ritson, quoted by Collier, Crowley's epigram on the *Collier of Croydon* was printed in 1550 or 1551. The phrase which gives its title to the play occurs as a proverbial expression (scurrilously applied to the 'precise crew' of the godly) in Bunyan's *Life and Death of Mr. Badman* (1680).

[3] Hangman's drunkenness manifests itself in an original Leonine hexameter, and in his dancing 'as evil-favoured as may be devised.'

[4] Printed in vol. ii. of Hazlitt's Dodsley.

and sensible; and there is a genuine enthusiasm about the tone of the work which deserves the sympathy of every real student.

The Marriage of Wit and Wisdom [1] seems likewise to belong to the Elisabethan moralities. It is divided into acts and scenes, and is decidedly one of the liveliest productions of its class. There is considerable reality about several of the personages, among whom are *Snatch* and *Catch*, two vagabond 'soldiares' who have 'come from Flushing to the English port'—characters well known to the comic drama of the Elisabethan age. *Idleness*, who on one occasion appears as a priest, is the Vice, who introduces himself as 'the flower of the frying-pan,' and describes his parentage and antecedents in the following nonsense rimes:— *(The Marriage of Wit and Wisdom (temp. Elisabeth).)*

> ' My mother had ij. whelps at one litter,
>   Both borne in Lent ;
> So we ware both put into a musselbote,
>   And came sailing in a sowes yeare ouer sea into Kent.'

The *Contention between Liberalitie and Prodigalitie* [2] was in its present form acted before Queen Elisabeth in 1600 [3], but may very possibly be a revision of an earlier work. In any case, the style is unequal, the incidental lyrics being in general superior to the dialogue. The action, in which several concrete personages take a subsidiary part, is upon the whole brisk, showing how after *Prodigality* had gained possession of *Master Money*, son of *Dame Fortune*, he lost his prize by his recklessness ; how *Money* then fell into the hands of *Tenacity* (i. e. Avarice, who talks the usual peasant's dialect of the stage); how *Prodigality* then set upon *Tenacity* in the high-road and robbed him of *Money* ; and how *Money* was finally delivered out of the hands of his tormentors and entrusted to the care of *Liberality* ; *(The Contention between Liberality and Prodigality (acted 1600).)*

---

[1] Edited by Halliwell-Phillipps for the *Shakesp. Soc. Publ.* (1846). In the tragedy of *Sir Thomas More* (*vide infra*), this morality is selected for performance before a banquet, as a play within the play, from a list including with it *The Cradle of Securitie, Hit nayle o' th' Head, Impatient Poverty,* [Heywood's] *The Four P's, Dives and Lazarus,* and *Lusty Juventus.* See Collier, ii. 194.

[2] Printed in vol. viii. of Hazlitt's Dodsley.

[3] See Act v. Sc. 5.

while *Prodigality* (this is the effective bit of realism in the play) was tried and sentenced in due form, but in mercy forgiven part of the penalty. This morality, besides being written (or revised) by a scholar evidently desirous of showing his scholarship, is not devoid of a rude kind of intrinsic merit; but it is not a little curious to find such a relic of the early drama performed before Queen Elisabeth at a time when Shakspere had probably produced more than half his plays.

Moralities bearing on the religious controversy. Although during the Tudor period, from the first introduction of changes into ecclesiastical affairs down to the settlement of them under Elisabeth, the prohibitions were numerous which sought to prevent the popular stage from taking part in religious controversy, yet it was not in the nature of things that occasional use should fail to be made of so convenient an organ of public opinion or sentiment in connexion with topics occupying them above all others. Several interludes were produced in the latter part of the reign of Henry VIII bearing upon the religious questions of the day; but none of these has been preserved to us [1]. King Edward VI is said himself to have composed an 'elegant comedy' which took for its title the most opprobrious allegorical designation ever bestowed by her enemies upon the Church of Rome [2]. And at the very commencement of Queen Mary's reign a morality called *Respublica* was represented at Court which was bitterly anti-protestant in sentiment, and introduced Queen Mary herself in the character of Nemesis [3]. As a matter of course the same controversial tendency manifested itself in the productions of the earlier part of Elisabeth's reign. It introduces itself

---

[1] See the letter addressed to Cromwell soon after 1535 by Thomas Wylley, vicar of Yoxford in Suffolk, *ap.* Collier, i. 128–130, in which the writer complains of not being allowed to preach in most of the other churches in the county because he had made a play 'agaynst the popys Counselers, Error, Colle Clogger of Conscyens, and Incredulyte.' He adds that he has made ' a playe caulyd A Rude Commynawlte,' and is making another ' caulyd The Woman on the Rokke, yn the fyer of faythe a fynyng, and a purgyng in the trewe purgatory.' The last however was 'never to be seen but of' Cromwell's ' eye.'

[2] *The Whore of Babylon.* See Collier, ii. 408.

[3] She appears, though in humbler guise, in much the same character in John Heywood's epical allegory of *The Spider and the Flie.*

into W. Wager's *The longer thou livest the more Foole thou
art*[1]; but it is the pervading element of two moralities of
the Elisabethan age which from this point of view call for
special notice.

The anonymous play of *New Custome*[2], printed in 1573, *New
is, then, a purely controversial production ; its characters, Custom
which are so arranged as to admit of being performed by (pr. 1573).
four players, representing respectively the Church of Rome
and her allies, and the Reformation and its supporters.
The allies of Rome are '*Perverse Doctrine*, an old Popish
priest,' and '*Ignorance*, another but elder,' whose friends
are '*Hypocrisie*, an olde woman,' and '*Creweltie* and
Avarice, two Rufflers' (i. e. bullies). On the other side
stand *New Custome* and *Light of the Gospell*, who are
called ' Ministers,' '*Edification*, a Sage,' '*Assauraunce*,
a Virtue,' and '*Goddes Felicitie*, a Sage.' The contention
between these adversaries is carried on with great ardour ;
Perverse Doctrine reprobates the spread of the Bible among
the people as 'casting perles to an hogge'; *New Custome*
quotes ' Paule to the Corinthians,' declares the Mass, Popery,
Purgatory and pardons to be 'flatt against Godde's woorde,'
and vindicates to himself his proper appellation of *Primitive
Constitution*. While *Light of the Gospell* cheers on the
representative of the recovered simplicity and purity of the
early Church, *Perverse Doctrine*, after consulting with
Hypocrisie, declares that

' Since these Genevian doctours came so fast into this lande,
  Since that time it was never merie with Englande.'

Creweltie and *Avarice* then come on the scene ; and the
latter, in order to vindicate his power against the bluster

---

[1] This morality, which I have not seen, is described by Collier, ii. 332–8,
cf. n. e.). Its hero is Moros ; and it contains the 'foote' or refrain of several
old songs.—Wager was also author of *The Cruel Detter* (entered in Stationers'
Registers in 1565 or 1566), a play partly written in seven-line stanzas, of
which further fragments have been recently discovered by Mr. Edmund
Gosse (*The Academy*, March 9, 1878), and of '*Tis good sleeping in a whole
skin*. See *New Shakspere Society's Transactions*, i. 2*.

[2] Printed in vol. iii. of Hazlitt's Dodsley. One of the 'auncient plays'
known to Captain Cox was, according to Robert Laneham, *Nu Gize* (*New
Guise*), which Dr. Furnivall, *u. s.* cxxii–iv, indentifies as the play in the
text.

of his companion, relates a cheering precedent from ' the daies of queene Marie' of the foul betrayal of a brother. But in the end *Perverse Doctrine* is converted by *Light of the Gospell*, and *Edification, Assuraunce* and *Godde's Felicitie* consummate the triumph of the righteous cause. The morality ends with a prayer for Queen Elisabeth, and a song—the latter not extant.

The other work which I have to notice in this connexion is additionally curious as containing a character taken from actual history, though the whole contrivance of the piece allows us still to class it among the moralities. The incident which suggested Nathaniel Woodes' *The Conflict of Conscience* (originally printed in 1581 [1]), viz. the abandonment of the Protestant for the Catholic faith by an Italian lawyer of the name of Francis Spira or Spiera, had indeed taken place about the middle of the century; but unless the play was kept concealed by the author for some time after its composition, it can hardly have been written before Protestantism had been definitively re-established in England. The author, who is stated to have been a clergyman of Norwich, seems to bear the Marian persecution in fresh remembrance, and perhaps the Cardinal Legate whose proceedings he holds up to abhorrence may be intended for Reginald Pole, Rome's emissary for the work of reunion [2]. But the play is devoid of any allusions which can be directly brought home to the national history. Its hero Philologus is represented as a learned man who, by the agency of allegorical personages, of whom *Hypocrisy* is the most prominent and *Sensual Suggestion* the most effective, is lured away from the truth of the Gospel into the toils of Rome. *Conscience* in vain seeks to hold him back; and *Horror* inflicts upon him the pangs—described with some degree of power—of remorse and despair. In

N. Woodes' The Conflict of Conscience (pr. 1581).

---

[1] Reprinted from the edition published for the Roxburghe Club by Collier in 1851 in vol. ii. of Hazlitt's Dodsley, with Collier's Introduction to this and the other plays included in his volume.

[2] See iii. 3. It is strange, by the bye, that the priest Caconos who rejoices over the restoration of the Pope's authority and the revival of saints' days, ' pilgrimage, reliques, trentals, and pardons' (iii. 4), should be made to talk what seems intended for Scotch.

the end, the credit of the good cause is saved by a short
sixth act or epilogue, in which a *Nuntius* describes Philologus
as having been reconverted at the last, and died in peace
with God.

The tone of this work is bitterly controversial ; and the
fulness with which it enters into its subject, as well as the
lengthiness of its speeches, is that of a clerical author.
Nearly the whole of it is written in the seven-line stanza ;
and although this metre is not unfrequently used in our
early plays, this can hardly have been intended for representation.   The blind intolerance which it exhibits almost
surpasses that of any other production not professedly
theological with which I am acquainted.

The solitary political morality which has come down to *Political*
us has unfortunately been preserved in a fragment only. *moralities.*
To what extent elements of political controversy or invective intermingled with that of religious vituperation in the
plays dating from the reigns of Henry VIII and Edward VI,
and in the *Respublica* performed at Court on Queen Mary's
accession, on which I have already touched [1], is of course
unknown.   Towards the end of Mary's reign—in 1557—
a play called *The Sackful of News* is stated to have been
prohibited by order of the Privy Council.   It may be
surmised to have been unambitious from a literary point
of view, although it would be interesting to know more of
this attempt—the earliest on record—in the direction of the
purely secular drama [2].   But the ' mery Playe both pythy
and pleasaunt of *Albyon Knight* ' [3] may be unhesitatingly *Albyon*
described as a political morality, inasmuch as all the *Knight*
characters appearing in it represent either political ideas or *(entered*
political institutions, after the fashion of Lyndsay's dramatic *1565–6).*
Satyre.   The hero is of course a personification of England,
as *Johne the Common-weill* is of the sister country in the
Scottish play.   To judge from the fragment which remains

[1] *Ante*, p. 136.
[2] According to Collier, ii. 408, this is, so far as we know, the ' single play
anterior to the reign of Elizabeth, which, from its name, looks like an original
composition of a profane kind.'
[3] Printed by Collier in vol. i. of *The Shakespeare Society's Papers*, pp. 55 *seqq.*,
in *Publications*, 1844.

of the work, its purpose would seem to have been to allay the ill-feeling on the part of the commonalty against the nobility, as well as the jealousy between the lords spiritual and the lords temporal. It would be unsafe to speculate on the particular relations with which *Albyon Knight* concerned itself ; nor are we justified in assuming this to have been the particular play of which the performance was abruptly stopped at Court in 1559. But *Albyon Knight* was in all probability written not later than 1565–6, when it was entered on the Registers of the Stationers' Company. This was a period of notable uncertainty in the policy of Queen Elisabeth, when among the chief nobles intrigue and counter-intrigue were at their height, particularly in connexion with the aspirations of Leicester, and when the great Catholic houses could not yet have reconciled themselves to the newly-made bishops of the existing reign. Considerable boldness was required for the implied admonition to *Principalytie*—in other words, to the Queen—not to suppose the people unwilling to grant supplies. In general, however, the bearing of the text is not enough to suggest that it contains allusions to particular occasions or persons. The main characters of this morality seem to be, besides *Albyon Knight* himself, *Injuri* (who at first appears under the false name of *Manhode*) and *Justice* ; and their contention reminds us of that between the δίκαιος and the ἄδικος λόγος in the *Clouds* of Aristophanes. The chief ally of *Injuri* is *Divisio* ; and the moral of the piece is the evil result of discord [1].

[1] I add a reference to two productions which may be most conveniently noticed here, as in fact moral-plays by the nature of their design as well as execution. ' R. W.,' the author of *The Three Ladies of London* (printed in 1584 ' as it hath been publiquely played ') and the *The Three Lordes and Three Ladies of London* (printed in 1590), has been conjectured by Collier to have been an actor of the name of Robert Wilson (who was one of the Earl of Leicester's players in 1574, was adopted into the Queen's company in 1583, and was buried at Cripplegate in 1600) and a different person from the dramatist of the same name mentioned *infra*. See Collier's *Memoirs of the Principal Actors in the Plays of Shakespeare* (*Shakesp. Soc. Publ.*, 1846), Introduction, p. xviii, *note*, and p. 131. (According to Collier, i. 361, *note*, a play with this title was printed in the same year 1590 by one Paul Bucke, cf.) ' R. W.' was in any case a writer of considerable fluency, and, as the second of these plays shows, able to accommodate himself to the fashion of

The moralities proper survived in England to the close *Moralities*
of the sixteenth century, and even into the early years of *resembling*
comedy and
the seventeenth[1]. But the regular drama had flourished *tragedy.*
from a period long preceding these dates, and to it the
moralities in the end could not but give way. The tran-

lively prose dialogue which Lyly had brought into favour. The plots of
these moralities are little if at all in advance of those of earlier compositions
of the kind. The Three Ladies are *Lucre, Love,* and *Conscience,* of whom the
two latter are in the first piece perverted by the machinations of Lucre and
Dissimulation, and the rest of her servants ; while in the second the three
are wooed by three series of gallants, respectively Lords of London (*Policy,
Pomp,* and *Pleasure*), Lords of Spain (*Pride, Ambition,* and *Tyranny*), and
Lords of Lincoln (*Desire, Delight,* and *Devotion*). The London and Spanish
Lords (each of whom has an appropriate Page—indeed the *dramatis personae*
of this piece are bewildering in their multiplicity) engage in a contest manifestly intended to refer to the times of the Spanish Armada, in which this
play must have been written. In its predecessor one or two concrete
personages are introduced by the side of the allegorical abstractions ; one of
these (Judge Nemo) plays a less important part in the second piece ; another
(the Jew Gerontus) is curious as the representation of an honest Jew, who
is favourably contrasted with his Christian adversary Mercatore :
' One may judge and speak truth, as appears by this ;
Jews seek to excel in Christianity and Christians in Jewishness.'
The name Gerontus, as Collier observes, cannot fail to recall that of ' Gernutus, the Jew of Venice,' the hero of the ballad referred to *infra.* See also
Mr. Sidney Lee's letter on Shylock and his Predecessors printed in *The
Academy,* May 14, 1887. There is no resemblance in the characters of
Gernutus, Barabas, or Shylock to that of Gerontus ; but there are some odd
similarities of expression between the scene in *The Three Ladies* and the
trial-scene in *The Merchant of Venice* (' reverend judge ' . . . ' most puissant
judge ' . . . ' Pay me the principal '). In both of the plays *Simplicity* supplies
the place of clown; in the first singing an appropriate song, with the
burden,
' Simplicity sings it, and 'sperience doth prove,
No dwelling in London, no biding in London, for Conscience and Love ';
and in the second paying a tribute to the memory of Tarlton as the prince
of merry fellows. (Cf. *infra.*) The main distinction between these two works
and the older moralities lies in a greater ease of style ; in conception and in
construction they mark no advance whatever. As to *The Playe of Playes,*
a morality described by Gosson in his *Playes confuted in five Actions* (1581
or 2\, see Collier, ii. 197–8.
[1] Thomas Nash, in his verses *The Choosing of Valentines,* which must
belong to about the last decad of the sixteenth century, refers to
' A play of straunge moralitee
Shewen by bachelrie of *Manning-tree.*'
See Nash's *Works,* edited by Dr. Grosart, vol. i. *Memorial Introduction,*
p. lx. In his *Apology for Actors* (1612), bk. iii. p. 53 (*Shakesp. Soc. Publ.*
1841), Thomas Heywood speaks of ' moralls ' as a still existing variety of the
drama.

sitions by which the mysteries and the moralities respectively
grew into branches of the regular drama in this country
will be indicated below; here it may be noted in conclusion,
that we possess a considerable number of plays, dating
chiefly from the latter half of the sixteenth century, which
may be said to occupy a doubtful position on the boundary-
line between moralities on the one hand, and comedies
or tragedies on the other. In these pieces the tendency,
observable already in some of the moralities described
above, to introduce real human personages of a typical kind
by the side of allegorical abstractions, is more fully and
systematically pursued. Those among them in which both
action and characters are still in the main allegorical may
be classed with the moralities rather than with our earliest
comedies and tragedies. In this category should perhaps
be placed the play of *Tom Tiler and his Wife*[1] (1578),
where allegorical characters, including *Desire* the Vice,
mix with *Tom Tiler* and *Tom Tailor*, while the former
Tom's wife, named *Strife*, is half an abstraction, half a
type. George Wapull's *Tide tarrieth no Man*, already
cited as introducing a Vice called *Courage*, out of whom the
humour has gone with the wickedness, seems to have been
a composition of a similar description[2]. In *The Nice
Wanton*[3] (1560), 'ye may see Three branches of an ill tree:
The mother and her children three, Two naught and one
godly,'—real human types; but the action is as simple
as that of any morality, and *Iniquity* plays his usual part.
In certain productions of a more ambitious cast, such as
Apius and Virginia, *King Cambises* and Bale's *Kyng Johan*,
and in the play called *A Knack to know a Knave* (1594 cf.),
although allegorical personages still appear, the action and
the main characters are historical, and the 'moral' element
is secondary only. The same is the relation between the
latter and the element of romantic narrative in *Common
Conditions* (printed about 1568), and in *Sir Clyomon and*

---

[1] Collier, ii.—Tom Tiler and his wife are referred to in Fletcher's *The
Woman's Prize, or The Tamer Tamed* (ii. 6).
[2] Collier, ii. 296-8. Cf. *ante*, p. 110, *note*.
[3] Printed in vol. ii. of Hazlitt's Dodsley.

Sir Clamydes[1]. Thus by a natural process was reached, as we shall see, the stage of the Interludes, and of the Chronicle Histories proper, at which the allegorical characters were altogether dropped.

I have thus pursued to the point at which it seems warrantable to speak of the beginnings of the regular English drama the two main growths from which it took its origin. Before concluding this chapter I have only in addition to advert very briefly to a third species of entertainment, not properly speaking dramatic, but containing dramatic elements, which may be said to have existed almost from the first by the side of the other two. The *Pageants.* origin of the term *pageants* has been already explained [2]. The expression originally referred to the movable scaffolds on which both miracle-plays and moralities were represented, and (as has been repeatedly seen) was freely used of the plays themselves that were performed on these structures. As in the case of some of the plays connected with the symbols and services of the Church already noticed [3], so in that of a few popular productions, essentially or altogether secular in theme, it would be useless to seek to discriminate too nicely between such processional and spectacular features on the one hand, and dramatic on the other, as we may conclude them to have severally presented. Thus we hear of a play of *St. George*, which enjoyed a long-lived popularity in various parts of the country as an open-air summer entertainment. While at times its presentment may have in no respect differed from that of an ordinary miracle-play [4], it was very frequently accompanied by processional pageantry, and on at least one memorable occasion—at Windsor, in 1416—seems to have been expanded into a magnificent dumb-show, fit to be put before King Henry V and his guest the Emperor Sigismund [5]. Other entertainments—half play, half show—seem in many *Festival* localities to have been exhibited in connexion with particular *plays.*

---

[1] Collier, ii. 425 *seqq.* As to these two plays, see below.
[2] *Ante*, p. 58.
[3] *Ante*, p. 97.
[4] Collier, i. 16; ten Brink, ii. 305.
[5] Collier, i. 29.

festivals, or with particular seasons of the year [1]. The custom
of kindling fires and setting watches on the Eves of St. John
(Midsummer Eve) and St. Peter lasted into the Elisabethan
age [2]; and readers of Shakspere need no reminder as to the
fact that on such occasions some sort of plays were at
times performed in connexion with the shows furnished by
town gilds and other bodies. The perennially popular
festivities of Mayday have preserved, even in the forms
which they wear at the present time, some reminiscences
of their traditional association with the legends of Robin
Hood and his companions [3]; and although the first extant
dramatic elaboration of this connexion seems to belong
to an advanced period of the sixteenth century, Robin Hood,
Maid Marian, Friar Tuck, and the rest, had no doubt been
known for many generations to the votaries of the merry
month of May [4]. A mixed entertainment of an exceptional
character, and perhaps of a historical origin, was the so-
called *Hox* or *Hock Tuesday Play*, which is known to have
been exhibited at Coventry from the year 1416 onwards,
and in 1575 was witnessed by Queen Elisabeth as part
of the entertainments provided for her at Kenilworth. This
'olld storial shew,' which was in the main a mirthful representation of a fight, showing among other things 'how
valiantly our English women for looue of their cuntree,
behaued themseluez' on the occasion, was 'expressed in'
both 'actionz and rymez [5],' and therefore seems, notwith-

*Hox Tues-
day Play.*

[1] It is needless to cite surviving instances—such as the Westmoreland
rush-bearing, the Devonshire harvest-play, &c., which point to the frequency in earlier times of popular usages of this description.

[2] Cf. Sharp, *u. s.*, pp. 174 *seqq.*

[3] *The newe Playe of Robyn Hoode, for to be played in Maye games, very
plesaunte to behold* was printed with *A mery geste of Robyn Hoode*, &c.,
about 1561. It is a dramatisation, with certain changes, of the ballads of
'Robin Hood and Friar Tuck,' and 'Robin Hood and the Potter.' See
Furnivall, *Forewords to Laneham's Letter*, pp. li–liv, and cf., as to this and
other early plays on the same subject, Halliwell's *Dictionary of Old English
Plays*, p. 213. Friar Tuck is referred to in Skelton's *Magnyfycence.*

[4] See a curious reference to these diversions in the *Convocation Books of the
Corporation of Wells*, vol. ii, noticed in the *First Report of the Historical MSS.
Commission*, 1874, p. 107.

[5] See the quotation from Laneham in Sharp's full description of the play,
u. s., pp. 125 *seqq.* The performance at Kenilworth was that in which

standing Collier's supposition [1], to have been something
more than 'merely a dumb shew.' It commemorated the
overthrow of the Danes; but whether its historical origin
was the massacre of St. Brice or the death of Hardicanute,
and what is the true etymology of its singular name, I will
not pretend to determine.

Apart, however, from these mixed productions, attention
must be directed to those pageants, in the generally accepted
later and narrower sense of the term, which consisted of
moving shows devoid of either action or dialogue, or at
least only employing the aid of these incidentally, by way
of supplementing and explaining the living figures or groups
of figures brought before the eyes of the spectators. These
exhibitions formed an important part of the public life
of the later Middle Ages, and, in accordance with tastes
and tendencies which have already been sufficiently commented on, were to a large extent allegorical in character—
yet were so devised and arranged that their significance
and intention, both in whole and in part, could as a rule
be divined without much searching by those whom they were
intended to delight and to impress [2]. In England, and
more especially in London, this pageantry obtained an

Pageants proper.

Captain Cox took a leading part, whose ghost, 'mounted in his hobby-horse,
delivered the so-called *Masque of Owls*, at Kenelworth, written by Ben
Jonson, in 1624 :—

> "And being a little man,
> When the skirmish began
> 'Twixt the Saxon and the Dane
> (For thence the story was ta'en)
> He was not so well seen
> As he would have been o' the Queen." '

It appears from *The Academy* of January 10, 1873, that a play by Captain
Cox bearing the title of *Impacient Poverty* was discovered by Mr. Halliwell-
Phillipps.—It would not be difficult, were it worth while, to find analogies
for the *Hox-Tuesday* play among the early popular festivals of ancient Rome.

[1] i. 225.

[2] Similar exhibitions were, again, known to the Romans of the Empire,
among whom they had doubtless grown out of the triumphal processions.
The *ingentes Rheni* mentioned by Persius (*Sat.* vi. 47) were typical if not
precisely allegorical figures; at a later date it seems to have been more
usual to bear along on gigantic scaffoldings pictorial and sculptured illustrations of the glories of a campaign. See the extract from Josephus (vii. 5)
quoted by Friedländer, *Sittengeschichte Roms*, ii. 145.

extraordinary hold over the popular taste, which the usages
of the Church and the institutions and instincts of the feudal
monarchy of course tended in every way to confirm. The
refining fancies of chivalry introduced in the Norman
period gave variety to these exhibitions, but their fuller
developement was owing to our commercial intercourse with
Flanders, which began and rose to its height in the Plantagenet reigns. The Low Countries were the favourite
home of spectacular as of almost every other kind of luxury
in the later Middle Ages, and among these cities Antwerp,
which kept up the most constant intercourse with England,
was from an early date specially famous for its procession
of the trades (*de groote Ommeganck*)[1]. But other countries
—France and Italy in particular—were subject to the
influences of the same tastes, and communicated them to
Englishmen, more especially when in the Renascence age
classical mythology was pressed into the service of these
entertainments[2].

Earliest English pageants.

City pageants.

The first of these shows on record in England[3] is that
described by Matthew Paris as having taken place in 1236,
on the occasion of the passage of King Henry III and
Eleanor of Provence through the City to Westminster.

[1] See, in general, the picturesque descriptions of Flemish pageantry in
vol. i. of Kirk's *History of Charles the Bold* (1863), where much attention is
given to this theme. As to Antwerp, cf. K. Hegel's description, suggested
by Makart's picture, of the entry of Charles V as witnessed by Albrecht
Dürer, in Sybel's *Historische Zeitschrift*, viii. 3 (1880). See also an engraving
and description of an Antwerp pageant of 1594 *ap.* Sharp, *u.s.*, p. 25.

[2] In France the *entremets* and *tableaux*, the figures in which were taken
from Scripture story or religious legend, or were allegorical, were popular
from an early to a relatively late date. In the sixteenth century figures
from classical mythology were introduced. See Ebert, *u.s.*, 37–8. In Italy
too we hear of these pageants; see *e.g.* Machiavelli, *History of Florence*, vii.
5. For a striking account of the *trionfi* and other Italian pageants of the
Renascence period, see Burckhardt, *Die Cultur der Renaissance in Italien*
(2nd ed. 1869), sec. 5. The Bishop of Peterborough, in his *History of the
Papacy during the period of the Reformation*, ii. 438–440, very vividly describes
an ecclesiastical pageant which Pope Pius II caused to be arranged at
Viterbo for Corpus Christi, 1462, and which bears a certain resemblance to
a collective mystery, each of the Cardinals in turn furnishing forth an
allegory illustrating some portion of the faith.

[3] A full account of the London pageants, from which I have borrowed in
the text, will be found in F. W. Fairholt's *Lord Mayor's Pageants, Percy
Society's Publications*, vol. x.

On the return of Edward I from his victory over the Scots in 1298 occurred the earliest exhibition of shows connected with the City trades. These processions were in England frequently called *ridings* [1].

To about the same period belongs the first detailed description which we possess of a pageant in the more modern sense of the term—Walsingham's account of the reception of Richard II by the citizens in 1377. There were pageants under Henry IV, one on Henry V's return from Agincourt [2], and another on Henry VI's return from France after his coronation. The Lord Mayor's annual procession on the day of his entrance upon the duties of his office from the City to Westminster, which had formerly been a 'riding,' from 1454 onwards was conducted by water [3]; and the first description of it dates from 1533 [4]. Similar gratulatory pageants were exhibited in other cities [5]; the Lord Mayor's pageants, however, of course remained pre-eminent [6]. Many of our early dramatists exercised their ingenuity upon them; Peele's *Descensus Astraeae*, and several productions by Munday, Dekker, Thomas Heywood, and Middleton belong to this class. They dealt in patriotic and moral allegories, as well as in direct illustrations of the glories of the City or of the particular City Company

---

[1] So Chaucer relates of the idle apprentice, Perkin Revelour, that
> 'whan ther any riding was in Chepe
> Out of the shoppe thider wold he lepe,
> And til that he had all the sight ysein,
> And danced wel, he would not come agein.' (*The Coke's Tale.*)

[2] Described by Lydgate (who probably wrote the songs for the occasion).

[3] 'This yere' (1454) 'the ridynge of the Mayres to Westmester was for done, and John Norman, Draper, was the first maire that went to Westmester by barge.' *A Short English Chronicle, &c.*, ed. by J. Gairdner for the Camden Society, 1880.

[4] In this year Queen Anne Boleyn was by royal command welcomed in the City 'likewyse as they use to dooe when the Maior is presented on the morrow after Symon and Jude.'

[5] Queen Margaret was welcomed to Coventry in 1455 by a pageant, of which the scheme has been preserved, and which introduces Scriptural, historical, and allegorical personages, several of whom speak a few lines of obeisance. (See Sharp, *u. s.*, p. 145 *seqq.*)

[6] 'I do not think,' says Spendall in Green's *Tu Quoque* (pr. 1614), 'but to be Lord Mayor of London before I die, and have three pageants carried before me, besides a ship and an unicorn.'

to which the Lord Mayor belonged, such as the *Triumphs of Old Drapery, or The Rich Clothing of England*, and *Chrysanaleia ; the Golden Fishing, or The Honour of Fishmongers* [1]. These City pageants continued in favour till the outbreak of the Great Civil War, when the very maypoles were extirpated by command of Parliament. They were revived shortly before the Restoration, but without recovering their former dignity ; and about the beginning of the eighteenth century sank to the level at which they still await their complete extinction. The pageantry of other towns has had a history analogous to, though of course less ample than, that of London [2].

The public pageantry on which I have touched has but little importance for the earlier history of our dramatic literature. It served, however, to encourage that love of spectacle which has at different times fostered the cultivation of the dramatic art, even when it has imperilled its higher purposes; and it helped to attach those popular tastes over which our drama was in its most glorious period to assert its mastery to the interests of national history and public life [3].

Court entertainments.

Lastly, the amusements of the Court and of the great houses of the nobility from a very early date consisted of entertainments partaking to a greater or less degree of a dramatic character. These entertainments were conducted partly by paid servants,—the survivors of the minstrels whose name they still occasionally retained,—partly by members of the Court and of the noble families themselves. Dances or other ordered appearances in costume, no doubt

[1] Both by Munday. A humorous description of the ' Marchant Taylers ' pageants will be found in the second part of the old play of *Promos and Cassandra*, Act i. Sc. 5.

[2] See e.g. Sharp's account of the ' Pageants on particular occasions ' at Coventry, *u.s.*, 145 *seqq.*

[3] The use of the term *pageant* was not altogether confined to exhibitions in which living personages took part. We find it also applied to hangings of cloth and tapestry, presenting pictures of an allegorical character accompanied by inscriptions. See the account of the ' nyne pageantes devised by Mayster Thomas More in his youth ' in his father's house, and the verses inscribed by him upon them, in Roper's *Life of Sir Thomas More*, ed. Singer (1822), *Appendix*, p. xxi.

often of a figurative character, were in vogue at Court from the time of Edward III;—these came to be known as ‘disguisings’ or ‘mummings,’ and possibly a distinction was sooner or later drawn between these two designations[1].

We have already seen that Henry V exhibited on the occasion of the visit of the Emperor Sigismund something in the nature of a pantomimic representation of the *Life of St. George*[2]. Thomas Heywood cites from Stowe the statement that ‘when Edward IV would shew himselfe in publicke state to the view of the people, hee repaired to his palace at St Johnes, where he was accustomed to see the citty actors; and since then,’ he adds, ‘that house by the prince’s free gift hath belonged to the Office of the Revels[3].’ Under the same sovereign the Duke of Gloucester (afterwards Richard III) kept a certain number of ‘players,’ and there are indications that this was no solitary instance[4]. In the reign of Henry VII we hear, in addition to the ‘Gentlemen of the King’s Chapel,’ who are also called ‘the players of the Chapel,’ of the King’s and of Prince Arthur’s ‘players of interludes’; and some of the great nobles—the Duke of Buckingham, and the Earls of Oxford and Northumberland—likewise had their companies of players[5]. There can be no doubt that the amusements of the Court herein only kept pace with those of the country at large, where about this time companies of players regularly appeared in a variety of places, more especially in London and its neighbourhood[6].

[1] Collier, i. 24, says that ‘in what respects a “disguising” differed from a “mumming” is a point which it is now impossible to settle with precision’; but *ib.* p. 26, he asserts that ‘there is little doubt that a “mumming” was a dumb shew,’ whereas a ‘disguising’ of the early Tudor period of which he quotes a description seems to have been merely an ordered dance or masque. Cf. the passage cited below from *A Tale of a Tub.*

[2] *Ante*, p. 143.

[3] *Apology for Actors*, Bk. ii. (*Shakspeare Society’s Publications*, 1841, p. 40).

[4] See Collier’s extracts from the Household Book of John Lord Howard, afterwards Duke of Norfolk, i. 36 *seqq.* The Austrian and Bavarian minstrels who were in England in the reign of Richard III may have been the first German comedians who visited this country. *Per contra*, Richard III appears to have been the first of our kings who appointed a ‘royal bearward.’ *Ib.* 42.   [5] *Ib.* i. 47.

[6] According to Collier, i. 37, London, Coventry, Wycombe, Mile-end,

But a new impulse was given in England to whatever
implied the enjoyment of life and of what, whether really
or seemingly, makes it worth living, by the accession to the
throne of a prince born and bred in the very midst of the
European Renascence. Henry VIII was the heir of endless
opportunities; nor was he blind to many of them. As
he began his reign after the most appropriate fashion—i. e.
in the way in which he was expected to begin it—by
amusing himself with great energy, a new era opened for
Masques.   the entertainments at Court. Early in this reign (1512–3)
there was introduced, as a new form of entertainment
recommended by its Italian origin, the *masque*, which very
probably at first differed from the 'mummings' or 'disguisings' customary before by nothing except the fanciful
adjunct of a mask to the costume worn by the participants[1].
The innovation was of the sort which Fashion loves—startling
at its first introduction[2], and meaningless before long.
Practically, however, the 'masque' was merely a more
elaborate and (so to speak) accentuated form of the old
'disguising.' Such an entertainment is that described by
Cavendish in his *Life of Wolsey*, and introduced with
notable effect into the play of *Henry VIII*. But we may
rest assured that, even supposing the use of the term
'masque' to have been from the first more or less accurately
restricted, the variety of which this and other forms of
entertainment (including dramatic elements) partook at the
Court and among the surroundings of King Henry VIII

Wimborne Minster, and Kingston. It strikes me as not impossible that the
companies of players which appeared in these localities were identical with
the companies attached to royal and noble personages, who were licensed
to this extent, as according to Collier, i. 84 and *note*, they were in the next
reign.—In the Household Book of King Henry VII, 'Frenche Players' are
more than once mentioned. *Ib.* 51 *note*.

[1] Cf. *A Tale of a Tub*, v. 2:
> '*Pan.*   A masque, what's that?
> *Scriben.*   A mumming, or a shew,
>   With vizards and fine clothes.
> *Clench.*   A disguise, neighbour,
>   Is the true word.'

[2] See the curious passage in Barclay's *Ship of Fools* (ii. 271), protesting
against the use of masks, and the original *passus* in Brant (sec. '*Fastnachts-
narren.*'

was already very considerable. We know that (in 1515) two so-called 'interludes' were represented there which were in point of fact moralities, one of which was written by 'Mayster Cornyshe of the Chapel' and the other by 'Mayster Midwell,' and which were acted respectively by the children of the Chapel and by the King's players. The latter of these has been already incidentally noticed[1]; in the former it seems probable that two ladies of the Court performed the attractive parts of 'Venus' and 'Bewte,' while a morris-dance, in which gentlemen of the Court took part, wound up the entertainment[2]. On the other hand, we hear of the performance (in 1520) of a 'goodly comedy of Plautus,' doubtless in Latin, and again (in 1527) of a satirical Latin play, in which Martin Luther and his wife were derisively introduced, and *per contra* (about 1533) of 'a comedy represented at Court to the no little defamation of certain Cardinals[3].' The performers in these rather hazardous attempts to meet King Henry's changes of mood may not always have been persons attached to the royal household, and there are indications that the players who appeared before him were occasionally tradesmen trained by tradesmen[4]. It is, however, certain that in this reign the King, the Queen and the Prince of Wales, as well as several of the great nobles, kept players of their own, and that these were at times allowed to travel about the country on their own account[5]. This 'extension' movement, implying a natural desire to utilise popular tastes for the profit of existing interests, may have contributed to spread the feeling that the State should regulate amusements, which had long outgrown the control of the Church

---

[1] *Ante*, p. 117.

[2] Collier, i. 69 *seqq.*—In 1527-8 a moral play was performed at Gray's Inn in the presence of Cardinal Wolsey, who, taking it to be directed against himself, consigned its author and one of the young gentlemen players to the Fleet, whence however they were released on his ascertaining that he had fitted on the cap too quickly. *Ib.* 104.

[3] *Ib.* 107. This was the year in which Pope Clement VII pronounced against the divorce.

[4] See the note of Mr. G. H. Overend *On the Dispute between the Glazier and the Tailer* in *New Shakspere Society's Transactions*, i. 7, 425 *seqq.*

[5] Collier, i. 84 and *note*.

Restrictions
upon
dramatic
perform-
ances.
A Proclamation of the year 1533, and an Act of Parliament of 1543 (the first statute of the realm known to have
taken notice of the stage), prohibited, among other manifestations of misplaced independence of opinion, the former
the playing of interludes 'concerning doctrines now in
question and controversie,' the latter (more explicitly) the
introduction into the same of any matter 'contrary to the
doctrines of the Church of Rome[1].'   Of greater importance,
however, than this ebullition of royal orthodoxy, was the
endeavour to impose suitable restrictions *in loco* upon the
entertainments at Court, which contained so large a share
of dramatic elements.   In the later Plantagenet period
these diversions were superintended by an Abbot, or Lord
of Misrule, whose primary duty was of course to provide
rather than to control them.   The appointment, in 1546,
of Sir Thomas Cawarden as *Magister Jocorum Revellorum
et Mascorum* at Court was possibly neither the first of its
kind, nor one in which the censorial functions were predominant[2].   Nor does 'the wise gentleman and learned,'
George Ferrers, who in 1551 became 'master of the
pastimes' of King Edward VI, appear to have owed his
appointment to his political so much as to his literary and
dramaturgical abilities, which, although a Protestant, he
was afterwards found ready to devote alike to the service
of the Catholic Queen Mary[3].   But an authoritative supervision of dramatic performances became more and more
a matter of course in these troublous times.   Although at
the beginning of King Edward's reign a reduced number
of players was retained in the royal service and the Duke
of Somerset had a company of his own[4], his downfall in
1549 was preceded (in August) by a prohibition for a
period of three months of the representation of all plays
and interludes throughout the realm on account of their
seditious tendency; and after his overthrow the special
license of the Privy Council was in 1551 declared necessary
for the performances of players attached to the households

---

[1] Collier, i. 118–119; 127–128.   [2] *Ib.* i. 131 *seqq.*
[3] See Mr. Sidney Lee's article on Ferrers in vol. xviii. of the *Dictionary of
National Biography.*   [4] Collier, i. 136–9.

of noblemen, and in 1552 (as part of a general restriction) made requisite for all players in the English tongue[1]. Performances at Court, or in connexion with Court society, seem however to have continued occasionally to take place[2]. On the accession of Mary in 1553 a proclamation against 'busy medlers in matters of Religion' included 'players,' together with 'prechars' and 'pryntars,' requiring them alike to obtain the Queen's license for any of their productions[3]. But, as has been seen, a morality which treated of these matters, although of course in an approved vein, was acted at Court in this very year; and at Hatfield the Princess Elisabeth was, as she had been already in the previous reign, indulged with dramatic entertainments that may be supposed to have commended themselves to her preferences[4]. Before very long popular representations of plays likewise revived, and dramatic performances had in 1556 to be prohibited throughout the country, the City of London being in some way exempted from the general regulation, inasmuch as plays were here, when licensed by the bishop, allowed to be played between All Saints and Shrovetide[5]. At Court the amusements of the age continued in more or less languid favour; the Queen maintained eight 'Players of Enterludes,' and furnished forth a 'maske of Almaynes Pilgrymes, and Irishemen,' possibly for the diversion of King Philip, when he should at last come from Flanders[6]. Thus, without noticing incidental recurrences to the old religious drama, we have reached the reign of Elisabeth. In the earlier years much the same twofold system prevailed that had been carried on under her sister. After in April, 1559, issuing a general prohibition of stage-plays, the new Queen's government in the month of May ensuing ordered that they should be permitted, if licensed by the mayors of towns, by lord-lieutenants of counties, or by two justices of peace, provided that they refrained from handling 'either matters of religion or of the governaunce

---

[1] Collier, i. 143–5.   [2] *Ib.* 141 *note* and 153 *note.*
[3] *Ib.* 155.
[4] *Ib.* 156–7. One was entitled *The Hanging of Antioch,* and the other *Holophernes.*   [5] Collier, i. 160.   [6] *Ib.* 163.

of the state of the common weale[1].' But at Court, and in the spheres of life connected with or subservient to the Court, the list of plays, masques and other entertainments is continuous from the same year. This conflict between policy of State and privileged practice seems a strange preface to the period of our dramatic history which, like the corresponding period of our national history at large, glories in calling itself by the name of Elisabeth.

Queen Elisabeth's patronage of plays and entertainments.
As a matter of fact the popular drama, consisting as it did of remnants of the miracle-plays and survivals of the moralities,—the latter presenting themselves, no doubt, in divers novel and curtailed forms,—would have run a serious risk of drying up, if not of being extinguished, had it not been for the patronage which was above the law. The need of amusing the Royal household (a body of men and women at all times deserving of special consideration), the unavoidable rivalry between the great nobles whose way to power led along the paths of fashion, and the marked personal likings of the Queen herself, alike kept up the dramatic entertainments of the Court. Queen Elisabeth could not be without them in town or country; and while there seems no reason to suppose that the players of her household themselves contributed in any notable measure to the progress of our drama, or indirectly to that of our dramatic literature, it may be concluded that in the early years of her reign players of all kinds, and the patrons upon whom they subsisted, looked up to the Royal favour as the ultimate object of their endeavours. The players of the great nobles and the boy-performers, who were either choristers of the Royal chapels or pupils of some of the larger London grammar-schools, acted their plays in inn-yards—which, as will be seen below, were in point of fact the earliest London theatres[2]. The process by which these companies of players sought to settle down in their London

---

[1] Collier, i. 167.

[2] See Fleay, *Chronicle History of the London Stage* (1890), chap. i. Section A (*Introduction*).—For some notes on the companies of players from Henry VIII to Elizabeth see notice of contents of *libri rationales* in Bowtell MSS. at Downing College, Cambridge, in *Historical MSS. Commission*, vol. iii. pp. 321 *seqq.*

houses, and the conflicts between them and the authorities of the City, together with the solution found (in the year 1576) in the erection of two theatres immediately outside the City walls, will be more conveniently described in a later passage of this book. Here it is more to the purpose to note that the Queen's fondness for dramatic exhibitions, or for the pageantry which contained dramatic elements, asserted itself both at her own expense and at that of her subjects from the early years of her reign. In and near London at her own palaces, at the Inns of Court, and at the seats of influential or ambitious nobles; in the country on her progresses at great houses, and in the Universities, a lavish expenditure upon her favourite amusement was incurred both by her and for her[1]. The climax of these entertainments was reached in those *Princely Pleasures of Kenilworth* which were exhibited in the year 1575 by the favourite who cherished the futile hope of dazzling the Queen into bestowing upon him the highest of the favours at her disposal[2]. It may be added that not only self-seeking ambition in the person of Leicester and of his less enduringly successful competitors for the smiles of the Queen, but also political wisdom as incarnate in Cecil, sought to turn to account her fondness for these diversions.

---

[1] The attempt at economy, or profession of a wish for it, in 1560 was succeeded by increased expenditure in 1561, when between April and September revels were held at a long series of palaces, and more than £3,000 was expended on Court amusements. Collier, i. 170–3. For details of the Queen's progresses see Nichols' *Progresses and Public Processions of Queen Elizabeth* (1823).

[2] The amusing letter of Robert Laneham descriptive of the Kenilworth entertainments, familiar to all readers of Scott's enchanting novel, was edited by Dr. Furnivall, with Introduction and Notes, for the Ballad Society in 1871, and this edition was republished for the New Shakspere Society (Series VI, No. 14) in 1887. The editor states a desire to investigate the 'library of Captain Cox' to have been the *raison d'être* of this treasury of delectable learning, and students of drama owe him particular thanks for his notes on the 'ancient plays' familiarly known to the Coventry worthy.— Laneham's letter is reprinted in the *Shakespeare Jahrbuch* for 1892.—One of the literary contributors to the Kenilworth entertainments was George Gascoigne (*vide infra*), whose verses and masques were published with those of other poets in 1576, under the title of *The Princelye Pleasures at the Courte of Kenelworthe* (reprinted 1821). See also Nichols' *Progresses of Elizabeth* and Dugdale's *Antiquities of Warwickshire* (1730).

Among the papers of the great minister is said to be a scheme for a masque to be performed at a meeting between Queen Elisabeth and Mary Queen of Scots, which was to be brought about in 1562, but which never actually took place [1].

Summary.   In my next chapter it will be necessary to go back once more to a rather earlier date in sketching the beginnings of the English regular drama ; and a few notes will then be in place as to the history of the stage on which it was performed.   Here I may in conclusion attempt to summarise the various growths, differing in origin though at many points in contact with and under the influence of one another, out of which that drama sprang.

In England no accurate distinction was ever drawn between *mysteries* and *miracle-plays*, and the latter term was employed as including the former.   But literary terminology, without affecting absolute accuracy, must distinguish between the miracle-play and the mystery as differing not only in themes, but also in origin.   While the miracle-play was of a more mixed derivation, the primary source of the mystery was religious, i.e. liturgical. The two growths took root in England soon after the Norman Conquest, and, with the incidental co-operation of the professional entertainers brought over by that event, and of their descendants, became the English religious drama.   Though the mystery bore the name of the miracle, it was the latter which was absorbed by the former.   In the hands, first of ecclesiastics, then of laymen, it became a popular form of dramatic entertainment, and, especially in the developed shape of the collective mystery, as performed by the gilds of English towns, survived with little material alteration to the close of the sixteenth century.

The English *moralities* cannot be traced back further than the middle of the fifteenth century, though the distinctive elements of this species of production are to be occasionally noticed in every stage of the religious drama. They were the result of tastes partly indigenous to the

---

[1] The scheme of the masque, by an unknown poet, is printed *ap*. Collier, i. 178–181.

English soil, partly due to the influence of French literature. Their form they borrowed in England from the popular religious drama ; but they never attained to the same degree of influence as that which it had reached, because it was not till the period of the Reformation that they concerned themselves with questions of immediate and lively interest to the nation at large.   Even then they could only fitfully, and at times under grave risks, address themselves to such topics.   And in this period they had already begun to lose their distinctive character by admitting among their *dramatis personae* real types of humanity by the side of personified abstractions.   In this modified form they too survived to about the close of the sixteenth century.

The *pageants* (using the term in a more restricted sense), *masques*, and similar entertainments had been introduced as early as the thirteenth century, and, receiving a fresh impulse in the Renascence age, continued down to the seventeenth to enjoy the favour of their patrons.   These were in the first instance the Court and its society, but also the civic authorities of London and other great towns, and the populace wherever it had a chance.   But though containing dramatic elements, these pageants, as lacking the essential element of a real dramatic action, could never assume genuinely dramatic forms.   They continued by the side of the regular drama, as they had existed by the side of its progenitors, influencing its course, but having no real part in it.   In the days of its first decline they combined with it into a hybrid species, which, under the old name, applied in a more specific sense, of the *masque*, will claim separate attention as an illegitimate outgrowth of our dramatic literature.

Such, then, were the phenomena of the origin of the modern drama, as they presented themselves on English soil.   The transitions which led directly to the beginnings of the regular English drama, and those beginnings themselves, will form the subject of my second chapter.

CHAPTER II.

THE BEGINNINGS OF THE ENGLISH REGULAR DRAMA.

BY the term 'the beginnings of the regular drama,' I mean the birth of the two species into which all dramatic literature divides itself, their frequent intermixture notwithstanding.

The tragic and the comic. The broad distinction between the tragic and the comic is peculiar neither to dramatic literature nor to literature in general among the intellectual activities of mankind. Ignorance and dulness indeed pass through the world without any clear consciousness of either the tragic or the comic elements which life contains ; for apathy is the unenviable privilege of the empty or unawakened mind. But wherever the power of sympathy or that of antipathy is knowingly possessed, the mind is necessarily alive to the difference upon which the only satisfactory definitions of the tragic and the comic, and of tragedy and comedy, depend. The difference is primarily one of subject, as was in point of fact shown by English linguistic usage in the Elisabethan age without any special reference to the drama [1]. But inasmuch as the secret of all true art lies in appropriate, and therefore pleasing, treatment, it is a difference of treat-

---

[1] Thus, I may instance from Robert Greene's works the application of the term 'tragedies' to narrative tales of a sad sort (*Planetomachia*, Grosart's edition, vol. v), and again 'Vlisses Tale, A Tragedy' (*Euphues' Censure to Philautus, ib.* vol. vi). This usage was not of English origin, but based on Greek precedent. So, in the fifth century of our era, Nestorius wrote a history of the controversy excited by his doctrines, and of its consequences for his fortunes, which he entitled his *Tragedy*; and his friend Irenaeus composed under the same title a work treating of the persecutions undergone by Nestorius and of the history of the Church in his times. See Neander, *History of the Christian Religion and Church* (English Translation), iv. 190 and *note*.—The title of *the Spanish Tragedy* signifies, not a tragic play taken from the Spanish, but a series of deadly deeds done by Spaniards.

ment also. It therefore applies to the entire character and effect of a dramatic work, and is most assuredly not to be determined by the mere accident of the nature of its conclusion. The distinction which is supported by the official authority of Philostrate, and has largely obtained, must therefore be rejected as inadequate. The circumstance that the hero of a play ' kills himself,' or is killed by somebody else, does not constitute it a tragedy ; and, conversely, the happy ending of a play does not establish it as a comedy [1].

Aristotle's definitions [2] will better serve the purpose. According to his theory, that which distinguishes tragedy as a dramatic species is the importance and magnitude of the action constituting its theme, together with the adequate elevation of its literary form, and the power of the emotions— pity and terror—by means of which it produces its effects [3].

---

[1] Although the serious drama which ends happily has been frequently treated as a sort of third species, co-ordinate with tragedy and comedy and called by some colourless name of its own—*drame, Schauspiel*—it is in reality nothing but a subordinate branch of tragedy. This has been well shown by the late Gustav Freytag in his admirable *Technik des Dramas* (2nd edition), pp. 96–7. He reminds us how 'already in the times of Aeschylus and Sophocles a gloomy ending was by no means indispensable to tragedy ; of seven extant plays by Sophocles, two, the *Ajax* and the *Philoctetes*, and according to Athenian conceptions even the *Oedipus Coloneus*, have a peaceful ending which gives a turn for the better to the destiny of the hero. Even in ' most tragic' Euripides, to whom the *Poetics* ascribe a love of a gloomy ending, among seven tragedies (exclusively of the *Alcestis*) four (*Helena, Iphigenia in Tauris, Andromeda*) end like a modern *Schauspiel*; in several others the unhappy ending seems accidental and not accounted for by dramatic motives.' Freytag concludes that the Athenian public resembled that of our own days in preferring a happy ending to a play. He might have referred to the still more striking instance of the Indian drama, where a positive rule prohibits a fatal conclusion. I have spoken in the text of the loose use of the terms ' tragedy' and ' tragical'; it is curious that, in a *glose* of his own in his Translation of Boëthius *de Consolatione Philosophiae* (Bk. II. Prose ii), Chaucer should adopt the following limitation : ' Tragedie is to seyne a dite of a prosperite for a time that endith in wretchednesse.' The same notion was in his mind when towards the close of his *Troilus and Creseide* (Bk. V), in which he had recurred to the philosophy of Boëthius, he thus apostrophised his poem :

> ' Go, little booke, go, my little tragedie,
> There God my maker yet ere that I die,
> So send me might to make some comedie ! '

[2] *Poet.* c. vi.

[3] I have thought it sufficient for my purpose to leave aside the question as

Comedy, on the other hand, imitates characters and actions of less elevated or intense interest ('neither painful nor destructive [1] '), which appeal to the sense of the ridiculous,— or, in other words, touch the springs of laughter by exciting our contempt for the meaner vices and the more common

to the proper interpretation of the famous concluding clause of this passage :
—' δι' ἐλέου καὶ φόβου περαίνουσα τὴν τῶν τοιούτων παθημάτων κάθαρσιν.'
Donaldson's translation ' effecting, through pity and terror, the correction and refinement of such passions,' implies the correctness of Lessing's explanation, according to which tragedy by exciting the emotions or passions of pity and terror purifies them, changing them into virtuous qualities. But even if this interpretation could be accepted as correct from the point of view of language—a question which scholars must decide—it would be open to the grave objection that it makes Aristotle ascribe to the tragic drama a distinctly moral function, viz. that of regulating the passions in question to a certain level or amount desirable as the due mean between excess and insufficiency. But this is quite foreign to Aristotle's—or to any true—conception of art; added to which, although tragedy may by exciting the passions of pity and terror be said to ennoble or elevate the mind, taking the latter as it were out of itself and away from the atmosphere of common things, it can in no reasonable sense be said to remove what is excessive or add what is deficient in these passions themselves. Goethe, giving utterance to what we all perceive, viz. that ' tragedy and tragic romances by no means appease the mind, but rather disquiet it,' could not bring himself to accept Lessing's interpretation of the tragic *catharsis* ; but it was left to Jacob Bernays to suggest an explanation which with all deference to the critical insight of Lessing and the scholarship of Donaldson and others, I venture to think irrefutable. Understanding κάθαρσις in the sense of a medical term familiar to Aristotle, he showed that it referred to the relief of the mind from the trouble caused in it by these very passions when excited by tragedy. That sympathy which is made up of pity and terror and which so heavily burdens the human soul, is drawn forth by tragedy, which suggests an object to these emotions and concentrates the working of them upon it ; and having as it were elicited them and occupied the mind which is full of them, it leaves behind it a sense of relief and calm. Humble as this interpretation may seem, yet, unlike Lessing's, which even were it correct would suggest a process familiar to only a very select few from personal experience, it brings home to all of us the very condition of mind which we know ourselves to have passed through on reading a tragic masterpiece. Who is a stranger to the process, whereby in the first instance everything that the soul contains of vague pity for the weaknesses and failings of our kind, and of terror for the snares besetting the path of life, is brought into a *focus* ; or again to the experience which, as we have walked out of the theatre or laid down the book, has left us the lighter, the purer, in a sense the better, for the mental effort undergone.

This note may seem both long and unnecessary; but having formerly written in a different sense, I have thought that it might at all events be permitted by way of a recantation.

[1] *Poet.* c. 5.

weaknesses of human nature or social habits.   As is well
known, the classical term ' comedy [1] ' covered a wider variety
of species than that included under the name in modern
dramatic classification, where it is usually reserved for the
more elaborate type of comic play.   The briefer sort, which,
as such, is allowed a more unrestricted licence of fun and
a stronger demand upon the sense of probability, we call
farce ; while *burlesque* (or, if more refined in manner, *extravaganza*) is the ironic species of which Aristophanes was
the unequalled master, and in which the characters stand in
laughable contrast to the action that they carry on, or even
to the diction that they use.

Obviously, quite apart from the facility with which these *Mixed
species.* different kinds of effects admit of being exhibited side by
side in the course of a single dramatic action, they may
easily be intermingled with, or, so to speak, shaded off into,
one another.   Pity, for example, if akin to love, not unfrequently seems to take her birth from ridicule, and there
is a touch of pathos in many a form of folly.   Even the
ancients were not absolutely consistent in their endeavour
to keep tragedy and comedy apart from one another,
although in the classical period of the Attic drama this
endeavour was facilitated not only by accepted outward
distinctions, but also by the wide difference between the
simple severity of the system of tragic composition and the
unbridled licence allowed to comedy [2].   Certain modern
dramatic schools—among them, the English in one period
of its history—have with more or less of success contrived
to hedge round tragedy with artificial safeguards of form
or treatment.   But wherever, as in a large majority of those
plays of which we are about to consider the growth, the
effects are mixed, it is the nature of the main action and
of the most important characters which must determine

[1] The vague use of the term ' comedy' for *any* kind of play is too common
in the Renascence literature of all countries to need special illustration.

[2] Thus in his English version of the *Antigone* (see his edition of the play,
1848) Donaldson ventured to translate the first speech of the Sentinel
(vv. 223-236), whom he calls a semi-grotesque character, into prose.   The
treatment of the character of Heracles in the *Alcestis* is hardly in point, if
this play was the satyr-drama of a tetralogy.

the classification of a drama (if we desire so to classify it) as tragic or as comic. Between the two species there lies a large variety of transitions, for which at different times different names have been invented ; we shall see how *tragi-comedy* (a term since used in a very different sense), in which both tragic and comic effects were sought in the course of the same action or combination of actions, was a mixed species much cultivated in Italy in the later Renascence age, and in England more especially under Italian influence. But, on the whole, the English drama while maintaining a remarkable freedom from rigour or straitness of any kind in the intermixture of species which it has permitted and exemplified, has likewise shown itself singularly indifferent to accuracy of terminology.

Elements of tragic and comic effect in the miracles and moralities.

Now, from what has already been said, it must have become abundantly manifest that elements of both tragic and comic effect existed in those early compositions of which the origin and progress have been traced in the preceding chapter. Nay, more, in the period when the so-called miracles and the moralities were simultaneously flourishing in England, and had in point of fact attained to the highest stage of developement which they were destined at any time to reach,—in the former half of the sixteenth century, the age of the English Reformation,—both these species had advanced a considerable way in the direction of those effects which it is possible for tragedy and comedy respectively to achieve. The religious plays, to begin with, habitually dealt with subjects of unequalled and, in the eyes of the age which produced them, of virtually unrivalled importance, challenging the deepest sympathies and the keenest antipathies of their audiences. In order further to rivet popular favour, they had introduced a growing amount of ludicrous characters, passages and scenes, and had constituted this admixture to all intents and purposes an integral part of their action. The moralities, on the other hand, had familiarised their spectators with personifications of the most admired of virtues, as well as of the most familiar and ridiculous kinds of vices. They had likewise given bodily form to numerous conceptions involving the

highest ideals of their public, or again coming closely home
to the interests of their business and bosoms.

But from an æsthetic point of view the miracles had,
unless in incidental passages, failed to rise in dignity of
form to the sublimity of their subjects.   The action of a
collective mystery was indeed, if regarded as a whole, of the
utmost magnitude; but as a matter of fact the connexion
between the several ' pageants ' was all but lost in the often
fragmentary action of each.   The endless repetition of the
well-known episodes of the Sacred Narrative must in some
measure have deprived them of freshness of interest; nor
could the circumstances of the case permit, even had the
art of the writers been equal to adopting, a treatment of
their themes resembling the loyal freedom with which the
Attic tragedians renewed the ancestral myths.   So stereotyped had the characters become, that it can no longer
have been easy by means of them to arouse pity or terror,
except in a very modified degree, in the breast of a fairly
experienced spectator.   The cohesion between the several
plays having become practically little more than formal
(more especially as they were respectively presented by
different sets of performers), the interest of each must have
as a rule centred in itself; and this interest can often have
amounted to little more than a curiosity which it was
attempted to stimulate by interpolations damaging the
total impression, or by mere external devices belonging to
the sphere of what we call stage-management.

The moralities, artificial in their origin, had a harder task
in seeking to produce powerful results by their *dramatis
personæ* of didactic abstractions, which, ringing the changes
on a not very flexible system of arguments, appealed to
the moral sympathies of their audiences in the first instance
through the medium of their intellectual faculties.   With
no associations of biblical or legendary narrative at their
command, as in the case of the miracles, they had to be
constructed on a scheme which admitted of comparatively
little variation ;   and their success accordingly depended
upon conditions which could not, as with the miracles, be
in a large measure assumed.   Thus, if men and women

*Limits of
their opera-
tions.*

were to be moved into something beyond a pupillary acquiescence in indisputable moral truths, it was necessary either to bring the truths in question to bear directly upon their personal interests, or to make the representatives of abstract qualities and ideas types of their most familiar human embodiments. Thus, unless in exceptional instances when the lesson was brought home to every man with a swiftness as of lightning, or when a fool in his folly made a whole audience kin, the moralities had to content themselves with slower processes and more gradual effects; pity and terror on the one hand, and contemptuous laughter on the other, could not be excited continuously or in a high degree by adhering to the lines on which the moralities as a species had been built up.

The transitions to the regular drama suggested by these defects. In itself, therefore, nothing might seem more natural than that a desire should have gradually arisen to remedy the defects which the miracles and the moralities alike cannot have failed to reveal to the eye of common sense, and which sooner or later must have become perceptible to the performers. To apply a dramatic treatment resembling that customary in the miracles to personages and passages of profane history, and to exchange the abstractions of the moralities for actual types of contemporary life, might seem to have been an advance of its nature inevitable. All classes of the population were familiar with the characters and events of Bible history and Christian legend; it was only necessary that a similar acquaintance, or something approaching to it, should come to prevail with regard to personages of profane history and their achievements,—and these could not fail to gain a footing on the popular stage. In the first place, however, the religious themes of their pageants might well to a large proportion of both performers and spectators seem inseparably associated with the very notion of a stage-play; and, again, the national history (and *a fortiori* all other secular history) was a field concerning which the public at large was in profound ignorance and in which it took an extremely restricted interest. In England as elsewhere the influence of the Renascence was to bring about a change in this respect; but the process was necessarily slow, and in its earlier steps feeble. On the other hand, the tendency towards substituting on the stage real human types for personified abstractions had long been asserting itself in particular instances. Some such types had found their way into the mysteries from the very first, or rather the mysteries had found them ready to hand in the Sacred Narrative on which they had been founded [1]; but their introduction had become more and more frequent and specific; and in the moralities the *Vice* was but the most prominent and popular example of the concrete beings whose presence in the eyes of a large proportion of the spectators atoned for a host of abstractions. In general, moreover, it will not be forgotten that the miracles and the moralities had never been kept absolutely distinct; both had alike been religious plays, and the manner and method of their performance had been in all essentials identical. Thus there was every likelihood that, should any new species of dramatic composition form themselves, they would contain elements of both the one and the other primitive species.

As a matter of fact, however, although the beginnings of both tragedy and comedy in England associate themselves distinctly with the moralities, while with the beginnings of tragedy the mysteries likewise must be brought into connexion, the first English comedy and the first English tragedy alike were direct reproductions of foreign (classical) models. Inasmuch as this fact stands undisputed and indisputable, there seems little advantage in speculating as to whether the regular drama or drama proper—as distinct from productions in which the essential demands of the drama are imperfectly met, although the works may be cast in the dramatic form and abound in elements of dramatic effect—could in England have sprung into being without the extraneous impulse which I now proceed to consider. At the same time no estimate of the force of this impulse—in other words, of the influence of the Renascence movement—can succeed in showing, *either*, that

The direct impulse an extraneous one.

---

[1] I refer to such characters as the *Shepherds, Soldiers, Tortores,* &c.

the Renascence first implanted the love of the drama in the English people and thus made our English stage a chosen home for the genius of dramatic literature; *or*, that the primitive but long-lived species of productions which I have been up to this point considering lacked the possibilities of a self-developement such as might have resulted in a national drama.

The Renascence movement in England.

The impulse in question was supplied by classical examples, and by the literature of that incomparable land which was not only to all intents and purposes the birthplace, but long the favourite home of the Renascence. It would be quite superfluous to attempt to trace here the first appearances in England of an active interest in, or communication with, Italian scholarship; since there is no gainsaying the fact that these early instances of contact between Italian culture and our own Teutonic nation were isolated in character. Down to a late period of the fifteenth century, during the calamitous reign of Henry VI and those of the sovereigns of the House of York which followed, this country was once more insulated from ready and productive contact with the other nations of Europe, and the mass of its inhabitants stagnated in apathy even as towards the interests of the civil conflicts which desolated their fields and homesteads. As the numbers of the population remained nearly stationary, so neither was the wealth of the country increased, nor, unless very gradually, were fresh routes of trade and intercourse with other countries opened. Fearful at times even of her security within her own seas, England in arts as well as in arms seemed for a time likely to lapse into the isolation of insignificance. Thus English civilisation remained in essentials unaffected by the current of the Renascence after individual Englishmen had become subject to its influence, or had even, in exceptional cases, been overpowered by it[1]. Perhaps England's 'trust to her Universities,' and her dislike of accepting articles of consumption not 'manufactured by the old-

---

[1] For instance, Battista Guarino's pupil John Tiptoft, Earl of Worcester, an early illustration of the force of the well-known proverb—*Inglese Italianato e un diavolo incarnato.*

established firms,' may have alike retarded and regulated the process of the introduction of the new learning among us [1]: and these institutions had fallen into a lassitude that was fast approaching a condition of torpor, not directly counteracted by the multiplication of endowed colleges. Still, the existence of these colleges contributed to the decline of the custom of sending young gentlemen to the monasteries for their education; and, again, the connexion between the colleges and dependent schools made for the growth of a clearer distinction than had hitherto prevailed between undergraduate and schoolboy; while on the other hand the wealthiness of the colleges encouraged residence under more liberal (or, if the term be preferred), more luxurious conditions of life [2]. Although students of this sort were not likely to prove specially awake to the dawn of a more eager spirit of study in our great seats of learning, yet it is unmistakeable that a closer connexion was gradually being established between these institutions and the well-to-do classes of the laity. More especially the lesser gentry—the class on which for many reasons the future of the country was from the close of the Wars of the Roses onwards so largely to depend—were brought into a closer relation than they had previously maintained with the best extant form of literary culture. Nor should it be forgotten that the sixteenth century has been called the golden age of legal education, and that in our London Inns of Court the processes by which this education was conducted were organically associated with the revels (including both singing and dancing) deemed indispensable by the spirit of the age. A closer continuity—or at least a more special one—than has been known to subsequent times, prevailed between the student life of the Universities and that of the Inns of Court, and made itself felt in their most authoritative spheres. Thus, while as a matter of

---

[1] I quote from the Bishop of Peterborough's Rede Lecture on *The Early Renaissance in England* (Cambridge, 1895).

[2] A fair type of this species of student is Walter Paston, of the *Paston Letters*, who did mediocre Latin composition at Eton, and was afterwards sent to both Oxford and Cambridge, whence he dutifully wrote home for supplies to enable him to live like other men.

course the passivities of which our country has at all times been a kindly nurse remained powerful forces to reckon with, a special public was gradually forming itself such as could not escape the influences of the Renascence, when they reached our shores in stronger and ampler currents. To none of these influences, whether pure or mixed in their relations to literature and art, was the English academical public (if I may so call it) of the period which may be roughly described as the third quarter of the sixteenth century, more susceptible than to that of the Classical and its scion the early Italian drama, together with the narrative sources from which the latter was constantly fed. It must remain a subsidiary matter of speculation how far the earliest visits of Italian actors to this country contributed to the beginnings of our regular drama [1].

These hints may suffice to introduce a brief account of the beginnings of English tragedy and comedy respectively. Though it was comedy which first established itself as a perfected growth in our national literature, tragedy claims her natural precedence in the ensuing outline.

The early Italian drama and its themes. Many generations before the influence of the Renascence movement made itself felt in the progress of the English drama, Italian tragedy had seized on themes of national interest, and treated them in a form imitating the Latin classical model—Seneca—of whom I shall immediately have to speak at length. Alberto Mussato's *Eccerinis* was the work of a Paduan born not more than three years after

---

[1] According to Collier, i. 226, a company of 'Italian players' performed before the Queen at Windsor in 1577; but one of these was evidently a tumbler or vaulter. In Whetstone's *Heptameron of Civil Discourses* (1582) are mentioned ' comedians of Ravenna,' who were not 'tied to any written device,' but who had ' certain grounds or principles ' (i. e. outlines of performance) ' of their own.' It can hardly be doubted that these were the actors alluded to a few years later in *The Spanish Tragedy* (Act V) :—
'The Italian Tragedians were so sharp of wit
That in one hour's meditation
They would perform any thing in action.'
Yet although these Italian actors probably for the most part presented the improvised comedies known as *commedie dell' arte*, to which reference will be made below, they may also have carried with them regular plays—so-called *commedie erudite*—which the performers had to get by heart. Cf. with Collier, iii. 201, Klein, iv 560.

the death of the tyrant Ezzelino himself[1]; and though the play is written in Latin, and is a close imitation of Seneca, from whose *Thyestes* it even borrows a passage *verbatim*, its subject is one of immediately national interest. Another Latin drama of the same century treats a contemporary event, the *Capture of Cesena*[2]; and Landivio, a poet of the fifteenth century, commemorates in another Latin tragedy the *Captivity* and death of a famous captain of its times[3]. But long after the Italian tragic poets had begun to compose in their own tongue their subservience to Seneca led them to prefer classical subjects, although we meet with a *Rosmunda*[4]; so that by the time when the English drama came into contact with the Italian, the example of the latter no longer pointed in a direction which our playwriters had already in an earlier period come to pursue of its own accord.

Of the influence of Italian models it would therefore at this stage be misleading to speak. We may, however, wonder why it should not have independently suggested itself to the minds of many of the authors of our later miracle-plays to widen their range of subjects so as to include dramatic versions of secular narrative. When historical figures such as Octavian and Tiberius Caesar found their way into the religious plays, and Pompey the Great and other heroes of profane lore made their appearance in the pageants, the step to the dramatic treatment of an entire *passus* of secular history or of pseudo-historical romance might seem to have been so easy, that the only wonder is that it should hardly ever have have taken[5]. An exception

Isolated English plays of an early date on secular themes.

---

[1] Mussato was born in 1261 and died in 1330 (Klein, v. 235). For an abstract of the *Eccerinis*, see J. Cooper Walker, *An Historical and Critical Essay on the Revival of the Drama in Italy* (1805), pp. 20 *seqq.*

[2] A.D. 1357 (Klein, v. 251).

[3] *De Captivitate Ducis Jacobi tragoedia.* Jacopo Piccinino was executed in 1464 (*ib.*). Cf. Walker, *u.s.*, pp. 56–8.

[4] By G. Rucellai, 1516. The earliest tragedy in Italian is Galeotto del Carretto's *Sofonisba*, acted 1502; Trissino's *Sofonisba* (1515), Martelli's *Tullia*, and Rucellai's *Rosmunda* followed. See Klein, v. 251. For an enumeration of other Italian tragedies of the same epoch and of the next two decades see Symonds, *Shakspere's Predecessors*, 217; and cf. Walker, *An Historical Memoir of Italian Tragedy* (1799).

[5] One or two French 'profane mysteries' have been already noted.

Robert Cicill (1529).

may perhaps be noted in the instance of a play acted at the market-cross of Chester in 1529, the title of which was *Robert Cicill, i.e.* King Robert of Sicily. It was doubtless founded on the old romance of that name, which although certainly not identical with the romance of Robert the Devil, may connect itself with the same cycle of Norman legend. The romance tells how the proud King Robert was subjected to a severe penance by an angel of God, who assumed the king's place, and changed him into the 'fool of the hall.' In this degraded capacity King Robert had to accompany his impersonation on a visit to the Pope of Rome; nor was he restored to his royalty till after their return to Sicily. Collier alleged that he had discovered a letter addressed to Thomas Cromwell by the Mayor and Corporation of Chester, in which they gave an account of the plot of the play closely corresponding to the story of the romance[1]. If so, this was to all intents and purposes a miracle-play, and should be classed with productions of this kind rather than regarded as a precocious attempt in the direction of historical tragedy.

Three plays founded on romance, *Patient Grisilde,* a *Titus and Gesippus* and a *Melibeus,* together with a fourth on a subject of modern history, the *Burning of John Huss,* are stated by Bale to have been among those seen by him in the library of their author, Ralph Radcliffe. This worthy was a learned man who in 1538 opened a school at Hitchin, having obtained a grant of the dissolved Carmelite friary in that town, and his plays were performed by his pupils in what had formerly been the refectory of the monks. We know nothing concerning these early efforts of our scholastic drama besides their titles; some of Radcliffe's plays are said to have been in English, others in Latin[2].

[1] See Collier, i. 116: 'It is callyd Kynge Robart of Cicylye, the whiche was warned by an Aungell whiche went to Rome, and shewyd Kyng Robart all the powre of God, and what thynge yt was to be a pore man; and thanne, after sondrye wanderynges, ledde hym backe agayne to his kingdome of Cicylye, where he lyved and raygned many yeres.'—For an account of the romance see Warton, ii. 174–6, with Price's *note.*

[2] See Warton, iii. 308–9; cf. Collier, i. 114 *note.* The names of the remaining plays by Radcliffe seen by Bale were *Dives and Lazarus; The Delivery of Susannah; Job's Sufferings; Jonas,* and *The Fortitude of Judith.*—

For many a long day our national history had remained *The begin-* a sealed work to our people at large. Although chronicles *nings of the study* had been composed in a long succession which even the *of our* Wars of the Roses had been unable altogether to break, *national history.* their authors had been chiefly ecclesiastics, nor had it ever formed part of their design to gratify such interest in the national past as might here or there exist in the general public. But the Renascence brought to England, from Italy in the first instance, a taste for historical study. In the first place, the reawakened enthusiasm for the great classical authors themselves was in some measure an enthusiasm for historians. In Italy the age of the Renascence opens the epoch of critical history, and in the fifteenth century the histories of the great Italian cities were already being written in a spirit to which the chroniclers of northern countries, with their *naïf* mingling of fact and fiction, as yet remained strangers. In France, Comines in historic insight excels Froissart, almost in the same measure in which he falls short of the earlier writer in purely literary excellence. The earlier phase, at least, of the German Renascence called forth, in Elsass more particularly, a taste for patriotic history. In England, both antiquarian and literary tendencies likewise began to turn to this field of study[1]. It was an Italian, Polydore Virgil, who, under the first two Tudors, made the first attempt to write English history after a fashion designed to be attractive from a literary point of view—of course in Latin; and already Henry VII's reign produced in Fabyan's Chronicle, or *Concordance of Histories*,

Bale likewise mentions, as having written 'tragedies and comedies' in the reign of Henry VIII, Henry Parker, Lord Morley, whose only extant work is a version of the *Triumphs* of Petrarch.

[1] As to the former, see in John Leland's *New Year's Gift to King Henry VIII*, published by Bale with his commentary two (or possibly rather more) years after the king's death, such passages as the following: 'O that we had now the floryshyng workes of Gildas, surnamed Cambrius, that most noble Poete and Historyane of the Britaines, which wrote in the tyme of Kynge Aruiragus, when S. Peter yet preached to the dispersed bretherne. The Venecyans more than lxxxviii yeares ago for theyr commodite could fatche them out of Irelande, and haue them yet commen both at Venys and Rome, accounting them a very specyal treasure.'—I quote from the charming reprint of this interesting relic, recently (1895) issued by my friend Dr. Copinger from his Priory Press at Manchester.

the earliest of a series of efforts at historical composition in the native tongue destined to exercise an enduring effect upon the patriotic sentiments of our people. The policy of Henry VIII necessarily rendered him unwilling to employ the art of printing, as it was used by the German reformers, for the encouragement of a spirit which should be at once national and anti-Roman ; but of the 'new learning' spread by the Renascence and the Reformation movements, some study of the national history, and a concomitant endeavour to compose historical works in a widely acceptable literary form, inevitably became part. It was impossible, especially in a people so conservative at bottom as the English, that a great political as well as religious transformation should accomplish itself without a conscious appeal on the part of its advocates to the historical past of the nation. The Tudor dynasty availed itself of the beginnings of our modern historical literature to blacken its adversaries and to glorify itself; and the Reformers, when advocating their doctrines and attacking the practices of the Church of Rome, were as a matter of course led to recur to the memory of controversies and struggles waged of old, if not for the same ends, at all events against the same resisting powers.

While therefore, as has been already seen, the mysteries did not remain wholly unaffected by the spirit of the Reformation [1], and while some of the moralities were designedly made vehicles for the inculcations of its principles and tenets, the attempt to call in the aid of national history for the purposes of dramatic effect could hardly fail to be made in a more comprehensive and a more systematic form. With the help of the existing chronicles of past reigns, practical lessons might conveniently be conveyed to the living genera-

---

[1] One would like to know how far this spirit manifested itself in some of the later, or latest, survivals of the religious plays of the ancient type. There can of course be no doubt, from this point of view, as to *Abraham's Sacrifice*, a translation from Beza by A. G. (Arthur Golding) which appeared in 1575. But we have no information concerning *Abrame and Lotte* except that at three performances of it on January 9, 17, and 31, 1593, Henslowe received lijs., xxxs. and xijs. respectively, or as to *Absolome*, except that on the occasion of its performance in October, 1602, he disbursed ' for poleyes and workmanshipp for to hang Absolome' xiiijd. (Henslowe's *Diary*, pp. 32, 33, 241).

tion ; and of all the forms of the controversial morality, if I may use the expression, that of the historical morality seemed most to recommend itself by its impressiveness, its interest, and its comparative safety.   It was at once more effective than the morality pure and simple, and less dangerous in days of sudden shifts and changes, than the political morality in the stricter sense of the term.

Something of the kind suggested must have been the *Origin of the Chronicle history.* origin of the so-called *Chronicle History*, of which the earliest specimen remaining to us closely connects itself with the moral-plays.   This is the *Kyng Johan* of Bishop Bale.

John Bale lived in times when alike for the sake of one's *Bishop Bale (1495–1563).* conscience and for the sake of one's career it is imperative to choose a side ; and his was chosen with promptitude and with decision.   Born in Suffolk in 1495, he was educated partly in a monastery at Norwich, partly at St. John's College, Cambridge (thus being the earliest of the *alumni* of that famous college to connect its history with the annals of the English drama).   At Cambridge he became a Protestant and, avowedly in order to dissever himself for ever from the service of Rome, married a wife.   He was in due course favoured by Cromwell, on whose downfall he withdrew into the Low Countries, where he resided for eight years, naturally finding ample time for literary occupation.   On the accession of Edward VI, he obtained first a living, then the Irish bishopric of Ossory.   His consecration, however, was speedily followed by the accession of Mary ; and after many troubles he once more fled to the Continent, not to return thence till after the death of the Queen.   He was now comforted for the remainder of his days by a prebendal stall at Canterbury.   He had actively served the cause of the Reformation with his pen, consistently seconding the policy of its most advanced political champions, Cromwell and Somerset and Northumberland ; knowing no measure in the violence of his partisanship, and pouring forth in extraordinary abundance, literature which can in no sense be called ' pure.'   His incontinence as a writer has caused him to be vituperated even by latter-day upholders of the interests to which he devoted his pen ; his diligence as a compiler has brought blessings on his head, such as have fallen to the lot of few of his contemporary craftsmen [1]. For my purpose it suffices to point out that we have in this instance to do with a man of strong opinions, and accustomed to express them with a vehemence in default of which listeners were not easily to be secured in so clamorous an age. Such a man neither puzzles nor refines before suiting words to his thoughts, shows scant scruple about putting new wine into old bottles, and leaves contents and continents to arrange things between them as best they may. Thus, for instance, the dramatic forms of the mysteries and moralities that he found ready to his hands, commended themselves to him without further ado for the controversial uses which were the business of his life. Among the plays from his hand preserved to us, only a single one is devoid of controversial elements.

Of those which have been lost the titles enable us to guess the contexts. He states that he translated *Pammachii tragoedias*, a phrase which Warton thinks may perhaps refer to the play called *Pammachius*, performed at Christ's College, Cambridge, in 1544, and afterwards laid before the Privy Council as a libel [2]. Bale's own dramatic pieces were, according to his account, extremely numerous, comprising a series of 'comedies,' which appear to form a sort of collective mystery concerning the life of Christ, from His boyhood to His Resurrection, together with other single plays both religious and secular. The titles of some of the latter group are in harmony with the political and religious opinions advocated by their author : *Upon both Marriages of the King* (Henry VIII) ; *The Treacheries of the Papists ;*

---

[1] Mr. Froude calls him 'the noisiest, the most profane, the most indecent of the movement party,' and, more tersely, 'a foul-mouthed ruffian.'— I remember the late Mr. Henry Bradshaw observing to me in the Cambridge University Library, that in certain lines of research everybody falls back on Bale.

[2] Warton, iv. 74. A reference to the account of this Latin comedy, *ib.* iii. 302, will show that Warton's expression 'a libel on the Reformation' must be a slip of the pen. Gardiner, the Chancellor of the University, denounced *Pammachius* as containing offensive reflexions on those papistical ceremonies which had not been abolished. It was originally dedicated to Luther. See K. Hase, *Miracle Plays, &c.* (*English Translation*), p. 57.

Of the Impostures of Thomas a Beckett[1]. Of this class of
plays by Bale, *Kyng Johan* (which will be noticed at length)
and *The Three Laws of Nature, Moses and Christ, corrupted
by the Sodomites, Pharisees, and Papists.* Unfortunately,
the latter production (printed about 1538 and reprinted in
1562) is not easily accessible ; but it is described by Warton
as 'a satirical play against popery, and perhaps the first of
the kind in our language.' *Infydelyte* is the parent of six
Vyces, who, according to the directions given, are to be
apparelled as follows : ' Let Idolatry be decked lyke an
olde wytche, Sodomey lyke a monke of all sectes, Ambycyon
lyke a byshop, Covetousnesse lyke a Pharisee or spyrituall
lawer, False Doctrine lyke a popysh doctour, and Hypo-
cresy lyke a graye fryre. The rest of the partes,' the direction adds, ' are easye ynough to conjecture.' At the opening
of a scene in Act ii *Infidelity* intones a Latin prayer of
unspeakable profanity and obscenity[2]. Of Bale's miracle-
plays which, using an ambiguous expression, he states
himself to have 'compiled,' four have been preserved ; and
of these, as belonging to a class of compositions already
sufficiently described, a passing notice will suffice.

God's   *God's Promises*[3], written in 1538, is a mystery of the
Promises   simplest kind of construction, and was, as its author himself
(1538).   informs us[4], like his *John the Baptist*, acted by the youths
upon a Sunday at the market-cross of Kilkenny. Its
diction, however, is that of a learned writer, and the theological argument or concatenation is developed with precision and strict consecutiveness. The 'Promises' are those
made by God to Adam, Noah, Abraham, Moses, David,
Isaiah, and John the Baptist, each of whom in turn, and
in an *Actus* devoted to him, holds discourse with *Pater
Coelestis.* Each of the seven 'Acts' concludes with an
Antiphon sung by the particular interlocutor, and a prologue and epilogue are spoken by the author, Balaeus
himself. The object of this composition (unless the general

---

[1] See the list given by Bale himself in his *Scriptorum illustrium Majoris
Britanniae Catalogus* (1549), and cited ap. Collier, ii. 160 *note,* from the Basel
folio of 1577.   [2] Warton, iv. 73–4 : cf. Froude, iv. 300.
[3] Printed in Dodsley's *Old Plays,* vol. i.
[4] In his *Vocacyon to the Bishoprick of Ossory.* (Warton, iv. 74.)

reference in the epilogue to the doctrine of Justification by
Faith be insisted upon) may therefore be said to be edification pure and simple—

> ' No tryfeling sporte
> In fantasyes fayned, nor soche like gaudysh gere,
> But the thyngs that shall your inward stomake chear,
> To rejoice in God for your justyfycacyon,
> And alone in Christ to hope for your salvacyon.'

The Temp-
tacyon of
our Lorde
(1538).

The Temptacyon of our Lorde [1], written in the same year,
distinctly describes itself as an 'Acte,' or portion of a series.
Although well and vigorously written, it is not otherwise
remarkable except as containing very unmistakeable references of a controversial character to some of the institutions upon which the Reformation made war.   The moral
of the whole piece is, not to condemn fasting, but to show
that its value lies merely in its being a fruit of faith; in
addition to which the opposition to the general reading of
Scripture, and the preference shown by 'relygyouse men'
for 'contemplacyon' rather than the study of the Scrip-
tures, are directly or indirectly inveighed against.   And
the Tempter, who in the first instance assumes the habit
of a hermit, explicitly expresses his conviction that, as the
'vycar at Rome' will be his friend, he may defy the
Saviour himself.

Johan
Baptyste
(1538).

A fourth mystery by Bale belongs in date of composition
to the same year 1538.   It is the 'brefe comedy or enterlude' of *Johan Baptystes preachynge in the Wyldernesse, &c.* [2]
Its characters are the sacred personages of the passages in
the Gospel which it paraphrases, and the typical figures
of *Publicanus, Pharisaeus, Turba vulgaris, Miles armatus,*
and *Sadducaeus.*   Prologue and epilogue are here too supposed to be spoken by the author himself; and there are
again references to the rupture with Rome.   The Pharisee
inveighs against the 'new lcrnynge' introduced by St. John
(the term employed in *Kyng Johan* to signify the teaching
of the Reformation), and all ambiguity is removed by the

---

[1] Edited by Dr. A. B. Grosart among the *Miscellanies of the Fuller
Worthies' Library*, vol. i. (1870).

[2] Printed in the *Harleian Miscellany*, vol. i.

direct admonition of the Prologue not to listen to saints
and founders of monastic orders, and to

> ' Beleve neither Pope, nor prest of hys consent.'

Even in the above group of plays, however, we cannot
recognise any very substantial advance upon the religious
and political moralities described in the previous chapter.
In *Kynge Johan*[1], which accordingly calls for a more special
and detailed notice, we perceive that a very remarkable
step in advance has been taken towards those chronicle
histories from which English historical tragedy was to
take its beginning. This work was not made known to
students until its discovery, some time between 1831 and
1838, among old papers belonging to the Corporation of
Ipswich, whence it found its way into the library of the
Duke of Devonshire. It contains a reference to King John's
charitable foundations there and in the neighbourhood—

> ' Great monymentes are in Yppeswych, Donwych and Berye,
>   Which noteth hym to be a man of notable mercye;'

and the editor of the play, the late J. P. Collier, conjectures
with much probability that it was performed by the guilds
or trades of Ipswich.

About half of this production, including all the latter
portion, is in Bale's handwriting, while the remainder is
throughout carefully corrected by him, various passages being
inserted for the sake of greater completeness, or for other
reasons. The name of Bale nowhere occurs, but as he enumerates a play under the title *De Joanne Anglorum Rege*
among his dramatic works, and describes it as *in idiomate
materno*, and as his handwriting is identifiable by other evidence, Collier thinks that no doubt can exist as to his authorship. Yet I cannot perceive any proof of the earlier part of
Kynge Johan having been Bale's own production, although,
on the other hand, there is likewise no proof of the contrary
assumption. The work is at the close of the MS. described
as *two playes*; but it remains doubtful where No. I ended
and No. II began. It might be surmised that No. I ended
where we read *Finit Actus I*, about the middle of the

Kynge Johan (1548 c.).

---

[1] Edited by Collier for the *Camden Society*, 1838.

whole, after a summary of what has gone before in stanzas by the *Interpretour* (who here appears as a kind of chorus). If, however, such is not the case, and if the second play begins, as Collier thinks, at a considerably later point, where some confusion or omission occurs in the MS., and where Bale's own handwriting commences, it may be that only the second part was by him. In support of this possibility, it may be noticed, first, which is of little importance, that Bale in his *Summarium* gives, as a translation of the beginning of his play, Latin words to which the actual beginning only very vaguely corresponds [1]; secondly, that a considerable difference seems noticeable between the earlier and the later portions, the earlier being (I think) at once more vigorous and effective in the serious, and coarser in the comic, passages. Internal evidence sufficiently shows the play to have been written either in or soon after Henry VIII's reign, and before, not after, that of Queen Mary. It is most probably a product of the early years of the reign of Edward VI [2]. The conclusion, with an adulatory reference to Queen Elisabeth, is obviously a later addition ; and may, as Mr. Fleay ingeniously conjectures, have been introduced, with certain other modifications, on the occasion of the play being performed before the Queen during her visit to Ipswich in August, 1561 [3].

In ages nearer to our own the reign of Queen Mary, who in 1548 was still but a persecuted princess, has been apt to furnish the most glaring illustrations required by Protestant partisanship when appealing to the antipathies of popular audiences. The contemporaries of Edward VI could hardly have found any period of English history so useful for

---

[1] See Collier's edition, Note I.

[2] Even granting that *Imperial Majesty*, as Mr. Fleay puts it, is ' ostensibly Henry VIII,' this would not show that the play was written before his death. On the other hand, the reference to 'our late Kynge Henrye' (see below) might of course have been introduced in the reign of Elisabeth.

[3] *Chronicle History of the London Stage*, 62–3, where it is pointed out that *Imperial Majesty* is repeatedly styled 'Governour'—the title assumed by Elisabeth in lieu of that of 'Head' of the Church. Cf. the same author's *Biographical Chronicle of the English Drama*, i. 28. Bale, who died in 1563, is supposed by Mr. Fleay to have himself been the corrector.

a similar purpose as the reign of King John. Had not
Wyclif begun his public career as the literary mouthpiece
of the English Parliament which rejected the impolitic
demand of Pope Urban V, that the arrears of the tribute
agreed upon between King John and Pandulph should be
paid up at once? With all the hatred of Papal exactions
and Papal interference, and of the arrogance characterising
it in manner as well as matter, there of course coexisted in
the popular English mind much ignorance as to many parts
of King John's story, and as to the individuality of King
John himself. Thus, although he could not well be vene-
rated as a hero, he might be sympathised with as a victim;
it might even be insinuated or asserted, that this treacherous
prince, whose homage done to the Pope for his two king-
doms was in truth a political manœuvre dictated by
desperation, and whose mind was visited by glimmerings
of Protestant doctrines just about as much as that of his
brother Richard, withstood proud Pharaoh—the Pope—as
a faithful Moses on behalf of his poor Israel—England;
while the now glorified name 'Lollard' might be applied
to him without any scruple as to its appropriateness.

Possibly, *Kynge Johan* was one of the publications against
which Bishop Gardiner protested in a letter to the Protector
Somerset written in the first year of Edward VI's reign[1],
when the Visitation had begun which was almost literally
to change the face of the land, and which, while received
with very different feelings elsewhere, may be supposed to
have found friends at Ipswich[2]. Cardinal Wolsey's birthplace had benefited by the abolition of some of the smaller
monasteries in the reign of Henry VIII, and its grammar-
school was to be endowed, probably from similar sources,
by Queen Elisabeth. Some of the charitable foundations
of this borough or its vicinity, as was mentioned above,
happened to date back to the reign of King John, whose
name had therefore a good sound in this part of the country.
But the choice of theme might have naturally suggested

---

[1] See Froude, iv. 300.
[2] Less isolated than the offender who had suffered there in the days of
the Six Articles (1539). Cf. Froude, iii. 188.

itself on more general grounds; and indeed a previous dramatic attempt on the subject seems to have been produced in the shape of 'an enterlude concernyng King John,' acted 'at my Lorde of Canterbury's' (Cranmer's) on January 2nd, 1540 [1].

The play of *Kynge Johan* (for I must treat it as a single one) breathes the very spirit of the period of its composition—an emphatic defiance of the Pope and of Popery, thoroughly in consonance with the tendencies which animated the sway of Somerset and the Calvinistic reformers. These were the men who made war upon the relics of Roman ritual and Church wealth spared by Henry VIII, against which the author of *Kynge Johan* inveighs with the utmost bitterness and vehemence. At no other time in the Tudor period was so 'thorough' a view in the ascendant in the reforming circles as to the authority of the temporal sovereign in Church as well as State; and it is this view which the play enforces with reiterated energy. The royal supremacy is repeatedly insisted upon in terms one may almost say of *gusto*, such as Cranmer would have heartily approved. It is curious, by the bye (and incidentally likewise points to an early date), that though the author vigorously denounces the absurdity of employing the Latin tongue in the services of the Church, he almost invariably makes his own quotations from Scripture (which are very copious) in Latin, as if that were the tongue after all most familiar to him as the language of the Bible.

The drama begins with a speech from King John himself, declaring his lineage and position, and announcing his intention to do his duty by his people. To him enter 'Ynglond *vidua*'—a personification of the country as a widow, who at once beseeches the King to protect her from her oppressors [2]. 'Who are these?' inquires the King. Her answer suggests the keynote to all that follows, in these plain-spoken words—

---

[1] See the document in the State-Paper Office as quoted by Collier, i. 123 *seqq.*

[2] Readers of *The Faerie Queene* will call to mind the allegory of the desolate widow Belgè in Bk. i, Canto v of that poem.

' Suche lubbers as hath dysgysed heads in their hoodes
Whych in ydlenes do lyve by other menns goodes,
Monkes, chanons and nones in dyvers coloure and shappe,
Bothe whyght blacke and pyed, God send their increase yll happe.'

The conference is interrupted by *Sedwsyon* (Sedition [1]),
who certainly proves deserving of the epithet of a 'lewde
person,' speedily applied to him by the King. *Sedition*
is in fact at once the main agent in the conduct of the play,
and its solitary comic character. While therefore he represents the Vice of the moralities, he not only by his
humorous (and ineffably coarse) sallies enlivens the progress of the action, but is the spirit of evil as well as
the spirit of mockery. He makes very clear to King John
the source of the mischief which is abroad in the realm,
and in no measured terms exposes the iniquitous designs
of the Pope, as well as the arts by which his emissaries
have mastered the minds of the nobles, the clergy, and the
lawyers, upon whom the King had imagined he could rely.
Personifications representing these three orders of men—
Nobilyte, the Clargy, and *Syvill* (Civil) *Order*—are then
introduced to prove that *Sedition* has spoken the truth,
but are constrained by the King to promise such obedience
as he may demand from them. Hereupon the plot is
hatched by *Sedition* and *Dissimulation* (' dan Davy Dyssy-
mulacyon '), who recognise one another as cousins :—

' *S.* Knowest thou not thi cosyn Sedycyon ?
 D. I have ever loved both the and thy condycyon.
 S. Thow must nedes, I trowe, for we cum of ij bretherne :
   If thou remēber owr fathers were on mans chylderne.
   Thou comyst of Falshed and I of Prevy Treason.
 D. Then Infydelyte our granfather ys by reson.
 S. Mary, that ys trewe and his begyner Antycrist,
   The great pope of Rome, or fyrst veyne popysh prist.'

After comparing their antecedents and principles, and finding them mutually satisfactory, these two worthies agree
to summon to their aid *Pryvat Welth* and *Usurpyd Power*,
who enter singing a canticle, and join in the conspiracy.
The conspirators now severally assume the characters

---

[1] The spelling of the MS. is unusually wild.

which are supposed to typify the qualities they represent, viz. *Dissimulation* becomes Raymundus [1], *Sedition* Stephen Langton Archbishop of Canterbury, *Private Wealth* Cardinal Pandulphus, and *Usurped Power* the Pope. They agree that an Interdict shall be issued, and the rule of Popery fully established.

Thus ends the ' first act,' after the ' Interpretour ' has summed up the position in the following stanzas, which may be quoted, as they will render unnecessary any close account of the remainder of the play:—

> ' In thys present acte we have to yow declaréd,
> As in a mirrour, the begynnynge of Kynge Johan,
> How he was of God a magistrate appoyntéd
> To the governaunce of thys same noble regyon,
> ·To see mayntayned the true faythe and relygyon ;
> But Satan the Devylle, which that time was at large,
> Had so great a swaye that he coulde it not discharge.
>
> Upon a good zele he attempted very farre
> For welthe of thys realme to provyde reformacyon
> In the Churche thereof, but they ded hym debarre
> Of that good purpose ; for by excommunycacyon
> The space of vij yeares they interdyct thys nacyon.
> These bloudsuppers thus of crueltie and spyght
> Subdued thys good Kynge for executynge ryght.
>
> In the second acte wylle apeare more playne,
> Wherein Pandulphus shall hym excommunycate
> Within thys hys lande, and depose hym from hys reigne.
> All other princes they shall move hym to hate,
> And to persecute after most cruell rate.
> They wyll hym poison in their malygnyte
> And cause yll report of hym alwayes to be.
>
> This noble Kynge Johan, as a faythfull Moyses
> Withstode proude Pharao for hys poore Israel,
> Myndynge to brynge yt owt of the lande of darknesse,
> But the Egyptanes did agaynst hym so rebell,
> That hys poore people ded styll in the desart dwell,
> *Tyll that duke Josue, whych was our late Kynge Henrye,*
> *Clerely brought us out in to the lande of mylke and honye.*

---

[1] The reference seems to be to John's brother-in-law, Raymond IV of Toulouse.

As a strong David, at the voyce of verytie,
Great Golye, the pope, he strake downe with hys slynge,
Restorynge agayne to a Crysten lybertie
Hys land and people, lyke a most vyctoryouse Kynge;
To hir first bewtye intendynge the Churche to brynge
From ceremonyes dead to the lyvynge wurde of the Lorde.
Thys the seconde acte wyll plenteously recorde.'

The view of King John's motives indicated in the above
pervades the play, in one passage of which he is called
a 'Loller,' *i. e.* Lollard.

Under the pressure of the Interdict, *Nobility*, *Clergy*, and
Civil Order, in spite of the remonstrances of the King,
bend their knees before Langton and Pandulphus; then
Commynalte, the personification of the suffering commons,
who is blind as well as poor, and in whom, as the son
of widowed *England*, the King had placed his last trust,
tremblingly submits to the arrogant Cardinal; the forsaken King receives news that enemies from abroad are
threatening him on every side; and thus at last he gives
way and delivers up his crown.

The rest of the play (which from this point is in Bale's
handwriting) is far less dramatically effective; the real dramatic climax being past. Further concessions are forced
out of the King, whose enemies finally determine to
make away with him by poison. *Dissimulation*, on being
promised eternal bliss as his reward, assumes to himself
the responsibility of the deed and its consequences. To
the King, who is athirst, he enters in the guise of a
monk, bearing a cup in his hand and singing a wassail-
song [1]; and after himself swallowing half the poisoned
draught, persuades the King to drink the remainder. The
treacherous monk hereupon goes to his death, comforted by

---

[1] Perhaps the oldest in our language. It runs thus:—

'Wassayle, wassayle out of the mylke payle,
Wassayle, wassayle, as whyte as my nayle,
Wassayle, wassayle in snowe froste and hayle,
Wassayle, wassayle with partrich and rayle.
Wassayle, wassayle that muche doth avayle,
Wassayle, wassayle that never wyll fayle.'

It may be worthy of remark that the poisoning of King John at Swineshead
monastery, accepted by Shakspere, is a doubtful tradition.

the belief that he 'dies for the Church with S. Thomas of
Canterbury;' and then his royal victim dies (not on the
stage), after forgiving his foes and uttering a farewell to
England:—

> 'Farwell, swete Englonde, now last of all to the;
> I am ryght sorye I coulde do for the no more.
> Farwell ones agayne, yes, farwell for evermore.'

The whole of what follows may, in the irreverent language of the modern stage, be described as a *tag*. *Veryte*
(Verity) expatiates on the King's virtues and good deeds [1],
and on the lies which partisan historians have uttered
against his memory, and inculcates at great length the
doctrine of absolute obedience to princes. *Nobility, Clergy,*
and *Civil Order* promise to amend their ways; and here
at last the play might have come to a close, but the
author could not forbear from bringing in, to wind up the
action, what may be almost called a *deus ex machinâ* in
the shape of one more personification—*Imperyall Majestie.*
This abstraction, beyond doubt, very thinly veils the royal
or 'imperial' (for he liked that style) figure of Henry VIII,
with whose sentiments the oration in favour of the royal
supremacy is in very complete accordance. *Sedition* is
called to account by *Imperial Majesty,* and though promised pardon if he will make a full confession is consigned
to the hands of *Civil Order* for the expiation of his sins:—

> 'Have hym fourth, Cyvyle Order, and hang hym tyll he be dead,
> And on London brydge loke ye bestowe his head.'

This worthy having been taken away, after begging that
some one will tell the Pope, so that he may be put in the
litany and prayed to 'with candels' like Thomas Becket,
there remains nothing to be said beyond some final words
of admonition against sedition and popery. The exhortation against anabaptism (a term of very elastic application

---

[1] They consist in London Bridge having been built in his reign, and in
his zeal 'as towchynge Christes religyon' having been proved by the expulsion of the Jews out of the realm. The list is not long, but Bale might
have found it difficult to enlarge it, unless he had foreseen the greatness of
Liverpool, to which King John gave its first charter.

in the Reformation age) and the tribute of praise to Queen Elisabeth, as to the sovereign who may be a light to all other princes, are, as has been seen, later additions.

As a matter of course, this play is written in anything but a historical spirit, and it would be of little advantage to criticise it from a historical point of view. Indeed, expert controversialist as he was, the author falls back on ' abusing the plaintiff's attorney' both in the passage of the *Interpretour's* speech cited above [1], and in the assertion of *Nobility* (which for the rest does not lack point), that

> ' You pristes are the cawse that chronycles doth defame
> So many prynces, and men of notable name,
> For yow take upon yow to wryght them evermore,
> And therfore Kyng Johan is lyke to rew it sore
> When ye wryte his time, for vexing of the Clargy [2].'

In other words, this earliest example of a species which was soon to develope into the *Chronicle Histories*, pretended to bid defiance to the *Chronicles*, because they were written by priests ; nor was it until a new generation of historical writers arose who were in sympathy with the sentiments of a large body of the laity that a national historical drama could draw its materials from congenial sources. It so happens that with the reign of King John began a new school of ecclesiastical chroniclers, associated with the monastery of St. Albans, who reflected the change in the clergy of the age from political neutrality to active partisanship on behalf of the claims of the Church [3]. Authorities of this description Bale was not very likely to follow ; and indeed even in the later Chronicle History of *The Troublesome Raigne of John King of England* (printed in 1591), to be mentioned below, mediaeval historical tradition was treated with scant courtesy. Yet for the main series of his facts Bale had, notwithstanding, to depend upon the narrative of the Chroniclers. This furnished the outline of the action of his play and suggested the dramatic idea that lay at the root of the two later dramatic treatments of the same subject—

[1] *Ante*, p. 182.   [2] *Act I.*
[3] Cf. Bishop Stubbs, *ap.* Gardiner and Mullinger, *Introduction to English History* (1881), pp. 270-1.

viz. the fatal influence of the Roman Church. Thus the
king became in his eyes a national hero, although, as perhaps
was natural in an admirer of so arbitrary a 'duke,' he overlooked what we should term the constitutional significance
of John's reign, and utterly ignored *Magna Charta*[1].

I have treated this production at what may perhaps seem
disproportionate length, because of the importance attaching
to it in the history of our dramatic literature on account of
its theme, which was at once (in a sense) religious and
national, and which accordingly places the work midway
between the early religious and the active beginnings
of our national historical drama. Yet, as must have
become sufficiently obvious, it has in form nothing of
moment to distinguish it from the moralities, to which by
the allegorical nature of most of its characters and by its
general method of treatment it properly speaking belongs.
As in so many of the moralities, a very limited number of
actors seems to have been contemplated for its performance.
The *exits* and entrances of the principal characters (with
the single exception of King John himself) are so arranged
as to admit of four, three or two of them respectively being
played by the same persons; and stage directions frequently occur such as '*Go out Ynglond, and drese for
Clargy.*'

In a prolific controversialist such as Bishop Bale it would
be odd to look for literary merit of the poetical kind. As
we shall see hereafter, the dramatist and the pamphleteer
were in the annals of our literature more than once combined
in the same individual,—but such writers only very exceptionally attain to loftier flights. There is however some
dramatic force in the struggle of King John as his catastrophe
draws near [2], and a touch of pathos may perhaps be found
in the figure of the poor 'Commonalty'—which Lyndsay

---

[1] So did the author of *The Troublesome Raigne* and (virtually) Shakspere,
to both of whom, as may be worth mentioning here, Bale's play seems to
have been altogether unknown.

[2] The earlier part of the play also has some vigorous passages; see *e. g.*
that in which *Clergy* interprets the text of the Queen's 'vesture of gold,
wrought about with divers colours' (*Psalm* xlv. 10) as referring to the

had made the central personage of his political morality [1],
but which was to be often conspicuous by its absence from
the actions of our English historical dramas.

The staple metre of *Kynge Johan* consists of rimed
Alexandrines, very irregular as to the number of syllables;
quatrains and triplets are frequently introduced; the stanza-
form of the *Interpretour's* speech is Chaucerian.

It should perhaps be pointed out that we possess no
evidence as to Bale's *Kynge Johan* having actually served
as a transition from the Moralities to the Chronicle Histories,
and by means of these to the regular drama of the tragic
or serious kind. Indeed, there is every indication to the
contrary; for the earliest Chronicle History proper known
to us belongs in date to the last decade but one of the
sixteenth century [2]; and to the author of the second in
date (*The Troublesome Raigne*, already noted), which was
printed in 1591, Bale's play was, as has been seen, unknown.
After its composition, succeeded perhaps by one or more
performances of it under King Edward VI, Queen Mary's
reign had intervened, during which there were the best of
reasons for keeping the MS. hidden away among the papers
of the Corporation at Ipswich. Thence it only emerged on
a single occasion early in Queen Elisabeth's reign, when if
not actually performed it was certainly revised for some
such purpose. The death of its author two years afterwards
(1563) may help to account for its having, so far as we
know, remained unprinted. At all events the fact of its
existence fell back into an oblivion from which it was not
rescued until its discovery some threescore years ago. In
the first decade of the reign of Elisabeth, as will be shown

*Its signifi-
cance in the
history
of our
dramatic
literature.*

various monastic orders, which he enumerates with extraordinary volubility;
whereupon King John remarks :—

> 'Davyd meanyth vertuys by the same diversitye
> As in the sayd psalme yt is evydent to se,
> And not munkysh sects; but it is ever yowr cast
> For yowr advauncement the scripturs for to wrast.'

[1] *Ante*, p. 132, *note*.

[2] *The Famous Victories of Henry V* was certainly performed before 1588.
See below. Mr. Fleay, but I am not sure on what evidence, dates the production of the *True Tragedie of Richard III* as early as 1587.

immediately, the beginnings of English tragedy were, with the utmost distinctness, to attach themselves to examples of a very different kind of dramatic writing. Yet the fact of the composition and existence of *Kynge Johan*, whatever were the actual fortunes of the work, remains not the less of great significance. An age which could produce a play of this description could not fail before long to find writers who would abandon the worn ways of the moralities and their abstract characters, and appeal to a range of ideas and feelings no longer to be satisfied by the allegorical inculcation of ethical commonplaces, or by the repetition of familiar Bible stories and anecdotes of saints.

Classical studies under Mary and Elisabeth. Queen Mary's reign, which (although only for a time[1]) swept away the creations of reforming or innovating zeal, likewise sought, in the ordinary spirit of Tudor despotism, to suppress by all the means in its power that freedom of public utterance of which stage and printing-press were already becoming joint agents[2]. But Mary likewise shared with her brother and sister, as well as with her father, a genuine love of learning; and the learning of the Renascence had its root and inmost being in the study of the two classical languages. Whatever may be the fortunes of this branch of research and study in future periods of civilisation, it may be confidently asserted that the classics can never again become to any portion or section of the public interested in intellectual effort what they were to the 'humanists' of the fifteenth and sixteenth centuries. To these men and women (for a representative bevy of the female sex was wanting neither in Italy nor in England) the languages and literatures of ancient Greece and Rome furnished the exemplars, which neither time could affect nor decay could befall, of whatever was wise in meaning and beautiful in form; and modern tongues and literatures were but the serving-maids of their privileged and more perfect elder sisters. And as in what may be called the technical parlance of the Renascence 'poets' and 'poetry' often meant the composers and composition of Latin verse, so in England translation from the Classics was reckoned the choicest—I had almost

[1] Cf. *ante*, p. 153.　　　[2] *Ante*, p. 153.

said 'the most respectable'—kind of literary productivity. No substantial difference is noticeable as to the general aspects of our literature between the reign of Mary and the earlier years of the reign of Elisabeth; at least, it would need a very nice sense of discrimination to distinguish between the lyrical collections of the one and those of the other; *Tottel's Miscellany* (1557) seems but the first of a long series of similars. All these anthologies display an *Transla-* unquenchable ardour in the pursuit of classical study that *tions.* finds its natural outlet in translation. English versions of classical poetry were produced in a continuous flow during the reign of Queen Mary and during the greater part of the reign of her successor. Even when the great period of our Elisabethan literature had already set in, when the *Faerie Queene* was on the eve of publication and when Shakspere was already known as a successful dramatist, one of the foremost of his earlier competitors, himself a writer of some original power, is found ranking by the side of the great English poets of old, a translator of the *Aeneid,* whose name is now known to none but professed literary students [1].

In the history of the literature of translations no fact is more familiar than this, that at particular times particular authors command, or even monopolise, the attention of both writers and readers. Among the classical authors who *The* attained to this kind of popularity in the early days of *tragedies* Elisabeth, the tragic poet Seneca [2] for very manifest reasons *of Seneca.* held a prominent place. To begin with, he wrote in Latin and not in Greek, and the history of the scholarship of the early Elisabethan age attests the fact, that it was the

---

[1] Peele, in the *Prologue* to *The Honour of the Garter* (1593), ranks Phaer, the translator of the *Aeneid* (1558), with Chaucer and Gower :—
> 'Why thither post not all good wits from hence,
> To Chaucer, Gower, and to the fairest *Phaer*
> That ever ventur'd on great Virgil's works ? '
In the same poem he refers with enthusiasm to
> ' our English *Fraunce,*
> A peerless sweet translator of our time.'

[2] The question cannot be discussed here whether or not the tragic poet L. or M. Annaeus Seneca, to whom are ascribed nine tragedies which are preserved complete, and a tenth, the grievously mutilated *Thebaïs,* was the same person as the philosopher, L. Annaeus Seneca, the tutor and adviser, and

'Latinists,' and not the 'auncient Grecians,' who were 'of the greatest fame and most obvious' in the eyes of the literary public of the period [1]. Secondly, Seneca the tragedian was a writer whose works, while enveloped by the glamour that was the due of the ancients, had little in them of the kind of difficulty that repels the modern. Nay, in a sense he was himself a modern, more especially as compared with the tragic poets who had preceded him. The reign of Nero has been justly characterised by one of its latest historians [2] as exhibiting the climax of a literary cosmopolitanism which had begun with Imperialism and which ignored any special connexion with a national life and a national religion that were themselves fast melting away. A Spaniard by descent, Seneca had inherited rhetorical gifts with his paternal blood. As a tragic poet he had no choice but to follow the models of the Attic drama, while evincing what originality or desire of originality there was in him, by his treatment of details, and more especially in matters of diction and versification. Among the Attic tragedians Euripides would naturally commend himself

afterwards the victim, of the Emperor Nero. Merivale thought that there was strong evidence of the latter having been the author of some at least of these plays. Conington inclined to the same opinion. See Merivale, *History of the Romans under the Empire* (ed. 1865), vi. 382, and Conington's Essay, *Seneca, Poet and Philosopher*, in vol. i. of his *Miscellaneous Writings* (1892), for a notice of the various theories which have been held as to the authorship of the 'Senecan' tragedies, including the theory of Nisard that the several plays were written by different members of the same family, and that of Bernhardy, who held them to have been the work of a school of rhetoricians. For a note on the Seneca family, see Merivale, v. 93.

[1] See the passage cited by Dr. Cunliffe, p. 10, from William Webbe's *Discourse of English Poetrie* (1586). Ascham, the pupil of Sir John Cheke, has been justly regarded as an exception proving the rule; but it is noticeable that even he gives at least nominal precedence to Seneca among 'the best authors' as to whose claims 'for learnyng of tonges and sciences' there rises 'amonges proude and envious wittes a great controversie, whether one or many are to be folowed : and if one, who is that one; *Seneca, Cicero, Salust,* or *Cesar,* and so forth, in *Greeke* and *Latin*.' (*The Schole Master*, Bk. II.) No genuine translation of a Greek play appeared in the sixteenth century, or long afterwards, in England. On the other hand, the *Plutus* of Aristophanes is said to have been performed in Greek before Queen Elisabeth. (Symonds, *Shakspere's Predecessors*, p. 222, *note*.)

[2] H. Schiller, *Geschichte des römischen Kaiserreichs unter der Regierung des Nero* (1872).

above the rest for imitation, both in his bolder and freer treatment of mythical characters and situations, and in his elaborate, artificial, and highly-seasoned effects of diction. What the old-fashioned Attic critics—or those who like Aristophanes pretended to be old-fashioned—found fault with in Euripides, most attracted the dramatist who catered for the Romans of the decadence. But Euripides was an Athenian whose earlier triumphs had fallen within the greatest age of the art to which he ministered; even those very excesses beyond what was held seemly in the treatment of his themes were due to the uncontrollable impetus of genius to create new problems for itself to master, and their very choice was determined by an idio-syncrasy with whose claims criticism could only quarrel at its peril. And if, 'haunted on the stage by the dæmon of Socrates,' he found too frequent outlets in the conjunctures of his dramas or the developement of their characters for philosophical speculation,—still, who would venture to assert of the 'most tragic of poets' that he composed his tragedies for the purpose of introducing into them subtle observa-tions, pregnant apophthegms, or familiar quotations *in posse*? Finally, his innovations in the familiar forms of Attic tragedy, such, above all, as his reduction of the *chorus* to a position of often vanishing importance in the action, and his consequent elaboration of its lyrical effects, were natural steps in a process of developement neither begun nor carried to its ultimate issue by himself.

Seneca possibly represents a phase of Roman tragedy in its artificiality and decline in which he did not stand alone; but as to this, whether fortunately or unfortunately for his poetic reputation, we know nothing. He borrows his sub-jects from the time-honoured themes of Greek mythology with a single-minded preference for what may in a word be called the most sensational in the list. The horrid banquet placed by Atreus before Thyestes, the murder of Agamen-non by his adulterous wife and her paramour, the incestuous love of Phaedra, the revenge of the disenchanted Medea— all these and others of the same kind are served up once more. But his pains are spent neither on the contrivance of the action nor in the evolution of its characters. In the former respect he is only notable for a proneness to gratifying the eyes as well as the ears of his public with the horrors of blood and iron, and for a specially free use of 'Charon's stairs.' Seneca's ghosts were in the Elisabethan age regarded as the most characteristic part of his tragic machinery, though in this respect as in others no very careful distinction was always drawn between himself and his master Euripides[1]. His treatment of the *chorus*, a more distinct advance upon the Euripidean precedent, facilitated the general conduct of the action of his plays, and enabled him more freely to ignore those so-called unities of time and place of which in the Attic drama the continuous presence of interlocutory and commentating witnesses on the orchestra was the actual cause. A convenient outward expression of this greater independence of dramatic construction was his habitual division of his tragedies into five acts—a system which (whether or not due to his own invention) was derived from him by the modern drama at large. But the chief attention of the Roman poet is devoted to matters other than choice of theme or method of construction. His versification has the facile fluency to which only a late age of any poetic literature can attain. His own literary genius, together with the influences of his age, show themselves in his diction, highly coloured by a brilliant rhetoric and studded with philosophical sentiments and gnomic phrases to which his Stoic training frequently lent a deeper significance, and which at times intensified the force of his action and characters themselves. His dialogue bristles with antithesis, to which effect is added by the device of *stichomythia*, and even by that of breaking up a single line into thrust and parry; but he is not invariably so far master of his art as to be able to leave a striking

---

[1] The summons 'Up grieslie ghostes' in *The Shepheardes Calendar*, November, v. 55, is thus annotated by 'E. K.': 'The maner of Tragicall Poetes, to call for helpe of Furies, and damned ghostes: so is Hecuba of Euripides, and Tantalus brought in of Seneca. And the rest of the rest.' As Dr. Herford observes (in his edition of the *Calendar*, 1895, p. 184), 'the ghost of Tantalus appears in Seneca's *Thyestes*, that of Polydorus in Euripides' *Hecuba*. Kirke's statement is somewhat confused.'

utterance alone when it has once been delivered. He is neither altogether commonplace nor altogether artificial; but his style so largely combines elements of both defects as to have all the imitability of bombast [1].

From all this we may perceive why among the ancient tragic poets Seneca pre-eminently commended himself to the sympathies of the Renascence age. It was to Italy that English writers in this period looked for their immediate models, and, in the emphatic words of a writer who on this subject may be described as authoritative, 'every tragic scene which the Italians of the Renaissance set forth upon the boards of Rome or Florence or Ferrara, was a transcript from Seneca. Following this lead,' he continues, 'our English scholars went to school with Seneca beneath the ferule of Italian ushers [2].' From Alberto Mussato, who wrote in Latin [3], downwards to the prolific school of Italian tragedies of the earlier half of the sixteenth century, all adhered to a model the atmosphere of whose themes and whose literary manner was alike congenial to them [4]. French tragedy began in 1552 with the *Cléopatre Captive* of Étienne Jodelle, a tragedy entirely in the manner of Seneca, devoid of action, but furnished with a *chorus* and not wanting a ghost. The long-enduring sway of the Latin tragedian over the French, and his influence upon other modern dramas, it would be superfluous in this place to illustrate [5]. I cannot say whether the four tragedies composed by

Their influence on Renascence literature.

---

[1] 'Ercles' vein' (*Midsummer Night's Dream*, i. 2) may immediately allude to the play of *Hercules*, of which Part I was produced in May 1595, and both Parts of which are stated to have been the work of Martin Slater, Slather, Slatier or Slaughter (see Henslowe's *Diary, passim*). But the existence of this bipartite drama only furnishes additional evidence of the influence of the *Hercules Furens* and the *Hercules Oetaeus*.

[2] Symonds, *Shakspere's Predecessors*, 217.   [3] *Ante*, p. 168.

[4] An account of the Italian tragedians who wrote under the influence of Seneca will be found in Klein, v. 341 *seqq.*; cf. Symonds, *u. s.*

[5] As to the commanding influence of Seneca upon a long period of the French drama, and upon more isolated phenomena in the Spanish and German, see Cunliffe, p. 8. Ludwig Uhland left behind him a play called *Thyest*—in the main a version of Seneca. The classical Dutch dramatists of the seventeenth century, Hooft and Vondel in particular, based their efforts upon a close study of the characteristic features of Seneca as a dramatist, and thus succeeded in expelling from the stage the allegorical figures which

George Buchanan while resident at Bordeaux during the years 1540 to 1545 (or thereabouts), which were acted by the students there—including a youth destined to become illustrious in the literature of the world—were based on Seneca, or more directly on Seneca's model Euripides; but they were expressly designed to encourage a transition from the old allegories to the imitation of classical models[1]. What is certain is that in the first three decades of Elisabeth's reign the tragedies of Seneca were a favourite study of English scholars and men of letters, more especially of course when connected by their present or past training with the Universities. Thus this author came to form the chief connecting link between the learning of the English Renascence and the growth of the English drama[2].

Seneca's Tenne Tragedies translated into English (1559–1581).   Between the years 1559 and 1581 all the ten tragedies written by Seneca, or attributed to his authorship, were successively translated into English by five scholars, one of whom, Thomas Newton, in 1581, collected the efforts of all these 'laudable Authors[3]' into a single volume, under the title of *Seneca his tenne Tragedies translated into Englysh*[4]. The earliest of these Translations was that of the *Troades*

had held sway in the plays exhibited in the *Rederijker-Kammern*. (See a notice of J. A. Worp, *De invloed van Seneca's Treurspelen op ons tonneel*, by E. Martin, in *Deutsche Litteraturzeitung*, February 11th, 1893; cf. a notice of the same work in *Archiv der neueren Sprachen und Litteraturen*, November 1894.)

[1] See Prof. A. Mackay's notice of Buchanan in the *Dictionary of National Biography*, vol. vii. p. 187: Ascham (*The Scholemaster*, Bk. II) describes one of these tragedies, ' *Jephthe*,' as 'able to abyde the trew touche of *Aristotle's* preceptes and *Euripides*' examples.'

[2] Both in the preceding passage and in what follows concerning the early translations into English of Seneca's tragedies, as well as in subsequent references to their influence upon our drama, I have made free use of an exhaustive essay by an old fellow-student of my own, Dr. J. W. Cunliffe, *The Influence of Seneca upon Elizabethan Tragedy* (1893). See also T. Vatke's essay, *Shakespeare und Euripides*, in *Shakespeare Jahrbuch*, vol. iv. (1869), and a note by W. Wagner, *ib.* vol. xi. (1876). I have already incidentally referred to the admirable passage concerning Seneca and his 'paramount authority' in the Renascence period in chap. vi. of Symonds' *Shakspere's Predecessors* (1884).

[3] They are so called by William Webbe, himself a Cambridge graduate, in his *Discourse of English Poetrie* (1586).

[4] This quarto was reprinted by the Spenser Society in 1887 with an *Introduction* by the President of the Society, Mr. Joseph Leigh.

in 1559 (reprinted in 1563) by Jasper Heywood, who also published in 1560 a translation of the *Thyestes*, and in 1561 one of the *Hercules Furens*. In 1560 Alexander Neville composed a translation of the *Oedipus*, first published in 1563. In 1561 Thomas Nuce published a translation of the *Octavia*. John Studley followed with the *Medea* (1563); and the complete edition by Thomas Newton (1581) included besides his own version of the *Thebais*, Studley's translations of the *Agamemnon*, the *Hercules Oetaeus*, and the *Hippolytus*.

All these writers were University men and professed scholars. The first of the band, Jasper Heywood (1535–1598), who specially interests us as a son of John Heywood, the author of interludes and epigrammatist, and who as a boy had been page of honour to the Princess Elisabeth, was under Queen Mary successively a fellow of Merton and of All Souls College. At Merton he had to resign his fellowship on account of misdemeanours[1]; All Souls he was obliged to leave because of his non-compliance with the changes in religion that followed on the accession of Queen Elisabeth. Being already in priest's orders, he repaired to Rome, where, in 1562, he was admitted a member of the Society of Jesus ; but his subsequent promotions (including a degree of D.D.) and strange experiences must here be passed by. He is supposed to have translated some portion of Vergil ; he put together a compendium of Hebrew grammar ; and he contributed several English poems to the *Paradyse of Daynty Deuises* (1578)[2]. Alexander Neville (1544–1614), Thomas Nuce (d. 1617), and John Studley (said to have been killed at the siege of Breda in 1587[3]) were all three Cambridge men. Neville, who was successively in the service of three Archbishops of Canterbury, belonged to the literary world of his day ; he was a nephew of Barnaby Googe and a friend of George Gascoigne, and edited the

---

[1] He had very successfully filled the office of lord of misrule in his College, and possibly forgot that Christmas comes but once a year.

[2] See the biographical notice by Mr. Thompson Cooper in vol. xxvi. of the *Dictionary of National Biography*, pp. 329–331; cf. Mr. Joseph Leigh's Introduction, pp. v–vi.

[3] *Biographica Dramatica* (1812), i. 696.

collection of Cambridge verses on the death of Sir Philip Sidney. He also wrote a Latin history of Kitt's rebellion [1]. Thomas Nuce, who, after holding a fellowship at Pembroke Hall, died as a Prebend of Ely, composed Latin as well as English verse [2]. Finally, Thomas Newton (d. 1607), who published all the ten tragedies in a single volume, was educated both at Oxford and at Cambridge, and after (probably) practising as a physician and teaching as a schoolmaster, settled down as a country rector. The long list of his works includes writings on historical, medical, and theological subjects, and he was, in addition, a skilled writer of both English and more especially of Latin verse, by which latter he excited the admiration of his contemporaries [3].

Men of letters of so liberal and many-sided a culture were as translators likely to err on the side of freedom rather than on that of a too servile fidelity to their original; and a seductive example was set by Jasper Heywood in the earliest of these versions, that of the *Troades*. Here not only are verses and stanzas freely added to the choric parts, and other alterations made in them, but an entire chorus is added at the end of Act I, and at the beginning of Act II is introduced a soliloquy by the 'Spright of Achilles'— both scene and character being the inventions of the translator. To the *Thyestes* he likewise added, at the end of Act V, a soliloquy into which Thyestes strives to condense all the horrors of the play [4]. The most anxious among the translators for fidelity seems to have been Thomas Newton,

---

[1] See Mr. S. Lee's notice in *Dictionary of National Biography*, xi. 244–5; and Mr. Joseph Leigh, *u. s.*, iii–iv.

[2] See Mr. Donald Bayne's notice in *Dictionary of National Biography*, xii. 256; and Mr. Joseph Leigh, *u. s.*, iii.

[3] See the late Mr. J. P. Earwaker's notice in *Dictionary of National Biography*, xl. 402–3, and Mr. Joseph Leigh, *u. s.* Although a Puritan in his tendencies, Newton was in Phillips' *Theatrum Poetarum* credited with the authorship of *Tamburlaine*.

[4] It begins with an invocation of Pluto, much in the style of the mysteries :—

'O Kyng of Dytis dungeon darke and grysly Ghosts of hell,
That in the deepe and dredfull Denne of blackest Tartare dwell;
Where leane and pale dyseases lye, where feare and famyne are,
Where discord stands with bleeding browes, where euery kynde of care.'

but it is very likely that he merely added a version of the *Thebais* in order to make the collection complete, instead of being attracted by preference to this play, which moreover is at best a fragment.

Both in diction and in versification these translations attest the period of their origin ; they contain no blank verse ; and while the stanza-forms and metres of the choruses are necessarily more varied, the favourite metre of the dialogue consists of those rimed couplets of fourteen syllables with seven accents, of which the best-known example is to be found in Chapman's *Iliad*.

The direct influence of the tragedies of Seneca—exercised no doubt chiefly through the medium of these translations— upon the beginnings of regular English tragedy will become abundantly manifest as we review in their sequence its earliest productions. Here it will suffice to state that in external form, as well as with respect to less tangible characteristics, these productions unmistakeably imitated Seneca and no other model—taking over his five acts separated from one another by choruses, his use and treat-ment of the chorus itself as detached from the action, and his occasional, but by no means obligatory, resort to the Messenger as the narrator of a catastrophe—for in Seneca and on the early English tragic stage much business of this kind is transacted before the eyes of the public[1]. The writers of our early tragedies likewise took over from Seneca other stock-characters of his scene, including the faithful servant and the confidential nurse, and above all they took over from him his ghosts and his supernatural devices in general. Not less certainly was he their chief (although not their only) guide in their choice of startling and often revolt-ing themes, as well as in their use of sententious speech and rapidly antithetical dialogue. Of these characteristic features—more especially of the last-named—our English tragic drama continued in varying measure to exhibit the influence in the works of Shakspere's predecessors, in those of Shakspere himself, and even in those of the later

Their direct in-fluence upon early English tragedy.

---

[1] Cunliffe, pp. 32 *seqq*.

Elisabethans; in addition to which isolated writers of high
classical training at various times in the course of this
period essayed a close and consistent imitation of Senecan
tragedy [1]. But as a matter of course the height of Seneca's
dominion over English tragedy belongs to its earliest days,
which may be regarded as very nearly coincident with
those over which the production of the translations noticed
above extended, and with the few years following upon
their collective publication [2].

The circumstance that earlier and contemporary Italian
tragedy stood wholly under the influence of Seneca, and
itself contributed to strengthen and intensify that influence,
more especially in the choice of themes, will therefore
not warrant us in representing as a primary what was but
a secondary channel. It was not from the Italian tragedians more or less contemporary with themselves, such as
Speron Sperone or Lodovico Dolce, that the writers of our
earliest English tragedies derived their method and manner,
but from Seneca in his original or in his translated form.
Before long, indeed (as it will be most convenient to show
in particular cases), but not in the first instance, the progress
of English tragedy was affected by the later Italian imitators of Seneca, many of whom seasoned their plays with
novelties in the way of the horrible due to personal tastes
vitiated by a continued decadence in public morals.

Gorboduc (Ferrex and Por- rex) the earliest English tragedy (1562).

To the influence, then, of the last eminent tragic writer of
classical antiquity, are to be ascribed the main characteristics,
as well as the fact of the composition of the earliest English
tragedy either preserved or known to us. This is the
tragedy of *Ferrex and Porrex*, as it is called in the only
genuine impression of 1570, or *Gorboduc* [3], under which

---

[1] See below as to Gascoigne, David and the Earl of Stirling (William
Alexander), and the reference to Fulke Greville, Lord Brooke.

[2] In Nash's Prefatory Letter to Greene's *Menaphon* addressed *to the
Gentlemen Students of the Universities* (Grosart's edition of Greene's *Works*,
vol. vi) there is a curious reference to the translators of Seneca who will
'affoord you whole *Hamlets*, I should say handfulls of tragical speaches';
but, the letter continues, all things come to an end, 'and Seneca let blood
line by line and page by page, at length must needs die to our stage.'

[3] Edited by W. D. Cooper for the (Old) Shakespeare Society, 1847, and

title it was printed in 1565, 1569, 1571 and 1590, and first
acted on January 18, 1562 by the gentlemen of the Inner
Temple before the Queen[1]. The unauthorised editions of
1565 and 1590 state that the first three acts of this play
were written by Thomas Norton ; the rest of the play at
all events was written by Thomas Sackville, afterwards
Lord Buckhurst and Earl of Dorset, with whose name the
authorship of the work at large is traditionally associated.
Norton, who was born in 1532 at Sharpenhoe in Bedford-
shire, and after being educated at Oxford was called to
the Bar from the Inner Temple, made himself useful to
the powers that were in both Church and State, while
adhering to his own Calvinistic views. He appears to have
been erroneously credited with the authorship of a treatise
in favour of the Puritans against Whitgift ; but he wrote
other Calvinistic pamphlets, translated Calvin's *Institutes*,
and was associated with Sternhold and Hopkins in their
version of the Psalms, while he seems also to have occasionally composed original verse[2]. He is said to have
been at one time counsel to the Stationers' Company, and
Warton believes that he filled the post of licenser of
publications under the bishop of London. His coadjutor
filled a notable place in both our political and literary
history. Under Queen Elisabeth he was concerned in
some of the most important and difficult affairs of state ;
it was he who conveyed her sentence of death to Mary
Queen of Scots at Fotheringay, and he was afterwards sent
to the Netherlands to fill the place of Leicester. The
office of Lord High Treasurer which he held at the close
of Elisabeth's reign was confirmed to him for life by her
successor, and he died full of honours in 1608.

At the time of the production of *Gorboduc* he was still
a young man (he was born about 1527), and as a barrister
of the Inner Temple divided his time between attendance

by Miss L. Toulmin Smith, Heilbronn, 1883; also printed in vol. ii. of
Hawkins' *Origin of the English Drama* and in vol. i. of the *Ancient British
Drama*.

[1] Cf. Fleay, *English Drama*, ii. 174, 149.

[2] See the lines 'A man may live thrice Nestor's life,' &c. in Ellis'
Specimens, ii. 108. Cf. Warton, iv. 213, and *ib*. 130, 255.

upon the Queen ' by her particular choice and liking,' and diversions among which literary pursuits must have held a conspicuous place. An early tradition asserted that he originally contemplated the composition of the entire earlier portion of the *Mirror for Magistrates*, of which the first edition appeared in 1559 ; to the second edition of 1563 his hand contributed the solemn and Dantesque *Induction* and the *Complaint of the Duke of Buckingham* [1]. On these his literary fame must chiefly rest ; yet neither is *Gorboduc*, as think will appear, devoid of literary merit.

The plot is thus stated in the *Argument of the Tragedie* :—

'Gorboduc King of Britain divided his realm in his life-time to his two sons Ferrex and Porrex. The sons fell to dissension. The younger killed the elder. The mother, that more dearly loved the elder, for revenge killed the younger. The people, moved with the cruelty of the fact, rose in rebellion and slew father and mother. The nobility assembled and most terribly destroyed the rebels ; and afterwards, for want of issue of the prince, whereby the succession to the crown became uncertain, they fell to civil war, in which both they and many of their issue were slain, and the land for a long time almost desolate and miserably wasted.'

Manifestly, this is an expansion of the ancient Theban story of the sons of Œdipus and Iocasta and their fatal strife ; although of course the antecedents of the Œdipodean legend are omitted, and the father and mother play a different part in the action. The immediate source of the story is a tale belonging to ancient British legend, which was afterwards treated by William Warner in his *Albion's England* [2], a work which is to be regarded as a successor of the *Mirror for Magistrates*. The dramatic idea of a fatal fratricidal rivalry recurs in many later dramas in different literatures, which it would be superfluous here to seek to enumerate [3].

Although this plot in some respects resembles the argu-

---

[1] See as to these, Warton, iv. 170 *seqq.*

[2] Book iii. canto 15.

[3] The opening in some measure recalls that of *King Lear*; for Gorboduc relinquishes his royal authority under the influence of an unwise generosity.

ment of an epic poem rather than the action of a drama, yet it must be allowed to cohere well, besides leading up to strong situations. No doubt these situations are not always sufficiently prepared ; in other words Gorboduc, like the tragedies of Seneca which served as models to its author, is deficient in characterisation[1]. As has been well remarked[2], although the personages of the action fall because of the wrong they have themselves committed, yet we are very insufficiently shown how the passions which bring about the catastrophe are developed in the individual characters. (Seneca, it will be remembered, was described above as weak, even among ancient tragedians, in characterisation.) On the other hand the play is strong in its construction, as to the management of which the authors, in the true spirit of the English drama, assume the right of declining to follow, except at their own pleasure, arbitrary rules. In formal matters, indeed, the authors of *Gorboduc* adhere to the usages of Seneca. The play is divided into five acts. Each of the first four acts closes with a chorus, of its essence superfluous, recited by a company of not more than four ' ancient and sage men of Britain.' The murders do not take place on the stage, but are announced to the audience by messengers. But while they borrow both chorus and messenger from the ancient classical drama, our authors have nothing to say to the supposed law of the unities of time and place ; their plot covers an epoch of history and involves frequent changes of scene. It must be allowed that the fifth act of the play is of the nature of an epilogue, and accordingly adds to the heaviness of the movement.

Enough has perhaps already been said to vindicate the tragedy of *Gorboduc* against the censures of A. W. von

---

[1] Thus, as Warton has acutely pointed out, the awful narrative in Act iv. of Marcella, who relates how the mother Vidua, who had loved Ferrex best, revenged his death at the hands of his brother Porrex by entering the chamber of the latter in the night, and murdering him in his sleep, introduces this murder without preparing the audience by any previous disclosure as to the character of Vidua.

[2] By Professor Wülcker, in a review of the first edition of the present work.

Schlegel, who declares Pope's 'praise of the regularity of this work, as fitting it to be one of the first of a school of classical dramas,' as only proving Pope's own ignorance of the primary elements of dramatic art, and inveighs against the utter monotony of its versification and diction [1]. To its own generation, its style seemed so excellent that in his *Apology for Poetry* (which was probably written between 1579 and 1581) Sidney extols it as full of 'notable moralitie,' i. e. of moral maxims deserving attention on their own account. Of course the readiest opportunities for such rhetorical reflexion are furnished by the choral odes (or tags). The dialogue moves with a grave and solemn march, but here and there deviates into sober imagery. Nor can it be denied that certain passages of the play, which dwell upon the evils of civil discord and disloyalty, seem to possess a force not altogether due to the influence of association. A protest against discord as the chief curse of the lives of both rulers and ruled may be said to form the leading motive of the work [2].

The metre of the dialogue is blank-verse—the first known to have been declaimed on an English stage— of a solid and slow movement throughout, with single-syllable endings. Thus early was the experiment tried

---

[1] *Ueber dramatische Kunst und Literatur* (1811) ii, ii, 266-7. Ulrici, too, judges *Gorboduc* with severity.

[2] In addition, we may detect a direct allusion to contemporary affairs in such a passage as the following (Act V, Sc. 2):—

> 'For right will last, and wrong cannot endure;
> Right mean I his *or hers* upon whose name
> The people rest, by means of native line
> Or by the virtue of some former law
> Already made their title to advance.
> Such one, my lords, let be your chosen King,
> Such one so born within your native land,
> Such one prefer, and in *no wise admit*
> *The heavy yoke of foreign governaunce.*'

Of the suits of foreign princes for the hand of the Virgin Queen, one (that of Eric of Sweden) was in this very year (1562) brought to an end by her own suggestion, while that of Philip of Spain had been previously staved off. At this period Dudley's ambition was still directed to sharing Elisabeth's throne, and Sackville (who was afterwards employed in the negotiations concerning the French marriage) belonged to the Protestant party.—Cf. as to the political allusions in this play, Miss L. Toulmin Smith, *Introduction*, xxii-xxiii.

in dramatic composition, which only a few years previously (in 1557) Surrey had first introduced into English verse from Italian examples, in his translation of
the Second and Fourth Books of the *Æneid*[1]. Its use
on the popular stage will more appropriately be discussed
hereafter.

In conclusion, mention should be made of the employment
in this tragedy of a device peculiar to the early period of
our drama, and familiar from its use in the 'play within the
play' of *Hamlet*. This is the prefiguring *dumb-show*,
which sets forth by pantomime (action without words) the
contents of the coming play, or—as in *Gorboduc*—of each
ensuing portion or act of it. This device, unnecessary in
a drama which like Attic tragedy treated legends familiar
to every spectator, in so far made for refinement, that after
satisfying the grosser craving of mere curiosity, it left the
attention of the spectator to fix itself upon the artistic treatment rather than upon the mere material incidents of
the action. When, as in *Gorboduc*, instead of representing the
incidents that were to follow in a mere pantomimical summary, it allegorised them under mythological types, it was
clearly suited for none but a learned audience. This kind
of dumb-show must therefore be distinguished from that
which, in some of our early plays, merely presented in
rapid action incidents which the author was unwilling to
protract with the aid of dialogue[2]. In general, it is
obvious that this device could not be maintained in a more
developed condition of the drama ; it belongs to the infancy
of dramatic construction, or, like the Euripidean Prologue,
implies a neglect of the requirement that a dramatic action
should be complete in itself.

After dwelling on a literary production of pretensions so *Other early*
advanced as those of *Gorboduc*, it seems like going back to *tragedies.*
note two dramatic efforts, contemporary with it, or nearly
so, but in form still closely associated with a phase of our
drama on which the scholarly and courtly authors of the

---

[1] Milton, as is known, loftily ignored the effort of his predecessor.
[2] E. g. the death of Guiscard and the preservation of his heart in *Tancred
and Gismunda*; cf. Cunliffe, p. 42.

first English tragedy would have looked down with lofty scorn.

Yet I should distinctly be inclined to class both *Apius and Virginia* and *King Cambises* among our earliest tragedies rather than among our later moralities, to which such plays as *King Darius, Godly Queene Hester*, and *Jacob and Esau* [1] essentially belong. Of the moralities they indeed still present some of the principal features: a considerable number of personified abstractions make their appearance in both, nor is the character of the Vice more important or prominent in any other of our early dramas. But the main interest which both these plays excite is historical and real, and their leading personages are actual —and supposed to be historical—human beings. Moreover, in *King Cambises* at least, it is not always easy to distinguish between abstract and concrete: 'Common Cry,' for instance, may be regarded as a type or representative of the oppressed commons, and 'Execution,' though wearing the name of an abstraction, is actually summoned by the King as a concrete being, the 'execution man.'

The date of both these plays is probably very nearly contemporary with that of our earliest English tragedy proper ; but from a literary point of view they may still be regarded as marking a transition rather than a consummated change. The *Tragical Comedy of Apius and Virginia* [2] is by an unknown author, or at least by one whose identity cannot be determined, designated under the initials R. B. It was probably acted as early as 1563, though it was not printed till 1575. The subject is one which has commended itself to various periods of our drama [3] ; from the beginnings of tragedy to Webster, and from Webster to Sheridan Knowles. The main plot of Lessing's *Emilia Galotti* is but a modern version of the same story. R. B.'s effort is of a very rude description, though it shows

Apius and Virginia (1563 circ.).

---

[1] *Ante*, 112 *note.* The Vice, 'Iniquity,' is a prominent personage in *King Darius*, and the fool Hardy-Dardy in *Godly Queene Hester* is a representative of the same type.

[2] Printed in vol. iv. of Hazlitt's *Dodsley.*

[3] Mr. Fleay (*History of the Stage*, 61) thinks that it was probably presented by the Westminster scholars.

some sense of dramatic construction. The tragedy opens
with an exhibition of the domestic bliss of Virginius and
his wife and daughter, which they celebrate not only
in dialogue, but in a song or refrain several times repeated :—

> ' The trustiest treasure in earth as wee see
> Is man, wife and children in one to agree ;
> Then friendly and kindly let measure be mixed
> With reason in season, where friendship is fixed.'

The criminal lust of Apius therefore mars a fair picture
of happiness with which the spectator has been previously
led to sympathise, and the action progresses simply and
effectively, without the allegorical personages playing any
important part in it. 'Haphazard,' the Vice, is a general
mischief-maker, but is himself, not less than the Mansipulus
and Mansipula with whom he holds converse, redundant to
the action. At the close of the play, Doctrina, Memorie,
and Virginius bring in a tome, wherein Memorie, Justice,
Rewarde, and Fame inscribe the honour of Virginia's name[1].
The Epilogue prays 'God save the Queen,' but makes no
reference to what later Elisabethan poets would have joyed
to find an occasion of celebrating,—her renown for the
virtue which is the subject of the play.

While the author of *Apius and Virginia* varies his tone *Preston's*
as he varies his metres, a higher degree of literary merit *Cambises*
seems to belong to the *Lamentable Tragedy mixed ful of* *(1569-70).*
pleasant mirth, conteyning the Life of Cambises King of
Percia—his one good deed, his many wicked deeds, and
(I condense) his odious death[2]. It was entered in the
Stationers' Registers, 1569–70, probably immediately after
its production. Its author was Thomas Preston, who is
said, when a fellow of King's College, Cambridge, to have
performed so well in the tragedy of *Dido* before Queen
Elisabeth, that, on account of this excellence and his
prowess in disputation, she, with unusual generosity, granted
him an annual allowance of £20. He afterwards became

---

[1] This is at least as effective as the introduction in Sheridan Knowles' play
of an urn superscribed *Virginia*, and supposed to contain the victim's ashes.

[2] Printed in Hawkins' *Origin of the English Drama*, vol. i., and in vol. iv.
of Hazlitt's *Dodsley*.

Master of Trinity Hall. His tragedy or comedy (as it
seems indifferently to call itself), besides being clearly constructed, is generally well written—chiefly in the so-called
' common metre.' King Cambises' one good deed is his
condemnation to death of the wicked judge Sisamnes, who
has misgoverned the realm during the King's absence in
Egypt; on the other side of the account stands his doing
to death of his too-outspoken counsellor Praxantes, after—
according to the famous anecdote, in order to prove his own
sobriety—shooting the minister's son in the heart, of his
brother Smirdis, and of his own consort, whom he had
married in defiance of the divine law. The King falls by
a divine Nemesis, as has been predicted by Ambidexter
the Vice, who opines that the King was ' akin to Bishop
Bonner [1].' The participation of this Vice in the action is
ingeniously managed; but room is also found for much
low fun and interchange of ribaldry between the Vice and
three ruffians, Huf, Snuf, and Ruf [2], and two ' country
patches,' Hob and Lob [3], who speak the usual rustic dialect
of the stage. On the other hand, some of the scenes (such
as that between the condemned Sisamnes and his son, and
that of the mother's lament over her murdered boy) display
touches of real pathos; and though ' Cambyses' vein ' has,
in consequence of its being cited by Shakspere [4], become
proverbial for rant, the language of the play is in no instance
specially obnoxious to this charge.

The simplicity which must have still characterised the
performance of these plays is illustrated by some of the

---

[1] Bonner was imprisoned in 1559; hence, so far as this indication goes,
the early date of 1561 sometimes assigned to the play is not impossible.
He died in 1569.

[2] These names are introduced by Lyly into the Dedication of his *Pappe
with an Hatchet* (1589 c.).

[3] There is some resemblance here to the scene in the *Winter's Tale* between the Peasants and Autolycus, who is a genuine descendant of the
Vice.

[4] 1 Henry IV, ii. 4. Mr. Fleay (*Life of Shakespeare*, 185) further supposes the intermixture of ' pleasant mirth ' in the title of *King Cambises* to
be alluded to in the ' tragical mirth' of the 'tedious brief scene of young
Piramus' (*Midsummer Night's Dream*, v. 1), and Prestor's pension in the
' sixpence a day' given by the Duke for playing the chief character (*ib.* iv. 2).

stage-directions. 'Here let Virginius go about the scaffold'—so that the stage was still that of the mystery-
dramas and moralities; and in *Cambises*, 'Smite him in
the neck with a sword to signify death,' and 'Flea with him
a false skin,' so that in this classical drama there was no
attempt to practise the classical abstinence from the introduction of death on the stage. Though *Cambises* is full
of characters, they are so arranged as to be capable of
performance by seven men and a boy.

In subject, at all events, both these plays attest the
influence of classical literature upon the beginnings of
English tragedy. A still more striking proof of this influence would be furnished by the performance at court,
less than a month after the production of *Gorboduc*, of
a play called *Julius Sesyar*, could we affirm with certainty
that the entry under February 1, 1562, in the diary of the
worthy citizen and undertaker Henry Machyn, establishes
the fact of such a performance. If it actually took place,
it was indisputably the earliest among many English
dramatic treatments of this theme[1].

Between the years 1567 and 1580 a large proportion of
the plays presented at court by the choir-boys of St. Paul's,
the Chapel Royal, and St. George's, Windsor, by the schoolboys of Westminster and Merchant Taylors', as well as by
various companies, were on classical subjects[3]. These
subjects are partly mythological, partly historical—although
this is a distinction which not many of the authors of the
plays in question would have been at much pains to draw.
To the plays treating themes of the former description
belongs John Pickering's *New interlude of Vice concerning*

*Other tra-
gedies on
classical
subjects
(1567-80).*

---

[1] The last words in the entry, 'and Julyus Sesar played,' are in another,
possibly a later, hand. See Machyn's *Diary*, 276, and *note.*—The line in
Shakspere's *Julius Caesar*, iii. 1 :
        'How many times shall Caesar bleed in sport'—
is by Mr. A. W. Verity (in his edition, 1895) ingeniously interpreted as
referring to the many dramatic representations of the theme.—A French
César, by Jacques Grévin, had appeared in 1560, eight years later than the
first French tragedy proper, Jodelle's *Cléopatre*. See A. Ebert, *Entwicklungsgeschichte der französischen Tragödie.*

[3] See Collier, i. 187-234 *passim*; and cf. the lists *ap.* Fleay, *Chronicle of
the English Drama*, ii. 287 *seqq.*

the history of Horestes (printed in 1567), the extant copy
of which seems to be an alteration for the public stage of
a version previously performed at Court [1]. This piece
curiously intermixes the personages of the classical myth,
a number of abstractions (Truth, Fame, &c.), three typical
half-concretes (Haltersick, Hempstring, and Hodge), and—
if I understand Collier's account correctly—a Vice in the
character of *Nuntius*, not so much the Euripidean or
Senecan messenger, as a self-licensed interviewer. This
play contains, besides a long ditty on the story of Paris
and Helen, a soldiers' song which, if it be the earliest of its
kind in our literature, must be regarded as the prototype
of Dorset's delightful ' To all you ladies, now on land.'
Other plays on mythological subjects performed in the
course of these years were *Iphigenia* [2], *Ajax and Ulysses,
Narcissus,* and *Paris and Vienna* [3] (all produced 1570–1),
Alcmaeon and *Perseus and 'Anthomeris'* (1573–4), and the
History of ' Serpedon' (1579–80). The plays on subjects
from ancient history seem to have been almost, if not
entirely, inspired by Livy; we meet with a *Toolie* (1576–7),
whom I conjecture to have been the impious daughter and
not the pious father [4], a *Mutius Scevola* (of the same date),
a *Quintus Fabius* (1573–4) and a *History of the Foure
Sonnes of Fabyous* (1579–80), and a *Cipio Africanus* (of
the same date). Stephen Gosson, who in 1579 came
forward as an adversary of the stage, had himself been

---

[1] Mr. Fleay's demonstration on this head (*History of the Stage,* 61–2)
seems to me convincing.   Collier, ii. 413, is not clear as to the *Nuntius.*

[2] This ' *Effigenia*,' performed by the ' children of Powles,' must of course
be distinguished from Peele's (non-extant) version of one of the *Iphigeniae*
of Euripides.

[3] Mr. Fleay (*English Drama,* ii. 288) is indisputably right in saying,
' these are characters, not towns.'   But what character is ' Vienna'—unless
this be thought as near Œnone as ' Anthomeris' is near Andromeda?

[4] Cicero has not, so far as I am aware, ever had a tragedy to himself—in
this respect less fortunate than Catiline.   In addition to Gosson's piece,
mentioned in the text, another play was performed at Gray's Inn before
Lord Burghley in 1587–8, in which Catiline was a character (Collier,
i. 260).   But I agree with Mr. Fleay (*History of the Stage,* 92) that, as shown
by the list of characters cited by Collier, he can only have been a subordinate character.   Probably he was expressly introduced for the sake of
an allusion to the conspiracies of which the air was then full.

a dramatic author; and among the plays 'tollerable at sometime' excepted by him from his general censure, is one which he terms a 'pig of his owne Sowe,' i. e. a piece written by himself, called *Catiline's Conspiracies*[1].

The nature of these works we can only conjecture; George Gascoigne's *Jocasta*, in the composition of which he was assisted by Francis Kinwelmarsh (who wrote acts i. and iv.), is a very free adaptation of the *Phoenissae* of Euripides, or rather a version of a free Italian adaptation of this tragedy. Mr. Symonds has proved that in certain passages at all events Ludovico Dolce, and not Euripides, was the direct original of the English writers[2]. I cannot say how far the English choral odes, which in part are independent of the Greek, correspond to the Italian; that which concludes the play was contributed by Christopher Yelverton (afterwards a judge and knighted), who is associated by Jasper Heywood with Sackville and Norton as one of the young lions of his times[3]. This tragedy was presented at Gray's Inn in 1566, and is notable as the second English play composed in blank verse. Dumb-shows and 'musickes' introduce each act; two of the former allegorically represent the doom of Curtius, and the conflict between the Horatii and the Curiatii.

Gascoigne's Jocasta (1566).

This enumeration shows how the choice of classical subjects and the imitation, direct or indirect, of classical models were exercising their influence upon the early progress of English tragedy. It is not of course in all cases possible to decide whether a play should strictly be classed under the head of tragedy or of comedy; and, to judge from the instance of a play preserved from the hand

Tragicomedies.

---

[1] *Schoole of Abuse*, p. 30 (*Shakspeare Society's Publications*, 1841). In subsequent publications he refers to *Pompey* and *The Fabii* as subjects treated by contemporary dramatists. Cf. Fleay, *Chronicle History of the English Drama*, i. 248–9.

[2] *Shakspere's Predecessors*, 221–2. L. Dolce's *Giocasta* ('già di Euripide invenzione e ora nuovo parto mio') was printed in 1549. Klein, v. 408.

[3] See the quotation from the *Introduction* to Seneca's *Thyestes*, *ap.* Collier, ii. 398. Cf. as to the play in general Warton's *History of English Poetry*, iv. 266 *seqq.* He notes that among the Hatton MSS. in the Bodleian is a long blank verse translation from the *Hercules Oetaeus* of Seneca by Queen Elisabeth.

of one of the most popular dramatists of his day, the two
species were at times so intermingled as to leave us almost
at liberty to call productions belonging to either by either
name. Upon the whole, however, *Damon and Pithias* will
be most appropriately mentioned by the side of the plays
enumerated above, although it would be more correctly
classed as a *tragicomedy*, a species much cultivated in the
Italian drama of the sixteenth century, and not without
classical precedents.   Unfortunately we have but one
classical play which satisfactorily exemplifies the Attic
conception of *tragicomedy*, as a species ' resembling the
regular *tragedy* in its outward form, but containing some
comic characters, and always having a happy termination[1].'
This is the *Alcestis* of Euripides (which we know to have
been performed as the satyr-drama of a tetralogy ; perhaps
the *Orestes* of the some poet may be regarded as another)[2].
We can hardly, on the strength of Mercury's accommodating
nomenclature, agree to call the *Amphitruo* of Plautus a
tragicomedy, because ' gods and kings ' do not appear in
comedies[3].   On the precise nature of the later so-called
hilarotragedies of Rhinthon of Tarentum, and one or two
other writers, it seems unsafe to speculate ; I incline, however, to think that they were rather of the nature of
burlesques[4].   Italian examples of the type of Bernardo
Accolti's *Virginia* (1513) doubtless directly influenced the
cultivation by our early English dramatists of the mixed
species which came to be called (but by no consistent
usage) *tragicomedy*, and which represents an unconscious
revolt against the monotony of Senecan tragedy.   To
assume the influence of Spanish tragicomedy to have already
largely co-operated, would probably be premature[5].

[1] Donaldson's *Theatre of the Greeks* (seventh edition), 75.

[2] *Ib.* 142, 148.

[3] See the amusing prologue to the play, in which Mercury, after calling
it a tragedy, offers to call it a comedy, if the spectators prefer, and then
concludes to call it a ' tragico-comedy ' :

> ' Nam me perpetuo facere ut sit comoedia,
> Reges quo veniant et Dii, non par arbitror.'

[4] Donaldson, pp. 75, 204, is not very definite on the subject.   These
plays were also called *phlyacographies*, from φλύαξ (chatter).

[5] As to Accolti's *Virginia,* see Klein, iv. 546 *seqq.* In the preface *to the*

To the author of *Damon and Pithias* a special measure of favour appears to have been accorded by his contemporaries. Richard Edwardes, born in Somersetshire in 1523, was a scholar of Corpus Christi College, Oxford, and afterwards a student of Christ Church ; in 1559 he was appointed master of the Children of the Chapel Royal, who performed a 'tragedy' by him (which was possibly no other play than *Damon and Pithias* itself) before the Queen at Christmas, 1564–5. In 1566, the year in which another play by him, *Palamon and Arcyte* [1] (in two parts), was acted before the Queen at Christ Church, he died. On the evidence of the solitary play known to have been preserved from his hand [2], he appears to have been overpraised by his admirers, one of whom terms him

'the flower of our realm
And phoenix of our age [3].'

Damon and Pithias (licensed 1566, and first printed, so far

Reader prefixed by Fletcher to his *Faithful Shepherdess* (which he designated as a 'pastoral tragi-comedy'), he says : 'A tragi-comedy is not so called in respect of mirth and killing, but in respect it wants deaths, which is enough to make it no tragedy, yet brings some near it, which is enough to make it no comedy, which must be a representation of familiar people, with such kind of trouble as no life to be questioned ; so that a god is as lawful in this as in a tragedy, and mean people as in a comedy.' It was this free intermingling of characters of the loftier and of the lowlier type to which our drama was to be so infinitely indebted. Alois Brandl (*Zu Lillo's Kaufmann von London* in *Vierteljahrschrift für Litteraturgeschichte*, iii. 55, 1890) has drawn a suggestive comparison between the growth of tragi-comedy adverted to in my text and that of domestic tragedy in Lillo's day, as a revolt respectively against the domination of classical (Senecan) and of 'heroic' tragedy. He notices as yet another analogy, the rise of melodrama about the beginning of the present century ; but on this head it is unnecessary for me to commit myself here.

[1] Collier, i. 183. Towards the end of this piece Dionysius tells the two fiends that the gods have made them play 'this tragedy' for his behoof ; but this of course refers not to the play, but to the self-sacrifice which is its serious theme.

[2] Mr. Fleay (*History of the Stage*, 60–1), on evidence which does not to me seem conclusive, considers Edwardes to have been the author of the anonymous early comedy *Misogonus*, and with the aid of this supposition builds up a plausible theory of a quarrel, of which the 'personalities' in *Damon and Pithias* are supposed to have formed the climax.

[3] For other compliments, see Warton, iv. 213 *seqq.*

Damon and Pithias (1564–5 ?).

as is known in 1571)[1], which calls itself a 'tragical comedy,'
but without apparently attaching any special significance
to the combined term [2], seems to me one of the clumsiest
of our early plays, in both action and language, and above
all in the management of the metre.   The lines are rimed,
but vary in length and neglect in *caesura*.   If, as has been
supposed, the object of this licence was to avoid monotony,
the gain in question was purchased at the cost of euphony.
As for the action of the play, the 'comic business' is of the
nature of the broadest and grossest farce, although the
episode of the shaving of the Collier Grim (who is brought
all the way from Croydon to the court of the Sicilian
Dionysius, and 'singeth Basse' for the delectation of the
lackeys there[3]) may have made the injudicious roar.   While
this entertainment proceeds two months are supposed to
'elapse,' during which Damon is absent, his friend's life in
peril, and the serious interest of the play in suspense.

Plays on Italian and other Romance subjects.

Ancient classical history and mythology were, however,
very far from monopolising the attention of our early playwrights, when in search of dramatic subjects of serious
interest.   Stories borrowed from the history, or more frequently borrowed from the legends and romances, in verse
and prose, of contemporary Western peoples, were finding
their way in increasing numbers to English readers, many
of whom still crossed the Alps to bring home with them
these with other trophies of their travels.   For more than
a century past the charm had been at work, which in the
opinion of sober—not necessarily sour—censors contained
so large an ingredient of poison.   And now there were
added to the tales, instinct alike with passion and with wit,
of Boccaccio and his school, the brilliant epical efforts, to
which he had himself furnished something of a model, and

[1] Printed in Hazlitt's *Dodsley*, vol. iv. (with a Preface found among the
papers of the elder Hazlitt), and in *Ancient British Drama*, vol. i.

[2] It occurs in the last line of the *Prologue*, near the beginning of which
the author speaks of 'comedies' simply.

[3] As Mr. Fleay shows to be probable, this episode and the allusions
contained in it were suggested by Ulpian Fulwell's *Like will to Like*, &c.,
concerning which see below.   The previous comic quarrel between Jack
and Will is made fun of in *Bartholomew Fair*, v. 3.

which form the chief boasts of the last phase of the Italian Renascence[1]. Many of the Italian epical and lyrical poets and novelists of the sixteenth century were also dramatists ; and there were doubtless not a few who, like Giraldi Cinthio, founded more than one of their plays upon novels of their own inditing[2]. The titles of a considerable proportion of our early English tragedies suggest a distinctly Italian origin. It would be pleasant to assert, could the assertion be made good on other than subjective grounds, that the first English tragedy on a subject taken, directly or indirectly, from an Italian novel, was the earliest known English dramatic version of the immortal story of *Romeo and Juliet*. In 1562, Arthur Brooke printed a metrical paraphrase of Bandello's story of *Romeo and Juliet* (1554), which Boisteau had shortly afterwards reproduced in a French version. Bandello's novel had itself been preceded by Luigi da Porto's on the same theme. Inasmuch as Brooke, at the close of his address *to the Reader*, states that he had seen 'the same argument lately set forth on stage with more commendation' than he could expect for his poem, it has been supposed that a play on the subject had in or before 1562 been performed in this country[3]. But no positive conclusion can be arrived at whether the play seen by Brooke was English or Italian, and it would therefore be superfluous to discuss a further conjecture identifying it with an early Italian drama akin to it in plot, and full of resemblances in details[4].

Thus the tragedy of *Tancred and Gismunda*[5], presented in its original form under the title of *Gismonde of Salerne* before the Queen at the Inner Temple in 1568, may still claim to be designated the oldest known English play

Tancred and Gismunda (acted 1598).

---

[1] I say 'the last,' thinking it unnecessary to include in the movement of the Italian Renascence its *rococo* and largely burlesque epilogue.

[2] So the *Orbecche* (Klein, v. 324 *seqq.*), and again the *Epitia* (*ib.* 353).

[3] For conflicting opinions on the question as to whether Brooke refers to an English play, or to one which he had seen abroad, see Furness' *Romeo and Juliet* (*Variorum Shakespeare* edition, 1873), Appendix, 397 *seqq.*

[4] Viz. Luigi Groto's *Hadriana* (1540–50) ; see Klein, v. 423 *seqq.*

[5] Printed in Dodsley's *Old Plays*, vol. ii, and in Hazlitt's *Dodsley*, vol. vii. The Introduction (*ib.*) gives a specimen of the earlier version.

of which the plot is certainly taken from an Italian novel
—a class of works that was afterwards to prove so fertile
a source of subjects for Shakspere and his fellow-dramatists.
And yet this play likewise connects itself with *Gorboduc*,
inasmuch as its authors endeavoured to follow ancient
models, each act commencing with a dumb-show (for which
at the opening of the play is substituted a kind of pageant
introduced in a long speech by Cupid), and ending with
a series of choruses (of which at the close an epilogue
takes the place). It was originally written, in rimed deca-
syllabic quatrains, by five gentlemen, probably all members
of the Inner Temple[1], where its performance was witnessed
by Queen Elisabeth and her 'Maidens of Honour,' to whom
the later edition commended itself by Prefaces in both
prose and verse. Of this later edition, which was not
printed till 1591, and was 'polished according to the decorum of these days,' i. e. put into blank verse, the author
was Robert Wilmot, the writer of the original fifth act.
He had then come to be a man of some literary repute[2],
and held the living of North Okenham in Essex.

The subject of this tragedy belongs to the most passionate kind of romance. King Tancred, after surprising
his daughter Gismunda with her lover, causes him to be put
to death, and his heart, placed in a golden cup, to be presented to his daughter. She fills the cup with poison,
and drinks her death from it; and her dying wish to be
reunited to her lover in the tomb is carried out by the
broken-hearted father, who slays himself with his own
hands. The story, which is taken from Boccaccio, served
as the theme of several dramas in the Italian and other
languages, and was retold by Dryden in some of his latest
and most characteristic verse[3].

---

[1] Their names are signed, in abbreviated forms, at the end of the several
acts. '*Ch. Hat.*' at the end of Act iv. is supposed to stand for Christopher
Hatton, whose dancing, so much admired by the Queen, is supposed to
have made him Lord Keeper.

[2] He is mentioned as a poet in Webbe's *Discourse* (1586).

[3] *Sigismonda and Guiscardo* is included in the *Fables*, which were published in November, 1699, a few months before Dryden's death. According
to Klein, v. 461-2, there were several Italian plays on the subject. Silvano

The most noteworthy feature of this play is beyond
doubt the struggle which it exhibits between the classical
tastes of its authors and the romantic character of their
subject. Through the first four acts everything proceeds
classically enough ; Cupid speaks as Prologue ; choruses
of maidens intersperse reflexive relics and calmly intervene
in the action, the real incidents of which are carefully kept
behind the scene. But, in the last act, though the death
and doom of the ' Countie ' has been decently narrated by
an eye-witness, the situation becomes too strong for the
classicism of the writer, and Gismunda and her father both
die on the stage. The speeches of this play are of inordinate length, though *stichomythia* in the Greek antithetical
manner is also introduced. The lyrical passages strike me
as graceful ; and, altogether, I should say that the play,
which in its revised version had no doubt been put together
with unusual care, possesses no mean literary merit. The
inevitable compliment to Queen Elisabeth here occurs, not
at the end, but in the middle of the piece [1].

A more enduring interest attaches, in the history of our
dramatic literature, to the next play founded on a subject

*G. Whet-
stone's
Promos*

de' Razzi's *Gismonda* was printed in 1569. Pomponio Torelli (d. 1608)
wrote a tragedy on the subject, and Federico Asinari another (printed
1588). The latter appeared in Paris in 1587, under the title *Gismonda*, as
a work by Torquato Tasso. The theme was once more treated by Ridolfo
Campeggi in 1614 (Walker, *Historical Memoir of Italian Tragedy*, 175).
A tragedy on this story, written by Sir Henry Wotton, probably in Latin,
was never printed, but read by Guarini in Italy in MS. (*ib.* 101 *note*).
Thompson's tragedy of *Tancred and Sigismunda* (1745) was made use of
by Whigs and Jacobites for a political demonstration and counter-demon-
stration like those which accompanied the production of Addison's *Cato*
(Doran, *London in the Jacobite Times*, ii. 108-9). The plot of this play,
Genest informs us (iv. 149), was however taken from *Gil Blas*. The
catastrophe of the play resembles that of Keats' *Pot of Basil*, the
story of which poem appears to be treated dramatically in Hans Sachs'
Lisabetha.

[1] Act ii. *ad fin.* :—
> ' Yet let not us maidens condemn our kind,
> Because our virtues are not all so rare :
> For we may freshly yet recall in mind,
> There lives a virgin, one without compare,
> Who of all graces hath her heavenly share ;
> In whose renown, and for whose happy days,
> Let us record this Paean of her praise.'

and Cassandra
(pr. 1578).

from Italian story. George Whetstone's *Promos and Cassandra*[1], from which Shakspere took the story of his *Measure for Measure*, was printed in 1578; and its subject is a novel of Giraldi Cinthio's, which Whetstone himself translated in his *Heptameron of Civil Discourses* (1582). Cinthio himself dramatised the story in a work of earlier date[2]. The author of this play was a writer of considerable productivity, who moreover gained varied experience of life as a courtier, soldier, and farmer, besides taking part in one of Sir Humphrey Gilbert's expeditions for Newfoundland[3]. According to a ghastly conjecture, he ended his days in Bedlam[4]. In the Dedication of *Promos and Cassandra*, Whetstone exhibits a highly critical spirit, condemning for various reasons the dramatic tastes of the principal literary nations of Europe, his own among the number[5]. But although he takes lofty ground with reference to both diction and construction, it cannot be said that he was in practice highly successful in either respect. Consideration of '*Decorum*' preventing him from 'convaying' his whole story in a single play of five acts, he

---

[1] Printed in vol. i. of the *Six Old Plays on which Sh. founded his Measure for Measure*, &c. (published by Nichols in 1779).

[2] *Epitia*; cf. Klein, v. 353 *seqq*. Cinthio died in 1573.

[3] Fleay, *English Drama*, ii. 274.

[4] See Cunningham's note to the passage in *Bartholomew Fair*, i. 1 : 'Good Lord, how sharp you are, with being at Bedlam yesterday! *Whetstone has set an edge upon you, has he?*' Of course there may be no meaning in this beyond a pun; as the same editor conjectures, Whetstone had possibly published something in the nature of a jest-book.

[5] The passage is worth quoting :—'At this daye, the Italian is so lascivious in his Commedies, that honest hearers are greeved at his actions : the *Frenchman* and *Spaniarde* folows the *Italians* humor: the *Germaine* is too holye; for he presents on every common Stage what Preachers should pronounce in Pulpets. The *Englishman*, in this qualitie, is most vaine, indiscrete, and out of order : he first groundes his worke on impossibilities : then in three howers ronnes he throwe the world: marryes, gets children, makes children men, men to conquer kingdomes, murder monsters, and bringeth Gods from Heaven, and fetcheth divels from Hel.' But the gravest objection to English playwrights is, that they do not make the speech of each character appropriate to it, but use one order of speech for all kinds of persons. The objection to the *Germaine* is the same as that brought against English plays by Northbrooke in his nearly contemporary *Treatise against Dicing, Dancing, Plays and Interludes* (1577 *circ.*). See *Shakesp. Society's Publ.*, 1843, p. 92.

distributed it over two—but very unequally as to the serious interest of the argument, which is wholly absorbed by the first part. And to 'work kindly' the action of his characters, he made his low comedy very low, and his grosser characters very gross. The moral struggle in his heroine is brought to a conclusion too rapidly to keep the reader or spectator in an effective condition of suspense; while the intrigues of a courtesan and the ribaldries of a pimp relieve after their fashion the cumbrous progress of an in itself offensive plot. It was something different from mere condensation which converted *Promos and Cassandra* into *Measure for Measure*[1].

The titles of a considerable number of other Early English tragedies, which have not been preserved, suggest a direct Italian origin—as in the case of *The Duke of Milan and the Marquis of Mantua* (1579)—while no mistake is possible as to the literary genealogy of a play called *Ariodante and Geneuora* (1582)[2]. Two years before he was moved to denounce the English stage, Stephen Gosson had composed the comedy of *Captain Mario* (1579), which he describes as 'a cast of Italian devices' and which may be assumed to have been founded on some Italian novel or novels. In a rather later tract, the same censor of the stage asserts that the doubtful novels of Latin, French, Italian and Spanish writers have been 'thoroughly ransacked to furnish the playhouses in London[3].' Already in this period of our literary history, France was becoming the natural purveyor to the English literary market of light wares produced by herself or adapted from the productions of her Romance neighbours. English translators seized with avidity upon all these exotic materials, and spread them forth before the eager eyes of our dramatists in search of themes[4].

Other early tragedies of Italian origin.

---

[1] Mr. Fleay notes that a scene from *Promos and Cassandra* (Part i, v. 5) was utilised by Chapman in his *Mayday*.

[2] Cf. Fleay, *English Drama*, ii. 290 and 288. The subject of the latter play is from the *Orlando Furioso*, whence the episode in question had been shortly before translated by Peter Beverley (Collier, i. 241 *note*).

[3] Collier, ii. 327 *seqq.* The earlier quotation is from *The School of Abuse*, the latter from *Plays compiled in Five Actions*.

[4] The first volume of Paynter's *Pallace of Pleasure* (sixty novels from Boccaccio) appeared in 1566; a translation of *Les Cent Nouvelles Nouvelles* in

Plays on subjects from national history.

From the twofold danger which threatened the English drama in the days of its infancy—that it might seek to dwell on the glacial heights of classical mythology or history, or might dissolve its vigour in the glowing heat of Italian stories of passion and crime—it was freed, more than by any other cause, by association, gradually growing closer, with the traditions of our own national history. The direction in which a sound instinct had turned the controversial ardour of Bishop Bale was that in which English tragedy was, not indeed to find a sphere sufficiently wide to absorb its energies, but to be imbued by influences at once invigorating and enduring. The *Chronicle History*, that species of the early tragic drama which was based upon the historical records of the nation's own past, was the healthiest developement to which it attained within the period when no great dramatist had as yet arisen, and was likewise the most productive in animating the early efforts of several among the great dramatists themselves.

It was, however, without any clear sense of the limits of national history that our early tragic drama widened its range from subjects of classical or foreign origin. The next tragedy which in chronological order has to be noted, belongs in truth rather to the plays founded on romantic legend than to those deriving their themes from national historical traditions. It associates itself directly with *Gorboduc* rather than with the *Chronicle Histories* of which I have immediately to treat.

T. Hughes' Misfortunes of Arthur (1587).

The *Misfortunes of Arthur* [1], acted before Queen Elisabeth at Greenwich in February, 1588, is in many respects one of the most remarkable of our early tragedies. Eight members of the Society of Gray's Inn co-operated in its composition, among whom Thomas Hughes was author of the whole body of the play. Nicholas Trotter furnished the Introduction, which in no very light-handed fashion apologises for the poetic effort of legal hands. The choruses

1557. See for further examples, Warton's *History of English Poetry*, Section lx.

[1] Printed in Collier's *Five Old Plays*, forming a supplement to Dodsley's collection (1833) ; and in vol. iv. of Hazlitt's *Dodsley*.

of acts i. and ii. (which are in rimed stanzas, while those appended to the remaining acts are, like the body of the piece, in blank verse [1]), were composed by Francis Flower. William Fulbeck contributed two speeches. Three other gentlemen of the Inn devised the dumb-shows introducing the several acts, and allegorising them with elaborate ingenuity. Of these three, one was 'Maister Francis Bacon,' who was at that time already a bencher of Gray's Inn, and had sat in Parliament [2]. Bacon, as is proved by the various 'devices' to which he contributed or which he 'contrived' or 'encouraged [3],' as well as by his essay *On Masques and Triumphs*, had considerable insight into the principles of dramatic effect, albeit at the close of that essay he dismisses as 'toys' the kind of productions which form its theme.

The circumstance of Bacon's co-operation, however slight it may have been, in this piece, would suffice to attach a special value to it; but it claims consideration on its own account. Its subject is taken, apparently without the intervention of any later literary treatment [4], from that *Morte d'Arthur* which, according to a well-known statement by Roger Ascham, had, in his 'forefathers' time' formed the staple literary entertainment of the English Court [5]. The Arthurian legend had derived a fresh senti-

---

[1] The Chorus to Act ii. is well written; see especially the stanza—

> 'Who sawe the griefe engraven in a crowne,
> Or knew the bad and bane whereto 'tis bound,
> Would never sticke to throwe and fling it downe,
> Nor once vouchsafe to heave it from the ground.
> Such is the sweete of this ambitious powre,
> No sooner had, then turnes eftsoones to sowre:
> Atchiev'd with envie, exercisde with hate,
> Garded with feare, supported with debate.'

[2] Parliament had been dissolved about a year before the production of this play. See Spedding's *Works of Bacon*, viii. 67.

[3] For a list of these see Fleay, *English Drama*, i. 27–8.

[4] No interest of the kind, of course, attaches to John Bourchier Lord Berners' 'comedy,' called *Ite in vineam*, or *The Parable of the Vineyard* (translated from the French *History of Arthur*), of which an edition, supposed to date from 1540, is extant. Lord Berners died in 1532. See Warton, iv. 66.

[5] *The Scholemaster*, Bk. i. Cf. the striking sarcasm in Ben Jonson's *New*

mental interest from the Welsh origin of the founder of the
Tudor dynasty, who bore the dragon on his flag when he
started on his march from Milford Haven, and who gave to
his heir the name of 'the Briton Prince.' But although the
Arthurian cycle of legend furnished the argument of more
than one Elisabethan drama [1], the figures of this misty and
migratory body of romance were not to become endeared
to English popular sympathies until after they had floated
down the stream of a long literary history. Thomas
Hughes, who 'reduced into tragical notes' the story of
' Uther Pendragon's son,' and of whom nothing is personally
known except that, before he came to London, he was an
undergraduate and fellow of Queens' College, Cambridge [2],
was unmistakeably attracted to the subject of the play
which he composed for the purpose of the 'devices and
shows' to be presented to the Queen by his Inn, by its
resemblance to the themes of the classical tragedies then so
constantly in the hands of learned students. He knew his
Seneca by heart, and the first act of his play has been
shown to be ' little more than a mosaic of extracts from
Seneca, pieced together with lines of Hughes' own invention, cast in the style of his model [3].' He viewed the story
of Arthur's fall as the wreaking of a curse due in its origin
to Arthur's sin ; and the Ghost of Gorlois, whom in life
Uther Pendragon, Arthur's father, had so cruelly wronged,
opens the play just as the *Umbra Tantali* opens the *Thyestes*
of the Latin tragedian [4]. The terrible complication of
adultery and incest which avenges itself on Arthur and his
son Mordred, resembles that with which the whole Senecan
cycle is familiar ; and the merits, as well as the limits, of

Inn, i. 1. Ben Jonson, by the way, himself effectively uses the Arthurian
legend in the *Speeches at Prince Henry's Barriers.*

[1] See more especially below as to *The Birth of Merlin,* attributed to
Shakspere and William Rowley.

[2] See the brief notice by Mr. A. H. Bullen in *The Dictionary of National
Biography,* vol. xxviii. p. 188.

[3] Cunliffe, *u. s.,* 52-4 ; cf. the striking comparison of passages in Dr.
Cunliffe's *Appendix II,* pp. 130-155.

[4] The *Ombra di Selina* in Cinthio's *Orbecche* (Klein, v. 326) has the same
origin, but no similar moral claim to assume the position.

the dramatic treatment are those of the writer's model. It is possible that as a classical scholar Hughes was acquainted with the *Agamemnon* of Aeschylus as well as with that of Seneca; but there is probably no necessity for the assumption. In general, the methods of the Senecan tragedy—including the use of messenger and chorus—are here carefully observed as in *Gorboduc*. In style the later is at least equal to the earlier play; the *stichomythia* is managed with considerable force and effect; and there is no lack of vigour in some of the speeches. Thus *e.g.* the address of Arthur to his soldiers (act iii. sc. 3), in which he bids defiance to his rebel son—

> ' Nay, let that Princocke come,
> That knowes not yet himselfe, nor Arthur's force ;
> That n'er yet waged warres ; that's yet to learne
> To give the charge : yea, let that Princocke come,
> With sodaine souldiers pamper'd up in peace,
> And gownèd troupes and wantons worne with ease ;
> With sluggish Saxon crewe, and Irish kernes
> And Scottish aide, and false redshankèd Picts '—

is extremely spirited, and contrasts powerfully with the subdued melancholy of the King's previous speeches. The last stanza of the chorus to act iii. ('O base yet happy boores!' &c.) will recall a familiar Shaksperian passage ; and the mysterious disappearance of Arthur in death ends the action with peculiar effectiveness:—

> ' This onely now I crave (O fortune, erst
> My faithfull friend) let it be soone forgot,
> Nor long in minde, nor mouth, where Arthur fell :
> Yea, though I conqueror die, and full of fame,
> Yet let my death and parture rest obscure.
> No grave I neede (O fates) nor buriall rights
> Nor stately hearce, nor tombe with haughty toppe ;
> But let my carcasse lurke ; yea, let my death
> Be ay unknowen, so that in every coast
> I still be feard, and lookt for every houre !
> 　　　　　　　　　　　*[Exeunt.'*

But Arthurian legend is not, and never has been, to the English national mind what the myths which supplied the subjects of Attic tragedy were to the Greek. British mythology in general had no relation to the historic consciousness of our people ; and the Arthurian cycle in particular had only come back to our shores after being impregnated with the romantic elements of a foreign literary atmosphere. Thus the meritorious, and within its limits successful, attempt of Hughes was beset by the radical weakness of an artificial origin, and belongs to a passing early phase in the history of English tragedy, instead of having caught a breath of the genuine national life with which our tragic drama was already associating itself.

Chronicle Histories. The dates of our earliest tragedies on subjects from national history, properly so called, are more or less uncertain. This uncertainty is largely owing to the fact that the dates in question practically fall within a period of dramatic authorship, including several of Shakspere's earlier contemporaries, and possibly Shakspere himself. Mr. Fleay [1] comprehensively avers this kind of drama to have 'arisen with the Armada, and died with Elisabeth.' Obviously, however, the chief interest attaching to it as a literary species contributing to the genesis of our regular tragic drama connects itself with those earlier productions which asserted their right to be regarded, in the words of the same literary historian, as 'a variant of tragedy,' usually marking its claim to a distinctive historical character by the assumption of the title of 'True Tragedy.' Among these plays the prerogative of seniority is, so far as we know, due *The Famous Victories of Henry V (acted before 1588).* to *The Famous Victories of Henry V* [2]. This drama cannot have been produced later than 1588, the year of the death of Richard Tarleton, who performed in it the part of Derrick the clown, very probably as composed by himself [3]. This play, written partly in prose, partly in blank verse, frequently of a rude description [4], is neither divided into

[1] *History of the Stage,* 75.

[2] Printed in the *Six Old Plays* (v. *ante*) and in the *Publications of the New Shakspere Society.*

[3] Cf. Fleay, *English Drama,* ii. 259.

[4] *E. g.* King Henry's not very perspicuous computation of the French and English forces before the battle of Agincourt :—

'They threescore thousand,	And we twelve thousand.
And we but two thousand,	They are a hundred thousand,
They threescore thousand footmen,	And we forty thousand, ten to one.'

acts and scenes, nor otherwise constructed with any perceptible measure of dramatic skill.   But its general vigour
and freshness are considerable ; and in many of its situations and characters we recognise the familiar scenes and
favourite figures of Shakspere's *Henry IV* and *Henry V*.
For the action opens with the end of the reign of the
founder of the dynasty, and introduces not only the wild
doings of Prince Hal and his merry companions, among
whom Sir John Oldcastle puts in a passing appearance, but
also the Prince's interview with his dying father, and his
premature seizure of the crown.   Hereupon follow, in a rapid
succession of scenes, the victorious campaign of the young
King up to Agincourt, and his marriage with the Princess
Katherine—the scene between whom and Henry contains
many of the best points of that in Shakspere, without
being disfigured by the unpardonable element of grossness
afterwards added for the benefit of the groundlings.

Another of these Chronicle Histories is *The Troublesome
Raigne of King John*, in two parts[1].   Like the *Famous
Victories*, it is partly in prose, partly in verse—the latter
being frequently rimed.   It is not divided into acts, and
the scenes follow one another without any attempt at
dramatic construction.   Nor is there, except perhaps in
the case of the Bastard Faulconbridge, any endeavour to
develope character out of the situations.   The facts, or
supposed facts, of history are allowed to speak for themselves ; and it is most instructive to compare this faithful
reproduction on the stage of an epically consecutive narrative with Bale's didactic effort on the one hand, and
Shakspere's compact drama on the other.   It is, perhaps,
in such a play as the *Troublesome Raigne* that we may
find the best example of the *Chronicle History* pure and
simple.   Its author, at one time carelessly thought to be
Shakspere himself[2], is at the same time fully alive to the
political lessons—such as he conceives them to be—of
his subject, so far as it relates to the struggle with

*The
Trouble-
some
Raigne of
King John
(pr.* 1591).

---

[1] Printed in the *Six Old Plays* (v. *ante*).

[2] In deference to Pope's 'hasty and inconsiderate opinion.'   See Malone's
Shaksp., vol. xviii. p. 593.

Rome [1]. But his facts are upon the whole drily given; only here and there a fine passage, and more frequently a Latin phrase [2], varies the progress of the dialogue. The incidents are the same as in Shakspere; but the old play introduces, with a large admixture of comic ribaldry, an incident omitted by Shakspere, viz. the plunder of a Franciscan abbey by Faulconbridge.

Of an early *Life and Death of Harry I* (acted in 1597) we know nothing but the title [3].

Quite manifestly, when the vein of these *Chronicle Histories* had once been opened, it was speedily and energetically worked by eager and competing playwrights. But it would be futile to attempt in the present connexion to discuss the dates of the earliest dramatic versions of the fall of *Richard III* and the *Contention* between the houses of York and Lancaster.

The True Chronicle History of King Leir (acted 1593).

The question of authorship is less entangled with regard to *The True Chronicle History of King Leir and his Three Daughters, Gonorill, Ragan, and Cordella* [4], acted in 1593 (but apparently not as a new play), which in its form is of the same kind as the Chronicle Histories founded on English history already mentioned. Its resemblance to Shakspere's tragedy is not more striking than its difference

---

[1] 'Tell thy master so from me,' says the King to Cardinal Pandulph, in Part I, 'and say, *John* of *England* said it, that never an Italian priest of them all, shal either have tythe, tole, or poling peny out of *England*; but as I am king, so will I raigne next under God, supreame head both over spiritual and temporall; and he that contradicts me in this, Ile make him hop headlesse.' And again, Part II :—
     'If my dying heart deceive me not,
  From out these loynes shall spring a kingly braunch
  Whose arms shall reach unto the gates of *Rome*,
  And with his feete treade downe the strumpet's pride
  That sits upon the chaire of *Babylon*.'

[2] *E. g.* '*Essex.* *Philip* speake I say, who was thy father?
  John.   Young man how now, what art thou in a trance?
  Elianor. *Philip* awake, the man is in a dreame.
  Philip. *Philippus atavis aedite Regibus.* [*sic.*]
      What saist thou *Philip*, sprung of auncient kings?
      Quo me rapit tempestas?
      What winde of honour blowes this furie forth?' &c.

[3] Fleay, *English Drama*, ii. 306.

[4] Printed in the *Six Old Plays*, &c., vol. ii.

from that masterpiece of tragedy—the dramatic form working by pity and terror. For not only is the powerful bye-plot of Gloucester and his sons absent from the Chronicle History, but the latter is far from developing the dramatic capabilities of the subject common to both these plays, after a fashion corresponding to that of Shakspere's tragedy. Mr. Fleay thinks himself able to distinguish between two divisions, of which, on evidence to my mind insufficient, he assigns the latter part to Lodge, while the earlier he guesses to have been written by Kyd. Whether the work of one or more authors, the play has the defects of an earlier phase of workmanship than that of Shakspere and his contemporaries. The influence of Lear's heartrending experiences upon his own mind and its powers is left aside, and even the ingratitude of Goneril and Regan is exhibited with comparatively slight skill and effect. On the other hand, the uninteresting episode of the wooing of 'Cordella' by the king of France, who with his comic companion Lord 'Mumford' meets her in disguise, is long drawn out. Yet with all its shortcomings, the play seems but to await the touch of a powerful hand to be converted into a tragedy of supreme effectiveness[1]. Even of the attractive minor character of Shakspere's Kent, the germ is here perceptible in the character of Perillus.

The birth of Comedy, as has already been hinted[2], in the history of the English drama slightly precedes that of Tragedy. As a matter of fact, the transition from the Moralities was in the former case a matter perfectly easy of accomplishment. Concrete figures, largely comic in effect, if not in design, had, as we have seen, been introduced with increasing freedom among the *dramatis personae* of the Moralities, and admitted to an organic share in the conduct of their action. The Vice and his various *aliases*, in particular, were hail-fellows well-met with any Dick or Tom in the audience. The difficulty—if indeed any such existed—attending the first and essential step in the transition was a negative rather than a positive one. It was not to be found

Comedy.

---

[1] See below as to *King Lear*.   [2] *Ante*, p. 168.

in any obstacle against the introduction of figures from real life, such as might present themselves as palpable human examples of particular virtues and vices, or of particular virtuous and vicious tendencies. What seemed to require the slow hand of time to accomplish, was rather the work of making a riddance, before the new dramatic chapter could be begun, of the antiquated machinery which had so long satisfied the public. Mediaeval taste had adhered with extraordinary persistency—and by no means in the sphere of dramatic compositions only—to its fondness for personified abstractions. And our wonder at the length of time that was required in England for the accomplishment of the simple process in question is heightened, when we notice the early dates, speaking relatively, at which the thought of effecting this change had been carried out by other Western peoples. Something has already been said,

Its pre-liminary growths in France; not only of the *débats* and *disputations* of the French *trouvères*[1], but also of the early *sotties* and *farces*, which, together with the moralities proper, in the fourteenth and fifteenth centuries competed with the French religious drama[2]. The *sotties* consisted of short comic scenes representing contemporary popular life, but interspersed with allegorical figures. Before long, however, the admixture of such abstractions among figures of living men and women was abandoned, both in the *sotties* and in the cognate growth of the *farces*. Nothing could be simpler than the scheme of many of these entertainments, in which husband and wife, husband and wife and mother-in-law, husband and wife and lover, make up the *dramatis personae*; but in others we already feel ourselves within the range of comedy

and in Italy. proper[3]. In Italy, the early efforts in the same direction were of a similar description, but of course were more directly stimulated by precedents or reminiscences of classical antiquity. The Italian term *farsa* was indeed

---

[1] *Ante*, p. 25.

[2] *Ante*, pp. 107–8. The *farces* were properly acted by the *Basoche*, who also performed the moralities, and the sotties by the *enfans sans souci*, but they mutually conceded to one another the privilege of poaching on one another's manor.

[3] Cf. above, p. 108, as to *Maître Pathelin*, acted in 1480 by the *Basoche*.

applied indiscriminately to a variety of entertainments, including religious, as well as profane and comic plays ; and in the hands of the famous Neapolitan poet, Giacopo Sannazaro (who flourished at the close of the fifteenth century), the court-*farsa* gained a new literary, as well as social, significance [1]. But it was the comic plays which attained to a peculiarly vigorous popular growth, accounted for by their derivation from the *atellanae* and *mimi* of ancient Italy. Various names were given to the earlier efforts in this direction. The *contrasti*, of which many titles are preserved from the close of the fifteenth and from the sixteenth century [2], were disputations or contentions, inevitably containing a considerable comic element, between abstract or allegorical figures [3]. The *frottola* (literally a comic ditty) marks a step in advance. Here types take the place of abstractions, and more characters than two are introduced ; we are, however, still among dramatised dialogues rather than in view of dramatic action. The Roman *carri* (comic disputations held on waggons during the Carnival) must have been of a similar class. Italian attempts, probably belonging to the fifteenth century, which already call themselves *commedie*, were doubtless still little or nothing more than lively dialogues [4]. But all these

---

[1] According to Collier, i. 71, *note*, it was not unusual for the great ladies of the French court, about the earlier part of the sixteenth century, to appear in what were termed '*farces*,' and the word is used by Sir William Paget, when giving an account of such an entertainment at the court of France to Henry VIII in 1542. *Farsa* and *farce* are from the non-classical Latin *farcita*, which has much the same meaning as *satura*.

[2] The term ' contentions ' remains in use in English dramatic literature as late as 1602, when Sir John Davies' *Contention betwixt a Wife, a Widow, and a Maid* was presented before Queen Elisabeth at Sir Robert Cecil's house in the Strand. It was afterwards printed in Davison's *Poetical Rhapsody* (2nd Ed., 1608). See *Dictionary of National Biography*, xiv. 241.

[3] The following titles will sufficiently illustrate the nature of the *contrasti*: *il contrasto di carnesciale et la quaresima* (Carnival and Fasting) ; *il c. degli uomini e dell donne* (men and women) ; *il c. del vivo et del morto ; c. del Denaro e dell' Uomo* (money and man) ; *contenzione della Povertà contra la Richezza ; el contrasto de l' Aqua et del Vino ;* and of the *frottole: la contenzione di Mona Gostanza* (Dame G.) *et di Biagio ; frottola d' un padre che haveva dua figliuoli* (one good and one bad) ; *f. da dua vecchi fattori di monache.* Cf. Klein, iv. 233–6. As to the *carri*, see *ib.* 239.

[4] So the *Commedia di due Contadini* (peasants) and the *C. d'un Villano e*

elements being in existence, it needed only the impulse
of example, which was here supplied by the Renascence at
a much earlier date than elsewhere, to call forth fruits from
the expectant soil. The schools, as a matter of course,
here came to the aid of life, as having never altogether
ceased forming, or claiming to form, part of it. In the
fourteenth and fifteenth centuries, Latin comedies were composed by Italian writers; but of these little remain beyond
the names, among them that of Petrarch's *Philologia*. In
the latter part of the fifteenth century, however, comedies
by the two representative authors of Roman *palliatae* were
performed in Italian translations as well as in the Latin
'originals.' Pomponio Leto, who has been credited with
the revival of the stage at Rome, produced comedies of
Plautus and Terence as entertainments in the courtyards
of the palaces of great prelates of the Church, and Dukes
Hercules I and II of Ferrara caused Italian translations
from the same writers to be performed at their court[1].

The designation of the first original comedy is probably
due to Bojardo's *Timone*, produced before the year 1494
(Nardi's *Amicizia* was not written till that year), in which
Bojardo died; the date of the celebrated *Calandria* by
Bernardo Divizio (afterwards Cardinal de Bibbiena) is more
or less uncertain, although we may grant the author's boast
that, notwithstanding his debt to the *Menaechmi*, his play is
not from Plautus[2]. This Italian *Timone* is founded on the
dialogue of Lucian, who accordingly speaks the prologue,
while Boëthius, a national figure, as he may almost be
called, of Italian literature and its outgrowths, similarly
moralises the last act; and the play as a whole, with its
conjunction of allegorical and mythological figures (Wealth,
Poverty, Wisdom, Mercury, and Jove), is still of its kind

---

di una Zingara. (Klein, iv. 243.) *Zingaresche* or gypsy-dialogues were
a standing species of dialogues. The Roman *Carri* were sometimes called
Giudati, because they systematically victimised the Jews. *Ib.* 239.

[1] *I Menecmi,* 1486; *Anfitrione,* 1487. He also caused the *Casina* and the
Mostellaria to be translated into Italian *terza rima*. Pomponio Leto brought
out the *Asinaria* and other Roman comedies, apparently in Latin, about the
same time. Klein, iv. 248–251.

[2] It was represented in 1508.

transitional. Within a generation, however, the first great
writer of modern comedy was busily at work; and with the
plays of Ariosto, composed in the first quarter of the sixteenth century, Italian comedy had established itself as an
independent literary growth. Although two of Ariosto's
plays are adapted from the Latin comic poets who had
served the same purpose for his predecessors, yet even in
these a native ease and grace of form apprise us that we
are concerned with products of a modern literature of
independent growth.

The influence exercised by Italian comedy upon the progress of the younger English sister will be best illustrated
by particular examples in the course of the following pages.
Perhaps, however, the general remark may be worth making
at once, that although Ariosto, and also Aretino (who with
Machiavelli is his chief rival among early Italian comic
dramatists), wrote plays in which much attention was devoted
to characterisation, it was the comedy of intrigue or adventure,
where character and manners are incidentally delineated
rather than made the principal subject of treatment, which
found particular favour in Italy in the age of the later Renascence. To these examples the luxuriant growth of our
own romantic comedy was to be very specially indebted.
At the same time, however, the peculiarly Italian species of *The Com-*
the so-called *commedia dell' arte* renewed a vitality, trace- *media*
dell' arte.
able no doubt in its origin to Oscan traditions imported
from Campania to Rome[1]. The figures of this popular
form of comedy, which derived its name from the secondary,
though significant fact that it was as a rule performed by
professional actors, trained members of a craft or guild,
underwent various modifications. But, down to their last
tremulous *epigoni*, who still prolong the dubious days of English pantomime, *Arlecchino* and his confederates reveal their
descent from *Maccus* and his inseparable companions. The

---

[1] The *atellanae* have already been referred to above. As to their origin see
Teuffel, *Geschichte der römischen Literatur*, § 9. Very possibly the chief characters of the *commedia dell' arte*, and even their traditional costumes, were
more or less traceable to a primitive source. The revival of this species, in
its modern frame, and under its modern name, has been ascribed to Francesco
(called Terenziano) Cherea, the favourite player of Pope Leo X.

scenes of the *commedia dell' arte* were merely the successive
parts or articles of a scheme drawn up beforehand, in which
the dialogue was filled up by improvisation (hence *commedia
all' improviso*). This feature marked out the species in
question as peculiar to the country of its birth ; although
attempts were made in England and elsewhere to imitate
the 'sharpness of wit' which enabled the Italian actors to
invent their own dialogue, to all intents and purposes, as
they went along[1]. Less distinctive in kind was the device
of connecting the scenes of these plays by means of the
lazzi (ligatures or links) furnished by the facile tongue or
limbs of *Arlecchino*. He was as a matter of course transferred into the stereotyped elaboration of the same species
of composition, which was distinguished by its action being
carried on by certain typical figures in masks—standing
varieties associated in the matter of speech with particular
local dialects. The invention of this new developement is
ascribed to Angelo Beolco of Padua, who called himself
Ruzante (joker), and who was born in 1502. The figures of
his pieces represented local types (*Pantalone* the Venetian
merchant, the *Dottore* from Bologna, &c.). He, and others
who followed his example, wrote down the text of their
plays[2]. The occasional influence upon the English comic
drama of the *commedia dell' arte*, which at home in Italy
popular sentiment has cherished by the side of a long series
of more purely literary growths, will be incidentally illustrated as we proceed[3].

----

[1] See Collier's chapter on *Extemporal Plays and Plots*, iii. 197 *seqq.* The
term *platt* (platform) was used of outlines or schemes of performances, in
which at least the greater part of the dialogue must have been extempo-
raneous ; and Collier cites at length the *platt* of the *Second Part of the Seven
Deadlie Sins,* found at Dulwich.—Italian *extempore* actors are repeatedly mentioned by English writers, and Collier thinks it possible that performances
of this kind were given by an Italian actor Drousiano, whose company
visited London in 1578.—In Germany, improvised comedy endured long
after tragedy had attained a regular character, and many actors of
Schroeder's company, perhaps Schroeder himself, had performed *extempore.*
See Uhde, *Denkwürdigkeiten von F. L. Schmidt* (1875), i. 12. As to the
commedia dell' arte, see an interesting essay by J. A. Symonds in his Translation of the *Memoirs of Count Carlo Gozzi* (1889).

[2] Klein, iv. 904 *seqq.*

[3] For the history of the important connexion between this species and

Lastly, it may be noted that the pastoral drama, which *The Italian* was, at first, nothing but the bucolic idyll in a dramatic *pastoral drama.* form, and which freely lent itself to the admission of both mythological and allegorical elements, flourished in Italy from as early a date as the close of the fifteenth century. Its origin was purely literary, and marks it as one of the most characteristic products of the Renascence. The renowned scholar Agnolo Poliziano's *Orfeo* (1472) begins a series, of which Tasso's *Aminta* (1573) and Guarini's *Pastor Fido* (1583, first printed 1590) may be held to represent the most exquisite flower[1]. The artificial character of this delicate combination commended it for imitation to the fancy and wit of our Elisabethan poets, who recognised in it an incomparable vehicle for the display of learning and imagination, suiting itself with equal facility to the intention of allegorical compliment and to that of satire ; and in both directions its influence will be perceptible at almost every stage in the progress of our sixteenth and seventeenth century drama, more especially in its comic branches.

The beginnings of the Spanish comic drama in the main *Beginnings* followed a course analogous to those of the Italian. The *of Comedy in Spain ;* first *entremeses* (interludes), to be sure, connect themselves directly with the mysteries and moralities in which, from an early date, it had been usual to insert them ; but in the celebrated *Couplets of Mingo Revulgo* (1472) we have a dialogue in character after the fashion of the Italian *contrasti.* The personages of the dialogue are *Mingo Revulgo* (Domingo Vulgus), who represents the common folk, and *Gil Arribato*, who belongs to the 'classes'[2]. *A Dialogue between Love and an Old Man*, dating from the same period, is a composition of the same kind. Of both

French comedy, see L. Moland, *Molière et la Comédie Italienne* (2ᵐᵉ éd.), Paris, 1867.

[1] For a characterisation of the *Orfeo*, see J. Mähly, *Angelus Politianus* (1864), pp. 108–143. The *Orfeo*, which the Italians are said to regard as the beginning of their opera, was despised by its author, who wished it to be treated as weakling children were dealt with by their Spartan parents. To the *Pastor Fido* I shall have repeated occasion of returning.

[2] A play called *Myngo* is mentioned among other plays of which the names are otherwise unknown, performed at Bristol in 1578. (Collier, i. 223 *note*.)

these species the authorship has been attributed to Rodrigo Cota the elder, who is also held to have begun, about the year 1480, a famous dramatic composition finished, not later than 1499, by Fernando de Rojas. This was *Calisto and Meliboea*, a dramatic novel of intrigue and character, which, under the name of *Celestina*, afterwards achieved a success extending far beyond the borders of Spain [1]. Before its adaptation for the stage by Romero de Zepeda (1582) it cannot, with its twenty-one acts, be regarded as having been intended for representation. The earliest dramatic compositions known to have been performed in Spain by actors, who were neither priests nor cavaliers, were the *Representaciones* of Juan de la Enzina (born 1468-9), which, under the title of *Eclogues*, were dramatic dialogues, partly of a religious, partly of a pastoral, character. Both in Spain and in Portugal these entertainments developed slowly in the direction of the regular drama, under the influence of Italian, and occasionally of ancient classical, examples; but a national drama had not formed itself in Spain, before it was already rising into life in England. The early Spanish theatre is chiefly remarkable for its mixture of styles, and the first great Spanish dramatists, Cervantes and Lope de Vega, are very unfixed in form [2].

and in Germany.   In Germany, on the other hand, although the first growths of the comic drama were by no means belated, the process was a far simpler one. Here, no doubt, under the influence of the dialogue - literature, to the remarkable growth of which in the Reformation age reference will immediately be made, it was the religious drama proper that suggested the comic exuberance of the *Fastnachtsspiele* (Shrove-Tuesday plays), dating in their earliest known speci-

---

[1] It was frequently translated, and, in 1632, was published in an English version by ' Don Diego Puedeser ' (James Mabbe) under a vernacular first title.   See *The Celestina, &c., in James Mabbe's version* ; with Introduction by J. Fitzmaurice Kelly (*Tudor Translations Series*).   For a translation of acts xix and xx of the *Celestina* (with the catastrophe of the ladder), see M. A. Fée's *Études sur l'ancien Théâtre Espagnol* (1873), pp. 417 *seqq.*

[2] Cf. Ticknor's *History of Spanish Literature*, Period I, chaps. xiii and xiv, and Period II, chaps. vii and viii.   For a sketch of the Spanish theatre before Cervantes, and of the changes introduced into it by him, see the essay on Cervantes in Mérimée's *Portraits historiques et littéraires* (2me éd., 1874).

mens from the middle of the fifteenth century[1]. At first these entertainments appear to have been little more than comic dialogues, diversified only by the occasional use of imported elements ; and it was natural that a strong impulse should be given towards this kind of production by the dialogues which form one of the most characteristic features of the earlier years of the sixteenth century in German literature. The masters of this form of composition were two of the chief leaders in the German Renascence movement, and of the most potent factors in the cognate movement of the Reformation, towards which their idiosyncrasies ultimately induced them to assume attitudes directly antagonistic to one another. In the dialogues of Erasmus and of Hutten the influences of classical culture and of national sentiment are respectively predominant, but by no means to the exclusion of other diversifying motives. In addition to these, a third group of German dialogues has been distinguished in this age by Dr. Herford, and happily described by him as that which exhibits the dialogue 'turning into what is perhaps best called the *drama of debate*[2].' To this species, which is apt to exhibit a succession of detached scenes and a crowd of contributory characters, Swiss writers particularly inclined.

It seems unnecessary to refer to the early efforts of the comic drama among other cognate peoples ; though it is perhaps noticeable that in the Low Countries comic as well as serious dramatic pieces, moving in the sphere of real life, are stated to have been produced as early as the fourteenth century[3].

---

[1] Cf. Devrient, *Geschichte der Schauspielkunst*, i. 93 *seqq.* As to the *Fastnachtsspiele*, see the instructive Introduction by Julius Tittmann to Part iii. of *Dichtungen von Hans Sachs* (in vol. vi. of Gödeke and Tittmann's *Deutsche Dichter des 16. Jahrhunderts*), Leipzig, 1871. The two chief authors of *Fastnachtsspiele* in the fifteenth century were Hans Rosenblüt, a 'minstrel' of the later type, and Hans Folz, both Nürnbergers, although Folz was a native of Worms.

[2] The second chapter of Dr. C. H. Herford's *Studies in the Literary Relations of England and Germany* (1886) brings out with admirable force the literary characteristics and influence of German dialogue literature in the Reformation Age.

[3] As to the Dutch *sotternie*, cf. F. v. Hellwald, *Geschichte des holländischen Theaters* (1874), p. 2.

These general notes will help to indicate the precedents and examples that affected the beginnings of English comedy before the Renascence movement, in this country with more of suddenness than elsewhere, brought them into direct contact with classical models.   In the period with which we are immediately concerned—the early Tudor period—these germs were still slumbering beneath the cumbrous folds of the moralities ; yet at home, too, there were not a few influences already in operation which, when combined, might seem to have been well capable of awakening them.   It should not be overlooked that in a quite different branch of literary composition, a work of long-continued and widespread popularity in this very age brought home to English, as it had to continental, hearers and readers the advantage and pleasure to be found in a concrete treatment of the vices and foibles exemplified to them by their neighbours.   Sebastian Brant's famous *Ship of Fools*, of which the English version by Alexander Barklay was published in the first year of Henry VIII's reign (1509), transmuted abstractions into human realities, calling down scorn and indignation, instead of upon Improvidence, Pretentious Incompetence, and the like, upon real *Folys without Provysyon*, *Folyshe Fesycyans*, and so forth—all of them more or less successful *facsimiles* of persons living next door or in the next street to your worship's self.   Such books, in the earliest as in later periods of our comic drama, have materially helped, not only to suggest effective types of character, but also to enforce the uses of comparison between them. Again, as has been seen, our literature had, from an early date, furnished examples of interlocutory poems which, as wholly lacking action, cannot be called dramatic, but which comprise efforts in the direction of characterisation—an

important branch of dramatic effort.   Under the influence of foreign examples, to which reference was made above, English dialogue-literature entered upon a new phase, which may be said to have lasted from the earlier days of Henry VIII into the great times of Elisabeth.   We are not concerned here with those of its productions which have no direct contact with the drama, and which include, together

with examples of didactic or satirical prose, headed by
More's *Utopia* in its English dress, the fierce polemical
verse of William Roy and Jerome Barlow[1], and the controversial aftermath which followed on the accession of
Edward VI. English writers utilised the time-honoured
'contrast' form for such productions in the manner of Hans
Sachs as *John Bon and Mast' Parson*, a disputation between
a peasant and a priest on the Sacrament, which the former,
in his rustic ignorance, calls 'Corpsy-cursty[2].' *Robyn Conscience*, a disputation in seven-line stanzas between a son
and his father, who is an abstract personage called Covetous-
ness, and represents, oddly enough, the ἄδικος λόγος of the
old generation, is justly regarded by Dr. Herford as a composition of the same class[3]. Dr. William Turner's *Examination of the Mass* (1547 c.) and a rather later composition
of similar conception, entitled *The Endightment* (Indictment)
against Mother Masse[4], add an element of novelty by
arranging the disputation for and against the Mass and the
dogma involved in the rite under the ever popular form of
judicial trials, carried on in the one instance by concrete
agents in the familiar locality of a London sessions-house,
in the other before a personified *God's Word* as judge
and the Twelve Apostles as jurymen. The liking for
controversial dialogue was not extinguished under Mary,
but came to an end under Elisabeth, when a religious
settlement was effected, against which it gradually became
either needless, or futile, to struggle. Isolated examples of
the dialogue or disputation of the non-controversial type,

---

[1] The *Dialogue between Watkyn and Jeffroye* follows upon the mock *Lamen-
tacion for the decease of the Mass* in the invective, published by the two
fugitive Franciscan Friars against Cardinal Wolsey and the orthodox Church
at home under the heading *Rede me and be nott wrothe* (1528). See Arber's
English Reprints (1871). Dr. Herford, *u. s.*, p. 43, shows that there is no
reason for supposing the authors to have been acquainted with the Bernese
poet Nicholas Manuel's more elaborate satire on (virtually) the same theme
of *The Sickness of the Mass*.

[2] Herford, *u. s.*, p. 54. This dialogue, printed in 1548, is reprinted *ap.*
W. C. Hazlitt's *Remains of Early English Poetry*.

[3] Herford, p. 55. A sufficient account of this piece will be found *ap.*
Collier, ii. 316–319. It is in the library of the Duke of Devonshire.

[4] Described by Herford, pp. 63–6, from the originals, preserved respectively in the British Museum and at Lambeth.

in which an argument is carried on merely or mainly for the intellectual pleasure to be derived from it, recur at different times in the Tudor period of our literature.

'Dialogue of Death' (1564–5).

A very celebrated dialogue, or rather series of dialogues, combining precept with example, and enforcing the effect of the latter with much picturesque vivacity, by William Bulleyn, was published in 1564–5, and is often cited under the title of a *Dialogue of Death*. Its full title better displays its double purpose, which is that of indicating 'a goodly regimente' (regimen) 'against the fever Pestilence, with a consolation and comfort against death.' Its author was a learned scholar, born under Henry VIII, who held clerical preferment in the early years of Edward VI, and then travelled abroad. On his return he published a variety of medical treatises, partly in dialogue form, and led a life of chequered fortunes till his death in 1576[1]. The *Dialogue* on account of which he is most generally remembered, and on the bibliographical history of which a vast amount of learning has been expended, is still, so far as I know, only accessible in fragments[2]. They show the author to have had a large and varied knowledge of both books and men, and to have possessed the art of imparting a lifelike colour of reality to such pictures as that which he introduces of the citizen and his wife riding forth from London to escape the plague. But I cannot perceive that this interesting relic of an interesting man has any special value for the early history of our drama.

Dialogue of Gentylnes and Nobilitye (*pr.* 1533 *c.*).

Of other Tudor dialogues I need only mention here, by the side of John Heywood's *Dialogue of Wit and Folly*, noted among his works below, a similar piece printed about the same time (1533 *c.*, according to Mr. Bullen's conjecture) by John Rastell, who was possibly its author.

---

[1] See Mr. A. H. Bullen's notice of William Bulleyn in vol. vii of the *Dictionary of National Biography*.

[2] See the note, pp. xc–xcii of the *Notice of the Life and Writings of Alexander Barclay*, in Jamieson's edition of *The Ship of Fools* (1874), vol. i. The fullest series of extracts known to me is that in the Appendix to Waldron's *Sad Shepherd* (1783), pp. 185–223. The scene in which the 'Pothicaire' and the doctor attend upon the sick rich man Antonius contains the much-quoted passage on our early English poets.

It has also been attributed, but without apparent reason, to John Heywood. This is a dialogue bearing the title *Of gentylnes and nobilitye*[1], and addressing itself to a question which has in its time been illustrated by both wit and wisdom, and not unfrequently reiterated without much of either,—' Who is a verey gentleman[2] ? ' The discussion is carried on between ' the Marchaunt, the Knyght and the Plowman,' and the piece professes to be ' compiled after the maner of an enterlude, with divers toys and gestis addyd therto to make mery pastyme and disport'; but there is no action to differentiate it from the type of the Italian *contrasti*. A similar production seems to have been that mentioned in Hall's *Chronicle* (*s. a.* 1527) as having served to entertain the King and Court; in it, we are told, ' two persones plaied a dialog, theffect whereof was whether riches were better than love[3].'

It must not, however, be forgotten that already at a much earlier date there are traces in England of a species of entertainment in which an element of action was included, and which, unlike the disputations and dialogues to which I have adverted, may therefore be rightly described as dramatic. These early *interludes*, as they were called, were in point of fact dramatised anecdotes of the type of the French or Italian comic farce, which from the Plantagenet times onwards seem to have not unfrequently been produced to diversify or fill up the pauses of the banquets ensuing in great houses upon the more substantial part of the repast. One such composition has been preserved, although in a fragmentary condition ; but though the *Interludium de clerico et puella*, which probably dates from the reign of Edward I, was founded on the English tale of *Dame Sirith*, there are indications that the author of the English farce had (like so many of his successors) a French model in his

Early interludes.

---

[1] Cf. Collier, ii. 310 *seqq.*

[2] The best answer, I suppose, is Chaucer's, professedly rather than actually founding itself on a passage in Dante, in *The Wife of Bath's Tale*.

[3] Collier, ii. 307 *note*. Francis Thynn's *Debate between Pride and Lowliness* (edited by Collier for the Old Shakespeare Society's Publications, 1841), which Robert Greene reproduced under the title of *A Quip for an Upstart Courtier*, is, on the other hand, not dramatic even in form.

hands [1].   It is unlikely that similar 'interludes' should not
have continued in England, as they did in France, to divert
the leisure of those who had so much of it on their hands.
What was needed was that some dramatic writer of ingenuity
and power should be bold enough to take a lesson from
such neglected trifles, and break with the usage long imposed by literary custom.   To effect a transition from the
moralities, upon which literary effort of the dramatic kind
had in England so long concentrated itself, he would have
to throw overboard the time-honoured agency of personified
abstractions which they had preserved with so wearisome
a persistency, and to confine the characters of plays pursuing
the same ends as the moralities themselves to those human
types which had hitherto been only occasionally or fitfully
introduced in these.   But although it may seem an easy
matter to take a step of this description, the resolute
freedom proper to genius frequently has to come into play
before such a step is actually taken.   The real beginner of
English comedy had been long awaited in the man who
should definitively establish the practice of combining, in an
easy and amusing dramatic action, clearly marked and
contrasted types of ordinary human life.   This man was
John Heywood, whom I thus have no scruple in accounting
a man of genius, and whose series of *Interludes* possesses
a distinctive significance for the history of our national
drama.

Transition from the Moralities.

JOHN HEYWOOD [2], the date and place of whose birth are
alike uncertain, was in his boyhood very possibly employed
in the choir of the chapel-royal, and, according to his own
statement, was afterwards, for a long time, one of King
Henry VIII's 'singing-men.'   It may be that between

John Heywood (b. 1497 c., d. 1580 c.).

---

[1] Ten Brinck, ii. 308-9.   This curious fragment is printed in Wright and
Halliwell's *Reliquiae Antiquae*, vol. ii. p. 145.   It consists of two scenes of
a farce, written in short couplets, of which the diction has a strong dialect
colouring.   The second scene unluckily breaks off in the middle, after
'Mome Ellwis,' a homely Celestina by her calling, has testified to her
religious sentiments.

[2] For the known data of Heywood's life, and for references to the authorities concerning it, see my article on him in vol. xxvi of the *Dictionary of
National Biography*.

these two stages of his life he spent some time at Broadgates Hall, now Pembroke College, Oxford, of which he is
traditionally said to have been a member.   In 1526 he was
officially known as 'player of the virginals' at court, and
it is conjectured that a reduction in his wages as such was
due to his appointment, some time before 1538, as master
of a company of children who performed plays before the
court.   The Princess Mary, to whom Heywood was introduced by his patron Sir Thomas More, witnessed one of
these performances, and to her he became attached with
a loyal devotion to which his writings repeatedly testify,
and which was unmistakeably enhanced by his sympathy
with her subsequent policy in matters of both Church and
State.   Under Edward VI he is said to have escaped 'the
jerke of the six-string'd whip'; as a matter of fact he had
already, in 1544, avoided a charge of having denied the
Royal Supremacy by a public recantation, and it must be
the Supremacy, not the Six Articles, Act against which
he had again offended in the new reign.   His literary
reputation, already considerable under Edward, rose to its
height under Mary, who took an intelligent delight in his
accomplishments and in his wit, which is said to have
amused her even on her death-bed.   She granted him a lease
of the manor of Bolmer and other lands in Yorkshire.
After the accession of Elisabeth, although he had enjoyed
her favour in former days, he thought it more prudent to
withdraw to the continent, where (at Malines) he is supposed
to have passed the remainder of his days.   He was certainly
alive early in 1577, when his name occurs in a return of
Catholic fugitives; but in 1587 he is spoken of [1] as 'dead
and gone.'   Of his two sons, the younger, Jasper, has been
previously mentioned as one of the translators of Seneca's
Tragedies [2].

John Heywood's personal position at the courts of the
sovereigns whom he so loyally served was not completely
defined by his official duties as trainer of boy-players,
conductor of their performances, and writer of the pieces

---

[1] By Thomas Newton, in his *Epilogue or Conclusion to Heywood's Works*.
[2] *Ante*, p. 195.

presented by them. Upon these duties he appears to have
entered at some time between 1514, when Henry VIII enlarged his establishment of players (to which Heywood did
not belong), and 1520 or thereabouts, the probable date of
his earliest extant interlude. He cannot be supposed to have
held the place of court jester or fool [1], but he was certainly
expected to amuse by his conversation as well as to interest
by his writings and by their reputation. His *Epigrams*
were probably considered by himself, as well as by his contemporaries and by near generations, to constitute his foremost title to literary fame ; and indeed the collection is
full of flashes of wit and humour, and here and there even
has touches of pathos, which it needs no great alertness to
discern amidst inevitably dull surroundings. The store of
Proverbs, cleverly fitted by a *tour de force* into the framework of a single *Dialogue,* redounds to the credit of his
learning rather than of his wit, although displaying an
aptness in the art of quotation which is rightly held to
partake of the quality of wit itself. But the *Epigrams*—
six hundred in number—would, even if nothing else were
preserved from their author's hand, prove their author to
have been possessed of a vein of wit and humour such
as no difference of times or manners can altogether
obscure, and to have moreover had in him a vein of
sentiment occasionally approaching the confines of poetical power [2]. Of even more importance, perhaps, in the
present connexion, is the fact that as an epigrammatist
he may be said to be free from the pedantry which has
beset so many more richly endowed humourists, and is
quite content to use a cross-bow instead of a catapult in
dealing with folly as it flies [3]. I do not think that this
estimate is contradicted by his elaborate allegory on the

---

[1] The dagger worn by him in the woodcut portrait which appears in
editions both of *The Spider and the Flie* and of *Epigrams upon Proverbs* can
hardly be adduced as an argument to the contrary.

[2] I may instance the epigram *Of weeping :*
'Better children weepe then olde men, say wyse men.
But olde men weepe when children laugh, now and then.'

[3] 'This write I not to teache but to touche; for why,
Men know this as well or better than I.'

affairs of Church and State—the burlesque epos of *The Spider and the Flie*,—which has been generally condemned as wearisome, although its general lucidity and relative variety of treatment to my mind redeem some of the tediousness inherent in the literary species to which it belongs. Of his remaining non-dramatic writings, I need here only mention the *Willow Garland* ballad, the refrain of which was known to Desdemona [1].

Such a humourist as John Heywood was manifestly fitted for the task which, doubtless without much consciousness of its importance, he undertook in connexion with the progress of our comic drama. Frank and open-minded, he is at the same time a really modest writer, who, in the matter of characterisation, for instance, unaffectedly rates his powers at the very lowest [2]. Yet it was precisely the vivacity of his genius which, in a more advanced age of the English drama, would probably have secured to him a far more prominent position in its history than is usually accorded to him. His humour is of a kind perhaps peculiarly characteristic of those minds which, while strongly conservative at bottom, claim a wide personal liberty in the expression of opinion, and are radically adverse to all shams. Such a mind was that of Aristophanes, who, I am convinced, went through no such changes of religious opinion as have been attributed to him by modern criticism, but who consistently indulged in a license of expression quite compatible with the maintenance of fixed principles in religion and in politics. Such a mind was that of Canning, who, under the influence of personal feeling, could satirise a Tory premier as happily as he could ridicule a revolutionary Radical. Heywood was a convinced orthodox Roman Catholic, as he was an upholder of legitimate authority in the realm; to quarrel with the foundations of spiritual authority (such as they seemed to him) was in his eyes alike foolish and criminal; but he saw

---

[1] Reprinted in the (Old) *Shakespeare Society's Papers*, 1844, i. 44–6.
[2] ' Were I, in portraiying persons dead or alive
    As cunnyng and as quicke to touche them at full,
    As in that feate I am ignorant and dull.'
        Dialogue of Prouerbes &c., Part i.

no reason for sparing priests, pardoners, or pilgrims the lash
of his ' mad, mery wit.'

 For both the wit and the humour of Heywood are not
only undeniable, but exceedingly striking, especially in the
midst of the literature, tame and tedious as a whole, of our
English moralities.   The manifestation of these qualities
by Heywood redeems the youthful period of the English
comic drama from the charge of utter inferiority to that
of the French ; and proves that neither had Chaucer
written in vain, nor were Shakspere and Ben Jonson in
this respect without a true predecessor.   If the form of
Heywood's interludes is extremely simple, this only increases our admiration for the fact that he found it possible
within so limited an area to display comic faculties which
would have been equal to far ampler opportunities.   He
tells a merry tale with Chaucerian *verve* ; and contrives in
his simple scenes to introduce touches of character of irresistible effectiveness.   And, so far as it is possible to judge,
his fondness for a joke is merely the ripple on a broad sur-
face of good sense, and never at issue with the fundamental
principles of a sound morality.   Lastly, he is possessed of
what, considering the age in which he wrote, may be described
as the most exceptional of his literary gifts, viz. genuine
lightness of hand ; while all his writings are interesting, his
interludes may be described as thoroughly enjoyable.

 Not all the productions of Heywood which I am about
to notice are properly described as *interludes*, if that name
is, in its more precise application to a distinct literary
species, to be confined to short comic pieces containing an
element of action that entitles them to be called dramatic.
But, as it is these which constitute his claim to a conspicuous
place in a survey of our dramatic literature, and as they
appear to have preceded the rest in chronological order of
production, they may here be noticed first.

A Mery Play be-tween the Pardoner, &c. (pr. 1533).

 The *Mery Play between the Pardoner and the Frere, the
Curate and Neybour Pratte*, was printed by Rastell in
1533 [1], but the internal evidence of a reference to Pope

---

[1] A unique copy of this is to be found in the library of the Duke of Devonshire, and was reproduced in facsimile in 1820.   It has been reprinted in

Leo X (who died in 1521) shows it to have been written at least twelve years before this date. The construction of this easy dramatic satire is even slighter than that of its successors, the idea being simply that of a ludicrous rivalry between the Friar and the Pardoner to gain the ear of a parish which could do very well without the presence of either. The Friar having secured the use of the Curate's pulpit sets out upon his begging sermon, in which he is interrupted by the Pardoner, intent upon extolling his relics [1]. They carry on their oratorical efforts in alternate lines, with the ludicrous effect of such an alternation so well known to later days of the comic stage. Ultimately they fall to blows, and are engaged in a furious scuffle, when the Curate (or Parson) appears on the scene to preserve his church, as he incisively puts it, from 'pollution.' He thus appeals to the lay-element, in the person of neighbour Pratte, to second him in this endeavour :

> 'Neighbour, ye be constable; stand ye near,
> Take ye that lay knave, and let me alone
> With this gentleman. By God and by Saint John,
> I shall borrow upon priesthood somewhat ;
> For I may say to thee, neighbour Pratte,
> It is a good deed to punish such, to th' ensample
> Of such other, how that they shall [not] mell
> In like fashion, as these caitiffs do.'

It proves, however, a difficult task, especially for the Curate, to quell such determined intruders, and in the end they are allowed to depart in peace, although without a benediction :

> '*Friar.* Will ye leave, then, and let us in peace depart ?
> *Curate and Pratte.* Yea, by our lady, even with all our heart.
> *Friar and Pardoner.* Then adieu to the devil, till we come again !
> *Curate and Pratte.* And a mischief go with you both twain !'

The Mery Play between Johan the Husbande, Tyb the Wife, and Syr Jhon the Priest [2], was likewise printed by

A Mery Play between Johan

Four Old Plays, edited by Child (Cambridge, U. S. A., 1848), and in Hazlitt's *Dodsley*, vol. i.

[1] Collier, ii. 301 note, mentions that a Proclamation, issued in 1537 against erroneous writings and books, contains a warning against ' dyvers and sundry light persons called Pardoners,' which denounces their evil ways in very explicit terms.

[2] Reprinted at the Chiswick Press (1819), from the unique copy in the

the Hus-
bande, Tyb
the Wife,
and Syr
Jhon the
Priest.

Rastell in 1533. It treats of a triple relationship, which the later Middle Ages and the Renascence period 'analyse' as persistently as our novelists of the nineteenth century. Johan commences the action by a soliloquy, in which, because it *is* a soliloquy, he proclaims with heroic boldness his determination to exercise his martial authority by 'beting' his wife. But after he has reviewed and confuted all possible arguments against such a procedure, the real argument soon appears in the person of his wife Tyb herself. She meets her husband's suspicions as to her relations with the parish priest by constraining him to invite her ghostly friend to partake of a 'pye,' which constitutes the central point of interest in the drama. The notion that to suffer injury is much, but that to be in addition deprived of one's dinner by the destroyer of one's peace is *too* much, is immortal in farce; but never has it been worked out with more 'convincing' humour than in this *Mery Play*. While the priest and Tyb are consuming the pie, the husband is set to 'chafe wax' at the fire, in order to stop up a hole in a pail, which, there is but too much reason to believe, was not strange in its origin to Tyb[1]. In the end, the long-suffering husband's patience gives way, and with a courage born from despair he suddenly attacks the priest 'with his fyst,' ending the play with an expression of forebodings that excuse if they do not justify his conduct. In a farcical sketch such as this there is, of course, not very much room for characterisation, or for any very special depiction of manners. In his third and most celebrated interlude, the author returns to the more elaborate kind of satire which he had attempted in his first extant piece.

The Four
P's (pr.
1545 c.).

The Four P's, a Mery Interlude of a Palmer, a Pardoner, a Potycary, and a Pedlar, was printed, without date, by William Myddleton, but as no dated publication was issued from his press before 1543 or after 1547, the precise time

---

Ashmolean Museum, Oxford.   'Sir' is of course the usual prefix allowed to a priest, as representing the 'dominus' attesting his (actual or supposed) B.A. degree.

[1] Cf. in the *Farce de Pernet* (*Ancien Théatre Français*, i. 211):

   'C'est ung très pouvre passetemps
   De chauffer la cire quant on digne.'

of the printing of this play must fall between these years, although its composition was probably more or less contemporaneous with that of the interludes previously noticed [1]. This piece [2] is in its details extremely entertaining, while it thoroughly succeeds in conveying a moral quite distinct from the tendency which might, by a natural mistake, be imputed to it. We may therefore unaffectedly regret that its most humorous passages are unfit for modern ears. The Palmer and the Pardoner begin by a contest as to the superior efficacy of the processes of salvation which they respectively practise ; the 'Poticary asserts that if *they* teach men how to prepare for death, *he* can facilitate death itself; while the task of the Pedlar is to judge which is the greatest liar of the three. The competition consists in the telling of two stories by the Palmer and the Pardoner, and the outbidding of their lies circumstantial by a monstrously extravagant assertion on the part of the 'Poticary [3]. The humour of the whole is inimitable, but at the end the author takes occasion to show that it is the abuse and not the use of means of edification which he has been satirising. This interlude is in many respects curious as an illustration of manners as well as character ; the Pardoner's list of his relics being only equalled by the Palmer's enumeration of his pilgrimages, of which his rival thus sums up the result :

> 'And when ye have gone as far as ye can,
> For all your labour and gostely entente,
> Ye will come home as wyse as ye wente.'

Heywood's lines often possess the felicity of the above ;

---

[1] Reprinted in vol. i. of Dodsley's *Select Old Plays* ; in vol. i. of the *Ancient British Drama* ; and in vol. i. of Hazlitt's *Dodsley*.

[2] The alliterative title of *The Four P's* either was already popular, or was made such by Heywood's interlude.   On the dismissal of Coke, Chamberlain writes to Carleton (Nov. 18, 1621) : 'The common speech is that four PP's have overthrown and put him down, that is, Pride, Prohibitions, Praemunire, and Prerogative.' (*Court and Times of James I*, 1848, i. 427.)

[3]   'And this I wolde ye shulde understande,
I have sene women v hundred thousande :
And oft with them have longe tyme taried ;
Yet in all places where I have ben,
Of all the women that I have sene,
I never sawe nor knewe in my conscyens,
Any one woman out of paciens.'

he had all the power of condensing and pointing expression which became second nature to him as an epigrammatist; and there is a really gnomic force in the use to which he puts his power in the few serious words at the close of this interlude. Or is there not strength of meaning, as well as of expression, in the admonition—

> 'But where ye dout, the truthe nat knowynge,
> Belevynge the beste, good may be growynge,
> In judgynge the best, no harme at the leste;
> In judgynge the worste, no good at the beste'—

whatever may be thought of the corollary, which exhibits the author's orthodoxy:

> 'But beste in these thynges it semeth to me,
> To take no judgement upon ye;
> But as the churche doth judge or take them,
> So do ye receyve or forsake them.
> And so be you sure ye cannat erre,
> But may be a frutfull folower'?

The Play of the Wether (pr. 1533).

Besides these *Interludes*, in the more special sense of the term which they may be said to have themselves succeeded in establishing for it, John Heywood composed other pieces more or less resembling earlier types, but not unmarked with the originality which rarely deserted him. *The Play of the Wether, a new and a very mery interlude of all maner of Wethers* (printed in 1533)[1], is a highly ingenious composition, of which the plot has a more didactic design than can with sincerity be ascribed to any of the interludes noticed above. The introduction of personages from classical mythology interests us, as indicating the influence of Renascence tastes, which kept alive a liking for such agency in the more fanciful spheres of our drama down to a very late date[2].

[1] A copy of this exists at St. John's College, Oxford. There is another edition, printed by Robert Wyer. A full account of this play by Dr. Bliss is reproduced by Fairholt in his essay on Heywood and his writings in *Percy Society's Publications*, vol. xx (1846).

[2] Robert Greene's *Debate between Follie and Love*, professedly translated out of French (printed 1587, and reprinted in Dr. Grosart's edition of Greene's *Works*, iv. 45–223), comprises a long disputation between these personages 'of their power, dignitie and superioritie,' followed by action. Folly, having made herself invisible, puts out Love's eyes, and Venus carries the complaint of Love before Jupiter, who appoints Apollo and Mercury as counsel. They make long speeches full of ancient instances, and Jupiter's

The divinities who superintend the several phenomena of the weather—Phoebus, Saturn, Aeolus, and Phoebe—prefer complaints against one another at the throne of Jupiter, who thereupon, through Merry Report, the 'Vice' of the play, summons before the supreme tribunal a set of human witnesses, types of classes specially interested in different sorts of weather, such as the Ranger, the Water-miller, the Wind-miller. The variety of their requests, to which Jupiter undertakes to respond one by one, inasmuch as to respond to them simultaneously is impossible, proves the absurdity of demanding more than what is in the end beneficial to the human community at large. If, as Collier suggests [1], intended for a court show, this mythological morality was certainly a refined as well as genial specimen of its class.

The *Play of Love*, of which the extant copy [2] is without date, was perhaps an earlier production of the same versatile author. One may best compare it to an Italian *frottola*, comprising, as it does, as many as four characters, although the contention between them is in the form of a disputation rather than of a dramatic action. These characters consist of 'the Lover not beloved — the Woman beloved, not loving—the Lover beloved—and one Neither lover nor loved.' This last unlucky wight makes his appearance as the Vice, who 'cometh in ronnynge sodenly aboute the place among the audiens, with a huge coppyr tank on his head, full of squybs, fyred, crying "Watere, water; fyre, fyre, fyre; water, water; fyre;" till the fyre in the squybs be spent.' A certain measure of action is thus introduced, inasmuch as the Lover nervously imagines his mistress to be aflame. But finally argument settles, or rather harmonises, the difficulty in dispute, and the closing speech gives a religious turn to the sentiment conveyed. *The Play of Love.*

The Dialogue of Wit and Folly, in conclusion, of which the MS. [3] likewise bears no date, is, as its title implies, a mere dialogue, and not therefore to be included among Heywood's *The Dialogue of Wit and Folly.*

sentence is postponement, Folly to undertake the guidance in the meantime of blind Love.

[1] ii. 307.
[2] In the Bodleian. It is described at length by Fairholt, *u. s.*
[3] In the British Museum. Reprinted by Fairholt, *u. s.*

dramatic works. The disputation on the question whether the life of a wise man or that of a fool be superior to the other, is conducted by two persons named John and James, and decided by a third, bearing the authoritative name of Jerome. The piece appears to have been recited before the king, and repeatedly refers to his majesty's fool, Will Somers or Summer, as illustrating the advantage of being unencumbered by either understanding or education [1].

Other early Tudor interludes.　One or two other plays may be conveniently mentioned here, which, whether or not designated as 'interludes' by their authors or printers, can hardly be classed among regular comedies, and exhibit features of treatment or style connecting them with earlier species which were passing away [2]. *A new Enterlude called Thersytes* [3], which announces its purpose to be to 'declare howe that the greatest boesters are not the greatest doers,' must have been first performed in or very soon after 1537, the year of the birth of the prince who afterwards reigned as King Edward VI; for to this auspicious event the play expressly refers at its close [4]. As it was printed at some date not earlier than 1561, it may have been revived under Queen Elisabeth. Although in its design resembling Heywood's interludes, it differs from them both in its method of treatment, which is that of a rather childish kind of burlesque, and in its style, which is manifestly, and not altogether unsuccessfully, modelled on the Skeltonical [5]. Although the chief character bears a name taken from classical story, and there is some further display of classical learning, the fun is of the most

[1] Collier, ii. 307–9. This dialogue ends in an epilogue of four stanzas which extol the king's wit, but which 'in his absens are voyde,' i. e. to be omitted.

[2] A few other pieces of this class which, however, contain so large an allegorical element as to admit on the whole of being reckoned among the moralities, have been mentioned *ante*, p. 142.

[3] Printed in Hazlitt's *Dodsley*, vol. i. Both this and the following play were published by Haslewood in 1820, with an Introduction, reprinted by Mr. Hazlitt.

[4] 'Beseech ye also, that God may save his queen,
　　Lovely Lady Jane, and the prince that he hath sent them between.'

[5] Cf. p. 129, *ante*. One of the speeches of Thersites contains a long string of onomatopoeic names, in the fashion which *Ralph Roister Doister* and other comedies took over from the moralities.

straightforward kind, and occasionally, as observed, borders on the infantile. (Thersites ' must fight with his sword against the snail, and the snail draweth her horns in.') *A new Enterlude for children to playe, named Jacke Juggler* [1], on the other hand, though intended to be performed by children, is extremely gross in expression, while we must grant that its plot, or shred of a plot, is a most innocent adaptation of an original very differently treated by later hands [2]. It is, in point of fact, taken from the *Amphitruo* of Plautus, ' without the part of Amphitruo'; and resembles those ' drolls' of a later period which consist of a farcical episode taken from a play of established reputation. The hero and other personages bear typical names (Mayster Boungrace, Dame Coye, Ales trype and go, &c.) [3]. Of a far more advanced kind is the interlude of *Calisto and Meliboea* [4], printed by John Rastell about 1530, with a long and edifying title [5], for which it seems ungracious to have substituted one merely conveying the origin of the piece. But, in point of fact, the circumstance of this origin accounts for the relatively developed nature of both action and diction, which no occasional defects of detail can conceal. We have here the earliest English version of part of the *Celestina*, the significance of which, although here reduced to the proportions of the action of an interlude, seems to anticipate many later developements in the history of our drama [6].

[1] Printed in Hazlitt's *Dodsley*, vol. i.
[2] See below as to Dryden's *Amphitryon*.
[3]   ' And a maid we have at home, Alison Trip-and-go ;
        Not all London can show such other two ;
        She simpereth, and pranketh,' &c.
[4] Reprinted in vol. i. of Hazlitt's *Dodsley*.
[5] ' *A new comedy in English in manner of an interlude right elegant and full of rhetoric ; wherein is shewed and described as well the beauty and good properties of women, as their vices and evil conditions, with a moral conclusion and exhortation to virtue.*'
[6] Cf. Klein, iv. 591, in the connexion between the *Celestina* with the Italian, and indirectly with the English romantic drama. As to mere diction, I content myself with citing a passage which (quite early in the play) expresses the longing of Calisto for Meliboea:
        ' Oh, what woeful wight with me can compare ?
        The thirst of sorrow is my mixèd wine
        Which daily I drink with deep draughts of care.'

The Disobedient Child[1], an interlude by Thomas Ingelend, described on the title-page as ' late student in Cambridge,' where he appears to have been a member of Christ's College, may probably be assigned to the reign of Edward VI, or even to that of Henry VIII ; but it was not printed till 1560, and concludes with the praise of Queen Elisabeth. I mention it here, because, though in manner belonging to the moralities, and introducing the Devil with his ' O, ho, ho, what a felowe am I,' in the old-fashioned style, it possesses a real dramatic fable, however simple, while its characters are all human types, not personified abstractions. Its story is that of a rich man's son in the city of London, who, instead of following the admonitions of his kind parent, leads a life of wantonness, and crowns his follies by an imprudent early marriage. This crime brings with itself its own punishment in the shape of a shrewish wife ; and the Prodigal returns repentant to his father. The play straightforwardly teaches its homely lesson, and the characters (including, besides father and son and the young woman, a priest, and as comic personages, a Man Cooke and a Woman Cooke) are distinctly drawn. But the whole manner of the play bespeaks the style of dramatic composition to which the age of its production was accustomed.

There can be no doubt that so soon as the *Interludes* of John Heywood, and compositions more or less resembling these in kind, had established themselves in popular favour as an accepted dramatic species, the required transition from the moralities to comedy had, to all intents and purposes, been effected. There can be no mistake whatever as to the facility with which the Interlude might have been expanded so as to fill the larger mould of comedy; indeed, as will be seen, the second in date of our extant English comedies[2] differs from such a piece as *The Four P's* merely by its larger number of characters and by its rather nearer approach to the *minimum* in the matter of plot. In the

[1] Edited by Halliwell for the Percy Society (*Publications*, vol. xxii). This play appears to be alluded to in Will Summer's sarcastic remarks on ' the prodigal child in his doublet and hose all greasy,' in *Summer's Last Will and Testament*.

[2] See below as to *Gammer Gurton's Needle*.

meantime, however, a direct influence from the outside had actually ripened the earliest fruit on the tree. As a matter of fact, not only was the progress of English comedy from the first materially facilitated by examples from other modern literatures which the Renascence movement had already stimulated to efforts in this branch of literature, but its own actual beginning was due to the promptings of that movement. Yet, while so much is admitted as indisputable, it would be an error to ignore either the co-operation of a free creative spirit, due to the consciousness of the national literary developement which I have attempted to trace, or the circumstance that the classical examples on which the earliest English comedy, and not a few of its successors, were immediately modelled, themselves attested the informing power of a similar influence.

Plautus and Terence, with whom, like the Italian before them, our English comic dramatists were brought into direct contact by the current of the Renascence, belonged to a very different period of Roman literary and social life from that in which Seneca, the direct exemplar of modern tragedy, had his being [1].   It is true that, like Seneca, these writers were almost entirely indebted to Greek originals for their subjects, which they borrowed all but exclusively from the masters of the so-called New Comedy—Menander and Philemon in particular—either adapting single plays, or ' contaminating,' i. e. blending into one, parts or portions of single plays.   But, in the first place, the Roman *comoedia palliata* was, properly speaking, not a literary imitation, but the Greek comic stage bodily transferred to Rome, at a time when its productions were still gratifying Greek audiences as a living and continuous growth [2].   And, again, Plautus at least was so genuine a Roman that his plays without effort

Plautus and Terence as models of Renascence comedy ;

---

[1] *Ante*, p. 190.

[2] See K. O. Müller, *History of the Literature of Ancient Greece* (English Translation), ii. 63. Although Menander died as early as 291 B. C., and Philemon (who had been his contemporary) in 262, yet they were followed by a younger Philemon and other comic poets, whose plays, inferior examples of the same school, amused the Greek public by the side of their own. The dates of the lives of Plautus and Terence are 254-185, and 193-160 B. C. respectively.

adapted themselves to the atmosphere in which they were produced, and in manner and style presented themselves as thoroughly Roman and thoroughly popular. Terence, who was born a few years before the death of Plautus, is, to be sure, as far inferior to his predecessor in comic power as he excelled him in refinement of manner and elegance of form; yet his comedies have only the possible faintest smell of the lamp, while their intrinsic attractiveness has left them in little need of changes of importance at various times and in various literatures to accompany their assumption of the garb of a modern tongue [1]. Without, then, dwelling in this place either on the merits or on the short-comings of these two poets, whose fate (for reasons perhaps of a more or less incidental kind) has certainly not been undue neglect, we may regard them as precursors whom the Italian, and afterwards the English, comic dramatists of the Renascence age might easily follow. Now, the chief merits of these Latin adapters of the New Attic Comedy consisted in a deft construction of plots and in a diction at once terse and sententious. Their range of characters was by no means wide, and in its selection of types illustrated the decay of contemporary Greek civilisation, rather than the still abounding vigour and solid coherence of Roman public and private life [2].

---

[1] The English adaptations of comedies by both these poets are, as is well known, extremely numerous; in the case of Terence this is the less astonishing, when we note the long series of English translations of his plays. (See Halliwell's *Dictionary*, sub voc. *Adelphis* and *Eunuchus*.)

[2] The lines are well known in which M. Manilius (*Astronomica*, v. 467–471) summarised these types, and paid a tribute to their literary creator Menander as an artistic painter of real life:

> '*Ardentes juvenes, raptasque in amore puellas,*
> *Elusosque senes, agilesque per omnia servos;*
> *Queis in cuncta suam produxit saecula vitam*
> *Doctor in urbe suâ linguae sub flore Menander,*
> *Qui vitae ostendit vitam, chartisque sacravit.*'

I venture on a paraphrase of the first two of these lines:

> '*Young men in love the livelong day;*
> *Young girls with whom they run away;*
> *With guardians or parents old,*
> *Of tricks the victims manifold;*
> *And slaves for ever on the wing,*
> *Who deftly manage everything.*'

By the end of the first quarter of the sixteenth century, *in England.* Italian comedy had, as has been already seen, vindicated to itself an independent literary existence of its own, while the English comic drama was still, as it were, striving by its own strength to free itself from the fetters encumbering its growth. Yet just as the literary parentage of our earliest English tragedy is to be sought in the tragic poetry of Seneca, so our earliest extant English comedy is a direct imitation of the *comoedia palliata* of the Romans, without the intervention of any Italian or other modern agency. We have already met, in the case of the interlude *Jack Juggler*, with a plot borrowed from the *Amphitruo* of Plautus[1]. A version of the *Andria*, under the title of *Terens in English*, was printed some time before 1530, which, although not pretending to be anything more than a translation, expressly insists on the expediency of English plays being composed in the English tongue, and moves in this direction by introducing occasional allusions to things of its own day. The authors (for there was more than one) must have been men of taste as well as learning, since their prologue pays a tribute, which recalls that of Bulleyn's celebrated *Dialogue*, to Chaucer and other illustrious English poets[2]. A purely scholastic purpose, as I may take this opportunity of noting, was that of the English version of the Dutch scholar William Fullonius' so-called 'comedy,' *Acolastus*, printed in 1540 by the learned John Palsgrave, who was one of the earliest professors of modern languages in England, and to the excellence of whose training witness was borne by the linguistic accomplishments of his pupil, afterwards Queen Mary. *Acolastus* dramatises the parable of *The Prodigal Son*, but its purpose was more restricted than that of even the ordinary scholastic drama[3]. For the translation was

[1] *Ante*, p. 249. As early as 1520 Henry VIII had provided 'a goodly comedy of Plautus' for the entertainment of certain hostages left in this country for the payment of the indemnity agreed upon as the condition of the restoration of Tournay in the previous year; but inasmuch as these strangers were Frenchmen, the play was doubtless acted in the original. See Collier, i. 89.

[2] *Ib.* ii. 278 *note*.

[3] I remember a version of the same parable on the modern stage in the form of a melodrama, by the late Mr. Edward Fitzball.

arranged 'after such maner as chylderne are taught in the grammar-schole, fyrst, worde for worde, as the Latyne lyeth, and afterwarde, accordynge to the sense and meanyng of the Latin sentences,' and was accompanied by a variety of marginal 'admonitions' concerning grammar, diction, and metre[1]. A very different significance attaches to the play of which I am about to speak, although its author was likewise a schoolmaster, whom internal not less conclusively than external evidence shows to have intended this piece for performance by his pupils.

The first extant English comedy.

Nicholas Udall, the author of *Ralph Roister Doister*, is known to have been head master of Eton School during the years 1534–41. He had been educated at Corpus Christi College, Oxford, where his Lutheran views had for several years delayed his proceeding to the M.A. degree. Already previously to that period, his literary pretensions must have been well known, or he would not have been associated with his Oxford contemporary John Leland in the composition of a pageant designed to celebrate the entry into London, after her marriage, of the new Queen Anne Boleyn[2]. In the following year he published a Latin anthology, which included three comedies of Terence. It would be futile to discuss the scandals connected with his dismissal from Eton, followed by his consignment to the Marshalsea prison. He seems afterwards to have been for a time vicar of Braintree in Essex. His most important literary production, the Translation of Erasmus' *Paraphrase of St. Luke*, was dedicated to Henry VIII's last, and Protestant, Queen ; but in the tripartite *Introduction to the Gospels*, published by him under Edward VI, he found occasion to pay a fervid tribute of praise to the Princess Mary, who had in her turn translated the *Paraphrase of the Gospel of St. John*. Our literary history, as has been already seen in the case of John Heywood, shows how our

Udall's Ralph Roister Doister (1552 or 1553).

---

[1] See the elaborate title of this curious publication in Halliwell's *Dictionary of Old English Plays*. Palsgrave's treatise, *L'Esclaircissement de la langue Française*, was printed by Pynson in 1530 (Warton, iv. 335).

[2] See Collier, ii. 353, for an extract from this pageant, offering to Queen Anne the same hyperbolical tribute as that paid to her daughter Queen Elisabeth at the close of *The Arraignment of Paris*.

Tudor sovereigns at times rewarded attachment to their family without too close a personal enquiry, and Udall seems to have known how to please the whole dynasty in turn. Under Edward VI he was presented to a prebendary's stall at Windsor, and to a rectory (Calbourne) in the Isle of Wight. Under Mary he is officially named as one of the Queen's purveyors of dramatic entertainments, who set forth in her presence both dialogues and interludes; so that the *tragoedia de Papatu*, which Bale in 1548 notes him as having composed, must have been overlooked in consideration of his dramaturgic capabilities, as well as of his scholarly reputation. In 1555, or possibly even a year or two earlier, he was headmaster of Westminster School, and at Westminster he died in 1556. His play called *Ezechias in English*, doubtless founded upon 2 Kings xviii–xx, which was performed before Queen Elisabeth at King's College, Cambridge, on her visit to the University in 1564, was therefore a posthumous work [1].

The supposition, generally entertained, that Udall wrote *Ralph Roister Doister* for performance by the Eton boys during his tenure of the headmastership of this school, would fix the date of our earliest English comedy between the years 1534 and 1541 [2]. This supposition derives colour, not from the accidental fact that the single old copy of the play extant was in 1818 presented to Eton College Library, but from the explicit statement, cited by Warton from the Eton *Consuetudinary* drawn up about the year 1560, that in addition to the best and most suitable plays being publicly acted by the Eton boys in the Christmas holidays, *plays written in English* were occasionally exhibited by them, when any were to be found of sufficient wit and attractiveness [3]. But recent researches have established on

---

[1] As to *Ezechias*, see Collier, i. 183. For the data of Udall's life, see W. D. Cooper's *Introductory Memoir, u. s.*, and cf. Warton, iii. 308 *et al.*, and Professor J. W. Hales, *The Date of the First English Comedy*, in *Englicche Studien* (1893). 'Nicolas Yevedall' was registered as buried in St. Margaret's parish, on December 23, 1556.

[2] It was some time before 1543 that Thomas Tusser, the author of *Five Hundreth Pointes of Good Husbandrie*, was at Eton, and received from Udall the flogging of fifty-three stripes recorded by him in the *Author's Life*. See Warton, iv. 222.　　　　　　　　[3] Warton, iv. 308.

direct evidence of a very striking character the extreme
probability that the play was written in 1552 or 1553, in
which case there is every likelihood that it was composed by
Udall for performance at Westminster School, either during
or just before his tenure of the headmastership there, which
may have commenced as early as the latter of the two
above-mentioned years [1]. And it has at the same time been
shown to be even less open to dispute that the comedy
cannot have been written before 1546, inasmuch as it contains a number of more or less unmistakeable coincidences
with John Heywood's *Proverbs*, which were published in
that year [2]. The result seems to be that the date of our
earliest English comedy falls at least eleven years later
than has hitherto been assumed, and therefore in closer
proximity to those of its next successors.

Ralph Roister Doister [3] is an adaptation of the *Miles
Gloriosus* of Plautus, itself in all probability an adaptation
from Menander, from whose *Colax* Terence, in his *Eunuchus*,
borrowed the figures of Thraso the soldier and Gnatho the
parasite [4]. But although both Plautus and Terence are duly
mentioned in the prologue, the scene of the action is laid
in London, and the characters were doubtless both intended
and represented as types of contemporary manners. Thus,
though both the literary origin of the play, and the 'mirth
with modesty' which it preserves through all its rollicking

---

[1] See Hales, *u. s.* The third edition of the *Rule of Reason*, by Thomas
Wilson, an old pupil of Udall's, published in 1553 (or, though less probably,
in 1554), makes use of Ralph Roister Doister's celebrated mispunctuated
love-letter to Mistress Custance for the purpose of illustrating 'antiquity.'
The first and second editions of the same book (1550–1 and 1552) do not
contain this reference. The obvious conclusion is strengthened by the
possibility of an allusion in the play to another of Wilson's works, the *Art
of Rhetoric*, of which Udall, who contributed commendatory verses to it,
certainly knew in 1553, the year of its publication.

[2] I do not refer to Professor Hales' additional argument from the dates of
the Usury Acts (1546 or 1552), which appears to me less convincing. Taken
as a whole, his demonstration is irresistible.

[3] Printed by F. Marshall, 1821, edited for the (old) Shakespeare Society,
with Introductory Memoir, by W. D. Cooper, 1847; again reprinted in
Arber's *English Reprints*, 1869, and in vol. iv. of Hazlitt's *Dodsley*.

[4] The notion of professional military arrogance is better suited to the
Macedonian period of Greek than to any age of Roman history before the
Civil Wars.

fun, mark it as an example of the scholastic drama, intended for the delectation of a special kind of audience, it is to all intents and purposes a popular play, resting its effects broadly and directly upon its genuine comic qualities.

The names of the *dramatis personae* are onomatopoeic, i. e. they are made to suit the characters, after a fashion of which we have already met with abundant examples. The hero's name, which recurs in a morality of rather later date[1] and elsewhere, signifies swaggerer; and the type[2] became a standing one on the stages of most modern nations. He is a vain-glorious, cowardly blockhead, of whom the *Pyrgopolinices* of the Latin comedy is the precise prototype. Matthew Merygreeke (who opens the play with an account of his skill in the art of living at the expense of somebody else, into which he introduces a whole gallery of alliterative shadows[3]) is the *Artotrogos* or Loafer of Plautus, the standing figure of the parasite in Greek New Comedy and its Latin reproductions. His name was, or became, proverbial for proficiency in the kind of talk which is the stock-in-trade of such hangers-on[4]. Besides these, there are Gawyn Goodluck, Tristram Trusty, Dobinet Doughty, Harpax, Truepenny, Sim Suresby, Dame Christian Custance (Constance), the heroine—too pretty a name for

---

[1] Ulpian Fulwel's *Like will to Like* (1568). Cf. *ante.*

[2] Nares quotes from the *Mirror for Magistrates*:
'In peace, at home they swear, stare, foist, roist, fight and jar.'
Cf. the French *rustre.*

[3] 'My living lieth here and there, of God's grace,
Sometime with this good man, sometime in that place;
Sometime Lewis Loytrer biddeth me come near;
Sometime Watkin Waster maketh us good cheer;
Sometime Davy Diceplayer when he hath well cast
Maketh revel rout, as long as it will last;
Sometime Tom Titivile maketh us a feast;
Sometime with Sir Hugh Pye I am a bidden guest;
Sometime at Nickol Neverthrive's I get a sop;
Sometime I am feasted with Bryan Blinkinsoppe;
Sometime I hang on Hankin Hoddydodie's sleeve,
But this day on Ralph Royster Doyster's, by his leave,' &c.
I have quoted the passage, in order to show once again how near our early comedies are in manner to the later moralities.

[4] Dick Litchfield, the Trinity barber, to whom Nashe dedicates his entertaining tractate, *Haue with you to Saffron Walden*, is there described as 'a rare ingenuous old merry Greeke' (Nashe's *Works*, ed. Grosart, iii. 47).

the swaggering Ralph to hang his erotics on [1]—and the
less attractive trio of Madge Mumblecheek, Tibet Talkapace,
and Annot Alyface.   The dialogue carried on by these
worthies is vigorous in texture and interlarded with an
unconscionable number of strange oaths, but, in accordance
with the author's promise, free from a worse kind of indecency. The lyrics, too, for which this early comedy, as well
as *Gammer Gurton's Needle*, freely found room, thereby
setting an example of some importance to the later drama,
although they cannot lay claim to elegance, are harmless in
tone. The construction of the plot is both ingenious and
clear ; and the device, already noticed, of the letter which,
through the parasite's false interpunctuation, conveys to the
heroine the directly opposite meaning to that which his
master intended it to bear, is amusing enough, even though
the trick may slightly smack of the schoolroom [2]. A bit
of broader fun, and one that doubtless commended itself
highly to the Westminster actors, is the free fight between
the men and the women [3]. At the end, all the characters
unite in a ' tag ' in honour of Queen Elisabeth, not forgetting
to dwell upon her royal task of protecting the Gospel ; this,
however, must in any case have been a later addition.

A comparison between this comedy, written by a schoolmaster for schoolboys, and its first known successor, will
show that, like *Gorboduc*, when compared with *Apius and
Virginia* or *Cambises*, *Ralph Roister Doister* has already
with true academical freedom cast off certain of the traditions still slavishly obeyed by the writers of plays designed
to win the favour of an ordinary audience. This implies
a testimony to the liberating spirit of the Renascence, in

[1] ' Christian Custance have I found ;
    Christian Custance have I found ;
    A widow with a thousand pound !
    I maun be married a Sunday.'

[2] The same humourous notion constitutes the fun of the Prologue to
the Tradesmen's Play in *A Midsummer Night's Dream*, the speaker of which
does not 'stand upon points, rides his prologue like a rough colt, and minds
not the stops,' thereby effectually mangling the meaning of his text, ' nothing
impaired, but all disordered.'

[3] Rapp (*Englisches Theater*, p. 126) has pointed out the resemblance of
this episode to an infinitely funny (and also infinitely coarse) passage in
Aristophanes' *Lysistrata*.

a quarter where at first sight the operation of its influence might have not been expected to go beyond the mere imitation of ancient models.   In literary as in historical movements, the school or the academy not unfrequently anticipates the market-place; their habitual failing lies in too close an adherence to their own first estimate of the required measure of reform, in their unresponsiveness, in other words to the ever-fresh demands of life.

Misogonus, which a singularly convincing piece of internal evidence proves to have been written as early as 1560 [1], although the date of the MS. in which it is preserved to us falls as late as 1577, may, in the opinion of a high authority [2], claim to rank as our earliest English comedy.   It must, however, be later in date of composition than *Ralph Roister Doister*, even on the hypothesis adopted above; while (which is of more real importance) it contains a more considerable admixture of the manner of the moralities, so far as can be judged from the copious extracts of the play printed by Collier [3].   Rather pedantically introduced by a prologue spoken by an actor in the character of Homer, the action of the play is simple, and the versification ordinarily in long four-line stanzas.   Among the characters, which bear Greek or Latin names indicative of their qualities, the most notable is the Vice of the play, who describes himself in a long speech, in Skeltonical verse, as a domestic fool out of place:

Misogonus (1560).

> 'Small wages I will aske;
> A cap only once bith' yeare,
> And some prety cullerd geare,
> And drink whense'er I wull,
> And eat my belly full.'

His ordinary name is *Cacurgus*, but in allusion to King Henry VIII's jester he is by himself and others frequently called 'Will Summer [4].'   While there seems no reason for

---

[1] A reference to the 'rising rection i' the north,' as having occurred twenty-four years before the date of the play.   The allusion must be to the Pilgrimage of Grace (1536).

[2] Fleay, *History of the Stage*, i. 58.   [3] ii. 369 *seqq.*

[4] 'Ha, ha! now will I goe playe Will Sommer agayne,
And seme as verie a gose as I was before.'

assigning the authorship of this play to one Thomas Rychardes, who wrote the prologue, I cannot think that a sufficient case is made out by Mr. Fleay for assigning it to Richard Edwardes, or for supposing that a polemical intention connects *Misogonus* with the play designated as the first English comedy[1]. For the rest, inasmuch as the scene of *Misogonus* is laid in Italy, and the name of Laurentius Bariωna [*sic*] is mentioned on the title-page, this piece may be based on some Italian work or drama. It is, however, written in a bitterly anti-Papal spirit.

Still's (?)
Gammer
Gurton's
Needle
(*pr.* 1575).

Gammer Gurton's Needle[2], long regarded as the earliest of all English comedies, was printed in 1575, with a statement that it had been acted 'not long ago in Christ's College, Cambridge.' Its authorship is attributed, on evidence which cannot be deemed quite conclusive, to Dr. John Still, a scholar and ecclesiastic of some distinction[3]. He was in turn Lady Margaret Professor of Divinity (succeeding Cartwright, to whose tenets his own were directly opposed), and Master of St. John's and Trinity Colleges, Cambridge, and died as Bishop of Bath and Wells in 1607. A rare charm appears to have attached to his personality, as one combining moral force with intellectual culture[4]. He was in any case a remarkable man, belonging to a phase of the English Reformation and Renascence distinct from Udall's, with whose name his own is brought into so close a contact in the history of our drama. The

---

[1] Cf. *ante*, p. 211, *note* 2.

[2] Printed in Dodsley's *Old Plays*, vol. ii., and in vol. iv. of Hazlitt's *Dodsley*.

[3] See Fleay, *English Drama*, ii. 253, 254, as to the doubtfulness of the claim. From a passage in *Martin Marprelate's Epistle* (1588), it would appear that Dr. Bridges, Dean of Salisbury, the author of *The Defence of Church Government*, attacked in that celebrated libel, had been supposed to be the author of this play. But M. M. holds that the internal evidence of 'some witte and invention' in it disproves the supposition. See *Epistle*, p. 13 (*Puritan Tracts* edition, 1843) ; and cf. an allusion in the *Epitome*, p. 55.

[4] Of ' Divine Still ' there is a sympathetic biographical sketch in *A Brief View of the State of the Church of England*, by Sir John Harington, whom Still examined for his B.A. degree. See *Nugae Antiquae*, ed. Park, ii. 157 *seqq*. Cf. as to the facts of his career, Mullinger, *History of the University of Cambridge*, ii. 264-267.

performance of Latin plays, both tragedies and comedies, had become frequent in the English Universities by the time of the production of *Gammer Gurton's Needle* in a Cambridge college hall; and it is curious, though not in any way contradictory to the supposition of authorship of an English academical play seventeen years before, that during Dr. Still's Vice-Chancellorship in 1592, he headed a supplication to the Queen, requesting that a Christmas play ordered by Her Majesty from Cambridge, in consequence of the Plague having rendered impossible a performance by her own actors, should be in Latin, as 'more beseeming the students,' there being, moreover, no English plays at hand [1].

The chief difference between *Ralph Roister Doister* and *Gammer Gurton's Needle*, which undoubtedly marks an advance on the part of the latter play, lies in the fact that its plot is so far as we know of original invention. It is, to be sure, not only slighter than that of the adapted comedy, but on the whole childish in its general texture. At the same time the central notion of basing the action on the fortunes of an inanimate piece of goods is felicitous in conception, and not without noteworthy analogues in later dramatic literature [2]. In other respects *Gammer Gurton's Needle* compares by no means favourably with its predecessor. Its plot is slighter, and its language coarser, than those of the earlier play. All the characters, gaffer and gammer, priest and justice, talk in the same unelevated strain. The parson is particularly wanting in refinement, and is treated with the most undisguised contempt both by characters and by author. Diccon (*i. e.* Richard) is the evil genius of the action, whose machinations create every

---

[1] Collier, i. 284. The excuse appears to have been ungraciously received, and a *posse* (or *non-posse*) of Cambridge students was ordered to Oxford, to witness the superior facilities of the sister university.

[2] Two occur to me in German: the charming rustic comedy of *Der zerbrochene Krug*, by that true dramatic genius, Heinrich von Kleist, and Platen's Aristophanic burlesque on the Destiny-tragedies, *Die verhängnissvolle Gabel.* V. Sardou's capital comedy, so well known to English audiences through its adaptation, *A Scrap of Paper*, partakes of the same character; to the Chinese judicial dramas of the type of *The Speaking Platter* (Klein, iii. 478, 479) it may be well to refer with more diffidence.

successive complication, but who in the end is subjected to a merely mock penalty. He is of course merely the Vice of the old moralities slightly modified. The diction, which is held to be in the Midland dialect, seems more antiquated than that of *Ralph Roister Doister*. The touches of humour are only occasional [1], and it has been not unjustly remarked, that the song in praise of ale, which is still occasionally heard in convivial spheres ('Back and syde go bare, go bare,' &c.), is the best thing in the play. It is, however, merely an adaptation of an older original [2].

The scene of *Misogonus*, as we saw, was laid in Italy, and there are other indications that the story of this play was of Italian derivation. That the English comic stage was beginning, like the tragic, to turn its attention in this direction, is however proved with certainty by George Gascoigne's *Supposes* [3] (acted at Gray's Inn in the same year as his *Iocasta*, 1566). This comedy is a translation of *I Suppositi* of Ariosto, acted in 1519 [4]. The literary genius of the author of the *Steele-glasse*, one of our most effective didactic satires, was well employed in reproducing, in flowing and facile English prose, the liquid iambics, with a dactyl at the end of the line, of his Italian original. Gascoigne's cleverness as a translator is manifest already from the Prologue or Argument, which plays with graceful lightness on the title of the comedy [5]. Its fable is a very

Gascoigne's Supposes (acted 1566).

---

[1] *E. g.* in Hodge's account to the vicar of the grievance of the lost needle, where, after the manner of the uneducated of all times, he cannot bring out a single clause without the support of an expletive :

> 'My Gammer Gurton here, see now,
> Sat her down at the door, see now,
> And as she began to slisher, see now,
> Her needle fell on the floor, see now,
> And while her staff she took, see now,
> At Tyb her cat to fling, see now,
> Her needle was lost in the floor, see now,
> Is not this a wondrous thing, see now.'

[2] See Warton, iv. 159.

[3] Printed in Hawkins's *Origin of the English Drama*, vol. iii.

[4] For a notice of the performance of *I Suppositi* at Rome, see Gregorovius, *Geschichte der Stadt Rom im Mittelalter*, viii. 350.

[5] 'I suppose you are assembled here, supposing to reap the fruit of my travails ; and, to be plain, I mean presently to present you with a comedy,

ingenious combination of Terence and Plautus, and suggested to Shakspere part of the plot of his *Taming of the Shrew*, as well as (possibly) the name Petruchio.

Italian plays and novels were now largely resorted to by the writers of English comedies ; in his *School of Abuse* Gosson mentions *Captain Mario* as a ' cast of Italian devises'; and in the list of plays acted at Court from 1568 to 1580 we recognise the influence of Italian reading. Native subjects were however also treated—the *History of the Collier* is of course a dramatic representation of the famous Croydon worthy[1]; and the hero of *Tooley* (1576) was possibly the player of that name. At the same time English writers continued to resort directly to Classical sources. A *Historie of Error*, which may have been the foundation of Shakspere's *Comedy of Errors*, was acted at Court in 1577, and was possibly, like the Shaksperean piece, founded on that Plautine comedy, the *Menaechmi*, which has produced so endless a crop of imitations[2]. In 1595 was printed the *Menaechmi taken out of Plautus*, by 'W. W.' (at one time supposed to have been William Warner), who states that it was by him ' chosen purposely from out the rest, as least harmefull, and yet most delightfull'; while in the previous year was printed that old

Other early comedies on Italian, Classical, and native subjects.

called *Supposes*; the very name whereof may, peradventure, drive into every of your heads a sundry suppose, to suppose the meaning of our supposes,' &c. Cf. Klein, iv. 326 *seqq.*, for an analysis of Ariosto's play. As to Gascoigne's strange and by no means wholly reputable personal and literary career, see Fleay, *English Drama*, i. 237 *seqq.*

[1] Possibly this was Ulpian Fulwell's morality. (*Ante*, p. 134.) The extant play of *Grim the Collier of Croydon* is stated to have been printed under the name of *The Devil and his Dame* in 1600, and is assigned by Fleay, *English Drama*, i. 273, to William Haughton. It was probably written at an earlier date, subsequently, however, to the publication of the *Faërie Queen*. See Hazlitt's *Dodsley*, vol. viii.

[2] The *Menaechmi* of Plautus is itself from a Greek original, of which the title was doubtless Δίδυμοι, like that of all Greek comedies turning on the deceptive likeness of twins. Plays of this name by not less than six authors are actually mentioned. The variations of the same idea in both ancient and modern plays are too numerous for mention. See Brix, *Einleitung zu ausgw. Komödien des Plautus*, Bd. iii. He considers that the author of the play imitated by Plautus was not Epicharmus, as used to be supposed, but Posidippus; Teuffel, however (*History of Roman Literature*, Engl. tr., i. 120), holds that this conjecture is likewise extremely doubtful.

Taming of the Shrew, of which the main action was in
some way derived from a novel of Straparola (1550), and
which was, with altered names and scenes (for it plays at
Athens), at a doubtless early period of his career adapted
by Shakspere[1]. The beginnings of romantic comedy were
foreshadowed by such a play as *The Rare Triumphs of
Love and Fortune* (printed in 1589), a court entertainment
presented before Queen Elisabeth, and consisting of a mythological Induction and an action apparently founded on some
Italian tale; but to this play I shall immediately have
special occasion for returning. A mere reference to these
examples of the variously derived themes of our early
English comedies must suffice for our present purpose.

Thus easy and natural had, with the animating aid of
Classical and Italian models, proved the transition from the
moralities to comedy in England. Flexible by its nature,
this branch of dramatic literature sprang into vigorous and
varied activity almost immediately after it had been called
into being; and in reviewing its further progress we shall
find one of our chief difficulties in having to select out of
a superabundance of productivity those authors and works
that possess a distinctive significance.

*Summary
of the
beginnings
of English
Tragedy*

Henceforth then, in treating of the progress of our
dramatic literature, I shall endeavour to confine my remarks
to works of literary mark or special historical interest. In
the present chapter I have sought to trace the beginnings of
the regular English drama in its two species through their
connexion with earlier forms of native dramatic composition, and with Classical and Italian models. TRAGEDY
was derived from the mysteries and moralities through the
transitional phase of the chronicle histories, with the immediate aid of the examples of Seneca, and secondarily of
his Italian imitators. Italian romance, but not this exclusively, suggested a wider variety of subjects, of a cast
dealing by preference with horrible and exciting events.
These subjects were partly historical and political, partly

---

[1] Both these old comedies are printed in vol. i. of the *Six Old Plays*
published by J. Nichols in 1779. See below as to the sources of the
Shaksperean plays.

domestic; and both kinds were seized upon by our early tragic dramatists. But our national history likewise continued to furnish subjects; and the *Chronicle History* remained a favourite species of dramatic composition. COMEDY sprang more easily from the moralities through *and Comedy.* the transitional phase of the interludes, by the direct impulse of the examples of Plautus and Terence, and secondarily of the Italian comic dramatists. The association of marked characters, often of a typical kind, with complicated and interesting plots, which these dramatists loved, pointed in the direction of comedies of incident as well as of comedies of character. The mixture of tragic with comic motives produced *Tragicomedy*; of which the Spanish as well as the Italian theatre furnished some contemporary examples; and the precedent of the Italian pastoral drama encouraged the introduction of figures and stories from Classical mythology. The vivacities of the *commedia dell' arte* and of the *masked comedy* suggested to our English writers many hints; but it was in the literature of *regular* Italian comedy that they continued to find the most numerous examples for direct imitation.

Under these more immediate influences opened, in the *The period* third decade of Elisabeth's reign, the great age of English *opening the great age* dramatic literature. The period was in almost every *of our* respect a momentous epoch in the history of the nation. *dramatic literature* The die had been cast in the great struggle between Spain *under its* and Rome on the one side and the Protestant North on the *general historical* other. England had assumed her position in the van, and *aspect.* the hesitating hands of Elisabeth had at last thrown away the scabbard. Her people felt more distinctly than herself the necessity for a full and sustained effort; and fortune crowned the national hopes by the dissipation of the Spanish Armada, by the gradually established success (to which England's direct aid had contributed little or nothing) of the revolt of the Netherlands, and by the overthrow of the cause of the Catholic League, and of the ascendancy of the Spanish party, in France.

It was in the period of Elisabeth's reign which may be *Our litera-* considered to date from the execution of Mary Queen of *ture be-comes thoroughly national.* Scots (1587) and the destruction of the Spanish Armada (1588), that Elisabethan literature accomplished its great works, and testified to the greatness of the age which produced it. Still subject to the influence of the Classical Renascence, and pursuing with increasing rather than abated ardour the study of foreign, especially Italian, models, our literature became thoroughly national as it became really great. Spenser is at once one of the most scholarly and one of the most English of our poets [1]. Neither the pedantic influence of such a friend as Gabriel Harvey, nor the antiquated tastes of such a patroness as Queen Elisabeth, could prevent his mighty muse from identifying herself with the genius of an aspiring nation.

In every direction literature was contending for the smiles of royal favour which typified the acquisition of national popularity. The seminaries of learning and the homes of law were full of literary adventurers, the success of whose efforts made them national poets, just as the achievements of the sea-rovers of Devon made them national heroes. Often, as in the case of Ralegh, the double venture was made by the same person. And the born favourites of fortune were as eager in the strife as those whose ambition prompted them to become the authors of their own greatness. The tears of the Muses bedewed the laurels which Sidney had gained by a hero's death.

The dignity of the drama begins to be recognised. At such a time genius, if it turned its creative powers in the direction of the stage, could hardly fail to make that vehicle serve the highest purposes which it is capable of fulfilling. Hitherto, dramatic entertainments had been mainly regarded as the toys of an hour, suited to beguile the everlasting tedium of fashionable amusements, or to

---

[1] The union of these characteristics is already perceptible in the *Shepheard's Calender,* with the publication of which in 1579 the great Elisabethan age of our literature may be fairly said to begin. Ten years later Spenser presented to the Queen the first three books of his master-piece, a poem equally national in spirit and in colouring. Coleridge has admirably illustrated this latter characteristic. Sidney's *Arcadia* was written in 1580-1; Warner's *Albion's England* was published in 1586; Daniel began his original literary career in 1592; Drayton in 1591; Davies in 1596. With the above dates coincide those of the earliest of Ralegh's literary labours, and that of Hooker's great work, the noblest monument of Elisabethan prose.

stimulate the passing curiosity of the multitude. The dramatic performances at Court, and more especially during the progresses of the Queen, in the houses of the nobility, were mere appendages of other entertainments; the London playhouses were the resort of idlers, and in general of the least sober-minded elements of the population. The civic authorities looked with dislike upon the drama; a grave clergyman, such as Northbrooke, condemned it together with dicing, dancing, and 'other idle pastimes'; a repentant play-writer, such as Gosson, hurled against it all the epithets of righteous abuse.

Yet it was inevitable that, as the royal sanction continued to favour the production of dramatic entertainments—and Elisabeth's love of stage-plays was, like that of all born 'patrons of the drama,' in a word insatiable—and as the establishment of permanent theatres encouraged the growth of experience in their public, a connexion should establish itself between the drama and the highest aims of contemporary literature. The fact that the study of Classical and Italian dramatists had induced writers so talented as were Sackville and Gascoigne to compose English plays, was in itself full of promise for the growth of a dramatic literature which should be entitled to take an equal place by the side of the branches of literary composition holding an acknowledged place in the national literature. Those reflecting minds which were beginning to survey critically, by means more especially of systematic comparison, the entire field of poetic literature, whether as cultivated at large in the past, or at home in more recent times, were not blind to the claims of its dramatic branch. Sir Philip Sidney, in his *Apology for Poetry* (written about 1583), upholds the cause of Comedy and Tragedy, together with that of other species of poetry. He allows that 'naughty play-makers and stage-keepers' have 'justly made odious' the Comic; but, taking his examples from the Latin drama, he insists upon the irresistible force of the comic poet's art. Still less will he consent to a depreciation of Tragedy, for 'it were too absurd to cast out so excellent a representation of whatsoever is most worthy to be learned [1].' George Puttenham, in his *Arte of English Poesie* (written about 1585, published in 1589), not only discusses the objects of Comedy and Tragedy at length, but in his enumeration of those ' who in any age have bene the most commended writers in our English tongue,' gives it as his 'censure' that 'for Tragedie, the Lord of Buckhurst, and Maister *Edward Ferrys* for such doings as' he has 'sene of theirs do deserue the hyest price : Th' Earle of Oxford and Maister *Edwardes* of her Maiesties Chappell for Comedy and Enterlude [2].' William Webbe, in a work of a rather earlier date (*A Discourse of English Poesie*, 1584), confesses that ' the profitte or discommoditie which aryseth by the vse of tragedies and comedies, hath beene long in controuersie, and is sore vrged among vs at these dayes [3],' but himself discusses the drama at length as an advocate of its claims.

That the stage should soon throw itself with eagerness into the political and religious agitations of the times, was unavoidable; and in the earliest day of its flower we shall find it at once the instrument and the subject of ardent and bitter controversy. But it was not herein or hereby that *Literary genius devotes itself to the drama.* lay its path to greatness. The one thing needed was that literary genius should apply itself to this form of literary composition. Every stimulus and theoretical as well as practical encouragement combined to bring about this result. The great opportunity was therefore consciously seized ; and it is no mere phrase to say, that in seizing it our first great Elisabethan dramatists addressed themselves to a national task, as men understanding their age, its signs, and its needs.

Had it been otherwise, had the creative activity of Elisabethan genius failed to find in dramatic composition its

---

[1] Sir P. Sidney's *Works* (1724), vol. iii. pp. 25–27. Some reference will be made below to Sidney's own high-spirited masque, *The Lady of May*, presented before Queen Elisabeth in 1578.

[2] Bk. I, chaps. xiv. and xxxi.

[3] P. 30 in vol. ii. of Haslewood's *Ancient Critical Essays upon English Poets and Poësy*, in which collection Puttenham's treatise is also printed. The quotations made above refer solely to works written before plays of high literary merit had been produced.

most attractive and its most appropriate sphere, our literature would have been shorn of its most splendid and its
most peculiar growth. At the same time, the incomparable
resources of our language would never have had to meet
so exacting, because so varied, a series of demands.
Lastly, our national history and national life would have
missed their most faithful, most complete, and most effective
interpretation. Both in the judgment and in the sentiment
of subsequent generations the great Elisabethan age would
have remained, so to speak, isolated from its predecessors
and its successors, had not its dramatic literature, with
a vividness beyond the reach of any other literary form,
held up to itself the mirror of the past, and transmitted
its own picture of itself to posterity.

What, then, the genius of the Elisabethan age accomplished in dramatic literature, before the consummation of
its glories was achieved in the works of its master-mind,
I shall seek to indicate in my Third Chapter.

CHAPTER III.

SHAKSPERE'S PREDECESSORS.

John Lyly (1554–1606).

IN the group of dramatists of whom I propose to treat under the title of ' Shakspere's Predecessors,' the first place in order of chronology belongs to JOHN LYLY[1]. The relation in time between the dates of his life and Shakspere's illustrates the inaccuracy, in one sense, of the title in question ; on the other hand, the nature of the work of no other dramatist more strikingly justifies the aptness, in a wider sense, of the present application of the term. Although he was connected personally with at least one of the dramatists to be subsequently noticed in this chapter, and exercised a marked influence upon the literary growth of all these predecessors of Shakspere, as well as on that of

[1] *The Dramatic Works of John Lilly. With notes and some account of his Life and Writings.* By F. W. Fairholt. 2 vols. 1858. This edition includes, besides the plays printed in the first collected edition of Lyly's dramatic works, the *Sixe Court Comedies*, published by Edward Blount in 1632, *The Woman in the Moone*, and *Love's Metamorphosis.*—See also Collier's chapter, iii. 1 *seqq.*, On John Lyly and his Works, and Fleay, *English Drama*, ii. 36 *seqq.*, and cf. J. A. Symonds' *Shakspere's Predecessors*, chap. xiii, and, as to the stylistic qualities of Lyly's comedies, the two essays by C. C. Hense on John Lilly and Shakespeare in the *Jahrbuch der deutschen Shakespeare-Gesellschaft*, vols. vii. and viii. (1872 and 1873), and the very careful treatise, *John Lyly and Euphuism*, by Clarence Griffin Child, *Münchener Beiträge*, &c., Erlangen and Leipzig, 1894. References to Lyly's plays will of course be found in most of the other literature concerning Euphuism, and in the articles on him by Mrs. Humphry Ward in vol. xv. of the ninth edition of the *Encyclopaedia Britannica*, and by Mr. Sidney Lee in vol. xxxiv of the *Dictionary of National Biography.* The most recent essay on Lyly, in the *Quarterly Review*, No. 365, January 1896, devotes special attention to his plays.—The *Biographical Introduction* in Mr. G. P. Baker's edition of *Endymion* (New York, 1894) contains much that is of value concerning Lyly's dramatic works at large and their connexion with his literary labours in general and with his personal career.

Shakspere himself, yet Lyly occupies in the history of our literature a position apart from the rest of our dramatists, and is more easily at all events than any of his contemporaries in this branch of composition distinguishable by characteristics of his own.

John Lyly (whose name it seems preferable to write as *His life.* he seems to have written it himself) was born in the Weald of Kent [1] in the year 1553 or 1554, of well-to-do parents. He passed, not without interruptions, through an undergraduate course at Magdalen College, Oxford [2], but having in vain sought to obtain a Fellowship there by asking for letters of commendation from Lord Burghley [3], he seems to have continued his studies at Cambridge, and at all events ultimately, like his follower Robert Greene, became *utriusque Academiae in Artibus magister.* Some time before 1578 he went up to London to try his fortune at Court, where he seems in some fashion to have entered the Queen's service in connexion with the Revels, and where he was patronised by Burghley's son-in-law, the Earl of Oxford. His literary reputation was established with extraordinary

---

[1] This and other biographical data are derived from the tale of Fidus in *Euphues and his England.* Elsewhere in the same work the Kentish men are described as 'most civilest,' and the whole county as differing ' not greatly from the maner of France.'

[2] 'Which house,' says Anthony à Wood, as if inspired by his subject, 'was seldom or never without a Lilye (understand me, not that it bears three lilyes for its arms) from the first foundation thereof to the latter end of Queen Elizabeth.'— From a passage in the address *To my verie good friends the Gentlemen Schollers of Oxford* prefixed to *Euphues* it has been concluded that Lyly was rusticated for three years soon after entering into residence at Magdalen. If this were so, how could he, having entered in 1569, have taken his B.A. degree in April 1573 ? Possibly, in accordance with the suggestion of Mr. Baker (*Introduction,* p. xli), the plague of 1571, which relegated both tutors and scholars from Oxford into the country, may have something to do with the matter.

[3] In Lyly's letter to the Lord Treasurer, which is printed by Fairholt in his *Introduction,* pp. xii–xiv, the petitioner prays, ' *ut tua celsitudo dignetur serenissimae regiae majestati literas (ut minus latine dicam) mandatorias extorquere, ut ad Magdalenses deferantur quo in eorum societatem te duce possim obrepere.*' Burghley, who had evidently shown some previous kindness to Lyly, seems to have taken notice of him at a subsequent date, and to have given him some employment ; but the Fellows of Magdalen either were not approached, or proved as inflexible as they did on a later occasion, more famous in English history.

rapidity by the work which he published in the winter
1578-9, the famous *Euphues, the Anatomy of Wit.* Its
continuation, *Euphues and his England,* in which academical
satire is superseded by courtly flattery, followed in 1580.
Not less than five editions of the original *Euphues* were
printed during the seven years ensuing upon its issue ; but
neither the popularity so speedily achieved by Lyly among
a public which had its centre in the Court, nor the series
of comedies produced by him for its delectation from about
the time of the publication of *Euphues* onwards, obtained
for him the office—the Mastership of the Revels—on which,
sooner or later, his heart had become set. It is conceivable
that, as has been conjectured by the latest editor of his
comedy of *Endimion,* that by identifying himself in that
play with Leicester's interest, he had as early as 1580
become attached to the service of the Queen, in which
capacity he presents himself in a petition to her probably
belonging to the year 1585. Both this letter, and another
to the same address written in 1588, testify to his disap-
pointment in missing the desired meed of his multifarious
labours. As vice-master of the St. Paul's and Savoy companies of children players, he toiled both in the teaching of
histrionics, and possibly in the minor duties of custodian
of properties and censor of copy; while all the time he was
undergoing that experience of Court-service and Court-
suitorship to the tediousness of which the parsimony of the
Virgin Queen imparted so exceptionally bitter a flavour.
It may very conceivably have been a delight to him to
take part in the *Marprelate* controversy, to which further
reference will be made below, and in which, apart from its
general bearings upon the relations between the stage and
its adversaries, his personal quarrel with his former friend
Gabriel Harvey must have made him eager to break a lance.
He was, it can hardly be doubted [1], the author, possibly in
conjunction with Thomas Nashe, of the anonymous pamphlet
Pappe with a Hatchet, alias this and that, directed against
Harvey (probably in 1589), who had offended Lyly's patron
the Earl of Oxford, and who may have been in some way

[1] See Baker, *u. s.,* pp. cxxxvii *seqq.*

connected with his dismissal from that nobleman's service
or favour[1]. Harvey's reply was in its turn answered by
Nashe[2], who took the opportunity of paying a high compliment to his friend Lyly's literary ability (and incidentally
to his power of taking tobacco), and who promised a retaliation from his pen. This, however, was so far as is
known never attempted. In 1589 Lyly became a member
of Parliament, where he represented three different con-
stituencies in succession[3]; but notwithstanding these services
and his literary reputation, to which his contemporaries
whether friendly or adverse to it abundantly testify[4], he
obtained no satisfactory mark of the royal favour, and the
Mastership of the Revels continued to elude his grasp.
Two doleful letters addressed by him to the Queen, about
1590 and 1593 respectively, remain as records of his heart-
sickness at hopes deferred ; in the second of these he begs
permission to dedicate to Her Majesty *Lillie de Tristibus*,
and adds a petition that if born to have nothing, he might
have a protection to pay nothing, ' which suite is like his,
that having followed the Court ten years for recompence
of his seruis committed a Robberie and tooke it out in
a pardon.' The statement of Edward Blount, the publisher
of the first collected edition of his plays, that some kind of
reward was granted to him by the Queen, has been thought
to account for his having settled in his later years in the
parish of St. Bartholomew the Less, where three children

---

[1] See Introduction to *Plaine Percevall*, p. x, *Puritan Discipline Tracts*, 1860.
The tract forms part of this collection. The meaning of its title (a proverbial expression signifying, in Fairholt's words, ' the roughest mode of
doing a necessary service ') is well illustrated by a passage in Lyly's comedy
Mother Bombie, act i. sc. 3.—His authorship of *An Almonde for a Parrott*
appears to be more than doubtful.

[2] In the tract *Have with you to Saffron Walden*.

[3] Viz. Hindon (in Wiltshire), Aylesbury, Appleby, and again Aylesbury.
The identification of the dramatist with the John Lyly who represented
these places is, of course, not a matter of absolute certainty.

[4] Among his encomiasts are William Webbe, in his *Discourse of English
Poetrie* (1586), and Francis Meres, in his *Wit's Treasury* (1598). According
to Harvey, in his *Pierce's Supererogation* (1593), ' Euphues similes ' were,
among other literary favourites of the day, ' too well known to go unknown.'
The most charming tribute came in the next generation from Ben Jonson:
		' And tell, how far thou didst our Lilly outshine.'
For a complete *catena*, see C. G. Child, pp. 6–9.

were born to him [1]; but he had his erratic holidays [2], and is said to have hovered about the Court even in the decline of his days, although the tradition that Shakspere portrayed him as a genial old lord admitted by his sovereign to intimate converse and comment, strikes me as intrinsically absurd [3]. He died, according to the evidence of the register of St. Bartholomew the Less, in November, 1606.

Euphues and Euphuism.

Euphues—to speak of the two books which included that name in their titles as of a single work. although in matter and treatment each has a character of its own—was the delight of its own age, and suggested the designation of a distinct style or manner in English prose composition. Even more largely and enduringly than is the usual fate of specific fashions, whether in letters or other forms of art, *Euphuism* has in turn been extolled, ridiculed, and misinterpreted. It may suit the convenience of literary historians, and of critics in search of names and phrases, to give to such terms applications of unwarranted width, and, for instance, to denounce as Euphuism all the affectations which from the *Petrarchisti* downwards to certain mannerists of our own age have emphasised literary pretentiousness or self-conceit. But all such phraseology is wide of the mark where historical accuracy of nomenclature is held of value. Euphuism, from this point of view, can only mean the style of *Euphues* and of other works by the same author in so far as in them also its essential characteristics are traceable [4].

---

[1] If their parentage be rightly identified. See Fleay, ii. 38–9; Baker, *u.s.*, p. clxxiv. The entries were discovered by the late Mr. Collier.

[2] Bishop Hall, in his narrative of *Some Specialities of his Life,* mentions that after his acceptance of the living of Halstead in Essex, he 'found there a dangerous opposite to the success of his ministry, a witty and bold atheist, one Mr. Lilly, who by reason of his travels and abilities of discourse and behaviour' had hopelessly prejudiced the patron of the living against the incumbent. Ultimately, as he states, 'this malicious man going hastily to London to exasperate my patron against me, was then and there swept away by the pestilence, and never returned to do any farther mischief.' See *Satires by Joseph Hall,* Warton and Singer's edition, 1824, pp. xxxvii–viii.

[3] Lord Lafeu in *All's Well that Ends Well* has been supposed to have been intended as a portrait of Lyly.

[4] In the connexion hinted at, and on which it is difficult to forbear the temptation to enlarge, I need only refer to J. A. Symonds' excellent passage on the mannerism, bred in the premature decay of the Renascence movement in Italy, 'which pervaded every country where Italian culture

It cannot, of course, be disputed that Euphuism shares *Euphuism* many of its most salient characteristics with kindred forms *and kindred* of style, both in our own and in other modern literatures. *forms of* And, again, some of these features are most largely notice- *style.* able in fashions of composition belonging to the literary periods immediately preceding or following upon that over which *Euphues* exerted its influence.   No style is made in a day, or (in spite of a famous maxim) altogether by one man.   Moreover, in connexion with the question of this particular literary manner or fashion, we are perhaps apt to overlook the relative tardiness with which the Renascence movement asserted its full effect in our own country.   Thus, while in one sense Euphuism was an aftergrowth drawing its nourishment from mediaeval notions which swathed poetic invention in the bands of allegory and of metaphorical conceits, in another sense it is alive with the instincts of a new era ; it moves freely through the range of thought and fancy opened by the rediscovery of classical antiquity through the now victorious Renascence ; and it attests its indebtedness by means of an imitation, sometimes servile and not always legitimate, of the ancient models.

To have made clear this cohesion between Euphuism and the general movement of modern and more especially of English literature, and to have thus redeemed Lyly from the imputation of having sought notoriety by thrusting more or less arbitrary perversions of his own into the growth of English prose, is perhaps the most striking merit of the late Henry Morley's celebrated essay[1], which vindi- cated to *Euphues* and Euphuism their true importance in the history of our literature.   But I am here concerned, not with a comparison between particular fashions of style and Euphuism, but only with Euphuism itself.   Nothing need therefore be said about Marinism—a later growth in point of time than Euphuism—or of the schools of the

penetrated.'   This accomplished critic, though he ' dwells upon the generic rather than the specific characteristics of this *lues litteraria*,' holds that ' Euphuism may claim to be a separate type.'   (*Shakespere's Predecessors*, 506 *seqq.*)   Nothing more or less is what is contended for in the text.

[1] Published in the *Quarterly Review*, No. CIX, for 1861.

Précieux in France and of the Fantastic Poets in England, upon which it incontestably exerted an influence[1]. On the other hand, Gongorism—a designation which has been applied to the inflated and highly figurative speech introduced at the contemporary Spanish court by Luis de Gongora—has been frequently confounded with Euphuism[2]. Gongora and his style were the models of Don Adriano de Armado in *Love's Labour's Lost*, and to them, not to Lyly and his perfectly clear English, applies Sir Walter Scott's caricature, the pedantic Sir Piercie Shafton in *The Monastery*, who builds up compound verbal phrases quite out of keeping with Lyly's balanced elegance. So, again, the well-known style of Sidney in his *Arcadia* stands virtually apart from Euphuism, of which it manifestly had no intention of reproducing the distinctive characteristics; although the *Arcadia* and *Euphues*, of which the dates of composition all but coincide, may share with one another a tendency to alliteration and to a general elevation of diction[3].

The distinctive characteristics of Euphuism. In any attempt, then, to analyse the principal ingredients in the style of English prose to which Lyly's two novels, and in a minor measure the body of his plays, gave so notable a vogue in letters as well as in fashionable life, care should be taken to distinguish between what was, and what was not, peculiar to itself[4]. Lyly, to begin with, is fond

[1] The date of Marini's *Adone* was 1623. For a specific comparison between Euphuism and Marinism, see Symonds' *Renaissance in Italy*, vol. vii. pp. 302-5.

[2] As to Luis de Gongora and his style, see Ticknor, iii. 21-2. It is described as consisting almost entirely of metaphors, and further signalised by a vocabulary full of new words coined from the classical languages and of old Castilian words with new meanings, as well as by involved and unnatural constructions, foreign to the genius of the language.

[3] It is well pointed out by the writer in the *Quarterly Review* (1896), already cited, that though Master Fastidious Brisk in *Every Man out of his Humour* (see below) may be a satirical sketch of Lyly himself, his use of fine words to lend a dignity to the most simple actions may be abundantly illustrated from the *Arcadia*, but that this habit is not at all a mark of *Euphues*. Cf. Child, p. 112.

[4] The most noteworthy attempts of the kind are the monographs of Dr. R. F. Weymouth in the *Philological Society's Transactions*, 1870-2, and of Dr. F. Landmann (Giessen, 1881, and *New Shakspere Society's Transactions*, 1880-2; see also the Introduction to his edition of *Euphues* and chap. i. of

of classical references and allusions ; he borrowed the felicitous word *Euphues* from Plato, and the whole of an appendix from a treatise by Plutarch [1] ; he conveyed the queer details of his apparatus of ' natural history ' without disguise from Pliny ; and he was in various ways and degrees indebted in style and in matter to Ovid, Virgil and Homer, and to Caesar, Cicero and Seneca. Yet there is no evidence either in his novels or elsewhere to show him to have been either a widely or a deeply read classical scholar, nor can his diction and vocabulary in themselves, and as apart from quotations, be fairly described as impregnated by classicism. A more important effect, because more novel of its kind, might be expected to have been exerted upon his style by confluent impressions derived from other modern literatures with which our own was in more or less active contact. Yet although, as will be seen immediately, Lyly found a model of prose composition in a Spanish writer belonging to an earlier period of the Renascence age, he had too sound and too sincere a literary sense to Hispaniolise, Italianate, or Gallicise his English either in vocabulary or in syntax.

Thus, no *a priori* suppositions will account for the distinctive features of Euphuism. The most important, indeed the cardinal, characteristic among these is the particular use of antithesis. While Euphuism is free from the more violent varieties of the figure, which indeed would have jarred against what may be called the placid force of the author's manner, he is consistently and consciously addicted to the purely formal antithesis which depends on the arrangement of sentences and the selection of words. Thus is brought about that balance between sentence and sentence, clause and clause, vocable and vocable, which is of its nature unique as compared with what had in English prose gone before or what (Lyly's direct imitators apart) came

the *Arcadia*, Heilbronn, 1887), together with those of Mr. C. G. Child and Dr. C. C. Hense, already cited.

[1] The *Euphues and his Ephoebus*, appended to *Euphues, the Anatomy of Wit*, is an almost literal translation of Plutarch's tractate *de Educatione Liberorum*. One of the epistles from Euphues that follow is a translation of the same writer's *de Exilio*.

after it. Antithesis of this sort inevitably calls to its aid alliteration—in which figure he out-Heroded Herod and the other rhetoricians of our early mysteries, moralities, and comedies—assonance, rime, and pun. In all these processes it is purely an effect of sound which the author has at heart, and if I may so say a total rather than a particular effect. This may be illustrated from his use of the last and humblest of those aids which I have just enumerated. Lyly's puns are of the feeblest sort of that frequently feeble sort of wit, precisely because it is the similarity of sound— mere consonance as a rule sufficing—which satisfies his purpose, instead of the surprise evoked by the sudden discovery of a new pair of paronyms in our paronymous tongue.

In making prose the arena of these gymnastics, Lyly indisputably gave a very remarkable impulse to the progress of that branch of English literary composition. On the effect of his endeavours in the special sphere of the drama I will touch immediately ; as to other fields of prose composition, it may be said that the writers of non-dramatic English prose who preceded him were in truth so few, and the productions of his contemporaries and immediate successors comparatively so numerous, and from many points of view so important, that the temptation is strong to exaggerate the results of individual influence. Apart from Roger Ascham, and perhaps a few orators of whom Latimer is one of the few transmitted examples, what effective prose-writers did our Renascence age produce before the author of *Euphues*? We are so generally prone to neglect the essential merits of a literary style while discussing the points in which it strives to differentiate itself, that in the present instance we run the risk of overlooking the chief merits of Lyly's prose while seeking to trace the origin of its mannerisms. Yet his style, so far as I can judge, is remarkably lucid, and free from the fatal defect of involution. Aided by a carefully chosen diction, and a perfectly correct syntax, it has in it nothing that is either ambiguous or obscure—a praise which cannot be given to Lyly's most conspicuous imitators.

There yet remains to notice one special feature of Euphuism, which has not escaped the censure or satire of its critics, from Falstaff downwards[1]. This is the mannerism or trick which, I am still inclined to think, the late Mr. Collier very happily described as 'the employment of a species of fabulous or unnatutal natural philosophy, in which the existence of certain animals, vegetables, and minerals with peculiar properties is presumed, in order to afford similes and illustrations.' No doubt some of these illustrations are of a very homely kind, but this (as in the case of the anecdotes in Oliver Goldsmith's *Animated Nature*) does not prove them to be as correct as they are humble. But the real objection to these instances is not to be found in the violence which they may do to scientific truth, or possibly even to the text of Pliny from which they were borrowed. It really consists in Lyly's taking no trouble to assimilate his facts or fancies concerning birds, fishes and amphibia, trees, shrubs and precious stones to the circumstances under which he applies them,—herein showing himself very unlike Shakspere, who when he either borrowed or unconsciously appropriated certain of these similes, justified as true poetic ornaments what in *Euphues* had been mere formal and fictitious appendages[2].

Although the present is not the place for a full re-statement of results that may now be regarded as definitively ascertained, a word may, finally, seem called for, as to the *Their special sources.*

[1] 'Harry, I do not only marvel, where thou spendest thy time, but also how thou art accompanied; for though the camomile, the more it is trodden on, the faster it grows, yet youth, the more it is wasted, the sooner it wears.' (1 *Henry IV*, ii. 4.) This passage, as has been correctly pointed out, is the only one in which Shakspere makes fun of the Euphuistic style proper. Drayton's well-known commendation (in his poem to his friend H. Reynolds, *Of Poets and Poesie*) of Sidney as the author who
'did first reduce
Our tongue from Lyly's writing then in use,
Talking of stones, stars, plants, of fishes, flies'—
furnishes a further illustration of the fact, insisted upon above, that Euphuism and 'Arcadianism' both are, and were regarded as, styles quite distinct from one another.

[2] See, amidst some doubtful matter, the examples of this in W. L. Rushton, *Shakespeare's Euphuism*, above all the immortal instance of Shakspere's famous adaptation in *As you like It* (ii. 1) of Lyly's *dictum*, 'the foule Toade hath a faire stone in his head.'

sources that suggested to Lyly the peculiarities which, as
elaborated by himself, together constitute the distinctive-
ness of the Euphuistic style. Whence did he borrow or
assimilate the characteristic artificialities of Euphuism?
The answer seems to be that these characteristics are
traceable in their origin to the influence of a particular
Spanish prosaist, and after being transmitted through the
medium of an English translator, and exhibited with more
distinctness in a popular English collection of stories, were
developed with refinements of his own by Lyly himself.
The Spanish prose-writer in question was the Biscayan-born
Don Antonio de Guevara, whom the favour of the Emperor
Charles V transformed from a monk into a courtier, and
who became court preacher, Imperial historiographer, and
bishop of two Spanish sees. He died in 1545, but the
work of which the *alto estilo* or 'grand style' had so
inspiring an effect, was first published in 1529. This was
the *Libro de Marco Aurelio*, a species of *Cyropaedia*, designed
at the same time to exhibit the model of a prince trained
in ideas partly copied from the Emperor's own unpublished
meditations, and to appeal to classical examples raised high
above the associations of degenerate romance[1]. This
essentially didactic work was repeatedly translated and
imitated by English writers during the sixteenth century;
but the version of his *Marco Aurelio*, which appears to have
created by far the most notable impression among English
readers, was that published some time before 1568, under
the title of *The Dial of Princes*, by Sir Thomas North, who
more closely than any of his predecessors imitated the style
of his original. This, however, he did in his own way.
Guevara's style has the balanced effect of Euphuism, but
to his use of consonance and rime towards the attainment
of this effect, North and the other English predecessors of
Lyly added the use of alliteration[2]. Of these the most

---

[1] For an account of Guevara, see Ticknor, ii. 14–18; Warton only mentions
him incidentally. The credit of having first demonstrated his influence upon
Lyly belongs to Dr. Landmann, whose conclusions were summarised by
Mrs. Humphry Ward, an accomplished Spanish scholar, in her article on
Lyly in the last edition of the *Encyclopaedia Britannica*.

[2] Landmann and Child, *u. s.*

notable was George Pettie, author of the *Petite Pallace of
Pettie his Pleasure* (licensed 1576), a collection of tales of
which the first actually came through Guevara from Plutarch.
In general manner of diction, even including the illustrations fetched from accommodating repertories of strange
facts in the natural world, Pettie, so far as I can judge, is
the precise exemplar of *Euphues*. There remain niceties of
stylistic modulation, traceable no doubt in their turn partly
to a reaction of matter upon manner, in which Lyly goes
back most directly upon Guevara, while his indebtedness
to the latter as to the actual contents of the earlier part of
his novel must be regarded as established [1].

It will suffice to add in the present connexion, that *Imitators
of Euphues.* Euphuism did not die out with Lyly, even if viewed as
a combination of stylistic elements dictated by his proper
choice.   He had not only his continuators proper, whose
stock-in-trade was confined to his own suggestions of subject
and tricks of style, but also his imitators of the type of
Robert Greene and Thomas Lodge, who elaborated his
turns of thought and manner for the enjoyment of the
cognoscenti [2].   Shakspere's general indebtedness to Lyly as
a writer of dramatic prose dialogue will be dwelt on below ;
as to the special characteristics of the Euphuistic style,
however, he was alike too catholic in his appreciation and
too eclectic in his appropriation of exotic excellence to
imitate Lyly otherwise than incidentally, or (so to speak)
as it might suit himself.   On the other hand, as has been
already mentioned, Shakspere cannot be shown to have
satirised Euphuism more than once, when he made fun of
it in the way of harmless parody [3].   Towards the close of
the century, and the end of Lyly's own life, we may
conclude the special charms of his style to have begun

---

[1] Landmann, Introduction to *Euphues, u. s.*, xxii. *seqq.*

[2] Of course, as is pointed out in the chapter entitled 'Lyly's Legatees' in
Jusserand's *English Novel in the time of Shakespere* (Miss E. Lee's English
Translation, 1890), none of these authors copied Lyly's 'style in all its
peculiarities, at any rate in all their works.'

[3] The relation of Shakspere to Euphuism seems to me well defined in the
article in the *Quarterly Review* (for January, 1896), already cited, where will
also be found a long list of 'reminiscences' of *Euphues* in Shakspere's plays.

wearing themselves out, as is the doom of everything in literature or art that is lightly rooted in assumption or affectation [1].

Prose domesti- cated in English comedy by Lyly.

In the branch of our national literature with which this book is alone directly concerned, the influence of Lyly, though inseparable from that of the features of his general style on which I have accordingly dwelt at a perhaps disproportionate length [2], possessed intrinsic importance. As a dramatic writer, Lyly exercised an influence upon his contemporaries and successors in this particular field of composition, which is by no means to be summed up by a review of the distinctive characteristics of his prose style as a novelist.   To begin with, his great service to dramatic literature lies in the plain fact that although he was not actually the first English author who wrote plays in prose [3], he was the first to set the example of dramatic prose which was enjoyable and effective.   Plays in prose were no actual innovation on the English stage at the time of the production of Lyly's earliest comedy ; for Gascoigne's *Supposes* was acted in 1566 [3], and the *Famous Victories of Henry V*, which is partly in prose [4], as well as 'two *prose* books' of name unknown, showing 'how seditious estates with their own devices, false friends with their own swords, and rebellious commons with their own snares, are overthrown,' mentioned by Gosson in his *School of Abuse* (1579) among plays acted in London inn-yards [5], probably likewise pre-

---

[1] A sure sign of approaching decay in any kind of *mode* or fashion is the eager adoption of it on a lower rung of, as the case may be, the social or the intellectual scale.   Thus it is a city lady who in Ben Jonson's *Every Man out of his Humour*, v. 7, seeking to form her speech upon the fashions of the Court, apostrophises a supposed representation of those fashions : 'O Master Brisk, as 'tis in *Euphues*, " Hard is the choice, when one is compelled either by silence to die with grief, or by speaking to live with shame." '   I cannot say that I am aware of any conscious allusions to Euphuism or its influence in later Elisabethan literature.

[2] I am free to confess that I have been anxious on a topic of so much general interest, to make use of the comments of critics who have been at the pains of correcting, instead of merely reprehending, misapprehensions in the earlier edition of this work.   I refer especially to the essay of Mr. C. G. Child, to which I am also indebted for valuable suggestions on 'the Euphuism of Lyly's Plays.'

[3] *Ante*, p. 262.   [4] *Ante*, p. 222.   [5] Collier, ii. 329.

ceded Lyly's first dramatic work. But these were merely
incidental productions, and cannot be held to interfere with
his claim to having domesticated prose in English comedy.
Whatever ridicule has in times more or less remote from
his own been poured upon him because of his affectations [1],
has failed to obscure this memorable service to our dramatic
literature ; and when we delight in the flow of wit, the flash
of repartee, and the dialectical brilliancy of some of the
most famous comic scenes in Shakspere, Ben Jonson and
Fletcher, we should not forget that the path trodden by
them had been opened by the writer whom they ' so much
outshone.'

The more general as well as the distinctive characteristics
of Lyly's prose style are reproduced in that of his plays,
but in a form more or less modified by the conditions of
dramatic composition. The plays, acted before fashionable
audiences at a time when classical learning was in fashion,
performed by boys whose scholastic training prepared
them for court service with an interval, in some cases [2], of
a period of University life, and written by an author whose
main object in life was to gain the goodwill of a learned
Queen, of course reflect the classicism which he was
anxious to display. With a single exception (*Mother
Bombie*) the subjects of all his plays are derived from
classical history or legend. The names of their personages,
even where not directly derived from a particular classical
story, recall classical originals and episodes derived immediately from classical sources are repeatedly interwoven
with the main action. The shepherds in *Gallathea* have
Horatian names ; the story of Erisicthon in *Love's
Metamorphosis* is from Ovid ; Sir Tophas in *Endimion* has

*The Eu-
phuism
of Lyly's
plays.*

---

[1] '*Euphues*, Anglus, verbivendulus et caerimoniarum magister,' is a character in *Senile Odium*, a Latin comedy by Peter Hausted, acted at Queen's
College, Cambridge, in 1633. In the life of Lyly, in the *Lives of the Poets*,
compiled (or edited) by Theophilus Cibber in 1753 (i. 122), the writer
acknowledges that he has not read *Euphues*, but quotes the author of *The
British Theatre*, who has, and who describes its style as 'an unnatural
affected jargon.' ' With this nonsense,' he continues, ' the court of Queen
Elizabeth became miserably infected, and [*sic*] greatly help'd to let in all the
vile pedantries of language in the two following reigns.'

[2] Such as that of John Heywood. Cf. *ante*, pp. 238–9.

far more assuredly a prototype in the *Miles Gloriosus*
of Plautus than Falstaff has such in Sir Tophas. But
it is quite needless to multiply examples ; they crowd
every one of Lyly's dramas[1]. Still more obvious is his
fondness for classical allusions, taken from a fair but
not very wide range of reading, and above all for Latin
quotations, which are far more common in the plays than
in *Euphues*[2].

Lyly, whose classical reading was, as has been seen, in
the main confined to a few Latin poets and prose-writers
(although in *Campaspe* he was able to give his audience
a passing taste of Aristotle and Plato), was as a dramatist
specially attracted to Ovid. The reason of this may doubtless be sought in the prevailing taste for allegory, to which
so strong an impulse had been given by the pageants and
masques. Certainly, neither Lyly, nor any of the earlier
writers who contributed to the formation of the Euphuistic
style, invented the fashion of introducing the deities and
other figures of classical mythology as the representatives
of moral qualities, vices and virtues, emotions and affections.
But he carried the tendency to an extreme limit, and was
especially adventurous in introducing in combination with
it a species of allegory which had hitherto hardly ventured
beyond its merest beginnings on the stage[3]. Compliments
to Queen Elisabeth, under the designation of Diana, did not
satisfy his ambition ; he actually apprised his audience that
there was a hidden meaning in the plot of at least one of
his plays, and unless (which in the case in question seems
unlikely) the ingenuity of commentators has laboured in
vain, that meaning was in more than one instance the

---

[1] Cf. Hense, *u. s.*, vii. 241 *seqq.*

[2] See *Campaspe* ; *Sapho and Phao* ; *Mydas* ; *Love's Metamorphosis* ;
apart from the quotations of Sir Tophas in *Endimion*, who when in love
can 'speak nothing but verses' and 'feels all *Ovid de arte amandi* as heavy
at his heart as a load of logges.'

[3] Nothing can exceed the difficulty and delicacy of the task of discerning
without excess of zeal the element of personal, which of course is very often
political, meaning in a literary work. Our first English tragedy is most
assuredly not devoid of political intentions; our first English comedy, as has
been seen, is held by Mr. Fleay to have formed part of a sustained controversy between two rival dramaturgists. Cf. *ante*, p. 260.

reverse of trifling or vague [1]. Lyly's boldness in this respect
remains very striking, although it may be partially accounted
for by the strong current of fashion in favour of allusive-
ness of this sort and by the special charm it seems to have
possessed for the Virgin Queen, and although his imaginative
power as an allegorical poet seems small by the side of
that of his great contemporary Spenser. And while even
in the hands of a master allegory is prone at times to
become frosty, or to wither away into lifelessness, with
Lyly it is often the merest external machinery, which
readily lends itself to use, and when used is with equally
little difficulty cast aside. After all, however, he was in
this respect only a more hardened offender against the
demands of nature and good taste than his most illustrious
non-dramatic competitors in the same direction. If Lyly's
allegories are cold and tame, it would be difficult to
characterise by kindlier epithets the staple of those in
Sidney's *Arcadia*, or even many of those contained in the
later books of the *Faerie Queene*. On the other hand, it
may be doubted whether without the example of Lyly,
Jonson [2], Marston, and others would have attempted the
composition of those allegorical dramas into which, for the
delectation of the initiated, they crowded so much cryptic
sentiment and criticism ; or whether Shakspere himself
would have thought of elaborating in the same fashion one
of the most exquisite poetical passages to be found in any
of his romantic comedies [3].

As to the style of Lyly's comedies, while there can be
no doubt but that it exhibits all the special characteristics
of Euphuism which have been discussed at sufficient
length above, and while in a greater or less degree these
characteristics are to be found in all kinds of scenes and in
the mouths of all kinds of personages, it has been well

---

[1] See the observations below as to *Endimion, Sapho and Phao*, and *Mydas*.
Allegorical allusions of a personal kind are probably intended in one or two
of the remaining plays.

[2] That *Cynthia's Revels* is not a satire on Euphuism, but written in much
the same critical temper as the *Anatomy of Wit* itself, is pointed out in the
article in the *Quarterly Review*, January 1896, already cited.

[3] See below as to the passage in *A Midsummer Night's Dream*, ii. 2.

pointed out that 'the Euphuism of the plays in a word
is simplified Euphuism [1].' This was, of course, a result of
conditions of dramatic composition inevitable at all events
in the case of plays intended for representation on the
stage. The extent of the sentences,—the length, so to speak,
of the swing of the pendulum,—is necessarily contracted, and
the elaboration of the artifices of illustration is more sparing.
But, including the allusions to natural history (though they
are introduced as metaphors, not as similes), these artifices
are all to be found in the dialogue of the plays—naturally
most abundantly in the more sustained and serious passages,
and in purely rhetorical additions such as the Prologues
and Epilogues. The sameness which, though again in
a modified measure, thus attaches to Lyly's dramatic as
well as to his narrative style, is the more marked in consequence of his chief defect as a dramatist—his lack of
a real power of characterisation.

His verse. What has to be noted concerning Lyly's blank verse will
most appropriately be said in connexion with the play professing to have been his earliest,—the only one of the series
which is written in metre. The lyrics interspersed in his
dramas are many in number, probably largely in consequence of the fact that his actors were choir-boys. Few of
them are gems of so pure a water as the famous song from
Campaspe ; but many deserve Mr. Symonds' praise of being
' as neat and delicate as French songs [2].'

A brief survey of Lyly's dramatic works will best
exemplify the foregoing remarks.

The A passage in the Prologue to *The Woman in the Moone*
Woman in seems unmistakeably to ascribe to that play the position of
the Moone
(pr. 1597). the earliest among its author's dramatic productions. The
grave objections to this conclusion would, no doubt, be
obviated could we suppose this passage [3] to mean merely

---

[1] C. G. Child, *u. s.*, 88. I am inclined, however, to demur to Mr. Child's
assertion, safeguarded as it is in a way which renders it difficult to reply by
quotations, that ' low comedy dialogue shows little trace of Euphuism,
though hints and gleams break through it by an unavoidable mannerism.'

[2] *Shakspere's Predecessors*, p. 516. Cf. Baker, *u. s.*, p. clxxxvi.

[3] ' Remember all is but a poet's dreame,
 The first he had in Phoebus' holy bowre,
 But not the last, unlesse the first displease.'

that this was Lyly's 'first verse-play, but not his first play[1].' But there seems no sufficient reason for putting such an interpretation on the words, more especially as it would imply the existence in Lyly's mind of a distinction between the claims of verse and of prose composition which it would be specially unfair to impute to him. The difficulties, at the same time, remain. *The Woman in the Moone* was not entered on the Stationers' Registers till 1595, and does not appear to have been actually published till 1597. Its title seems to suggest a parodistic allusion to that of the same author's *Endimion, or the Man in the Moone,* of which, as will be immediately seen, the date may be almost conclusively assigned to the years 1579–80. The plays are so different in style that the one can be hardly supposed to have immediately followed upon the other ; besides which, the *Man* could in the way of title hardly have been preceded by the *Woman.* Of far more consequence is the cavil, that the blank-verse in which this play is written can hardly date from as early a year as 1579 or 1580, when no blank-verse of Marlowe's or of any similar build was as yet known to English literature. It cannot be denied that the firm but at the same time remarkably elastic texture of the blank-verse in this play, which accommodates itself without manifest effort to the sequence of the diction, is not easily to be reconciled with the assumption of a date before 1587, or a not very much earlier year[2].

As for the diction itself, it is fairly simple and straightforward, with only a few classical quotations and reminiscences of more or less natural history, and here and there a play on words or alliterative antithesis, to remind the reader of the capabilities of the author. The plot of this pastoral comedy is very simple, and its construction the reverse of elaborate. Nature, with the assistance of Concord

[1] Fleay, *English Drama*, ii. 42.
[2] I cite as an example the lines in act iv. sc. 1 :
> 'O Stesias, what a heavenly love hast thou,—
> A love as chaste as is Apollo's tree ;
> As ardent as a vestall Virgin's eye,
> And yet as bright as glow-worms in the night,
> With which the morning decks her lover's hayre !'

and Discord, in answer to the demand of the shepherds
for a representative of the female sex, creates Pandora, the
heroine of the play. She is successively exposed to the influence of the several gods, under which she acts as a mere
puppet. Saturn makes her 'sullen,' and Jove 'proud';
Mars 'bloody-minded' and exceedingly demonstrative of
a tendency to lay hands upon whomsoever she meets; Sol
'a Puritan,' though a Puritan after the fashion of Gabriel
Harvey, inasmuch as she is 'inspyrd' to an exercise in
Latin verse composition [1]. After this she proves only too
apt an automaton in the hands of Venus, and involves herself in a maze of intrigue, from which she next seeks to
escape under the guidance of Mercury. Finally, she goes
mad under the influence of Luna; and is by Nature
banished into the Moon for a perpetual dwelling-place.
Hither her unfortunate husband, Stesias, is bidden follow
her, so as to become the Man in the Moon; and to revenge
himself on Gunophilus, Pandora's servant and the clown of
the play, who for his ready subservience to her frailties has
been changed into a 'hathorne,' the Man in the Moon
undertakes to

> 'rend this hathorne with my furious hands,
> And beare this bush, if eare she looke but backe,
> I'le scratch her face that was so false to me [2].'

The device of *Prologus'* introducing the whole of this
play as the poet's dream is familiar enough to Chaucer
and his successors, and was adopted, very possibly on the
suggestion of this production of Lyly's, by Shakspere in
his early fairy-drama [3]. That an allegorical meaning of

---

[1] See the odd scene, act iii. sc. 2, in which Pandora puts Stesias through
a lesson in poetry very similar to that undergone by M. Jourdain in *Le
Bourgeois Gentilhomme.*

[2] As to the relation of this device to the popular fable of the Man in the
Moon, see Fairholt's note, ii. 282. For further information on the subject of
the popular farce he refers to Halliwell's remarks on *A Midsummer Night's
Dream*, in his folio edition of Shakspere, where by the bye 'Moonshine' is
far less communicative of elucidatory learning than his commentator: 'All
that I have to say, is to tell you, that the lantern is the moon; I, the man
in the moon; this thorn-bush, my thorn-bush; and this dog, my dog.'

[3] See Fairholt's note, ii. 278; where the resemblance is pointed out

a personal kind underlies Lyly's play, seems to me, with all deference, out of the question. It would have been a sorry compliment to Queen Elisabeth to designate her under the name of Luna as the final refuge of the errant Pandora [1].

In noticing the remaining comedies by Lyly, there seems no reason for diverging from the order of sequence adopted in the first collective edition (which however did not include *Love's Metamorphosis*), except in a single instance. This is, however, that of the play which may for more reasons than one claim to be regarded as the most notable of Lyly's dramatic works.

Endimion, the Man in the Moone, can only by internal evidence be shown to have preceded in date of production the other earlier plays of its author, which share with it a more marked adherence to the Euphuistic qualities of style. But this internal evidence is peculiarly strong, and turns on an interpretation of its plot and characters as to the substantial correctness of which no reasonable doubt can be said to remain. It was not printed till 1591 [2].

Endimion (acted 1579, pr. 1591).

between the thought in the lines quoted above at the close of Lyly's prologue, and Shakespere's—

> 'If we shadows have offended,
> Think but this (and all is mended),
> That you have but slumber'd here
> While these visions did appear.'

The same idea recurs, with an even closer resemblance to the Shaksperean passage, at the close of the *Prologue at the Court* to *Sapho and Phao*: 'In all humblenesse we all, and I on knee for all, intreat, that your Highnesse imagine your selfe to be in a deepe dreame, that staying the conclusion, in your rising your Majesty vouchsafe but to say, *and so you awakt.*'

The original suggestion of the machinery of a dream was of course due to the *Somnium Scipionis*, as narrated by Cicero, *de Republ.* lib. vi. *ad fin.* (where he uses the phrase, '*Ego somno solutus sum*'). The tenacity with which the fancy was repeated was a consequence of the popularity of the *Roman de la Rose*.

[1] This is rightly seen by Hense, *u. s.*, vii. 248. The notion seems to have been suggested by Mézières as the 'most piquant' thing in the play. Mr. Fleay, though of course he recognizes the 'indirect' satire, is guarded as to its effects. Mr. Baker, *Introduction*, p. clxxiii, offers the conjecture that the play was privately produced before the Queen.

[2] Apart from its appearance in the collective editions already cited, it has been reprinted in Dilke's *Old Plays* (vol. ii. 1814), and more recently in the edition, already cited, by Mr. G. P. Baker, to whose *Introduction* I am

Although in the Prologue to this comedy its author expresses a hope that 'none will apply pastimes, because they are fancies[1],' and facetiously adds that 'there liveth none under the sunne, that knoweth what to make of the Man in the Moone,' in the Epilogue he claims the Queen's protection against 'the malicious that seeke to overthrow us with threats,' yet 'do but stiffen our thoughts.' It is thus obvious, that he desired a particular meaning of his play to be accepted, if approved by the authority to whose commendation it was addressed.

Now, a very interesting attempt has been made to furnish the key to this meaning. In a highly elaborate argument, which I shall again have occasion to notice in connexion with Shakspere's *Midsummer Night's Dream,* the late Mr. N. J. Halpin, a distinguished Irish man of letters[2], examined the story of Lyly's comedy, and came to the conclusion that in all probability it is a dramatic representation of the disgrace brought upon Leicester (Endymion) by his clandestine marriage with the Countess of Sheffield (Tellus), which incurred the anger of his royal mistress (Cynthia), to whose hand he had previously aspired. Endymion's forty years' sleep upon the bank of lunary[3] signifies

indebted for the opportunity of revising my former remarks concerning this play and Mr. Halpin's view of its allegorical significance.

[1] Cf. the proverbial sarcasm cited by Lyly in another play (*Sapho and Phao,* act iii. sc. 2, where see Fairholt's note, i. 294). Ben Jonson has more than one humorous attack upon this kind of ultra-ingenuity; see *e.g. The Magnetic Lady,* act ii. *ad fin.,* and above all the well-known reference in the *Induction* to *Bartholomew Fair* to 'state-decypherers, or politic picklocks of the scene, so solemnly ridiculous as to search out who was meant by the gingerbread woman, who by the hobby-horseman, who by the costard-monger, who by their wares.' The well-known experiments of Süvern upon Aristophanes illustrate the fact, that the danger of such attempts lies chiefly in the want of self-restraint, which often accompanies really remarkable hermeneutical ability.

[2] *Oberon's Vision in the Midsummer Night's Dream, illustrated by a comparison with Lylie's Endymion.* By the Rev. N. J. Halpin, (Old) *Shakespeare Society's Publications,* 1843.

[3] Endymion's resolution, because 'on yonder banke never grew anything but lunary,' never hereafter to 'have any bed but that banke,' is a genuine bit of Euphuism. It reminds the editor of the *Continuation of Dodsley* (1814) (ii. 3) of the *Humorous Lieutenant* of Beaumont and Fletcher, who, 'when, by magical delusions, he falls in love with the old *King,* determines to lodge in *King-street.'*

his imprisonment in the castle of Greenwich (the Queen's favourite residence); the friendly intervention of Eumenides refers to the good offices of the Earl of Sussex; and the marriage of Tellus to Corsites, which solves the difficulty, is the marriage of Lady Sheffield to Sir Edmund Stafford. There are other identifications of characters of secondary importance in the action to which it is unnecessary to refer. But, though Mr. Halpin's investigation began on something like the right track, it does not appear to have led him home. Cynthia, of course, is Queen Elisabeth, and that Leicester is Endymion seems almost equally certain. But the secret marriage with Lady Sheffield took place in 1573, two years before the famous festivities at Kenilworth saw Leicester at the height of the royal favour, and his imprisonment at Greenwich did not take place till 1579, and was due to the revelation by the French ambassador de Simier of Leicester's secret marriage in the previous year (1578) to another widowed Countess, Lettice Countess of Essex. It will be seen at a glance that not only do these circumstances [1] better correspond to the action of the play than the incidents which Mr. Halpin has intermixed from two different dates, but that Lyly, whose play cannot in any case have been written long before 1579, could hardly have made an event dating back as far as 1573 the main subject of his plot.

But this plot is in the play carried to a very decisive issue. After forty years' slumber Endymion is awakened by Cynthia's kiss [2], and after he has related his dream, in

[1] See Baker, xliv. *seqq.* He cites Camden as showing that Sussex (Eumenides), notwithstanding his enmity to Leicester, deprecated the Queen's wrath against him.

[2] Mr. Symonds has admirably depicted this scene, as enacted before Queen Elisabeth at Greenwich. 'Lords, ladies, and ambassadors watch her face, as courtiers watch a queen. On the stage lies no Hellenic shepherd in the bloom of youth, but a boy attired in sylvan style to represent an aged man with flowing beard. Cynthia—not the solitary maiden goddess, led by Cupid, wafting her long raiment to the breeze of night, but a queen among her ladies, a boy disguised to personate Elisabeth herself—bends over him. And Endymion's dream, when he awakes, has been no fair romance of love revealed in slumber, but a vision of treason, envy, ingratitude, assassination, threatening his sovereign' (*Shakspere's Predecessors*, p. 521).

itself not devoid of significance [1], Endymion's marriage is
made the best of, and he is restored to Cynthia's favour.
Leicester's imprisonment, we know, lasted little more than
a month; but after his release he again fell into disfavour,
and was not finally restored to the Queen's good graces
till nearly a year had elapsed after the disclosure of his
marriage and his confinement.   The probability certainly
seems to be that his release is one of the incidents included
in the allegory, so that it cannot have been produced before
September, 1579.   On the other hand, it is difficult to
suppose Lyly to have been bold enough to plead in
Leicester's behalf when he was again in disgrace, and this
excludes any date after the beginning of November, 1579,
unless we are to assume one later than July, 1580.   This,
however, would not only imply that Lyly then revived
what at court would already have become a piece of ancient
history [2]; but it would remove the date of the composition
of *Endimion* out of the close proximity to the dates of
publication of the two books of *Euphues*, of which the
diction of the play furnishes specific as well as general
proofs in a measure reached by no second among Lyly's
comedies [3].   On the whole, therefore, the conclusion may be
accepted with confidence, that *Endimion* was first performed
in September or October, 1579.

   While, then, exhibiting the style and sentiment of its
author's contemporary non-dramatic work [4], *Endimion*,

----

[1] See the preceding note. There is no perceptible allusion in Endymion's
narrative to the French marriage-scheme.

[2] Such, of course, it would have yet more emphatically been, were it
necessary to accept Mr. Fleay's assumption (*u.s.* p. 41 ; cf. *History of the Stage*,
p. 76) that *Endimion* was first performed in 1588. This supposition rests on
the statement on the title-page of the original edition, that the play was
performed ' at Candlemas at Greenwich,' about which time the children of
Paul's are known to have acted there.   But we do not know what play
they acted at Candlemas, or supposing it to have been *Endimion*, that this
was the first performance of that comedy.

[3] See Baker, *u.s.*, lxxviii. *seqq.* The differences between the Euphuism
of *Endimion* and that of *Campaspe* and *Sapho and Phao*, which are dwelt
on by Child, *u. s.*, 93-4, will hardly be thought to tell against either the
above statement or the hypothesis which it supports.

[4] See the contrast drawn between friendship and love by Geron, act iii.
sc. 4, which quite accords with the social philosophy of *Euphues*.

instead of leaning closely on any classical original, derives
a semblance of life from the contact between its action and
the real experiences of real personages. It would have
been out of keeping with the purpose of the play, even had
it been in Lyly's power, to infuse much human passion
into the amorous declamations of his hero, but they are not
wholly devoid of charm ; while the laughable character of
the 'bragging soldier' and foolish pedant, Sir Tophas,
happily supplies the comic element in an action which it
would perhaps have been a mistake to sustain in too continuous a key of sentiment [1]. That Shakspere was familiar
with *Endimion* is, apart from the relation already mentioned,
obvious from unmistakeable resemblances between passages
in this comedy and two at least of his plays [2].

Lyly's second play (if the above conclusions be accepted)
was the ' moste excellent Comedie of *Alexander, Campaspe
and Diogenes*, played before the Queene's Majestie on twelfe
day at night, by her Maiestie's Children and the Children
of Paules,' also played at the Blackfriars, and first printed
in 1584. Although we have in this instance no internal
evidence to fix the actual date of first production (for
I cannot, with Mr. Fleay, suppose Lyly to have been bold
enough to have thought of 'shadowing forth' Leicester's
marriage with the Countess of Essex under the union of
Apelles and Campaspe, to which Alexander (Elisabeth)
magnanimously consents), it is obvious, from the style of
the piece, that it came fresh from the hand which had
recently written *Euphues* ; and this agrees with Mr. Fleay's

*Campaspe
acted 1581?
(pr. 1584).*

---

[1] Some of the dialogue in which Sir Tophas takes part is pleasant
fooling. See *e.g.* act iii. sc. 2, where, on Tophas sighing 'Hey ho,' his
attendant ' Epi' replies 'What's that?' 'An interjection, whereof some
are of mourning, as eho, vah.' ' I understand you not.' 'Thou seest me?'
'I' (*i.e.* Aye). ' No.' 'Thou hearest me?' ' I.' ' Thou feelest me?' ' I.'
'And not understandst me?' ' No.' ' Then am I but three quarters of
a nowne substantive. But also, *Epi*, to tell thee troth, I am a nowne
adjective.' ' Why?' ' Because I cannot stand without another.' ' Who is
that?' ' Dipsas,' &c. Mr. Halpin thinks Sir Tophas may have been intended
for Gabriel Harvey, with whom, as has been seen, Lyly was, or was to be,
at feud.

[2] See act iv. sc. 2—'Enter the Watch'; and act iv. sc. 3—'Song by
fairies' ; and *Much Ado about Nothing* (Dogberry and Verges) and the *Merry
Wives of Windsor*, act v. sc. 5.

supposition[1], based on the Court accounts, that it was
first performed on New Year's Eve, 1581.   The euphuism
of *Campaspe* pervades the entire play, with the exception of
but one or two scenes, and well suits a method of treatment
which has incurred the censure of Schlegel, unanswerable
in itself, that this comedy furnishes a warning example, how
incapable anecdotes and conceits are of forming a dramatic
whole.   Indeed, *Campaspe* is little more than a dramatic
anecdote; but within the limits thus indicated it is a singularly entertaining production; nor is it difficult to understand how it served to gratify the tastes both of the Court
and of the popular audience before which it was repeated.
It has accordingly two prologues and epilogues, addressed
severally to the two audiences.   The slight substructure of
the story is borrowed straight away from Pliny, who relates
it in a very few words, but in a very impressive way[2].
Alexander and Apelles—the King and the painter—both
love the Theban captive Campaspe; but in the end the
King resigns her to his rival, and starts to woo another
mistress, Glory, in the Persian Wars.   Round these personages, interesting in themselves, are grouped the soldiers
and courtiers of Alexander, with the philosophers of the
Court and the philosopher of the street, Diogenes[3].   Thus
the ingenious author is easily enabled, as he says in one of
the prologues, to mix 'mirth with councell, and discipline
with delight, thinking it not amisse in the same garden to
sow pot-hearbes, that wee set flowers.'   To continue the
antithesis, I think the 'pot-hearbes' will be generally preferred to the 'flowers,'—the ready retorts of Diogenes to
the profundity of Aristotle and Plato and the harangues of
Hephaestion, and the charming song of Apelles[4] to the

---

[1] ii. 39.

[2] *Nat. Hist.* lib. xxxv. cap. x. §§ 85-87.   He says that Alexander, by re-
signing 'Pancaste' (from whose name that of *Campaspe* seems to have been
formed by a curious kind of metathesis), showed himself to be '*magnus
animo, maior imperio sui, nec minor hoc facto quam victoriâ aliquâ.*'   We
again recall *Edward III* in the fine play attributed to Shakspere.

[3] 'Diogenes, I think, means Lyly himself.' (Fleay.)   *Quaere?*

[4] This song (act iii. sc. 5) is the celebrated 'Cupid and my Campaspe
played,' which has justly attracted the praise of generations of critics, and
was printed by Bishop Percy in his *Reliques.*   The play contains another

long soliloquy which precedes it, steeped in allusions to natural philosophy and medicine. There is in this play, besides a great amount of far-fetched ingenuity, much real wit; and the 'quips' of Diogenes could not easily be surpassed in swiftness and smartness. He remains victor in all the contests, except perhaps in a brief bout with his servant Manes[1]; and the speech is not without power which he addresses to the Athenians, assembled to see him fly, while he contents himself with the experiment of 'flying over their disordered lives[2].'

Even slighter in texture than *Campaspe* is the comedy of *Sapho and Phao*, which like the former was acted both at the Court and at Blackfriars, and was printed in 1584. *Sapho and Phao (acted 1582 ? pr. 1584).* Indeed, notwithstanding an abundant display of the favourite features of Euphuism (including natural history similes), showing clearly enough to which period of its author's literary life it belongs, *Sapho and Phao* could hardly have engaged the attention of its audiences, but for references in its plot, which at the same time go far to establish the date of the play. There can be little doubt that Phao's departure from Sicily, of whose princess Sapho[3] he is enamoured (while Venus herself is in love with him), points (notwithstanding the awkwardness involved in the last-

charming song of a different kind (act v. sc. 1), cited by Symonds, in which occurs the passage (concerning the lark):—
> 'How at Heaven's gates she claps her wings,
>   The morning waiting till she sings.'

Cf. the opening line of the song in *Cymbeline*, act ii. sc. 3.

[1] See act ii. sc. 1. Manes (named, as Psyllus says, 'Manes, a Manendo, because he runneth away') is a kind of philosophical Launcelot Gobbo. 'I did not run away, but retire,' he says in answer to Psyllus' jest. And when Diogenes announces his determination to put him away and serve himself, '*quia non egeo tui vel te*,' he replies that he means to run away again, '*quia scio tibi non esse argentum*.' Manes' definition of a 'quip' may be worth quoting (act iii. sc. 2) : 'Wee great girders call it a short saying of a sharpe wit, with a bitter sense in a sweet word.'

[2] Act iv. sc. 1 : 'All conscience is sealed at Athens. Swearing cometh of a hot mettle ; lying of a quick wit ; flattery of a flowing tongue ; indecent talke of a merry disposition. All things are lawfull at Athens.' 'Allusions' of this sort, although they may happen to hit the mark in the England of Euphues or of any other censor, have a general gnomic force worth recognising.

[3] This *Sapho* has nothing in common with the poetess of Lesbos, whom among moderns Grillparzer has made the subject of a tragedy of some interest.

named complication) at the departure from England, in February, 1682, of Francis Duke of Anjou. Otherwise, the breaking-off of the action of the play with so lame a conclusion would hardly admit of explanation. Mr. Fleay, who has a further reason for assigning this date to the production of *Sapho and Phao*, holds that the inhibition of performances by the Children of St. Paul's was due to the offence given by this play and its predecessor[1]. If so, Lyly might have spared himself the mixture of deprecation and *innuendo* into which he thought fit to conclude this play[2]. We, who may be presumed to have outlived the taste for scandal about Queen Elisabeth or her suitors, may be excused for indulging other artificial tastes which such a production as *Sapho and Phao* gratifies. As Mr. Symonds hints, the Dresden china style of love-making has a certain attractiveness of its own[3].

Gallathea (pr. 1592).　The date of the production at Court of *Gallathea*, first printed in 1592, might, in accordance with a very striking piece of internal evidence, seem assignable to the beginning of 1588[4]. But so simple a solution has been held, while agreeing with the freedom of the dialogue of this play from the Euphuistic peculiarities of style common to the earlier group of Lyly's dramas, to be out of keeping with their manifest presence in much of the remaining part of the comedy[5]. A chorizontic solution of the difficulty has therefore been thought necessary; and we are invited to assign the composition of the earlier version of *Gallathea*, of which the subsidiary action concerning the pages and their masters formed no part, to 1584, and the production of the play in

---

[1] *English Drama*, ii. 40.

[2] See the speech of *Sybilla* at the end of the comedy; and cf. the vague 'wish' at the end of the *Epilogue*.

[3] *U. s.*, 523–4. I add a later illustration : ' "Shall I feed my pretty Princess with *bonbons*?" Arthur Pendennis enquired sarcastically of Miss Blanche Amory. " *Mais j'adore les bonbons, moi*," said the little Sylphide.'

[4] See the references, cited by Fleay, to *octogesimus octavus mirabilis annus* in act iii. sc. 3, and act v. sc. 1. These allusions to a current astrological superstition are in harmony with the general drift of the play. Fleay thinks the particular character of the 'astronomer' identifiable with the famous Dr. Dee, &c.

[5] Child, *u. s.*, p. 95.

its present entirety to 1588, 'the wonderful year[1].' The conclusion involves no actual improbability; but I must confess that I can perceive no such distinction between the several portions of the play—dialogues and soliloquies—as has been freely assumed.

The scene of the action is laid in Lincolnshire, and some comic personages of a modern cast are introduced; indeed, the comic element vindicates to itself a considerable importance in the progress of the play. 'Raffe,' with his anything but far-fetched puns[2], is a promising specimen of the clown of Elisabethan comedy, while the figures of the 'Alcumist' and the 'Astronomer' directly satirise the false science of the day. The plot, which involves the disguise of two maidens as boys, and their consequent passion for one another, may have been suggested by an inversion of a lascivious tale in Ovid[3]; but in the play little is made either of the pathetic or of the comic side of the situation. On the other hand, there is some pretty toying with the fancy of the capture of Cupid by Diana's nymphs, who subject him to a series of penalties in revenge for his misdeeds, first making proclamation as follows:

> 'O yes, O yes, if any maid
> Whom loving Cupid has betraid
> To frownes of spite, to eyes of scorne,
> And would in madness now see torne
> The boy in pieces—
>   Let her come
> Hither, and lay him to his doome.'

The frolic spirit of this, which recalls the gaiety of Theocritean pastoral in its English dress[4], is more amusing than the harangue to her nymphs of Diana, the accepted type of royal virginity[5].

Curiously enough, the next play in the list of Lyly's comedies, where there is no reason to suppose but that it *Mydas* (*pr.* 1592).

---

[1] Baker, *u. s.*, pp. xcvi. *seqq.*

[2] '*Concurre? Condogge!* I will away,' &c.

[3] The story of Iphis and Ianthe in Ov. *Metamorph.* bk. ix. The *Quarterly Reviewer* has pointed out this and another classical reminiscence in the play.

[4] Cf. *The Shepheards Calendar*, March.

[5] Cf. Symonds, *u. s.*, p. 529. Her 'Now, ladies,' indeed, is in a more modern feminine style.

occupies its proper place in chronological order, exhibits a marked falling-off in some of the characteristics of style which are so manifest in his earlier dramas. It may be that a certain consciousness of higher and more serious purpose pervades the allegorical passages in *Mydas* (first printed in 1592, and unmistakeably written in those later years of the reign of Philip II of Spain, when England was beginning to confront him as the avowed representative of the cause whose ruin he had spent his life in essaying to compass [1]). It may be also that Lyly, as years went on, had become weary of the more 'mechanical devices' [2] of his favourite earlier manner, while adhering to the use of its most essential characteristics, and, where the large comic admixture in the action did not interfere, effectively making use of the *alto estilo* which was so particularly in harmony with the allegorical significance of his argument.   For although it may be difficult to convince oneself that *Mydas* is like *Endimion,* a more or less complete allegory in dramatic form [3], the course of the play is beyond dispute abundantly seasoned by political allusions.   The time of its production was favourable to a free delivery of hits at Philip of Spain, who is repeatedly [4] satirised as Mydas, and to an indulgence in exultation over the achievements of

---

[1] A passage in act iii. sc. 1 undeniably shows that the play was written after the dissipation of the Armada. 'Have not I,' exclaims Mydas, 'made the sea to groane under the number of my ships; and have they not perished, that there was not two left to make a number?' And another passage, act iv. sc. 4, while apparently alluding to the same catastrophe, appears to refer not less distinctly to the various English attempts against the Spanish power that preceded the expedition to Cadiz : 'I see all his expeditions for warres are laid in water; for now, when he should execute, he begins to consult, and suffers the enemies to bid us good morrow at our owne doores, to whom wee long since might have given the last good night in their owne beds.'

[2] Cf. Child, *u. s.,* p. 96.

[3] So Mr. Halpin (*Oberon's Vision,* p. 123) seems to think, who supplies a key, 'conjectural and incomplete,' as he avows, but sufficiently ingenious, to many of its characters and passages. Cf. Fleay, *u. s.,* p. 42. In a 'Concluding Note' to this play in vol. i. of the *Continuation of Dodsley* (1814), the editor solemnly leaves it to the future to decide whether a historical parallel drawn by him between Midas and another ambitious sovereign will be completely borne out by the termination of the career of—Napoleon!

[4] Act iii. sc. 1 ; act iv. sc. 1 ; act v. sc. 3.

England, here extolled under the name of Lesbos, which
'the gods have pitched out of the world, as not to be
controlled by any in the world[1].' It is on stretching his
hands to Lesbos, that Mydas has become conscious, and
prepared to confess to Diana, that his affection is grown
'unnaturall[2],' or, as one should say, obsolete. Among other
incidental references is one to Philip's supposed anxiety for
the inherited rights of his daughter, the Infanta Clara
Isabella Eugenia, but herein Lyly appears to have fallen
into a mistake[3]. In any case, it may be confessed that
the play stood in some need of such incidental appeals
to patriotic sympathies; for it is in substance a dull
production. In the conduct of his story, the dramatist
imitates neither Apuleius' fable nor Lucian's earlier
dialogue version of its theme, but his favourite Ovid[4].
Possibly because the resources of the stage 'in Pauls[5]'
were unequal to such an effort, the crucial incident of
turning all objects into gold forms no part of the course of
the action presented; and the opportunity is thus foregone
of displaying the folly of Mydas' wish. On the other hand,
the second part of the action, which reproduces the story of
the ass's ears, is more lively in effect, although it is difficult
not to sympathise with Mydas for preferring Pan's song,
poor as it is, to Apollo's, which is still poorer. The barber
Motto and Dello his boy (who says that his master has
taught him 'Tully *de oratore*, the very art of trimming')
are fairly amusing[6]. The diction, as usual with Lyly, suffers
from an excess of cadences, and there is an abundance
of puns and Latinity of the quotable sort[7].

[1] Act v. sc. 3; and cf. act iv. sc. 4, and *ib.* sc. 1, the cry of Midas, when
his ass's ears are discovered : 'What will they say in Lesbos?'

[2] Act v. sc. 3.

[3] See act v. sc. 3. Philip put forward her claims (through her mother) to
the French, not to the Spanish, crown.

[4] *Metam.* xi. 90 *seqq.*

[5] *Prologue.*

[6] O'Hara's 'burletta' on the subject of *Midas* is well known, and still,
I believe, keeps the stage. It was first acted in Ireland, and appeared on
the English stage in 1764.

[7] Mr. C. G. Child, *u.s.*, 82-3, refers to the rhythm of the oracle of Apollo
in this play, act v. sc. 3. It is indeed a curious mixture ; but a novel sort
of trochaic basis is its most interesting characteristic.

Fortune-telling, a favourite practice of the age to which
Lyly elsewhere makes reference, suggested the eponymous
character in his ' pleasant conceited comedie, called *Mother
Bombie* ' (first printed in 1594). No derivation from any
classical source has been suggested in the case of this play,
and, in accordance with probable date, as well as with its
broadly comic matter and manner, it is not pervaded by
the Euphuism of its predecessors. Yet the cunning old
woman of Rochester has little to say or do in the play,
although her intervention helps to bring about the solution
of its plot. This plot shows considerable skill of invention,
and an audacious symmetry unsurpassed in any of our old
comedies founded on ' errors ' (mistakes of identity). It
will suffice to summarise the argument of *Mother Bombie* in
the words of two of its agents [1] :—

' *Memphio* had a foole to his sonne, which *Stellio* knew not ; *Stellio*
a foole to his daughter, unknowne to *Memphio ;* to coosen each other
they dealt with their boies [i. e. servants] for a match [in other
words, they tried with the help of their servants each to palm off his
foolish child upon the supposed sensible child of the other] ; wee [the
servants] met with *Lucio* and *Halfepenie* [two other serving-men]
who told the love betweene their master's children [Accius and Silena],
the youth deeply in love, the fathers unwitting to consent . . . then wee
foure met, which argued wee were no mountaines ; and in a taverne
wee met, which argued wee were mortall ; and everie one in his wine
told his dayes worke, which was a signe wee forgot not our businesse ;
and seeing all our masters troubled with devises, we determined
a little to trouble the water before they drunke ; so that in the attire
of your children, our masters' wise children bewrayed their good
natures [i. e. proved themselves the fools they were] ; and in the
garments of our masters' children yours made a marriage ; this all
stood upon us poore children, and your young children, to shew that
old folkes may be overtaken by children.'

To which it has only to be added, that the two foolish
children, Accius and Silena, in the end turn out to be brother
and sister, changelings foisted upon Memphio and Stellio,
by Vicina, who has brought up their actual children,
Maestius and Serena, as her own, and as brother and sister,
and has thus impeded the solution which satisfies the actual
state of the case.

Such is the sufficiently ingenious contrivance of the plot

[1] Act v. sc. 3.

of *Mother Bombie.* The diction of the play, in consequence
no doubt of the relative freedom of its style, is by no means
deficient in humour; although the author is nowhere so
much himself as in the scene where the two clever children
display their wit,—Livia by displaying a sampler stitched
with an emblematic anthology of ' flowers, fowles, beastes,
fishes, trees, plants, stones and what not,' and Candius by
quoting (in the original tongue) a certain ' fine pleasant poet
who intreateth of the art of love, and of the remedie[1].'

Finally, in the last of the plays which can with certainty
be ascribed to Lyly, the ' wittie and courtly Pastorall ' of
Love's Metamorphosis (first printed in 1601), we are, as the
description implies, once more transplanted into the more
special atmosphere of the author's earlier efforts. Its
allegorical element (if it exists at all) is indeed comparatively faint ; on the other hand there is no admixture of
low-comedy or farcial matter. While the diction is often
more dramatically direct, we elsewhere have to recognise
the copious industry with which similes and conceits are
as usual accumulated round an unsubstantial plot. The
characters are of the familiar cast—Ceres and her nymphs,
' cruell,' ' coy,' and ' wavering,' the shepherds their lovers,
and Cupid, who in anger at their coldness metamorphoses
them into a stone, a rose, and a bird, and only releases them
at the conclusion of the play. In a bye-plot, not very
skilfully interwoven with the main action, the savage Erisicthon is by reason of his destruction of the holy tree of
Ceres, and with it of the life of the unhappy Fidelia who
had been metamorphosed into the tree, visited by Famine[2],
to escape whose inflictions he is willing to sell his daughter
Protea to ' a merchant.' Protea escapes by changing her
aspect (in accordance with her name), and returns under the
fresh disguise of the revengeful ghost of ' Ulisses,' in time to
save her lover Petulius from the wiles of the ' Syren.' Thus
the materials employed by the author are more abundant

Love's Metamor-phosis (pr. 1601).

---

[1] Act i. sc. 3.

[2] The fancy of the tree 'pouring out blood' and giving forth a human
voice may have been suggested by *The Faerie Queene,* bk. i. canto ii.
stanza xxx. *seqq.* ; the description of the personified Famine, act ii. sc. 1, by
' the griesly shape ' of Famine in Sackville's *Induction,* stanzas 50-55.

than usual. The comparative lack of vivacity is partly accounted for by the absence of the farcical element; both cause and effect may be due to the fact that this play was probably a production of Lyly's latest years.

Plays ascribed to Lyly.

Two other plays have been ascribed to Lyly, but neither of them with any reasonable degree of probability. His authorship of *A Warning for Faire Women* (printed 1599, but probably written shortly after 1590) is indeed altogether out of the question. This play, as its second title indicates[1], is one of those domestic tragedies founded directly on incidents of real life, which, as will be seen below[2], had a special vogue in the last decade of the sixteenth century. Its *Induction*, in which Tragedy, History (i. e. the Historical Drama of the early type), and Comedy dispute against one another the possession of the stage, is not without interest for the early history of our regular drama, but it would be hazardous to apply too definitely the satirical invective of the mutual recriminations[3]. The second of these plays is the very charming pastoral drama, *The Maid's Metamorphosis*, printed 1600, 'as it hath been sundrie times acted by the children of Powles[4].' This circumstance no doubt led to its being usually attributed to Lyly; but its manner is singularly unlike his at any period of his career, and the difference is more marked by this play being throughout in rime. The quaint simplicity of its verse has a charm of its own, which reminds one eminent critic of the style of John Day; among the moderns, Leigh Hunt occasionally wrote in a not very dissimilar fashion. Passages here and there may recall Lyly; but he cannot conceivably have been the author of a work which is not only free from his favourite affectations, but in spite of the Ovidian lubricity of its main theme (the change of maid into man, followed by a happy

---

[1] *The most tragical and lamentable Murther of Master George Sanders, of London, Merchant, nigh Shooter's Hill; consented unto by his owne Wife, and acted by Mr. Brown, Mrs. Drewry, and Trusty Roger, Agents therein; with their several Ends.*

[2] Under *Arden of Feversham*, in the chapter on *Shakspere*.

[3] See Collier, ii. 345 *seqq.*

[4] Edited, with an *Introduction*, by Mr. A. H. Bullen, in vol. i. of his *Collection of Old English Plays* (4 vols., 1882).

restoration), has a certain *naïveté* of pathos, particularly in its earlier scenes, to which he was assuredly a stranger. The humour of the three pages, Mopso, Frisco, and Jomlo, may be thought nearer to Lyly's way; but even here there is no salient likeness[1].

Before passing to the small but illustrious group of English dramatic poets, whose undisputed works closely ally their fame with Shakspere's own, we may fitly make mention of a writer whose long-established reputation as the author of one original play of marked individuality cannot be held to exhaust his claims upon the attention of literary students. Their estimate of his influence upon his contemporaries and immediate successors—including Shakspere himself—must depend upon the latitude allowed to conjecture in helping to determine the list of his extant achievements as a playwright.

Thomas Kyd (1557 c.– 1595 c.).

THOMAS KYD[2], the author of *The Spanish Tragedy*, has the honour of being ranked by Ben Jonson, with Lyly and Marlowe, among the dramatists whom Shakspere 'outshone.' Jonson calls him 'Sporting Kyd'—manifestly by way of nothing more than a facile, and probably familiar, pun. There is sufficient reason for supposing him to have been trained for the profession (paternal, it would seem) of a law scrivener, before he diverged into literary activity. He published in 1588 a translation of one of Tasso's prose tractates, and followed it up by at least one pamphlet narrating a contemporary case of 'secret' murder—a theme entirely in agreement with the tastes of the period, and,

---

[1] It is hardly worth while pointing out the affinities between the character and antecedents of Amaranthus in this play and those of Prospero in *The Tempest*. In act iv. sc. 1, Echo makes one of her many appearances in the pastoral or romantic drama as a mocking interlocution.

[2] The four plays, of which two were certainly written by Kyd, while the other two have with more or less plausibility been attributed to him, are printed in Hazlitt's *Dodsley*, vols. iv. and v. Mr. Fleay's arguments for assigning to Kyd a longer list of dramatic productions will be found in his *English Drama*, ii. 26-35. An elaborate research on Kyd's dramatic writings has been published by G. Sarrazin, under the title of *Thomas Kyd und sein Kreis*, Berlin, 1882. See also Mr. S. Lee's article on Kyd in vol. xxxi. of the *Dictionary of National Biography*.

one may venture to add, of the writer himself. His authorship of *The Spanish Tragedy*, which was licensed in 1592,
and printed at all events as early as 1594, is established on
sufficient authority [1]; but he published nothing with his
name except a translation of Robert Garnier's tragedy of
Cornélie, printed in 1594, and reprinted in the following
year under the title of *Pompey the Great, his faire Cornelias
Tragedie, effected by her Father* (Q. Metellus Scipio) *and
Husbandes* (the younger Crassus' and Pompeius Magnus')
downe-cast, death and fortune. Whether or not because in
the latter part of his career Kyd's personal repute suffered,
as it seems to have done, from reports as to his participation
in the recently dead Marlowe's vagaries of opinion, he was
manifestly anxious to establish a sort of literary orthodoxy,
undertaking in the Dedication of his *Cornelia* to the Countess
of Sussex to 'assure her his next summer's better travel
with the tragedy of *Portia*,' a version of the *Julius Caesar*
theme which is thought to surpass the *Cornelia* in power [2].
For Kyd is said to have died in 1595. His *Cornelia* carries
us back, like all the earlier of Garnier's tragedies, to a phase
of the drama antecedent to that which is represented by
Kyd himself as an original poet. Not only is Seneca, with
his ghosts and the rest of his machinery, still master of the
method, but the drama, with its endless speeches and
generally retrospective procedure, is still in the embrace of
the epos. Kyd seems here to be doing penance for the
spasmodic extravagances as well as for the freer movement
of his earlier efforts.

Among these it seems to me imperative to mention first
the famous *Spanish Tragedy, or, Hieronimo is mad again* [3],
not because of its fame, but because of the fact that on the
evidence contained in it rests the argument as to Kyd's

---

[1] Thomas Heywood's, in his *Apology for Actors*, (Old) *Shakspere Society's
Publications*, 1841, p. 45.

[2] Kyd's *Cornelia* is printed in Dodsley's *Old Plays*, vol. ii., and in vol. v. of
Hazlitt's *Dodsley*. Ebert, *Entw. d. französ. Tragödie*, p. 155, describes *Cornélie*
as a feeble replica of *Porcie*. The background of both plays seems to have
been intended to refer to the civil troubles recently undergone by France.

[3] Printed in vol. iii. of Dodsley's *Old Plays*, and in vol. v. of Mr. Hazlitt's
Dodsley; also in vol. ii. of Hawkins' *Origin of the English Drama*, and in
vol. i. of the *Ancient British Drama*.

claim to the authorship of any other plays. The excep- The Spanish Tragedy (1588 ?).
tional popularity of this piece is attested by the frequency
with which it was performed after its first appearance on
the stage in 1588, or a year or two earlier [1]. It was, moreover,
frequently reprinted after the first extant edition, which itself
refers to an earlier impression. The edition of 1602 purports
to have received 'new additions of the Painter's part and
others,' with which it had been of late several times performed; and Henslowe's *Diary* contains two entries of sums
paid to 'Bengemen Johnson,' *alias* 'Bengemy Johnsone,'
for 'additions' and for 'new additions' to this play [2].
Charles Lamb is sceptical as to Ben Jonson's authorship of
certain of the additions, which he terms 'the salt of the
old play'—an expression that appears rather too strong,
although Lamb's extracts no doubt comprise the most
highly-wrought passages, especially in the great scene
which another critic of rare insight agrees in thinking
beyond Ben Jonson's powers [3]. Jonson himself was at no
pains to conceal his opinion of the value of the additions;
for in the *Induction* to his *Cynthia's Revels* he ridicules the
man who, 'furnished with more beard than wit,' 'prunes
his mustachio, lisps and swears "that the old *Hieronimo*, as
it was first acted, was the only best and judiciously penned

[1] The date of the first performance of *The Spanish Tragedy* and of
The First Part of Jeronimo rests on the humorous declaration in the
Induction to *Bartholomew Fair* (1614), that ' he that will swear *Jeronimo* or
Andronicus are the best plays yet, shall pass unexcepted at here, as a man
whose judgment shows it is constant, and hath stood still these five and
twenty or thirty years. Though it be an ignorance, it is a virtuous and
staid ignorance.' As to the early performances of *The Spanish Comedy* see
Henslowe's *Diary*, where it is mentioned under the alternating designations
of *The Comedy of Jeronymo*, *The Spanish Comedy* and *Don Oracoe* (from the
character of Horatio). *Jeronymo* usually signifies the *First Part of
Jeronimo*, but in the case of the 'additions' by Ben Jonson clearly means
The Spanish Tragedy.
[2] See Henslowe's *Diary*, under the dates of September 21, 1601, and
June 24, 1602. (Collier's edition, printed for the (Old) Shakspere Society,
1845, pp. 201 and 223.)
[3] See the scene from act iv. in Lamb's *Specimens*. Edward Fitzgerald
writes to Fanny Kemble : ' Nobody knows who wrote this one scene : it
was thought Ben Jonson, who could no more have written it than I who
read it : for what else of his is it like ? Whereas, Webster one fancies
might have done it.' (*Letters of Edward Fitzgerald to Fanny Kemble*,
1895, p. 63.) The same suggestion had been made by Charles Lamb.

play of Europe."' For the rest, although perhaps no other play received so ample a recognition as *The Spanish Tragedy* in the way of quotation by dramatists contemporary with its author or belonging to the generation next ensuing [1], yet it is obvious that they largely regarded it as the type of antiquated extravagance. They may be excused for having overlooked the notable advance which *The Spanish Tragedy*, with its direct and forcible, if excessive, presentment of human passions, represents in comparison with our earlier English tragedies modelled on Seneca [2], and as yet lacking the impulse towards freedom of movement which is unmistakeably present in Kyd's work. Its influence, I may add, was by no means confined to our own national drama [3].

A notion of the plot of *The Spanish Tragedy* will perhaps be most easily gathered from a ballad which must

---

[1] See Shakspere, *King John*, act ii. sc. 1 ('You are the hare,' &c.), and 3 *Henry VI*, act v. sc. 6 ('If any spark of life be yet remaining'). Cf. *The Taming of the Shrew, Induction*, sc. 1 ('Go by, Jeronimy ; go to thy cold bed and warm thee'). The quotations from or allusions to *The Spanish Tragedy* in Ben Jonson are very numerous : see *Every Man in His Humour*, act i. sc. 1 ; *The Alchemist*, act iv. sc. 4 ; *The Poetaster*, act iii. sc. 1 ; *The New Inn*, act ii. sc. 2 ; *The Tale of a Tub*, act iv. sc. 4.

[2] I do not of course for a moment pretend that the influence of Seneca is absent from *The Spanish Tragedy*, any more than from the other plays connected with it in subject, while Kyd, as has been seen, did indirect homage to the Roman tragedian by his *Cornelia*. His reading as a classical scholar has been illustrated in the Dean of Canterbury's (Dr. Farrar) early essay *On the Revival of Classical Learning, &c.* (1856), more especially with reference to *The Spanish Tragedy*.

[3] Jacob Ayrer's *Tragedia von dem Griegischen Keyser zu Constantinopel und seiner Tochter Pelimperia* (1595-8) follows the form of *The Spanish Tragedy* previous to the 'additions.' Kyd's play seems to have been a stock-piece of the English comedians in Germany, and was acted at Dresden as late as 1626. See the *Introductory Note* on Ayrer in Julius Tittmann's *Schauspiele aus dem 16. Jahrhundert* (1868), ii. 133 *seqq.* ; cf. Cohn, *Shakspeare in Germany*, Pt. I., p. lxvi. A curious literary discovery by Mr. J. A. Worp is described by him in vol. xxix-xxx. of the *Jahrbuch der deutschen Shakespeare-Gesellschaft* (1894). He found the whole story, as dramatised in *The Spanish Tragedy* up to the end of act iv., inserted into the text of a Dutch verse translation by Everaert Syceram of Brussels, published at Antwerp in 1615. The fact that this inserted narrative is largely a literal version of Kyd's play precludes any doubt but that its text was in Syceram's hands ; possibly the visit of the English comedians to Brussels in 1612 may have first suggested to him the use of the story. *The Spanish Tragedy* itself was acted in the Netherlands in a Dutch version in 1621 and 1638.

have been composed after the production of the play, and
which thus adds one more to the many testimonies to its
popularity[1]. A terrific woodcut depicts the most sensational situation in the story. In the play itself the
introductory speech of the *Ghost of Andrea* and the narrative of the *General* briefly explain what may be called the
antecedents of the action; but inasmuch as these antecedents
themselves form the action of another and shorter play,
now usually called *The First Part of Jeronimo*, but
apparently referred to by Henslowe under the title of
Jeronimo pure and simple, the relation between this and
The Spanish Tragedy becomes a problem of interest. Was
the shorter as well as the longer play the work of Kyd,
and if so, which of the two was the earlier in date of
composition? *The First Part* is unmistakeably slighter in
construction (so much so that it has been actually conjectured to have merely formed the first act of *The Spanish
Tragedy*[2]) as well as less forcible in diction, and altogether
less characteristic of Kyd's special manner than the more
important work. That manner is not easily described,
since so many reminiscences of an earlier form of tragic
writing still adhere to it. But as is justly observed by
Schlegel, when comparing the whole of *The Spanish Tragedy*
to the drawings of children, scribbled down by an uncertain
hand without regard to perspective or proportion[3], the tone
of the dialogue, notwithstanding the large quantity of bombast, possesses a certain naturalness, and the changes of scene
impart to the action an attractive lightness of movement.
Thus, no clogging influence upon the action is exercised even
by the superhuman machinery of the *Ghost of Andrea* (the
first lover of the heroine, enamoured in *The Spanish Tragedy*
of Horatio, the son of Hieronimo) and the abstraction of
Revenge, who reappear at the end of Acts i. and iv. and at
the close of the play[4], and accordingly, in the words of

---

[1] Reprinted in the old edition of *Dodsley.*
[2] See Sarrazin, *u.s.,* p. 57. I do not think this a probable explanation.
[3] *Lectures on Dramatic Art and Literature,* No. xiii. (In the original.)
[4] That results are achieved adequate to the cravings of the most resentful
ghost, will appear from his final summary :—

Revenge, serve 'for Chorus' in this tragedy, and during its course we feel ourselves transplanted into the region of real human emotion, powerfully and on occasion even pathetically depicted. The sensuous charm of the love-scene between Belimperia and Horatio (written in rimed couplets of no ordinary beauty) cannot be gainsaid, although the author's chief effort (heightened by the later additions) is reserved for what ensues. After Horatio has been hanged on the stage by his enemies, the body is discovered by his father, the brave old Marshal Hieronimo, whose desperate grief and craving for revenge become the keynote of the climax and catastrophe of the action at large. Here is introduced the striking device of the play within the play,—in its main features the same as that employed in *Hamlet*, although in Kyd's tragedy it is more directly interwoven with the action. And, indeed, the whole dramatic idea of *The Spanish Tragedy* needs nothing but inversion to resemble that of *Hamlet* itself; for the main theme of the former is the effect of the murder of a son upon the mind of his father, whose slowly prepared revenge at last wreaks itself as a Nemesis upon the authors of the original wrong, as well as upon the contrivers of the actual process of retaliation.

The First Part of Jeronimo (1587?).

The First Part of Jeronimo [1], which, as already observed, is a far slighter production, and while not wanting in vehemence and even extravagance of diction, lacks both the peculiar *afflatus* and a certain flacidity of style, aided by a tendency to 'return' word or phrase, characteristic of *The Spanish Tragedy*, may or may not have been the work of

> 'Aye, now my hopes have end in their effects
> When blood and sorrow finish my desires.
> Horatio murder'd in his father's bower;
> Vile Serberine by Pedringano slain;
> False Pedringano hang'd by quaint device;
> Fair Isabella by herself undone;
> Prince Balthasar by Belimperia stabb'd;
> The Duke of Castile and his wicked son
> Both done to death by old Hieronimo;
> My Belimperia fall'n, as Dido fell,
> And good Hieronimo slain by himself:—
> Aye, these were spectacles to please my soul.'

[1] Printed in *Dodsley*, vol. iii, and in vol. iv. of Hazlitt's *Dodsley*.

the same hand ; to me it seems on the whole most probable
that it was a play of rather earlier date, written perhaps
under the effects of the first appearance of Marlowe's
Tamburlaine[1], i. e. about the year 1587 ; and that its
subsequent popularity was due to the continuation of its
theme in *The Spanish Tragedy*, whence it became customary
to perform the two plays on successive days.   It is in
Jeronimo, and not in the longer play, that occur the
repeated allusions to the small size of the hero[2], from which
it may be inferred that the part was originally written for
a particular actor.   The tradition[3] that Ben Jonson ' took
mad Jeronymo's part' (which would have been in *The
Spanish Tragedy*) ill accords with this particular association.

The authorship of the tragedy of *Solyman and Perseda*[4]
is, as it seems to me, a much more interesting question than
that of a production which can in no case be regarded as
more than an adjunct of *The Spanish Tragedy*, its nominal
continuation.   The 'play within the play,' introduced in
the last act of Kyd's famous tragedy, treats the story of
Erastus and Perseda, which is that of the piece now in question; but it merely follows in abstract, so to speak, the general
course of the action which in *Solyman and Perseda* fills
a larger canvas, while diverging from the latter in details of
incident, and only occasionally recalling its actual diction.
Solyman and Perseda, which was first printed in 1599, though
licensed as early as 1592, is itself founded in plot upon a story
forming part of a collection published in 1578 by Sir Henry
Wotton, under the title of *A Courtlie Controversie of Cupid's
Cautels*[5]; a noteworthy passage in it, descriptive of the

Solyman and Perseda (pr. 1599).

---

[1] Cf. Sarrazin, p. 57. At the same time, as is here pointed out, *Jeronimo*
contains an abundance of rime.

[2] 'My mind's a giant, though my bulk be small.'
'Little Jeronimo Marshal.'
'Thou inch of Spain . . . .
Thou very little longer than thy beard, &c.'

[3] Thrown in Jonson's teeth in Dekker's *Satiro-mastix*—no very convincing authority. (See below.) In the same play there is a sneer at
Jonson's 'villanous broad backe.'

[4] Printed in Hawkins, *u. s.*, vol. ii, and in vol. v. of Hazlitt's *Dodsley*.

[5] The text of the story has been reprinted, with a few omissions, by
Sarrazin, *u. s.*, pp. 12-40.

beauty of Perseda, is partly borrowed from a sonnet in Watson's *Ecatompathia* (1582)[1]. It is a tale containing varied ingredients—a chivalrous opening, an episode of sheer chance put to base use by intriguing guile (the episode of the gold chain given by Perseda to Erastus, that finds its way into the possession of Lucina), a romantic developement which places the fate of the lovers in the hands of Sultan Solyman, and a tragic catastrophe which involves their doom, together with that of Christian Rhodes. This story is modified, while the characters are partly elaborated, partly altered, in the play, where an allegorical element is introduced in the personages of Love, Fortune, and Death, who prologise and ' serve as chorus,' and a comic element is added to meet the demands of the groundlings. The action is full of interest, and the indebtedness of Shakspere to this drama is by no means limited to reminiscences of particular passages[2].

The question as to Kyd's authorship of this remarkable work cannot be determined by inferences drawn from the fact that the 'play within the play' in *The Spanish Tragedy* was derived from the same source as *Solyman and Perseda*, more especially as that drama and the abstract differ in the contrivance of the final catastrophe. The answer depends on the general evidence as to agreement in construction and style between the two tragedies; and this evidence must be allowed to be strong, though not overwhelming. The use made in both plays of the abstract figures that ' serve as chorus,' though not precisely peculiar to these two dramas, is yet somewhat different from the employment of similar impersonations in any earlier drama ; possibly, as will be seen, the suggestion may be due to a third play, of

---

[1] The author of *The Spanish Tragedy* imitates another passage in the same collection of sonnets.

[2] Of these the most striking is Perseda's speech (act v):

> ' What, dar'st thou not ? Give me the dagger then—
> There's a reward for all thy treasons past.
> *Then* PERSEDA *kills* LUCINA.'

Piston's foolery with the dead body of Ferdinando (slain by Erastus) in act ii. must have in no happy moment suggested the dealings of Falstaff with the corpse of Hotspur, while the same captain's famous speech (1 Henry IV, act v. sc. 1) betrays obscurer reminiscences of Basilisco's soliloquy in act v.

which the framework bears a general resemblance to that
of the two plays in question, and which has likewise been
attributed to Kyd. Of more importance are the very
striking similarities of style. Not only is there in the two
plays an undeniably frequent recurrence of the same sorts
of quotations and allusions, and a remarkable parallelism—
at times an actual identity—of more or less unusual phrases
and collocations of words[1]; but in both we find mannerisms
such as it is not usual for two authors to share in common—
such as the usage, indulged in so largely as to become
a characteristic feature, of repeating a catch-word from
the line preceding, and of bandying back as it were the
half or the whole of a line from speaker to speaker[2]. Both
plays were unmistakeably written by the hand of a Euphuist,
and on the whole I am inclined to think that hand, in the
case of *Solyman and Perseda* as well as in that of *The
Spanish Tragedy*, to have been Thomas Kyd's[3].

There appears to me to be no sufficient reason for accepting
the supposition that the curious old play entitled *The Rare
Triumphs of Love and Fortune*, printed in 1589, but doubtless performed several years earlier, was written by Kyd[4].
The Induction is occupied with a 'debate' or 'mutiny' among
the divinities of Olympus, due to the endeavour of Venus to
destroy the power of Fortune, in order to assert her own
supreme authority. At the bidding of Jupiter, Mercury

*Plays attri-
buted to
Kyd:
The Rare
Triumphs
of Love and
Fortune
(pr. 1589).*

---

[1] The most out-of-the-way is the 'translucent breast' to be found in both
plays.

[2] For examples I must refer to Sarrazin, *u. s.*, pp. 2 *seqq.* I am bound to
say that the impression made upon me by his argument was confirmed by
a consecutive re-reading of these two plays.

[3] The versification of this play is less finished than that of *The Spanish
Tragedy*; but it must not be overlooked that the printer of *Solyman and
Perseda* turned a good deal of prose into verse. I am not aware, by the
way, whether it has ever been noticed that in the passage in Dekker's
Satiro-mastix referred to above (p. 309, note 3), in which 'Horace' (Jonson)
is taunted with having 'taken mad Jeronymo's part,' he replies (to Tucca's
flourish and enquiry, 'My name's Hamlet Revenge; thou hast been at
Paris Garden, hast not?') 'Yes, Captaine, I ha' played Zulziman there.'
This must refer to *Solyman and Perseda* itself, not to the 'play within' *The
Spanish Tragedy*.

[4] For an account of this play, of which the only extant copy is in the collection at Bridgewater House, see Collier, ii. 432–7. Cf. as to the probability of Kyd's authorship, Fleay, ii. 26.

hereupon exhibits a series of dumb-shows of persons slain by
Love or Fortune; after which the action of the play itself
begins, accompanied by musical demonstrations of the alternating successes of the two contending deities in aiding or
defeating the purposes of the lovers Hermione and Fidelia,
with whose story it is concerned. In the body of the play,
of which the greater part is written in a rimed twelve-syllable
measure, there seems nothing to connect it with a writer so
comparatively advanced in manner as Kyd; of the Induction
part is in blank verse, but rimes are here also frequent.

Other early plays have been attributed to Kyd by
Mr. Fleay and earlier writers, among them the *Taming of
a Shrew* (1594), on which Shakspere founded his comedy,
Titus Andronicus, which similarity of theme and treatment
naturally associated with *The Spanish Tragedy*, and (on the
evidence of a few parallel passages) *Arden of Feversham*.

*An early
Hamlet.*

Of more interest, and supported by certain specious considerations partaking of the nature of both external and
internal evidence [1], is the hypothesis, first offered by Malone
and since adopted by Widgery, Fleay, and others, that Kyd
was the author of an early tragedy of *Hamlet*, lost to us but
known to Shakspere. The extent and depth of the interest
which such a hypothesis involves may be illustrated by the
statement of one of its more recent supporters, that 'whatever
in *Hamlet* is relatively out of harmony with Shakspere's
taste, may be more or less [2] interpreted to be due to Kyd.'
But to examine from such a point of view the conjecture in
question would be foreign to the purpose of a historical
sketch, while an attempt to indicate its bearing upon the
genesis of Shakspere's *Hamlet* will find a more appropriate

---

[1] Nashe's *Epistle to the Gentlemen Students* (1589) pictures a playwright
who for many reasons (not the least among them the University man's
contempt for Latin not learnt on Cam or Isis) may be concluded to be Kyd.
In a later passage of the letter the 'famisht followers' of Sencca are said to
imitate 'the Kidde in *Aesop*,' who leapt into a new occupation, as they take
to Italian translations. Between these amenities occurs the suggestion,
that 'if you intreate' the playright in question, 'in a frostie morning, he will
afford you whole *Hamlets*, I should say handfulls of tragicall speeches.' See
also the passage cited above from Dekker's *Satiro-mastix*.

[2] '*Ungezwungen*.' Sarrazin, p. 119. I am aware that this word is itself
open to diplomatic interpretation.

place below[1]. Resemblance—or let us say cognateness—
of theme furnishes no proof of identity of authorship—still
less is the latter demonstrated by incidental similarities of
treatment. For my part, I am unable, in dealing with a lost
caput, to reach conviction except by way of external
evidence, which in this instance appears to me inadequate.

The author of *The Spanish Tragedy* was a contemporary   *Kyd's
of dramatists who were greater than himself, in whatever   claims to re-
degree he may have directly or indirectly influenced their   cognition as
endeavours. But, to whatever extent he may in his turn   an original
have profited from the productions of his fellow-playwrights,   dramatist.*
he was himself a dramatic poet of high and original capacity
for dealing with both the matter and the form of the branch
of literature to which he devoted his labours. He proved
himself capable of presenting, without servile adherence to
Senecan models,

> ' *Tragoedia cothurnata*, fitting kings,
>   Containing matter, and not common things[2]; '

and he was at the same time able to exhibit with natural
force the operation of incidents upon character, and to make
a direct and irresistible appeal to the passions that move all
men, and are felt by generation after generation. Herein
lies the great difference between him and the authors of
Gorboduc; nor will he, because of the ridicule which was
his recompense from some of those to whom he had helped
to point the way, be refused the tribute due to original
power.

CHRISTOPHER or Kit, MARLOWE[3], the son of John   *Christopher
Marlowe, shoemaker, ' clerk ' of St. Mary's, and of his wife   Marlowe
(1564–93).*

[1] See the chapter on *Shakspere*.
[2] *The Spanish Tragedy*, act v.
[3] *The Works of Christopher Marlowe. With some Account of the Author,
and Notes.* By the Rev. Alexander Dyce, 1850 and 1870.—*The Works of
Marlowe.* Edited by A. H. Bullen, 3 vols., 1885.—*The Works of Christopher
Marlowe,* edited with Notes and Introduction, by Lt. - Col. Francis
Cuningham, 1870.—*Christopher Marlowe.* Edited by Havelock Ellis ; with
a General Introduction, &c., by J. A. Symonds, 1887 ; see also chap. xv.
(*Marlowe*) of the same writer's *Shakspere's Predecessors.* An edition of
Marlowe's plays by H. Breymann and A. Wagner is now in course of
publication at Heilbronn, and several have already been published.—Arts.
on *Marlowe* by A. C. Swinburne in vol. xv. of the *Encyclopaedia Britannica*,

Catherine, apparently the daughter of Christopher Arthur, rector of St. Peter's, Canterbury, was born in that city in February, 1564. He received his early education at the King's School in his native city; and proceeded thence early in 1581 to Bene't (Corpus Christi) College, Cambridge, where he graduated B.A. and M.A. in 1583 and 1587. He was probably intended for the Church, or at all events for one of the learned professions; of his classical training so far as the usual Latin classics are concerned, there is evidence enough in the quotations freely introduced by him into his dramatic works, more especially *The Jew of Malta*, *Edward II*, and, as a matter of course, *Dido*. His translation of Ovid's *Amores* (the blunders in which have met with severe censure) seems to date from his Cambridge days, and shows that they were not devoted to close or accurate classical studies.

It must have been at an early date, and before the nominal completion of his University career, that Marlowe became seized by a passion for the stage. Possibly, as has been conjectured on grounds in themselves inadequate, he may, in the stormy years immediately preceding 1587, have served in the Netherlands; as to his anti-Spanish and anti-Catholic sentiments, at least, there can be no doubt. But it seems most likely that before 1587 he went up to London from Cambridge, where, possibly under other influences[1] besides that of his own fermenting genius, he had come to abandon the notion of entering the clerical or any other regular profession. In London he at once began to write for the stage; the supposition that he combined

9th ed., 1883, and by Sidney Lee, in vol. xxxvi. of the *Dictionary of National Biography*, 1893.—Cf. Collier, ii. 487 *seqq.*; Fleay, *English Drama*, ii. 57 *seqq.*; and *Life and Work of Shakspere*, and *History of the Stage*, passim; Ulrici, *Shakspere's Dramatic Art*, Sec. i. and art. *Christopher Marlowe u. Shakspere's Verhältniss zu ihm* in *Shakspere-Jahrbuch*, vol. i. (1865). For editions of particular plays see subsequent notes. An elaborate analysis of Marlowe's diction will be found in O. Fischer's dissertation *Zur Charakteristik der Dramen Marlowe's* (Munich, 1889).

[1] The supposition that Marlowe imbibed the theological views of Francis Kett, a fellow and tutor of his college, who was burnt for heresy at Norwich in 1589, presumes, what must be considered doubtful, that Marlowe had any theological views at all. However undergraduate and even postgraduate, minds are easily encouraged to 'give up' theology.

with the playwright's occupation that of the player, rests on
the evidence of a ballad called *The Atheist's Tragedy*, in
which he is said during a performance at the Curtain in
Shoreditch to have broken his leg

'in one lewd scene
When in his early age.'

But the genuineness of these verses is open to the gravest
doubts [1]. He appears to have attached himself as
a playwright to the Lord Admiral's company, by which
most of his plays were produced, with Edward Alleyn
as the principal actor; and he is supposed towards the
end of his life to have transferred his services to Lord
Strange's company, and thus to have entered into direct
co-operation with Shakspere [2]. That he was in close
personal connexion with all the chief theatrical writers of his
age, is in any case obvious, even were the fact not attested
by the passages to be immediately cited, containing cordial
tributes from several of them to his genius; his familiar
relations with at least one eminent personage whose literary
efforts were only part of his public activity are proved by
an almost unique monument of literary association [3]. He
was not without other friends and patrons of high social
standing; in the *Dedication* of his posthumous poem of
Hero and Leander, Marlowe's publisher speaks of Sir Thomas
Walsingham of Chiselhurst (the son of Sir Francis, connected
by marriage with a Canterbury family to which Marlowe
certainly entertained sentiments of attachment) as 'one who
had bestowed upon the author many kind favours'; and
Walsingham's house was indicated as a place where
Marlowe might be found in the warrant issued against him
shortly before his death.

It would, however, be idle to shut our eyes to the

[1] See the late Dr. Ingleby's trenchant letter to *The Academy*, April 1,
1876; and cf. Mr. Lee's statement, with which Mr. Bullen is in accord, that
'the ballad is in all probability one of Mr. Collier's forgeries,' and Mr. Fleay's
contemptuous silence with regard to it.

[2] Fleay, *History of the Stage*, p. 74.

[3] The famous lyric by Marlowe, *The Passionate Shepherd to his Love*,
which called forth Sir Walter Raleigh's *Reply* (as well as '*Another of the
same Nature*'), is quoted by Marlowe himself in a comic speech in *The Jew
of Malta*, act iv. sc. 4.

general bearing of the evidence as to Marlowe's personal
ways of life and thought during his career as a playwright
and man of letters in London.   It is manifest that, during
the short six years of that career, he reached a very high
point of popularity on the stage, where his *Tamburlaine*
and *Doctor Faustus* at all events were extraordinarily
successful.   It is also obvious that this popularity, and the
personal admiration called forth among his brother-wits by
his extraordinary powers, cannot have failed to affect the
moral balance of so young a man.   When the intellectual
agitations of the times in which he lived and the specially
overcharged atmosphere in which he worked are taken
into account, it seems only in the nature of things that
he should have demeaned himself as a rebel.   Very manifestly he led a loose life, and in all probability it tickled
his fancy, as it has that of others who have not proved
weaklings in the end, to let self-indulgence wear the
semblance of intellectual revolt.   His published works—
Doctor Faustus included—contain no evidence of a personal
struggle between doubt and faith.   When Robert Greene
died in want and misery in September 1592, he left behind
him the celebrated tract (to which frequent references will
have to be made in these pages) entitled *A Groats-worth of
Wit bought with a Million of Repentance*.   This pamphlet
contained a violent overt invective against Marlowe's professed atheism, with a warning to him to repent ere it was
too late.   Henry Chettle, who published Greene's tract,
immediately after his death, thought it well, in the preface to
his tract of *Kind Hart's Dream*, to disclaim any personal
acquaintance with Marlowe, while professing a reverence
for his learning, and stating that he had thought it well to
omit passages of Greene's attack [1].   We are, of course, anything but constrained to place reliance upon accusations
forming part of the lees of such a life as Greene's, who,
moreover, was probably actuated by bitter jealousy as
a playwright.   We are still less called upon to accept the

---

[1] The side-issue as to Nashe's supposed authorship of *A Groatsworth of Wit*,
and Gabriel Harvey's charge against him of disloyalty to Marlowe among
other friends, may be neglected here. See Bullen's *Introduction*, pp. lxi–lxii.

farrago of charges concerning Marlowe's opinions on religion put forward against him by one Richard Bame (possibly the person who was hanged in the following year), which led to the institution of inquisitorial proceedings, involving among others Thomas Kyd and Sir Walter Raleigh. But there are sufficient other indications that he had made himself notorious by licentious talk as well as by loose living; and the closing scene of his life, which followed while a warrant of the Privy Council was actually out against him, cannot be detached from the rest of the circumstantial evidence. On June 1, 1593, he was stabbed to death in a tavern brawl at Deptford, the revolting details of which may be fitly passed by, especially as their truth or falsehood, or the nature of the mixture in them of both, is not to be ascertained [1].

Of Marlowe's contemporaries—or of writers belonging to a generation by which the personal features of his career were still freshly remembered—not a few mention him with sincere and generous admiration for his genius. So Peele, in the *Prologue to the Honour of the Garter*, published in the year of Marlowe's death, addresses him as *Tributes from his contemporaries.*

> ' Unhappy in thine end,
> Marley, the Muse's darling for thy verse,
> Fit to write passions for the souls below,
> If any wretched souls in passion speak.'

Drayton, in his epistle *To my dear friend Henry Reynolds of Poets and Poesy* (1627), speaks of him in lines of singular beauty, recalling in their final turn of thought a well-known Shaksperean passage :—

---

[1] The entry in the burial-register of St. Nicholas' Church, Deptford, merely states that he was 'slain by Francis Archer' on the date mentioned. Gabriel Harvey was unfortunate enough to be without information, and concluded that Marlowe had died of the plague. (See Bullen on the *Glosse* at the end of Harvey's *Newe Letter of Notable Contests*, 1893, *u. s.* lxvi–lxvii; for versions of the actual catastrophe, including the Puritan Beard's (1597) and Meres' reference in *Palladis Tamia* (1598), see *ib.* lxiii–lxv.)—A remarkable specimen of anecdotical mendacity is to be found in Aubrey's assertion (quoted by Gifford) that 'Ben Jonson killed Mr. Marlowe the poet, coming from the Green Curtain playhouse.' This invention may have arisen out of a mistaken remembrance of the fact that Ben Jonson killed in a duel 'Gabriel,' a member of Henslowe's company of players, in Hoxton Fields. This, to be sure, was in 1598. (See *Memoirs of E. Alleyn*, p. 50.)

> ' Next Marlowe, bathèd in the Thespian springs,
>   Had in him those brave translunáry things
>   That the first poets had; his raptures were
>   All air and fire, which made his verses clere ;
>   For that fine madnes still he did retaine,
>   Which rightly should possess a poet's braine ' ;

and this tribute is doubly noteworthy as proceeding from a poet whose own life was well-ordered, and free from the ' Bohemianism ' which, in later days than those of Queen Elisabeth, many excellent people have deemed inseparable from the successful pursuit of literature [1]. Ben Jonson, in his verses *To the Memory of Shakspere* (in which I for one confess myself unable to discover any trace of irony), reckons Marlowe among those peers of Shakspere who were by him surpassed, and, in a phrase which has become immortal, refers to ' Marlowe's mighty line [2].' The Cambridge author of Part II of *The Returne from Parnassus* (printed 1606, but acted some years earlier) describes Marlowe as

> ' happy in his buskin'd Muse,'

although

> ' unhappy in his life and end ;
>   Pity it is that wit so ill should dwell,—
>   Wit lent from Heaven, but vices sent from Hell.'

The two poets who, with very different pretensions, took upon themselves to continue Marlowe's *Hero and Leander*, both apostrophised their predecessor,—Petowe at the close of a long set of doggerel lines hailing him as ' the prince of poetrie,' Chapman interrupting the first section of the

---

[1] ' He wants,' says the author of Part II of *The Returne from Parnassus*, referring to Drayton, ' one true note of a poet of our own times, and that is this : He cannot swagger it well in a tavern, or domineer in a pot-house.'

[2] Jonson is, however, thought by Gifford to indicate Marlowe among others in speaking, in the *Induction* to *Cynthia's Revels*, of poets who are ' promoters of other men's jests, and way-lay all the stale apophthegms, or other books, they can hear of, in print or otherwise, to farce their scenes withal.' The late Mr. Halpin (*Oberon's Vision*, &c.) says that Ben Jonson decried Marlowe in his *Poetaster* as well as in his *Cynthia's Revels*. I should doubt both these assertions. In the *Poetaster* (act i. sc. 1) Jonson certainly borrowed, with certain modifications, Marlowe's version of one of Ovid's Elegies (*Amor.* bk. i. el. xv.), though Gifford tried to turn the tables on Marlowe. (See Cuningham's *Jonson*, i. 210, *note*, and cf. Fleay, *English Drama*, i. 367.

poem written by himself in order to depict his desire of being in full accord with

> ' His free soul, whose living subject stood
> Up to the chin in the Pierian flood [1].'

Nashe, who completed Marlowe's tragedy of *Dido*, prefixed to the first edition (1594) an elegy full of praise, which is unfortunately lost [2]. Thomas Heywood, in his *Hierarchie of the Blessed Angels* (1634), speaks of Marlowe as

> ' renown'd for his rare art and wit,'

making special reference to his *Hero and Leander*. Lastly, Shakspere has a brief but kindly allusion to his deceased fellow-poet in the passage in *As You Like It* (act iii. sc. 5), which introduces a line from *Hero and Leander* :

> ' Dead shepherd ! now I find thy saw of might :
> "Who ever lov'd, that lov'd not at first sight [3] ?" '

For us, unable as we are to penetrate through the foul mists that obscured the career of this mighty genius, it remains only to lament the loss to the world's literature of a maturity, whose mere promise excels the achievements of any other but one among all our Elisabethan poets. A poet of our own times has met a challenge thrown out by Hartley Coleridge, in finding a poetic form for the tragedy of Marlowe's death. The late Mr. R. H. Horne's *Death of Marlowe* [4], a piece conceived and executed with genuine power, closes with the exquisite lines from the poet's own *Doctor Faustus* :

> ' Cut is the branch that might have grown full straight,
> And wither'd is Apollo's laurel bough.'

It is not Art which is guilty of the fall of such victims as this,—not genius which is chargeable with a share in such

---

[1] *Hero and Leander, Third Sestiad.* For Petowe's effort, cf. Dyce, *Some Account*, &c., p. xlii, and Bullen's Introduction, pp. lxx–lxxi. See *ib.* as to the reference in a poem by ' J. M.' (1600) to ' Kynde Kit Marloe.'

[2] Cf. *ib.*

[3] There is no evidence that the references to the story of *Hero and Leander* in *The Two Gentlemen of Verona* were due to Marlowe's poem. See Delius' *Shakspere*, i. 41, *note* 7 ; and cf. below as to the date of this comedy.

[4] This one-act play, first published in 1837, was reprinted in 1875.

a catastrophe. And, while drawing from it a homely moral,
yet one such as Thackeray might not have disdained to
draw, we may, at the same time, bow before the blessed
healthfulness of spirit that enabled Shakspere to come
forth unscathed from the temptations with which his time,
his life, and his surroundings, as it were resistlessly, overwhelmed Marlowe.

Marlowe's non-dra-matic works.   Besides the unfinished tragedy *Dido, Queen of Carthage*
(of which below), Marlowe left behind him certain transla-
tions and epigrams, and so much as he had written of the
paraphrase (for such it is rather than a translation) of
Musaeus' *Hero and Leander*. It is beyond my purpose to
dwell on the beauties of both the descriptive and the
passionate parts of this work of Marlowe's. The tributes
to his powers cited above have sufficiently illustrated the
fact that, in the eyes of his own generation, his poetic fame
largely, if not principally, rested on this achievement.
Indeed, even in a *Prologue* to a posthumous reproduction
of one of his plays, Marlowe is said to have gained 'a lasting
memory' by his English version of Musaeus' *epopoeia*, while
his plays and their renown are chiefly associated with that of
a popular actor [1]. Yet, since a comparison between Marlowe
and Shakspere, in so far as their careers ran more or less
parallel in dates, is legitimate, the fact cannot be overlooked
that, so far as Marlowe's share in it is concerned, *Hero and
Leander* is as superior to *Venus and Adonis* in general
poetic effect as it is in that special force of sensuous passion
which dries up critical comment. In the matter of luxurious
Renascence foliage, who could claim the preference for
either youthful artist? In the same connexion, a reference
cannot be omitted to Marlowe's famous lyric, *The Passionate
Shepherd to his Love*, first published in a collection of poems
(*The Passionate Pilgrim*, 1599), purporting to be wholly

---

[1] See Dyce's note, p. 142, to the *Prologue to the Stage, at the Cock-Pit*,
prefixed to the *Jew of Malta*, in special compliment to Edward Alleyn, the
representative of 'the Jew.'—*Hero and Leander* is quoted as a popular
work in *Greene's Tu Quoque*, printed in 1614—the year in which Jonson
burlesqued the myth in the puppet-show of his *Bartholomew Fair*. In
Middleton's *A Mad World, my Masters* (i. 2), Harebrain couples *Hero
and Leander* and *Venus and Adonis* as 'wanton pamphlets.' *Hero and
Leander* is also alluded to in Middleton's *The Family of Love* (iii. 2).

Shakspere's. The first stanza of Raleigh's reply was likewise printed in this collection [1]. Other English lyric poets
have, more or less consciously, imitated a masterpiece which
suffices to prove Marlowe's rare endowment for a species
of composition which he only exceptionally essayed.

Marlowe's earliest play, there is every reason for assuming,
was the tragedy of *Tamburlaine the Great*, in two Parts,
each of five acts [2]. His authorship of this work cannot
underlie a moment's doubt, although the only external
evidence of a direct kind attesting it is to be found
in a sonnet, and the 'glosse' accompanying it, already
noticed as published by Gabriel Harvey in 1593. The
'crude notion' of Malone that not Marlowe, but Nashe, was
the author of *Tamburlaine*, is refuted by the fact that in
the *Epistle to the Gentlemen Students of Both Universities*
prefixed by Nashe to Greene's *Menaphon* (1589, or possibly
as early as 1587) he inveighs, in obvious allusion to the
defiance in the Prologue to *Tamburlaine*, against the
endeavour of 'idiote art-masters' to 'outbrave better pens
with the swelling bumbast of a bragging blank verse.'
This passage, taken together with another attack upon the
introduction of blank verse, which is accompanied by an
express reference to 'that atheist *Tamburlan*' in the address
'To the Gentlemen Readers,' prefixed by Greene to his *Perimedes the Blacke-Smith*, further proves that *Tamburlaine*
was brought on the stage as early as 1588; probably it
was first acted by the Lord Admiral's company, as
Mr. Fleay says, 'on stages in the City of London as early
as 1587.' It was printed in 1590 [3].

*Tambur-
laine the
Great*
(1587).

[1] Dyce, *u. s.*, xlv. Marlowe himself alludes to 'Come live with me' in
a comic speech in *The Jew of Malta*, act iv.

[2] Besides the English editions, reference should be made to that of
A. Wagner, in the series already mentioned (Heilbronn, 1885).—The full
title of the 4to edition of 1590 may be worth citing: '*Tamburlaine the Great.
Who, from a Scythian Shephearde by his rare and wonderfull Conquests, became
a most puissant and mightye Monarque. And (for his tyranny, and terrour in
Warre) was tearmed, The Scourge of God.*' Nothing but the title-page is left of
this edition. The full title of *Part II* in the 8vo edition of both Parts, bearing
the same date, of which a copy is in the Bodleian, runs: '*The Second Part
of The bloody Conqueste of Tamburlaine. With his impassionate fury, for the
death of his Lady and loue faire Zenocrate; his fourme of exhortacion and discipline to his three sons, and the maner of his own death.*' (Dyce.)

[3] See Bullen's *Introduction*, pp. xv-xviii. Cf. Collier, ii. 491-4. Collier

The sources of this play have been detected by its most recent Editor and Dr. C. H. Herford, who have shown [1] that a Spanish account of Timour the Tartar conqueror, by Pedro Mexia, in a *Silva* of which one among many versions was an English translation known as Fortescue's *The Foreste*, and printed in 1571, may be concluded to have among various more or less contemporary narratives suggested to Marlowe the theme of his tragedy.   They further show that his general arrangement of the argument of his ten acts seems to have resulted from his use, together with Mexia's biography, of the Latin life of Timour published at Florence by the Italian scholar Perondinus in 1551, to which are due, among a number of incidental details, some of those making up the authentic portrait of the hero [2]. The question as to the authenticity of the statements in these narratives, or in others at which his eye may have glanced [3], cannot be supposed to have exercised Marlowe

adduces two other supposed proofs of Marlowe's authorship of *Tamburlaine*. But the first of these, viz. the entry in Henslowe's *Diary* of two payments to 'Thomas Dickers' (Dekker) on December 20, 1597, for 'adycyons' to *Doctor Faustus* and 'a prolog to Marloes Tamberlen' is unhappily discredited.   The second is a passage in the *Prologue* written by Thomas Heywood for the performance of *The Jew of Malta* at the Cock-pit in 1633, which Collier misunderstood, although it may be held to suggest, by association, that *Tamburlaine* was written by Marlowe.   See Dyce's note to this *Prologue*.—As to the date of the composition of *Tamburlaine*, the simile of the almond-tree in Part II. act iv. sc. 4, was certainly not only suggested by, but in part copied from, *The Faerie Queene*, I. vii. 32; and since the first three books of Spenser's poem were not published till the beginning of 1590, the passage must have been seen by Marlowe in MS.; possibly Raleigh may have acted as intermediary.—If Marlowe obtained his knowledge of a passage in the *Orlando Furioso* (see below as to the episode of Olympia's death) from Sir John Harington's translation, he must have seen this also in MS., as it was not published till 1591. (Collier, ii. 497.)

[1] See their letter on *The Sources of Marlowe's Tamburlaine* in *The Academy*, October 20, 1883.   It may be worth mentioning that the story of Tamerlane was dramatically treated by the Spaniard Luis Velez de Guevara (1570–1644) in his *La nueva era de Dios, y Tamerlan de Persia*.   See Klein, x. 725 note.

[2] See the speech of Menaphon, Part I. act ii. sc. 1:
'Of stature tall, and straightly fashionèd,' &c.

[3] These cannot have included the Abbé du Bec's *Histoire du Grand Tamerlan*, which (for the first time largely utilising Arabic sources) sought to humanise and rationalise the conduct of the hero.   This book, which Warton supposes to have introduced the story of Tamerlane into English literature, was not published till 1595, or translated into English till 1597.

severely; and I perceive no proof in or apart from his
sonorous but as a rule perfunctory references to ancient
names and places that he was possessed of the illustrative
resources of true classical scholarship. As a matter of course,
any sceptical hesitation with regard to the statements which
he found in his sources was still less to be expected from
him[1]. *Tamburlaine* neither called itself a *History* (as the
Elisabethan dramatists applied the word[2]), nor is it in any
but the vaguest sense of the term to be described as a historical drama. Strict historical propriety would of course in
no case have been expected in it; and even the passage in
which Tamburlaine imparts to his sons a notion of the science
of military engineering, odd as it may seem in the mouth of
a warrior whose opportunities of technical training had been
so limited, calls for no exceptional comment[3]. But there is
no attempt to furnish that 'poetical image of historical
truth[4]' which Shakspere kept in view in the midst of constant
violations of historical accuracy; and it is on purely internal
grounds that the poet's free and fantastic treatment of his
theme is called upon to vindicate itself.

Now, it would be idle to deny that the appalling—or
should I say 'sensational'—nature of some of the situations
in this play constitutes a more salient feature in it than the
measure of power exhibited by its general method of construction. Bajazeth, brought out of his cage to serve as his
conqueror's footstool[5]; the same ex-potentate, and afterwards

---

[1] I cannot say how far they provoked, or justified the *caveat* of Sir Thomas
Browne (*Vulgar Errors*, Bk. II. ch. 16): 'That Tamerlane was a Scythian
shepherd . . . we have reason to deny.'

[2] The two Parts are called 'Tragicall Discourses' on the title-pages of the
editions of both 1590 and 1592.

[3] Among the things he would have them learn is

'the way to fortify your men;
In champion grounds, what figure serves you best
For which the quinque-angle is meet,
Because the corners there may fall more flat,
Whereas the fort may fittest be assailed,
And sharpest where the assault is desperate,' &c. &c.

Artillery effects are more than once alluded to in the play.

[4] Ulrici.

[5] Part I. act iv. scene 2. In the 'cage' itself there was nothing
specially Oriental. Unless my memory deceives me, I have myself seen

his wife, 'braining' themselves against his prison-bars[1];
Tamburlaine cutting his arm in order to show his hopeful
sons that a 'wound is nothing,' although he restrains the
most aspiring among them from immediately imitating his
example[2]; and, above all, his famous entry in his chariot
drawn by captive kings[3],—in the presence of such effects as
these it is indeed difficult to admit any other impressions.
Yet, considering the general nature of the action, which resembles an avalanche proceedng on its irresistible course, some
skill must be allowed to be shown in its conduct. The movement of the action, notwithstanding its essential sameness and
its extension over ten successive acts, rises instead of falling
off, and its climax is marked not only by the entrance on
the scene of the pampered jades, but also by the magnificent
defiance hurled by the conqueror at Mahomet, the reputed
assessor of the Almighty[4].   Opportunity is moreover found

swinging from the Cathedral tower at Munster, the cage to which some
of the Anabaptist leaders were consigned A. D. 1536.   The story of Bajazet's
cage, and of his treatment by Timour in general, is critically examined in
ch. lxiv of Gibbon's *Decline and Fall.*—The governor of Babylon, Part II.
act v. scene 1, is merely hung up in chains on his own walls to be shot to
death by the victorious soldiery.

[1] Part I. act v. sc. 2.
[2] Part II. act iii. sc. 2.
[3] Part II. act iv. sc. 4, *et post.*   The following is the stage-direction:—
'*Enter* TAMBURLAINE *drawn in his chariot by the Kings of Trebizond and
Soria, with bits in their mouths, reins in his left hand, and in his right hand a
whip, with which he scourgeth them. . . . Kings of Natolia and Jerusalem*'
[they are afterwards termed the '*two spare Kings*'] '*led by five or six common
Soldiers.*'—This famous passage, with Tamburlaine's 'Holla, ye pampered
jades of Asia,' which Shakspere ridiculed in 2 *Henry IV,* act ii. sc. 4, is also
derided by a host of other writers, including Beaumont and Fletcher (*The
Coxcomb,* act ii. sc. 2) and Chapman and his associates (*Eastward Hoe,*
act ii); also in Edward Sharpham's *The Fleire,* a play first printed in 1607
(Collier, ii. 502 note).   It was however imitated by Lodge in his *Wounds of
Civil War* (cf. *ib.* iii. 37).
[4] The conclusion of this speech does not to my mind warrant Greene's
denunciatory phrase of 'daring God out of heaven with that atheist *Tamburlan*' :

> 'Well, soldiers, Mahomet remains in hell,
> He cannot hear the voice of Tamburlaine ;
> Seek out another Godhead to adore,—
> The God that sits in heaven, if any God ;
> For he is God alone, and none but he.'
>
> (Act v. sc. 1.)

Marlowe was doubtless thinking of St. Matthew, iv. 10.

for a few love-scenes not devoid of a certain rough charm;
there is genuine passion, though defaced by extravagance,
in Tamburlaine's lament over Zenocrate, and true pathos in
the appeal of the virgins of Damascus on behalf of their
menaced city. The episode of Olympia's death, although, to
be sure, not original but borrowed from Ariosto [1], cannot have
left many readers unmoved ; and if the scenes in which Tamburlaine's boys take part are not specially pleasing, they
at least help to vary the progress of the drama. It should
be added that the play was not printed as it was acted,
many omissions of 'fond and frivolous gestures' having
been made by its first editor—passages, it has been conjectured, comprising the buffoonery of the clown, whose
absence from the printed tragedy is certainly no matter for
regret [2].

Of even greater importance, however, than the substance *The blank*
of this tragedy is its form. The proposition indeed that *verse and*
Marlowe was the first to introduce blank verse upon the *the diction*
English stage will not bear examination, and cannot be *of Tam-*
sustained even in the sense that most of the plays before *burlaine.*
Tamburlaine in which blank verse was employed were
intended for performance at Court, like *Gorboduc*, or at all
events before select and cultivated audiences. The innovation lies rather in the quality of the verse, which harmonised
with the vigorous movement of the action, the stir of life
in the characters, and the exuberant passion of the diction [3].
To meet such a demand as this—to suit his metre to the
tragic themes and the tragic treatment commending themselves to his genius—Marlowe had to give the go-by to rime,
to which the popular drama, even where it did not indulge in
the seven-foot metre or in stanza-forms, had on the whole
continued to adhere. Rimed stanzas were, except as lyrical
intermezzos, doomed as a metre of the English drama so soon

---

[1] Cf. *ante*, p. 322 note. In Book xxix. of the *Orlando Furioso* Isabella
defeats the desires of Rodomonte by precisely the same stratagem as that
employed by Olympia against Theridamas.

[2] Traces of these fond features remain in the fragments of prose scattered
through the piece. See e. g. Part II. act iii. sc. 4.

[3] 'It is,' says Mr. Swinburne, 'the first poem ever written in English
blank verse, as distinguished from mere rhymeless decasyllabics.'

as the latter became a living representation of human action. The case was not so clear with rimed couplets, but except where the practice of running-in (*enjambement*) is adopted and the natural effect of the couplet is accordingly taken away, this kind of verse both lends itself to, and in return encourages, an artificial arrangement of thoughts, while interfering with the continuity which is part of the naturalness of dramatic movement[1]. Perceiving this, Marlowe so to speak at once and completely threw in his lot with blank verse; but though his lines from the first had the same combination of strength, ease and majesty which remained characteristic of them to the last[2], yet the metrification of *Tamburlaine* still shows some signs of uncertainty. To begin with, the occurrence of rime, in the middle as well as at the end of speeches, is not at all uncommon[3]; double-endings, on the other hand, are only very occasionally admitted, though they became more common in Marlowe's later plays. Prose, as has been seen, is not entirely banished from this buskined tragedy. But more noteworthy is the fact that, half doubtful of the inherent power of the blank verse which came forth from his hands, the author of *Tamburlaine* thought it well to compensate his hearers for the loss of rime by providing them with unprecedented effects of diction[4]. Hence, though not solely hence, the 'high-astounding terms' for which *Tamburlaine* became proverbial. They comprised much bombast, but with it also much new material (if I may use the phrase) of poetic diction that, though not always inspired by a genius such as Marlowe's, became part and parcel of the endowment of a whole generation of

---

[1] This of course is not the case where special emphasis is required, as above all at the close of a speech of greater length.

[2] A Miltonic delight in the subjugation of magnificent proper names— 'Usumcasane and Theridamas '—is likewise largely perceptible.

[3] In *Part I* there are fifteen (possibly more) instances of rime, in *Part II* twenty-six or thereabouts, with at least two cases of triplets in addition.

[4] 'From jigging veins of rhyming mother-wits,
And such conceits as clownage keeps in pay,
We'll lead you to the stately tent of war,
Where you shall hear the Scythian Tamburlaine
Threatening the world with high astounding terms,' &c.
(*Prologue.*)

dramatists. Nowhere else, however, do we find all the
elements of out-of-the-way effect mixed and stirred up
together in a diction so recklessly and yet of set purpose
extravagant as is that of *Tamburlaine*. The accumulation
of strange personal and local appellatives is the most superficial among these ingredients, but not necessarily that in
which the author took the smallest amount of pride[1]. Of
more consequence is the boundless fury of the invective
rhetoric which victor and vanquished bandy to and fro,
without respite or remorse, and always in the same key of
supreme but sustained excitement[2]. And I cannot but
add a reference to the excessive use of ornate similes
drawn from a limited range of classical mythology more or
less at haphazard, although among them are to be found
already in this play some of the choicest gems of Marlowe's
poetry[3]. In course of time, no doubt, as an examination of
the works subsequently produced by Marlowe during the
very brief limits of his career as a playwright will show,
practice brought home to him the supreme excellence of
the instrument of versification he had chosen—which is no
other than its incomparable flexibility; so that, while
adhering to the preference for single-syllable endings which
was a characteristic of his earlier blank verse, that of his later
plays is far more varied in rhythm and cadence[4]. Upon
his contemporaries the example set by him had the effect of

---

[1] If *Limnasphaltis, Zona Mundi*, &c., were terms derived from the
author's researches, this fact is not likely to have diminished his zest in
employing them.

[2] Mr. Swinburne's description of the diction of *Tamburlaine* is classical,—
'the stormy monotony of Titanic truculence which blusters like a Simoom
through the noisy course of its ten fierce acts.'

[3] I need only mention the famous apostrophe to Zenocrate (Part I. act v.
sc. 1) which contains the immortal lines on ' Beauty, mother to the Muses.'—
How uncontrollably these similes ran from the poet's pen, may be seen
from the passage (Part II. act iii. sc. 4) introducing Cynthia and Thetis,
which, unless it be supposed that Cynthia is meant for Queen Elisabeth,
contains a curious involution of comparisons.

[4] It is not easy to say whether we should apply to the substance or to the
form of Marlowe's plays the remark said to have been often made by Ben
Jonson, that ' Marlowe's mighty lines were examples fitter for admiration
than for parallel.' (R. C.'s *Address to the Reader* prefixed to William
Bosworth's *Chast and Lost Lovers*, &c. (1651), a poem partly based on *Hero
and Leander*.)

the beacon which lights up the chain of flame; and the establishment of blank verse as the metre of English tragedy was not less rapid than its endurance has proved secure.

Of the commanding popularity of *Tamburlaine* the evidence is overpowering, being made up of the factors of recognition, censure, reminiscence, and parody[1]. Of its enduring influence the one fact is the criterion, that it created the style of Elisabethan tragedy.

Marlowe's second play, as may without hesitation be

---

[1] In Peele's *Battle of Alcazar*, act i. sc. 2, we have a recognition of the Napoleonic type represented by the hero:—

> 'Convey Tamburlaine into our Afric here,
> To chastise and to menace lawful kings:
> Tamburlaine, triumph not, for thou must die,
> As Philip did, Cæsar, and Cæsar's peers.'

Per contra, Greene, in his *Menaphon*, sneeringly guesses that 'mightie *Tamburlaine* after his wife Zenocrate (the world's fair eye) past out of the Theater of this mortall life'—*avait des maitresses*. Tamerlane is twice mentioned as a proverbial bugbear in the same author's *Tu Quoque*. In his *Discoveries*, Jonson reprobates language which flies 'from all humanity, with the Tamerlanes and Tamer-Chams, which had nothing in them but the scenical strutting and furious vociferation to warrant them to the ignorant gapers.'—Of imitations of the play as a whole it would lead me too far to speak; Tamburlaine is twice mentioned in the play of *The Tragicall Raigne of Selimus, sometime Emperour of the Turkes* (pr. 1594), in which Mr. Fleay (*English Drama*, ii. 315) is convinced that Greene had a hand, although he supposes the greater part of it to have been written by Lodge. The *First Part* of this play concludes by holding out the promise that

> 'If this First Part, Gentles, do like you well,
> The Second Part shall greater murthers tell.'

(Halliwell's *Dictionary*, &c., p. 223.) The parodistic allusions to the 'pampered jades of Asia' have already been noticed; another phrase which lent itself to quotation was 'Awake, ye men of Memphis' at the opening of act iv. of Part I.—Among reminiscences (as distinct from parodies) of passages in *Tamburlaine* to be found in Shakspere by far the most striking is the famous description of Death in *Richard II*, act iii. sc. 2 ('There the antic sits,' &c.; cf. *Tamburlaine*, Part I. act v. sc. 1; the 'antic Death' occurs also in *Henry VI*, Part I. act iv. sc. 7, which has been ascribed to Marlowe). Of less moment is the resemblance between *Macbeth*, act v. sc. 5 ('Hang out our banners,' &c.) and *Tamburlaine*, Part I. act iv. sc. 4 (one of the several passages in which Marlowe makes effective use of the story of Tamburlaine's use of white, vermilion and black standards with graduated significance); and that between *King John*, act iii. sc. 1 ('Nature and Fortune join'd to make you great') and *Tamburlaine*, Part I. act ii. sc. 1.— Mr. Bullen, p. xxii, has noted some later references to *Tamburlaine*, and its revival on the stage about 1650. As to Rowe's *Tamerlane*, and the curious contrast between this play and Marlowe's, see below.

concluded, was *The Tragical History of Doctor Faustus*[1]. The internal evidence which points to 1588, or to the very beginning of the following year, as the date of the earliest performance of this tragedy, is remarkably strong, the arguments from details being reinforced by the general conclusion as to the progress noticeable in its versification as compared with that of *Tamburlaine*. And a further corroboration by external evidence is furnished by the date (February, 1589) at which the ballad of the *Life and Death of Doctor Faustus the great Conjurer* was entered upon the Stationers' Registers, inasmuch as this ballad, if it was the same as that which has been preserved, may be held to have been in all probability composed after, and not before, the production of Marlowe's tragedy[2]. The first extant edition of the play is the quarto of 1604; but before this date it had been subjected to at least one revision[3]. The edition of 1616 contains further comic matter of a supplementary kind; and much controversy has inevitably arisen as to the authorship of the comic scenes in both the one and the other of these versions of the play. Here it must suffice to say that while Marlowe cannot possibly be held responsible for the additions of 1616[4], no such certainty obtains as to the buffoonery contained in the earliest edition. This may, as Mr. Fleay holds, be the invention of Dekker, to whom the fabricated entry in Henslowe's *Diary* assigned it; on the other hand, more especially as we know that *Tamburlaine* originally contained a similar admixture, it may be Marlowe's own. Even those who incline to the

The Tragical History of Doctor Faustus (1588).

---

[1] Recent editions of Marlowe's *Faustus* are those of the late Professor W. Wagner (1877), the present writer (1878, since revised), and Professor H. Breymann (Heilbronn, 1889). Concerning the multitudinous literature connected with this play I may perhaps be excused for making a general reference to my edition, while conscious how vainly it toils after the exigences of such a theme. The translations of Marlowe's *Faustus* with which I am acquainted are the German by Wilhelm Müller (1818) and A. von der Velde (1870) and the French by F. V. Hugo (1858).

[2] See also Mr. Fleay's conclusions as to the date of performance derived from the history of the actors' companies in *Appendix A* to the *Introduction* to my second and third editions.

[3] 'Adicyones' by William Birde (or Borne) and Samuel Rowley are mentioned in the (genuine) entry in Henslowe's *Diary* of November 22, 1602.

[4] Whatever view may be taken as to the rest of the text of this quarto.

former view cannot escape the unwelcome conclusion, that
the first performance of this immortal work was accompanied by deplorable drolleries differing not very materially
from those of which the origin has been discussed by so
many learned men.

Its theme,   The undying interest attaching to Marlowe's *Doctor
Faustus* lies, for once in almost equal proportions, in the
theme of the tragedy, and in that tragedy itself. The theme
which the great English poet was the first to treat in an
adequate dramatic form, has occupied modern European
literature from its beginnings to its most modern developements. Its original source (although even this expression
may seem to need modification) may be sought in those
conflicts between Christianity and magic to which already
the *Acts of the Apostles* bear testimony. The specific notion,
however, of the sale of his soul by a human being to the
Devil—followed in all these early instances by the ultimate
annihilation of the contract through the Divine Grace—can
be traced as far back as the sixth century, when the story of
Theophilus was supposed to have been related in Greek by
his pupil Eutychianus; it spread in a variety of versions
through Eastern and Western Christendom ; was narrated in
Leonine hexameters by the learned abbess Hrotsvitha ; was
introduced into the *Golden Legend*; and besides finding its
way to the miracle-stage through Rutebeuf, a French *trouvère*
of the thirteenth century, re-appeared in early English narrative and in Low-German dramatic literature. Two Icelandic
versions of the story are likewise mentioned. Finally, it was
made the subject of an English poem by the Catholic priest
William Forrest in 1572, and of two seventeenth-century
Jesuit ' comedies.' In other legends the object of the contract
with the Evil One is the prolongation of a life of pleasure ;
in the story of Cyprian of Antioch, which so far as we
know is even earlier in origin than that of Theophilus, and
which afterwards furnished the materials for Calderon's *El
Magico Prodigioso* (1637), the thirst for knowledge appears
as the first suggestion, though not as the actual motive, of
the understanding. Here the virgin purity of a human
maiden defeats the wiles of Satan ; in an Italian *Miracolo*

de Nostra Donna, belonging to the close of the fourteenth or
the beginning of the fifteenth century, the influence of the
Blessed Virgin is directly victorious.

The mediaeval conception which associated with magic
and witchcraft scientific enquiry, more especially those
kinds of it in which, as in astrology and alchemy,
science and imposture were inextricably intermixed,—the
inclination to theosophic and cabbalistic studies which
was characteristic of the earlier Renascence age, and was
industriously fostered by the migratory professors of this
branch of learning,—and finally the superstitious fears of
the Reformation age, which had cast off its leading-
strings before it had learnt to walk alone,—these were
the influences jointly responsible for the creation of the
particular type of Doctor Faustus. That the original
Faust was a real personage—not of course the printer Fust,
as was at one time frequently supposed, but a wandering
necromant and medical quack, who flourished after his
fashion in the South-West of the Empire, as well as
in Thuringia, Saxony, and adjoining countries, somewhere
between the years 1510 and 1540—may at the same time
held to be established. His birthplace, according to
Melanchthon, was Knittlingen in Württemberg ; but various
other places contended for the honour of his nativity, among
others Roda in the Duchy of Saxe-Altenburg ; hence
Marlowe [1] speaks of his Doctor Faustus as born

'In Germany, within a town call'd Rhodes.'

Very soon references to this worthy found their way into contemporary German literature ; and it should not be overlooked
that not only was the English public in this period peculiarly
susceptible to all stories of sorcery and witchcraft [2], but
that its craving in this direction was largely fed by ' news

[1] Opening *Chorus*.

[2] We shall have many opportunities of noticing the testimonies to the
truth of the above statement furnished by our drama in the Elisabethan and
Jacobæan ages. Witchcraft is an important element of the interest of the
action in *Macbeth*, in Middleton's *The Witch*, and in Thomas Heywood and
Brome's *The Lancashire Witches*, not to mention Jonson's *The Sad Shepherd*
and *The Masque of Queens*. I need not refer to plays introducing with
a satirical purpose the figures of astrologers or alchemists. The story of

and sources.

out of Germany,' which came over with all kinds of literature in unprecedented quantities from the home of the Reformation and the printing-press. When, accordingly, the story of Dr. Faustus was, in the year 1587, made the theme of a popular story-book (the so-called old *Faustbuch*, printed by Johann Spiess at Frankfort-on-the-Main), which speedily ran through several editions, besides being continued, elaborated and imitated in various ways, it naturally found its way to England without much delay. An English translation very soon made its appearance under the title of *The History of the Damnable Life and deserved Death of Doctor Johann Faustus;* but unfortunately this has not come down to us in an earlier edition than that of 1592, which describes itself as ' newly printed and amended.' Thus the question whether Marlowe founded his tragedy upon one of the early editions of the German original, or upon the English version, can only be determined by internal evidence; and not many questions of the kind have been debated with more persevering assiduity and minuteness. My own opinion inclines to the conclusion that the English *History* was used for the first extant edition of Marlowe's play ; although it cannot I think be regarded as absolutely certain whether the edition so used was that of 1592. This conclusion does not put out of court the possibility that the German original as well as the English version was referred to by Marlowe. There is, for the rest, no proof of the existence of any German drama on the story of Faustus which the English poet might have used in conjunction with the popular narrative [1].

The agreement in essentials between Marlowe's tragedy and the old popular book, whether in its German or in its English form, is in any case incontestable, and of these

a contract with the Devil appears in *The Divil's Charter* (1607). In *The Merry Devil of Edmonton* and in Jonson's *The Devil is an Ass* it serves a comic purpose.

[1] This was supposed to have been the case by Simrock, because the figures of *the Good* and *the Evil Angel*, which are not in the *Faustbuch* but occur in an early German (not in the English) ballad, are familiar to the German puppet-plays, based in all probability upon an early German drama or dramas, on the subject of Faust.

essentials that which possesses the deepest interest for us is
the motive of Faustus' fall. Herein Marlowe's tragedy is
at one with the popular legend, representing Faustus as
impelled towards the fatal contract by the arrogance of his
intellectual self-consciousness. Knowing so much, he must
know all, do all, dare all [1]. I am quite ready to concede
that neither Marlowe nor the popular books represented
Faustus as selling his soul in order to compass knowledge
for its own sake ;—such was not even Goethe's conception,
notwithstanding its far greater complexity ; it does appear,
in the first instance at all events, to have been Lessing's.
But although the sentiment that ' knowledge is power ' was
applied with unaffected directness by the child of an age
whose philosophers strove to make gold and to read the fate
of kings in the stars, I cannot on the late Mr. Lewes' own
showing [2] agree with him that Marlowe has ' given his hero
the vulgarest of motives.'

It has, however, been pointed out with indisputable truth *Marlowe's*
by Goethe's English biographer, that the resemblance *treatment*
of his sub-
between Marlowe's tragedy and the loftiest poetic repro- *ject.*
duction which the Faust-legend has at any time experienced,
ceases, or all but ceases, after the first scene, where Faustus,
in his study at Wittenberg, declares himself at the end of
all science, and craves for something more [3]. The something
more which Marlowe's Faustus desires, he feels, quite in
the spirit of the age to which he belongs, absolutely certain
of finding in magic [4]. The spirit who obeys the call of
Faustus is ' Mephistophilis.' Notwithstanding the pretended

[1]   ' Unlawful things,
        Whose deepness doth entice such forward wits,
        To practise more than heavenly power permits.'
    [2] *Life of Goethe* (ed. 1864), p. 470.
    [3] The character of Wagner, Faust's *famulus*, is also in Marlowe, with
certain of the touches which make it so lifelike in Goethe's work.—The
Wagnerbuch of 1593, which sought to carry on the experiences of Faust in
the person of his assistant, was of course guiltless of influence upon Marlowe's play.
    [4] ' A sound magician is a mighty god.'—Nothing in the early scenes of
Goethe's *Faust* is more powerful than the hero's recognition of the insufficiency of the mere vision which his skill has enabled him to summon, and
which for a moment made him doubt, while bathed in its flood of light,
whether he was not ' a god.'

accuracy of magical terminology, it would be as absurd to
define the place of Marlowe's Mephistophilis in the hierarchy
of hell, as to assign his proper position in it to his namesake
in Goethe.   Neither is intended to represent the Prince of
Darkness himself; but though Marlowe's Mephistophilis is
but 'a servant to great Lucifer,' he is capable of rising above
his functions [1]. Of far more importance is the deeply spiritual
conception of a future state revealed by Marlowe's Mephistophilis, in reply to the query of Faustus how it comes to pass
that if his visitor is damned in Hell he is out of it :

> 'Why, this is Hell, nor am I out of it.
> Think'st thou that I that saw the face of God
> And tasted the eternal joys of Heaven,
> Am not tormented with ten thousand Hills
> In being deprived of everlasting bliss?' [2]

The same depth of moral meaning reveals itself elsewhere
in the earlier part of the play.   No sooner has he formed
his resolution, than Faustus is distracted by the conflicting
monitions of the *Good* and the *Evil Angel;* but he decides
to sign the document which consigns his soul to perdition in
payment of four-and-twenty years' service on the part of
Mephistophilis.   Just before the execution of the deed the
following colloquy takes place between the pair :

> '*F.* Stay, Mephistophilis, and tell me what good will my soul do
> thy lord ?
> *M.* Enlarge his kingdom.
> *F.* Is this the reason why he tempts me thus?
> *M.* *Solamen miseris socios habuisse malorum.*
> *F.* Why, have you any pain that torture others?
> *M.* As great as have the human souls of man [3].'

But the action, thus powerfully begun, soon loses its strength
of purpose.   Faustus—and this is finely conceived, though
quite inadequately carried out—falls into vain and irresolute
repentance immediately after he has overtly sinned against
high Heaven ; his Good Angel tells him that it is 'never too
late if Faustus will repent'; but his heart is hardened, and

---

[1] See the fine lines, sc. xiii. 79–81.—In sc. vi. Lucifer (with Belzebub)
asserts his royal position.

[2] Sc. iii ; cf. sc. v.   [3] Sc. v.

he launches recklessly upon the career which now lies open
before him. The successive scenes representing the period
of his command over the services of Mephistophilis are
extremely wearisome ; and critics are of course at liberty to
accept or reject as Marlowe's so much or so little of these as
they choose. But it is at least unsafe to pronounce those
passages not to be his which are directly based on the
narrative that he must have used as the main foundation
of his play. From this point of view, part of the buffoonery
may, and part may not, be regarded as probably Marlowe's
composition. The examination in natural philosophy to
which Faustus subjects his servant deviates from the popular
books in details which may or may not have been inserted
by Marlowe himself. The introduction of the Seven Deadly
Sins, favourite characters of both mediaeval and Renascence
literature[1], seems to me both appropriate and in its way
effective.   On the other hand, Faustus' endeavours to put
his new powers to the proof are calculated (as they are presented to us) upon simply astonishing the spectators. They
commence (this however off the scene) with an aërial voyage
by Faustus to view the secrets of astronomy, and his return
to earth ' to prove cosmography '; but these scientific researches are speedily succeeded by doings of a different sort
at Rome and at the imperial court in Germany. The
incidents here consist in a display by Faustus of his magical
powers, partly in practical jokes, impartially played upon
Pope and horse-dealer, partly in the summoning up of the
dead (Alexander and his Paramour).   A higher interest is
only revived in the fifth act, when Faustus, at the request of
his students at Wittenberg, calls up the vision of fair Helen
—the figure invested with so mysterious a significance in
the *Second Part* of Goethe's *Faust*. The lines in which
the magician addresses the beauteous apparition are

---

[1] The Procession of the Deadly Sins in *The Faerie Queene*, Bk. I. canto iv.
stanzas 17–37, Marlowe could have only seen in MS.; Dekker's tractate, *The
Seven Deadly Sinnes of London*, was not published till 1606. Tarleton's ex-
tempora play (mentioned in 1592) on the subject, of which the 'plott' (or
skeleton sketch fixed on a board for consultation by the performers) is
reprinted by Collier, iii. 198 *seqq.*, may possibly have been suggested by
Doctor Faustus.

famous as an incomparably beautiful example of a strain of passionate poetry, of which *Tamburlaine* had offered but very imperfect anticipations. Hereupon, after the climax, comes the catastrophe, which is presented with tremendous tragic force. The anxious students and the Angels Bad and Good prepare us for the end—and then, as the hand of the clock slowly moves on to the midnight hour ('*O lente, lente, currite noctis equi*'), Faustus tremblingly awaits his certain doom. When it has been wrought, the students reappear, and undertake with pathetic fidelity to bury their master's mangled limbs. As they go out, the Chorus enters, and in lines of great beauty preaches the simple moral of the tragedy. It is simple enough,—'unlawful things' are to be wondered at but not to be practised; yet it had its meaning for Marlowe's age[1], and for Marlowe's mind. His age believed that there were such possibilities of temptation as those before which Faustus succumbed ; and to his mind the temptation of tampering with the inscrutable was doubtless a real seduction. No solution of the problem is proposed, or even hinted at ; any such was beyond both the poet and his times; but a subjective as well as an objective significance underlies his theme, though his treatment of it is crude, and his endeavour to work it out dramatically (whatever may be the extent of interpolations by other hands in his tragedy) is imperfect.

For the additions which appeared in the edition of 1616 and in subsequent editions Marlowe cannot, as a matter of course, be held responsible, though it is quite possible that the edition of 1616 restored some of the original readings of Marlowe's text. The exceptional popularity of his play is shown both by the frequency with which it was reprinted, and by its having suggested two other successful plays which have been already incidentally noticed[2]. Its influence upon a popular play, derived like it from German legend and written by the very playwright to whom the first comic additions to *Doctor Faustus* are supposed to

---

[1] See e.g. Raleigh's section 'Of the Divers Kinds of Unlawful Magic' in his *History of the World*, Bk. I. chap. xi.

[2] *The Divil's Charter* and *The Merry Devil of Edmonton.*

have been due—Dekker's *Olde Fortunatus*—is likewise unmistakeable; and the allusions to Doctor Faustus, Mephistophilis, and their doings in Elisabethan and Jacobaean literature are numerous[1]. The play was carried across to Germany by the English comedians who visited that country in the last years of the sixteenth and the earlier part of the seventeenth century, and thus, while itself derived from a German source, influenced, if it did not actually give rise, to the treatment of the same theme by the German popular drama[2]. In England, on the other hand, Marlowe's tragedy, fragmentary though it is, has never been supplemented by any other direct literary treatment of its theme. After being revived, apparently in no effective fashion, on the Restoration stage[3], *Doctor Faustus* in the next generation was transmuted into a half-harlequinade[4], and in the eighteenth century was altogether turned into pantomime upon pantomime. The English theatre of our own century, which has never wearied of truncating or travestying Goethe's poem in one form or another, has wisely shrunk from the tragic terrors, intermixed with passages of rare imaginative beauty, of Marlowe's Titanic work.

The Famous Tragedy of the Rich Jew of Malta[5] must

The Jew of Malta (1589-90).

---

[1] They include Ancient Pistol's 'How now, Mephistophilus,' and Bardolph's allusion in the Horse-courser's scene in his account of the flight of the horses that 'set spurs and away, like three German devils, three Doctor Faustuses.' (*The Merry Wives of Windsor*, act i. sc. 1 and act iv. sc. 5.)— A very different indication of Shakspere's familiarity with *Doctor Faustus* is the line in *Troilus and Cressida*, act ii. sc. 1:

'She is a pearl,
Whose price has launch'd above a thousand ships
And turn'd crown'd Kings to merchants.'

[2] The relations between *Puppenspiele* and *Volksbuch* on the one hand, and Goethe's *Faust* on the other, cannot be discussed here. Goethe's direct debt to Marlowe is, as already indicated, trifling; all the more notable is his acknowledgment of the poetic merits of his predecessor: 'How greatly is it all planned. . . . Shakspere, it is certain, did not stand alone.'—What little Byron's *Manfred* owed to Marlowe, came indirectly through Goethe.

[3] See Pepys' *Diary*, under May 26, 1688.

[4] William Mountfort's *Life and Death of Doctor Faustus*, produced between 1684 and 1688, was first printed in 1694.

[5] An edition has been published by A. Wagner (Heilbronn, 1889), with an *Introduction*, which specially dwells on the causes accounting for the corruptness of the text. I am not aware of any other separate modern edition

have been produced after the end of December 1588 [1], and was familiar to the stage from February 1591. The internal evidence of style places it unmistakeably between the tragedies already noticed, and the historical tragedy of *Edward II*. It seems probable that *The Jew of Malta* preceded *The Massacre at Paris*, of which 'the Guise' is the central figure.

As a dramatic composition, the third of Marlowe's tragedies shows a considerable advance upon its predecessors. The popularity of *The Jew of Malta*, which on the evidence of Henslowe's *Diary* exceeded that of any contemporary play [2], was no doubt due in the first instance to the breadth and distinctness of its principal character, and was sustained by a favourite actor's (Edward Alleyn) masterly impersonation. Yet now that the extraordinary accumulation of villainies perpetrated by the hero has lost its fascination while the character as a whole attracts us as a curiosity rather than as a masterpiece, there remains much to admire in the ingenuity of the construction of the plot, which, notwithstanding its elaborateness, is remarkably clear and intelligible. Although the action proceeds from startling to more startling scenes, in the course of which it must be allowed that the lifelike characterisation of the earlier part of the play is exchanged for caricature [3], a climax of effect is reserved for the close. And in form this work deserves high praise ; for the vigour and ease of its versification are

of this interesting play. In 1813 S. Penley published *Marlowe's Celebrated Tragedy of the Jew of Malta, with Alterations and Additions.*

[1] The passage in the *Prologue*—

'And now the Guise is dead'—

cannot well have been interpolated. Henry Duke of Guise was murdered December 23, 1588.

[2] See the series of entries, beginning with February 26, 1590 (O.S.). The extant version was that edited by Thomas Heywood in 1633 after its revival at Court and at the Cock-pit. In the *Prologue* for the latter performance occur the lines :

'By the best of poets in that age
The Malta-Jew had being and was made,
And he then by the best of actors play'd.'

The episode of the two mutually hostile friars in Heywood's *The Captives* appears to have been suggested by act iv. sc. 2 of Marlowe's play.

[3] Bullen, *Introduction*, pp. xl–xliii.

alike undeniable. Indeed, there are passages in the earlier part of the play in which the exquisite beauty of Marlowe's verse, heightened by that imaginative use of classical similes which was peculiarly his own, overcomes every other impression [1]. How far the grosser portions of the last three acts are due to later insertions by other hands—perhaps by that of the facile playwright who edited the play for its first known appearance in print (1633)[2],—I cannot pretend to decide.

The *Prologue* to the play is spoken by Machiavel [3]   Of

[1] *E.g.* act i. sc. 1 :
> 'One sole daughter, whom I hold as dear
> As Agamemnon did his Iphigene :
> And all I have is hers.'

[2] 'In the scenes with Bellamira and Pilia Borza there is a good deal not by Marlowe. This is not due to original collaboration, but to alteration by Heywood, c. 1632.' Fleay, *English Drama*, ii. 61, where the resemblance to Heywood's *Captives*, which had struck me independently, is also noted.

[3] The interest taken in Macchiavelli by English writers was curiously great, if we may judge from the numerous references made to him and his writings, in and out of season. Very possibly it had been fed by the publication in English (in 1537) of the *Vindication* (see *Harleian Miscellany*, vol. i). Apart from the circumstances, that a play called by him '*Matchavell*' was produced by Henslowe in 1591, that in 1613 Robert Daborne was in treaty with him for a revival of this with additions, or for a new play, under the name of *Machiavell and the Devil* (*Henslowe's Diary*, ed. Collier, p. 22 and *note*), and that in 1597 a Latin drama by D. Wiburne called *Machiavellus, of which the hero was a Jew*, was acted at Cambridge (a transcript of this is in the Bodleian ; see S. Lee, *u.s.*, p. 147, and cf. Halliwell's *Dictionary*), I have traced the recurrence of allusions to Macchiavelli through a large number of our dramatists. Proverbial use is made of his name in plays treating of events which happened before his time ; see *Henry VI*, Part I, act v. sc. 4 : 'Alençon ! that notorious Machiavel'; and cf. Steevens' note citing a passage from *The Valiant Welchman* (1615, ascribed to Armin), where Caradoc (Caractacus) is rather unreasonably bidden 'read Machiavel'; also *Henry VI*, Part III, act iii. sc. 3, where 'Machiavel' is substituted for 'Catiline.' He is referred to in *The Merry Wives*, act iii. sc. 2 ; in Greene's *James IV*, where 'annotations upon Machiavel' are found in the pocket of the villain Ateukin; in Nashe's *Summer's Last Will and Testament*, where it is declared that 'the art of murder Machiavel hath penn'd'; in Jonson's *Every Man out of his Humour* (act ii. sc. 2), and in his *Magnetic Lady* (act i. sc. 1). Jonson, as a passage in his *Discoveries* proves, had read the author whose name his age was so fond of evoking. While it is interesting to observe with what tenacity popular literature clings to personified conceptions, we may be glad that Englishmen have done something for the memory of the great Italian besides helping to keep alive an oblique view of it ; the English visitor to Florence learns with pride that the monument to Macchiavelli in the Church of Sta. Croce was raised by a subscription set on foot (in 1787) by an

course this personage (the historical Machiavel had died in
1527), as the allusion to his having inhabited the body of
the Guise 'now dead' shows, is intended to bear a typical
significance only. 'Machiavel' introduces the Jew of Malta
as one whose wealth had not been amassed 'without my
means.' In other words, the villain with whom the play is
concerned is no common villain, but a politic schemer acting
on a well-considered system; and Barabas fully redeems
the promise thus made on his behalf; one at least of his
speeches (act v. line 117 *seqq.*) has something like the true
ring of the *Principe* itself, by which Macchiavelli's name
was chiefly known to the foreign world.

This play is so noteworthy, both on its own account and
because of the comparison which inevitably suggests itself
with Shakspere's *Merchant of Venice*, that it may be well to
indicate briefly the nature of its plot. Barabas is discovered
at the outset counting his wealth, when at the height of his
prosperity as a merchant of Malta. But the rulers of the
islands, the Knights of St. John, being suddenly called upon
by a Turkish force to pay a heavy outstanding tribute, the
expedient occurs to them of making the rich Jews pay the
money, and thus free the island from the danger threatening
it. Every Jew is to surrender half his wealth; if he refuses,
he is straight to become a Christian; and if he declines
conversion, he is to lose the whole of his property. Barabas
having refused both the first and the second demand, is
sentenced to the ultimate penalty and apparently reduced
to beggary, his house being at the same time turned into
a nunnery. As, however, he has in this house concealed
a large part of his wealth, he instructs his daughter Abigail
to ask admission into the nunnery, feigning herself a Christian
convert, so that she may secure for him his secret hoard.
The device succeeds; but a complication arises from the

Englishman (Earl Cowper). It is noticeable that already in 1734 (in *The
Craftsman*, No. 431) Macchiavelli is introduced as the writer of 'a letter
from the dead' in his true character as a 'friend to the Cause of Liberty.'
It is curious that Goethe in his *Egmont* should have thought fit to give the
name of Macchiavelli to Margaret of Parma's secretary,—of course a palpable
anachronism, had not Goethe in his turn intended simply to indicate a type of
the policy represented by the character in question.

circumstance of two young nobles of the island being
enamoured of Abigail, who returns the love of one of them,
the governor's son. Barabas persuades her to inveigle her
other admirer by pretending to return his passion ; and by
sending forged challenges to the rivals as from each to each,
he stirs up a quarrel between them which ends in their killing
one another. Filled with anguish and remorse, Abigail confesses to a friar her connivance in her father's murderous
scheme, and dies. Barabas hereupon contrives to rid himself
both of the inconvenient confessor, and of another friar, by
pretending a desire to become a Christian. He invites both
the friars into his house, kills the one and makes the other
believe himself guilty of the deed. Having again become
rich, he seems likely to reap the reward of his ingenuity,
when he is betrayed by the accomplice of his misdeeds,
a rascally Turkish slave, whose services he had secured on
the strength of his evil looks and antecedents. This Ithamore
having betrayed everything to a courtesan, who reveals the
villanies of Barabas to the governor, the Jew (not, however,
before he has managed to take vengeance by poison on
those who had ruined him) is thrown over the walls as
a dead man. But his career is not yet at an end. The
Turks are again besieging Malta ; and Barabas (for he had
merely feigned death) becomes their guide into the fortress,
after having been promised the governorship in case of success.
The citadel is taken; governor and people are in his hands;
and he is master of the situation. But his politic cunning
now suggests to him the necessity of making friends with
his former foes ; he therefore proposes to entertain the
departing Turks at a farewell banquet, in the course of
which he will contrive to put them all to death. Thus
he will assure to himself the gratitude of the Christians,
remain governor, and be master of the future as well as of the
present. The Christians pretend to fall in with this Macchia-
vellian scheme,—but only in order to catch the Jew in his own
trap, of which he has revealed the secret. Thus, instead of the
Turkish leaders being crushed by the fall of the banquetting-
room, Barabas alone is precipitated into a cauldron of fire
held in readiness beneath ; and, foiled at last, expires

with a curse, of which it is sufficient to state that it very adequately marks the conclusion of the play.

It has not escaped the observation of critics, that in this work the first two acts are greatly superior in execution to the remainder. Not that the play in the slightest degree abates either in rapidity of dramatic movement or in vigour of language in its latter part ; but the colouring grows much coarser, the human element in the character of Barabas is altogether lost sight of, and if the story becomes more striking, its execution becomes less pleasing. I doubt whether the extraordinary dialogue in which Barabas secures the services of Ithamore, by giving him an insight into his own character and intentions, is to be taken to imply that Barabas really has been all he says he has been—in a word, a very fiend. But he certainly acts up to this self-drawn sketch in what follows ; and inasmuch as he is no longer sinned against as well as sinning, we lose all those elements of sympathy with him which the earlier part of the play had allowed to operate. Of the remaining characters, Ithamore, though very coarsely drawn, is a most effective picture of the basest kind of villain [1] ; the friars are satirical pictures of monkish selfishness and debauchery, at which it is easy for us to shake our heads,—but we should remember how the passions and prejudices of the age persistently encouraged their reflexion in whatever kind of literature was, or desired to be, in accord with popular sentiment [2].

---

[1] Ithamore bears some resemblance to the very effective figure of the Moor in Schiller's *Fiesco*.

[2] The Middle Ages, no doubt, had shown little or no compunction in illustrating human frailty by examples drawn (often with a successful concealment of the *a fortiori* intention) from the lives of the regular clergy. But the Reformation age imported an unprecedented acrimony into the use to which it put ecclesiastical figures of this sort in its literature. I have given some examples of this in my edition of Marlowe's *Doctor Faustus*, where Mephistophilis first appears in the habit of a monk. Without touching on other instances here, I may remind readers of Spenser that in *The Faerie Queene* Idleness appears as a monk (I. iv. 19) and the Devil himself as a hermit (I. i. 29). Schlegel has pointed out how Shakspere, when he has occasion to bring monks on the scene, prefers to dwell on the nobler aspects of their lives and duties. A corresponding sentiment may have induced him to omit in *King John* the ribald scene in *The Troublesome Raigne*, descriptive of the looting of Swineshead Abbey.

The special interest attaching to the chief character in *The Jew of Malta and The Merchant of Venice.* this play is not solely or even mainly due to the resemblances which it presents to Shakspere's Shylock. For inasmuch as Barabas certainly preceded Shylock on the stage, it is the former character which more directly suggests the question, how and why it came to pass that a Jew should be presented there as a type intended to excite popular antipathy, at a time when, whether or not Jews were to be found in England [1], their presence could hardly have been regarded or apprehended as a religious, political, or social grievance. For it may be well to premise that, whatever may have been the effect originally produced by the character of Shylock (although I am convinced that the sympathy aroused by this character is merely the result of the unconscious tact with which it was incidentally humanised by Shakspere), Barabas [2] was assuredly never intended to secure either the respect or (*sit venia verbo!*) the sneaking kindness of a single spectator. To be sure, just as Shakspere, in working out the relations between character and action, could not fail on occasion to imply his consciousness of counter-arguments *ad Christianos*, so Marlowe puts into the mouth of Barabas the following specious plea in defence of his own practice:

> ' It's no sin to deceive a Christian;
> For they themselves hold it a principle:
> Faith is not to be kept with heretics.—
> But all are heretics that are not Jews.
> This follows well [3].'

Apart, moreover, from the much grosser developement of

---

[1] There can be no doubt but that Mr. S. Lee has proved in his admirable paper on Elizabethan England and the Jews, in New Shakspere Society's Transactions, 1888, that this question should be answered in the affirmative.

[2] I cannot remember any instance in the old mystery-drama in which the figure of Barabbas has comic touches such as are said to have been given to it at one time in the Oberammergau passion-play (they had been removed when I witnessed its performance in 1871). But the name was at all events the most odious that could have been chosen by Marlowe for his Jew.—By the bye it is odd (though in the style of the mysteries) that Barabas, who is learned enough to quote Terence ('*Ego mihimet sum semper proximus*'), should forget himself into a Christian oath (*Corpo di Dio*).

[3] Act ii. sc. 3.

the evil tendencies of the character (whether or not 'racial' or personal, the frequenters of Rose or Cockpit would be hardly expected to distinguish), there are passages in *The Jew of Malta*[1] proving that in external appearance, too, Barabas was intended to be held up to the ridicule as well as to the disgust of the pensive public. It cannot, of course, be for a moment supposed that any traditional conception of the Jew, such as afterwards dominated the drama of more than one nation, had thus early definitely formed itself on the English stage, and was accepted accordingly by Marlowe and by Shakspere after him. Of the early play of *The Jew*, commended by Stephen Gosson[2] at as early a date as 1579, we know indeed that its argument included 'the bloody minds of usurers'; and if, as seems extremely probable, a playful passage in a letter written in the same year by Spenser to Gabriel Harvey contains an allusion to this play, we may further conjecture that it already contained the story of a bond[3]. But in his next appearance on the stage, in an episode introduced into Robert Wilson's late morality, *The Three Ladies of London* (printed in 1590)[4], the Jew, Gerontus, plays a highly honourable part, preferring to be cheated of the debt due to him than to approve of the Christian Mercatore's interested conversion; and the commendation of the Jew's conduct uttered by the judge upon the stage must be supposed to have been echoed by the audience. Why then should Marlowe have fallen upon such a type as Barabas, who cannot be called in any sense a study of the Jewish nature, mind, or character,

---

[1] *E.g.* act ii. sc. 3 (*Ithanos* to *Barabas*): 'O brave! master, I worship your nose for this.' The character was rendered grotesque and hideous on the stage by means of a false nose, which (as Dyce and Bullen point out) is referred to in Samuel Rowley's *Search for Money* (1609) as 'the artificiall Jewe of Maltaes nose.'

[2] *Ante*, p. 209.

[3] In this letter, printed in Harvey's *Letter-book* (printed for the Camden Society, 1884), Spenser signs himself 'he that is fast bownde to the in more obligations than any marchant of Italy to any Jew there.' Cf. Lee, *u.s.*, p. 143.

[4] Cf. the notice of play and episode, *ante*, p. 140, *note*. See also Dr. H. Fernow's dissertation *The Three Lords and Three Ladies of London* (Hamburg, 1885), where the significance of the episode between Gerontus and Mercatore is admirably elucidated.

but who was conceived in so resolute a spirit of Anti-Semitism as to call forth a whole line of successors [1]. It is indeed evident from incidental allusions to Jews in the Elisabethan drama, both that when mentioned they were mentioned with contempt and dislike, and that they were commonly connected in the popular mind with the practice of usury. But there is nothing in these allusions to warrant such a conception as that of Marlowe's Barabas, and whatever may be the case with Shylock, his predecessor on the stage can have nothing to do with Roderigo Lopez, the Portuguese physician who in 1594 was, on evidence which seems more than doubtful, hanged for a supposed design upon the life of Queen Elisabeth [2].

Barabas, the Jew of Malta, is then to all intents and purposes the child of Marlowe's imagination, although it is not to be denied that certain suggestions were ready to his hand that could be easily used to heighten the odiousness of his monstrous conception. To Marlowe's mind a Jew was fair game, his diabolical hatred of everything Christian a matter of course, and his love of money an axiom. He was wholly innocent of any design of producing a typical study of Judaism—least of all by introducing into the character the one softening element of paternal affection.

The resemblances of detail between *The Jew of Malta* and *The Merchant of Venice*, of which it may be worth while

---

[1] Among these, apart from Shylock, Mr. Lee notes Abraham 'a cunning Jew' and a physician well seen in poisons, in the tragedy of *Selimus* mentioned above, p. 328, note 1, as an imitation of *Tamburlaine*, and below among the plays attributed to Greene; the Cambridge *Machiavellus*; 'Mammon the Usurer with a great nose' in *Jacke Drum's Entertainment* (1601), Zariph in Day's *Travels of the Three English Brothers* (*Shirley*) (1607), Zabulon in Beaumont and Fletcher's *Custom of the Country* (1622), and the chief figures in two lost plays by Dekker and by Brome.

[2] See below as to Shylock. There is an allusion to 'Dr. Lopus' in *Doctor Faustus*, sc. xi, which cannot have been from the hand of Marlowe, who died in 1593. It is conceivable that the long-continued popularity of *The Jew of Malta* may have owed something to the effect of the trial and execution of Lopez. But Dr. Honigmann's conjecture (in an article on the character of Shylock in *Jahrbuch*, vol. xvii, 1882) that Marlowe, who he says exhibits in the diction of Barabas, interspersed as it is with bits of Spanish and Italian, a close acquaintance with the Jewish jargon, had studied it in the speech of London Jews, *perhaps even in that of Dr. Lopez* himself, must be respectfully dismissed.

to note some, without pretending to exhaust their number [1], are such as to leave no doubt with regard to the debt owing by the later to the earlier play [2].   As it seems to me, they prove conclusively that Marlowe's *Jew of Malta* was present to

[1] *Jew of Malta.*	*Merchant of Venice.*
Act I. Sc. 1.	Act I. Sc. 3.
First appearance of B. He enumerates his argosies.	First appearance of S. He enumerates the argosies of Antonio.
Ib.	*Ib.*
' These are the blessings promised to the Jews, And herein was old Abraham's happiness,' &c.	Passage about Jacob, with a reference to Abraham, ending : ' This was a way to thrive, and he was bless'd ; And *thrift* is blessing, if men steal it not.'
Act I. Sc. 2.	Act IV. Sc. 1.
' You have my goods, my money, and my wealth, &c. . . . you can request no more ' (Unless you wish to take my life).	Greatly improved in Shylock's speech : ' Nay take my life and all,' &c.
Ib.	Act I. Sc. 3.
' What, bring you Scriptures to confirm your wrongs ? '	' The devil can cite Scripture for his purpose.'
Act II. Sc. 1. ' Oh my girl, My gold, my fortune, my felicity.	Act II. Sc. 8. ' My daughter !—O my ducats !—O my daughter !
. . . . . .	. . . . . .
Oh, girl, oh, gold, oh, beauty, oh, my bliss.'	Justice ! the law ! my ducats, and my daughter * ! '
Act II. Sc. 2.	Act II. Sc. 5.
Barabas and Slave (against hearty feeders in general).	Shylock and Launcelot Gobbo.

* There is a strong resemblance to both these passages in Ben Jonson's *The Case is Altered*, act v. sc. 2.

[2] See several others (some not very striking) in Waldron's edition of Ben Jonson's *Sad Shepherd*, Appendix, p. 209 *seqq.*; among them the following speech of Barabas, to which I need not supply the Shaksperean parallel :

> ' I learn'd in Florence how to kiss my hand,
> Heave up my shoulders when they call me dog,
> And duck as low as any barefoot friar.'

It may be added that the passage in the *Jew of Malta,*

> ' What sight is this ? my Lodovico slain !
> These arms of mine shall be thy sepulchre,'

Shakspere's mind when he wrote his *Merchant of Venice.*
Yet the transforming power of his genius is evident in this as
in almost every instance where he made use of the labours
of his predecessors. The artistic difference between the
plays needs no comment. The psychological distinction
in the treatment of the two principal characters lies, not
in the nature of the ingredients of which they are com-
pounded—avarice, cruelty, revengefulness, with no mitigating
element but that of paternal love, and this only till it is
quenched in the sense of a daughter's desertion—but in the
way in which these elements are fused. The art of
Shakspere is immeasurably superior to that of Marlowe in
allowing neither avarice nor lust of vengeance to attain
to such a pitch in his Jew as to take the character out of
the range of human nature. In contrast with the un-
relieved blackness of Barabas, Shylock remains both
truly human and within the limits of dramatic probability.
A comparison of the last three with the first two acts of the
Jew of Malta may indeed suggest that haste of execution
was the chief cause which prevented Marlowe from achieving
a character instead of a caricature; but it remains not the
less certain that he failed in this instance, as in those of
the heroes of *Tamburlaine* and of *Doctor Faustus,* to achieve
in actual literary presentment the highest part of the
dramatist's task.

Marlowe unmistakeably attained to his highest point as *Edward II*
a dramatist in *The Troublesome Raigne and Lamentable* (1590-1).
Death of Edward the Second, King of England[1]. Apart

doubtless suggested one in *Henry VI,* Part III, act ii. sc. 5; and the beautiful
simile,
  ' But stay: what star shines yonder in the east?
  The loadstar of my life, if Abigail,' &c.,
cannot have been far from Shakspere's memory when he wrote the still more
beautiful passage in *Romeo and Juliet,* act ii. sc. 2. These two similarities
are pointed out by Dyce.

[1] The full title of the quarto of 1598 continues : ' *With the tragicall fall of
proud Mortimer : and also the life and death of Peirs Gaueston, the great Earle
of Cornewall, and mighty favourite of King Edward the second.*' A copy of
an edition of *Edward II* dated 1594 was discovered some years ago by
R. Genée in the State Library of the Museum Fridericianum at Cassel; its
presence there he thought might be explained by a visit of English
comedians to the court of Cassel towards the end of the sixteenth century.

from the high poetic merits of its diction and verse, which place it on a level with the finest creations of his genius, while no other of his plays in the form in which we possess it is so sustained and (if I may use the expression) so equal to itself, *Edward II* marks a distinct progress in the developement of an entire species of our dramatic literature. If, as is probable, Marlowe's play was preceded in date of performance by Peele's *Famous Chronicle History of Edward I*, which was printed in 1593, it must be acknowledged that a considerable advance had here already been effected in the direction of freeing the historical drama from the relation of absolute dependence and complete subserviency in which it had hitherto stood towards the chronicles. Even so, however, the process of self-emancipation was carried further by Marlowe, and by the authors of the two old plays from which the *Second and Third Parts of Henry VI* were elaborated, and of that now called *The First Part of Henry VI*. The question as to the authorship of *The First Part of the Contention betwixt the two famous Houses of York and Lancaster*, of *The True Tragedie of Richard Duke of York*, of the two Parts of *Henry VI* founded upon them, and of *The First Part of Henry VI*, will be most conveniently discussed in a later passage of this volume, where it is desirable to avoid unnecessary repetitions ; but whatever may have been the share of Marlowe in the composition of these works, the similarity between a number of passages in *Henry VI*, more especially in *Parts II* and *III* of the trilogy as it is now printed, and a corresponding series in *Edward II* must be noted at once. Ulrici, who rejected the hypothesis of Marlowe's authorship of *The Contention* and *The True Tragedie*, was content to assume that in his *Edward II* he freely borrowed from the plays in question. But there can be no doubt that this solution at least may be unhesitatingly rejected. It assumes the priority in date of production of

---

This earlier edition wants a scene occurring in that of 1598 ; but the other differences between the two editions are merely matters of spelling or stage-directing. See *The Examiner*, November 25, 1876.—Recent separate editions of *Edward II* are those of the late Dr. W. Wagner (Hamburg, 1871); of Mr. Fleay (London and Glasgow, 1877), and of Mr. O. W. Tancock (Oxford, 1887) ; and I see announced yet another by Professor E. T. McLaughlin of Yale.

the two plays of disputed authorship, although they unmistakeably represent in some respects, more especially in
the treatment of the humorous element, an advance which
had not been reached in *Edward II*. And it contradicts the
ordinary practice of a dramatic poet who cannot in any of
his acknowledged works be convicted of having borrowed
from his fellows, while he certainly on occasion repeats
phrases or similes of his own. Whatever conclusion may
be formed as to the authorship of the other plays referred
to, the originality of the vexed passages in *Edward II* is
practically beyond cavil [1].

Marlowe based his tragedy, so far as can be ascertained,
upon no single chronicle or annalistic history, although he
seems to have made special use of the narrative of Sir
Thomas de la Moor, which was probably written in the
reign of Edward III and shows much sympathy for his
unfortunate father [2]. He had, however, before him Robert
Fabyan's *Chronicle* or *Concordance of Histories*, written
some time within the years 1485 to 1490, in which, according
to the author's fashion, was inserted a verse *Complaint of
Edward II* (translated from a Latin poem, probably by

---

[1] Ulrici, *Shakespeare's Dramatic Art*, &c., pp. 69 *seqq.*—The list of parallel
passages cited by Dyce in his *Introduction* has been enlarged by Fleay, in
the *Introduction* to his edition, pp. 15 *seqq.*, where he further adds (what
does not immediately concern us here) a number of instances of uses of
words peculiar to *Edward II* and *Henry VI*, and not occurring in any other
play attributed to Shakspere except, in one or two instances, in *The Taming
of the Shrew* and *Titus Andronicus.*—One of the most remarkable of the
parallel passages had already been pointed out by Halliwell-Phillips; see (Old)
Shakespeare Society's Papers, vol. i. pp. 5-7.—The indebtedness of Shakspere,
in plays of which his sole authorship is undisputed, has already been abundantly illustrated. The famous passage in *Romeo and Juliet*, act iii. sc. 2:
'Gallop apace, ye fiery-footed steeds,
.   .   .   .   .   .
And bring in cloudy night immediately,'
can hardly have been suggested by that in *Edward II*, act iv. sc. 3:
'Gallop, apace, bright Phœbus, through the sky,
And dusky night in rusty iron car,' &c.
(where, by the way, both Cunningham and Wagner print the epithet of
night as 'dusty'). Other reminiscences of *Edward II* in Shakspere are
pointed out by Mr. Bullen in his edition.

[2] See Pauli, *Geschichte von England*, vol. iv. p. 721. Sir Thomas de la
Moor, who was an eyewitness of Edward II's resignation, appears to have
been Marlowe's authority for the story of the oracularly ambiguous
'*Edwardum occidere nolite timere bonum est.*' See *ib.* p. 303.

William of Worcester), in which the unhappy king, after
the fashion of the personages in Boccaccio's *Falls of Illustrious Men*, followed by the authors of *The Mirror for
Magistrates*, recites his own misfortunes. (Other early
poems on the same subject were extant; in one of them[1]
the corruption of the law-courts is attacked together with
the morals of the clergy; the Chancellor of the time was
the Robert de Baldock who plays a part in Marlowe's
tragedy.) But the worthy Fabyan, whose work in general
has the stiffness and steadiness of the municipal dignity he
held, cannot be shown to have been directly used by Marlowe
even for the main conduct of his action, which owes more to
Stow's *Annals* and Holinshed's *Chronicles*, although neither
of these was its exclusive source[2]. In fact, neither in the last
act, of which the actual source has not been ascertained,
nor in the preceding part of the play, has Marlowe slavishly
followed any authorities known to us; nor was he so unconscious as has been sometimes thought of the necessity of
assigning dramatic motives—causes, that is to say, by which
the dramatist in the course of the action itself explains its
successive incidents, and the part taken in them by his
personages, to the spectator. Thus, the idea of the passage
in act i. sc. 4, where, in order to gratify Queen Isabel,
Young Mortimer consents to bring about the return of his
enemy Gaveston, seems to be Marlowe's own invention—
a felicitous one, since it accounts at the same time for
Gaveston's return and for the growth of the Queen's guilty
passion for Mortimer. This is a well-devised addition;
elsewhere compression is not less successfully applied.
Altogether, the subject must be allowed to have been
as skilfully treated as it was fortunately chosen[3].

[1] In Peterhouse Library, Cambridge; and edited by the late Archdeacon
Hardwick for the Percy Society (*Publications*, vol. xxviii). It may be
regarded as in some sense a precursor of the *Vision concerning Piers
Plowman*.

[2] See the extracts from Fabyan, Stow and Holinshed, *ap.* Fleay, pp.
18–44.—I have not verified the statement of another writer, that one
passage of Marlowe's play is directly based on Capgrave—I presume on
his *Chronicle*.

[3] To the impression created by Marlowe's *Edward II* may perhaps be
traceable the passage in Peele's *Order of the Garter* (1593), referring to

The dramatic merits, then, as well as the poetic beauties of *Edward II* are extremely great. The construction of the play is upon the whole very clear, infinitely superior *e.g.* to that of Peele's *Edward I.* The two divisions into which the reign of Edward II naturally falls, viz. the period of the ascendancy of Gaveston and that of the ascendancy of the Spensers, are skilfully interwoven ; and after the catastrophe of the fourth act (the victory of the King's adversaries and his capture) the interest in an issue that can no longer be regarded as uncertain, viz. the ultimate fate of the King, is most powerfully sustained. The characters too are mostly well drawn ; there is no ignobility about the King, whose passionate love for his favourites is itself traced to a generous motive [1]; he is not without courage and spirit in the face of danger ; but his weakness is his doom. Misfortune utterly breaks him ; and never have the 'drowsiness of woe' (to use Charles Lamb's expression), and, after a last struggle between pride and necessity, the lingering expectation of a certain doom, been painted with more tragic power. The scene in act iv, where the King seeks refuge with the monks of Neath Abbey, possesses singular pathos; but it is perhaps even more remarkable how in the last scene of all the unutterable horror of the situation is depicted without arousing the sense of the loathsome ; and how pity and terror are mingled in a degree to which Shakspere himself only on occasion attains [2]. For the combined power and delicacy of treatment, the murder of Edward II may be compared to the murder of Desdemona in *Othello* ; for the fearful suspense in which the spectator is kept, I know no parallel except that

Edward's 'tragic cry.' I think that allusions to Marlowe's play are also recognisable in the brief *History of Edward II* by the first Lord Falkland, not printed till long after its author's death (1633) in 1680, apparently with the design of injuring the Government, and containing some very judicious reflexions on Edward II's downfall. Gaveston is here spoken of as 'the Ganymede of the King's affections,' and the image of a fallen cedar is applied to the dismissed favourite, perhaps in loose remembrance of the passage in act ii. sc. 2.

[1] ' *Y. M.* Why should you love him whom the world hates so ?
  Edw. Because he loves me more than all the world.'
[2] 'The death-scene of Marlowe's King moves pity and terror beyond any scene, ancient or modern, with which I am acquainted.'—*Charles Lamb.*

which precedes the catastrophe of Aeschylus' *Agamemnon*. But even here the effort is inferior, since in the Greek play the suspense and the apprehension of its inevitable termination are not imposed upon the spectator in the presence of the sufferer on the stage. On the other characters I will not dwell; but they are not mere figures from the Chronicle. It may be worth while to note the skill with which the character of young Edward (afterwards Edward III) is drawn, and how our good-will is preserved for him, even though his name is put forward by his father's enemies, till in the closing scene he proves himself every inch a King. Gaveston's insolence is admirably reproduced; he is a Frenchman, full of brightness and resource[1], and preserves an air of lightheartedness to the last, when he expresses his indifference as to the precise *manner* of his death:

> ' I thank you all, my lords : then I perceive
> That heading's one, and hanging is the other,
> And death is all[2].'

The imperious haughtiness of Young Mortimer—a Hotspur in germ—is equally well depicted; in the character of the Queen alone I miss any indication of the transition from her faithful but despairing attachment to the King to a guilty love for Mortimer. The dignity of the tragedy remains unmarred by any comic scenes,—which is well, for humour was not Marlowe's strong point; but there is some wit in the sketch of Baldock as an unscrupulous upstart,—albeit of University 'culture'[3]—who fawns upon the great, and gains

---

[1] See, in the opening scene, his brilliant *programme* of the system by means of which he will sustain himself as a favourite. The courts of Elisabeth and Henry III seem to revive in this luxurious passage.

[2] Unlike both 'the Spanish malefactor who claimed the privilege of a Roman,' and was accordingly 'executed by the command of Galba on a fairer and more lofty cross' (Gibbon, xliv), and the nobleman who requested George III to allow him to be hanged in a gilt chain, the sovereign however replying that it should be done in 'the usual way.' In the play of *Sir John Oldcastle* there is an Irishman who insists upon being hanged in the Irish way. Ulrici oddly censures this speech of Gaveston's as 'the answer of a condemned robber or murderer, but not of the favourite, however unworthy, of a king.'

[3] He presents himself to the King, act ii. sc. 2, with typical humbleness:
> ' My name is Baldock, and my gentry
> I fetch from Oxford, not from heraldry.'

influence by means of his ability to find for everything reasons, or, as his interlocutor terms them, *Quandoquidems*.

The play is written in blank verse, of a flowing as well as vigorous description ; rimes only occasionally occur, and there is no prose. Marlowe's love of classical allusions is as active as ever, and suggests passages of singular charm— in the present instance harmonising with the general treatment of the subject, although we may be rather overwhelmed by meeting, besides Leander and Ganymede, who from different reasons were naturally in the poet's mind, with Circe, the Cyclops, Proteus, Danaë, Helen, Atlas, Pluto, Charon, and Tisiphone, as well as with Catiline and other historical parallels. Seneca and Pliny's *Natural History* are cited ; it is, in short, as if the poet had poured all the resources of his training as well as of his genius into the cup.

In conclusion, there seems no necessity for dwelling on the obvious resemblance between this tragedy and Shakspere's *Richard II*, except in so far as to suggest the narrowness of the limits to which this resemblance, after all, reduces itself. Charles Lamb observes that the ' reluctant pangs of abdicating royalty in *Edward* furnished hints which Shakspere scarcely improved in his *Richard II* '; and if this observation be taken *cum grano*, it must be allowed to furnish a sufficient summary of the relation between the two tragedies. We may, however, remember that while Marlowe's play covers nearly the whole reign of Edward II, Shakspere treats of little more than the last two years of Richard II. But although Shakspere is thus far less tied down by the mere historical facts than Marlowe, he cannot be said in this instance to have drawn his characters with greater fullness and detail than his predecessor ; it is rather in the elaboration of sentiment and reflexion that he has allowed himself ampler latitude in this, the most eloquent of all his tragedies. On the other hand, Marlowe's subject was in

*Edward
II and
Richard II.*

When a lonely fugitive in act iv. sc. 6, the king thus addresses Baldock :
  ' Come, Baldock, come, sit down by me,
  Make trial now of that philosophy,
  That in our famous nurseries of arts
  Thou suck'dst from Plato and from Aristotle.'

some respects the more promising; for the favourites of
Edward II, or at all events Pierce Gaveston, have a distinct
individuality, such as cannot be ascribed to Green, Busby,
and Bagot. Again, while Marlowe was under no necessity
of reconciling with other considerations the rebellious arrogance of Young Mortimer, Shakspere was obliged to deal
tenderly with his rebel-in-chief and usurper, Bolingbroke,
as the progenitor of the Lancaster and Tudor sovereigns.
Thus his play is more elaborate,—as e. g. in the striking
death-bed scene of John of Gaunt and in the prison scenes
of the King,—but can hardly be termed more effective than
Marlowe's; and with regard to the essential point in the
comparison, viz. the character and conduct of the two kings,
it is not easy to decide which of the two poets has the
advantage. Shakspere's *Richard* is certainly more of a
piece than Marlowe's *Edward*,—more fundamentally and
persistently a man prone to hopeless lapses into desultory
self-comment and futile meditation, and therefore more manifestly unfit for action. But, then, Shakspere's unavowed
but unmistakeable purpose was to represent Richard's downfall as a more or less inevitable result of the defects of
character in the King himself; whereas in Marlowe's case
it was permissible for the tragic poet to assert his prerogative right, and to exhibit in Edward's doom a calamity
terrible and pitiful enough to redeem the blind folly of his
past. In the closing scenes, Marlowe, without ever approaching the grandeur and abundance of the associations concentrated by Shakspere upon the situation and its central
figure, compels the emotions of horror and compassion with
far more potent directness; and the death of the victim,
which in Shakspere is swiftly consummated, in Marlowe
seems gradually to stifle and stamp down our sobs with
those of the expiring King. I know of no second scene like
this in tragedy.

The Massacre at Paris (1593).

Of the *Massacre at Paris* it is unnecessary to say much.
It appears to have been produced as a new play in January,
1593; but the one printed early edition, which bears no
date, is not merely corrupt, but defective in a measure of
which we are fortunately enabled to form an estimate by

the evidence of a particular truncated passage[1]. Few critics, however, will be found to deny that, after making every allowance for the condition in which it has come down to us, this must be pronounced to be among Marlowe's dramas the least worthy of his genius. Its chief interest for us may be said to consist in considerations of historical rather than literary interest. It certainly shows what an English Protestant of Marlowe's fervid type thought—even when the lapse of ten years or so had cooled down the first gloss of indignant wrath excited by the event—of the Massacre, its authors and abettors, and the principal personages of French and European political life whom it concerned; or, at least, it shows what view on these matters he thought would be acceptable to an English popular audience[2]. Sober historians may form a more considerate or composite judgment of Catherine de' Medici than that presented by Marlowe; on the other hand they may be slower in displaying sympathy with the fate of Henry III, perhaps the most wretched member of a wretched brood, but, it must not be forgotten, a prince who at one time had been Queen Elisabeth's suitor. Marlowe accordingly makes him send his dying salutations to England's Queen; and King Henry's death, it will be remembered, had happened as late as 1589, and was therefore still fresh in the remembrance of men. There is no disputing the dramatic capabilities of the theme, which were fully recognised by Elisabethan and later playwrights[3]. Marlowe's argument, had opportunity or patience

[1] See Collier, iii. 510–2, where it is shown that three-fourths of a verse tirade, besides much of a prose speech, recovered in MS., have been omitted in the print. The MS turns ' Mugeron,' the name of one of the characters, into the familiar ' Minion '; but ' Mugeron' seems to be a corruption of ' Maugiron,' whom the dramatist confused with Saint-Mégrim, another of the king's minions.

[2] It would of course be diametrically opposite to that favoured at Madrid, where the Massacre was, by command of King Philip II, celebrated by the performance of a festival play called *The Triumph of Faith*. (K. Hase, *Miracle Plays and Sacred Dramas* (Engl. Tr.), p. 60.)

[3] Webster's (non-extant) play of *The Guise* is held by Collier (ii. 482) to be identical with that mentioned elsewhere as *The Masaker of France*. A *Duke of Guise* was entered on the Stationers' books in 1653 in the name of Henry Shirley; and in the Restoration age Lee contributed to the political play of *The Duke of Guise* (1682) by Dryden and himself some scenes and passages of an earlier unfinished play by himself on the Massacre.—In M. J. de Chénier's

been given to him for working it out with care, might have proved productive of a very powerful effect, resembling in its developement that of an Aeschylean trilogy. For it should be observed that the consequences of the Massacre, rather than the Massacre itself (which occupies the first act, and is thus merely the starting-point of the play), constitute the real subject of the action. Its central figure is the Guise, with the queen-mother in the background. Marlowe, who loved to paint black in black, was unlikely to forego the opportunity of presenting on the English stage a monster of the deepest hue. From the beginning, where Guise procures from an 'apothecary' a pair of perfumed gloves, with which to poison the old Queen of Navarre, down to his dying exclamation,

> '*Vive la Messe!* perish Huguenots!
> Thus Caesar did go forth, and thus he dies'—

there is no redeeming feature about him; indeed, in one passage ('Religion! *O Diabole*,' &c.) it is suggested that he is a hypocrite as well as a fanatic. But, though there is force, and in one instance[1] imaginative *afflatus*, in Guise's speeches, Marlowe again fails in motivation of character; and fails to account psychologically, as Shakspere in *Richard III* at least sought to do, for the deadly determination of his hero. Even as conceived by the author, the hurried succession of scenes could have left no room for any such attempt in this breathless play[2].

Dido Queen of Carthage (pr. 1594).　In *The Tragedy of Dido Queen of Carthage* (printed 1594), Marlowe was assisted, or his unfinished work was completed, by Thomas Nashe, with whom he was on friendly terms in the latter part of his career. I am inclined to think that so far as *Dido* was written by Marlowe, it must be regarded as a juvenile work, very probably

---

tragedy of *Charles IX, ou L'École des Rois* (1789), Talma achieved his first great success. A notable agitation was caused by the withdrawal of this play from the stage of the Comédie Française.—In 1878 was published (posthumously) Charles de Rémusat's drama, *Saint-Barthélemy*.

[1] Sc. 2.

[2] The application of the term 'Puritans' to the French Protestants, which occurs more than once in this tragedy, may perhaps be worth noticing.

composed before he left Cambridge [1]. On the other hand,
in the absence of any proof that Marlowe and Nashe were in
co-operation at so early a date, or that this play was ever
acted in the lifetime of the former, it seems most likely
that this unfinished juvenile work was completed by Nashe
not long before its publication, which may itself in all
probability be attributed to the interest excited by Marlowe's death in the previous year. While the play rarely,
if at all, rises to the passionate force which is so characteristic of his tragic genius in the brief period of its maturity,
and although we are only now and then in its course
thrilled by an exquisite epithet or an inimitable cadence,
the work must be allowed to show no signs of incom-
pleteness, and few of what can properly be called uneven-
ness. It is a very charming version of the oft-told tale of
Dido's unhappy passion for Aeneas, which follows Vergil
with remarkable fidelity, even quoting, in salient passages,
lines from him in the original Latin. But so infinite are
the opportunities in this immortal story for the depiction
of strong human emotions, that the two English writers
could, without going much out of their way to elaborate
or vary the details of their subject, treat it anew in
a dramatic poem which it is impossible to read without
sympathetic interest. In all that concerns the relations
between the characters, the construction of this tragedy is
neat and firm. Anna loves Iarbas, and Iarbas Dido; Dido
loves Aeneas ; Aeneas loves glory, or, it would be more
correct to say, his duty to his destiny, better than he loves

[1] Mr. Fleay, *English Drama*, ii. 147, suggests that Marlowe and Nashe's
tragedy was possibly founded on the Latin *Dido* by Edward Halliwell
(whose namesake in the *Dictionary* however supposes it to have been by
John Rightwise), which was acted before Queen Elisabeth at King's
College, Cambridge, in 1564; and that their production was intended in
rivalry to William Gager's *Dido*, presented in magnificent style in the hall of
Christ Church, Oxford, in 1583, before the Polish Prince Palatine, Albertus
de Alasco.—Besides an unprinted *Didone* by Alessandro de' Pazzi, a nephew
of Pope Leo X, there were two early Italian tragedies on the subject, by
Giraldi Cintio (Klein, v. 350) and by Ludovico Dolce (*ib.* pp. 399 *seqq.*).
Jodelle's *Didon se sacrifiant* was written by 1558 (it is printed in *Ancien
Théâtre Français*, vol. iv). As to the *Elisa Dido* of Cristoval de Virues
(printed 1579–1581), see Ticknor, ii. 65.—The best-known later *Dido* is
Metastasio's.

Dido. The intervention of the gods is very successfully,
and so to speak naturally, managed ; Juno and Venus only
interfere at critical moments ; at the beginning of the play
a sensuous but finely-written scene accounts for Juno's
jealousy of Jupiter; and near the close Hermes appears as
the *deus ex machinâ* to cut the knot of a difficulty which
admits of no solution. The comic character of the Nurse,
touched like her betters by the dart of Cupid, whom she has
unconsciously been tending under the shape of Ascanius [1],
irresistibly recalls Shakspere's more elaborately comic Nurse
in *Romeo and Juliet*; and there are one or two other
passages that remind us of Shakspere [2]. It is impossible
to determine how much of this tragedy is Marlowe's,
although it is tolerably easy to lay one's finger on what
must be Nashe's. The vein of tenderness, although undoubtedly of a sensuous cast, which runs through the play
(see in particular the moving scene in the cave) is that of
the poet of *Hero and Leander*, nor is there any female
figure in the rest of Marlowe's tragedies who may claim to
approach so nearly to the heroine of that lovely poem [3].

Plays at-
tributed to
Marlowe.

The question as to Marlowe's supposed authorship of the
two old plays on which *Parts II* and *III* of *Henry VI*
were founded, and of those Parts themselves as containing
passages that have been held attributable to him, but are
wanting in the *Contention* and the *True Tragedie* re-

---

[1] How charming is her description of the orchard and garden to which
she thinks she is luring the boy away !

[2] So Dido's gallery of rejected suitors (act iii. sc. 1) recalls Portia's
enumeration. Such reviews seem to have been popular; perhaps it was
usual to apply them to Queen Elisabeth and her rejected suitors, and the
parallel of Dido would be particularly appropriate to the Virgin Queen.—
With all deference to Mr. Bullen, I cannot persuade myself that Shakspere
in *Hamlet*, act ii. sc. 2, ' burlesqued' passages in the narrative of Aeneas in
our play (act ii. sc. 1)—by means of what would have been neither a parody
nor a caricature, but merely a sort of rival version. It seems more likely
·that he had some other play in his mind—perhaps (if this was not merely
a revision of Marlowe and Nashe's) the *Dido and Aeneas* mentioned by
Henslowe in 1597. Hamlet's preliminary praise, which could not be applied
except in irony to such fustian as that which follows, would have suited our
Dido well enough, as a production which would not have ' pleased the
million,' and which would have been ' cavaire to the general.'—The closing
line of *Dido* falls on the ear like the last line of Juliet's speech after drinking
the potion.   [3] Cf. W. Wagner in *Jahrbuch*, vol. xi. (1876), p. 75.

spectively, and, finally, as to his share, if any, in the *First Part of Henry VI*, must be reserved for discussion in the next chapter of this book. I may there prove unable to summon strength enough for subscribing to Mr. Swinburne's conclusion[1] that ' it is nearly as certain as anything can be which depends chiefly upon cumulative and collateral evidence, that the better part of what is best in the serious scenes of *Henry VI* is from the hand of Marlowe'; but I shall not lightly set my judgment against the *consensus* of authority which attributes to Marlowe a large share in the *Second* or *Third Part*, whether in their earlier or later forms. Of other plays within the now but slightly reverenced Shaksperean canon, *Titus Andronicus* has with some show of reason been attributed to Marlowe[2]. The evidence consists in resemblances of diction, which to my mind are by no means absolutely convincing, and in the powerfulness of both the conception and the execution of the character of Aaron, which certainly is not in the manner of any known dramatist of Marlowe's age besides himself. The supposition, on the other hand, that he was the author of the old *Taming of a Shrew*, remodelled by Shakspere, rests on the entirely fallacious evidence of the plagiarisms from Marlowe which it undoubtedly contains ; the comic humour which this play possesses in a singularly marked degree was beyond all dispute foreign to the bent of Marlowe's genius. He has been similarly supposed, on the strength of one or two coincident passages, and of a reference in the *Prologue* to *Tamburlaine*, which however is obviously intended to imply the author's wish to supplant the Scythian Shepherd's popularity by his own presentment of a Christian Englishman, to have written the *Troublesome Raigne of King John*, the early Chronicle History of which mention has already been made[3]. In a different connexion, which will be more suitably brought under examination in my chapter on Shakspere, Mr. Fleay holds that the basis of the play of

---

[1] In his article on Marlowe in the *Encyclopaedia Britannica*, already cited.

[2] See Bullen, *Introduction*, pp. lxxvi. *seqq.* Mr. Fleay, for whose ingenious conjectures as to the history of this play see *English Drama*, ii. 299–300, ' fears it is Marlowe's.'   [3] *Ante*, p. 223.

Edward III was supplied by Marlowe to its conjectural author Shakspere [1], who incurred a similar debt to his contemporary in the case of the tragedy of *Richard III* [2]. Marlowe has also been charged with the authorship of *Locrine* and of *Lust's Dominion*; the former imputation must be left to destroy itself; the latter is satisfactorily refuted by the circumstance that the King Philip who dies in act i. is Philip II of Spain, whose decease took place five years after Marlowe's own [3]. He is likewise stated to have 'had a hand' in the *Alarum for London, or Siege of Antwerp*, the modern editor of which [4] play considers that Shakspere may have exercised some general superintendence over its composition, which he believes to have been the work of Marston. The lost comedy of *The Maiden's Holiday* was entered on the Stationers' Registers in 1654 as by Marlowe and Day. Finally, Mr. Fleay [5] has suggested as the obvious interpretation of an ill-natured query by Gabriel Harvey in the course of his expectoration, already cited, on receiving the news of Marlowe's death, that he was the author of a tragedy called *The True History of George Scanderbage*—an early version of a theme repeatedly treated in later days on the English stage—which was entered on the Stationers' Registers in 1601, and doubtless performed before that date.

Marlowe's services to our dramatic literature. The services of Marlowe to our dramatic literature are in the main twofold. To the author whose example gave to blank verse its not indeed unassailed, but in point of fact unassailable position as the chosen metre of the English

---

[1] The design at least of a play on this subject may well have been present to the mind of the author of the last act of *Edward II*. See above, p. 352.

[2] See section v. of Mr. Fleay's *Life of Shakspere*, entitled *The Marlowe Group of Plays*, to which I propose to recur. He observes, p. 281: 'Mr. Dyce has warned us against attributing too many plays to the short career of Marlowe, but he did not consider that Marlowe probably wrote two plays a year from 1587-1593, and that we have at present only seven acknowledged as his.'

[3] See the note in Dodsley's *Old Plays*, vol. ii. p. 311. Several passages in the play are here shown to be founded on a tract descriptive of Philip's death, published in London in 1599. Collier, Henslowe's *Diary*, p. 165 *note*, thinks this play was very probably identical with *The Spanish Moor's Tragedy*, for which payments were made in February, 1600, to Dekker, Haughton and Day. Cf. Dekker's *Dramatic Works*, vol. i., *Introduction*, p. xii. *note*.   [4] The late Mr. R. Simpson.   [5] *English Drama*, ii. 64-5.

drama, that drama owed an inestimable debt. The experi- *The estab-*
ment on which Surrey had ventured nearly half a century *lishment by*
before in his translation of the *Second* and *Fourth Books* *blank verse*
of the *Aeneid* (1557), had a few years later been applied by *as the*
English
the authors of *Gorboduc* to their English version, intended *dramatic*
for lettered ears, of Seneca's Latin tragedy. But though *metre.*
attempts had hereupon been repeatedly made in the same
metre by writers for the popular stage, it was Marlowe who
first vindicated to blank verse the sovereignty which it has
since retained among English dramatic metres, together with
the ascendancy which it has acquired among metres employed in other branches of English poetic composition.
This he achieved with a rapidity and completeness to which
it would be difficult, if not impossible, to find a parallel in
literary history. Brief as was his career, it was long
enough to demonstrate the flexibility as well as the force of
his chosen metre, and to establish its ascendancy among the
whole body of dramatists contemporary with him [1]. The
English drama never returned to rime, except in a transitory
phase of its history which must be regarded as a conscious
aberration from its national and natural course; and it
soon afterwards relinquished an endeavour forced upon it by
extraneous influences lightly adopted, to be before long as
lightly cast off, by the foremost of the English writers of the
age [2]. But Marlowe established the commanding position
in question, not only for blank verse, but for the kind of
blank verse of which he and he alone was the originator.
' He first, and he alone,' says the greatest modern master of
English metre, referring to Marlowe's literary achievements
as a whole, ' guided Shakspere into the right way of work ;
his music, in which there is no echo of any man's before
him, found its own echo in the more prolonged and hardly
more exalted harmony of Milton's. . . . Before him there
was neither genuine blank verse nor a genuine tragedy in

---

[1] Of course there were at first oscillations, such as that referred to by
Thomas Heywood in the *Prologue* to his *Royal King and Loyal Subject* (1600):
        ' (And not long since) there was a time
    Strong lines were not looked after ; but if *rime*,
    Oh then 'twas excellent ! '
[2] See below, the remarks on Dryden's views and practice on this head.

our language. After his arrival the way was prepared, the paths were made straight, for Skakspere [1].' To the force and charm of Marlowe's metre—so entirely had it become part of him as a poet—the wondrous graces of his diction, aided by the resources of his slender but select classical learning, were subservient ; his often wondrously beautiful similes themselves are but so many jewels ornamenting the royal robe of his verse.

The in-fusion of passion into dra-matic com-position.

But Marlowe's second service to the progress of our dramatic literature, adverted to in the above quotation, although it may perhaps not admit of being stated with precision like the other, was of even more commanding importance. His genius, as it displays itself in the few works which, on the most liberal computation, have come down to us as the undoubted products of his brief career as a dramatic author, fails to satisfy all the demands of his art. In dramatic construction, although by no means unskilful and at times signally successful, he is as a rule careless ; the condition in which some of his plays have come down to us must however in some degree be taken into account in this particular censure. It is but rarely that he applies himself to the gradual unfolding of character ; even in the *Jew of Malta* his patience proves unequal to carrying out an admirable con-ception. It is not just to say of the author of *Edward II*— or on a lower plane of the joint author of *Dido*—that he never draws a picture of any dramatic conflicts save those between human impatience of all control and of all limits, and that necessity of control and limits which the conditions of human life impose. It is not just to deny that he is capable of moving the springs of pity as well as those of terror, or that he can paint other and gentler passions besides those of boundless ambition, hunger for knowledge of all things and power over all things, insatiable greed of gold, and cruelty that hardens its heart against God and man. But during his brief labours he had not compassed the art of showing, except now and then, or as it were incidentally, how other human motives of action co-operate and mingle their influence with those on which his ardent spirit loved to dwell ; while of the divine gift

[1] Swinburne, *u. s.*

of humour which lies so close to that of pathos, of which he was not devoid, he exhibits at the most only occasional signs. The element in which as a poet he lived was passion; and it was he who first inspired with true poetic passion the form of literature to which his chief efforts were consecrated. For with few and faint exceptions this element had hitherto been strange to English tragedy, and where our tragic drama seemed to have been touched by the divine fire, this was only borrowed heat from Seneca or some of the Italians. After Marlowe had written, the days of cold horrors and soulless declaration had alike been left behind; the stage was peopled with living men and women, full of hatred and love, of desire and remorse, of aspiration and despair, whose language was the confession of their souls. 'His raptures were all ayre and fire'; and it is this gift of passion, which filled our drama full of it, even to the brim, that in intimate conjunction with his services to the outward form of the drama, whereby it was first enabled to find beautiful expression for beautiful things, places Marlowe at the head of Shakspere's predecessors and proclaim him the earliest of our great English dramatists.

GEORGE PEELE [1], who was born about 1558, a few years before Marlowe, and outlived him by a rather shorter space of time, occupies a lower, but still very important position, among our Elisabethan dramatists. The family from which he sprang is supposed to have been of Devonshire origin, but his father was clerk of Christ's Hospital in London, where George Peele received his early education. At Oxford, where he was successively a member of Broadgates Hall (now Pembroke College) and Christ Church, he took the usual degrees, and is said to have been noted for his poetical productions. These included, besides perhaps his *Tale of*

George Peele (1558 c.–1597 c.).

---

[1] *The Dramatic Works of George Peele, with Life*, by A. Dyce. 3 vols., 1829–1839. *The Dramatic Works of R. Greene and G. Peele*, by the same editor, 1861. *The Works of Peele*, edited by A. H. Bullen, 2 vols., 1895.— Laemmerhirt, *Georg Peele, Untersuchungen über sein Leben und seine Werke*, Rostock, 1882. For as complete a list of Peele's writings as it was in my power to compile, see my article on him in vol. xliv. of the *Dictionary of National Biography*, 1895.

Troy, a version of one of the *Iphigenias* of Euripides, which was performed in Christ Church hall. The governors of Christ's Hospital, to whose bounty he had been indebted, having seen reason to turn the young Master of Arts out of their precincts, he became dependent on his wits, and though he chiefly lived in London, found his way back, at least on one occasion, to Oxford, where in June, 1558, he aided in the production of Dr. William Gager's Latin comedy *Rivales* and tragedy *Dido* [1]. He was, like Marlowe, well read in classical poetry, to the phrases and subjects of which he makes constant reference in his works, while his Latin quotations are likewise frequent, although perhaps not in quite the same measure as those of his brother-author. He made the most of the credentials of his Oxford career, and the 'Master of Arts' is duly appended to his name at the close of many of his publications. But his life was in the main that of a reckless London wit, alternating between labour and dissipation, and though he married early, and even seems to have acquired some land in his wife's right, he seems at no time to have settled down to regular ways. There is good reason to conclude that sooner or later he became a player as well as a playwright, and belonged in succession to the Lord Admiral's and Queen's companies. Among his private patrons were the Earl of Northumberland, the 'Maecenas' to whom he addressed the *Prologus* to *The Honour of the Garter* (1593), and the great Lord Burghley himself, in whose employ he composed certain verses for the Queen's visit to Theobalds in 1591, and to whom in 1596 he sent his *Tale of Troy*, a poem which he had already printed in 1589 and which he is supposed to have written when at Oxford. He was the author of a variety of gratulatory and occasional verse, among which his spirited *Farewell to Sir John Norris and Sir Francis Drake, &c.* (1589) deserves special notice as a characteristic memorial of Elisabethan enthusiam, and in addition to his labours as a playwright proper, which probably began with *The Arraignment of Paris* in 1581, he was from 1585 onwards employed on the devising and composition of pageants.

---

[1] Fleay, *English Drama*, ii. 171; and cf. *ib.* i. 236 and *ante*, 357, note.

The less decorous aspects of Peele's life call for little comment, although they became unusually notorious. So much it seems not unfair to conclude from the fact that a collection of disreputable practical jokes and loose adventures, repeatedly reprinted after its first known publication in 1607, was connected with his name under the title of the *Merry conceited Jests of George Peele, sometime a Student in Oxford*[1]*;* but he may be acquitted of any personal share in most of the escapades narrated in this collection, which after its kind largely consists of warmed-up anecdotes of more or less ancient origin, although here and there a personal touch suggests a real connexion with the hero of the whole. Unfortunately, other evidence remains as to his ways of life. Peele was one of the associates of Robert Greene, whom the latter in his *Groatsworth of Wit* (1592) admonished to turn from the vicious courses which had brought him low ; and in Dekker's tract, *A Knight's Conjuring* (1606), Peele appears with Greene and Marlowe under the suggestive 'shadow of a large vyne.' A more pleasing testimony to this companionship is furnished by Peele's tribute to the dead Marlowe, already cited ; on the other hand, he cannot be shown to have taken any direct part in the bitter literary feuds which occupied some of his fellow-dramatists, although Nashe, the most combative of them all, wrote of him with special warmth of praise[2]. Whatever may have been the course of Peele's life, his touching confession in his poem of *The Honour of the Garter* (1593) shows how it had filled his soul with weariness :

> 'I laid me down, laden with many cares,
> My bed-fellows almost these twenty years' ;

and in 1596, when supplicating Burghley's patronage, he described himself as enfeebled by long sickness. In 1598

---

[1] Reprinted by Dyce and Bullen, and in the *Publications of the Percy Society*. One of the *Jests* was dramatised in the comedy of *The Puritan, or The Widow of Watling Street*, absurdly attributed to Shakspere, of which the hero is George Pyeboard, *i. e.* George Peele,—'*peel* signifying a board with a long handle, with which bakers put things in and out of the oven' (*Dyce*). Collier and Fleay have also supposed that Peele is the 'humorous George' of the Prologue to *Wily Beguiled*, a play probably performed several years before its first known publication in 1606.

[2] See his *Address*, prefixed to Greene's *Menaphon* (1589).

Francis Meres in his *Palladis Tamia* spoke of him as dead of disease due to vice.

It was to Peele's first known dramatic work, *The Arraignment of Paris*, that Nashe specially pointed, when applying to its author, some years after its publication and probably even at a greater distance of time from the date of its first performance, the sonorous designations of 'the Atlas of Poetrie and *primus verborum artifex.*' This court entertainment, which was performed before the Queen by the Children of her Chapel, probably as early as 1581, and certainly not later than 1584, and which thus entered into direct competition with the earlier plays of Lyly, is certainly not the least attractive of its author's works. After the earlier part of the piece has treated the Ovidian story [1] of Paris and Oenone, and of the shepherd prince's judgment between the three contending goddesses, its novelty begins with the arraignment of Paris before Jupiter and the tribunal of Olympus for having adjudged the apple of Ate to Venus. Inasmuch as the act was committed in the vicinity of a place sacred to Diana, the final judgment is committed to her hands; and she solves the problem by awarding the apple to none of the rivals, but to a gracious nymph 'whose name Eliza is,' and whom Pallas with appropriate readiness of wit recognises to be the same as she 'whom some Zabeta call.' This turn of fancy, which both convicts Paris of an error of judgment and corrects this error in an unanswerable way, is uncommonly ingenious, although probably not altogether original; the nucleus of it may perhaps be traceable to a masque contributed by Gascoigne to the *Princely Pleasures of Kenilworth* [2]. The passage [3] in which Diana celebrates, and the other goddesses echo, the praises of the Queen, may be taken to represent the *non plus ultra* of Elisabethan flattery, while it is at the same time remarkably smooth and even delicate in form. The diction of *The Arraignment of Paris* in general already shows that mixture of affectation and audacity, and that romantic (or perhaps I might venture

---

[1] *Heroides, Epp.* v and xvi.

[2] Cf. *ante*, p. 155. See F. E. Schelling in *Modern Language Notes*, Baltimore, April, 1893. The form 'Zabeta' was doubtless suggested by Gascoigne's effort.   [3] In act v. sc. i.

to say, *rococo*) classicism which were characteristic of Peele. A still more noticeable feature of this pretty play is the extraordinary versatility of its metrification. While all considerations of correct or even of tolerable riming are ignored, the management of the blank verse, of which about a quarter of the text consists, at least occasionally shows considerable skill or power. The undeniable effectiveness of the entire composition is all the more striking, since it is an example of one of the most artificial of literary species; we may ascribe the result in part to the lusciousness of the language, and in part to the general *verve* or dash of the style. Some of the lyrics in the *Arraignment of Paris* became popular, and one of them, ' Fair and fair, and twice so fair [1],' is eulogised by Charles Lamb. Malone thought that in the episode between Colin and the cruel shepherdess, Peele referred to the Rosalynde whose identity has puzzled so many commentators, and her lover, and supposed Spenser to have taken his revenge by stigmatising the envious Peele as Palin in his *Colin Clout's Come Home Again* [2]. Mr. Fleay, who has discovered additional allegorical meanings in the play, concludes Colin and Hobbinol to stand as a matter of course for Spenser and Harvey ; and Thestylis to be Spenser's Rosalynde [3]. I mention these interpretations, chiefly because the fact that Peele's works contain more than one reminiscence to his great contemporary furnish a notable testimony to his own poetic taste, more especially as his personal friendships and partisanship associated him with very different literary companions [4].

Of another pastoral drama by Peele, licensed under the

[1] Act i. sc. 2.

[2] 'There eke is Palin, worthie of great praise,
Albe he cavil at my rustick quill.'
But this is doubted by Todd, and has not, I think, been accepted by later commentators.

[3] *English Drama*, ii. 152.

[4] See Dyce's note on the passage in the *Prologus* to the *Honour of the Garter* :   'Why thither speed not Hobbin and his feres,—
Great Hobbinol, on whom our shepherds gaze ' ;
also the passage in *David and Bethsabe*, sc. 7, traced by Collier, iii. 26-7, to *The Faërie Queene*, bk. i. canto v. st. 2 ; also the Spenserian figure of Magnanimity, occupying the place of honour in the *Pageant borne before Woolstone Dixi*.

title of *The Hunting of Cupid* in 1591, only a few fragments, chiefly lyrical and dispersed through the Elisabethan anthologies, remain. One may regret that, so far as can be ascertained, Peele made no further literary attempts in a direction which the peculiar admixture of light and serious elements in his genius might have naturally induced him to follow. His labours in the service of pure pageantry and show are less closely related to dramatic literature, but no doubt brought with them consolations of their own. Two of his pageants for Lord Mayor's Day are preserved to us. The earlier of them, which is at the same time the first known literary specimen of its kind, is *The Device of the Pageant borne before Woolstone Dixie*—who became Lord Mayor on October 29, 1585. In this pageant the praises of 'lovely London,' otherwise ' New Troy,' are coupled with tributes of Queen Elisabeth. The other pageant, *Descensus Astraeae*, was written for the mayoralty of William Webbe, which dated from 1591. Astraea is Queen Elisabeth, while Superstition and Ignorance figure under monastic disguises. Some special political significance may underlie this fantastic device; but the noble passage in honour of London, which shows Astraea confounding her enemies, makes a less evanescent appeal to patriotic memories. Peele's other extant efforts as a writer or director of pageants or shows, of the kind celebrated by him in his poem *Polyhymnia*, call for no further notice here[1].

Without pretending to determine the relative priority in date of the two historical dramas indisputably assignable to Peele, I am disposed to think that there are sufficient reasons for concluding *The Battle of Alcazar* to have been the earlier play of the pair. But *The Chronicle of Edward I* occupies so signal a position in the progress of our national historical drama, marking with unparallelled distinctness the transition from the Chronicle History, still fettered by the traditions of the Morality, to the 'true' dramatisation which, in the hands of Shakspere and his

---

[1] *The Device of the Pageant for Martin Calthorpe, Mayor*, entered on the Stationers' Registers in October, 1588, under Peele's name as author, is not preserved. Cf. Fleay, *English Drama*, ii. 154.

fellow-dramatists, became the ' History' proper, that its traditional precedence need not be here disturbed. Although
not printed, so far as we know, till 1593, this play, there is
good reason for believing, may have been acted two or three
years earlier [1]. In any case, its relation to the rest of Peele's
dramatic works is wholly different from that borne by
Marlowe's *Edward II* to the other undisputed plays of its
author. For once, there is in this case much in a name, and
no designation could better describe the method of composition adopted by Peele in this play than its compound
title of *The Famous Chronicle of Edward I, sirnamed
Edward Longshanks, with his returne from the holy land.
Also the life of Lleuellen rebell in Wales. Lastly, the sinking
of Queen Elinor, who sunck at Charing-crosse, and rose againe
at Potters-hith, now named Queenshith.* In fact, this *Chronicle
History*, calling itself by a name which we are in the habit
of assigning to a whole species or series among the products
of our national historical drama, although obviously a gap
separates *Edward I* from *Edward II* not less wide than
that which intervenes between *Kyng Johan* and *Edward I*,
is little more than a series of scenes or episodes, derived
mainly from Holinshed, and strung together without either
connecting care or assimilating art. For the large admixture
of prose, especially in the Welsh scenes, which are in-
sufferably tedious and trivial, the author or the stage which
he served must be held responsible. But while these scenes
are calculated to make the judicious grieve, the author has
incurred more serious blame by defacing the material part of
his work through a reckless introduction of scandal—of the
blackest and most mendacious sort. It concerns the good
Queen Eleanor, of Castilian birth—unluckily for her
reputation in the later Tudor age, whether we are to conclude the doggrel ballad from which Peele derived his lying
charges to have been a production of the griefs of Queen
Mary's reign, or an oblique reflexion of Elisabethan pseudo-
patriotism [2]. The poetical merits of the play are half

---

[1] Mr. Fleay's argument, that several lines in this play are also to be
found in *Polyhymnia* (1590), is not in itself convincing. But one is anxious
to believe *Edward I* to have been a relatively early production of its author's.

[2] The ballad is printed by both Dyce and Bullen.—The incident of the

buried by these obstructions ; they have been justly sought more especially in its first, which is also its finest, portion. The return of King Edward from the Holy Land is a striking incident strikingly represented; but this entry, which vaguely recalls that of the Aeschylean Agamemnon, has no similar dignified sequel. The King's speech at the close of the play possesses intrinsic dignity, in addition to the local interests to which it appropriately makes appeal [1] ; but, taken as a whole, while interesting by reason of its peculiar position in our dramatic history, this play, notwithstanding the ornamentation of both classical and Italian lore bestowed upon it by the author, is not only singularly unequal, but devoid of intrinsic value.

The Battle of Alcazar (1592 or ante).

The Battle of Alcazar, printed in 1594, was acted at all events as early as 1592, if we accept the hardly avoidable conclusion identifying it with the popular play designated by various permutations of the name of *Muley surnamed Abdelmilech* [2]. The incidents of the play, of which the central one belongs to the year 1578 (August 4th), no doubt acquired a living popular interest from the attempt made in 1589, and celebrated at its outset in Peele's *Farewell* [3], to place Don Antonio on the throne left empty by

King, in company with his brother, taking his wife's confession in friar's disguise, was very probably copied from some Italian novel.—The curious legend about the 'sinking' of Queen Eleanor is referred to in Middleton's *The Witch* (act i. sc. 1) :

'Amsterdam swallow thee up for a puritan,
And Geneva cast thee up again! like she that sunk
At Charing Cross, and rose again at Queenhithe.'

Cf. also *Anything for a Quiet Life*, act v. sc. 3.

[1] Viz. those associated with Queen Eleanor's crosses. Cf. Professor Tout's *Edward I* (in Macmillan's *Twelve English Statesmen* series, 1893), pp. 176-7, where reference is made to ' the chroniclers' who 'celebrate her piety, her modesty, her pitifulness, and above all her love for all good Englishmen, and her complete sympathy with the ways of her adopted country.' Milton in his *Animadversions upon the Remonstrants' Defence against Smectymnuus* (sec. v.) ridicules ' the old wife's tale of a certain queen of England that sunk at Charing-cross, and rose up at Queenhithe.' The phraseology of the allusion is curious ; see below as to *The Old Wives' Tale*.

[2] See *Henslowe's Diary*, ed. Collier, pp. 21 *et post*.

[3] Cf. *ante*, p. 364. The lines, which will have again to be referred to, are the following :

'Bid theatres and proud tragedians,
Bid Mahomet's Pow, and mighty Tamburlaine,

Don Sebastian; and it has been consequently supposed that the play mentioned in that poem under the name of *Tom Stukely* is no other than *The Battle of Alcazar* itself. This would no doubt add freshness to the allusion to the fate of the Great Armada which the play is supposed to contain [1]. As to Peele's authorship of *The Battle of Alcazar*, although it is corroborated by no external evidence earlier in date than 1600 [2], no reasonable doubt can be entertained. We can hardly err in concluding him to have seized upon a subject, commending itself to him both by the popularity of its associations and perhaps by the Devonian origin of the hero, in order to rival Marlowe's *Tamburlaine* in its own vein [3]. The central personage of Peele's play, who began his career as a cadet of an ancient family settled near Ilfracombe, and ended it by dying on the battle-field of Alcazar, in the company of three kings, had certainly a very different kind of interest for Englishmen than that which could be evoked by the 'Scythian Shepherd.' The events of Stukeley's career are vivaciously set forth in this drama, though it is put together in a more antique, not to say clumsy, fashion than Marlowe's much longer tragedy; and the moral which it is made to teach is obvious enough, while the praises of Queen Elisabeth and of loyalty have in this instance a real pregnancy of meaning [4]. A *Presenter* speaks a by no means superfluous prologue to each act, and a series of dumb-shows further elucidates the conduct

> King Charlemagne, Tom Stukely, and the rest
> Adieu. To arms, to arms, to glorious arms!'

A later play, *The Famous History of the Life and Death of Captain Thomas Stukely* (pr. 1605), was reprinted by the late Mr. Richard Simpson in vol. i. of his *School of Shakspere* (1878). As to the Latin *Historia de Bello Africano* (Nüremberg, 1580), whence Peele derived part of the materials of his play, see Dr. Brinsley Nicholson's note *ap*. Bullen, i. 221 *seqq*.—Stukely and the battle of Alcazar are mentioned in Beaumont and Fletcher's *Wit at several Weapons*, act i. sc. 2. In *Greene's Tu Quoque* Stukely is mentioned as a type of martial spirit and liberality.

[1] See act iii. sc. 1.

[2] When it was assigned to him in *England's Parnassus*.

[3] Ancient Pistol addresses to Mistress Doll a parody on the Moor's
    'Hold thee, Calipolis, feed, and faint no more.'
(Act ii. sc. 3.) The *Battle of Alcazar* is also ridiculed, together with other early plays, in Jonson's *Poetaster*, act iii. sc. 1.

[4] A savage sarcasm against Philip II occurs in act iii. sc. 2.

of the action.   It abounds with life, at all events from the
first appearance of the hero, intent upon bearding the
Portugals in their own capital ; the battle-scenes in especial
are full of stir [1] ; and the hero's dying speech, if not quite
true to its promise—

> 'Short be my tale, because my life is short,'—

for in point of fact, it gives a summary of his biography—is
not without a touch of pathos.   But we are still in the
infancy of the drama, and, while the diction is manifestly
Peele's, this play is in construction and characterisation one
of the least ambitious of his efforts, inasmuch as the
accumulation of striking incidents, dramatically reproduced
in forcible speech, seems to satisfy the author's conception
of his task.

The Old Wives' Tale (before 1595).   *The Old Wives' Tale*, printed 1595, was acted very
possibly several years earlier, although it contains no evidence
of animosity against Gabriel Harvey sufficient to suggest
any connexion between it and the much-complicated quarrel
between the latter and Nashe.   This play might be passed
by with a brief commendation of the homely humour of its
exordium, contrasting as it does with the labyrinthine but
manifestly undesigned intricacy of its main scenes, were it not
for the fact of its connexion in subject with one of the loftiest
productions of English poetical literature.   A glance at
Peele's farce, or interlude—for it is difficult to decide which
name to assign to it—places this connexion beyond doubt ;
and it may be noted that Milton's literary acquaintance
with Peele seems not to have been confined to this play [2].
The *Old Wives' Tale* begins with the entrance upon the
scene of three merry companions, Antick, Frolick, and
Fantastick, who in their wanderings in the woods have lost

---

[1] Cf. especially a passage which the author of *Richard III* may be supposed to have remembered :

> '*The Moor*. Villain, a horse !
> *Boy*. O, my lord, if you return, you lie !
> *The Moor*. Villain, I say, give me a horse to fly,
> To swim the river, villain, and to fly.'
> (Act v. sc. 1.)

[2] Cf. the allusions to *The Old Wives' Tale* and to *Edward I* in *Animadversions upon the Remonstrants' Defence against Smectymnuus*. (Todd.)

their way, without at the same time losing their good spirits. They are conducted by an old man (who appears with a 'lanthorn and candle,' and announces himself as 'Clunch the Smith') to his hut, where they are made welcome by the good-wife. She sends one of them to bed with her husband, and undertakes to entertain the two others with a merry winter's tale 'to drive away the time trimly[1].' The whole of this introduction is written with much natural freshness and humour, as indeed is the opening of the old wife's tale, which, like the beginnings of many another narrative, is neither very clear nor very concise. So soon as the old woman has involved herself and her hearers in a maze between what she remembers and what she forgets, her story is interrupted by the appearance of 'some that come to tell her tale for her.' In other words, from this point the 'tale' is no longer told but acted, the two Brothers, Sacrapant the conjuror (the son of the witch Meroe[2]), Delia the enchanted lady, and numerous other personages appearing in a swift and not always very perspicuously connected succession of scenes. A variety of comic characters are also introduced, among them Huanebango, who quotes Gabriel Harvey and ridicules his hexameters[3]; and the hero who makes an end of Sacrapant is Jack, the namesake and rival of the immortal Giant-Killer. Now, that Sacrapant, Delia, her Brothers, and Jack became in Milton's hands Comus, the Lady, her Brothers, and the Attendant Spirit, is open to no doubt, although the author of *Comus* also derived suggestions from Ariosto, and probably likewise from Apuleius and other classical sources. The difference

The Old Wives' Tale and Milton's Comus.

---

[1] Cf. Lyly's *Sapho and Phao*, act ii. sc. 1.

[2] 'Sacrapant King of Libia' appears in Greene's *Perimedes the Blacksmith* (1588), where by the bye is also to be found an old wife who tells stories. (See Greene's *Works*, ed. Grossart, vii. 83.)

[3] ' Phylyda, phylerydos, pamphylyda, floryda, flortos,
    Dub dub a dub, bounce quoth the guns, with a sulphurous huff snuff,' &c.

One of the ensuing lines is actually taken from Harvey's *Encomium Lauri*, where it occurs as the second in the following exquisite couplet :

'Faine wod I crave, might I so presume, some further acquaintance.
  O that I might? but I may not : woe to my destinie therefore.'

As to Harvey's quarrel with Greene, *vide infra*.

between the play of Peele and the poem of Milton is that between a farcical extravaganza, not devoid of occasional touches of a true poetic fancy, and one of the loftiest, most sustained, and most refined of moral allegories in poetic literature. But inasmuch as Milton was beyond doubt a reader of Peele, I cannot think that the expression, 'coincidences as regards the plan, the characters, and the imagery,' used by Mr. Masson [1] in discussing the origin of *Comus*, adequately represents the relation between Milton's sublime poem and Peele's fanciful creation. For the rest, the fresh and sparkling induction of the piece, together with the irresistible flow of high spirits that pervades it as a whole and atones for the considerable admixture of romance dissolved in nonsense, ought to suffice to make it delightful to readers open to the charms of desipience in season.

Plays attributed to Peele: *The Old Wives' Tale* is the last of Peele's plays that was ascertainably published in his lifetime. It may be regarded as indisputable that he wrote many plays now lost ; but their catalogue is not easy of construction [2]. The list may possibly include *The Turkish Mahomet and Hiren the Fair Greek*, which may be the play referred to in the celebrated passage in Peele's *Farewell* already cited, and which has also been thought identifiable with a play designated as *Mahomet* in 1594 [3]. His possible share in the *First and Second Parts of Henry VI* must be left open for the nonce ; of the other plays which have been supposed in whole or in part to be the product of his pen, none can be connected with his name by any but hazardous conjecture except the comedy of *Wily Beguiled* (not known to have been printed before 1606,

---

[1] *Life of Milton*, i. 586.

[2] I should be the last to impugn tests of phraseology which carry conviction to a scholar imbued with the study to which he has devoted his powers. Mr. Fleay thinks the expression 'sandy plain' Peele's sign-manual; but like Wouverman's white horse, the property seems to me to be one liable to falling into different hands.

[3] See *Henslowe's Diary*, p. 39.—The authority on which *The Turkish Mahomet and Hiren the faire Greek* is ascribed to Peele, is that of *The Jests of George Peele* (see *How George read a Play-book to a Gentleman*). Collier, ii. 411, suggests that the play in question was possibly only an adaptation of an earlier play, *The History of a Greek Maid*.

although an earlier version had been probably produced some years before). If Peele was the 'humorous George' of the Prologue to the later version of this play, he may very probably have been author at least in part of it in its original form [1]. On the other hand, I have no hesitation in subscribing to the opinion of both Fleay and Bullen, in refusing to burden Peele's reputation with the authorship of *Sir Clyomon and Sir Clamydes*, ascribed to him by Dyce on wholly unsatisfactory evidence [2]. This semi-epical production, notwithstanding a tediousness emphasised by the jogtrot 'common metre' in which it is composed, presents certain points of interest to the student of our early drama,— more especially the comic character of *Subtle-Shift*, unsavoury though his talk is from the moment when he first tumbles on the stage, as out of a ditch, and then runs off to look for one of his legs, which he fancies he has left behind him with the corresponding boot. He is, of course, no other than the Vice ; nor could any more instructive illustration be suggested of the transition from the Vice of the old moralities to the Fools of Shakspere. This is, too, one of the earliest play wherein a lady appears in the since time-honoured disguise of a page ; and a certain resemblance suggests itself between the pathetic situation of Neronis and that of Viola [3]. The play as a whole is based on some unknown romance—one of those queer tales of chivalry in which ancient and mediaeval times are wildly jumbled together ; the two heroes of the play, for instance, the sons respectively of the King of Denmark and the King of Swabia, meet at the court of Alexander the Great.

Sir Clyomon and Sir Clamydes (pr. 1599).

The play which I follow Dyce in thinking beyond all question Peele's masterpiece, was not printed till after his

David and Bethsabe (pr. 1599).

---

[1] Fleay, *English Drama*, ii. 158. See below.

[2] Viz. that of a MS. note in a very old-hand on the title-page of a copy. Laemmerhirt's list of parallel phrases in plays undoubtedly by Peele cannot in my judgment be regarded as evidence to the contrary. See as to this play, Collier, ii. 425 *seqq.*, and Fleay, *English Drama*, ii. 295-7, where it is attributed to the author of the old *Appius and Virginia (ante*, p. 204).

[3] See the lines 'How can the tree but wither'd be.' The name of the cowardly knight Brian *Sansfoy* in this play suggests a derivation from Spenser, with whose *Faërie Queene* Peele was familiar ; but too much should not be made of this.

death, in the year 1599. The date of its composition is
unknown — Mr. Fleay, who very unnecessarily, so far as
I can perceive, suspects an allegorical purpose in it which
would suit the date, places it as far back as 1588 [1]. In its
method of construction this play, as is indicated by its full
title, *The Love of King David and Fair Bethsabe. With the
Tragedie* (i. e. tragic fate) *of Absalom*, resembles *Edward I*.
It is, in fact, composed in the manner of a Chronicle History,
although the original text is, of course, that of Holy Writ,
or perhaps of some version of its narrative with which Peele
had met in an old religious play unknown to us. Collier
conjectured that Peele's play was printed in order to disarm
the strictures which had in the year 1599 been put forth
against the morality of stage-plays [2]. This hypothesis seems
far-fetched ; but it must be allowed that Peele not only
succeeded in assimilating (so to speak) the true spirit of
the Old Testament [3], but also managed to treat most of the
thorny passages of his subject without indelicacy [4], and the
whole of it with force. There is nothing that is really
offensive in this play, and much that comes home to both
heart and conscience. Peele's was not, in my judgment,
a sensuous genius, and I recognise in this work, in its earlier
part in especial, a sincerity of moral feeling to which many
of his dramatic contemporaries were strangers. On the other
hand it must be granted that *David and Bethsabe* exhibits
little evidence of power of dramatic characterisation, and still
less of any endeavour to balance or co-ordinate dramatic
effect. A great error of dramatic feeling (if I may use the

---

[1] See *English Drama*, ii. 153, where, to be sure, Mr. Fleay does not go
further than saying that 'the situations in the play are strikingly suggestive
of Elisabeth and Leicester as David and Bathsheba, Uriah as Leicester's
first wife, and Absalom as Mary Queen of Scots.' The play appears to have
been reproduced in 1602 (I do not suggest, with a fresh allegorical intention).

[2] Collier, iii. 26. In 1599 Dr. Rainolds published his *Overthrow of Stage-
plays*. As Collier points out, Peele was dead at the time, so that he at
least cannot be credited with a design which would have some resemblance
to that of Racine's endeavour to meet by means of his religious plays the
late awakening of his royal master, under the influence of Mme. de
Maintenon.   [3] Cf. Bullen, i. 11.

[4] It is true that the enumeration of the *dramatis personae* bears some
resemblance to a list of the offspring of Charles II. Perhaps the same thing
occurred to Dryden.

expression) is committed by the introduction of the scene in
which David steals Urias' wits with the aid of wine. Not that
the scene, the resemblance between which and a well-known
episode in *Othello* must strike every reader, is in itself
coarse in treatment; but a character for whom the strong
sympathies of the audience had been engaged should not
have been subjected to needless degradation.

The diction of the play, while generally pleasing and
suggestive of mature workmanship, here and there rises to
an impressiveness of form rare in a dramatist, who with all
his merits is of secondary rank. The aid of a scriptural (or
Oriental) tendency to parable may possibly have contributed
to this occasionally remarkable effect[1]. The blank verse,
although labouring under the defect of a rather monotonous
cadence, is on the whole fluent and agreeable.

Of Peele's pageants there are preserved to us *The Device*   Pageants
of the Pageant borne before Woolston Dixie[2] (Sir Woolston   (1585 and
Dixie became Lord Mayor on October 29, 1585), the earliest   1591).
extant city pageant. 'Lovely London' herself appears
under the designation of New Troy, accompanied by other
allegorical figures, of which the first is named *Magnanimity*.
In the *Descensus Astraeae* (in honour of the accession to the
Lord Mayoralty in 1591 of Sir William Webbe) Queen
Elisabeth herself is celebrated as Astraea; and since
Superstition confronts her as a friar and Ignorance as
a monk, a more special meaning may be supposed to underlie this fantastic device, in which the passage in praise of
London possesses considerable beauty, while the most is
made of the opportunity offered by the Lord Mayor's
patronymic. I need not return to Peele's other contributions to this species of literature. As is shown by the
multiplicity of non-dramatic productions of which he was
the author, as well as by the variety of the dramatic species
to which he set his ready hand, he shrank from no kind

---

[1] See the famous passage in the *Chorus* after sc. 3 (with the simile of the
Raven), and another in sc. 15 (with the simile of the Eagle). Cf. also
David's simile of the Roe in sc. 1. Collier has pointed out that the fine
comparison of David to the Sun coming forth like a bridegroom (sc. 7) was
borrowed directly from Spenser (*Fëarie Queene*, I. v. 2).

[2] Edited by Fairholt in the *Percy Society's Publications* (1843).

of literary labour which offered itself to him, and doubtless
he dissipated much of his creative energy in the process.

Peele's position among our dramatists.   At the same time he thus became one of the most prominent figures among the writers here classed as Shakspere's
predecessors ; and it is unavoidable that Shakspere's own
achievements should be more particularly compared with
those of a writer whose career, although relatively brief,
was not cut so short as that of Marlowe.   Undoubtedly
Peele was born eleven years before Shakspere, and this
slight chronological difference should count for much in
a literary period of so unparalleled a rapidity of developement.   It seems of slight significance to set against this the
fact of the literary training of which Peele availed, or might
have availed, himself.   The University culture to which he
like other gentlemen scholars of light equipment attached
so much importance—for he well remembered that he was
a Master of Arts—can scarcely be thought to count for
much in the substance of his qualities as a dramatist.   He
was able, both in and out of season, to introduce into his
writings classical allusions from a limited range of studies, and
to supplement them by illustrations of his familiarity with the
derived fragrance of Italian literature.   His use of such aids
as these was, it must be allowed, too liberal and frequently
too felicitous to admit of its being set down as essentially
pedantic.   Peele's method of literary workmanship as a whole
was assimilative rather than dependent ; and it may be more
than a coincidence that the greatest of literary assimilators
—Milton—seems to have entertained a predilection for his
works.   In any case, the difference between this predecessor of Shakspere ar̃d Shakspere himself remains almost
unmeasurable, from whatever aspect of the dramatic poet's art
it be viewed.   In the metrical manipulation of the English
language Peele was skilful and occasionally highly successful [1] ; his blank verse, as has been said above, rises now and
then to grandeur and power ; and scattered through his plays

---

[1] Peele's diction, as well as his versification, has been examined at
some length by Laemmerhirt, *u. s.* ; but the critic concludes that his
author's diction presents no features distinguishing it individually from
that of his contemporaries.

and pastorals we meet with a lyric or two of imperishable
charm. He had hardly mastered the treatment of rime in
its connexion with metre—though in truth, more especially
in view of the utter corruptness of so much of the text of the
plays indisputably his, this is a question on which it would
be unsafe to generalise. In constructive power, so far as
these plays are concerned, he made no perceptible advance
upon the dramatists who had preceded him or who were his
contemporaries [1]. His shortcomings, due to lack of example
perhaps rather than to want of ability, in the delineation
and developement of character, have been already noticed.
Even so, however, the vivacity of his fancy and the variety
of his imagery entitle him to an honourable position among
our Elisabethan dramatists; while the versatility of his
genius, attempered by patriotic sentiment and steadied by
enduring moral conviction, gives him his distinctive place in
our literature at large. If on the whole (though by no
means universally [2]) his merits have been overrated, it may
perhaps be urged on his behalf, that, neither in life nor
letters, was he ever (a slight infirmity of academical pretensions apart) desirous of presenting himself for more than
he was worth ; so that a just estimate of his merits is unlikely
to wane even beneath the blaze of inevitable comparison.

ROBERT GREENE [3], the most widely productive writer and
in certain respects the most notable dramatist among those

*Robert
Greene
(1560 c.–
1592).*

[1] It is chiefly in this sense that his influence upon the progress of our
drama has been rightly stated to have been inferior not only to Marlowe's,
but even to Lyly's or Greene's. See Symonds, *Shakspere's Predecessors*, 564.

[2] Charles Lamb is an eminent exception.

[3] *The Dramatic Works of Robert Greene.* With some Account of the Author,
and Notes. By Alexander Dyce. 2 vols., 1831.—*The Dramatic Works of
R. Greene and G. Peele.* By the same Editor, 1861.—*The Life and Complete
Works in Prose and Verse of Robert Greene.* Edited by Dr. A. B. Grosart
(*Huth Library*), 15 vols., 1881-6. (Vols. xiii–xiv. of this edition comprise the
plays ; vol. i. contains a Translation of Professor Storojenko's *Life of Greene*).
Fleay, *English Drama*, i. 250-266.—R. Simpson, *Account of Robert Greene,
his Prose Works and his Quarrel with Shakspere*, in vol. ii. of *The School of
Shakspere* (1878).—Jusserand's account of Greene's prose-tracts in *The Eng-
lish Novel* (Engl. Tr., 1890), pp. 167-192.—Dr. C. H. Herford, *On Greene's
Romances and Shakspere* (*Shakspere Society's Transactions*, 1888).—W.
Bernhardi, *Robert Greene's Leben und Schriften* (Leipzig, 1874.)—J. M. Brown,
An Early Rival of Shakspere (Auckland, 1877).—H. Conrad, *Robert Greene*

His life.   grouped in this chapter as Shakspere's predecessors, was born
in Norwich about the year 1560. The period of his birth can
only be calculated from the dates of his academical career.
He matriculated in 1575 at St. John's College, Cambridge,
towards which famous foundation, the nursing mother of
so many of the wits of his age and circle, he continued to
cherish a combative piety [1]. But after taking his B.A.
degree from this College in 1578–9, he migrated to Clare
Hall, whence he proceeded M.A. in 1583. In 1588 he was
incorporated at Oxford, thus acquiring the rather specious
privilege, of which he availed himself in not a few of
his title-pages, of styling himself '*utriusque Academiae
in Artibus Magister.*' Although at the end of one of
his publications [2] he further calls himself a 'Student in
Phisicke,' he does not appear to have proceeded to a medical
degree. After the termination of his undergraduate course
he appears to have for some time travelled abroad, and to
have indulged freely in the opportunities of dissipation
which came in his way [3]. His travels extended to Spain
and Italy, and probably also, besides France and Germany,
to Denmark and Poland ; and it seems most likely
that he went abroad on more than a single occasion.
There is no sufficient reason for supposing that on his
return from, or in an interval between these journeys, he
took Holy Orders ; he cannot well have been the Robert

als *Dramatiker* (*Shakespeare Jahrbuch*, vol. xxix. 1894).—Art. *Robert Greene*,
by A. H. Bullen, in *Dictionary of National Biography* (vol. xxiii., 1890).

  [1] See the passage in the letter *To the Gentlemen Students of both Universities*,
prefixed to *Menaphon*, in which he celebrates St. John's, of which Trinity
'was called by the University Orator a mere *colonia diducta*.'

  [2] *Planetomachia* (1585). This Euphuistic composition (printed in vol. v.
of Grosart's edition) may be regarded as a crude effort, which went beyond
the versatile powers of its author, at flavouring fiction with 'science.' A brief
apology for the Sacred Science of Astronomy prefaces a discourse in the
Decameronic manner among the Planets, interspersed with 'tragedies,'
i. e. narrative episodes of serious interest.

  [3] This as well as other statements in the brief biographical sketch in my
text, which I think will be generally accepted, rest on the assumption that the
experiences of Philador in the *Mourning Garment* (1590), and more especially
those of Francesco in *Never too Late* (1590), and of Roberto in the *Groatsworth
of Wit* (licensed 1592), are autobiographical reminiscences of Greene himself.
Further personal traits occur in *A Notable Discovery of Cosenage* (1591), and
in other of his tracts.

Greene who in 1576 was one of the Queen's Chaplains, and
was presented to the rectory of Walkington in Yorkshire ;
nor can he be surely identified with another namesake who
in 1584–5 was vicar, for one year only, of Tollesbury
in Essex. On the other hand, it is certain that in 1580 he
at least contemplated a literary venture in the shape of the
First Part of his *Mamillia, a Mirror or Looking-Glass for
the Ladies of England*, which was entered in the Stationers'
Register of that year. (It is not known to have been
published before 1583 ; the *Second Part*, licensed in that
year, is not known to have been printed till ten years
later.)   Inasmuch as he manifestly maintained some sort
of connexion with Cambridge till he proceeded M.A., the
conjecture seems justifiable that the unhappy experiences
of his early marriage life, which unmistakeably connect
themselves with the Eastern counties, began before his
taking to London life more or less definitively (for what
definitiveness attaches to the movements of a rolling stone?).
He left a wife and a child to shift for themselves at a distance,
while he after some brief attempts at conducting himself
respectably in London soon sank more and more deeply
into the mire [1]. Without insisting on the accuracy of every
detail recorded by himself or by his adversaries as to his
personal life, we may safely describe it as signally disreputable. But the strange thing is that as the fever of
his existence continued, dissipation and debauchery intermingling with literary labours both varied in character
and considerable in amount, he should have so steadily
accumulated the fund of repentance upon which he drew
liberally as a writer [2]. For, happily or otherwise, he was

---

[1] '. . . I married a gentleman's daughter of good account, with whom
I liued for a while ; but forasmuch as she would perswade me from my wilfull
wickednes, after I had a child by her, I cast her off, hauing spent vp the
marriage-money which I obtained by her.   Then left I her at six or seuen,
who went into Lincolneshire, and I to London ; where in short space I fell
into favor with such as were of honorable and good calling.   But heere
note, that though I knew how to get a friend, yet I had not the gift or
reason how to keepe a friend ; for hee that was my dearest friend, I would
bee sure so to behaue my selfe towards him, that he shoulde euer after
professe to bee my vtter enemie, or else vowe neuer after to come in my
company.'   *The Repentance of Robert Greene* (Grosart, xii. 177).

[2] There is considerable doubt as to the dates of publication of several of

gifted in a measure which leaves the sentimentalists of later
ages far behind, with the power of utilising for literary
purposes emotions which he had not the moral strength
to bring to bear upon the conduct of his life.   And this
practice the more readily became a sort of second nature
to him, since (to his credit be it said) he differed from many
other imaginative writers, both old and new, in that though
his life was 'jocund,' his Muse was chaste, and could thus
lend herself, without palpable inappropriateness, to his
copious moralisings.   On the other hand, he plunged with
hot eagerness into the professional rivalries between the
theatrical companies for which he wrote and those with
whose plays his own competed[1], pretending to maintain
himself on a superior level because of the academical *status*
by which he set so much store, and finally forswearing the
making of plays in the very pamphlet wherein his uncontrollable jealousy caused him to assail a fellow playwright[2]
in terms that posterity has been unable to forgive.   There
is, I may add, no satisfactory proof that Greene was himself
an actor[3].   The closing scenes of his career, with the

Greene's prose-works, of which the first editions are unknown; but whether
or not *Greene's Mourning Garment*, licensed in 1590, had been already published as early as 1587, it was at least written before the publication of
Greene's Farewell to Folly, which was registered in 1587 and published in
1591.   These, and *Greene's Never too late*, with the continuation *Francesco's
Fortunes*, published in 1590, constitute, together with the posthumous tracts,
his chief penitential issues. Cf. R. Simpson, *u. s.*, 344–350.

[1] On this head see Fleay, *u. s.*, 257 *seqq.*, and *Life of Shakespeare*, 96 *seqq.*
The particular conclusions arrived at by Mr. Fleay it would carry me out of
my depth to discuss.

[2] Whether or not the well-known passage in *A Groatsworth of Wit* as to
'the upstart crow, beautified with our feathers,' refers to Shakspere both
as a playwright and as a player, it is manifest that the 'bombasting out
a blank verse' and the rest of the sarcasms, reveal author's jealousy of
author.   This is well put by Mr. Fleay, *u. s.*, p. 110.

[3] Gabriel Harvey, in his *Fovre Letters* (1592), has some allusions implying
that Greene acted on the stage, and in one passage calls him a player.
And see the note on *George-a-Greene, the Pinner of Wakefield, infra.*—The
John Green who was famous in clowns' parts and who gave his name to
the play of *Greene's Tu Quoque*, in which he acted the part of Bubble, was
of course a different person.   A poet of the name of Thomas Greene, author
of *A Poet's Vision and a Prince's Glorie*, is likewise to be distinguished from
the dramatist.   In the passage in the *Groatsworth of Wit*, where Roberto
describes his town-life and speaks of himself as 'famoused for an arch-play-
making poet,' there is no mention of his having been a player.

depths of degradation and misery which they reveal, illustrate far more effectively than the declamations addressed
by him shortly before his death to the associates of his
labours and of his dissipations, or than the posthumous
records of his conversion to a better mind[1], the fatal weakness and corroding vice that had overcome his earlier
impulses towards self-amendment.   What imagination can
fail to be powerfully affected by the account of his last days,
given it is true by a hostile writer[2], but bearing on it the
unmistakeable signature of truth?   In an illness brought on
by a crapulous surfeit of 'Rhenish and red herrings,' he was
deserted by all his friends[3].   Lingering out the remnant of
his days with the compassionate aid of a shoemaker and his
wife, he lay in their house (in Dowgate) unvisited except by
two women—one of them the mother of his bastard son[4].
Shortly before the end, having given a bond to his host for
ten pounds due to him, the dying man wrote beneath it the
following words, addressed to his deserted wife[5]: 'Doll,
I charge thee by the love of our youth, and by my soules
rest, that thou wilte see this man paide ; for if hee and his
wife had not succoured me, I had died in the streets.'   The

---

[1] Viz. *Greene's Groatsworth of Wit, bought with a Million of Repentance ; The
Repentance of Robert Greene*, which I agree with Mr. Bullen in concluding to
have been 'edited,' and *Greene's Vision*, which if genuine was probably made
up from some earlier materials.

[2] Gabriel Harvey, in his *Fovre Letters, and certaine Sonnets : especially
touching Robert Greene and other parties, by him abused, &c.* (1592).

[3] Nashe, who admitted having been present at the banquet, which took
place a month before Greene's death, protested in his *Strange Newes, &c.*,
that 'Greene surfeted not of pickeld hearing, but of an exceeding
feare of his' [Harvey's] 'familiar epistles.'   Nashe was not anxious
to leave the impression that Greene and he had been very intimate.—
I need not here enter into the question, whether Nashe or Lodge was
intended by the 'young Juvenal' of the vexed passage in the *Groatsworth
of Wit*.   For the arguments on both sides, see Fleay, *English Drama*,
i. 260–1.

[4] This was the sister of the notorious bully 'Cutting' Ball.   The passage
in the *Groatsworth of Wit* referred to in a preceding note contains an unmistakable allusion to both brother and sister.—The child was buried in 1593,
under the name of Fortunatus Greene.

[5] This letter appears in Gabriel Harvey's pamphlet ; and, in a rather
different form, in *The Repentance of Robert Greene*.   A more elaborate (indeed
over-elaborate and doubtless genuine) epistle from Greene to his wife was
appended to *A Groatsworth of Wit*.

narrator adds, that Greene's dead body was, in accordance
with his own request, crowned by his hostess[1] with a garland
of bays.   His posthumous confessions, of which more
immediately, could not sensibly alter the impression made
upon all fair-judging minds by the all too open record of
his career.   A violent assault was at once delivered upon
his memory by Gabriel Harvey, whom in his lifetime he
had attacked in his *Quip for an Upstart Courtier*, and
wounded to the quick by calling him the son of a rope-
maker, and who now was able to take a full revenge[2].
'As Achilles,' says Meres in his *Palladis Tamia*, 'tortured
the dead body of Hector, and as Antonius and his wife
Fulvia tormented the lifeless corpse of Cicero, so Gabriel
Harvey hath shewn the same inhumanity to Greene, who
now lies full low in his grave.'   Among the taunts launched
by Harvey against Greene was that of having written for
his living.   In reply to his assailants Greene's friends had
little to say—or at all events said little—on his behalf; the
ablest advocate among his fellow-dramatists, Nashe, made
the attempt[3], but seems to have faltered in making it.
Yet there is wisdom in the question which he puts to the
poet's enemy, and with which this reference to a sickening
picture of sin and its punishment may be fitly concluded,
' *Why should Art answer for the infirmities of maners?* '
Were it not that this question implies an indisputable
though frequently overlooked truth, we should indeed be
well-advised if we turned away from the chapter of our
literature which contains, side by side with the works, the
biographies of such men as Greene and Marlowe.

The date of Greene's death was September 3, 1592;
he was buried in the New Churchyard, near Bethlehem
Hospital.   He was still young—at the most thirty-three
or thirty-four years of age—when he succumbed to the

---

[1] The good soul's name, Isam, has been preserved by Gabriel Harvey.

[2] In his *Fovre Letters, &c.*, already cited.—Greene's pamphlet against
Harvey was, as Mr. Collier showed, taken in substance from the old *Debate
between Pride and Loneliness* (by W. Francis Thynn).   See Introduction to
Debate, printed in (Old) *Shakespeare Society's Publications*, 1841.

[3] In his *Strange News, &c.* (1592), afterwards reprinted as *The Apologie
of Pierce Pennilesse, or Strange News, &c.* (1593).

consequences of his moral weakness. For we must not interpret literally his declaration in the year before his decease, that 'many yeeres had bitten him with experience, and age was growing on [1].' As in the case of two at least of the companions whom in his posthumous exhortation [2] he warned against yielding any longer to temptation— Marlowe and Peele—the antic Death might scoff at the *strength* of his manhood.

Greene's fame in English literature rests at least as much on his prose-tracts as on his dramas; indeed in one of his posthumous publications he describes it as having originated simultaneously in the popularity of his early efforts in both species of composition [3]. But while, as will be seen, the number of the plays which can be with certainty ascribed to him remains comparatively small, he was a most prolific producer of prose-writings which, taken as a whole, assure to him an unequalled pre-eminence in the early history of the English novel. Of the thirty (or possibly thirty-one [4]) tracts of which his authorship may be regarded as established, considerably more than half may be classified as romantic novels or, as we might nowadays call some of them, *novelettes*, their interest being distributed between incident, character, and style, and centring in the sovereign motive of love. Hence it is manifest upon which sex Greene could as a novelist most assuredly count as the upholders and promoters of his popularity; and we may accept the conjecture that it was he whom in the days of his early success his contemporary and associate Nashe designated

His non-dramatic writings, and their influence upon the progress of the English drama.

---

[1] Too much importance need not be attached to a poet's mention of his age. Thus Dekker speaks of himself as an old man when he can hardly have been more than fifty. (See *Memoir*, prefixed to vol. i. of his *Works*, p. viii.) Gervinus has adduced similar instances from Shakspere's *Sonnets* (lxxiii. *et al.*). In Coleridge's touching lines, *Youth and Age*, the poet, though then in truth only thirty-eight years of age, speaks of himself as an old man. Chaucer has been supposed to have wilfully told a falsehold in an opposite direction about his age; but the supposition is absurd.

[2] *A Groatsworth of Wit.*

[3] See the often-quoted passage in *The Repentance of Robert Greene* (Grosart, xii. 172-3) : 'I became an Author of Playes, and a penner of Loue Pamphlets, so that I soone grew famous in that qualite, that who for that trade growne so ordinary about London as *Robin Greene.*'

[4] If *Greene's Vision* be reckoned in the number.

with genial extravagance as 'the Homer of women[1].' In
style he was a follower or 'legatee' of the author of
Euphues, whom in certain peculiarities of diction he imitated
to the very last[2], and whom on occasion he contrived to
excel in the saliency of biological allusions that will no
doubt be verified as the specialisation of this branch of
studies continues to progress.   In one of his earliest works,
Euphues his Censure to Philautus (1587), he was contented
to appear as a novice gleaning in the rear of the car of
established success, hoping that these loose papers of
Euphues might 'for Euphues' sake' prove acceptable[3].
His *Menaphon* (1589), from several points of view one of the
most interesting of his romances, bore the sub-title of
*Camillas Alarvm to Slumbering Euphues in his Melancholie
Cell at Silexedra.*   But the circumstance that this very
work was reprinted in later editions (posthumous, no doubt)
under the title of *Greene's Arcadia, or Menaphon*, illustrates
the fact that, both as a novelist and as a dramatist, Greene's
literary talent was not of that subordinate kind which binds
itself in articles to a single master.   Except in the way of
an occasional *tour de force*, he never fell into complete
subserviency to the mannerisms either of *Euphues* or of the
Arcadia; and, as compared with Lyly in particular, he vindicated his claim to a popularity of his own by rarely
failing to command an interest beyond that excited by the
predecessor whose mantle he more or less conspicuously
wore.   His long series of tales, although generally artificial
in manner and not unfrequently in sentiment, are the reverse
of wearisome, even if subjected to an ordeal of consecutive
perusal such as these tracts were certainly not intended to
undergo.   His earliest prose fiction, *Mamillia*[4] (licensed

---

[1] See the passage cited from *The Anatomie of Absurditie, ap.* Jusserand,
169, note 2.

[2] See for instance the alliterative cadences in *The Repentance of Robert
Greene.*

[3] In point of fact, this piece is a series of four tales, strung together in
Decameronic fashion on the device of a *Sophomachia*, or philosophical word-
combat held during a thirty days' truce in the siege of Troy between Hector
and Achilles, accompanied each by some of the chief Trojan and Greek lords
and ladies.

[4] Grosart, vol. ii.

1580, but not known to have been printed before 1583; *Part II*, though not known to have been printed before 1593, must have been completed much earlier), was originally modelled on *Euphues* in construction as well as in style; but it possesses some intrinsic interest as a story, and the transition from the *First* to the *Second Part*, in which the constancy of the heroine is splendidly vindicated, is managed with a touch of Chaucer's half-ironical manner [1]. The story of *Gwydonius, the Carde of Fancie* (licensed and printed in 1584 [2]), of which the style with its alliteration and 'natural history' similes is thoroughly Euphuistic, the plot with its *Rustem and Sohrab dénouement*, is both lucid and telling, although interspersed with a great amount of incidental love-making, and contains an element of personal interest in the reference to the *jeunesse orageuse* of the hero [3]. *Arbasto* (licensed 1584) [4], in style extremely Euphuistic, is in construction clear and effective. Only a very few characters divide among them the interest of this tale of a hopeless conflict between a love which springs from passion, and an attachment suggested by self-interest and gratitude [5].

[1] The supplementary *Anatomie of Lovers Flatteries* (*ib.*, pp. 253 *seqq.*), while attesting the popularity of the work, reminds the reader of those reviews of suitors of which, perhaps in allusion to an august analogy, the Elisabethans were so fond, and of which the scene between Portia and Nerissa furnishes the most familiar example. In Sylandra's case the Englishman, a gentleman of great wit but very small wealth, wins the day. Greene, as a literary patriot, was quite up to Lyly's mark.

[2] Grosart, vol. iv.

[3] Cleophontes' advice to his son, when about to travel, recalls after a fashion the admonitions of Polonius to Laertes. This novel, curiously enough, contains an exhortation of a not very dissimilar kind from King Orlanio to an honoured old Widdowe, named Madam Melytta, whom he entrusts with the supervision of his daughter Castania.

[4] Grosart, vol. iii.

[5] The 'monstrous and mercilesse slaughter' of all but the whole of Arbasto's army, fifty thousand strong, is merely a passing incident.—I have not thought it necessary to refer to *Morando, the Tritameron of Love* (two parts, 1584-7), because it really contains nothing but a series of discourses (deadly dull to a modern reader) on favourite problems concerning Love and Friendship, although an attempt is made to introduce a personal interest by means of a love-affair between two of the interlocutors. Nor need I speak of *The Princely Mirrour of Peerles Modestie* (1584), which though narrative, is merely a long drawn-out version of the Scriptural story of Susanna and the Elders. Both these pieces are reprinted in Grosart, vol. iii.

Planetomachia (1585)[1] is made up of a framework of elaborate futility, and two tragedies, i. e. stories ending unhappily—the one, told by Venus, a rather clumsy tale of a feud of the Capulet-and-Montague type, the other, related by Saturn, a more effective and better told treatment of the Hippolytus-and-Phaedra motive, the scene being here laid in Egypt[2]. In *Penelope's Web* (1587)[3], a light but graceful device (Penelope endeavours to keep her maids awake by discourse, while, herself sleepless, she sits at her web), knits together three ancient instances showing obedience, chastity, and silence to be the cardinal virtues of a wife[4]. *Euphues his Censure to Philautus* (1587)[5] is, as has been already seen, constructed on similar lines; but in *Perimedes the Black-Smith* (1588), to which is prefixed an introductory Salutation to the Gentlemen Readers containing the reference already noticed to 'the Atheist *Tamburlan*[6],' the manner of the framework is pleasantly varied, and the three love-stories are narrated by a simple blacksmith of Memphis and his old wife Delia, who has declined to pass the evening over a pair of cards[7]. The first of these stories concerns a very melancholy Mariana, to whom however her children are restored at the last. A still greater interest attaches to *Pandosto, the Triumph of Time* (licensed in 1588)[8], of which the later editions bore the

---

[1] Grosart, vol. v.

[2] Elisabethan Egypt; for, after King Psammetichus has summoned a parliament to proclaim Rhodope his Queen, prince Philarkos falls in love with his stepmother after watching her *at barriers*.   [3] Grosart, vol. v.

[4] The foliage of historical precedents, illustrations, and comparisons in these tales overshadows the stories themselves, though they are intrinsically not uninteresting; and Penelope shows herself well acquainted with Roman history in particular.

[5] Grosart, vol. vi.—Dr. Herford, *u. s.*, 186 *seqq.*, has some suggestive remarks on the possible, or probable, influence of the Trojan framework of this tract upon Shakspere's (shall we say) modern treatment of the story of *Troilus and Cressida*.   [6] Cf. *ante*, p. 321.

[7] Cf. *ante*, p. 373, note 2. The occurrence in this tract of the names Delia and Sacrapant is curious, inasmuch as the framework has a certain resemblance to that of *The Old Wives' Tale*. See also below.

[8] Grosart, vol. iv.—Dyce reprinted the story in his *Introduction*, and it has been since reprinted in Collier's *Shakespeare's Library*. The tale was many times reprinted in the seventeenth and in the early part of the eighteenth century, and was twice translated into French.

running title of *Dorastus and Fawnia*. In this novel, as is well known, Shakspere found the substance of the plot, together with the suggestion of the principal characters of his *Winter's Tale*[1]. There is no reason to doubt that the story, the ingenuity of which is admirable, was due to Greene's own inventive power ; and though the contrast between ' modelling the clay ' and 'adding the soul[2]' may be warranted in itself, the labour of the earlier writer was not all mechanical. The pastoral fragrance of the loves of Perdita and Florizel is, to be sure, wholly wanting in the novel—although in one of his own dramas Greene was to prove himself capable of imparting to a not dissimilar episode something of the same charm[3]; and he unfortunately introduces into this part of his tale an unpleasant motive[4]. But the story is far less lengthy than are the majority of Greene's prose fictions, its character is essentially narrative, and the rhetorical element is kept under[5]. Its extraordinary popularity was thus in my judgment by no means only due to the exquisite fruit which it bore in the shape of its imperishable dramatic adaptation.

Passing by *Alcida, Greene's Metamorphosis* (licensed in 1588), the component stories of which are linked together as the confidences concerning herself and her daughters of a stranded old lady[6], we come to *Menaphon*, of which the

---

[1] The *dénouement* of the living statue, so charmingly imagined by Shakspere, is wanting in the novel, where the injured Queen dies on receipt of the false news of her son's decease, just when her innocence has been established, and her husband is seeking to obtain her forgiveness.—The characters of Paulina and Autolycus are absent from the novel; and the humour of the old shepherd's visit to Court can hardly be said to be even faintly suggested in it.

[2] Jusserand, *u. s.*, p. 179.

[3] See below as to *Friar Bacon and Friar Bungay*.

[4] The passion of King Egistus for his own daughter, when unknown to him as such. There can be less objection to King Pandosto's, equitably enough, ' falling into a melancholie fit, and to close up the Comedie with a Tragicall stratageme, slaying himself.'—Egistus' discovery that the maiden is loved by his son, is called a ' comicall ' event.

[5] Except in the cup-bearer Franion's Euphuistic discussion of the case of conscience, whether he shall poison his sovereign's guest or enrage his sovereign by refusing to meet his wishes.

[6] Grosart, vol. ix.—*Greene's Metamorphosis*, it may be noted, has nothing

earliest extant edition bears date 1589, and which was republished in several later editions under the first title of *Greene's Arcadia*[1]. Apart from the curious literary allusions, noticed elsewhere, contained in Nashe's *Letter to the Gentlemen Students of both Universities* prefixed to this novel, it possesses a twofold special interest for students of Greene's literary career. In the first place, it represents the deliberate invasion of Arcadia by this facile worker, to whom Sidney's occupation of a new literary territory seemed neither to be prohibitive of competition nor to require a more than allusive acknowledgment[2]. Secondly, the lyrics introduced into the text of this story form a feature which though not absent from his previous prose fictions, had not been prominent in them; these lyrics include Samela's charming lullaby to her infant[3]. Although the plot of the tale is obscured, not by any intricacy in itself, but by the rather inverted order in which it is worked out, the narrative is on the whole fresher in manner than most of Greene's productions, and the work is entitled to rank high among English pastoral romances[4]. In the style neither of this piece, nor of its successor *Ciceronis Amor, Tullies Love*[5], which first appeared in 1589 and was likewise frequently reprinted, is the Euphuistic element particularly prominent. *Tullies Love*, by the apposite longwindedness of its manner and the excessive nobility of its sentiments, seems almost to carry us beyond the Arcadian type of romance into the *Grand Cyrus* style of a later generation, to which no doubt Greene would have been found ready to adapt himself. Few of his compositions exhibit him in a more flexible mood[6]. It cannot be said that he surpassed

---

to do with Greene's *Metanoia*; the tales end with actual metamorphoses, more or less symbolical, but perfunctory.

[1] Grosart, vol. vi.

[2] The name of Samela must have been intended as a reminiscence of Pamela.

[3] 'Weep not my wanton, smile vpon my knee;
   When thou art olde, ther's grief inough for thee.'

[4] The late Mr. R. Simpson's attempt (*u. s.*) to identify the shepherd Doron in this tale with Shakspere is inadmissible. Mr. Fleay is clear that the person satirised was Kyd.   [5] Grosart, vol. vii.

[6] In the earlier part of the story Lentulus' love-making to Terentia is

himself in *Orpharion* (apparently published in 1590 [1]), the framework of which places the author and his readers among the gods and goddesses of Olympus, whom Orpheus and Orion entertain with tales of no humanly attractive sort [2]. The 'Venetian fiction' of *Philomela* [3], on the other hand, which Greene published in the year of his death with a dedication to Lady Fitzwater (hence its second title *Lady Fitzwaters Nightingale*), seems to have been composed at an earlier date. This tale of a husband's insane jealousy and a wife's heroic constancy, unless it was derived directly from an Italian source, was modelled on Italian examples, nor is the southern hardness of the harrowing narrative redeemed by any tender touch of unconscious pathos.

A word must be added as to the much smaller, but specially interesting, group of Greene's prose-writings, in which his own experiences are put to a more or less direct literary use, more especially as they too in their way distinctly contributed to the early progress of the English novel. To this group belong *Greene's Mourning Garment* (thought to have been published in 1590, the year in which it was licensed), and, more markedly, his *Neuer too late, or a Powder of Experience* (1590), of which the *Second Part*, describing Francesco's return to his faithful wife Isabella, is in a double sense of the term fiction, and the posthumous *Groatsworth of Wit bought with a Million of Repentance* (1592), with the story of Roberto, whose life, says the author, 'in most part agreeing with mine, found one selfe punishment as I have done [4].' It need not be held to include those tracts,

carried on both in verse and in prose, and in Latin as well as in English. The gallant soldier asks the accomplished orator to write his love-letters for him, with disastrous consequences, which he magnanimously accepts, to his own suit.

[1] Grosart, vol. xii.

[2] In the earlier, a cruel lady starves her valiant lover to death; in the second, a kinder heroine exposes her adorer to a similar trial, but ends it 'comically.'

[3] Grosart, vol. xi.

[4] 'The *Groatsworth of Wit* was published in 1592, after Greene's death, by Henry Chettle. It is reprinted in *Shakspere Allusion Books*, Part i, edited for the New Shakspere Society by the late Dr. Ingleby, 1874. To

in which Greene chose to hold himself up in his own person as an instructive or warning example of folly and vice ; the *Farewell to Folly* (1591 [1]), obviously furbished up from a manuscript of less retrospective days, might, except for this later 'gloss,' have been frankly included among the compositions modelled on the Decameronic scheme. A special interest attaches to the framework of this piece, as including 'wit-combats' of very probably undying suggestiveness [2]. *The Repentance of Robert Greene*, on the other hand, is in substance as well as in profession didactic. In the *Vision* Gower and Chaucer each contribute a tale; but the genuineness of the framework is open to serious doubt. I pass by, as of quite secondary importance for our purpose, those among Greene's non-dramatic publications which are merely pamphlets on topics of political interest or of contemporary social scandal [3]. But Greene's infusion of a personal, and therefore strongly realistic, thread into the texture of his fictions is not to be neglected in estimating the sources of their effectiveness. I should not have gone out of my way (as it may seem) to notice them in this place, were it not that, in the words of Dr. C. H. Herford, they 'were for his English-speaking contemporaries the most considerable body of English narrative which the language yet contained,' and together with the contemporary prose fiction of Lyly and Sydney, Lodge and (in one notable work) Nashe [4], either actually formed, or indicated in kind, a considerable part of the material of the Elisabethan drama. They thus rendered to English dramatic literature

the passage in this tract concerning Shakspere, and to Chettle's vindication of the latter in the same year from the aspersions he had thus helped to cast upon him, I shall have repeated occasions for returning. The *Groatsworth* long continued notorious. See Jonson's *Epicoene*, iv. 2.

[1] Grosart, vol. ix.

[2] See *Herford, u. s.*, 183, as to Benedict (in *Much Ado about Nothing*), whom I do not think it is at all 'going too far to attempt to attach' to Benedetto in Greene's tract.

[3] *The Spanish Masquerado* (1589) was generated by the *afflatus* that was supposed to have dissipated the Spanish Armada. The 'Conny-catching' series (1591–2), in so far as it can be brought home to Greene, concerns students of his writings chiefly from a biographical point of view, which cannot be further pursued here.

[4] *The Unfortunate Traveller* (v. *infra*).

the inestimable service of bringing it into living contact, not only with many of the chief interests or, as we should nowadays call them, 'problems' of the times, but also with the presentments of these by quickly impressionable agents in literary forms even more readily responsive and reflexive than its own.   Greene's services to the progress of our drama would therefore be very imperfectly measured by his own dramatic writings, of which I now proceed to add a rapid survey.

The chronological sequence of Greene's plays cannot be accurately determined, and we are therefore at liberty to follow Mr. Fleay in mentioning first among them *The Comicall History of Alphonsus, King of Arragon*.   Greene, both as a dramatist and as a novelist, was a man of many styles ; yet it was not less characteristic of him that he could as a rule keep well within the manner imitated, and refrain from exaggerating what, to be sure, often required no exaggeration.   In *Alphonsus, King of Arragon*, he unmistakeably set himself the task of rivalling, in all probability on the stage of the same theatrical company, the *Tamburlaine* of Marlowe, known to have been produced in 1587 [1]. If in addition we accept the ingenious conjecture which supposes this very play of Greene's to be alluded to by Peele, in direct association with *Tamburlaine*, in a popular set of verses which appeared in 1589 [2], the uncertainty surrounding the early date of *Alphonsus* will be much reduced.   Greene's play resembles *Tamburlaine* in subject

Alphonsus, King of Arragon (before 1589).

---

[1] See Fleay's *Life of Shakespeare*, 96–7.—The supposition that *Alphonsus* preceded *Tamburlaine* can hardly be maintained in earnest.

[2] In the celebrated *Farewell* addressed *To the famous and fortunate Generalls of our English forces, Sir John Norris and Sir Francis Drake, Knights, and all their brave and resolute followers*, he appeals to them to

' Bid theatres and proud tragedians,
  Bid Mahomet's Poo and mighty Tamburlaine,
  King Charlemagne, Tom Stukely, and the rest,
  Adieu.'

Mahomet's 'Poo' or 'Pow' is supposed by Fleay and others to refer to Mahomet's head which, as is noted in the text, plays a part in *Alphonsus*. The conjecture is not absolutely convincing, though decidedly better than Mitford's reading 'Mahomet, Scipio.' (A *Scipio Africanus* was acted at Whitehall by the children of St. Paul's in the year 1580, and there may of course have been other plays of the name.)

as well as in treatment, being in fact a stirring dramatic rehearsal of a series of conquering successes, in this case unbroken by catastrophe [1]. Hence it is called 'comical,' i.e. ending happily; we learn, however, from the concluding speech of Venus [2], that, as in the case of *Tamburlaine*, there was to have been a *Second Part* of the play. Even within comparatively restricted limits, however, Greene ran his model close; thus, the famous yoke of captive kings is fairly matched by Alphonsus in his chair, distributing crowns like so many baubles [3]. Regarded as a work of which the accumulated interest is epical rather than dramatic, *King Alphonsus* cannot be described as other than effective, and the progress of the action is so managed as to rise gradually in interest with the magnitude or difficulty of the deeds of its hero. It presents a noble confusion of the associations of different religious systems, subjugated by a free use of allusions derived from Graeco-Roman mythology; and the charms of a pseudo-classical Medea are grotesquely inter-mingled with the oracles of Mahomet, convey (no doubt with a remembrance of the popular tradition of Friar Bacon) through a brazen head; while the prologue and the connecting choruses are spoken by Venus, who both at the beginning and at the end of the play holds converse with the Muses. The stage-directions are numerous, and incidentally instructive as to the simplicity of the arrange-ments which rendered possible a succession of such scenes of combat as make up the staple of this play; at the close we find: 'Exit Venus, or, if you can conveniently, let a chair down from the top of the stage and draw her up.' Childish

---

[1] I presume the achievements of Alfonso I. of Aragon and Navarre, surnamed 'the Battler,' to have formed the substance of Greene's tragedy, doubtless through the medium of some (*translated*) chronicle which I am not prepared to specify. 'Alphonsus, the Prince of Aragon,' is mentioned at the outset of the Dedication of *The Carde of Fancie* (1587),—an additional indi-cation that Greene was about that time interested in the subject of the King's exploits.

[2] 'Meantime, dear Muses, wander you not far
Forth of the path of high Parnassus' hill;
That, when I come to finish up his life,
You may be ready to succour me.'

[3] Act iii.

as is the whole process of the action, partly in consequence
of the very variations of movement which the fancy of the
author has introduced into it, yet the effect produced is
not altogether inadequate to the design of impressing the
audience by the strangeness and grandeur of the subject.

The Historie of Orlando Furioso, one of the Twelve Peeres   Orlando
of France, was acted previously to the date of the earliest   *Furioso*
known impression of the play in the shape in which it was   *(before*
performed before the Queen (1594); very probably it was   1591).
produced even earlier than 1591 [1].   It is, of course, founded
on Ariosto's famous poem, the first edition of Sir John
Harington's version of which bears date 1591; but the
dramatic adaptation deals very freely with the romantic
epos that served as its original.   Collier, who, no doubt
correctly, considers the play to have been 'if not the
first, one of Greene's earliest dramatic productions,' rather
contemptuously describes the object of its author as having
been 'to compound a drama, which should exhibit an
unusual variety of characters in the dresses of Europeans,
Asiatics, and Africans, and to mix them up with as much
rivalship, love, jealousy and fighting as could be brought
within the compass of five acts.'   He allows that the
impression may inadequately represent the author's copy;
but even so I am not sure that the description quoted
conveys a fair estimate either of the character or of the
purpose of the play.   For the action of its lightly-strung
succession of scenes is after all arranged with sufficient
perspicuity, nor, speaking comparatively, is there any excess
of extravagance in the details of the composition—save in
certain passages, such as the dying speech of the wicked
Sacrapant, whose false devices prove the cause of Orlando's
madness [2].   The opening scene, in which the several suitors
of fair Angelica declare their love and elaborately establish
their claims, has a certain effective richness; but the more

---

[1] See Fleay, *English Drama*, i. 263, and cf. Collier, ii. 529.—I cannot
attach much value to the supposed identification of this play with the
Charlemagne referred to by Peele in the passage cited *ante*, p. 393, note 2.

[2] The name of Sacrapant recurs in Peele's *The Old Wives' Tale*, which, as
both Dyce and Fleay have pointed out, contains ampler reminiscences of
Greene's *Historie*. Cf. also *ante*, p. 388, note 7.

important incident of the madness of Orlando is presented without the requisite power of exposition. The diction of the play is ornamented with the usual redundance of imagery; and the versification, though under the control of no master-hand, is by no means so irredeemably obnoxious to the charges of 'tameness, lameness, and sameness' as Collier would have us to suppose. Latin as well as Italian quotations wantonly intermingle with the English text [1].

Friar Bacon and Friar Bungay (1589). A far more noticeable production than the foregoing is *The Honourable History of Friar Bacon and Friar Bungay*, which may with a reasonable degree of certainty be concluded to have been produced subsequently to the two plays previously noticed, and to date from the year 1589 [2]. The internal evidence is strong, though not irresistible, that the composition of this play was due to the success achieved by Marlowe's *Doctor Faustus*; and this conclusion is corroborated, although not raised to certainty, by the occurrence of hostile allusions to Marlowe in prose tracts by Greene assignable to the very period in question [3]. It would however be a mistake to regard Greene's play as a deliberate endeavour to outvie Marlowe's on its own ground. Supposing *Friar Bacon* to have been produced in close sequence upon *Doctor Faustus*, we may rather look upon it in the light of an attempt, made in conformity with the flexible and facile talent of its author, without loss of time to follow up a vein that had proved its popular effectiveness,

---

[1] In the Appendix to his *Memoirs of Edward Alleyn* (*Shakespeare Society's Publications*, 1841) Collier printed a large portion of the original part of Orlando, supposed to have been transcribed by the copyist of the theatre for the original actor (Alleyn), with the 'cues' regularly marked, according to the practice observed by theatrical transcribers down to the present day.

[2] See Mr. Fleay's *Appendix B* to the *Introduction* to my edition of this play and Marlowe's *Doctor Faustus*, second and third editions, Oxford, 1886 and 1892.

[3] Cf. *Perimedes the Black-Smith* (1588)—see the preliminary Address *To the Gentlemen Readers;* and *Menaphon* (1589), the very title of which is taken out of *Tamburlaine*, while the text contains an allusion to Marlowe's parentage and native city. Passages in Nashe's address *To the Gentlemen Students of both Universities* are likewise directed against Marlowe's play.

and to take the opportunity of dealing a lively hit or two at
the work of his predecessor that might enhance the success
of his own. There is no question here of parody, or even
of plagiarism ; but Greene was, I think, desirous of showing
that just as his English magician was capable of check-
mating mere German professors of his art on their own
ground, so an honest English story of the Black Art could
hold its own against imported German tales of devilry. In
any case, it should be remembered that the magic of Friar
Bacon and his brother-practitioner with the Suffolk patronymic, but likewise of historic Oxford fame, are hardly to
be regarded as constituting the essential subject of the plot
of Greene's play, in the sense in which the figure of Doctor
Faustus absorbs in itself the interest of Marlowe's tragedy.
So far as this part of Greene's *Historie* is concerned, it is
founded on a prose-tract of his own age, entitled *The
Famous Historie of frier Bacon : containing the wonderful
things that he did in his life : also the Manner of his death,
with the Lives and Deaths of the two Conjurers, Bungye
and Vandermast*[1]. The writer of this book was probably
no stranger to the German popular story-book of *Doctor
Faustus* or its English version, but his materials were in
main drawn from the native traditions which made up the
popular conception—or misconception—of Roger Bacon's
interesting personality. These are quite uncritically transferred into the play, towards the close of which Friar Bacon
breaks his magic glass and announces his intention to withdraw into the penitential retreat in which, according to the
story-book, he spent the last two years of his life. The
more attractive part of the action, however, is that concerned with the love of Edward Prince of Wales (afterwards King Edward I) for Margaret, 'the fair Maid of

---

[1] Reprinted in vol. ii. of Thoms' *Early Prose Romances*, and elsewhere.—
The extremely pleasing *Friar Bakon's Prophesie : a Satire on the Degeneracy
of the Times* (printed 1604, and edited for the Percy Society by the late Mr.
Halliwell-Phillips, 1844) has no connexion with the story of the Friar and
his Brazen Head except in its title, which was doubtless only adopted in
order to give popularity to the poem. The old story-book must have long
retained its reputation ; 'Bungy's dog' is mentioned in Ben Jonson's *Tale
of a Tub* (1633), ii. 1.

Fressingfield [1],' and daughter of the keeper there. Margaret's affections are captured by Edward's proxy wooer, the Earl of Lincoln—a notion familiar to Elisabethan as well as to more recent poetry [2]. The scenes in the Suffolk village are written with a loving hand ; they are pervaded by a delightful air of country freshness, not to be found in the works of any of Greene's fellow-dramatists save one, and there is much idyllic beauty in the picture of the maid, so 'lovely in her country-weeds.' From 'the country's sweet content' we are transplanted amidst the academic perturbations of Oxford, and are introduced to the magic studies of Friar Bacon in his cell at Brasenose. The description of Oxford has been often quoted ; its earlier lines exemplify the poetic license habitual to Greene, who in matters of illustrative statement, airily ignored mere questions of fact :

> '*Emperor.* Trust me, Plantagenet, these Oxford schools
> Are richly seated near the river side :
> The mountains full of fat and fallow deer,
> The battling pastures laid with kine and flocks,
> The town gorgeous with high-built Colleges,
> And scholars seemly in their grave attire,
> Learnèd in searching principles of art.
> What is thy judgment, Jacques Vandermast ?'

To which Vandermast, a German philosopher whose name was probably invented by Greene without much thought of High and Low German distinctions [3], and whom we are to suppose the Emperor to have brought with him to Oxford with the intent of confounding the wisdom and the self-

---

[1] This pretty title is appended to her name in a stage-direction of the edition of 1599. Compare '*the Fair Maid of Manchester,*' the heroine of *Fair Em.*

[2] It occurs in 1 *Henry VI*, where Suffolk woos Margaret for the King—and for himself; in *Faire Em,* where Lubeck finds himself in a similar dilemma, but prefers the claims of friendship to those of love ; in *A Knack to know a Knave* (printed 1594), and in Lord Orrery's *The History of Henry V*, where again Owen Tudor loyally renounces his passion for the Princess Catherine in the interests of his sovereign.—In later literature, Longfellow's treatment of the theme in his poem *The Courtship of Miles Standish* will be readily remembered.

[3] The nomenclature of Greene's prose-fictions often has the same casual character.

conceit of the great English University, replies with the
sceptical irreverence of 'the Belgic schools':

> ' That lordly are the dwellings of the town,
> Spacious the rooms, and full of pleasant walks ;
> But for the doctors, how that they be learned,
> It may be meanly, for aught I can hear.'

However, his exotic arrogance, which in disputation and
experiment completely overpowers Friar Bungay, proves no
match for Friar Bacon, whose magic art finally carries off
the insolent German by means of one of the ghostly
apparitions conjured up by his own charms. A very
diverting comic character is supplied in the person of
Bacon's servant Miles, a late type of the Vice in the old
moralities ; his drolleries, it may be remarked, are far more
closely connected with the action of the piece than are the
buffooneries of the clown in *Doctor Faustus*. Miles plays
the fool unabashed either by crowned monarchs or by supernatural phenomena, and in the end cheerfully consents to be
carried off by a devil, on being given to understand that in
the quarters for which he is bound he will find a lusty fire,
a pot of good ale, a 'pair' of cards, and other requisites for
a comfortable life. The underplot of the play has in the
meantime moved on, or rather been extended by a series of
complications—Lucy's trial of Margaret's faith (a variation
on the *Patient Grissil* motive), and the fatal enmity between
the two Suffolk squires, which Greene derived from the
same source as the story of Friar Bacon himself, but
ingeniously linked with the Fair Maid's story by constituting a rival passion for her the cause of the quarrel.
The play ends with a most gracefully conceived and truly
poetic compliment, delivered prophetically by the great
magician himself, to Queen Elisabeth, under the symbol of
a flower which shall overshadow Albion with its leaves,
until

> ' Apollo's heliotrope shall stoop,
> And Venus' hyacinth shall vail her top ;
> Juno shall shut her gilliflowers up,
> And Pallas' bay shall 'bash her brightest green ;

> Ceres' carnation in consort with those
> Shall stoop and wonder at Diana's rose[1].'

The whole of this play forms to my mind one of the most fascinating products of our old dramatic literature, in spite of its being put together without great pains, while its ornamentation resembles that of a rustic board covered with a tumbling profusion of flowers. As for the moral lessons which its subject is suited to enforce, it avoids them, or at least applies them with slight strenuousness or skill[2].

James IV,
&c.
(1590 c.).   Another very notable play, and in execution, I think, one of the happiest of its author's dramatic works, is *The Scottish Historie of James IV, slaine at Flodden. Intermixed with a pleasant Comedie, presented by Oboram King of Fayeries* (printed 1598). The title is deceptive, since the fatal field of Flodden is not included in the action, which ends happily by the reconciliation of King James with his Queen Dorothea. Indeed, the plot of the play has no historical foundation ; James IV's consort, though of course an English princess, as she is in the play, was named Margaret, not Dorothea ; and King Henry VII never undertook an expedition to avenge misdeeds committed against her by her husband[3]. But although the play is founded on fiction, such as we may be astonished to find to have been invented or accepted with regard to a historical period anything but remote from the writer, it is very interesting ; and, besides being symmetrically constructed, contains passages full of vigour and of pathos. The story turns on the passion of King James for Ida daughter of the Countess of Arran, to obtain whose hand he, at the suggestion of a villain called Ateukin[4],—

---

[1] ' Dian's bud ' in *A Midsummer Night's Dream* (act iv. sc. 1), if it refers to Queen Elisabeth, may have been borrowed from Greene's image. Cf. Halpin, *Oberon's Vision, u. s.*, pp. 12-13.

[2] It should however be noted that, in the words of Dr. Herford, ' the repentance-scene ' of Friar Bacon ' in the play is of altogether a more solemn cast than that of the story book.' (*Studies*, &c., p. 191.) Here, again, the influence of *Faustus* may be traceable.

[3] The King of England is in the play called *Arius*, an appellation which, but for Greene's many vagaries of this description, might excite some curiosity as to its origin.

[4] From one or two passages it would appear that Greene hesitated as to naming this personage thus, or by the Terentian name Gnatho. I cannot

a well-drawn character,— endeavours to make away with his Queen. Wounded by the dagger of the Frenchman Jaques, she however escapes ; and assuming the disguise of a squire, remains for a time in concealment, attended only by her dwarf Nano. To avenge her wrongs, her father makes war upon her husband, whose design upon Ida has been frustrated by her marriage, and whose nobles and people have deserted him [1]. Queen Dorothea intervenes to reconcile her father and her husband, whom she forgives ; so that, as observed, all ends happily. Thus, the play, besides being very well written throughout, is perspicuously and neatly constructed, and full advantage is taken of the opportunities offered by the plot for the introduction of naturally drawn characters as well as of genuinely powerful and effective situations. The fine character of the chaste lady, Ida, recalls that of the Countess of Salisbury in *Edward III*, a play in which I cannot help thinking that Shakspere had a hand.

But though the *Scottish History of James IV* is both effective in its serious and amusing in its comic scenes ('Slipper' is an excellent clown), Greene seems to have thought it necessary to furnish it with an adventitious attraction which can only be described as superfluous or futile. The title of the play describes it as 'intermixed with a pleasant comedy presented by Oboram King of Fairies '; but the 'pleasant comedy' in point of fact consists of nothing but a brief prelude, in which Oberon and a misanthropical Scotchman named Bohan introduce the ensuing play as a story of this Bohan's writing, together with dances and antics by the fairies between the acts, which are again perfectly supererogatory intermezzos. The 'history,' or body of the play itself, is represented by a set of players, 'guid fellows of Bohan's countrymen,' before 'Aster Oberon,'—the same personage as he who figures in the *Midsummer Night's Dream*, though very differently drawn, if indeed he can be said to be 'drawn' at all [2].

follow Mr. Fleay in supposing this to indicate that a second author (he conjectures Lodge) had a hand in the play.

[1] A curious dialogue on the sins of the times between the Merchant, the Lawyer, and the Divine in act v. should be noted. This, Mr. Fleay thinks, was written by Lodge.

[2] The *Midsummer Night's Dream* was probably not written till after

In *A Looking Glasse for London and England* (not known to have been printed before 1594), Greene certainly had the co-operation of Thomas Lodge. This play, which would interest us if only as a specimen of a peculiar Elisabethan variation on the manner of the old religious drama, begins with a picture of Rasni, King of Nineveh, in the fulness of his pride after the overthrow of Jeroboam, King of Israel. At an early point in its progress, an angel brings on the stage the prophet ' Oseas,' whose mission is to note the sins of Nineveh in order to preach from them a warning lesson to Jerusalem. But this warning addresses itself not to Jerusalem only, but, as already the title of the play has apprised us[1], to London also :

> ' London, look on, this matter nips thee near ;
> Leave off thy riot, pride, and sumptuous cheer,
> Spend less at board, and spare not at the door,
> But aid the infant, and relieve the poor,

Greene's death ; but in any case the borrowing of this solitary feather can hardly have anything to do with the much-vexed accusation in *A Groatsworth of Wit.*

[1] Compare the frequent use of the term ' *Mirrour*' as the title of a book, especially among the old French writers. (See Warton's *History of English Poetry*, sect. xlviii, on *The Mirrours for Magistrates*. The sub-title of Greene's *Mamillia* is *A Mirror or Looking-Glasse for the Ladies of England*.) Cf. also Euphues' *Glasse for Europe* in *Euphues and his England*. Nashe, in his prose-tract *Christ's Teares over Jerusalem*, says (Nashe's *Works*, ed. Grosart, v. 120) : ' Now to London must I turn. Whatsoever of Jerusalem I haue written, was but to lende her a Looking-glasse.' The first title of the old play *The Seige of Antwerp* is (in a rather different sense) *A Larum for London.*—The special comparison of Nineveh with London is at least as old as Latimer's *Sermons :* ' What then ? Sin must be rebuked ; sin must be plainly spoken against. And when should Jonas have preached against Ninive, if he should have forborne for the respects of the times, or the place, or the state of things there ? For what was Ninive ? A noble, rich and wealthy city. What is London to Ninive ? Like a village, as Islington, or such another, in comparison to London,' &c.—Cf. *Bartholomew Fair*, act v. sc. 1 : ' Jerusalem was a stately thing, and so was Nineveh, and the City of Norwich, and Sodom and Gomorrah.' Gifford says (in a note to *Every Man in his Humour*, act iii. sc. 2) that there is no puppet-show of which our old writers make so frequent mention as that of Nineveh. (Cf. the passages cited in Nares, s. v. *Nineveh.*) See also Marston, *The Dutch Courtezan*, act iii. sc. 1. Hence the term ' Ninevitical motions,' i. e. puppet-shows.—The suggestiveness of the comparison caused its endurance into the times of the Puritan ascendancy, when (in 1657) T. Reeve published *God's Plea for Nineveh, or London's Precedent for Mercy.*

Else seeking mercy, being merciless,
Thou be adjudg'd to endless heaviness.'

Usury [1] (a vice of which Greene, as has been seen, had some
personal experience), lust, and judicial corruption are
exemplified, as well as directly commented upon. Then
the Angel summons the prophet 'Jonas' to repair to
Nineveh. His attempt to fly to Tarsus gives Hosea an
opportunity for moralising on the presumption of prophets
'new inspired' and 'men of art.' But Jonah, after being
thrown overboard in the storm, and swallowed and cast up
by the whale, appears at Nineveh to preach repentance ;
Hosea applying the moral to London. At the close King
Rasni accepts the warning, and the play ends with a final
address by Jonah to London, and a fulsome compliment to
Queen Elisabeth, whose prayers are said alone to defer the
plague which otherwise would fall. This dramatic apologue,
after the fashion of the moralities, with which as already
observed it invites a suggestive comparison, exhibits a peculiar mixture of serious and comic elements. There is much
life in the comic scenes in which Adam, the clown of the
piece, is conspicuous ; while the verse of the dialogue is
distinguished by considerable fire and by copiousness of
imagery, apart from the solemn directness of the passages
delivered by Hosea, who, as taking no direct part in the
action, may be described as the chorus of the play.

Various other plays have been thought due, in whole
or in part, to Greene's authorship. Among these, the
temptation is great to claim for it, although the external
evidence is trifling [2], the delightful comedy of *George-a-*

*Plays at-
tributed to
Greene in
whole or
in part :*

[1] 'I borrowed of you forty pounds, whereof I had ten pounds in money,
and thirty pounds in lute-strings.' This substitution of 'commodities' for
cash, of which Thackeray used to make grim fun, is described by Ben
Jonson in *The Alchemist* (iii. 2), and elsewhere. Cf. also Dekker, in the
Seuen Deadly Sinnes of London: 'Vsurers: who for a little money, and
a greate deal of trash: (as Fire-Shouels, browne-paper, motley cloake-bags,
&c.) bring Yong Novices into a fooles Paradice till they have sealed the
Morgage of their lands, and then like Pedlers, goe they (or some Familiar
Spirit for them raizde by the *Vsurers*) vp and downe to cry *Commodities*,
which scarce yeeld the third part of the sum for which they take them vp.'

[2] A copy exists with two MS. notes in different hands: 'Ed. Juby
[a player] saith it was made by Ro. Greene,' and 'Written by . . a minister,
who acted the pinner's part in it himself. Teste W. Shakespeare.' See

Greene, the Pinner of Wakefield, acted in 1593 [1], but not known to have been printed before 1599. For it has one of Greene's most attractive notes—a native English freshness of colouring. It breathes the very spirit of the old ballads of the Robin Hood cycle, and is indeed founded partly on one of these [2], partly and mainly however on the old prose-history of *George-a-Greene*; for there is no reason to suppose an inversion in this case of the usual relation between popular romance and popular drama [3]. The dramatist, however, shifts the period in which the story plays from the reign of Richard I to that of Edward—I presume Edward III. The hero of his play is the valiant yeoman who gives to it his name, and whose figure is to be found in the *Robin Hood* legends down to their latest notable English dramatic adaptation [4]. He is the keeper of the *pinfolds* (or penfolds [5]) belonging to the common lands about Wakefield in the West Riding, and the strongest and bravest man in England to boot. We witness how by his valour and craft he quells single-handed the rebellion of the Earl of Kendal, and makes the Earl himself and his companions prisoners; how

Fleay, *English Drama*, i. 264; cf. *ante*, 382 and note. This statement, if authentic, would establish the twofold fact that Greene was a clergyman, and afterwards an actor. I am again unable to follow Mr. Fleay in his conclusion that the piece was written by two authors—he thinks, Greene and Peele.

[1] Henslowe's *Diary*, pp. 31 *seqq.* The pieces entered by him as *Gorge a Gren* and as *The Piner of Wiackefelld* must be supposed to be one and the same; but it is noticeable that Munday in his *Downfall of Robert Earl of Huntington* (act iii. sc. 1) mentions George-a-Greene and 'wanton Wakefield's Pinner' as two distinct personages. Cf. Collier's note, *Five Old Plays*, p. 49.

[2] The ballad of *Robin Hood and the Pinder of Wakefield*, of which Bishop Percy in his *Reliques* (in the prefatory note to *Sir Lancelot of the Lake*) quotes the first stanza, adding: 'that ballad may be found on every stall, and therefore is not here reprinted.' This would appear to be the ballad, with a passage from which—
              'And Robin Hood, Scarlet and John'—
Master Silence 'confronts the Helicons.' (2 *Henry IV*, act v. sc. 3.) Cf. R. Sachs, *George Green the Pinner of Wakefield*, in *Jahrbuch*, vol. xxvii (1892), pp. 192 *seqq.*

[3] Cf. Dyce's *Introduction*.

[4] He appears as one of Robin Hood's merry men in Jonson's *Sad Shepherd*.

[5] The 'Pinder's' office, according to Nares (*s. v.*) was 'to look after stray animals and put them into the pound, and to prevent trespassers.'

he then proves himself stronger than Robin Hood and his three merry men ; and how in the end he refuses all reward from the King, save a royal good word with the father of his sweetheart Bettris. The later part of the piece plays at Bradford, and much fun is made out of the local custom obliging every man who passes to vail his staff to the shoe-makers. To this custom the King himself, who with his royal Scottish prisoner (of immortal poetic fame) visits Bradford in disguise to see George-a-Greene, is fain to submit. This charming play, very national in spirit and singularly bright in manner, was at one time attributed to Shakspere ; nor was dishonour done to him by this untenable supposition [1].

The First Part of the Tragicall Raigne of Selimus (first printed, so far as is known, in 1594) is included in the Huth Library edition of Greene's *Works* [2], and the external evidence advanced by Dr. Grosart in favour of Greene's authorship is certainly striking. In *England's Parnassus*, a poetical anthology printed in 1600 with a Dedication and Address signed 'R. A.'—in all probability the publisher Robert Allott—not less than thirty-five passages cited are attributed to Greene. Of these all but ten appear to have been traced to this author's known works, six remain untraced, two belong to Spenser, and two are to be found in *Selimus* [3]. Allott was an assiduous collector, although perhaps not unusually discriminating as to the authorship of all that he collected [4] ; and no attempt has been made to bring home the two passages in question to any other author [5]. The play itself, when it appeared in a second edition in 1638, was said to be by 'T. G.' ; but the blunder which explained these letters to signify Thomas Goffe stands self-exposed [6]. The internal evidence in the play

The First Part of the Tragicall Raigne of Selimus (pr. 1594).

---

[1] Tieck, who suggested or entertained this notion, afterwards assigned the play to Greene (cf. Sachs, *u. s.*).

[2] Vol. xiv ; cf. the editor's observations in vol. i. pp. lxxi–lxxvii.

[3] Viz. the lines on '*Delaie*' (Grosart, p. 211), and those alluding to the story of Dionysius and Damocles (*ib.* p. 224).

[4] Cf. Mr. A. H. Bullen's notice of him in vol. i of *The Dictionary of National Biography* (1885).

[5] Moreover, Thos. Creede, who published *Selimus*, also printed *James IV* and *Alphonsus*.

[6] Thomas Goffe, the author of *The Raging Turk, or Bajazet the Second*, was born in 1592. (Cf. Fleay, *English Drama*, vol. i. p. 247.)

itself, however, in my judgment, fails to furnish adequate
support for Dr. Grosart's theory.   He is inclined to regard
Selimus as fulfilling, after a fashion, Greene's half-promise of
producing a Second Part to *Alphonsus*[1]; but this interpretation seems forced, all the more so that *Selimus* is itself
only a First Part.   Neither can I detect in the supposed
autobiographical—or quasi-autobiographical—passages that
personal flavour which Greene, when he entered upon any
attempt of the sort, was wont to impart to it; while the
parallelism between the lines concerning 'the sweet content'
of country life and a passage in Greene's *Farewell to Follie*
admits of a more obvious explanation.   As to the coincidences of words and phrases in *Selimus* and in undoubted
productions of Greene's, I am obliged to confess that they
leave me unconvinced; on the other hand, it must be
allowed that there is a certain analogy between *Selimus* and
Alphonsus in the intermixture of rime and blank verse in
both plays; but where in *Alphonsus*, or in any other of
Greene's plays, are to be found the old-fashioned stanza-
forms of the opening of *Selimus*?   In sum, the place which
Dr. Grosart has sought to vindicate to Greene is certainly
unoccupied by any other claimant; but for myself, I am
still inclined to adhere to the supposition of an author
belonging to a school less advanced than Greene's.   The
play, in any case, seems hardly to have been written, like
Alphonsus, in direct rivalry of Marlowe's *Tamburlaine*[2];
and it is noticeable that, while at least one passage contains
a direct imitation of one of the most peculiar features of
Euphuism, the style and diction of *Selimus* are modelled
to a very remarkable degree on those of the Senecan
tragedies, one passage of the dialogue being indeed directly
borrowed from the *Thyestes*[3].

---

[1] See the concluding speech of Venus in *Alphonsus*:
>   'That, when I come to finish up his life, &c.'
[3] Selimus is rather a sort of Machiavel.
[4] See Cunliffe, *u.s.*, pp. 62-6.—In the character of the Jewish physician and
poisoner Abraham an allusion has been sought to Lopez, the date of whose
trial (1594) would thus affect the chronology of the play; but the circumstances
of the poisoning of Bajazet II by his Jewish physician are historical.   See
Zinkeisen, *Geschichte des Osmanischen Reiches*, vol. ii. p. 565 and *note*.

A *History of Jobe* was entered as by Robert Greene in the Stationers' Registers in 1594, but is not known to have been printed.   Mr. Fleay also claims for him a share in *The Troublesome Raigne of King John* [1], and in the *First and Second Part of Henry VI*, but any comments on the latter supposition I reserve for the present.

The unusually violent oscillations which the reputation of Greene as a dramatist has undergone, and may be destined yet to undergo, are more easily explained than reconciled with one another.   With the pedantic champion of the self-satisfied clique who looked down with contempt upon such writers as himself he was at war, and the rancour of his adversary pursued him even beyond the grave.   But he was *Greene as a victim of plagiarism.* also at different times at issue with the most distinguished of his fellow-playwrights, and as it were with his dying breath asserted that one of them had committed (for so I think we are bound to understand his words) literary robbery upon him and his fellows.   The charge that he had suffered by such appropriations is echoed by his panegyrist 'R. B.,' who wrote of him after his death with an obvious reference to his own complaint:

> 'Greene is the pleasing object of an eie :
> Greene pleasde the eies of all that lookt vppon him.
> Greene is the ground of everie Painters die :
> Greene gave the ground to all that wrote vpon him.
> Nay more the men that so Eclipst his fame
> Purloynd his Plumes, can they deny the same ? [2]'

To the melancholy lesson which is taught by his personal life there is no necessity for returning ; but the remembrance *His merits as a dramatist.* of its errors should the less affect the judgment of posterity upon his genius as a dramatist, since its productions are wholly, and we can scarcely doubt intentionally, free from wantonness.   His felicity in the choice, and inventiveness in the treatment, of his dramatic themes are alike remarkable ;

[1] *Ante*, p. 223.
[2] Jonson's famous quip seems merely to point to the fact that Greene's prose fictions as a whole had rapidly fallen out of fashion. See *Every Man out of his Humour*, act ii. sc. 1 : ' She does use as choice figures in her ordinary conferences, as any be in the *Arcadia*.'   *Carlo :* ' Or rather in Greene's works, *whence she may steal with more security*.'

he deals with a great variety of materials in a spirit of rare buoyancy and freedom, and of that audacity which becomes a poet sure of himself.   Thus, notwithstanding that, as has been pointed out by Mr. Fleay, all those plays for which Greene assumed the sole responsibility, are called by the old name of *Histories*—implying dependence on extant narrative materials—his freedom and originality of treatment entitle his plays to a high rank in the early English romantic drama.   In regard to all that may be comprised under the word style, it is less easy to estimate the merits of an author who in his plays as in his more abundant non-dramatic writings was so ready to mould his manner upon that of other authors, if they had shown themselves capable of commanding success.   His versification never reached Marlowe's majestic level, or even that of Peele when at his best—in moments of tragic inspiration such as never visited Greene.   His diction often shone with ornament ; but this was rather of the accepted Parnassian sort, and rarely comprised images prompted by an inspiration of adaptation.   In humorous passages his large practice as a writer of prose enabled him to move with perfect ease, while the experiences of which he was periodically repentant imparted a certain variation of colour to his desipience.   He cannot, without hyperbole, be said in respect to his dramatic works to deserve the tribute paid to his writings at large by a French sonneteer, of having been a *raffineur de l'Anglois* [1] ; but as a dramatist hardly less than as a novelist, he rendered a distinct service to the growth of English prose.   Apart, therefore, from the important productivity displayed by him in other fields of literary composition, Robert Greene stands high among the predecessors of Shakspere in dramatic literature itself.   And although we may be indifferent as well as sceptical as to the nature of the debt with which he sought to burden the fame of Shakspere, yet we may allow that a different kind of debt was assuredly owed to the elder by the younger and infinitely

---

[1] *Greene et Lylli tous deux raffineurs de l'Anglois.*   See the sonnet prefixed to *Perimedes the Blacksmith*, by J. Eliote.   It is curious that this admirer should have caught the temper of Greene himself, in exhorting him to ' *mépriser des chiens et chathuans* [chats-huants, screech-owls] *la rage.*'

greater dramatist. In a greater measure perhaps than any
poet before Shakspere, Greene helped to wing the feet of
the English dramatic Muse, by giving liberty and lightness
to her movements; and more than one of his plays breathe
in some degree that undescribable freshness, that air blown
from over English homesteads and over English meads,
which we recognise as a Shaksperean characteristic, and
which belongs to none but a wholly and truly national art.

THOMAS LODGE [1], born at West Ham in Essex about *Thomas*
the year 1558, was the son of a London Lord Mayor of *Lodge*
substantial wealth and ancient family. He was educated at *(1558 c.–*
Trinity College, Oxford, where (since there is on this head *1625).*
no doubt as to identity) he may be stated to have taken his *His life*
degrees in due course. It is perhaps hardly fair to conclude *and literary*
from the experience which he shows of youth led astray by *labours.*
usurers that the personal difficulties of his own life began at
Lincoln's Inn, where he was admitted in 1578, although he
dwells on the temptations incident to the life of a young
student of the law. But it seems suspicious that his mother,
when on her death in 1579 she left him part of her property,
attached to his inheritance of other parts of it on her
husband's death the condition that he should have remained
what ' a good student ought to be '; and that, when the time
came (in 1584), Lodge, although or because he had married
a year or more previously, was left out of his father's will.

In any case, he must from a very early date have
renounced legal studies in favour of literary pursuits. In
1580 he came forward as a champion of the liberal arts of
poetry, music, and the drama, against their aspersor Stephen
Gosson, whose *Schoole of Abuse* had been published in the
previous year, with a dedication (which met with no gracious
acceptance) to Sir Philip Sidney. Lodge was not the first

---

[1] All the extant works of Lodge, with the exception of his translations of
Seneca, Josephus and Du Bartas, have been edited for the Hunterian Club,
Glasgow, 1878-82, by Mr. Edmund Gosse, with an introductory essay, since
reprinted by him in his *Seventeenth Century Studies* (1883). See also
D. Laing's Introduction to Lodge's *Defence of Poetry, Music and Stage-plays*
(*Shakespeare Society's Publications*, 1853) ; and cf. Mr. S. Lee's article on
Lodge in vol. xxxiv of the *Dictionary of National Biography* (1893).

to enter the lists against Gosson, and his pamphlet entitled *A Defence of Poetry, Music, and Stage-plays* [1] is not particularly interesting, being in fact rather commonplace in matter and academically pedantic in treatment.   Perhaps the interest which it aroused was increased by the fact that it had been refused a licence ; at all events, when the tract reached Gosson's hands, he deemed it of sufficient importance to answer it in his *Playes confuted in Five Actions* (1582).   To this Lodge afterwards replied in the preface to his *Alarum against Usurers* (1584) [2], a tract of which the title explains itself, and which is also dedicated to Sidney.

How far the charges of loose living, launched against Lodge by Gosson in his *Playes Confuted*, &c., were warranted by fact, need not be discussed ; the censor, who appears some time before to have withdrawn from town life, shows no knowledge of his adversary's private history [3].   Gosson does not state in this pamphlet, as he was by the late Mr. Collier asserted to have done, that Lodge had actually appeared on the stage as a player ; and the attempt made, with the aid not only of misquotation, but also of a grave falsification of documentary evidence, to substantiate the supposed statement, has, although dying hard, met with the ultimate fate of all such manœuvres [4].   On the other hand, the language of Gosson in *Playes Confuted* leaves no doubt as to the fact that before the publication of this pamphlet Lodge had become a 'playmaker,'—an occupation which his assailant readily couples with terms of the blackest

[1] See the edition already cited ; and cf. Collier in *Shakespeare Society's Papers*, ii. 162 *seqq.*

[2] Edited for the Shakespeare Society, with the *Defence*, &c., by D. Laing.

[3] Dr. Ingleby, in the tract cited below, points out that Gosson, when he wrote his *Apologie of the Schole of Abuse* (1579), did not know for certain who his opponent was, and that in *Playes Confuted*, &c., he misnames him *William* Lodge.

[4] I sincerely regret that, in the first edition of this book, I should have been misled into repeating this fiction, not being at the time acquainted with the complete exposure of it by the late Dr. C. M. Ingleby in his pamphlet, *Was Thomas Lodge an Actor?   An Exposition touching the Social Status of the Playwright in the time of Elizabeth* (1868), and by Dr. Furnivall in subsequent publications. Cf. as to the history of this fraud and its exposure, Ingleby's *General Introduction to Shakspere Allusion Books*, Part I. (*New Shakspere Society's Publications*, 1874), p. iv, *note*.

infamy[1]. Of his earlier plays, however, none remain. As
will be shown immediately, *The Wounds of Civil War*, the
only play of which the sole authorship is with certainty to
be attributed to Lodge, was probably produced about the
year 1587 ; in *The Looking Glasse for London*, and possibly
in other plays, he co-operated with Greene, who died in
1592, when Lodge had been for some months absent from
England ; the majority of the remaining dramas in which he
is supposed, on more or less specious grounds, to have had
a hand have (though in the same conjectural fashion[2]) likewise been assigned to the last few years of the ninth decade
of the century. But his connexion with the stage as a playwright was, on the most liberal assumption, of a transitory
nature only. His literary *début* fell in the heyday of
Euphuism, and the tractate against which he fleshed his
youthful rapier (*The Schoole of Abuse*) was itself a specimen
of the Euphuistic manner. What wonder that, instead of
confining his imitation of the style in fashion to didactic
pamphlets, he should himself have ventured into the con-
tiguous realm of fiction whither the master's example was
pointing the way? *The Delectable History of Forbonius
and Prisceria*[3] (1584) is, however, a very ordinary love-
pamphlet which could not pretend to enter into competition
with the efforts already made by Lodge's literary associate,
Robert Greene, in the same direction. In the very year of
its publication, Lodge, to use his own phrase, fell 'from
bookes to armes,' and accompanied Captain Clarke in
a patriotic investigation of the islands of Tercera and the
Canaries. It was to beguile the tedium of this voyage that,
according to his own account, Lodge composed by far the
most famous of his literary works, the prose-tale of *Rosalynde, Euphues' Golden Legacie, found in his cell at Silexdra*[4].
Written in the fashionable style, wherever the author thought

---

[1] 'No *Lodge*, no playmaker, no Epicure, no Atheiste, shall make you to
surfette with these delights' (*Playes Confuted*, &c., *ad fin.*).

[2] I refer to those enumerated by Mr. Fleay, *English Drama*, ii. 49 *seqq.*

[3] Edited for the Shakespeare Society with the *Defence*, &c., by D. Laing.

[4] Of this celebrated novel there are several reprints, including one in
vol. ii of Collier's *Shakespeare Library* (1843 and 1875) and another in
Cassell's *National Library* (1886).

it incumbent upon him to take particular pains, this story
secured to itself an exceptional vitality by the more certain
means of an interesting plot full of situations best described
by the French term *piquant*.   Shakspere in adapting it for
his comedy of *As You Like It*, added something besides the
characters of the melancholy Jacques and (in his mellower
phases, at all events) of the nobly desipient Touchstone ;
but of this below.   Lodge's novel is a felicitous example of
the transition towards life and action which was accom-
plishing itself in English prose fiction in the hands of Lyly's
followers, while in their artificiality of description, illustration, and phraseology, they jingled their gilded fetters with
a persistency almost equal to his own[1].   It will not be
overlooked that this book contains some very pleasing
attractive lyrics.

Rosalynde was published in 1590 ; on his return from his
sea-voyage in the previous year Lodge had put forth
a volume of verse entitled *Scillaes Metamorphosis, enter-
laced with the unfortunate love of Glaucus*[2].   We need not, in
this place at all events, concern ourselves with the question
as to the relations between this poem and Shakspere's
Venus and Adonis ; its significance for our purpose is rather
that Lodge seized the opportunity of his first presenting
himself in the full-fledged dignity of a 'poet' to renounce
his literary connexion with the stage, of which he had not
long since come forward as the defender.   At the close of
this poem he announces that he has been now bound by
oath—

> ' To write no more of that whence shame doth grow:
> Or tie my pen to penny-knaues delight,
> But liue with fame, and so for fame to write[3].'

Whether or not some similar feeling may have in passing

---

[1] See the criticism of *Rosalynde*, ap. Jusserand, *u. s.*, 204 ; and cf. Delius,
Lodge's Rosalynde and Shakspere's As You Like It, in *Jahrbuch*, vol. vi
(1872).—How far or in what sense the novel in its turn is to be described as
original, is a question which cannot occupy us here.

[2] Its later and better-known title is *The Most Pithie and Pleasant Historie
of Glaucus and Scilla* (1610). Reprinted, with preface by Singer, 1819.

[3] Cf. Ingleby, *Introduction* to *Shakspere Allusion Books, u. s.*   To the
significance of the passage cited by him from Shakspere's *Sonnet lxxii*
I may return below.

taken hold of Shakspere himself, when reflecting on the degradation which a personal connexion with the theatre seemed to involve or imply, we at all events know that he was not permanently mastered by it. Lodge, on the other hand, appears at this time to have, in his own case, put an end to this connexion, so that in point of fact the remainder of his long career falls outside the history of dramatic literature. If the conjecture which identifies Lodge with the 'young Juvenal' of Greene's *Groats-worth of Wit* could be maintained [1] we might attribute an influence upon his resolution, or rather upon his steady observance of it, to Greene's warning. In a very different literary sphere, Lodge's abandonment of play-writing for poetry was encouraged or applauded,—if we are to accept Malone's ingenious but not very safe interpretation of one of the many ambiguous allusions in Spenser's *Colin Clouts Come Home Againe* [2].

At the time of his unhappy associate's decease, Lodge was at sea again, having accompanied the famous navigator Cavendish on a long and ill-starred voyage. Before setting forth he had printed a species of historical romance, *The History of Robert, second Duke of Normandy, surnamed* (as Lodge says, 'for his youthful imperfections') *Robin the Divell* (1591) ; his *Euphues' Shadow the battaile of the sences*, of which the scene is laid in the days of Octavianus Augustus, and in which Lodge, as Mr. Gosse thinks, comes nearest to 'his great precursor' Lyly, was published for his absent friend by Greene (1592). On his return from his troubled travels, in which, however, he had carried himself

---

[1] This view, held by Malone and a series of Shaksperean scholars after him, still finds a champion in Mr. Fleay. See, however, Ingleby, *Supplement to General Introduction, u. s.*, and cf. R. Simpson, *The School of Shakspere*, ii. 382-3. — The person addressed as 'young Juvenal' by Greene is stated by him to have 'lastly with him together writ a comedy.' Mr. Fleay not very convincingly argues that this was *A Looking Glasse for London* (*English Drama*, ii. 53-4).

[2] 'And there is pleasing Alcon, could he raise
His tone from laies to matter of more skill.'

Lodge is supposed to have repaid the compliment in his *Phillis*. See Collier, *Memoirs of Alleyn*, p. 40.—A personage in *A Looking Glasse* is called Alcon ; but, although one pretty lyric is placed in his mouth, it would hardly have been complimentary to name after him one of the authors of the play.

with credit, Lodge printed in 1593, besides another 'historical' romance, *The Life and Death of William Longbeard, the most famous and witty English Traitor, borne in the Citty of London,* his *Phillis,* one of the most notable early Elisabethan books of sonnets; his two dramatic works, *The Tragedy of the Wounds of Civil War* and the *Looking-glass* (1594); and his *Fig for Momus,* a volume of verse comprising epistles addressed to distinguished friends, including Drayton, satires and eclogues, one of which is dedicated to Daniel (1595). It is by reason of this production that Bishop Hall's claim—

> 'I first adventure, follow me who list,
> And be the second English satirist'—

seems to admit of being challenged on behalf of Lodge [1]. His last contribution to imaginative literature was the highly ornate romance of *A Margarite* (i.e. pearl) *of America* (1596), which the writer professes to have discovered in its original Spanish in a Jesuit library visited by him on his expedition with Cavendish, and to have translated on shipboard in the Magellan Straits [2].

After this, Lodge betook himself to intellectual labours of a different cast. Possibly he had exhausted his original, and more especially his lyric, vein [3]. Possibly the licence of imaginative composition failed to suit itself easily to the discipline to which he now seems to have subjected himself as a convert to the Church of Rome [4]; and his second wife, herself a Roman Catholic, may have influenced him in the

---

[1] See Singer's preface to his edition of the *Satires of Joseph Hall* (1824).

[2] Reprinted by Halliwell-Phillips (1859).

[3] He contributed, however, to the poetical miscellany, *England's Helicon,* published in 1600 (Gosse, *u. s.,* p. 56). But these may have been verses written at an earlier date.

[4] He is supposed to have been the author of '*Prosopopeia,* containing the Teares of the holy, blessed and sanctified Marie, the Mother of God' (1596), to which the initials 'T. L.' are attached. (Reprinted by Collier in *Shakespeare's Library.*) Dr. Ingleby thinks that the self-accusation in the following passage in the preliminary epistle can only refer to his plays : 'Some will condemn me, and that justly, for a Galba (who begat foule children by night, and made faire children by daie ;) to whom I answere, that I paint things in the light of my meditation, who begot the foule fore-

same direction. He had too long, he says in the Preface
to his *Seneca*, 'surfeited upon time-pleasing'; and he now
settled down to professional work in London, though
usually residing on or near some family property at Low
Leyton. Some little time before the close of the century
he graduated as Doctor of Physic at Avignon, and was
incorporated with this degree at Oxford in 1602. He
rapidly attained to a high reputation as a physician, but his
personal difficulties were not altogether at an end, and for
some time before 1619 he resided abroad, practising at
Malines and probably elsewhere in the Spanish Netherlands. His works during this later period of his life were of
a sober cast, including, together with a *Treatise of the
Plague* and a popular manual of medicine called *The Poor
Man's Talent*, translations of Josephus and Seneca, and of
'a learned Summary upon the famous Poeme' of Du Bartas.
He died in Old Fish Street, London, in 1625.

The literary career of Lodge is full of interest, and taken
as a whole may be said to illustrate with a unique sort of
completeness the literary history of the score of years
covered by the period of his youth and earlier manhood.
He had, says a contemporary critic who usually hits the
mark, 'his oare in every paper boate'[1]; and even in
a writer who combined with a classical training of some
solidity a very remarkable productive power, such versatility
would call for admiration. But he was by no means an
imitator only, or chiefly; if he followed Lyly, he cannot for
a moment be set down as having followed him in the wake
of Greene, and in more than one branch of poetic composition
the credit of its origination may be successfully disputed in
his favour,—in one instance, even against Shakspere himself.

passed progenie of my thoughts in the night of mine error.' (*Was Thomas
Lodge an Actor?* p. 15.) This does not, however, seem to me quite so clear.

    [1] 'Lodge for his oare in euery paper boate,
      He that turnes ouer *Galen* euery day,
      To sit and simper *Euphues* legacy.'

The *Second Part* of the *Returne from Parnassus*, in which these lines occur,
was written for representation at Christmas in one of the years 1598–1600—
the very years in which Lodge was effecting his transition from romance
to respectability.

His lyrical gifts, moreover, are of a quality rare even among the English poets of his age[1]. We are, however, directly concerned only with his contributions to our dramatic literature, which, in so far as they can be with certainty assigned to his authorship, cannot be said to constitute a noteworthy part of his achievements.

Lodge's plays. The Wounds of Civil War (1587? pr. 1594).

The Wounds of Civil War, lively set forth in the True Tragedies of Marius and Sylla[2], first printed in 1594, was in all probability produced several years previously to this date. Apart from the evidence of the author's motto, there is in this play a manifest imitation of the celebrated entry of Tamburlaine; Sylla comes on the stage 'in triumph in his chair triumphant of gold, drawn by four Moors; before the chariot, his colours, his crest, his captains, his prisoners[3].' This points to a date of production not far distant from that of Marlowe's tragedy (1587); and Mr. Fleay pertinently observes that no year could have been more suitable than this[4] in which to enforce a warning against the evils of 'civil war.' Founded upon North's *Lives from Plutarch*, though as a competent scholar the author may very possibly have had recourse to their original, the play appears to have been put together chiefly with a view to producing a prolonged succession of stirring scenes; nor can the author be said to have fallen short of his intent. Many of the speeches are full of vigour, especially Sylla's address to his flying soldiery[5]. The piece,

---

[1] See, *e. g.*, the charming lines from the poem in commendation of a solitary life, *ap.* Laing, *u. s.* p. 1, and the charming erotic which relieves the tedium of *Forbonius and Prisceria*, reprinted in the same volume.

[2] Reprinted in Dodsley's *Old Plays*, vol. viii, and in Hazlitt's *Dodsley*, vol. vii. According to the *Biographia Dramatica*, this play was by Winstanley ascribed to Lodovick Carlell.

[3] At the commencement of act iv, according to one of the divisions in the quarto. Cf. Collier, iii. 37.

[4] The year of the execution of Mary Queen of Scots, followed by apprehensions of the Spanish Armada.

[5] Act i. *ad fin.* In this address we catch a tone of Shakspere's Roman plays, Caesar, of course, in particular. The stage-direction is suggestive of the simple materials out of which our old dramatists could construct powerful effects: '*A great alarum. Let young* MARIUS *chase* POMPEY *over the stage, and old* MARIUS *chase* LUCRETIUS. *Then let enter three or four Soldiers, and his ancient with his colours, and* SYLLA *after them with his hat in his hand: they offer to fly away.*'

in the versification of which an abundance of rimed lines
serves to vary a rather rigid form of blank verse, is enlivened
here and there by a farcical intermixture ; an anecdote in
Plutarch is made use of to introduce a clown who in his
drunkenness betrays his master, ' old Anthony '; while the
author's own inventive fancy must be held responsible for
the broken French talked by the Gaul[1] commissioned to
slay ' old Marius' in prison. When terrified by the glance
of the captive conqueror of the Cimbri, he cries out,
' *Me no dare kill Marius ; adieu Messieurs ; me be dead
si je touche Marius*'; and finally runs off the stage
shrieking forth a Christian oath[2]. Equally incongruous
with the historic dignity of the theme, although quite in
harmony with the artificialities of contemporary composition, is the purely fanciful treatment of one of the most
effective situations in the course of the action—the isolation
of the fugitive Marius among the ' Numidian mountains.'
The playwright seizes upon the opportunity in order to
make Marius utter his complaint to Echo, who answers him
by repeating the last word—or a pun upon it—in the several
lines of his lament. The device (or trick) here reproduced
is not of Euphuistic origin ; for the neatest and wittiest
example of it is to be found in the *Colloquia* of Erasmus[3].

Of a *Looking Glasse for London*, &c., written by Lodge

---

[1] He is called ' Pedro.'

[2] ' *Marius est un diable. Jesu Maria, sava moy.*' The striking anecdote
of which this scene is a version is of course in Plutarch.

[3] See the (prose) dialogue between *Juvenis* and *Echo*, carried on by the
latter entirely by means of echoes, largely of a punning nature, and playing
with Greek as well as Latin vocables.—Disraeli, in his *Curiosities of Literature*
(ed. 1865, i. 297, section *Literary Follies*), refers to the practice of *Echo
Verses*, affected by old French bards in the age of Marot, to Butler's ridicule
of this in *Hudibras* (bk. i. canto iii :

     'Quoth he, "O whither, wicked Bruin,
     Art thou fled to my "—Echo, *Ruin*'),

and to the modern French poet Pannard's imitation of the same fashion.
In a subsequent section (ii. 229 *seqq.*) he recurs to the subject of *Anagrams*
and *Echo Verses*, which he thinks to be at times capable of reflecting the
ingenuity of their authors—an assertion not holding good as to *acrostics*, and
cites a copy of *Echo Verses against the Roundheads* from an academical
play presented before Charles I at Trinity College, Cambridge, in March,
1641. I owe these references, both to the *Colloquia Familiaria* and to *The
Curiosities of Literature*, to a criticism by the late Dr. W. Wagner.

in conjunction with Greene, some account has already been given among the dramatic works of that author. Mr. Fleay believes Lodge to have likewise collaborated with Greene in *James IV* and in *George-a-Greene*, as well as in the *Second Part of Henry VI*. He is further inclined to assign to him the authorship of *Mucedorus*, *The True Chronicle History of King Leir*, and *The Troublesome Raigne of King John*[1]. I see no sufficient reason for noticing other conjectural attributions to Lodge of compositions usually assigned to dates that hardly fall within the period of his ascertained dramatic activity—including portions of *The True Tragedie of Richard III*[2] and *A Warning for Faire Women*. The temptation is no doubt great to suppose so facile a workmanship to have adapted itself to the demands of very different dramatic styles; but the ascertained share of Lodge in the progress of that branch of our literature with which we are alone directly concerned cannot be described as other than relatively unimportant and exiguous.

Thomas Nashe (1567–1601).

His life and non-dramatic writings;

The name of THOMAS NASHE[3] is so intimately connected with those of the dramatists previously mentioned in the present chapter, that some notice of him seems in its turn called for here, although his dramatic writings can in no case have formed more than a very slight part of his extraordinary literary activity. Born at Lowestoft in 1567, as the son of a 'minister' of Herefordshire descent, he became at a very early age a member of 'thrice fruitfull' St. John's College, Cambridge, 'which is and euer was the sweetest

---

[1] *English Drama*, ii. 49 *seqq.* Mr. Fleay is much impressed by the use in all these pieces and in *The True Tragedie of Richard III* of the phrase 'a cooling card,' which he supposes the medically disposed author of *The Wounds of Civil War* to have adopted as a kind of 'trade-mark.' Perhaps the learning of scholars blinds them in some cases to the probability that a phrase was appropriated for no reason but because it seemed telling.

[2] *Ib.*, 315–7.—Mr. Fleay is careful, in the instance of two 'doubtful' plays, to describe his own supposition of Lodge's authorship to be essentially conjectural.

[3] *The Complete Works of Thomas Nashe.* Edited by Dr. A. B. Grosart (*Huth Library*), 6 vols., 1883–5; cf. Fleay, *English Drama*, ii. 122-149, and Mr. S. Lee's article on Nashe in vol. xl. of *The Dictionary of National Biography* (1894).

nurse of knowledge in all that Vniversity[1].' Here he resided
for nearly seven years, but he seems to have left College
when of third year's standing as B.A., having according to
his subsequent chief enemy's account made himself too
prominent in the production of a *jeu d'esprit* offensive to the
authorities[2]. He is concluded to have paid a rapid visit to
France and Italy before beginning his literary life in London
in 1588.

Here he at once attached himself to the rising celebrity,
Robert Greene, prefacing his *Menaphon* (1589) by an
Epistle in which he took occasion while not very affably
reviewing contemporary literature in general to pour special
contempt upon a playwright who is with extreme probability
held to be identifiable with Kyd[3]. His first independent
literary venture, *The Anatomie of Absurditie* (1589), bore
a title which may have been imitated either from Greene, or
from Greene's own exemplar[4]. In any case, Nashe had
borrowed his methods of diction from neither Lyly nor
Greene, having as a born pamphleteer (or as we should
say journalist) made bold to set up a good plain, strong
and abusive prose-style of his own.

Fortunately (as the world goes) for the peculiar bent of
Nashe's genius, the year in which he was fairly launched
upon his life as a man of letters in London was also that in
which the turbulent sea of the *Mar-Prelate* controversy
was at full tide. As a matter of course he immediately
engaged in it, and with so much effect that he was both at
the time and afterwards (when Nashe's ghost' was repeatedly
appealed to as having settled the affair of the Martinists)
regarded as a protagonist in the struggle. Probably, however, his direct share in this war of pamphlets has been
considerably exaggerated. Anonymity—or pseudonymity,

controversial,

---

[1] See *Nashe's Lenten Stuffe* (Grosart, v. 241). Cf. *Strange Newes*, &c., and
the famous passage in praise of St. John's in the *Epistle to the Gentlemen
Students of both Universities* prefixed by Nashe to Greene's *Menaphon*.

[2] According to the supposition of Gabriel Harvey (*The Trimming of
Thomas Nashe*), he played the 'varlet of clubs' in a show called *Terminus et
non Terminus*.

[3] See Fleay, *u. s.*, p. 124. The evidence is practically irresistible.

[4] Dr. Furnivall, however, thinks that it was imitated from the title of
Stubbs' *Anatomie of Abuses*.

a more convenient form of the same device—was an indispensable condition of the fray ; there can at the same
time be little doubt that the ' Pasquil ' of the contention was
Nashe, from whose hand the celebrated *Returne of the
renowned Cavalerio Pasquil* (1589) in particular indisputably proceeded. His authorship of *An Almond for a
Parratt* (1590), dedicated to the actor William Kemp, has
notwithstanding some supposed biographical allusions, been
doubted in several quarters [1]. The course of the controversy,
while establishing the reputation of Nashe as a professed
satirist—a ' Young Juvenal,' if (as can hardly be doubted) he
earned this valedictory epithet from Greene [2] as a reward
and encouragement of his exertions,—involved him in a
personal quarrel of exceptional virulence. Of this he
sounded a loud note in one of the most notable of his
tracts, *Pierce Pennilesse his Supplication to the Divell*
(1592) [3], interesting both as a defence of poetry and plays,
and as a picture of the miseries of authorship. The
attack upon the brothers Harvey contained in this publication was taken up by Gabriel Harvey, whose traditional
eminence as the type of the scholar-pedant living near
the rose—nay in a rose-garden of associations ancient
and modern—but unable thence to perfume his native
vinegar—has not been lowered by recent opportunities of
closer acquaintance [4]. The most characteristic of Nashe's
appearances in this on the whole not very edifying series of
bouts is the last, his tract of *Haue with you to Saffron
Walden, or Gabriel Harvey's Hunt is Vp* (1596), which is
in dialogue-form, and full of allusions of interest to the
student of the *minutiae* of the history of our early dramatic
literature [5]. Gabriel Harvey retorted with the *Trimming
of Thomas Nashe* (1597), his adversary being at the time

---

[1] See Grosart, i. xlix, and cf. Fleay, 126-7.

[2] *A Groatsworth of Wit.* Cf. below, the reference to Meres.

[3] Edited by Collier for the (Old) Shakespeare Society, 1842. It is full of
references of interest for the history of our drama—of comedy in particular.

[4] Dr. Grosart's edition of his *Works* (*Huth Library*), 6 vols., 1883-5 ; and
Gabriel Harvey's Letter Book (1573-80), edited for the Camden Society by
Mr. E. J. L. Scott (1884).

[5] It opens with a very facetious dedication to Dick Litchfield, the Trinity
College barber.

a prisoner in the Fleet, and two years afterwards the combatants were silenced by archiepiscopal authority, and 'all the books' of each ordered to be suppressed.

During the seven years (more or less) through which this *and non-* war of libels had raged, Nashe's pen had been unceasingly *contro-* busy with compositions not falling under the description of *versial.* controversial; and, as has already been indicated, some of his controversial pamphlets themselves may at the same time be regarded as general satires and descriptive essays. Thus, in a more marked degree than those of any of his contemporaries, his writings were preparatory of some of the earlier efforts of the English novel, just as certain famous papers in *The Tatler* and the *Spectator* led up to some of its later developements. His social satires—of which *Pierce Pennilesse* and *Lenten Stuffe* may serve as types—display together with a great deal of queer learning a great deal of queer knowledge of life, and while crammed with anecdotes and witticisms of all kinds, are manifestly the work of a man of letters who was a keen observer of the world around him. At the same time he became master of an effective style, because from the first he allowed his own style to be formed by his matter, and scorned imitation, except to the innocuous extent of proving himself as good a scholar as his fellow-authors[1]. This freedom from affectation and mannerism distinguishes his way of writing even in pieces put together, like the two works just named, with an obvious purpose of creating an effect by eccentricity; it is only in the earlier and didactive portion of his solemnly-meant *Christ's Teares over Jerusalem* (1593) that he rather strains his style (though even here not unbearably), lest he

---

[1] 'Wherin haue I borrowed from *Greene* or *Tarlton, that I should thanke them for all I haue?* Is my stile like *Greenes,* or my ieasts like *Tarltons?* . . . This I will proudly boast . . . that the vaine which I haue . . . is of my own begetting, and cals no man father in England but my silfe, neyther *Euphues,* nor *Tarlton,* nor *Greene.* Not *Tarlton* nor *Greene* but haue beene contented to let my simple iudgement ouerrule them in some matters of wit. *Euphues* I readd when I was a little ape at Cambridge, and I then thought it was *Ipse ille*: it may be excellent good still, for ought I know, for I lookt not on it this ten yeare: but to imitate it I abhorre, otherwise than it imitates *Plutarch, Ouid* and the choicest Latine Authors' (*Foure Letters Confuted,* Grosart, ii. 267).

should fall short of being impressive[1]. The natural power of his style stood him in good stead in the most notable of all his works, *The Unfortunate Traveller* [2] (1594), in which we may unhesitatingly recognise the first English example of the *novela picaresca*—the novel of odd adventure—which was to attain to so notable a developement in the works of our eighteenth-century masters of fiction. To a novelist of Nashe's type no kind of adventure came amiss, and his hero is in turn practical joker, poet's confidant, and actor in a real drama of murderous intrigue. Historical personages, from Martin Luther to Pietro Aretino, are freely brought in to fill the canvas; and incident abounds so continually that we do not care to ask for a plot. The author boldly disclaims any intention of hidden allusions; his novel contains no cipher and requires no key; he can promise nothing but 'some reasonable conveyance of historie, and varietie of mirth.' Irregular and haphazard as it might seem in form, the product was racy of the soil whence it sprang, and not unworthy of the most famous of its successors.

Impression left by him upon his age. While it cannot be pretended that either in this novel or in any other of his works Nashe is a writer to whom genius of a high order should be ascribed, yet hardly anything remains from his hand unmarked by the fresh and vigorous vitality so conspicuous in *The Unfortunate Traveller*. Such was the impression left by him as a writer upon his contemporaries, after in 1601 his brief life of less than thirty-four years had come to a close. His personal career had been full of troubles of all sorts; a MS. epitaph states that he 'never in his life paid shoemaker or tailor'; Henslowe had to make him advances both when at large and when (as will be seen immediately) in prison; nor is there any reason for supposing that the storms had calmed when he sank beneath the waters. But although, as his own confessions would suffice to show, in frequent straits, and never out of a fray when he could be in the midst of one, he was so far as it is

[1] As to the general theme of this tract, cf. *ante*, p. 402, note.—In the address *To the Reader* prefixed to this tract, Nashe notices objections that have been made to his style as inflated and defaced by 'the often coyning of Italionate verbs which all end in Ize, as mummianize, tympanize, tirannize.'

[2] Edited by Mr. Gosse in *Chiswick Press Reprints* (1892).

possible to discern an honest partisan and a staunch friend, and one who in his writings at least was not wont to play fast and loose with truth and virtue. His ' ghost,' as already observed, did active work as a pamphleteer against the Martinists and their descendants long after his death ; but his associates and contemporaries, while they naturally recalled the sharpness and bitterness of his satirical wit as his most salient characteristic, cherished a kindly remembrance of the most eager and effective combatant of an unquiet age[1].

Nashe is only known with certainty to have composed two plays, besides co-operating in, or completing, Marlowe's *Dido Queen of Carthage*[2].   The earlier of these was his 'pleasant comedie' of *Summer's Last Will and Testament*[3], which was privately acted in 1592 at or near Croydon, but not printed till 1600.   It is something between a morality and a ' show '; but besides the seasons and other mythological figures, a real personage is by the easy expedient of an obvious pun upon his name introduced on the scene in the shape of Will Summer (Summers, or Somers), the celebrated jester of King Henry VIII[4].   This worthy ' sits

His dramatic works.

[1] See the tributes collected by Mr. Lee in his admirable biographical article, and more especially the passage in *The Returne from Pernassus* (part ii. act i. sc. 2), which it is pleasant to think of as spoken within the walls of St. John's College :—

> ' Let all his faultes sleepe with his mournfull chest,
> And [there] for euer with his ashes rest.
> His style was wittie, though [it] had some gal,
> Something he might haue mended,—so may all.
> Yet this I say, that for a mother witt,
> Few men haue euer seene the like of it.'

[2] *Ante*, pp. 356–8.

[3] Printed in Dodsley's *Old Plays*, vol. ix., and in Hazlitt's *Dodsley*, vol. viii. ; also in vol. vi. of Dr. Grosart's edition of *Nashe's Works*, which likewise contains *Dido*.   Dr. Grosart's volume contains an excessively ingenious series of conjectures by Dr. Brinsley Nicholson, as to when, where, by whom and on what occasion, the play was performed.   The most interesting of these argumentations is that concerning the supposed locality of the performance —the archiepiscopal palace at Croydon.   As to the date (1592, not 1593, as given by Dr. Grosart), see Fleay, *History of the Stage*, p. 78, and *English Drama*, ii. 148–9.   Mr. Lee, *u. s.*, says that the play was acted at Beddington near Croydon, the house of Sir George Carey, to whose wife and daughter respectively Nashe dedicated his *Christes Teares over Jerusalem* and his *Terrors of the Night* (1594).

[4] As to Will Summers, see R. Armin's *Nest of Ninnies*, (Old) *Shakespeare Society's Publications*, 1842, pp. 41 *seqq.*, and Collier's *Introduction and Notes*,

as chorus,' and, as he says, 'flouts the actors' after a fashion which Ben Jonson's *Every Man out of his Humour* and other Elisabethan plays bequeathed to *The Rehearsal, The Critic,* and to a host of later more or less successful appropriations of an all too seductive device. For the rest, there is but little plot in Nashe's piece, where 'because the plague reigns in most places in this latter end of Summer, Summer must come in sick, yield his throne to Autumn, make Winter his executor.' 'Summer' calls before him the other Seasons, with their offspring and companions, such as Orion, Bacchus, Harvest, Christmas, 'Backwinter,' and others; and in the dialogues consequently arising abundant opportunity occurs for both description and satire. The command of language characteristic of Nashe is admirably illustrated by a variety of passages; while at times his writing rises above mere ingenuity. Thus, Orion's praise of the Dog will commend itself to observers, and is very humorous to boot; while Ver's praise of poverty and Winter's assault upon Contemplation and the Liberal Arts deserve the credit of telling efforts of sophistry. A certain poetical charm will be allowed to attach to Sol's apology, and the song or litany prefacing the death of Summer in its epigrammatic melancholy mingles Ralegh's with an earlier Renascence manner [1]. The elaborate, if not always accurate erudition which this production displays, would probably have rendered it unsuitable for a 'common stage'; but if as

---

[1] *ib.,* pp. xix. and 63–5. He is several times referred to in John Heywood's *Play of the Wether* (cf. *ante,* p. 248); and his antics are mentioned proverbially in *The Death and Buriall of Martin Mar-Prelate,* a pamphlet (probably erroneously) attributed to Nashe: 'For first, like Wil Sommers, when you knowe not who bobd you, you strike him that first comes in your foolish head' (Grosart, i. 202).—In Gabriel Harvey's *Pierce's Supererogation* (1593) the following varieties are enumerated: 'Scoggin the Ioviall foole, or Skelton the Malancholy foole, or Elderton the bibbing foole, or Will Sommer the chollericke foole.'

[1] '. .   .   .   .   .

           Beauty is but a flower
           Which wrinkles will devour:
           Brightness falls from the air;
           Queens have died young and fair.
           Dust hath clos'd Helen's eye.
           I am sick, I must die.
              Lord have mercy on us!

   .   .   .   .

has been supposed Queen Elisabeth's own presence graced
the performance, her learned tastes were assuredly never
provided with a more cunningly seasoned banquet.

The Isle of Dogs, which has a very special interest for
Nashe's biography, was never printed. It appears from
Henslowe's *Diary* [1] that in the spring of 1597 Nashe was
engaged upon the composition of this piece when in circumstances of distress which the manager was fain to relieve ;
yet according to Nashe's own account [2], when the play was
actually produced, his own share in it, something like that
of Sackville in *The Mirror for Magistrates*, comprised
only the Induction and the first Act. But the offence given
by the piece was such that the license of the lord admiral's
company was withdrawn for some weeks, and that Nashe,
as the reputed author of the whole, was for an even longer
period confined in the Fleet prison. The incident, the effect
of which was heightened by the suggestive title of the
play, long remained a favourite reminiscence in connexion
with Nashe's name [3]; but we know nothing concerning the

*The Isle
of Dogs
(never
printed).*

> Hast therefore each degree
> To welcome destiny :
> Heaven is our heritage,
> Earth but a player's stage.
> Mount we unto the sky,
> I am sick, 1 must die.
> > Lord have mercy on us ! '—

By the bye, the unexplained ' Domingo ' in the song of Bacchus'
companions—
> 'Monsieur Mingo for quaffing doth surpass '—
of which the last two lines are quoted in *Henry 1V, Part II*, act v. sc. 2, may
owe its origin to the type of Mingo Revulgo (i. e. Domingo Vulgus) in the
famous Spanish *Coplas*. See Ticknor, *History of Spanish Literature*, i. 232–3 ;
and cf. *ante*, p. 231.—In *Nashe's Lenten Stuffe*, ' Domingo Rufus ' appears as
an *alter ego* of Master Redherring, the hero of the tract.

[1] Collier's edition, p. 94.

[2] See *Nashe's Lenten Stuffe* (Grosart, v. 200): ' That infortunate Embrion
(an imperfit Embrion I may well call it, for I hauing begun but the induction and first act of it, the other foure acts, without my consent, or the least
guesse of my drift or scope, by the players were supplied, which bred both
their trouble and mine to) of my idle houres, the Ile of Dogs before mentioned, breeding vnto me such bitter throwes in the teaming as it did . . . .
I was so terrifyed with my own encrease . . . that it was no sooner borne
but I was glad to runne from it.'

[3] It is referred to both by Meres in his *Palladis Tamia*, where he apostrophises Nashe as ' gallant young Juvenal,' and in *The Returne from Pernassus*.

piece, although we may safely suspect it to have had a special savour of the Thames and of 'lovely' London.

Nashe's genius not essentially dramatic.

The discursive element in Nashe's genius, although it undoubtedly contributed to the attractiveness of his lost as it does to that of his extant dramatic work, is in itself the reverse of a dramatic quality. Whether or not, as has been sympathetically suggested[1], he was the particular writer pictured under the character of *Ingenioso* by the author or authors of the *Pernassus Plays*, to whose charming personal tribute to himself I have already referred, he was the very incarnation of reckless wit—'academical' even in the special sense of the epithet that denotes the detachment of efforts like his from the immediate and what are very generally considered the serious purposes of life. It does not follow, however, that either human life or its mirror the drama would be anything but the poorer for the absence of such sallies as those by which he diversified their regular course of operations.

Henry Chettle (1564– 1607 or ante).

HENRY CHETTLE (1564–1607 or *ante*) should be mentioned here, as a writer closely connected with one at least of the above-mentioned dramatists, and thus placed in a peculiarly direct relation towards the early reputation of Shakspere himself. Having as editor of the posthumous publication of *Greene's Groatsworth of Wit* fallen under the suspicion (not, however, confined to himself) of manipulation of his text, Chettle published in self-defence his tract of *Kind-Hart's Dreame* (1593, or quite at the end of 1592)[2]. In this pamphlet he repudiated any such insinuation and took occasion to offer a very handsome testimonial to the playwright—unmistakeably Shakspere—whom the deceased author of the *Groatsworth* had gone out of his way to vilify. Chettle, who seems to have been in business as a printer before he contributed matter of his own to the press, claimed

---

[1] See articles by Professor Hales in *The Academy*, March 19, and in *Macmillan's Magazine*, May, 1887.

[2] Reprinted in *Part I* of *Shakspere Allusion Books*, edited by Dr. C. H. Ingleby for the (New) Shakspere Society, 1874. See, in the *Introduction*, Dr. Ingleby's argument as to Shakspere having been the person to whom Chettle's apology to this tractate was addressed.

to have done good service in his earlier craft both to
Nashe and to other 'advanced' scholars; and the extraordinary multiplicity of his own dramatic labours brought
him into direct association with a large number of the playwrights contemporary with himself. To him are attributed
the sole or joint authorship of plays amounting in numbers
to a total of two-score-and-nine, of which something like
one-fifth purport to have been of his own unassisted making[1].
Such a record, however, possesses no very solid statistical
value. Chettle's tract entitled *Englande's Mourning Garment*[2] (an elaborate tribute which, from its design, must
have been published very soon after the death of Queen
Elisabeth) has a more general literary interest as furnishing
his estimate of the chief literary influences acknowledged in
his earlier days—although the names of several of the writers
are veiled under fictitious appellations. His own life was
full of troubles, and few of Henslowe's most regular supporters seem to have required more systematic relief[3].

No play attributed to Chettle's single authorship has
been preserved, with the exception of the sanguinary but
not as a whole powerful tragedy of *Hoffman, or A Revenge
for a Father* (acted 1602, printed 1631[4]). It would be
futile to pretend to judge the dramatic talent of the author
from this particular example of his work, more especially
since Meres, in his *Palladis Tamia*, signals him out as
'one of the best for comedy'; on the other hand, so far
as one can judge from the titles of the plays with which he
is said to have been connected, his bent must be supposed
to have lain towards tragedy. It is difficult to escape
the conclusion, supported by the circumstance that in
the summer of 1592 Chettle had in view for Henslowe

*Hoffman
(acted
1602, pr.
1631).*

---

[1] For the various computations, see Collier, iii. 51 ; Fleay, *English Drama*,
i. 66 *seqq.* ; and Mr. Bullen's article on Chettle in vol. x. of the *Dictionary of
National Biography* (1887).

[2] Likewise reprinted by Dr. Ingleby, *u. s.*

[3] See *Henslowe's Diary*, 126, 141, 151.

[4] Edited, with an *Introduction*, by 'H. B. L.' (1852). The *Introduction*
contains a list of sixteen original plays attributed to Chettle, and of thirty-
one (twenty-seven of these being lost) in which he is stated to have collaborated.—Mr. Fleay considers Thomas Heywood to have had a share in
Hoffman. See *English Drama*, i. 70-71 ; 291.

the composition of a play called by the latter a *Danish tragedye* [1], that the author of *Hoffman* was acquainted with the theme of *Hamlet*, which was entered in the *Stationers' Registers* in this very year 1602 under the title of *The Revenge of Hamlet Prince of Denmark* [2]. Whether from this we are to conclude *Hoffman* to have been designed as a rival play to the production of a rival company, is a question on which it is unnecessary to pronounce [3]. If so, it was by coarser means that the 'Henslowe' tragedy sought to compass a more complete effect. The first act, notwithstanding its ghastliness, is perhaps the best portion of this play, the hero of which—nor vainly—boasts that the tragedy wreaked by him 'shall surpass those of Thyestes, Terens, Jocasta, or Medea.' The course of the action suggests either the determination of the author to lose sight of no suggestion of dramatic horror, or his use of some undiscovered local narrative source. But, although the strange jumble of German names and titles might favour the latter supposition, no such source has so much as been conjectured; and the tragedy remains, so far as we can see, a mass of theatrical motives of tragic effect rudely worked out.

Patient Grissil pr. 1603). Among the plays in which Chettle collaborated with other writers, it is pardonable to single out *The Pleasant Comedie of Patient Grissil* [4], in the composition of which Dekker and Haughton shared with him [5]. The special

[1] *Henslowe's Diary*, p. 224.

[2] *Stationers' Registers*, ed. Weber, vol. iii. p. 84 b. The 'booke' is entered ' as yt was latelie Acted by the Lord Chamberlayne his servantes.'

[3] See Delius' article *Chettle's Hoffman and Shakespeare's Hamlet* in *Jahrbuch, &c*, vol. ix. (1874).

[4] Edited for the (Old) Shakespeare Society by the late Mr. Collier (1841).

[5] As to Dekker, see below.—Of William Haughton personally very little is known, except that an attempt has been made to identify him with a namesake who, after graduating M.A. at Oxford, was incorporated at Cambridge in 1604. (See Mr. Bullen's notice in vol. xxv. of the *Dictionary of National Biography*, 1891.) His name is frequently mentioned in *Henslowe's Diary*, as concerned in all kinds of dramatic work, from a revision of *Ferrex and Porrex* to plays appealing directly to the tastes or interests of the day. On one occasion Henslowe records a loan to Haughton of ' x^s. to releace him owt of the clyncke' (the Clink prison in Southwark). His *Englishmen for my Money, or A Woman will have her Will* (reprinted in vol. x. of Hazlitt's *Dodsley*), entered in 1598 by Henslowe under the second of the above titles, but not extant in an earlier edition than that of 1616, appears to have been

history of the theme treated in this play covers a wider
ground than can here be surveyed ; suffice it therefore to
say that the story, for which Chaucer considered himself
indebted to Petrarch, although it had been previously—
probably not for the first time—treated by Boccaccio, at
a very early period commended itself to the stage. It
furnished the plot of one of the few French mysteries known
to have dealt with a semi-secular subject [1]. In the later
Renascence age (1546) Hans Sachs produced a 'comedi'
on the story of Griselda, in which according to his wont
the concluding moral was not stinted [2]. The subject has,
in various forms, continued to attract dramatic writers down
to our own day [3]. As to the play by Chettle and his
coadjutors, it was probably founded in the first instance
upon the prose tract reproducing this favourite story, from
which we may suppose the ballads on the same theme to
have been derived [4]. No immediate influence of Chaucer is
recognisable in the composition of the play under notice.
Indeed, the obvious necessity of compressing the limits of
time gives to the action of this drama a greater measure

a very popular play. It is a merry, bustling comedy of London life, showing
how the three daughters of a 'Portingal' usurer and their three English
lovers carried the day over their avaricious sire (whose nose, like that of
Barabas, betokens his style of business) and the three benighted foreigners
favoured by him—a Frenchman, an Italian, and a Dutchman. Anthony, an
intriguing schoolmaster, and Frisco, a bungling clown, help to carry on the
action, which is extremely animated.—*The Spanish Moor's Tragedy*, by
Chettle, Day, and Dekker (1600), is thought by Mr. Fleay, *English Drama*,
i. 272, to be identical with *Lust's Dominion*, published in 1657 as Marlowe's.
—The play of *Jane Shore*, by Chettle and Day, was probably much earlier
in date of composition than 1602, when it was acted, with alterations, by
Lord Worcester's company. (Halliwell's *Dictionary*, &c., 132.)

[1] See Collier's *Introduction*, *u. s.*, p. vi, and Ebert, *Entwicklungsgeschichte*,
&c., p. 33. The date is given by Collier as 1393, by Ebert as 1395.

[2] See Goedeke and Tittmann's *Dichtungen von Hans Sachs*, iii. 48 *seqq.*
Hans Sachs mentions Boccaccio as his original.

[3] 'Friedrich's Halm's' *Griseldis* was produced at Vienna in 1835 ; MM.
Silvestre and Morand's *Grisélidis* at the *Comédie Française* in 1891 ; and
Mr. H. A. Jones' *Patient Grizzle* (I think) in 1893.

[4] *The History of Patient Grissil*. Two early tracts in black letter. With
an Introduction and Notes (by J. P. Collier), *Percy Society's Publications*,
1342.—William Forrest's poem *The Second Gresyld* (completed in 1558),
a narrative in verse of the divorce of Queen Catherine of Aragon, testifies
to the popularity of the story. (See *Dictionary of National Biography*,
vol. xx. p. 5.)

of probability than can be attributed to that of *The Clerke's Tale*, extending as it does over a long series of years. And although even the spectators of the play may have found some difficulty in reconciling the proceedings of the 'thoughtful markis' with the demands of common sense, yet the playwrights must be allowed to have contrived with considerable skill to humanise his inhuman trial of his wife's obedience. *Patient Grissil*, which moreover contains two charming lyrics [1], appears to me to be a both effective and pleasing work. The character of the faithful Babulo, the clown of the piece, mingles with its broad fun some touches of true pathos [2]. On the other hand, the humour of the Welsh Sir Owen (whose shrewish charmer Gwenthyan is intended as a comic antitype to the patient heroine) has a stagey flavour; but the Tudor public seems never to have wearied of gibes against the Welsh compatriots of the founder of the reigning dynasty; and the union of Wales and England seems to have been deemed a standing popular joke long after it had been consummated as a political act. Shakspere, with his usual felicity, was able to give a sympathetic turn even to a national prejudice [3].

Among the dramatic authors with whom Chettle collaborated were, besides those already mentioned, John

[1] The song 'Art thou poor, yet hast thou golden slumbers' (act i. sc. 1), and the lullaby (act iv. sc. 2) have been ascribed to Dekker, by reason of his acknowledged lyrical gifts. But I know of nothing undoubtedly his that could be described as equal to the former of these two songs.

[2] See act iv. sc. 2: 'Enter Babulo, with a bundle of osiers in one arm, and a child in another; Grissil after him with another' (she has been expelled with her twins from her husband's house, and driven to seek refuge with her father). Babulo's speech offers an admirable opportunity for that mixture of low comedy and pathos which rarely misses its effect in the hands of a suitably gifted actor: 'A fig for care! old master, but now old grandsire, take this little Pope Innocent: we'll give over basket-making, and turn nurses. She has uncled Laureo. It's no matter, you shall go make a fire. Grandsire, you shall daudle them. Grissil shall go make pap, and I'll lick the skillet; but first I'll fetch a candle. It's a sign 'tis not a dear year, when they come by two at once. Here's a couple, quoth jackdaw. Art thou there? Sing grandsire.'

[3] Possibly Chettle took the same line in his play, in which Drayton was his collaborator, 'wherein is a part of a Welchman,' which has been supposed to be identical with *The Valiant Welchman* (Caradoc the Great) printed in 1615 as by 'R. A.,' and consequently attributed to Armia.

Day, of whom it seems more appropriate to speak in
a later chapter, and ANTHONY MUNDAY [1]. Munday's long
life (he was born in 1553) extended to 1633, but the most
characteristic phases of his extraordinary literary activity
proclaim his special partnership in the likings and labours
of the age with which this chapter is more immediately
concerned. The non-literary aspects of his life are not of
a nature to secure our sympathy. In his early manhood he
visited Rome in what seems to have been the secret
capacity of a Protestant spy, commissioned by two enterprising publishers, upon the English Jesuit College there.
(His experiences are described in *The English Romayne Life*,
in a style of which the literature of tracts furnishes only
too many examples [2].) Three years later he thrust himself
forward by means of a series of tracts purporting to clear
up the circumstances of the betrayal of Edmund Campion
into the hands of the Government, and discrediting the
Jesuits to the best of his ability. His reward seems to
have been the post of messenger of the Queen's chamber.
This may have rendered it unnecessary for him to return to
the actor's profession, in which he seems to have previously
engaged (perhaps even before his Italian journey), but from
1584 onwards to about the close of the reign he appears to
have been most actively employed in dramatic composition.
Commencing with *Fidele and Fortunio, or The Two Italian
Gentlemen*, a translation or adaptation seemingly never
brought on the stage, but containing a character, Captain
Crackstone, which achieved a passing celebrity [3], these
plays would seem to have chiefly treated themes derived
from historical or other romance. To his translations
of popular French and Spanish romances, including *Amadis
de Gaule* and the *Palmerin* family, Munday probably owed

*Anthony
Munday
(1553–
1633). His
life and
labours.*

[1] See Collier's Introduction to his *Five Old Plays*, in which *The Downfall
of Robert Earl of Huntingdon* is reprinted, and to his edition of *John a Kent
and John a Cumbre* (Shakespeare Society's Publications, 1851), and Mr. J.
Seccombe's article on Munday in vol. xxxix of *The Dictionary of National
Biography* (1894).

[2] Printed in 1582, and reprinted in vol. ii. of *The Harleian Miscellany*
(1809).

[3] It is alluded to in Nashe's *Haue with you to Saffron Walden*. Cf. Fleay,
ii. 113.

the chief part of his reputation. But he increased it by his plays, by his prose-tracts of various contents, and more especially by his ballads, fitted to popular tunes. In his later years, mindful of his own origin as 'a citizen and a draper,' and probably conscious of a personal agreement with the spirit of the times (so far at least as the City was concerned), he devoted himself largely to the composition of City Pageants. Both on account of his labours in this line of authorship, and as a writer of ballads, he incurred the ridicule of Ben Jonson, who made fun of him in the character of Antonio Balladino, and at the same time cast in Munday's teeth a compliment that had recently been paid to his constructive powers as a dramatist by a less exacting critic [1].

His plays.   Munday's lively comedy of *John a Kent and John a Cumber* (of which the MS. bears date 1595) exists only in an imperfect state. It is said to be founded upon an old ballad ; and its chief characters are two wizards of popular renown resembling the Friars Bacon and Bungay of Greene's play, likewise founded upon popular traditions ; the rustic orator Turnop is also amusing.

But a superior interest attaches to *The Downfall,* and to its sequel, *The Death, of Robert Earl of Huntington,* whom the title of the earlier play describes as '*afterwards called Robin Hoode of merrie Sherwodde* [2].' Both these plays were produced in 1598, and printed in 1601 ; the former, as we possess it, comprises the alterations introduced by Chettle into Munday's original play with a view to its performance at Court ; the latter seems to have been a collaboration between the two writers, to whom it is less easy to assign their respective shares [3].

Munday's Downfall of Robert Earl of   Neither taken individually nor viewed in conjunction do these plays bear out Munday's claim to have been 'the best plotter' of his age. Indeed, nothing could be looser

---

[1] See *The Case is Altered* (1598–9), act i. sc. 1 : 'You are not pageant poet to the city of Milan, sir, are you ?' and (in allusion to the praise of Munday in Meres' *Palladis Tamia,* 1598),' You are in print already for the best plotter.'— Munday is supposed to have taken part in the Marprelate controversy on the side of the Bishops, but whether as a ballad-writer or as a playwright is unknown.

[2] Both plays are printed in *Five Old Plays,* and in Hazlitt's *Dodsley,* vol. viii.

[3] Fleay, *English Drama,* i. 114-6.

than the construction of these pieces. The *Downfall* begins   *Hunting-
ton (acted
1598).*
with an Induction, in which the principal part is taken by
Skelton, who accompanies with an explanatory comment
a dumb-show shadowing forth the argument of the play.
Its subject is the overthrow from his high estate of the
Earl of Huntington, otherwise 'the poor man's patron,
Robin Hood,' by the violence of Prince John, the villainy
of the Earl's enemies, and the faithlessness of his steward
Warman, who afterwards becomes sheriff of Nottingham.
Prince John is enamoured of Marian or Matilda, daughter
to Earl Fitzwater, and betrothed to Robin ; and Queen
Elinor is enamoured of Robin himself. The wiles of his
foes force Robin to betake himself once more to an outlaw's
life with his merry men in Sherwood Forest ; but in the end
King Richard arrives as a *deus ex machinâ*, and restores the
hero and his friends to honourable estate.

The play however announces itself as incomplete, and   *Chettle and
Munday's
Death of
Robert
Earl of
Hunting-
ton (acted
1598).*
Skelton (who, after playing the part of Friar Tuck, and
being allowed 'a word or two besides the play' in act iv,
again comes forward as stage-manager and Epilogus at the
close) promises the continuation of the subject in another
tragedy. In the first act of the *Death* the hero is accordingly
killed by poison ; and the remainder of the tragedy is chiefly
occupied with King John's attempts to secure the love of
Matilda, Robin's virgin widow. She eludes him by seeking
refuge in an abbey ; but being pursued even there, willingly
takes poison from the hands of the agent of the baffled
tyrant. King John's remorse, aided by an insurrection
against his rule, induces him at the end of the play to
promise an amendment of his ways.

In all this there is of course neither historical truth nor
even a faithful adherence to popular tradition. In details
as well as in the general management of the action the
author or authors might easily be convicted of carelessness,
and upon the whole these plays are as hurriedly written
as they are put together. They abound (especially the
Downfall) in rimes, often of an indifferent kind ; quatrains
are largely interspersed ; and apart from the Skeltonical
verse (by no means good of its kind), the metre is varied

by short lines. Yet both plays contain passages of considerable vigour and spirit ; and nothing but care was needed in order to weld good materials into a satisfactory whole [1].

Munday and others' First Part of Sir John Oldcastle (1597–1600).

Munday was also joint author, with Michael Drayton, R. Wilson, and R. Hathwaye, of the *First Part of Sir John Oldcastle* [2], a play which, having been published in 1600 with the name of Shakspere on the title-page (though this would seem to have been afterwards removed), has naturally occupied the attention of sanguine critics. But already Malone placed its real authorship beyond doubt [3] ; and its merits must be discussed without reference to any supposed Shaksperean origin. Schlegel spoke of it as a model of the biographical drama ; Hazlitt, on the other hand, considered it a very indifferent composition. The latter opinion seems to me the nearer to the truth. Whether or not the lost *Second Part* may have been able to make the hero as interesting on the stage as he is in history, the *First* in my opinion fails to attain to this end. Sir John Oldcastle here appears as nothing more than an injured

---

[1] The speeches of Leicester, *Downfall,* iv. 1, are very effective ; the references to the *bear* were doubtless acceptable at court. In Bruce's speech, *Death,* v. 2, there is even a touch of imaginative descriptive power. The scene, immediately following, in which Maid Marian's dead body, clad in white, is borne on the stage, must have been very touching, and may remind the modern reader of a beautiful passage in the *Idylls of the King.* Warman's attempt at suicide (*Downfall,* v. 1), although an obvious reminiscence of the end of Judas in the mysteries, is very vigorous in its way. On the other hand, King John's vision, *Death,* i. 2, introduces abstract figures, as if the authors had remembered Bishop Bale's Chronicle History. I am convinced that Shakspere was acquainted with these plays. Mr. Collier has pointed out the resemblance between a famous line in *Macbeth* and one in *The Death :*
 ' The multitudes of seas dyed red with blood.'
The masque in ii. 2 did not of course suggest that in *Henry VIII*, which Shakspere took from Cavendish ; but the resemblance (with a difference) in the situations is striking. The song of Friar Tuck, when disguised as a pedlar (*Downfall.* iii. 1), should also be compared with that of Autolycus in *The Winter's Tale* (iv. 3).—As to earlier dramatic treatments of the Robin Hood legends, see *ante,* p. 144, and *ib.* note (as to Skelton's allusion to Friar Tuck).

[2] Printed in the *Ancient British Drama,* vol. i.

[3] *Inquiry,* p. 293. Its relation in *subject* to the *First Part of Henry IV* will be touched upon below. A passage in the Prologue, and two references to the Shaksperean Falstaff in iii. 4, prove *Henry IV* to have preceded the *First Part of Sir John Oldcastle.*

innocent. But the play is very stirring in its action; and
contains both situations and characters of a very vivacious
humour, such as the scene in which the servant of Sir John
forces the summoner to eat his writ, and the characters of
this servant, the faithful but irrepressible Harpool, and the
Irishman, who on being taken to the gallows to suffer for
his misdeeds, entreats the 'lord shudge' to let him be
'hang'd in a wyth after his own country, the Irish fashion.'
Nor should I pass by the very ungodly Sir John, the Parson
of Wrotham,—a character which, had it been drawn by
Shakspere, might indeed furnish us with a very distinct clue
as to the poet's opinions concerning the Church authorities of
his day. But it was not drawn by Shakspere ; and Anthony
Munday's views on the subject are more easily gauged.

The ROBERT WILSON, stated to have collaboratored *Robert*
with Munday in the last-mentioned play, and with Chettle *Wilson (the*
and others in several dramatic productions belonging to the *fl. 1598.* *younger ?),*
same period, should possibly be distinguished from the name-
sake who has been previously mentioned as the author of
works connecting themselves with an earlier phase in the
developement of our drama[1], and who was an actor first in
Lord Leicester's, and then in the Queen's, service. If so, we
must suppose it to have been the younger Robert Wilson
that was praised by Meres, although on what grounds we
are hardly in a position to estimate, as 'for learning and extemporal wit, without compare or compeer[2].'

ROBERT ARMIN[3], although the more settled part of his *Robert*
career both as player and as playwright falls in the reign of *Armin* *(1570 c.–* *1610 c.)*

---

[1] Cf. *ante,* 140 note; and see Fleay, *English Drama,* ii. 278 and 283 *seqq.*
Mr. Fleay attributes to the elder Wilson the authorship of *Fair Em* (see below).

[2] *Palladis Tamia.*   Cf. Collier's *Introduction,* reprinted in vol. vi. of
Hazlitt's *Dodsley,* where the non-identity of the two Robert Wilsons is
already suggested.

[3] See Collier, iii. 411–21 ; and cf. Fleay, i. 24 *seqq.,* and the notice by the
late Mr. Dutton Cook in vol. ii. of *The Dictionary of National Biography* (1885).
The authority as to his relations with Tarlton is the collection called *Tarlton's
Jests,* of which the earliest extant edition bears date 1611.   Gabriel Harvey
described Armin in 1593 as one of 'the common pamphleteers of London';
but his best-known tract, *A Nest of Ninnies,* edited by Collier for the (Old)
Shakespeare Society, 1842, was not published till 1608.   The probable date
of his death is 1611.—As to Tarlton and the 'Jests,' see below.

King James I, belongs by his training as a stage humourist and by his activity as a pamphleteer to the group of which I have noted the most prominent figures. He is said to have been apprenticed to the famous Richard Tarlton, who trained him to become his successor in the clown's parts by which he had earned the chief part of his popular renown. There is some doubt as to the origin of the only play by Armin which has been preserved, viz. the 'Chronicle History' of *The Valiant Welshman* [1].

Nobody and Somebody (1603 c.).

Another drama, by an unknown author, describing itself as of this species is *Nobody and Somebody. With the True Chronicle History of Elydure who was fortunately three seuerall times crowned King of England.* The 'historical' portion of this piece, which in the method of its satire follows the model of the old moralities, is borrowed from an episode in Geoffrey of Monmouth which was known to Spenser. It seems to have revived early in the reign of James I, and to have been one of the plays which found its way to Germany, where a translation of it was published in 1620 [2].

Michael Drayton (1563–1631).

I close these gleanings among the records of half or wholly forgotten writers by the mention of one distinguished name, to which, however, its connexion with the history of the Elisabethan drama adds no special lustre [3]. It has been

---

[1] Cf. *ante*, p. 430, note 3.

[2] Cf. Meissner, *Die Englischen Comoedianten, &c., in Oesterreich* (1884), pp. 96-7 *et al.* Trinculo in *The Tempest* (act iii. sc. 2) is supposed to allude to the engraving of the two principal characters prefixed to the printed play : ' This is the tune of our catch, played by the picture of Nobody.'—The play is reprinted with an *Introduction* in vol. i. of the late Mr. Simpson's *School of Shakspere.* ' Nobody,' unlike the Οὖτις of the Odyssey, is the virtuous man who bears all the blame of ' Somebody's ' misdeeds, and does all the good himself, without receiving any reward until the close of the piece.

[3] I do not here refer to Samuel Daniel, who has a notable place of his own in the history of our dramatic literature, and will be spoken of later— although his *Cleopatra* was printed in 1594, and written a few years earlier, as a companion-piece to the *Tragedy of Antonie*, by Mary Countess of Pembroke,—' Urania, sister unto Astrofell '—printed 1592, and written in 1590, which only professes to be ' done into English from the French.' All the principal speeches of *Antonie* are in blank verse,—a notably early attempt in this metre (Collier, iii. 73).—Like Daniel's *Cleopatra*, Samuel Brandon's *The Virtuous Octavia* (printed 1598) is interesting, if Collier, iii. 74-5, is correct in suggesting from the point of view of form that its compound epithets are

well observed [1] that the epical treatment of themes, partly
mythical, connected with English history after the Norman
Conquest which were usually termed *Legends*, 'form a kind
of little affluent to the *Mirror' for Magistrates* and the
literature associated with it, of which Warner's *Albion's
England* (1586) is a late popular example, 'and the chronicle
play; and the whole body of historic narrative verse must be
regarded as a defeated rival of the chronicle play, equally
popular perhaps for a while, but in true achievement far beyond it.'   Although of these *Legends* the earliest entered for
publication was David's *Complaint of Rosamond* (1592), it was
MICHAEL DRAYTON who, after printing his *Legend of Piers
Gaveston* in 1593 (the year in which Marlowe's *Edward II*
was entered on the Stationers' Registers), treated this and
cognate themes both in separate *Legends* and in the two
most important of his earlier poetic productions, the *Morti-
meriados* (1596), republished with large alterations under
the title of *The Barrons Wars* (1603) and in his *Heroicall
Epistles* (1597).   But Drayton was also directly connected
with the theatre, whose methods he thus attempted to rival
by his own.   Henslowe's *Diary* proves him to have been
actively engaged as a playwright from about the close of
the year 1597 to 1603, and to have had a share in the   *His plays.*
authorship of at least nineteen plays [2].   In the earlier part
of this period he co-operated with writers whose names
have been already mentioned in this chapter; in the later
also with Middleton and Webster.   Several of these plays
were of the nature of chronicle histories, or at all events
treated historical themes of patriotic interest; there is, at the
same time, no reason for doubting that Drayton readily put
his hand to whatever kind of work was imposed upon him
by his employer [3].   The solitary play of which so far

either modelled on those of Chapman's *Seven Books of the Iliad* and *Shield of
Achilles* (printed in the same year), or were Brandon's own stylistic invention.

[1] By Mr. Oliver Elton, in his admirable monograph on *Michael Drayton*,
printed for the Spenser Society, 1893, p. 15, where he refers to Mr. Fleay's
interesting list, i. 141-2, illustrating the connexion between Drayton's
Heroicall Epistles and other poems and plays.

[2] Cf. Elton, *u. s.*, 26-7, and Mr. Bullen's notice of Drayton in vol. xvi. of
The Dictionary of National Biography (1888).   See also Fleay, *u. s.*

[3] I regret not to see my way at present to accepting either Mr. Fleay's

as we know Drayton was the unassisted author, *William Longsword* (1599) [1], is unfortunately not extant. In point of fact, his contributions to the drama count for-nothing in the records of his literary achievements, which in the latter part of his career he was to crown by the publication of the *Polyolbion*. But it is pleasant to be able to associate with a branch of our literature that was on the eve of becoming one of its chief glories a name so dear to all lovers of the land, whose past and present were alike cherished by his refined but generous Muse. And this association is the more gratifying, because, as there is ample concurrent testimony to show, he was both respected and beloved by his contemporaries, of whom one of the most critically exacting honoured him with an epitaph which is in itself 'a lasting monument of his glory [2].'

The term 'Shakspere's Predecessors' defined.

I have spoken of the writers whose dramatic works, so far as they can be with more or less of certainty ascribed to them, have been briefly described in this chapter, under the general designation of the Predecessors of Shakspere. By this term, as a comparison of the dates furnished in the progress of this chapter will show, nothing is of course intended to be implied beyond the fact that these writers had as dramatists come before the public previously to the time when Shakspere himself may be concluded to have begun to work as an original dramatic author. This time, as will be shown more at length below, cannot be fixed with absolute certainty. There can, however, be no reasonable doubt but that Shakspere's connexion with the London stage had begun some few years before his first appearance as a dramatic author in his own right. This first appearance

theory as to Drayton's authorship of a series of plays by ' W. S.,' which were in consequence attributed to Shakspere, or the supposition, which constitutes one of the arguments for this theory, that he was the author of *The Merry Devil of Edmonton.*

[1] Henslowe's *Diary*, p. 95 (Drayton's receipt). In another entry, p. 142, the play—if it be the same—is called *William Longbeard*, the title of a novel published a few years previously by Lodge.

[2] See the noble *Epitaph on Michael Drayton* in Jonson's *Underwoods;* and cf. *ib. A Vision on the Muses of his Friend, Michael Drayton.*—In *The Returne from Pernassus* a very marked tribute is paid to the sober, dignity of Drayton's personal life.

we may with tolerable safety assume to have taken place
not later than the year 1590. Of the dramatic works noted
(unless incidentally) in the present chapter, the earliest can
hardly have been composed at dates falling much more
than a decade—or a year or two beyond—before that year ;
the majority of the dates range from slightly later years
onwards into a period when Shakspere was undoubtedly
active as an original dramatic writer. While therefore the
influence of Shakspere's productions may, and indeed must,
have affected the dramatic labours of all—or virtually all—
these writers, it may be asserted that they all—or virtually
all—began their careers as dramatic writers before he
began his own ; while of some the activity as dramatists
was nearing its close when his was only setting in.

Keeping these considerations of chronology (as to which
precision is manifestly out of the question) generally in view,
we may, before passing to the most consummate achievements of the Elisabethan drama—the works of Shakspere
himself—pause for a moment, in order to consider what
had been accomplished by Shakspere's more immediate
predecessors, and under what circumstances their labours
had been carried on.

The last decennium but one of the sixteenth century is, *Historical*
in our political history, the most critical as well as the most *aspects of*
glorious period of Elisabeth's reign. It was in the middle *of Shak-*
of this decennium—in the years 1584, 1585, and 1586,— *spere's Pre-*
that three conspiracies were discovered, the combined result *The great*
of which was at last to determine the Queen to consign her *European*
rival to the scaffold. In 1587 the unhappy Queen of *decided.*
Scots, 'the daughter of Debate,' as Elisabeth called her, fell
a victim, less to the accumulated apprehensions of the past,
than to the actual perils of the present, which had at last
reached the sticking-point. In 1588 the avenging Armada
was dissipated by England's allies, the winds and the waves,
and by the efforts of her own sons who had learnt in distant
waters how to overthrow Spanish invincibility. Already in
1589 the shores of the Pyrenean peninsula were visited by
an English expedition : and from this time forth England

no longer stood on the defensive in the great struggle, and
the efforts of her riper statesmen were directed rather to
curbing than to urging forward the national enthusiasm for
its continuance.   In its two chief phases on the European
continent, that great struggle was in this same period
virtually settled against the predominance of Spain and
Spanish policy.   The year 1590 may be regarded as a
turning-point both in the struggle of the Netherlands for
independence, and in the attempt of the League to make
itself the master of France.   English aid had been but
scantily given either to the United Provinces or to the
Huguenots; the expedition of Leicester had been worse
than useless, and the English volunteers who fought for
Henry of Navarre had been few in number.   But the
sympathies of the bulk of the English people had supported
the general bent of English policy; and the steady progress
of Maurice of Nassau, as well as the accession to the
French throne of Henry IV, left no doubt but that
the issue of the great European struggle was virtually
decided.   Those Englishmen who had taken a personal
part in the contest formed indeed no considerable proportion of the nation; but the sea-rovers who had become
national heroes had pointed the way to glory as well as
to gold, and the adventurous youth of the nation knew no
more stirring ambition than that of extending and multi-
plying the enterprises to which, across narrow or broad
seas, the enterprise of their predecessors had pointed the
way.   The volunteers and other soldiers who returned from
the Netherlands were thought by satirical observers to be perhaps more numerous than those who had proceeded thither;
but noble patriotic memories associated themselves with the
battle-fields of the Continent as well as with the naval
enterprises of the Channel and of the far Western waters.

*The Queen
the incar-
nation
of the
national
cause.*
          If the blood of the nation had thus been stirred by an
era of unprecedented significance in the relations between
the country and foreign powers, at home the change which
had come over the aspect of things had been not less
momentous.   Queen Elisabeth had now become in very
truth the incarnation of the national cause.   The season of

her coquetting with foreign proposals of marriage drew
gradually to its inevitable end; 'Monsieur's days[1]' were
coming to be remembered as a thing of the past; while
the doubtful prospect of a union between the Queen and
the favourite of her heart was closed, before his brilliant
but miserable life was extinguished amidst suspicions as
dark as those which beset his fame. So long as Elisabeth
chose to coquet with the possibility of marriage, and so long
as Leicester lived, loyal flattery was tuned to honour her
foibles and sympathise with her preference; and a false
note accordingly jars upon us in the contemporary tributes,
whether passing or elaborate, in honour of the Virgin
Queen. Gradually, however, she became to her subjects
less of a person and more of an idea; and fortunately may-
be for her fame, the woman was forgotten in the national
sovereign. Loyalty and patriotism became convertible
terms. Only the persecuted Catholics, political offenders
because the profession of their faith was identified with the
cause of the foes of Queen and nation, and the growing
number of those Protestants who could not reconcile their
system of religious life and doctrine with the established
forms of Church government, remained as discordant
elements in the concert of a politically united people. The
Catholics, if they were fortunate enough to escape persecution, remained isolated from their fellow-subjects. While
London audiences applauded the exposure on the stage of
the Massacre of St. Bartholomew, Catholic manor-houses
may have solaced themselves with the secret performance
of the anti-Reformation moralities of a past age[2]. Puritanism, on the other hand, was rapidly entering upon a new
phase of its history. At the beginning of this period Puritan
tendencies had still been observable among many of Elisabeth's leading statesmen; and her favourite Leicester himself had been regarded as the head of a party favouring

[1] 1581, when the Duke of Anjou (afterwards Henry III) resided in
England. See Middleton's *A Mad World, my Masters* (iv. 2), *et al.*

[2] See Disraeli's *Curiosities of Literature*, section on *Catholic and Protestant
Dramas*. Sir John Yorke was fined by the Star-Chamber as late as 1614
for allowing a play to be acted at his house containing 'many foul passages
to the vilifying of our religion and exacting of popery.'

views of this description. But as the movement assumed a wider scope, its significance became a totally new one; and, ruthlessly suppressed in its outward manifestations, it doggedly nursed for the future the seeds of a democratic revolution in Church and State [1].

General movement in literature.

It was in times thus widely and strangely stirred that our Elisabethan literature really began its glorious course. The most cursory glance will serve to recall the fact that not in the drama alone, but in a wide variety of other fields of literary productivity, the years of which I am speaking were full of exuberant life. In these years Spenser, with Ralegh by his side, was writing his great epic, the most magnificent monument of the aspirations as well as of the achievements of the age [2]. In them Sidney's prose-romance was received as a bequest by a mourning nation [3]. The earliest publications of Daniel, of Warner, of Drayton, of Davies and Constable are spanned by the same brief series of years. Hall was about to publish his Satires, which in date of composition had already been preceded by Donne's. Stowe was systematising the national annals; and the translation of Sir Thomas North was opening to English readers of history the great treasure-house of ancient examples. Hakluyt was describing the voyages and discoveries of Englishmen, and Ralegh was putting forth his narrative of the most marvellous 'Discoverie' of all.

Classical and Italian influences still operating.

Some of these efforts merely amounted to a continuation of previous literary tendencies; and by their side the circulation increased of an abundant popular literature of novels and tales from foreign sources, and of controversial and social tracts called forth by the multifarious activity of the national life. The worthy critics like George Puttenham who at this time [3] took stock of the

---

[1] The aggressors in the Mar-Prelate Controversy (see below), which forms so strange a pendant to the campaign against the Armada, may at first have found sympathisers among courtiers who cared more for Church property than for the Church ; but before the contention was at an end, the strength of the attack had been proved to lie in a very different quarter.

[2] The first three books of *The Faerie Queene* were published in 1590.

[3] He fell in 1586 ; *The Arcadia* was published in 1590.

[4] His *Arte of English Poesie* was published in 1589. Puttenham, by the bye, was himself a dramatist ; but his plays, none of which are preserved, seem

achievements of our national poetical literature, failed to
realise in its dimensions or in its scope the mighty change
which was in progress [1]. A very few years only passed, and
the selections of modern criticism seem already to be anticipated by a diligent observer of contemporary effort [2]. For
in truth a literature such as this had, if the expression be
permissible, justified itself of itself. It had outgrown the
trammels of mere fashion under which it had begun its
course,—even of a fashion imposed by a Court whose centre
was a sovereign sure of her learning and far from distrustful
of her powers of judgment. The tastes of the Tudor Court
remained true to the traditions of the Renascence. The
ancient classical models, or rather the half-accidental list of
them which had secured a species of literary prerogative, together with the examples derived from the nation to which
the revival of those models was primarily due,—the Italian,—
accordingly long remained on their pedestal of pre-eminence.
The learning of the Universities largely reflected the same
tastes. The euphuism of Lyly and his successors, though
primarily derived from Spanish models, accommodated
itself easily to the adaptation of Italian and French
materials; while the subjects of their dramas, and still
more the ornaments of their diction, continued to display
a fond belief in the inexhaustible resources of classic lore.
Gabriel Harvey sought to reform 'English versifying' on
un-English principles; and Daniel had to break a lance
against Sidney himself in defence of our English heritage
of rime. The unnatural vitality of Euphuistic, Arcadian,
and other affectations—'nothing,' says Ben Jonson [3], 'is

---

to have been mostly of an earlier type. They included, besides a comedy entitled *Ginecocratia*, two 'enterludes,' *Lusty London* and *Woer* (the latter
'yielding a specimen of female pertness'), and a series of *Triumphals* in
honour of Queen Elisabeth. See Haslewood, *Ancient Critical Essays*, i. xiii. *note.*

[1] See the well-known passage at the end of Bk. i.

[2] 'The English tongue,' says Meres in his *Palladis Tamia* (1598), 'is
mightily enriched, and gorgeouslie inuested in rare ornaments and resplen-
dent abiliments by sir *Philip Sidney, Spencer, Daniel, Drayton, Warner,
Shakespeare, Marlowe,* and *Chapman,'*—a judicious choice of names for
any survey of the poetical literature of the age. It is interesting to compare
with this list of English poets that suggested by Drayton in his *Epistle to
H. Reynolds* (1618); cf. Fleay, i. 141.

[3] *Discoveries* (*De vere argutis*).

fashionable till it be deformed '—supplies the best proof of
the power which belonged to the tastes of the Court. The
writers who addressed themselves directly or primarily to
courtly ears, Sidney himself among them, were all more or
less emphatically artificial. It was by the imitation of
classical models, or by efforts savouring of the ' Italianated '
taste of the Court, that great writers as well as small—
a Spenser, a Marlowe, a Peele, and a Shakspere—sought
in the first instance to commend themselves to the favour
of high personal patronage. Other dramatists, or their
admirers on their behalf, appealed to their classical epopees
and their ' sugared sonnets ' as their titles to literary reputation. The author of *Doctor Faustus* was remembered for
his *Hero and Leander*, Shakspere's first offering to his
patron was *Venus and Adonis;* and Meres cannot compare
our poets, in life or in death, to any parallels but Classical
or Italian predecessors.

The drama the main agent in nationalising Elisabethan literature. But our literature was fast broadening beyond such
bounds by dint of its fertility, diversity, and power. That
it swept these bounds away altogether, and in the end
compassed a range of achievement unprecedented and
unsurpassed in grandeur and breadth, was due in a signal
degree to the growth, wholly without parallel, of one among
its branches. And the branch in question was no other
than the drama.

To later generations this has, I think, become an incontestable fact. That the age which witnessed it should but
partially and gradually have become conscious of the extraordinary literary importance of the advance of the English
drama, may require some explanation; but there seems
little difficulty in suggesting reasons for the slowness of the
process of recognition. The importunity of secondary
aspects is, in the nature of things, apt for a time to preclude
a broad face-to-face estimate of the greatest issues of
literary, as of all other kinds of history.

The greatness of the Elisabethan drama not due to patronage. In the first place, then, the glories of the Elisabethan
drama were not essentially due to patronage,—often a neces-
sary nurse of literary success, but not indispensable for the
preservation of the vitality of genius.

'Poets,' says one of them [1] who was sustained from more enduring sources, 'should walk with princes.' Without having so broadly formulated her conceptions either of her royal dignity or its 'rewardfulness' to poets (dramatic or other), Queen Elisabeth most assuredly had a most genuine and enduring love of the drama. But it is obvious—and it must have been so even to the generations which exulted in the glamour of the Cynthian light—that neither was the impulse to the marvellous progress achieved by our dramatic literature in her reign of her giving, nor was it her favour that really sustained the growth upon which she smiled to the last [2]. All but insatiable as she was in her fondness for plays, expending sums which must be called considerable upon theatrical and musical entertainments at Court from the very commencement of her reign [3], and willing to be welcomed with such diversions at the houses of her nobles, at the colleges in the Universities, and at the Inns of Court, —she formed no exception to the rule, that the habitual playgoer is the most catholic of pleasure-seekers in his or her own line of amusement. It would prove difficult to discover any signs of personal discrimination in the best of plays recorded or supposed to have been performed in her presence. Her way was to see before she judged, and to preface by ambiguous utterances her ultimate censure. Moreover, one may take leave to doubt whether the most vehement of her appetites—the love of flattery—could ever have been gratified more completely than by the attempts made in the earlier dramatic productions of her reign to meet its demands, seasoned as they almost uniformly were by the classical imagery on which as a true child of the Tudor Renascence she had herself been nurtured.

The favour of Queen Elisabeth.

---

[1] Schiller.

[2] At as late a date as December 29, 1601, Dudley Carleton mentions the presence of the Queen 'with all her *candidae auditrices* at a dramatic performance at Blackfriars. (*Calendar of State Papers, Domestic Series, Elisabeth,* 1601-3, p. 130.)

[3] See Collier, i. 173 *seqq.* Collier cites, adding the requisite qualifications, the assertion of George Chalmers (*Apology for the Believers in the Shakspeare Papers,* 1797, p. 353) that 'the persecutions of preceding governments had left Elisabeth without a theatre, without dramas, and without players.'

Among the great nobles of Queen Elisabeth's reign many—including the Endymion who lingered out to the last such rays as he could catch from his Diana—kept companies of players; and the fashion unmistakeably contributed to the refinement of dramatic production in both matter and manner.   In each of these directions, the process of selection must have continued, as some of these players were drafted off into the royal service [1].   But, in the midst of all the researches which have been devoted to this period of dramaturgic effort, it is not easy to discover any evidence of a patronage, such as has been thought discernible in the case of Shakspere's own career, of a patronage directing itself to the consistent encouragement of literary merit in the productions of the stage, as apart from incidental personal 'protection.'   In other words, such aristocratic patronage as was enjoyed by the writers who have been discussed in this chapter was incidental or fitful, and to all appearance unproductive.   The association between the progress of our theatre and such names as Southampton and Pembroke was at the most beginning; while the days were yet distant when in the *élite* of the younger nobility of which Essex was at once the type and the leader, a genuine love became perceptible, not of the stage only, but of dramatic literature.

The requirements of the public and of the times.
Except, then, in the particular instances noted above, from Lyly downwards, in which our dramatists directly accommodated themselves to the known demands of Queen and Court, and of the circles of society following their tastes, the dramatic writers rather led their patrons than were directed by them.   If the adventurous volunteers

---

[1] See the passage from Stow's *Annals*, cited by Halliwell-Phillips in his Introduction to *Tarlton's Jests, &c. (Shakespeare Society's Publications,* 1844), p. x note : 'Comedians and stage-players were very poore and ignorant in respect of those of this time, but being more growne very skilfull and exquisite actors for all matters, they were entertained into the service of divers great Lords, out of which companies there were all, of the best chosen, and at the request of Sir Francis Walsingham, they were sworn the Queenes servants, and were allowed wages and liveries as groomes of the chamber : and until this yeere, 1583, the Queene had no players.'   Cf. *infra.*

apostrophised by Peele found it difficult to tear themselves
from 'Mahomet's Pow and mighty Tamburlaine,' they left
other audiences behind them to applaud these 'pagan
vaunts[1].' Dramatists, patrons, and public shared the influence of their times. A stirring age called for stirring
themes ; and these in their turn for a corresponding vigour
of treatment. If 'the style is the man,' so the style is also
the age ; and the general tension of men's minds manifested
itself in every branch of the form of art which most easily
and quickly reproduced it. Neatness and symmetry of
construction were neglected for fulness and variety of matter.
Novelty and grandeur of subject seemed suited by a swelling
amplitude and even reckless extravagance of diction. The
balance of rimed couplets gave way to the forward march
of a remodelled blank-verse, as if from an inner necessity ;
'strong lines' were as inevitably called for as strong situations and strong characters. Individuality determined
the degree in which, either in form or in matter, the several
writers were subject to such influences. A Greene could
not rise to the passion of a Marlowe, nor a Marlowe imitate
the flexible vivacity of a Greene ; but the stamp of the age
was impressed upon them all, and no less powerful an
influence than this could have marked them all, while
severally distinct in their poetic individualities, as forming
a homogeneous group of national writers.

But it would have been impossible for these dramatists *Peculiar*
thus to give full expression to the spirit of the age to which *conditions*
they belonged, had not the outward conditions of their *of the lives*
lives cast them into the very midst of the current, instead *of these*
of leaving them to lounge as bystanders on its banks, to *dramatists.*
note and speculate on its phenomena, or to indite letters
'touching the earthquake in April last, and our English
reformed versifying.'

I have narrated the lives of these dramatists very briefly,
but without seeking to cast a veil over their errors any
more than over their misfortunes. On these errors I need
not superfluously dwell. To suppose that at any time the

---

[1] Hall's *Satires*, i. I.

experience of folly and vice constitutes a necessary pro-gymnasium of intellectual labours, is to invert the rational system of human progress, in which all intellectual achieve-ments must find their legitimate place. Genius must have its years of journeying, as it must have its years of appren-ticeship; but misfortune only, not the operation of any inevitable law, so often causes those years of journeying to include a sojourn in the tangled woods of Bohemia. Not, however, in all periods of literary effort is it calmly carried on under the cheerful encouragement of the clear light of common day; and the lives of these men were beset by dangers and difficulties, as well as stimulated by opportunities, of an exceptional character. These dangers and difficulties sprang from the condition in which the dramatists found the very sphere of their endeavours, the stage.

The pro-fessions of playwright and actor in close contact.

To minds exalted and animated by an active imagination, and fed by the varied experience of men and books which we know these writers to have undergone at an early period of their lives, the literature of the drama offered the most obvious and the most promising outlet. But this particular literature of the drama had already so thoroughly estab-lished its natural union with the stage, and the possibility of gaining a livelihood as a playwright without entering into a personal connexion with the stage was so infinitesimal, that all the dramatic authors of whom this chapter has treated identified themselves at particular times of their lives with particular theatrical companies. The learned Lyly might pine for the dignified office of superintendent of the dramatic entertainments of the Court; Peele might eke out his rougher earnings by the dues received by him as managing *factotum* of royal and noblemen's entertain-ments; Munday might satisfy his aspirations in catering for the city; reasons of one kind or another might prevail with Lodge and Drayton to put an end to their dependence upon 'pennie-knaves' and the purveyors of their pleasures. But, permanently or temporarily, all these predecessors of Shakspere were the servants of the stage and its immediate public, and not a few of them—probably including Peele himself—were actors. This connexion, while, in ways on which there is no necessity for dwelling further, it affected the course of the personal lives of the dramatists, and the estimation in which they were held by their contemporaries, at the same time directly influenced the character of their dramatic works. It taught with incomparable certainty a keen insight into the laws of dramatic cause and effect, and imparted warm vitality to a dramatic literature produced, as the phrase is, for immediate consumption. On the other hand, it as inevitably constituted rapidity of workmanship an indispensable element in the qualifications of a successful playwright. Marvellous as was the productivity of many of these dramatists, and still more marvellous as it would appear were we aware of all they wrote, the very nature of the case suffices to account for it. *How* a play was produced, what number of hands had been at work upon it, what loans and what spoliations had occurred in the process, must ordinarily have seemed of less moment than *whether* it was produced, and whether it succeeded. Not literary criticism, but the verdict of popular applause, was in the first instance challenged. Plays were written to be acted ; and they were acted to please. For a dramatist to say of himself that he ' knew his art and not his trade' would have struck his fellow-actors and authors as a more than doubtful vaunt. The play was the property of the company ; and exposed to any alterations and ' additions,' which, while they 'made' it on the stage, might 'mar' it, as in the case of *Faustus*, for all future ages. This simple consideration accounts at once for many of the merits, and for many of the faults, common to a large proportion of the dramatic works discussed in this chapter [1].

Results of the conditions of production upon the plays themselves.

---

[1] The same considerations will of course, to a very large extent, have to be borne in mind in considering the dramatic work of Shakspere, Ben Jonson, and many of the later Elisabethans.—Analogies from the history of Greek dramatic literature are always fascinating, and it might thus be noticed here that the comic dramatist Plato, probably one of the most brilliant competitors of Aristophanes, described himself as having laboured for others, like an Arcadian mercenary. It is not however certain whether he meant that he was (*sit venia verbo*) 'sweated,' or that he began by representing his plays anonymously, like Aristophanes himself and Ameipsias. See Donaldson, *Theatre of the Greeks* (7th edition, 1860), p. 174.

Summary of the history of the stage in the earlier Elisabethan period.

It therefore becomes necessary to recall, however briefly, the conditions of the English stage in this period of our dramatic literature.   In the course of this period the theatre had, in the fullest sense of the term, become a popular institution.   This, however, by no means implies either a simultaneous rise of the stage in the esteem of classes and sections of the population whose interests and sentiments had little or no direct concern with literature or art, or a corresponding advance of the labours of playwright and player towards due recognition in those literary and artistic circles of which they in truth themselves formed part.   It must be remembered that up to the time when the first dramas of Marlowe and his fellows were produced there had been no example of men of University education (in those days far more exclusively than afterwards the representatives of higher intellectual training) addressing themselves to the composition of plays intended to be performed in a public theatre, and to profit those interested in its affairs[1]. I may notice, although not wishing to insist too much on the coincidence of dates, that the careers of the two most renowned tragic actors of this age, Edward Alleyn and Richard Burbage, seem to have begun very much about this time[2].   Which, if any, of the University playwrights themselves trod the boards, must, in the case of the more illustrious among them, remain a matter of pure supposition[3].

Influence of the patronage of the Queen,

Queen Elisabeth's fondness for dramatic performances, which had shown itself already before her accession to the throne and from that date onwards[4] steadily affected its

[1] This is of course the sense of Mr. Fleay's saying, *History of the Stage*, p. 72, that 'until 1587 educated men who made it the business of their lives to promote the interest of the stage by their plays or their playing were unknown.'

[2] Alleyn's name first occurs in a list of Lord Worcester's players in 1586; Richard Burbage had made himself some sort of theatrical reputation by 1588.   As to his *sobriquet* 'Roscio' and the association of him with Shakspere by contemporary writers, see Ingleby, *Shakespeare's Centurie of Prayse* (New Shakspere Society's Publications, 1879, pp. 27, 58 *et al.*). Richard Burbage was of course stage-born and bred; as to Alleyn, this is not so certain.   See Mr. J. T. Warner's notice of Alleyn in vol. i. of *The Dictionary of National Biography* (1885).

[3] Cf. *ante*, pp. 315, 382, 410.

[4] *Ante*, p. 153.   The proclamation of April, 1559, there noticed, was

strength, at first exercised no strongly perceptible influence upon the history of the theatre. The dramatic entertainments at court and on the royal progresses continued in accordance with the practice of Queen Elisabeth's predecessors; indeed, not a few of these performances seem to have been revivals of interludes which the Queen had applauded in the days of her brother King Edward VI, and one or more of the old players in which drew their Court pensions till late into her own reign[1]. Her own interlude players, who continued to perform during the earlier years of that reign, cannot have exercised much more influence than these veterans upon the advance of the drama[2].

But as year after year witnessed a continuance and an increase of the national confidence (foes and factions notwithstanding) in the stability of her *régime*, and as her liking for dramatic entertainments underwent no abatement, her position as supreme and general patron of the English drama became more and more fully established. In a sense all the writers or performers of plays, in the earlier half of the reign at all events, openly wore her colours and were eager to lay themselves at her feet[3].

From the beginning of the new reign onwards, the chief *and of the* noblemen and gentlemen connected with the Court—or per- *nobility.* haps it would be more correct to say, the more favoured and enterprising among their number—maintained companies of actors to which the privilege was allowed of performing plays in various counties[4], although it was not until 1574

obviously due to political considerations. Cf. T. F. Ordish, *Early London Theatres* (1894), p. 28.

[1] Fleay, *History of the Stage*, 42–4. [2] *Ib.* 10.

[3] These expressions are suggested by De Silva's account to King Philip II, July, 1564, how after a comedy at Court there was 'a masque of certain gentlemen, who entered dressed in black and white, which the Queen told me were her colours, and after dancing awhile, one of them approached and handed the Queen a sonnet in English, praising her.' *Calendar of Spanish State Papers* (*Elisabeth*), vol. i. (1892), p. 368.

[4] Fleay, *History of the Stage*, 34–5, distinguishes four stocks: (1) Lord Robert Dudley's (afterwards Earl of Leicester); (2) Sir Robert Rich's, succeeded by Sir Robert Lane's, and then by the company formed by the Duttons for the Earl of Oxford, and succeeded in its turn by the company of Henry Carey, Lord Hunsdon; (3) Lord Clinton's, succeeded by the Earl of Sussex' (Lord Chamberlain, 1576); on his death probably transferred to the

that the earliest of these companies in date of establishment
(the Earl of Leicester's) obtained a patent for performances
in every part of the kingdom, including therefore the City of
London, in 1574; but of the significance of this immediately. At the same time, whichsoever among the efforts
of these several companies attained to a conspicuous success,
were, as a matter of course, reproduced before the Queen
herself at her Court, Christmas or Shrovetide revels. On such
occasions the actors called themselves the Queen's players,
and we may well suppose masters as well as servants to have
eagerly sought these opportunities of distinction. It was not,
as will be seen immediately, until 1583, that a permanent
company of Queen's Players was selected for appointment.

Academical and scho-lastic uses. In much the same way, the two Universities and the Inns
of Court, as loyal corporations delighting in the visitations
of the royal presence, were ready to gratify the Queen by
dramatic performances specially suited to the scholarly
tastes and attainments which she could nowhere else so
appropriately air. The chief London schools, so far as their
relatively slender means extended, were fain to offer similar
dramatic exhibitions. More continuously, and with the aid
of a training of which the steadiness must have gone some
way towards making up for the immaturity of the acting
material, the choristers of the Queen's own Chapels Royal,
and of the cathedral and collegiate churches in or near
London [1], were on select occasions able to present before the
Queen plays more or less suitable for juvenile impersonation.

service of the Earl of Oxford: (4) Lord Charles Howard's (the Lord Admiral),
succeeded by the Earl of Derby's, who in their turn were succeeded by
the Earl of Arundel's (Philip Howard). These companies, according to the
results of Mr. Fleay's researches, cover a period extending from 1559 to
about 1584.—As to Dutton's company of actors, see the curious satirical
lines reflecting on their desertion of the service of the Earl of Warwick for
that of the Earl of Oxford—they 'wrot themselves his Comoedians, which
certayne gentlemen altered and made Camoelions'—in Wright and Halliwell's *Reliquiae Antiquae* (1843), ii. 122. A 'Dutton's play' is mentioned
as performed at Court in or about 1574; this mention of plays by the name
of the manager of the company is characteristic of Elisabethan straight-
forwardness. Cf. Collier, i. 226.

[1] Mr. Fleay, *u. s.* 34, enumerates as organised boys' companies in the
period 1559–1586, the choirs of St. Paul's, the Chapel Royal and Windsor
(or Eton), and Merchant Taylors' and Westminster Schools.

These boys enacted many of the plays mentioned in the present or in later chapters of this book; and their competition was much felt by the men actors and at times strongly complained of by their mouthpieces[1]. It would seem that in 1585 a royal warrant was issued for the impressing of children for the choir of St. Paul's anywhere in the kingdom; which implies that this company of 'little eyases' at the time enjoyed a monopoly as juvenile actors[2].

Thus it is obvious that in the earlier period of Queen Elisabeth's reign there could never have been a lack either of players or of plays to be presented before her, and consequently never a lack of playwrights to furnish forth the materials of her favourite diversion. When, accordingly, in 1583 the time was held to have arrived for selecting a regular company of players to Her Majesty, who henceforth bore

[1] Cf. *The English Drama and Stage, &c.*, 1543–1664, *illustrated by Documents, Treatises, and Poems* (Roxburghe Library, 1869); and Clark and Wright's edition of *Hamlet* (Clarendon Press), *Preface*, p. xv.

[2] Although perhaps anticipating rather too much in date, I may be here allowed in a note to translate a curious passage referring to these performances by children in the *Diary of the Duke* [Philip Julius] *of* [Pomerania-] *Stettin*, edited by Dr. G. von Bülow, assisted by Mr. Wilfred Powell, for the Royal Historical Society (*Transactions, New Series*, vol. vi. 1892). The date of his visit to England was 1602; but the general features of the description may be in part held applicable to these performances at a much earlier period of the Queen's reign. 'Thence we proceeded to the *Kindercomoedia*, which in its plot dealt with a *casta vidua*; it was a *historia* of a royal widow in England. Now this is the account of this *Kindercomoedia*: the Queen maintains many young boys, who are bound to apply themselves with diligence to the art of singing, and to learn how to perform on all instruments, and at the same time to pursue their studies. These boys have their special *praeceptores* in all arts, in especial very good *musicus*.

'Now in order that they may use courtly manners, they are obliged every week to perform a *comoedia*, for which purpose the Queen has caused to be built for them a particular *theatrum*, and has supplied them superabundantly with artistic dresses. Whoever desires to be a spectator of such a performance must pay as much as eight *sundische Schillinge* of our coinage; yet there is always to be found there a large audience including many decent women, because they expect, in accordance with what they heard from others, to have brought before them many interesting *argumenta* and many noble maxims; everything in the performance being done by candlelight (*bei Lichte*), which makes a great sensation (*Aufsehen*). For a whole hour previously, one listens to a costly *musica instrumentalis* of organs, cithers, pandores, mandores, fiddles and pipes; on the present occasion, indeed, a boy *cum voce tremula* sung in so lovely a fashion to a cello (*Basgeige*) that, unless the muses at Milan may have excelled him, we had not heard the like of him on our travels.'

the distinctive name of the Queen's men, although their efforts were by no means confined to performances in her presence, there could be no difficulty in finding a sufficient number of established favourites deserving of the coveted distinction. We know that those chosen included the famous clown Richard Tarlton, together with Robert Wilson, the supposed author of *The Three Lordes and Three Ladies of London*, and other popular favourites [1].

[1] See Fleay, *History of the Stage*, 54–5.—Of Richard Tarlton a full account will be found in Halliwell(-Phillips') *Introduction* to his edition of *Tarlton's Jests, and News out of Purgatory* (*Shakespeare Society's Publications*, 1844). Cf. a note to the life of Hall in Chalmers' *English Poets*, v. 254.—Tarlton was a 'prentice in his youth' in the City of London, and is said to have afterwards earned his living as a 'water-bearer.' Later in life he seems to have followed the more suitable avocation of a tavern-keeper. On the stage he became famous as a clown, and was above all admired for his extemporal riming (to 'Tarletonise' became synonymous with extemporising), and more especially for his 'jigs'—i. e. ludicrous 'topical' songs, often accompanied by a dance, introduced by the clown and usually invented by him. Of these a good example remains in *Tarlton's Jigge of a horse loade of Fooles*, printed by Halliwell-Phillips, *u. s.*, pp. xx–xxvi).—His popularity, fostered by his audacity, knew no bounds. Nashe says, with a touch true to human nature, that 'the people began exceedingly to laugh when Tarlton first peept out his head'; and Fuller records that 'the self-same words, spoken by another, would hardly move a merry man to smile, which, uttered by him, would force a sad soul to laughter.' Tarlton died in 1588, the year of the Spanish Armada. A warm tribute is paid to him in *The Three Lordes and Ladies of London*, a play probably written shortly after his decease and attributed to his fellow-actor Robert Wilson. (See *ante*, 140 note, and cf. 435. The 'extemporal' wit attributed to the supposed 'younger' Wilson by Meres, suggests at least a hereditary connexion with Tarlton's associate.) Long afterwards the portrait of Tarlton, with drum and fife, of which Mr. Halliwell-Phillips gives a *facsimile*, continued to ornament ale-houses and other places of public resort. For references to him, see among others the *Induction* to *Bartholomew Fair* (1614), and an epitaph of the year 1617, quoted by Waldron in his edition of *The Sad Shepherd*, p. 167, where he is apostrophised as 'the Lord of Mirth,' while 'all clownes since' are said to have been 'his apes.'—As for the productions that have been attributed to Tarlton, the authenticity of the *Jests* (of which the first known, but probably not the earliest, edition bears date 1611) is in several instances supported by external evidence; the remarkably ancient and flat flavour of others seems on the whole to add to the probability of their traditional origin. The medley of short stories called *Tarleton's Newes out of Purgatorie* was printed in or about 1590, but his name is generally thought to have been attached to this pamphlet merely by way of a catchpenny. He wrote, however, a good deal of verse (including a volume called *Tarlton's Toyes*), none of which except the above-mentioned 'jig' has been preserved. Of more interest for students of our dramatic literature is the statement of Gabriel Harvey (in his *Fovre Letters*, 1592, cited *ap.* Halliwell-Phillips, Introduction, p. xxxiv), that Tarlton

But the efforts of the earlier Elisabethan theatre, although concentrated in the way indicated upon the service of the Queen, were after all due in their origin to a popular demand for dramatic entertainments which was older than her dynasty or the forms of Church and State under which her government was carried on. In former days this demand had attached itself to localities consecrated by tradition to dramatic spectacle, or associated by immemorial usage with diversions of a dramatic character[1]. As it became customary for companies of players attached to the households of noblemen and gentlemen to travel from place to place in order to exhibit their performances, they naturally resorted to the inns, more especially in or about London ; the boy companies when intent upon profit followed suit ; and thus it came to pass that ' in the history of the London stage the immediate predecessor of the play-house was the inn-yard[2].' From the accession of Queen Elisabeth until the year 1576, when the first London theatre, properly so-called, was built, these inn-yards remained the chosen homes of the popular drama[3]. Among the hostelries known to have been frequented for this purpose were the Cross Keys[4] in Gracious (Gracechurch) Street, the Bull in Bishops-gate Street, the Belle Savage on Ludgate Hill, and others in Whitefriars, in Blackfriars, and elsewhere near St. Paul's[5]. In this very natural, and under the circumstances practically inevitable process, we may recognise the origin of a long

Popular demand for dramatic entertainments.

Dramatic performances in inn-yards.

was the author of the *platt* or outline of action (to be filled up with words by the performers) of *The Seven Deadlie Sins*, of which the *Second Part* was found by Malone at Dulwich, and has been printed by Collier. Cf. *ante*, p. 230, note 1.—After Tarlton's death, his mantle—or perhaps I should say his cap and bells—fell to William Kempe, of whom a word below.—The vogue of Edward Alleyn and Richard Burbage, as has been seen, had hardly begun by 1583 ; Richard's father James was a member of Leicester's company, probably from a very early period of its existence.

[1] Cf. *ante* as to the exhibition of religious plays in churches and chapels, or in their immediate vicinity, and in that of the ancient and sacred wells ; and see Mr. T. Fairman Ordish's *Early London Theatres* (1894) as to the amphitheatrical constructions for spectacular purposes, both in London and in other parts of the country.

[2] Ordish, p. 28.

[3] Fleay, *History of the Stage*, 35 *seqq.*

[4] According to Prynne, *ap.* Fleay, 36, this house was called the Bell.

[5] See Fleay, *u. s.*, and Ordish, 30.

series of conflicts which affected, together with the history
of the London, and therefore of the English stage, the
course of our dramatic, and with it that of many other 'rivers
of the blood' of our national literature. It will accordingly,
I think, best serve the purpose of this subsidiary reference to
the annals of the earlier Elisabethan stage, to connect the
chief incidents which remain to be noticed in them according
to chronological sequence with the most notable data of the
struggle in question [1].

*The City
and the
stage.*

Queen Elisabeth's proclamation of April 7, 1559, issued
probably for purely political reasons, had not affected the
acknowledged administrative principle that all dramatic
performances in the City of London remained under the
control of its Lord Mayor and Corporation. But the
increasing number of these performances in the London inn-
yards, fostered by the love of the theatre in which the Queen
was at one with her magnates and with a large proportion of
her people, continuously aggravated the aspect of a nuisance
in which they presented themselves to the fathers of the
City. Entertainments of the kind in question could not be
carried on without noise and disturbance of all sorts, more
particularly since, in accordance with the traditions of the
mediaeval drama [2], the performance of a play implied a *processus* with drums and trumpets to its performance; while
within the precincts of the inn-yards, the terribly real peril
of spreading infectious disease, and above all the Plague—
the curse of curses in this unsanitary and unscientific age—
speedily attained to proportions such as nothing short of
sheer blindness could have ignored and neglected. It was
under an exceptionally awful visitation of the Plague that in
1563 Archbishop Grindall (Spenser's 'good Algrind'), influenced by his Puritan antipathies against the stage, advised
Secretary Cecil to inhibit all plays for one whole year within
the City, 'and if it were for ever,' the Primate added, 'it were
not amiss [3].' We do not know whether his advice was taken;
but it was in any case momentous as at the same time pro-

---

[1] My main guide in this summary is Mr. Fleay, whose *History of the Stage*
has superseded all other treatments of the subject. See especially pp. 44 *seqq.*
[2] *Ante*, p. 44.   [3] Collier, i. 182.

testing against plays on religious and on social grounds, and appealing to the competence of the royal authority to exercise a control over their performance within as well as without the City of London.

Nine years later—in 1572, as we learn from Harrison's *Chronologie*[1]—plays were actually 'banished for a time out of London, lest the resort unto them should ingender a plague, or rather disperse it, being already begonne.' But by whatever authority (doubtless it was that of the City itself) this ordinance was issued, its result was not to check the popularity of dramatic performances. Not only did the Queen's high-handed bestowal, in 1574, upon Leicester's players of the privilege of performing plays within as well as without the City limits, whether for her own delectation or for that of her subjects at large, imply a defiance of the claim of the City authorities to manage their own affairs[2]; but, which was perhaps of even more practical importance, she had been met halfway by the inclinations of the London population, inasmuch as the temporary prohibition of plays within the walls was beginning to be evaded by a systematic increase of dramatic performances, both on the Surrey side of the river in Southwark,—a district devoted from of old to popular diversions of all sorts and descriptions,—and to the North of the Walls. In 1575 the actors of the several companies interested, assuming the *ad captandum* designation of 'Her Majesty's poor players,' ventured on a sort of ultimate attempt by petitioning the Privy Council for permissive letters to the Lord Mayor, and the City replied by a statement of its case against them, to

---

[1] See *Extracts* (Appendix I to Furnivall's *Forewords to Harrison's Description of England*, Bks. ii. and iii.), *New Shakspere Society's Publications*, 1877, pp. liv–lv, cited *ap.* Ordish, p. 31. Harrison inveighs against the signs of the times, when players could 'build such houses' as were by this edict emptied of their frequenters. But his meaning, as Dr. Furnivall allows, is ambiguous.

[2] Cf. *ante*, p. 452.—The name of James Burbage heads the list. He may be described as the father of the popular Elisabethan theatre, but of his own successes as an actor we possess no authentic record. Cf. Mr. S. Lee's notice of him in vol. vii. of *The Dictionary of National Biography* (1886).— For the patent in question, cf. Collier, i. 203-4, with Fleay's observations, *History of the Stage*, p. 45.

Earliest permanent theatres in London (from 1576 or 1577).

which the merit of exhaustiveness cannot be denied[1]. In 1576 or 1577 a new chapter in the history of the English stage may be said to have begun with the opening of *The Theatre* in Finsbury Fields, followed immediately afterwards by that of the Curtain hard-by in Shoreditch[2]. The history of the origin and progress of these playhouses ' in the fields,' and of others which sprang up after them in rapid succession, both within and without the City proper, must be left to the chroniclers of the stage;—the theatres in question included the Whitefriars[3], the Fortune in Golden or Golding Lane St. Giles, Cripplegate, and from 1596–7 the Blackfriars, a house purchased by James Burbage in 1596; together with, on the Bankside, the Rose (Henslowe's playhouse), the Swan[4], the Globe (from 1599; in the immediate neighbourhood of Paris Garden, which, though mainly a resort for bear-baiting and other sports, was itself also used for dramatic representations), the Hope and Newington Butts[5]. In 1583, as has been seen, a single company of Queen's players was constituted, and although the plague appears to have prevented it for a time from performing in London, its formation added a new element of stability to the English stage.

Literary attacks upon the theatre.

Meanwhile, the combination of moral sentiment, religious opinion, and practical grievance which had long sustained the endeavours of the City authorities towards staying, and if possible extinguishing, the activity of the stage, had begun and continued to find eager literary exponents.

---

[1] Cf. Fleay, *u. s.*, 46–7. The third article of the reply, as there condensed, is *sui generis* excellent: ' To play in plague-time increases the plague by infection; to play out of plague-time calls down the plague from God.'

[2] See Ordish, 32 *seqq.* and 76 *seqq.*—two exhaustive chapters, which render further references superfluous.

[3] See J. Greenstreet, *The Whitefriars Theatre in the time of Shakspere. New Shakspere Society's Transactions*, 1888, founded on information from documents connected with a Chancery suit of the year 1609.

[4] See as to the manuscript and drawing of the Swan Theatre, discovered by Dr. Guedertz of Berlin among the papers of John de Witt, Canon of Utrecht, who visited London about the year 1596, Dr. Gaedertz' publication on the subject (Bremen, 1888), and Mr. H. B. Wheatley's paper in *Transactions of the New Shakspere Society*, 1888.

[5] See as to the London Theatres of this period, Fleay, *History of the Stage*, 147 *seqq.*

Passing by published pulpit utterances of even earlier dates, we may notice in the first instance a treatise entered for publication in 1577, and printed at all events as early as 1579, by John Northbrooke, a divine whose Orders dated from the Elisabethan age, under a heading or motto which he adopted for a succession of tracts. This was the *Treatise wherein Dicing, Dauncing, vaine Playes or Enterluds, with other idle Pastimes, &c., commonly used on the Sabaoth Day, are reproved by the Authoritie of the Word of God and auntient Writers*[1]. The method of this tract is the exhaustive method proper to Puritan argument down to (and after) the days of Prynne, concerning which it would be rash to assert that it is ill calculated for effect upon the audience with which it is primarily concerned ; but, oddly enough, as Collier notices, the argument is conveyed in that dialogue-form which is akin to the dramatic, and which has the advantage of anticipating opposition by putting it into as weak as possible a position[2]. Moreover, the drama here figures as a mere adjunct to more enticing phases of popular debauchery. In 1579, Stephen Gosson, an Oxonian who had himself contributed both to dramatic literature and to its histrionic interpretation, but who was now on his way towards ecclesiastical preferment, found himself moved to put forth *The School of Abuse, conteining a pleasant inuective against Poets, Pipers, Plaiers, Jesters and such like Caterpillers of a Commonwealth*, which he dedicated to Sidney, and which, after it had been answered by Lodge, he followed up in 1581 or 1582 by a second diatribe entitled *Playes Confuted in five Actions*[3]. *The Schoole of Abuse*, written in euphuistic style and with an obvious consciousness of the author's academical pretensions, cannot be said to convey the impression that a deep spiritual indignation was the principal motive

North-brooke (1577-9).

Gosson (1579).

---

[1] Edited by Collier for the Shakspeare Society, with an Introduction, 1843. Cf. the biographical notice of Northbrooke by Mr. Ronald Bayne in vol. xli. of *The Dictionary of National Biography* (1895). The motto of the tract is ' *Spiritus est vicarius Christi in terra.*'

[2] The interlocutors are *Youth and Age*, of whom the former is an ἄδικος λόγος of remarkably ineffective improbity. As to the literary fashion followed by this tract, cf. *ante*, p. 234.

[3] See Collier's edition of *The Schoole of Abuse, Shakespeare Society's Publications*, 1843. Cf. *ante*, pp. 409 *seqq*.

of its composition; moveover, it exhibits a certain degree of eclecticism in its censures, describing 'some plays,' including 'a pig of mine owne Sowe[1],' as 'tollerable at some time.' It is, in short, on the author's part a note of transition into a camp whose standard did not disdain to adorn itself by *Other pamphlets (1581-2).* literary streamers. In 1580, a pamphlet was entered under the name of Henry Denham[2] by the title of *A Second and Third Blast of Retreat from Plays and Theatres*[3]; and I have noted the publication of an anonymous treatise *Stubbes (1583).* of similar purport in the following year (1581)[4]. In 1583— the very year in which a special remonstrance from the Lord Mayor against the dangers of promiscuous and infectious assemblies of theatrical spectators had been answered by the license granted to a special body of players as appropriated to Her Majesty's service—Philip Stubbes (over whose personal origin and identity a cloud of mystery still seems to hang) published his portentous *Anatomie of Abuses*, a survey of contemporary society and of the remedies needed by it, of which it would be difficult to overrate the interest and significance[5]. The general spirit of this work (which curiously enough is again in dialogue-form, besides being for appearance sake veiled beneath a transparent allegory[6]) will not be refused the recognition which it deserves, more especially since the force of its invective is proportioned to the gravity of the themes to which it in succession addresses itself[7]. Moreover, it frequently becomes

---

[1] *Catilins Conspiracies;* cf. *ante,* p. 209.

[2] Doubtless the active printer, of whom a short notice, by Mr. H. R. Tedder, will be found in vol. xiv. of *The Dictionary of National Biography* (1888).

[3] Cf. Fleay, *History of the Stage,* 51, where is also noticed the license of a ballad under the same telling title, which Mr. Fleay considers identifiable with 'a ballad against plays' attributed in 1581 to Antony Munday.

[4] *A Treatise of Daunses, wherein it is showed, that they are as it were accessories and dependants (or things annexed) to whoredom: where also by the way is touched and proved, that Playes are ioyned and knit together in a ranck or rowe with them. Anno* 1581. (*Chatsworth Library Catalogue.*)

[5] Reprinted in *Publications of the New Shakspere Society, Series VI,* 1876–1882, with *Forewords and Notes,* by Dr. Furnivall.

[6] The abuses censured are allocated to an anagrammatically named country *Ailgna,* and in several instances to its capital *Munidnol.*

[7] The later portions of *Part I* (*The Temporalty*) and virtually the whole of *Part II* (*The Spiritualty*) are concerned with religious, social and economical

obvious that the author, while pouring out without stint the stores of information gathered by his learning and application, was desirous of guarding himself against the onesidedness which is the bane of such diatribes. Unfortunately, however, the particular section of *Part I* of this book, which treats *Of Stage-Playes and Enterluds, with their wickednes*[1], while manifesting on the part of the author no very close or varied familiarity with the subject, is conceived in a spirit of uncompromising wrath, and written black in black. Religious plays are sacrilegious, profane are devilish; and a divine *praemunire* of eternal damnation lies against all who bear a part in their maintenance[2]. To the names of Gosson and Stubbes may be added those of George Whetstone, the author of *Promos and Cassandra*, and therefore like Gosson a 'repentant' dramatist, who in 1584 published his *Touchstone for the Time*, and of William Rankine, whose *Mirror of Monsters* appeared in 1587, and who, conversely, is said to have composed plays after inveighing against their production[3].

Other pamphlets (1584-7).

In what proportion the Puritan spirit, which inspired all these publications, was accountable for the opposition to the theatre so long and so sturdily maintained by the City authorities, it would be difficult with any degree of accuracy to determine. For prejudice alone, which is not always on

The opposition to the stage not wholly due to Puritan feeling.

problems of the highest importance, and often of great difficulty—and in the treatment of some of these Stubbes shows himself in advance of his age. The sections in Part I on *Abuses in Trade* and on *Abuses in Apparel and its Makers* are, as is well known, full of curious detail.

[1] Pp. 140 *seqq.*, *u. s.* Some extracts are given in *The English Drama and Stage* (Roxburghe Library), cited *ante*, p. 453, note 1.

[2] Nashe attacked the latter both in his *Anatomie of Absurditie* (which can hardly be said to have 'plagiarised' Stubbes' title, cf. *ante*, p. 419) and (if this tract was his) in *An Almond for a Parrat*. Gabriel Harvey of course took up the cudgels in Stubbes' defence. See the passages *ap.* Furnivall, *u. s.*, pp. 36 *seqq.*

[3] See Collier, *Introduction to the Schoole of Abuse*, pp. ix-x.—I have passed by minor literary efforts, such as the ballad provoked by the falling of a wooden gallery full of spectators during a Sunday bear-baiting at Paris Garden in January, 1583,—and the tract by 'John Field, Minister of the Word of God,' suggested by the same accident. See Collier, i. 243-6, where it is surmised that the result of this occurrence was that the order of the Privy Council against performances on Sundays, which had hitherto applied only to the City of London, was now made general.

one side (as is shown among other instances by the particular controversy to be immediately touched upon), could pretend to deny that the theatre, as it affected the life of London in the earlier Elisabethan age, had in it the elements of both a social and a moral nuisance of considerable magnitude. The question for its future in England, and implicitly for that of our dramatic literature, was in what degree these elements were essential to its continued existence as a popular institution. Meanwhile the opposition against the stage on the part of the City of London, and of those classes throughout the country of which its citizens were typical, continued, as will be noticed hereafter, throughout the reigns of Elizabeth and her successors, nor has it ever wholly ceased whenever there has been a stage to contend against.

The stage on its defence.

We have seen from the examples of Lodge and others, that the natural apologists of the stage had not been backward in defending it against these early attacks. The violence of its censors stimulated the boldness of their opponents, until at last the outbreak of a controversy originally unconnected with the stage [1] allowed them with unprecedented outspokenness to assume the offensive, and to identify themselves with the cause of allies whose sympathy with the theatre can at the most have been of but a very limited description.

The Mar-PrelateControversy (1588-90).

The details of the Mar-Prelate Controversy—the most famous literary quarrel of these libellous times [2]— surrounded as they are by an obscurity which laborious investigation is only gradually clearing up, and which in part will probably

---

[1] Such a charge as that implied in the anecdote told by Martin Marprelate in *Hay any work for Cooper* (1589), of the priest ' Gliberie of Hawsteade' in Essex (cf. Maskell, *u.i.*, 96-7), should be regarded as merely illustrative. This divine of the old school, who had formerly, 'symple as he now standes,' been 'a vice in a playe for want of a better,' on hearing a morris dance in progress outside the church of which he was occupying the pulpit, cut short his sermon and 'came down' among the dancers.

[2] 'Do you not see these Pamphlets, Libels, Rhimes,
These strange confusèd Tumults of the Mind,
Are grown to be the Sickness of these Times,
The great Disease inflicted on Mankind.'
Daniel's *Musophilus* (1599).

be never altogether removed, cannot occupy us in this place [1]. Its immediate motive cause was the sentiment of 'now or never' aroused by Whitgift's policy of repression after his acceptance of the Primacy in 1583 ; its intellectual parentage may be ascribed to Cartwright, the *antipous* of Whitgift in the religious history of the reign. But nothing is gained by widening until they lose themselves in dimness the circles of an enquiry into a subject bearing upon so wide a variety of connected interests, and the history of the Mar-Prelate controversy, properly so called, is in point of fact comprised within very definite limits. It begins with the publication of the famous *Epistle to the terrible Priests of the Confocation house*, which professed to be a mere introduction to a coming refutation of a defence of the Church of England, as it was, recently published by Dr. Bridges, Dean of Salisbury, and which, so far as is known, first introduced 'Martin Mar-Prelate, gentleman,' into the controversial arena. This pamphlet unmistakeably indicates the peculiar method of the controversy, which was that of bringing its issues home to the general public by means of familiar, and if necessary, comic illustration—in a word, the satiric method, never more effectively practised than in the Renascence age, from which exaggeration and misrepresentation are in point of fact inseparable [2]. Such was the method which, from

---

[1] By far the best survey of the Mar-Prelate controversy is, so far as I know, to be found in Professor E. Arber's *English Scholar's Library*, No. 8 (*An Introductory Sketch to the Martin Mar-Prelate Controversy*), 1879, with No. 9 (*Martin Marprelate, The Epistle*), 1880. Previously to this, the only compendious account extant was Maskell's *History of the Martin Marprelate Controversy*, &c. (1845), an interesting book, but manifestly tinged with prejudice. An earlier but discursive account will be found in the elder Disraeli's *Quarrels of Authors*, ii. 203–282. See also Neal's *History of the Puritans*, ii. 336 *seqq.*; and the articles on Penry by Mr. S. Lee, and on Barrowe by Dr. Grosart, in vols. xliv. and iii. of *The Dictionary of National Biography* (1895 and 1885).— Much information may be gleaned from the collection of *Puritan Discipline Tracts*, of which the reprinting and the circulation in America were deeply regretted by Mr. Maskell, on the ground that ' poison' should not be sold without its ' antidote.'

[2] There seems no reason for doubting that the personality of *Martin Marprelate*, as first introduced in the *Epistle*, was to all intents and purposes original. The best summary of the character is that offered in *Hay any Work for Cooper* (1589); cf. Grosart, *u. s.*, No. 8, 12–13. Thomas Cooper, Bishop of Winchester, had attempted a serious reply to the *Epistle* in a tract entitled *An Admonition to the People of England* (1589). As Disraeli points

motives which it is unnecessary here either to extol or to
impugn, had been determined upon by a secret clique of
writers against a system of church government which they
deemed obsolete and rotten, and consequently inimical to
the interests of religion.   They carried out their design with
extraordinary resolution and skill, by means of a secret
printing-press moved from place to place, and with the support of a popular sympathy of which the measure can only be
gauged by impartial historical enquiry.   Apart from local influences[1] and the growth of theological opinion in academical
spheres[2], a national problem—that of the emancipation of
a Protestant Church from its derived trammels—lent force
and fury to the struggle.   It ended, with the ready aid of the
State, in the martyrdom of its principal agents[3]; but the end
was the beginning of a movement which transformed the
religious life of the nation.

In this celebrated controversy, upon the more important
aspects of which I must abstain from further dwelling, the rail-
ing had not by any means been all on the side of the ' Martin-
mongers[4].'   Even academically-nurtured scholars, whose
sympathies leant to the Puritanising party in the Church,
were painfully affected by the onslaught upon ecclesiastical
dignitaries credited with the same way of thinking[5].   What

out, his name presented the inestimable advantage of lending itself to
punning retorts.

[1] Above all the feeling to which Penry had already given expression in
a previous tract, and which ended by consecrating him ' the father of Welsh
non-conformity.'

[2] Penry was of Peterhouse, and Barrowe of Clare Hall.

[3] Although John Penry was not put to death (1593) on the charge of
authorship of any of the Mar-Prelate tracts, his share in them and in their
publication seems established. ('Penry, son of Martin Marprelate, was
hanged lately.'   *Calendar of State Papers, Domestic Series, Elisabeth,* 1891–4,
p. 353).   Henry Barrowe, whom Dr. Dexter has sought to prove the author
of the chief tracts, was executed in the same year with John Greenwood
on a different indictment.   These, with John Udall, who died in prison,
and the Warwickshire country-gentleman Job Throckmorton, make up the
list of the suspected ' Martinist' authors.

[4] So they are called in Lyly's tract, *A Pappe with an Hatchet.*

[5] 'Spenser's attitude to Puritanism, after the fierce paper war of Mar-
prelate and his foes, is palpably changed.—The party of the saintly sufferer
Algrind is now represented by the Blatant Beast.'   C. H. Herford, Introduction to his edition of *Spenser's Shepheards Calendar* (1895), p. lxxiii.—

wonder that the prelates and their cause (the cause of the
existing state of things) should have found advocates
among writers fully prepared to meet a whole company
of 'Martins' on their own ground [1]. Lyly and Nashe were
drawn into the controversy by motives which it is unnecessary further to analyse ; and the latter took so active a part
in it that it long remained customary to father upon him the
entire series of the replies to the Martinists. But the notion
of answering these writers in their own popular satiric vein
seems to have originated with Richard Bancroft (afterwards
Archbishop of Canterbury), who early in 1589 preached a
violent sermon at St. Paul's Cross against the Martinists *eo
nomine ;* and it has even been thought not unlikely that he
had something to do with the composing of the tracts in question [2]. Nashe may with certainty be held responsible for at
least four of them, including *The Returne of the Renowned
Caualier Pasquill of England* (1589), and Lyly was undoubtedly the author of *A Pappe with an Hatchet* (1589) [3] ;
Munday, too, seems to have taken service on the same side [4].   *Martin
Lastly—and this is what principally concerns us here—the*   *Mar-Pre-
stage itself had at an early date in the controversy been made   late on the
use of by the opponents of Martin Mar-Prelate ; and, by   stage
1589, a play in the nature of a morality had been exhibited   (1589).*
in derision of the adversaries of the Establishment [5].   The

John Aylmer, Bishop of London (the ' Morrell of the *Calender*), is the ' dumb
John' upon whom the *Epistle* vents its most personal satire.
    [1] I use the neutral expression ' company'; the Anti-Martinists would have
said ' herd,' mindful as they were of the fact that ' Martin,' though the use
of the word was doubtless suggested by Luther's baptismal name, was the
popular appellation of the loudest-voiced of domestic animals.
    [2] Maskell, 167. Cf. Mr. Mullinger's notice of Bancroft in vol. iii. of *The
Dictionary of National Biography* (1885).
    [3] See for a list of anti-Martinist pamphlets forming an integral part of the
controversy, Arber, *u. s.*, No. 8, pp. 197-200; and cf. Maskell, 164 *seqq.*
    [4] At least in *An Almond for a Parrat* ' Martin ' is bid ' beware *Anthony
Munday* be not euen with you for calling him Iudas, and lay open your false
carding to the stage of all men's scorne.' (*Puritan Discipline Tracts*, p. 52.)
Plaine Percevall was, as Maskell shows, a late effort on the Puritan side in
favour of quiet, and has been most absurdly attributed to Nashe. There
seems every likelihood of its having been written, as Nashe asserts in his
Strange Newes, by Richard Harvey. See *Introduction to Puritan Discipline
Tracts.*
    [5] This piece is thus described by Nashe in his *Returne of Pasquill* :

Master of the Revels (Edmund Tylney) having in consequence made an adverse representation to the Lord
Treasurer (Burghley), the latter wrote to the Lord Mayor,
requiring him to put a stop to all theatrical exhibitions
Prohibitory within his jurisdiction.   The chief magistrate of the city
and restric- could only consign two refractory players 'to one of the
tive mea- Compters[1].'   Six days afterwards (November 12, 1589), how-
sures
(1589). ever, the Privy Council took the necessary measures to put
an end to the scandal.   The Archbishop of Canterbury was
required to name 'a person well learned in divinity,' and the
Lord Mayor 'a sufficient person learned and of judgment,'
who together with the Master of the Revels were to license all
plays acted in and about the City.   From the letters issued
by the Privy Council on this occasion, it would appear that
'certen matters of Divinytie and State' had been 'handled'
in more than one play of the day.   The stoppage of stage-
plays was accordingly only temporary; but the 'comedies'
against Martin Mar-Prelate, whether written or in preparation, had to be laid aside, greatly to Lyly's regret, who
thought they would have 'decyphered, and so perhaps

'Methought *Vetus Comoedia* began to pricke him at London in the right
vaine, when shee brought foorth *Divinitie* with a scratcht face, holding of
her hart, as if she were sicke, because *Martin* would have forced her; but
myssing of his purpose, he left the print of his nayles upon her cheekes, and
poysoned her with a vomit, which he ministred unto her to make her cast
uppe her dignities and promotions.' Collier, i. 273.   Lyly in the *Pappe
with an Hatchet* seems to describe the same, or a similar, play when he says
(of Martin): 'He shall not be brought in as whilom he was, and yet verie
well, with a cocks combe, an apes face, a wolfe's bellie, cats clawes,' &c.
Quoted by Maskell, p. 210.   Lyly adds: 'If he be showed at Paul's,' i. e.
by the Children of Paul's, it will cost you four pence, if at the Theatre two
pence, if at St. Thomas a Watrings' (the place of execution close to the
Theatre), 'nothing.'   (Cf. Fleay, *History of the Stage*, 92-3.)   See Collier,
i. 266-7, where a further passage is cited from the tract *A Countercuffe
given to Martin Junior*, referring to 'the *Anatomie* lately taken of him, the
blood and the humors that were taken from him by lancing and worming him
at London upon the common stage.'

[1] As Mr. Fleay, *Life of Shakespeare*, pp. 102-3, puts it, the Anti-Martinist
plays being, with the exception of those represented by the Paul's Boys,
performed outside the City, could not be silenced by the Lord Mayor, who
could only try to stop the Lord Admiral's and Lord Strange's companies;
whereupon, when the latter (Shakspere's) company persisted in playing,
two of its members were arrested.   Mr. Fleay thinks that the play acted
on this occasion was *Love's Labour's Lost*.

discouraged' the enemy. Nor was his playful proposal of a 'Tragedie,' in which 'Mardocheus' should play 'a Bishoppe' and Martin 'Hamman,' ever carried into execution [1].

We may rejoice that an attempt should have been nipped in the bud to make the popular stage a vehicle of contro- versial abuse and invective; since the result could not but have been to intensify the influences which were about this time tending to coarsen and degrade it. Very shortly after the transactions referred to—in 1590—the performances of the Children of Paul's were stopped on account of the per- sonal abuse and scurrility put into the mouths of these youthful actors, who thus came to be silenced for several years [2]. In 1592 'certaine players' are stated to have been 'suffered to scoffe and jeast at' the King of Spain 'upon their common stages,' and to have derided Popery by annexing a verse against it to one of 'the Psalmes of David [3].' In 1593 it was thought desirable, though on what specific grounds we are not informed, to interfere with the exhibition of interludes and plays by strolling performers in both the University towns [4]. The evidence of contemporary poets shows a vivid sense of the degradation of a form which even as it was had hitherto been only tentatively admitted into what might be called the inner circle of the literature repre- sented by them. Spenser, of whose own early essays in dramatic composition (manifestly of a purely literary kind) no notice is preserved beyond Gabriel Harvey's encomiastic mention [5], in his *Teares of the Muses* (printed 1591) adverts to the condition of both the tragic and the comic drama in a spirit of pessimism which may seem too compre-

Danger of a degrada- tion of the stage to contro- versial uses.

---

[1] See *A Pappe with an Hatchet*, p. 32 and note, pp. 47–50 ; cf. Collier, *u. s.*
[2] Collier, i. 271 *seqq.* ; cf. Fleay, *History of the Stage*, 93 ; and see Clark and Wright, *u. s.*, p. xiv.
[3] Collier, i. 279.   [4] *Ib.* 283–4.
[5] 'To be plaine, I am voyde of al judgment, if your nine Comoedies, whereunto, in imitation of Herodotus, you give the names of the Nine Muses, and (in one man's fansie not unworthily), come not neerer Ariosto's Comoedies, eyther for the fineness of plausible elocution, or the rareness of poetical invention, than that Elvish queen doth to his Orlando Furioso.' (April 7, 1580.) Quoted by Dr. Hales, *Introductory Memoir* to Globe Edition of Spenser's *Works*, p. xxvij.

hensive to admit of special application ; but his characterisation of ' the Comick Stage' can hardly be passed by as a mere
expression of contemptuous dislike for its ordinary methods :

> 'All places they with follie have possest,
> And with vaine toyes the vulgare entertaine;
> But me [1] have banishèd, with all the rest
> That whilome wont to wait upon my traine,
> Fine Counterfesaunce, and unhurtfull Sport,
> Delight, and Laughter, deckt in seemly sort [2].'

Hall, again, in his satirical attack upon the contemporary
stage, which though the *Sixe Bookes Virgidemiarum* were
not published till 1597, may be supposed to have been
composed or conceived at a rather earlier date, dwells upon
the vulgar comic mirth—the 'vile russetings'—that alter-
nated with the 'pot-fury' of popular tragedy [3]. But neither
critical censure nor authoritative restriction could bring
about a sudden reformation. In 1595 the Lord Mayor
complained of the reopening of the 'old haunts' of 'the
Theatre' and the Bankside, and in 1597 the Privy Council
made an abortive attempt to stop performances at theatres
within three miles of London, in consequence of the dis-
Consolida- orders and the 'lewd matters handled' there [4]. Probably,
tion of the however, nothing made so steadily, albeit slowly, for
companies improvement, as the gradual consolidation, and reduction
of actors. in number, of the companies of actors. The subject is too
complicated, and the evidence concerning it too fluid, to
admit of being dealt with here ; but it seems established
that from about 1593 onwards, not more than three
companies—with an occasional fourth—were regarded as
authorised to play in or about the City. These were the

---

[1] *i. e.* Thalia.

[2] To realise the full force of Spenser's invective, it would be necessary
to cite the complaints of Melpomene and Thalia in their entirety.—I
pass by, at all events for the present, the improbable conjecture that
the subsequent allusion to the 'death' of 'our pleasant Willy' refers to
Shakspere's supposed abstinence at this time from the writing of comedies.

[3] Book i, Satire iii.—In the curious Induction to the tragedy called
A Warning for Fair Women, which though not printed till 1599 must have
been acted several years earlier, Tragedy, Comedy, and History inveigh
against one another ; but the taunts directed against Comedy possess no
very special significance. See Collier, ii. 345-8.

[4] Fleay, *History of the Stage*, 157-8.

Lord Chamberlain's, the Lord Admiral's, and Lord Derby's (formerly Lord Strange's), which, after his death in 1594, was absorbed in the Lord Chamberlain's. The fourth company was Lord Pembroke's, which led a fitful existence till 1600. (In addition, there were the Chapel Children, who occupied the Globe from 1600, and after their reinstatement in that year, the Paul's boys[1].) In other words, instead of a more or less indefinite number of migratory companies attached to the households of great nobles, associations of actors were becoming established, which as domesticated in particular places and directed by business-like and reputable men, acquired the confidence, while they held fast the favour, of their public. Gradually the companies and with them the houses with which their performances were more or less identified, began 'to establish a history of their own[2]'—Alleyn and Henslowe, Burbage and Shakspere, became names with a solid ring. At the same time the playwrights were required to satisfy a steady demand, and to meet it quickly and under circumstances not always favourable to a very close discrimination of previous claims as to ideas or their presentment. For better and for worse—and the better had at last secured a basis for its endeavours—the progress of the English drama from the close of the period under discussion onwards connects itself intimately with the annals of the two most long-lived of the companies aforesaid; and Henslowe's *Diary*[3], though of course it contains the records only of the company of which he was joint manager, remains our *vademecum* for this chapter of our dramatic history.

Among dramatic authors who were, as we have seen, so intimately connected with the stage and the theatrical profession proper, a kindly sense of mutual good-will must

Mutual relations among the playwrights.

---

[1] Cf. Fleay, *History of the Stage*, 125 seqq., and *Shakespeare Manual* (1876), 76 *seqq.* As to the distribution of the companies in the several London theatres, see *History of the Stage*, 145.

[2] R. Simpson, *Introduction* to *A Larum for London, or The Seige of Antwerp* (1872), p. iv.

[3] In consequence of the discredit cast upon Collier's well-known edition of Henslowe's *Diary* (*Shakespeare Society's Publications*, 1845), Mr. Fleay has been at the pains of furnishing an abstract of the trustworthy materials contained in it. See his *History of the Stage*, pp. 94-116.

have perpetually asserted itself in the midst of conditions of eager competition. The utmost allowance should always be made for foibles which are practically inevitable; and when bread and fame were simultaneously involved in the question of comparative success, one might be fain to forgive even Greene's attack upon Shakspere. The general kindliness of tone which prevailed among the rival playwrights is, however, shown by many incidental touches of feeling, and no outward sign displays it more pleasantly than the usage that familiarly obtained among them of abbreviating the Christian names of authors, as well as of managers and actors. Even an eager follower of 'sweete Nedde' (Edward Alleyn), while sneering at 'Rossius Richard' (Burbage), disarms our disapproval of his jealous partisanship when he declares that when Ned acts,

> 'Willes new playe
> Shall be rehearst some other daye [1],'—

while at a rather later date, Thomas Heywood, who so chivalrously broke a lance in defence of the actor's art, testified in a score of genial lines to this memorable method of preserving the memory of good fellowship:

> 'Greene, who had in both Academies ta'ne
> Degree of Master, yet could never gaine
> To be call'd more than *Robin;* who, had he
> Profest aught but the Muse, serv'd and been free
> After a seven yeares' prenticeship, might have
> (With credit too) gone Robert to his grave.
> Marlo, renowned for his rare art and wit,
> Could ne're attaine beyond the name of *Kit,*
> Although his Hero and Leander did
> Merit addition rather. Famous Kid
> Was called but *Tom. Tom* Watson, though he wrote
> Able to make Apollo's selfe to dote
> Upon his Muse, for all that he could strive,
> Yet never could to his full name arrive.
> *Tom* Nash (in his time of no small esteeme)
> Could not a second syllable redeeme.

---

[1] So at least runs 'a paper in verse,' quoted by Collier, *Memoirs of Edward Alleyn,* p. 13.—As to Burbage's *sobriquet* of 'Roscio,' cf. Dr. Ingleby's note on Marston's use of it in *The Scourge of Villanie.* (*Shakespeare's Centurie of Prayse,* 2nd ed., p. 27, *New Shakspere Society's Publications,* 1879.)

Excellent Bewmont, in the foremost ranke
Of the rar'st wits, was never more than *Franck.*
Mellifluous Shakespeare, whose enchanting quill
Commanded mirth or passion, was but *Will* ;
And famous Johnson, though his learned pen
Be dipt in Castaly, is still but *Ben.*
Fletcher and Webster, of that learned packe
None of the mean'st, yet neither was but *Jacke.*
Dekker's but *Tom* ; nor May nor Middleton ;
And he's now but *Jacke* Foord that once was John[1].'

Before quitting the subject of the stage, as connected *Intercourse between the German and the English theatre.* with the dramatic literature of this period, I may advert in passing to a relation which has only recently received the attention it merits. Reference has already been incidentally made to the performances of Italian actors in England[2]; and the influence upon our own dramatic literature of that of Italy, Spain, and France, as well as of the prose fiction of those countries, has been or will be illustrated in various passages of this book. Until recently, however, it had been little noticed that in the particular period now under review a lively connexion prevailed between the English drama and the German theatre, which in its turn reacted notably upon the history of the former.

English actors had visited the Continent in the train of English bishops as early as 1417, when they played before the dignitaries assembled at the Council of Constance ; and thus had begun a connexion between the stages and early

---

[1] From T. Heywood's *Hierarchy of the Blessed Angels*, quoted in the Introduction to his *Apology for Actors, Shakesp. Soc. Publ.* 1841. It is perhaps worth remarking that this use of abbreviations is not *necessarily* to be understood as implying kind feeling. See Chapman, *The Gentleman Usher* (iii. 1):   'Nor yet call me Lord,
Nor my whole name Vincentio ; but Vince,
As they calle Jacke or Will, 'tis now in use,
'Twixt men of no equality or kindnesse.'—
In his *Apology* (p. 43), Heywood pays a graceful tribute to the chief actors whom he had known and who were now dead, and to Edward Alleyn who still survived. He adds a wish that 'such as are condemned for their licentiousnesse, might by a generall consent bee quite excluded our society.'

[2] *Ante*, p. 230. The extempore acting of French and Italian players is described, evidently from personal experience, by Middleton, *The Spanish Gipsy* (iv. 2).

dramatic literatures of England and Germany destined to exercise a very enduring influence. In the reign of Elisabeth, it became customary for German and Dutch princes to visit England; and the English stage necessarily attracted much of their attention. One of them—in 1596—speaks of four play-houses in London; the tutor of another mentions the theatres 'without the city' and their numerous audiences. On the other hand, Germany and the Netherlands were from the middle of the same century visited by English musicians and other entertainers in large numbers; and it is certain that Leicester took with him a company of players[1] when in 1585 he went over to the Netherlands to dazzle their inhabitants by his magnificence, and to disgust them by his weakness. In 1586 five Englishmen who had been sent by Leicester to King Frederick II of Denmark transferred their services to the Court of Christian I, Elector of Saxony; they are called 'instrumentalists,' but there were actors among them[2], or they were all actors as well as musicians. Finally, a whole company of English actors crossed the seas under the leadership of Robert Browne in 1590, and after visiting Holland, Zealand, and Friesland, repaired to Germany to exercise their profession.

We have evidence that English players visited Cologne

---

[1] They included, besides Thomas Pope and George Bryan, both of whom were afterwards members of Lord Strange's company, Robert Person, whom Mr. Fleay (*History of the Stage*, p. 83) daringly conjectures to have been Robert Greene (cf. *ante*, pp. 382, note 3, and 403, note 2), and 'jesting Wille,' who is with a greater degree of probability supposed to have been the celebrated actor William Kemp. As to Kemp, see the notice by Mr. S. Lee in vol. xxx. of *The Dictionary of National Biography* (1892), with Collier's revised account of him, iii. 330 *seqq.*, where he shows that Kemp was the original performer of the parts of Dogberry, in *Much Ado about Nothing*, and of Peter in *Romeo and Juliet*. His celebrated narrative entitled *Kemp's Nine Daies Wonder; performed in a Dannce from London to Norwich* (1600), was reprinted by Dyce, with a *Memoir*, for the Camden Society in 1840. In the tract of *An Almond for a Parrat*, Kemp is addressed as 'Vicegerent-generall to the Ghost of Dicke Tarlton,' to whose popularity alone his own stood second.—A very remarkable later tribute to his reputation is the introduction of him with Richard Burbage in *The Returne from Parnessus*, where these two actors as the acknowledged heads of their profession instruct the University students in their art.

[2] Thomas Pope and George Bryan were among them.

in 1592, and reappeared there in different years up to
1612[1]. English comedians are also found in the last years
of the sixteenth, or the early part of the seventeenth century
at Frankfort-on-Maine and at Cassel[2], in the Austrian
dominions[3], at Danzig and Königsberg[4], as well as in
Denmark and Sweden[5]. But the most noteworthy scene of
their performances was the Court of the accomplished Duke
Henry Julius of Brunswick, himself a dramatic author of
repute[6], before whom they played between the years 1602–
1617, and probably earlier. In 1617 English comedians
entered the service of the Elector of Brandenburg[7].

These facts, established on abundant and indisputable
evidence, prove the existence, already in the period here

[1] See a series of articles on *English Players in Cologne*, published by Dr.
L. Ennen in the *Stadt-Anzeiger der Kölnischen Zeitung* (cf. *The Academy*,
February 23, 1878). Cf. A. Cohn, *Englische Komoedianten in Koeln*, in *Jahr-buch*, &c., vol. xxi (1886).

[2] Cf. *Jahrbuch*, &c., vol. xviii. (1883), pp. 268–70; and *Sybel's Historische
Zeitschrift* (1884, 3. *Heft*), pp. 537-8.

[3] See J. Meissner, *Die Englischen Comoedianten zur Zeit Shakespeare's in
Oesterreich* (Vienna, 1884); cf. *Jahrbuch*, vol. xviii (1883). Meissner, who
found few traces of English comedians at Vienna, and none at Prague before
the Thirty Years' War, was extremely successful in his researches at Graz.
He prints in an Appendix a German version of *The Merchant of Venice*,
which can be shown to have been performed in the Styrian capital in the
lifetime of Shakspere (1608).

[4] See A. Hagen in *Jahrbuch*, &c., vol. xv (1880), pp. 325 *seqq.*, referring
for the documents to the same writer's *Geschichte des Theaters in Preussen*.

[5] See Thomas Heywood's *Apology for Actors*, bk. ii. (p. 40, *Shakespeare
Society's* edition); cf. J. Bolte, *Englische Comoedianten in Daenemark und
Schweden*, in *Jahrbuch*, &c., vol. xxiii (1888).

[6] The Brunswick exchequer accounts are missing from 1590 to 1601; the
reign of Henry Julius extended from 1589 to 1601.—A selection of his plays
was edited by Julius Tittmann for his and Goedeke's admirable series
(1880); cf. an essay on his plays in Hermann Grimm's *Fünfzehn Essays*
(*Neue Folge*), 1876.

[7] As to the whole of this notable relation, see A. Cohn, *Shakespeare in
Germany in the Sixteenth and Seventeenth Centuries* (1865); also chap. i. of
R. Genée's *Geschichte der Shakespeare'schen Dramen in Deutschland* (Leipzig,
1870); K. Elze's Introduction to his edition of Chapman's *Alphonsus*
(Leipzig, 1867); C. H. Herford, *u. s.*, p. 218.—Dr. Herford's studies on the
relations between the English and German school-drama will be noticed
below.—Julius Tittmann's edition of a select number of *Schauspiele der
Englischen Komoedianten in Deutschland* (1880) is full of literary interest; it
is based on an edition of these plays published in 1620, and republished in
1624.

designated as that of Shakspere's predecessors, of a close
intercourse between the German and the English stage.
This intercourse merely exemplified in a special way the
intimate connexion which the political as well as the literary
results of the Reformation had brought about between
England and Protestant Germany. The alliance which
Henry VIII had shrunk from drawing closely, had been as
a matter of course concluded by the scholars [1], and from them
had communicated itself to the peoples. The Reformers of
Edward's reign and the refugees of Mary's had derived much
of their intellectual nourishment from German sources; who
would have thought that the poor play-actors were to begin
the repayment of the debt [2]? Yet so it was ; for although
the beginnings of a new German dramatic literature were
not to prove an enduring national growth, they were productive of noteworthy literary fruits; and after the days
of desolation had passed, German literature was to draw
strength from ours in the very sphere where Henry Julius
of Brunswick and Jacob Ayrer had joined hands with
contemporary English dramatists.

It is not, however, of the influence of the English drama
upon the German that it behoves me here to speak. On
the other hand, the counter-influence of German writers and
German subjects, brought home with them by the English
comedians, or set in motion by means of their travels, was
not inconsiderable. We have seen an instance of it in
a work of Marlowe's, and we shall have to return to the
subject in connexion with Dekker's *Fortunatus* and with
other Elisabethan plays [3]. Whatever may be the value of

---

[1] The White Horse Inn at Cambridge, where in the third decade of the
sixteenth century the Reformers held their meetings, became known as
'Germany'; and its frequenters were called 'the Germans.' See Mullinger,
The University of Cambridge, i. (1893) pp. 572-3.

[2] Of Ralph Radclif's tragedy of *The Burning of John Huss*, which might
be regarded as directly connecting the German Reformation with the English
drama, we neither know whether it was in English or Latin, nor whether
it was founded on the German tragedy by J. Agricola. Radclif flourished
under Edward VI, and is mentioned by Bishop Bale in his *Scriptt. Illustt.
Catal*. Cf. Elze, *u. s.*, pp. 16-17.

[3] See, generally, chaps. iv. and v. of Dr. Herford's work, already repeatedly cited.

the evidence in the case of particular plays, the intercourse adverted to is noticeable as connecting our stage and our dramatic literature in its youthful days with those of a nation akin to our own not only in blood and speech, but in the spirit of its moral and intellectual development.

At the close of the period treated in this chapter, *The ex-* the stage, whose fortunes I do not propose further to pursue, *ternals of* was becoming a fashionable resort of the young nobility *the stage.* and their associates, and more especially of those whose amusements were coloured by literary tastes and tendencies. No great significance need, perhaps, be attached to the circumstance that a high-sounding name or two are to be found in the lists of personages credited with occasional contributions to our dramatic literature [1]. But the composition of its audience, which rarely fails to affect the critical reception of a play, usually exercises an anticipatory influence upon its character. In this age criticism, which in the next was in its cruder forms so deeply to vex a writer who like Ben Jonson knew his purpose—and others who may not have been equally sure of theirs—had not yet passed out of its infancy; but some tonic force must have been derived both from the opinion of the more aristocratic spectators, as they sat upon the stage attended by pages with tobacco and pipes [2], and even from the 'grounded judgment and grounded capacities' of the much-abused occupants of the roofless and rush-strewn pit. To describe the externals of the Elisabethan stage is no part of my task; and it must suffice to note only one or two circumstances directly bearing upon the composition of the plays exhibited upon it. In the first place, the construction and decorations of the theatre were of so extreme a simplicity that constant 'change of scene' neither required any effort on the part of the manager, nor interfered with the enjoyment of the spectators [3].' It was effected by drawing up

---

[1] The Earl of Oxford (1562–1604) wrote plays for his men, and is praised by Meres as one of 'the best for Comedy amongst us.' (Fleay, *History of the Stage*, p. 159.) I cannot lay my hand upon a similar tradition as to Lord Strange (Earl of Derby, 1593–4).

[2] Cf. Collier, iii. 157.

[3] Cf. as to the early methods of indicating locality and 'change of scene,'

and down the curtain, which covered the inner portion of
the stage only.   In front, it was requisite that all persons,
whether dead or alive, should be off the scene before it could
be supposed to change; again, no character could be 'discovered' on it in the middle of an act.   Hence the dramatists
found it necessary, to a degree hardly appreciable by writers
for the stage of later days, to make each situation complete
in itself from beginning to end.   On the other hand, the
frequent nominal change of scene constituted no such
irritating perpetual interruption to the progress of the action,
as it would seem if imposed upon a modern audience [1].

The imaginative powers of the spectators, consistently
kept on the stretch, were thus enfeebled by no adventitious
aids worth mentioning.   In the second place, as plays were
acted in the afternoon, the performance had to be com-
pressed into a short space of time ; Shakspere speaks of the
'two hours' traffic of our stage [2],' but probably a rather
more liberal measure of time may have been ordinarily

R. Koppel, *Scenen-Eintheilungen und Orts-Angaben in den Shakespeare'schen
Dramen* in *Jahrbuch, &c.*, vol. ix. (1874).   See also the reference to Haslewood's notes on the subject in the *Publications of the Roxburghe Society*, in
the *Journal of Sir Walter Scott* (1890), pp. 39–40.

[1] Cf. Freytag, *Die Technik des Dramas*, pp. 157 *seqq.*

[2] In the Prologue to *Romeo and Juliet*.   In Davies' sonnet *In Fuscum*
(Ellis's *Specimens*, ii. 37) the man of fashion

> ' first doth rise at ten, and at eleven
> He goes to Gill's where he doth eat till one,
> Then sees a play *till six* and sups at seven ;
> And after supper straight to bed is gone,
> And there till ten next day he doth remain,
> And then he dines and sees a comedy,
> And then he sups and goes to bed again,
> Thus runs he round without variety '—

but also, doubtless, at so leisurely a pace that the timing of his ' movements'
need not be taken quite literally.—Collier, iii. 180, concludes that three
o'clock was the usual hour for the commencement of a performance.   It
seems to have been unusual to perform more than one play in a single afternoon ; but occasionally the entertainment appears to have been prolonged
by a *jig*—a term defined by C. W. Dilke (*Continuation of Dodsley,* 6 vols.
1816, vi. 326), as signifying 'a dramatic performance in rime, every part of
which was *sung* by the performers, and one which was frequently exhibited
on the stage as an Afterpiece, as Farces are at present.'   Cf. *ante*, p. 454, *note*,
as to Tarlton's *Jigge of a horse loade of fooles.*—It seems to have been only on
private stages that performances were by candle, or torch-light ; the public
theatres lay open to the weather.   (Collier, iii. 141.)

allowed.   The fact that plays were performed at these hours of the day is likewise significant as indicating the usual composition of a theatrical audience ; for the busy citizens could hardly have made a practice of deserting their shops, even if they could have waived their principles.   Thus the regular frequenters of the theatre could not but chiefly belong to the idler sections of the population[1].   The prices of admission too seem to have been well adapted to the needs of 'habitual' playgoers[2].   Finally, no respectable woman might appear at a playhouse except with her face concealed under a mask,—a circumstance which, were it not for later experience, would help to account in return for the license that pervades so large a proportion of the Elisabethan drama.   Nor will it be forgotten that women's parts were invariably acted by boys.   This practice which, strange as it may seem to us, was in intention at least owing to a sense of propriety, implied at the same time a further demand upon the vigour of the imagination of the spectators[3].

But these details, and others of the same kind[4], must be left to the historians of the stage.   I have only borrowed from them what seemed necessary in order to illustrate the conditions under which the predecessors of Shakspere, and at the beginning of his professional career Shakspere himself, worked.   It remains to attempt in conclusion to draw the sum of the literary achievements as dramatists of the writers discussed in this chapter.   For the purposes of literary criticism the consideration of external conditions and circumstances of authorship is only of importance in so far as it helps to clear

---

[1] See *ib.* iii. 212 *seqq., On Audiences at Theatres.*   In private theatres plays were usually performed by candle-light, which was out of the question in public theatres, inasmuch as the latter lay partly open to the weather. *Ib.* pp. 140–1.

[2] See *ib.* iii. 146 *seqq., Price of Admission to Theatres.*

[3] Freytag, *u. s.*, p. 159.   In the Induction to *The Downfall of Robert, Earl of Huntington,* when the 'boys' come forward among the players, Skelton exclaims :   'What! our maid Marian, leaping like a lad !'

Julia's pretty pretence of having been made 'to play the woman's part' in the 'pageants of delight' at Pentecost will be remembered (*Two Gentlemen of Verona,* act iv. sc. 4).

[4] See Collier's section, *Properties, Apparel, and Furniture,* iii. 158 *seqq.*

the ground.   Only in what holds its place after this process
has been completed may we find the creations, not of time
and place, but of original genius,—the true parent of what
is immortal in the works of literary and all other art.

*The
measure
of original
genius in
Shakspere's
predeces-
sors.
Lyly.*
      By no means the whole of the dramatic works of
Shakspere's predecessors will bear a scrutiny of this description.   Lyly, unless a charming lyrical gift be taken into
account, has been aptly described as 'a *bel esprit,* but no
poet [1].'   Wit and ingenuity he possessed in abundance ; of
learning he had acquired a fair share; but even the most
characteristic features of the mannerism which made his
prose-romance fashionable and which he could not bring
himself to exclude from the dialogue of his dramas, were due
to an invention not his own.   The dexterity with which he
trod the 'lavoltas high and swift corantos' of his peculiar
style excited the admiration of his age and provoked
imitative efforts on the part of some of his contemporaries,
but his services to the national drama, as a branch of poetic
literature, were limited to the domestication of prose-dialogue
on the stage.   He has no claim to be regarded as occupying
such a position towards the great Elisabethan dramatists,
as e.g. Wieland (to whose literary endowment his own bears
a certain resemblance) holds towards the great classics of
modern German poetic literature.   In his treatment of his
dramatic themes his innate love of artificiality, coupled with
considerations foreign to artistic purpose, led him into an
aberration from the true principles of dramatic composition.
He ciphered personal allegories with so consummate a skill
on the background of classical or pseudo-classical mythology,
that a supreme enjoyment of his plays must be reserved
for the detectives of literary criticism.   Where their learning
has succeeded in finding something like a key, there are no
secrets of genius for it to unlock.   In this direction Lyly
doubtless taught something to the masque-writers of his own

---

[1] See Ulrici, *Shakespeare's Dramatic Art* (English Translation), p. 36.
Exception may, however, be taken to the antithetical oracle which follows,
'that while Tieck is right in maintaining that the commentators of Shakspeare have much to learn from Lyly, the assertion of Schlegel is equally
true, that Shakspeare himself can have learned little or nothing from him.'

age as well as of subsequent generations; but nothing that
really profited it to the legitimate drama. His influence
is traceable in most of his contemporaries, and even in
Shakspere himself; but, with the exception noted above, it
affected only transitory elements in their creations. Happily,
the conditions of the poetic art are such that influences of
this kind vanish from sight, as our attention fixes itself
upon more vital and more significant characteristics.

It was not by exaggerating in the direction of artificiality *English*
the traditions of our earlier drama that the predecessors *dramatic*
literature
of Shakspere began to make the dramatic branch of our *before these*
literature the greatest glory of its growth. They found *writers.*
a drama which, even where popular sources had contributed
to its origin, was artificial by reason of its imitation of
a limited class of models, and which at the same time
was still crude and inadequate in its form. Tragedy
had in choice of subjects and in method of construction
attached itself to the footsteps of Seneca and his Italian
followers; it was essentially epical in its treatment, the
lyrical elements remaining organically unconnected with
the epical; it occupied itself, so to speak, with the statement of an action rather than with its development out of
the characters of the agents. Such was the essential nature
of most of the tragedies described in my second chapter,
from *Gorboduc* to *Tancred and Gismund*, from *Promos and
Cassandra* to *The Misfortunes of Arthur*. The hopeful
beginnings of the historical drama on national subjects, the
Chronicle Histories, or as they were frequently called,
the *True Tragedies*[1], had from the nature of the case even
more distinctly exhibited the same characteristics. On
the other hand, their comparative warmth and energy
of manner had given them an advantage over plays
dissociated in subject from the national consciousness,
and moving in the less congenial spheres of Classical
history and legend, or of foreign romance. Comedy was
still hovering between the imitation of a late Classical
type, the reproduction of 'Italian devises,' the use of the
old mythological and revived pastoral machinery, and the

---

[1] Cf. Fleay, *History of the Stage*, p. 75.

irrepressible desire to introduce, with the incidental ease which comedy hardly ever fails to permit, types of existing manners and of the enduring varieties of human character. Where tragedy and comedy had been combined, their union had been of a perfunctory nature; the comic scenes introduced into the *Chronicle Histories* and cognate plays were manifestly foisted in to gratify inferior tastes; and tragicomedy, or (as Daniel writes it) 'tragic comedy,' was an avowed hybrid, struggling through the mischances which are apt at times to interrupt the orderly evolution of species.

Their preference for heroic tragedy. The genius of the predecessors of Shakspere threw itself with more especial ardour upon the advancement of the tragic stage. The greatness of the times made such a preference imperative in poetic capacities of eminent power. As the genius of Æschylus was in sympathy with the mighty movement of the great Persian wars, so Marlowe and his fellows, but Marlowe pre-eminently, claimed for tragedy the full grandeur of heroic themes. A vast canvas seemed needed for such purposes; and it was spread with no faltering impulse by the authors of *Tamburlaine* and *The Spanish Tragedy*, of *The Battle of Alcazar* and *The Wounds of Civil War*. Nor could subjects of national history fail to commend themselves to a constantly increasing sympathy and to be treated with a new vigour and impetus; in the hands of the author of *Edward II*, at all events, the Chronicle History made a mighty stride in advance towards historical tragedy; and as to the early Histories ascribed to Shakspere, the world is still in doubt whether they were written by him or by his 'predecessors.' However this may be, in the national historical drama of the English stage there is no gulf, there is hardly a gap, to interrupt its onward course. In this branch of their endeavours, the group of writers under discussion were fully adequate to the progressive demands of their literary task.

Sameness and limitation of their tragic themes. But to return. The choice of great themes, of which *Tamburlaine* set the example, in the first instance rather favoured than discouraged an epical manner of treatment, which the dramatic reproduction of the Chronicles seemed to make absolutely indispensable. The contemplation of actions mighty in their dimensions and marvellous in their results overpowered reflexion on their causes, and hindered a patient unfolding of events as the exemplification of moral laws. To will and to achieve seemed the sum of heroic action; to undertake and to fail the full significance of a tragic catastrophe. Marlowe's fiery genius inspired in him a poetic sympathy with passionate resolve, with victorious achievement, with fatal failure. Life in its historic aspect seemed a struggle of man against fate,—it might be said, against the conditions of human life itself. In a less impassioned degree, the view which the other dramatists—Kyd e. g. and Peele—took of the tragic conflict between heroism and circumstance is of the same kind.

Herein they saw but half—and only the smaller half—of the significance of true tragic effect. They knew how to mark with drastic force the great conditions of the conflict, how to express with overpowering energy the terror of the catastrophe. Hence the aberration, of which it is quite needless to cite instances, towards the horrible as a source of effect. Marlowe's want of humour made him a prominent offender in this direction[1]; Greene was of course anxious to outvie him wherever exaggeration was possible; and Kyd succeeded in establishing for himself a renown for efforts of the same kind which will endure with the history of our stage. But none of the dramatists of this period had learnt two of the great lessons taught by the highest examples of the tragic art. They had not learnt that 'vehement passion does not suffice to render a poetic character dramatic[2];' or again, that in the relation of the causation of a tragic conflict to its solution lies the really purifying force of its presentment.

Their extra-vagance in treatment.

Their failure in the former of these respects was the result

---

[1] Hence *Tamburlaine* is not unfairly treated by Hall in his well-known *Satire* (i. 3) as the type of contemporary tragedy, with its 'huff-cap terms and thundering threats.' Melpomene's lament in *The Teares of the Muses* seems to have the same meaning:

'But none more tragick matter I can finde
Than this, of men bereft of sense and minde.'

[2] I venture thus to apply the fine criticism of Gustav Freytag on Lessing; *u. s.*, p. 223.

Defective character- isation.

of an artistic shortcoming. Their obtuseness to the second of these truths sprang from a moral, which was at the same time an artistic, imperfection. The art of dramatic characterisation, in which lies the chief and crowning greatness of Shakspere, was not inherited by him from his predecessors, though in some of them—notably in Marlowe, but also in some measure in Greene and Peele—traces are to be found of its gradual beginnings. The conflict, not between man's power and his will, but between his nature and his will, is the real subject of the noblest dramatic art. Marlowe's Faustus perishes because he attempts more than it is allowed to human skill to attempt; Hamlet, because his will imposes on him a task to which his nature is unequal. What Marlowe only vaguely felt,—that his hero was the author of his own catastrophe,—Shakspere clearly perceived and distinctly expressed. A close study of character is the indispensable preliminary of its successful depiction as a dramatic reality. Marlowe is too impatient to allow the action of his play to develope itself as a logical result out of the nature of the characters taking part in it. Sometimes, as in the *Jew of Malta*, he begins with a powerful endeavour, which the progress of the action fails to sustain; sometimes, as in the *Massacre*, he eschews all efforts in this direction altogether. Among the other contemporary dramatists, Greene, though his hand is lighter, yet shows a surer touch. The natural bent of his genius, and the kind of training which so discursive a literary life as his had bestowed upon it, favoured anything rather than concentrated effort; but his powers of observation had been quickened by varied experience, and in his plays and in other of his works, as well as in those of certain other contemporary writers inferior to him in literary ability, the elements of real dramatic characterisation are distinctly perceptible.

Imperfect morality.

The second chief defect observable in these dramatists I have not scrupled to designate as primarily a moral shortcoming. Yet who can be blind to the truth that in literature—as in the plastic and the pictorial arts, and even in music—ethical laws cannot be ignored if a complete

canon of aesthetics is to be followed? Far from unconscious of the fact that a sequence of moral cause and
effect constitutes the most powerful kind of dramatic action
—as *Edward II, David and Bethsabe*, and other examples
prove,—these writers had not brought home to themselves,
and could not therefore bring home to their audiences,
the true relation between fate and human responsibility.
Revenge, e.g., which was not only so to speak the label of
a whole series of our early tragedies, but which actually
constitutes the main dramatic motive in a large proportion
of their number, is habitually treated as an inevitable law,
as a necessity of fate [1]. Herein ancient classical tragedy might
seem to have furnished a misleading precedent ; but Attic art,
unlike that of Marlowe and his fellows, was able to harmonise
the working of fate with the providence of the gods. For
the Greeks never abandoned the basis of a continuous body
of religious legend ; and even within the bounds of a single
trilogy (as in the Oedipodean of Sophocles, or the conjectured
Promethean of Aeschylus) their great masters were able to
make it clear that the tragic consummation is not fear but
hope. Victory is the goddess appealed to at the close of more
than one Greek tragedy; and none of its extant masterpieces preaches the dull, dead fallacy of the irresistible
power of circumstance.

But, apart from the question of such precedents, a tragedy
which is complete in itself can at all times indicate the
solution of its conflict, so long as it allows no doubt to remain
as to its true causation. The solution lies in the eternal
justice of the great moral laws, vindicated by the sufferings
which their violation entails and which call forth pity and
terror in the beholder. Who can fail to recognise this solution
in *Richard III*, in *Coriolanus*, in any of Shakspere's mature
tragedies ; who but will seek it in vain in most of the works
of his predecessors?

I have spoken of some of the main defects of these *Summary*
dramatists as tragedians ; but not, I trust, in any spirit of *of the advance*
depreciation or of futile cavil. The advance was, taken as *achieved*
a whole, enormous which they had made, in choosing great *in tragedy.*

---

[1] Cf. on this head Gervinus, *Shakespeare*, vol. i. p. 91.

subjects for tragic treatment,—in sustaining and developing the dramatic reproduction of important historical themes, more particularly such as were consecrated by national tradition,—in claiming for passion its right of adequate expression,— in essaying, however tentatively, the art of dramatic characterisation.   If we are justified, as later dramatists seem to have instinctively felt themselves justified [1], in regarding the age of Shakspere's predecessors as distinct from that of Shakspere himself, we shall not, I think, regard the former as one of mere crude effort, while recognising the latter as one of perfect consummation. Historical parallels are always dangerous ; and a comparison between Marlowe and Peele on the one hand, and Klinger and Lenz on the other, in their respective relations to Shakspere and to Goethe, would be delusive in spite of its speciousness.   The young men of the *Sturm und Drang* lacked what Marlowe and his fellows possessed in manifest abundance—creative genius.

Comedy.   In comedy the advance had been less decisive ; and in no branch of the drama is Shakspere's originality more marked than in the new spirit which he infused into the English comic drama, amidst difficulties to which his efforts seem to have temporarily succumbed.   Lyly had done much to facilitate freedom of form, and something (even though in a mistaken direction) to widen the range of subjects; the combination, in such writers as Greene, Lodge, and Nashe, of novelistic and pamphleteering with dramatic productivity, had enlarged the scope of our comic drama to an extent that will perhaps excuse the relative length at which I have dwelt upon the non-dramatic productions of these writers.

Dangers of a redundance of witty dialogue.   Yet a superabundance of wit and a keen interest in the more or less transitory ' problems ' of the times, serviceable as it is at all times to the essayist, and even to the novelist of certain kinds, is a danger and a snare to such writers when they essay the drama.   Unless the wit and the satirical

---

[1] So Thos. Heywood speaks of Marlowe as ' the best of poets *in that age*,' seeming, as the late Mr. Collier (*Memoirs of E. Alleyn*, p. 10) pointed out, to imply a distinction between it and the age of Shakspere, whom he can hardly have intended to rank beneath Marlowe.

purpose of the author are subordinated to his dramatic intention, his comic characterisation, in which lies the real secret of supreme comic effect, will suffer for the sake of mere brilliancy, or at least scintillation, of dialogue. A peculiar danger in this respect beset our earlier dramatists *The clowns.* in consequence of the usage allowing full license of comic extravagance to the clown, whose ambition it was to say very much more than was set down for him. Tarlton and Kemp were not 'hampered,' as a modern comic actor has humorously phrased it, by a prohibition against adding anything of their own [1].

The way out of the difficulty lay in the construction of *Beginnings* effective plots, for which a full storehouse was prepared in *of romantic comedy* the popular traditions preserved in national ballads, and in the growing literature of translated foreign fiction, or of native imitations of it. In the former, Greene at least found materials for comic dramatic writing of the highest promise ; Peele came perhaps nearest to him, nor should Munday's endeavours be overlooked. The aberration of the *in peril of* comic stage at the close of this period, towards an active *extinction.* participation in political and religious controversy, has probably been exaggerated in its significance ; but it marked a danger to which comedy is at all times peculiarly exposed.

To one further point it seems necessary to advert in con- *Blank verse* clusion. In no respect had a greater advance been made *and prose.* by Shakspere's predecessors than in that of the outward form of dramatic composition,—in diction and versification. Here again the most effective impulse had been given by Marlowe, when by his *Tamburlaine* he established blank verse as our English dramatic metre. Not long before—in his translation of Ariosto's *Suppositi*—Gascoigne had given

---

[1] Hall in the *Satire* already cited dwells with special anger on the antics of the clown, who ' comes leaping in,' and
　　' laughs, and grins, and frames his mimic face,
　　And justles straight into the prince's place.'—
See a curious paper by Dr. B. Nicholson in *New Shakspere Society's Transactions* (1880) as to the personal relations of Tarlton and Kemp to the play of *Hamlet*, which philosophises so decisively on the fool's place in the drama. As to the 'jigs,' cf. *ante*, p. 476, *note* 2.

the first example of the use of prose in comedy [1], and Lyly had by a series of works given permanency to the use in question. The two innovations taken together supplied the adequate formal materials for Shakspere's art. So long as rimed couplets (varied by artificial stanza-forms) and a monotonously inflexible kind of blank-verse were the only alternatives, true life was impossible to dramatic diction. Marlowe's original tendency was to let each line stand by itself, marking off the sense with the metre; and it was for this reason that he forged his lines with so redundant a vigour of expression. But this could only be a transitional phase of blank verse, and varied even in Marlowe's own practice. As to the management of the metre, Shakspere surpassed his predecessors in freedom; but this was now merely a question of degree; the process itself had been indicated to him by the greatest of his predecessors. Nor was the free use of prose in comic passages less favourable to the emancipation of the English drama from the trammels of tradition. Lyly who used prose in all—or nearly all—his plays, although he tortured his diction, like a rider twisting his horse when anxious to appear at his best, did good service by establishing the right of 'unbound speech' to be free of the stage. The great masters of dramatic comic dialogue, Shakspere and Ben Jonson, knew how to profit by the inheritance.

Shakspere's predecessors deserving of high individual consideration. The conclusion of which these brief remarks may help to illustrate the grounds, will, I think, be regarded as sufficiently established. The Elisabethan drama before Shakspere shares with his earliest works many characteristics, and some of them it shares with the masterpieces of his genius. No promise was ever followed by so marvellous a consummation; but neither has any other master of his art ever had predecessors so worthy of him. The mighty figures of Marlowe and his fellows—whether we call them by the title which has here been assigned by them, or whether we reverence them in their own right—occupy pedestals from which they will never be deposed in the House of Fame.

[1] Gervinus, *Shakespeare*, i. 98.

CHAPTER IV.

SHAKSPERE.

WE speak of a Homeric Age, thereby intending to indi- *Shakspere* cate very much more than merely the age in which the *not the* Homeric poems were produced, or the age to which their *representa-* narrative and descriptions relate. By the Homeric Age of *particular* Greece we mean an entire period in the history of country *age.* and people; Homer is to us the representative and the mirror of this period, as fully and thoroughly as Pericles is of another.

No such tribute has ever been paid by the most enthusiastic of his worshippers to the memory of Shakspere. A sound national instinct has preferred to designate the era of our literary as of our general history, on which his name sheds a brighter light than is reflected from that of any of his contemporaries, by an epithet comprehensive in its very vagueness and opportune in spite of its inaccuracy. In speaking of the Elisabethan Age, we think of a period of our national life animated by tendencies common to all its noteworthy forms of expression, and thus forming a whole by itself, though not in consequence cut off from connexion with its predecessors and its successors. Shakspere is not the microcosm of his age,—for this he was in a sense too great, and in another sense imperfectly qualified. On the one hand, a genius such as Shakspere's, be it fearlessly said though for the thousandth time, belongs to no age and to no country exclusively. On the other, the circumstances in which he was placed and to which his creative activity readily accommodated itself, were not of a kind to enable him to enter in every important respect into the full current of national progress, or to reach one hand forward into the phase of national life which was to succeed that of his own days. He was neither a Bacon nor a Ralegh, yet he became more to his nation than either of these. The legacy which he left to that nation was not one of which it could immediately enter into full possession; and it was long before the generations which succeeded him became fully or truly conscious of the wealth which he had bequeathed to them.

Shakspere as a national poet. And yet, in these latter days at all events, who would deny that Shakspere has become the property of the nation, not less than of the world at large? How many an Englishman has in a wider sense of the phrase done what the eloquent Hungarian patriot is said to have done literally, and taught himself the English language out of Shakspere's pages! How many a student, excluded by circumstances from experience of the world, has sought and found in Shakspere a richer and more varied knowledge of human life and character than could have been gained by long years of familiarity with Court and Senate, with camp and market-place! How many an imagination, in danger of being dulled and emasculated by the influence of a conventional selection of moral, or isolation of æsthetical, rules, has with the aid of Shakspere ranged far beyond and soared far above them! Him at least a wholly exceptional feeling of national reverence has consecrated against proscription; his name is placed on no Index of prudery or prejudice; he at least is allowed to teach our youth what a glorious and manysided thing is life, and how the wings of the mind were not meant to be demurely folded, for the drill-sergeant in the pay of tradition or fashion to examine and approve. Those who have some experience of the ordinary literary studies of Englishmen know that to many of our countrymen Shakspere is, besides the Bible, the only poetic literature worthy of the name which they possess. This national service at all events he has rendered to us; and were another Somerset to burn our libraries, and another Long Parliament to pull down our theatres, they could not destroy our poetic literature, because Shakspere at least has struck his roots into the people's heart.

But all this has been the work of centuries ; it was the achievement of Shakspere's genius, not of a Shaksperean age. In the period preceding the Elisabethan, there existed no higher secular literature which was, properly speaking, the possession of the English nation. Unacquainted with what it possessed, it therefore did not possess it. The leading poets were scholars and courtiers, trained on much Latin and a little Greek, or familiarised by travel or study with certain models of Italian literature. Chaucer and his school were mostly forgotten, even when the sources of ballads surviving or arising among the population might be found in their productions. Surrey and Wyatt and their successors, Sidney and even Spenser himself, with their sonnets and odes and allegories in prose and verse, had neither aimed at nor succeeded in popularising higher poetic literature. The chroniclers in prose and their adapters in verse followed the chapmen of more frivolous wares with no very buoyant or frequent step into the homes of the people. The stage had at last furnished a field for the growth of a literature which was of its nature essentially popular, while it admitted of the loftiest poetic aims. Men of talent, quite recently even men of genius, had begun to awake to so splendid an opportunity. But the labours of playwright, actor, and manager were still hopelessly mixed up in form as well as in fact ; and the excitement or amusement of the hour still seemed to constitute the main purpose of both authors and audiences. In the eyes of the age the drama had not yet made good its claim to be admitted into the domain of literature [1].

Uncertainty of the position of dramatic authors at the time of the beginning of Shakspere's career.

When, therefore, Shakspere came up to London as a youth ambitious of trying his fortune, there lay before him

The choice before him.

---

[1] Of this various illustrations have been already given ; a significant one may be found in the fact, noted by Malone, that only thirty-eight (or thirty-nine) original plays are extant which were printed in or before 1592. This need not exhaust, but probably approaches, the number of plays which either their authors deemed worthy of printing, or publishers thought likely to ensure success as printed works. See *Historical Account of the English Stage*, p. 6.

the choice of entering the old or the new sphere of literary life. If he desired literary fame, in the circles which regarded themselves and which were regarded by men of letters as its dispensers, he would have to seek it by such compositions as those which perhaps he brought with him in embryo to London, which at all events were early fruit, and which yet more than equalled in merit most of what poets of acknowledged reputation had produced for the entertainment of lords and ladies, and for the satisfaction of academical critics. How far such patronage and approval might bring bread as well as honour was of course a different question. On the other side there stood the stage, supported as a pastime by a rather different assortment of the same kind of patrons, or relying amidst dangers and difficulties upon its popularity among the lower orders. Here in return for hard toil, for a willingness and an aptitude to meet the tastes of various kinds of supporters (but nearly all staunch, according to the habit of playgoers), a prospect opened of modest gain, unaccompanied however by that of a dignified social position; and here too a golden opportunity of displaying the full vigour of conscious genius awaited him who would not shrink from the toils and troubles

He chooses the stage. of an inevitable apprenticeship. Shakspere, without by any means abandoning the design of pleasing by literary offerings of the other kind, chose the stage as his career in life, and the drama as his proper field of literary effort.

Result of this choice. The motives which determined this choice are unknown, but its effect was that Shakspere at once and for ever associated his genius with the current which popularised and nationalised our poetic literature.

Opinion of Shakspere as a dramatist among his literary contemporaries: The importance of the writer who had begun his labours among the rival playwrights gradually made itself felt among his contemporaries. At first, anxious above all to make his way, anxious therefore from the outset to be at work, he may be assumed to have addressed himself to what lay nearest to his hand; and as a theatrical adapter to have taught himself the secrets of his craft. Success may fairly be supposed to have waited upon his preliminary endeavours, and to have carried him rapidly forward into the sphere of original dramatic productivity[1]. The much-vext supposition—which indeed has with unspeakable persistency been turned round and round like the veriest cabbage—that in this the earliest stage of his activity as a playwright he incurred the charge of having unscrupulously seized upon the intellectual property of others, cannot be held to rest upon convincing proof. It has been expanded into conclusions as to Shakspere's ubiquitous activity as writer for the various companies of players then performing in London which find no support whatever in any known facts belonging to the contemporary history of the English stage. The notorious accusation preferred against Shakspere in *Greene's Groatsworth of Wit*, published in 1592, after the writer's death, is probably, though not quite certainly, the earliest extant contemporary notice of him. No shadow of doubt rests upon the conclusion that Shakspere was the object of this invective; there must be allowed to be less certainty whether it refers to him in his 'quality' as an actor only, an interpretation to which I for one am on the whole inclined to subscribe[2].

[1] The ensuing references to 'opinion upon Shakspere' have been revised with the aid, so far as the range of these collections extends, of the late Dr. Ingleby's *Shakespeare's Centurie of Prayse*, second edition, revised, with many additions, by Lucy Toulmin Smith, *New Shakspere Society's Publications*, 1879, in conjunction with Dr. Furnivall's *Some 300 Fresh Allusions to Shakspere, from 1594 to 1694 A.D.*, *New Shakspere Society's Publications*, 1886.

[2] See *Greene's Groatsworth of Wit* (1592), reprinted by Dr. Ingleby in *Part I* of *Shakspere Allusion-Books*, *New Shakspere Society's Publications*, 1874. The passage which forms part of the author's warning to his three fellow-playwrights (*ante*, p. 383, note 3) to abandon, as he had done, the composition of plays, runs as follows: 'Base minded men al three of you, if by my miserie ye be not warned: for vnto none of you (like me) sought those burres to cleaue: those Puppits (I meane) that speake in our mouths, those Articks garnisht in our colours. Is it not strange that I, to whom they al haue beene beholding: is it not like that you, to whom they al haue beene beholding, shall (were ye in case that I am now) be both at once of them forsaken? Yes, trust them not: for there is an vpstart Crow, beautified with our feathers, that with his *Tygers heart wrapt in a Players hide*, supposes he is as well able to bumbast out a blanke verse as the best of you, and being an absolute *Iohannes fac totum*, is in his owne conceit the onely Shakescene in a countrie.' The bearing of the allusion which this passage certainly contains to a line in *The True Tragedie of the Duke of Yorke, and the good King Henrie the Sixt*, which was transferred into *Part III* of *Henry VI*

In the following year (1593), a second contemporary dramatist who had been the agent of the publication of Greene's posthumous charge, proffered a kind of apology for such thoughtlessness as it might seem to imply in his own case, paying a tribute at the same time to the moral character, is reported to him on respectable authority, of the subject of this special libel, as well as to both his histrionic and his literary powers [1]. It thus appears that at a time when Shakspere was at the very beginning of his career as a dramatic writer he had already in this capacity conciliated the regard of estimable personages whom we

(act i. sc. 4), upon the question of the authorship of these plays, will be more appropriately discussed below; here it must suffice to point out that at the most it accentuates, or imparts a subsidiary sting to the general intention of the attack, by implying that the conceited actor had also been guilty of 'conveying' other men's property in his capacity as a playwright. For I feel convinced that alike the context of the passage (which for this reason I have been compelled to cite) and his general fashioning of this indictment, and in particular the obvious intention of the word *Shake-scene* (which Dr. Ingleby even, and I confess to my mind very plausibly, regards as a nick-name), are directed against the *actor*, and not against the *author*.

[1] See Chettle, *Kind-hartes Dreame* (*Shakspere Allusion Books, Part I, u. s.,* and *Percy Society's Publications,* vol. vi.). The Address *to the Gentlemen Readers* prefixed to this tract is dated December 8, 1592, but it was doubtless not published till early in the ensuing year. The passage referred to in the text runs as follows: 'The other, whome at that time I did not so much spare, as since I wish I had, for that as I have moderated the heate of living writers and might have usde my owne discretion (especially in such a case), the Author beeing dead, that I did not, I am as sory, as if the originall fault had beene my fault, because my selfe have seene his demeanor no lesse civill than he exelent in the qualitie he professes: Besides, divers of worship have reported his uprightnes of dealing, which argues his honesty, and his facetious grace in writing, that aprooves his Art.' The conclusion that the person thus praised was Shakspere, and not Nashe (as the late Mr. Staunton seems to have held), was I think clearly established by the late Mr. R. Simpson in a letter to *The Academy* (April 11, 1874) and may be said to command general assent. The term 'qualitie,' it may be added, is that constantly applied distinctively to the actor's profession. Hamlet (act ii, sc. 2) invites the players to give him 'a taste of their quality'; in Massinger's *The Roman Actor* (act i. sc. 3) Aretinus accuses 'the quality' of treason in the person of the tragedian Paris, 'the chief of his profession.' See Clark and Wright's note to their edition of *Hamlet,* p. 159; and cf. among numerous other examples, the address 'To my good Friends and Fellows the City-Actors,' prefixed by Thomas Heywood to his *Apology for Actors* (1612). Nashe is not known to have ever trod (or 'shaken') the boards; and the fact that he bestowed on Greene's pamphlet the epithets of 'scald, triviall, lying,' is not necessarily to the purpose.

shall certainly not shrink from describing as competent judges. In the following year (1595) at latest, and possibly already four years earlier, the most illustrious of his poetic contemporaries is believed to have paid to him the tribute of a sympathetic allusion. The supposition that the reference of Thalia, in Spenser's *Teares of the Muses*, to the recent 'death' of 'our pleasant Willy' as contributory to the downfall of the comic stage, may indeed be set aside as discredited [1]. But in *Colin Clouts come home again* (published in 1595, but held to have been written as early as 1591, though in a form afterwards amplified), one of Spenser's most striking personal allusions is couched in phraseology which certainly fits Shakspere better than any other contemporary poet [2]. If it is to him that the lines in question refer, the compliment they convey may however have been occasioned by one or more of his non-dramatic poems, the chief of which were by the year 1594 already before the public or circulating among personal and literary friends [3]. The earliest notice that can with tolerable certainty

Spenser (1595?).

Other early notices.

---

[1] I need not here enter into the question whether, as Mr. Fleay thinks is certain, the allusion is to Lyly.

[2]   'And there, though last not least is *Aetion*,
    A gentler shepheard may no where be found,
    Whose Muse, full of high thoughts invention,
    Doth like himselfe Heroically sound.'

Mr. Halliwell-Phillips' remark that 'the lines seem to apply with equal propriety to Warner' does not carry conviction ; nor can I subscribe to the late Professor Minto's opinion that a claim may be put in for Drayton, whose assumed poetic name 'Rowland' he thought 'sounded in those days much more heroically than *Shakespeare*.' Mr. Fleay supported this hypothesis with the aid of another, founded on an etymology of the word Aetion (αἴτιον), which I humbly conceive to be out of the question. If on the other hand the word is connected with ἀετός and signifies ' eaglet ' (as I think Professor Hales has sufficiently established), Mr. Fleay thought Marlowe might have been intended. But I have no space for entering into the minutiae of this delightful controversy.

[3] See the references to *The Rape of Lucrece* (printed 1594) in the anonymous verses prefixed to Henry Willobie's *Avisa* (1594), and in the lines attributed by Sir Egerton Brydges to Sir William Herbert (1594). The allusions to *Venus and Adonis* (printed 1593), by Robert Southwell (1594 ?), and to *Lucrece* in Drayton's *Legend of Matilda* (1594) cannot be convincingly brought home to Shakspere. (As to a later praise of Shakspere by Drayton, see below.) On the other hand I am inclined to think him the W. S. of the verse dialogue in the *Avisa* aforesaid, where (on the strength no doubt of his *Sonnets*) he appears as an expert in the tender passion, to whose

be stated to refer to a play undoubtedly Shakspere's belongs to this very year, when a *Comedy of Errors* was chosen as the chief part of their Christmas entertainment by the members of Gray's Inn[1]. We are thus justified in concluding that by this date his genius as a writer had, in one or another branch of his literary activity, inspired with sympathy some of the young and ambitious spirits on whom England's future seemed largely to depend. If, neglecting divers unmistakeable allusions to Shakspere's non-dramatic poems and the almost equally open flattery of manifest imitation from two of his plays in a comedy dating from the interval[2], we look a few years forward, we arrive at the testimony of a literary censor, who whether or not possessed of the gift of nice discrimination, was animated by what in the age to which he belonged was far more rare, viz. a wish to express his admiration of what he thought

Meres (1598). admirable. In 1598 Francis Meres, who very legitimately applied a method which becomes childish only when employed in the service of prejudice or whim[3], in his *Palladis Tamia* (*Wits Treasury*) mentioned Shakspere both as one of 'our best for Tragedie,' and as one of 'the best for Comedy amongst us,' besides including him in the list of 'the most passionate among us to bewaile and bemoane the perplexities of Love.' It is true that in 'Tragedy' he is here enumerated *pari passu* with 'the *Authour of the Mirrour for Magistrates*,' and with nearly all the writers, epical or dramatic, who in the Tudor age had with a more or less conspicuous success treated themes of a serious nature;

quality as an actor an allusion seems to be conveyed. *Centurie of Prayse,* *u. s.,* 1–14.

[1] See the account of the performance of 'a Comedy of Errors (like to *Plautus* his *Menaechmus*),' at Gray's Inn on the night of Innocents' Day, December 28, 1594, in Henry Helmes' MS. *Gesta Grayorum,* cited in Nichols' Progresses and in Furnivall's *Fresh Allusions, u. s.,* 1.

[2] See *Centurie of Prayse,* 15–20.—The passages in *Wily Beguiled* imitated from *The Merchant of Venice* and *Romeo and Juliet* are of importance on the assumption; as to which Mr. Fleay (*English Drama,* ii. 159) entertains no doubt that the original date of this play is 1596–7.

[3] Byron notoriously employed it in this way; but I do not know why he should be blamed for having done so, since he was guiltless of publishing the tables of poetic precedence which he must surely be allowed to have had the right of constructing for his own amusement.

while in 'Comedy' he is made to stand shoulder by shoulder with practitioners from Richard Edwardes down to Anthony Munday. But the proof remains that his reputation was at this early date established with a completeness to which it would be difficult to find anything in the nature of an analogy. During the progress of his literary career, of which his activity as a playwright was not always so liberally and distinctly acknowledged to form part as it had been in Meres' summary, a series of other writers, considerable or the reverse, supplemented his estimate by more or less perfunctory comparisons of their own [1].

During his lifetime not a few wholly personal tributes of praise were paid to his eminence in the various branches of his activity as an author. As early as 1599 John Weever printed among his *Epigrammes*, thought by Dyce [2] to have been written earlier, a set of lines *Ad Gulielmum Shakespeare*, possessing little or no intrinsic merit, but exhibiting

Weever (1599).

---

[1] See for all these the collections cited above. Richard Barnefeild (*Poems in divers humors*, 1598) compares Shakspere with Spenser, Daniel, and Drayton, but makes no allusion to his dramatic writings. John Bodenham (*Belvedere, or The Garden of the Muses*, 1600) asks the attention of his readers to the flowers which he has gathered into his works from a few 'Moderne and extant Poets,' among whom Shakspere finds a place not unworthy of his name.—Camden (*Remaines*, 1604) contents himself with including Shakspere in a not dissimilar list of 'the most pregnant witts of these our times.' In a more extensive list, arranged 'according to their' (chronological) 'priorities as neere as I could,' Edmund Howes (*Continuation of Stow's Chronicle*, 1615), sets down 'M. Willi. Shakespeare gentleman' between William Warner and Samuel Daniel. Drummond of Hawthornden (in a passage in his *Works* which internal evidence proves to have been written not earlier than 1614) assigned to Shakspere a late place, in more senses than one, among 'the authors he had seen on the subject of Love'; but on two earlier occasions (in 1606 and in 1611) he had noted several of Shakspere's plays or poems among books possessed by him. See also the *Life of Drummond*, by Professor Masson, p. 104, where it is noted that Drummond was 'one of Shakspere's earliest admirers in Scotland, and had his well-fingered copies of Shakespeare's Poems and three of his Plays on his bookshelves.' With direct reference to the merits as a dramatist of his great predecessor and contemporary, Webster (Dedication to *Vittoria Corombona*), 1612) extolled the prolific art, or as he phrased it, 'the right happy and copious industry' of Shakspere in terms equally felicitous and liberal, but made no distinction between his claims on either head, and those of Dekker and Thomas Heywood.

[2] *Life of Shakespeare*, p. lxv.

Chettle (1603).

a warm admiration for both plays and poems composed by this 'honie-tong'd' author. In similar phrase, Henry Chettle, who in 1593 had been so anxious to set himself with regard to his declared opinion of a rising young actor and writer, in a tract composed on the death of Queen Elisabeth and published in conjunction with an account of her burial (April 28, 1603), lamented that

'The silver tongèd Melicert,'

by whom as the context shows he meant Shakspere, should have as yet dropped 'from his honied muse' no 'sable teare'

> 'To mourne her death that gracèd his desert
> And to his laies opend her Royall eare[1].'

John Davies of Hereford (1611 c.).

During the last few years of Shakspere's life these tributes became more frequent. About 1611, John Davies of Hereford addressed one of the epigrams contained in *The Scourge of Folly*[2] to 'our English Terence, Mr. Will. Shakespeare.' Alluding, apparently, to his profession as an actor, and (though this may be a mere trick or phrase) to the jealousies excited by his talents, these lines pay a very notable tribute not only to his literary eminence, but to the high character maintained by him in all his dealings; for

> 'raile as they thinke fit,
> Thou hast no rayling, but a raigning Wit;
> And honesty thou sow'st, which they do reape.'

Freeman (1614).

In a collection of epigrams, published in 1614 under the title of *Runne and a Great Caste*[3], Thomas Freeman, in

---

[1] *Englandes Mourning Garment*, quoted by Collier in *Introduction* to *The Death of Robert, Earl of Huntington, u. s.*, p. 4, and in Ingleby's *Centurie of Prayse*. Dr. Hales pointed out long since (in a letter to *The Academy*, January 10, 1874) that the name Melicert was doubtless applied to Shakspere because of its supposed derivation from μέλι. As the late Mr. J. A. Symonds reminded the readers of the same Journal (January 24), the name is mentioned by Suidas as having been given to Simonides διὰ τὸ ἡδύ. Neither Hales nor Symonds, however, had any very satisfactory explanation of the -κέρτης to offer.

[2] Reprinted in his *Works*, edited by Dr. Grosart for his *Chertsey Worthies Library*, vol. xviii.

[3] Forming, apparently, Part II of *Rubbe and a great Caste*.

rather leaden-footed verse, lauded Shakspere's facility of poetic composition :

> 'At th' horse-foote fountain thou hast drunk full deepe,
> Vertues or vices theame to thee all one is';

and asserts that from his plays

> . . . 'needy new-composers borrow more
> Then *Terence* doth from *Plautus* or *Menander.*'

In the same year a more noted pen, that of Christopher Brooke, paid the following tribute to Shakspere's dramatic and poetic genius, supposed to be delivered by the hero of one of his most powerful historical tragedies (*Richard III*[1]) : *Brooke (1614).*

> 'To him that impt my fame with Clio's quill,
> Whose magick rais'd me from oblivion's den ;
> That writ my story on the Muses' hill,
> And with my actions dignifi'd his pen ;
> He that from Helicon sends many a rill,
> Whose nectared veines are drunke by thirstie men ;
>   Crown'd be his stile with fame, his head with bayes ;
>   And none detract, but gratulate his praise.'

Of the appreciation conveyed by allusion—occasionally trenching more or less closely upon imitation or reproduction —enough assuredly reached Shakspere even during his lifetime[2] to answer the first cause of so modest a stimulant. Criticism (in the true sense of the term) had scarcely dawned upon his age as a conscious form of intellectual effort ; and only a very faint impression could have been made upon him by casual cynicisms, such as those which in 1604 *Hamlet* suggested to a 'friendly' writer, who anticipated *Contemporary allusions to Shakspere's writings.*

---

[1] This poem, entitled *The Ghost of Richard III*, was reprinted by the late Mr. Collier for the Old Shakespeare Society, and by Dr. Grosart in his edition of Brooke's *Complete Poems* (*Fuller Worthies' Library*, 1872).

[2] Going over the passages in the authorities cited, one may gather that Shakspere would have been *primâ facie* justified in perceiving 'allusions' to his writings in passages contained in plays by Peele, Armin, Munday, Day, Henry Porter, Jonson, Beaumont and Fletcher, Dekker, Chapman, Middleton, Marston, Webster, Thomas Heywood, Lewis Machin, Edward Sharpham, Ludovic Barrey, and Robert Tailor ; or in passages of the published writings of authors to be classified so variously (if classified at all) is the following : Gabriel Harvey, Robert Tofte, John Lane, Samuel Nicholson, Thomas Rokesley, Nicholas Breton, and Richard Brathwaite. (I have omitted in this list names already mentioned in my text of writers who referred to Shakspere in his lifetime, as well as any reference to anonymous allusions.)

a very common, and often very shallow, censure of his general method as a tragic dramatist [1]. Yet I cannot but think that, whatever may have been Shakspere's personal relations to the author of the *Parnassus* plays (1597–1601), supposing that they came under his notice, he must have relished the element of true humour in their criticisms of his own productions. In Part ii. he has the dubious honour of being quoted by a fashionable fool as his favourite poet [2], but in Part iii., while in the famous review of poets his non-dramatic poems are described as at once irresistible in their charm and censurable because of the effeminacy of their themes [3], the audience of Cambridge students is told a home-truth about his plays and their excellence by ' one who knows'—one of the two famous actors who have come down to the University to instruct them in their art [4].

After Shakspere's death, occasional literary tributes were paid to his achievements by John Taylor, the Water Poet (1620 c.), William Basse (1622) [5], and others ; nor would it have been according to human nature had not allusive

---

[1] I refer to the passage in *The Epistle to the Reader*, prefixed by Anthony Scoloker to his *Daiphantus, or The Passion of Love* (1604), a work containing a notable allusion to *Hamlet*, in which, illustrating his observation by the chief personage of that play, the writer refers to '*Friendly Shakespeare's Tragedies*, where the *Commedian* rides, when the *Tragedian* stands on Tip-Toe' (*Centurie of Prayse*, p. 64).

[2] After Gallio's first quotation (from *Venus and Adonis*), Ingenioso exclaims : ' We shall have nothing but pure Shakspeare and shreds of poetrie that he hath gathered at the theatres ' (Act iii. sc. 1). ' Let this duncified worlde,' says Gallio himself further on, 'esteeme of Spencer and Chaucer, I'le worshipp sweet Mr. Shakespeare, and to honoure him will lay his Venus and Adonis under my pillowe,' &c. &c. (Act iv. sc. 1).

[3] '*William Shakespeare.*

> Who loues not Adons loue or Lucrece rape?
> His sweeter verse contains hart-throbbing line.
> Could but a grauer subiect him content,
> Without loues foolish lazy languishment.'—(Act i. sc. 2).

The reading of the last two words in the second of the above lines is uncertain.

[4] '*Kemp.* Few of the vniuersity [men] pen plaies well . . . Why heres our fellow Shakespeare puts them all downe, I and Ben Ionson too ' (Act iv. sc. 5). In the same scene Burbage bids one of the amateurs recite the opening lines of *Richard III*.

[5] Basse's elegy is alluded to in the famous lines of Ben Jonson mentioned below.

borrowings from his works increased rather than diminished in frequency. When in 1623 Shakspere's two fellow-actors, John Heminge and Henry Condell, ensured to themselves an imperishable remembrance[1] by publishing the first collective edition of his plays—the famous First Folio— four of his contemporaries, of whom besides Ben Jonson Leonard Digges[2] had made himself a literary name, contributed commendatory verses to the volume. Ben Jonson's judgment of Shakspere is a question of moment, more especially however as affecting our estimate of Jonson himself. For the present it will suffice to note the sympathetic appreciation pervading the lines,—in my judgment on the whole as just as they are beautiful,—*To the Memory of my beloved, the Author Mr. William Shakespeare, and what he hath left us*, written by Jonson together with the verses *On the Portrait of Shakespeare* for insertion in the First Folio, and reprinted in his *Underwoods*[3]. His criticism, probably written down not long before his own death (1637) and printed in *Timber, or Discoveries made upon Men and Matter*, as to certain 'defects of excess' in Shakspere's productivity, is not less kindly candid; as for his 'conversational' growls to Drummond (registered in 1619), they must go for what they are worth, which is in truth not very much[4]. Of the personal sentiments entertained towards Shakspere by other of his fellow-dramatists we have few traces, if we

Ben Jonson, Leonard Digges, and others (1623).

[1] Just as I am revising these sheets, I read of the unveiling by the Lord Mayor on Wednesday, July 8, 1896, of a monument to the editors of the First Folio at St. Mary the Virgin's, Aldermanbury.

[2] He was an accomplished modern as well as classical scholar, and the translator of several works. See the notice of him by Mr. S. Lee in vol. xv. of *The Dictionary of National Biography* (1888).—The remainder of these commendatory poems are signed by Hugh Holland and 'Z. M.'; the latter signature has been attributed to John Marston, Jasper Mayne, and James Mabbe—to the last-named with some little show of probability. See *Centurie of Prayse, u. s.*, p. 155.

[3] Pope says—and as it seems to me is perfectly justified in saying—'that he cannot for his own part find anything *Invidious* or *Sparing* in these verses, but wonders Mr. Dryden was of that opinion.' (See *Preface* to Pope's edition of Shakspere.)—Dr. Ingleby's observations on the nobly symmetrical structure of Jonson's poem (*Centurie of Prayse*, p. 150) should not be overlooked.

[4] As to these passages, and occasional allusions to Shakspere traceable in Ben Jonson's writings, see below, ch. v.

Drayton
(1627).

Thomas
Heywood
(1635).

Other
contempo-
rary dra-
matists.

Burton
(1624).

except a warm commendation of his genius as a comic dramatist in Drayton's lines to Henry Reynolds, *Of Poets and Poësie*, written at a time (1627 or rather earlier), when their author's own connexion with the stage had long ceased[1], and Thomas Heywood's graceful tribute, in his *Hierarchie of the Blessed Angells* (1635), to the 'enchanting' and versatile art of 'mellifluous Shakespeare,' already incidentally quoted[2]. On the other hand, his personal relations with Fletcher, the foremost of the younger generation of dramatic poets contemporary with himself, are matter of pure hypothesis or conjecture[3]. Passages in his plays are freely quoted or alluded to in those of most of these writers,—in none more notably than in Massinger's, whose genius in certain respects bore an affinity to Shakspere's own. Shirley, too, who has been called the last of the Elisabethans, as late as 1640, when the London stage was on the eve of its catastrophe, found occasion for paying a cordial tribute to the most potent of its early masters[4]. All these dramatists, and not a few other writers—including the author of the immortal *Anatomy of Melancholy*[5] —find abundant matter in Shakspere for quotation and

---

[1] 'Shakespeare, thou hadst as smooth a Comick vaine,
　　　Fitting the socke, and in thy natural braine
　　　As strong conception, and as Cleere a rage,
　　　As any one that trafiqu'd with the stage.'
The half-contemptuous turn of the last line will be noticed.
[2] *Ante*, p. 471.
[3] That Laurence Fletcher, the player with whom Shakspere was associated in the Lord Chamberlain's company, was an elder brother of the dramatist, seems an untenable supposition. See Dyce's *Introduction* to his edition of the *Works* of Beaumont and Fletcher, p. xvii. The question of Fletcher's supposed collaboration with Shakspere will be discussed below.
[4] *Prologue to the Sisters* (1640) :
　　　'. . . Shakespear . . . whose mirth did once beguile
　　　Dull hours and, buskin'd, made even sorrow smile ;
　　　So lovely were the wounds, that men would say
　　　They could endure the bleeding a whole day.'
[5] Burton here refers to '*Benedict* and *Belteris* in the Comedy,' and quotes the concluding couplet of *Romeo and Juliet*, besides four lines from *Venus and Adonis*. One might have thought that a suggestion would have been made as to the study of plays by Shakspere, or by Ben Jonson, whom Burton likewise quotes, by way of a remedy against melancholy, partaking neither of the danger of 'overmuch study' of learned works, nor of that of reading 'nothing but Play books, idle Poems, and Jests,' such as those mentioned in Part i. Sec. 2. No. 4 of the *Anatomy*.

illustration, setting an example which has been bettered by
the generations that have followed them.

If the favour which Shakspere's reputation experienced
during or immediately after the close of his life was more *the Court*
'patronage'
or less exceptional, and in some degree at least due to *received by*
an insight on the part of his contemporaries into the real *him.*
greatness of his genius, it remained within limits which it
is well to abstain from ignoring. *A priori*, of course,
there is everything to attract us in the picture of a great
Queen and her successor inciting by their example both
Court and nation to hold in honour the greatest of contemporary poets. But no proof is at hand of any personal
patronage extended to Shakspere by either Elisabeth
or James. In return, it must be allowed that of flattery,
the all but inevitable correlative of patronage, his plays
exhibit singularly few and faint signs. We may accept the
usual interpretation of a famous passage in the *Midsummer Night's Dream* as implying a tribute on the part
of the still youthful poet to the Vestal on the throne[1];
Portia's review of her suitors may imply an allusive compliment to the much-wooed princess; but the only direct
apostrophe to Elisabeth is to be found in the well-known
lines towards the close of *Henry VIII*, which were most
assuredly composed after the Queen's death. Doubtless
King James appreciated his share of the incense offered
in the same peroration (by whomsoever the passage was
penned), just as he must have been gratified by the *ex-post-
facto* tribute offered in *Macbeth* to his accomplishment of
the destinies of the line represented in his own person[2].

[1] Queen Elisabeth, it would be futile to doubt, liked the kind of incense of
which Shakspere was the reverse of profuse. When allusions were not forthcoming in plays performed in her presence, she appears to have occasionally
prepared to supply them herself. In 1564 the Spanish ambassador, de Silva,
describes her as interpreting to him the progress of a play, and adds that, as
'they generally deal with marriage in the comedies,' an opportunity soon
presented itself of discussing the proposed marriage of the Queen to Don
Carlos. (*Calendar of State Papers, Simancas*, vol. i. (1892) p. 368.)

[2] Professor Alfred Stern, in a most kindly criticism of the first edition of
this book, directed attention to two passages in the late Mr. E. Edwards's
Lives of the Founders of the British Museum (2 vols. 1870), pp. 155 and 157,
supposed to imply an acquaintance on the King's part with *A Midsummer
Night's Dream* (in 1594 the King forbade the introduction into a court pageant

But the fact that Shakspere now and then was found ready
to meet an inclination common to two sovereigns, by no means
implies that he was in any sense 'patronised' by either of them.
A letter ascribed to Southampton stating that several of
Shakspere's plays were 'most singularly liked of' Queen
Elisabeth when performed before her at Court, is apocryphal;
on the other hand, it is probable, though not proved, that
King James was a spectator of sundry of the poet's works.
But of any special or personal marks of goodwill towards
Shakspere on the part of ither sovereign there is no proof.
Credulity must be allowed to cling to the tradition that Elisa-
beth testified her desire to see Falstaff degraded from comedy
to farce, or to the equally apocryphal anecdote that James I
expressed his thanks for *Macbeth* in an autograph letter [1].
I remember a modern Italian play,—illuminated by the
acting of a great artist, the late Madame Ristori,—in which

of a live lion, ' because it would affright the ladies '), and a remembrance by
Shakspere, when writing Polonius' advice to Laertes, of James I's letter on
his accession to the English Crown to his son Henry Prince of Wales.

[1] See in reference to this Malone's *Inquiry*, p. 95, where he demolishes
the possibility of such a letter as that from Queen Elisabeth to Shakspere,
which had been forged by the ingenious Mr. Ireland. Malone incidentally
points out that Puttenham, whose *Arte of Poesie* appeared in 1589, and
who was one of the Gentlemen Pensioners, and therefore constantly near
the Queen's person, seems never to have heard of Shakspere, although he
discusses dramatic poets.—The generalities in the lines of Ben Jonson
(' those flights upon the banks of Thames, That so did take Eliza and our
James ') and Chettle appear to me to prove very little.   See, however,
Halliwell-Phillips' *Life of Shakespeare*, pp. 151-3.   A ballad called *A Mourn-
ful Dittie, entituled Elizabeth's Losse, together with a Welcome for King James*
(1603, printed in Collier's *Life of Shakespeare*, and reprinted in *Centurie of
Prayse*, p. 56), contains the lines :
> 'You Poets all, brave Shakspeare, Johnson, Greene,
>   Bestow your time to write for England's Queene ;
>   Lament, lament,' &c.

The Greene here mentioned is I suppose Thomas Greene, author of *A Poet's
Vision and a Prince's Glorie* (1603).—Reasons will be given below against
the supposition that Shakspere was in any way distinguished among his
fellow-actors (the King's actors) by James.   If he had been a courtly poet,
he would have less distinctly remembered the drinking habits of the Danish
Court, which on Christian IV's visit to England in 1606 so endeared
him to his brother-in-law.   Tieck's supposition that in *Timon of Athens*
(iv. 3) Shakspere directly flattered James in the passage where the hero proclaims but one honest man—'and he is a *steward*' (pronounce Stewart)—is
only less absurd than Ulrici's laborious apology (*Shakspeare's Dramatic
Art*, p. 245) for the 'extravagant flattery' in question.

Queen Elisabeth is represented as receiving a petition from Shakspere at the hands of Cecil, and graciously assenting to the prayer of her faithful poet. Other imaginative minds may have pictured to themselves analogous relations between the Queen and the poet; but romance must reckon with its own responsibilities.

The nature of the patronage extended to Shakspere by particular noblemen, and gentlemen of high rank, is more open to speculation. His relation, during many years of his life, to Southampton—although the measure of his patron's early munificence has doubtless been exaggerated, while the supposed manifestation of the nobleman's goodwill after the close of the actor's professional career may be regarded as mythical—forms an important chapter in Shakspere's life, and the dedications of two youthful poems have not more than an incidental significance in its history. According to one (nor the least plausible) among many theories intended to explain the *genesis* of Shakspere's *Sonnets*, the Earl of Pembroke too must have approached intimacy with the poet[1]. Among the later plays of Shakspere one is distinctly to be brought into connexion with speculations in foreign discovery in which both Southampton and Pembroke were interested[2]; and the conspiracy in which they were to some degree involved undoubtedly occupied the mind of the author of *Henry VIII*[3]. The Earl of Montgomery too, Pembroke's brother, seems to have admired and 'favoured' the poet[4]. But even after this has been said, it must be allowed to amount to very little. Among those whose patronage Shakspere sought and found in his early days were some noblemen of note, whose goodwill probably remained to him, and was prized by him, to the close of his theatrical career.

As to any appreciation of Shakspere by the master-minds

His noble patrons.

---

[1] Possibly *Much Ado about Nothing* may have some reference to the difficulty of inducing the same young nobleman to 'marry and settle.'

[2] Vide infra as to the subject of *The Tempest*.

[3] That it is actually adverted to in *Richard II* (*i. e.* in the passage added to the third or omitted from the first two editions of that play, iv. 1) is a more doubtful conjecture.

[4] The First Folio was dedicated to both the brothers.

No evidence of his having been appreciated by Ralegh or Bacon. of his age, except where, as in Ben Jonson's case, they were more or less his fellows in the same field of work, we are without convincing proofs.   It is hardly to be supposed that Ralegh was unacquainted with Shakspere, or that Bacon passed him by without notice [1].   But no evidence of a conclusive kind exists to show that either the most far-sighted man of action or the greatest thinker among the Elisabethans was aware of what it was to have, or to have had, a Shakspere by their side.

Extent of his general popularity as a dramatist. Lastly, there was the 'general public,' or rather that large section of the public which affected entertainments such as those provided by the genius of Shakspere.   That taken as a whole his plays, as compared with those of his fellow-playwrights, were during his lifetime pre-eminently popular, there seems no reason to doubt.   So much is proved by the ready testimony of his fellow-dramatists and of other contemporary writers—a testimony of which the strength grows almost from day to day with the progress of our acquaintance with Elisabethan literature.   It is supported by the fact that he wrote so much, though others (Thomas Heywood, *e.g.*) wrote more ; and by the certainty that he acquired through his interest in theatres to whose popularity his plays largely contributed, a comfortable income, sufficient to enable him to retire in fair case before old age had crippled his powers [2].   Lastly, it is borne out

---

[1] Although I shall be obliged to state on a subsequent page my view of the supposition that Shakspere's plays were written by Bacon, I must here at once express the opinion that the evidence even of Bacon's acquaintance with them is extremely slender.   All the learning and ingenuity expended by Mrs. Henry Pott upon the illustration by passages from Shakspere of Bacon's *Promus of Formularies and Elegancies,*—a common-place book kept by him somewhere between the years 1594 and 1596,—seems to me to fall short of proving even that the compiler had used for his purpose the knowledge of Shakspere's writings which by that time he might have acquired. (What Mrs. Pott's publication of this book (1883) intended to prove was, of course, something wholly different.)   The evidence of a few parallel passages in Bacon's *Essays* (first edition 1597, second 1612, third 1625) and in Shakspere's plays is, in my judgment, too slender to deserve discussion ; while it seems sheer absurdity to found any argument upon supposed resemblances between the action and characters of *The Tempest* and the parable of Pan in the *De Augmentis* (1623).

[2] Hence the amiable insinuation of Pope, that Shakspere
  'For gain, not glory, wing'd his roving flight,
  And grew immortal in his own despite.'

by the fact that when the stage fell under a cloud, Shakspere was among those remembered while others were
forgotten, and that when its life recommenced, his plays
were among the earliest and among the most rapidly successful in recovering possession of their ancient domain.

But to what extent was this enduring popularity within *Number of*
the walls of the play-house and among its patrons, reflected *his plays printed*
in the world of readers outside ?   Of the thirty-seven plays *during his*
in the Shaksperean canon [1], eighteen (or just one more than *lifetime.*
half) were printed in their author's lifetime ; and the average
number of impressions extant in each case from this period
is between two and three [2].   Of course this fails to exhaust
the number of quarto editions of single plays of Shakspere
printed during his lifetime ; but considering the facility of
surreptitious printing, and the freedom from blame enjoyed
by the practice except on the part of more sensitive playwrights, the calculation may assist in an enquiry as to the
demand for Shakspere's plays existing among contemporary
readers.   It may be added, that of the so-called 'doubtful
plays' which have been at any time ascribed to Shakspere,
eleven are known to have been printed in his lifetime [3].
Other reasons have no doubt been suggested for the paucity
of the number of plays by Shakspere which appeared in
print during his life [4]; but the demand for them on the
part of the public cannot have been in any sense large.
While the first volume of a collective edition of the works
of Ben Jonson was printed in the lifetime of their author [5],

[1] Counting them, as in the list arranged below, and reckoning each *Part*
as a play in the case of *Henry VI* and in that of *Henry IV*.   The First Folio
contains all these plays except *Pericles*.

[2] See the List of the Early Editions of Shakspeare in Malone's *Shakspeare*
(Boswell's edition of 1821, the edition quoted throughout this Chapter),
vol. ii. pp. 647 *seqq.*; and cf. Steevens' observations, *ib.* pp. 643 *seqq.*   See
also the *Table of Quarto Editions of Shakespeare's Plays*, forming *Appendix I*
to Mr. Fleay's *Life of Shakspeare*.

[3] See the list in Malone's *Shakspeare*, ii. 681–2.   Eight of these appear
in Mr. Fleay's List of *Quarto editions of other plays prepared by Shakespeare's
company*, *Appendix II, u. s.*

[4] The late Mr. W. Blades, in his *Shakspere and Typography* (1872), a
pamphlet in part intended as a *jeu d'esprit*, suggested that Shakspere was at
one time of his life a printer, and that it may accordingly be plausibly supposed that 'sickened with reading other people's proofs for a livelihood,
he shrunk from the same task on his own behalf.'   [5] In 1616.

Shakspere's works were not collected till seven years after his death (in the First Folio, 1623) ; and though the editors of this volume speak of 'diverse stolne, and surreptitious copies, maimed and deformed by the frauds and stealthes of injurious impostors,' yet they evidently by no means themselves expected a brisk sale of their folio, which was probably printed in a very limited number of copies [1].

Thus, the evidence which we possess on the subject tends to show that the reputation enjoyed by Shakspere in his lifetime was limited to a more or less genial recognition of his merits on the part of a few patrons and on that of some of his literary contemporaries,—chiefly fellow-dramatists,—and to what may be termed a general preference for his plays, as compared with those of other writers, on the part of the constituents of the theatrical public. But although this theatrical public must have largely increased in London during the earlier half of his career [2], the attacks upon the stage recommenced towards the close of the century [3], and indeed the spirit which prompted them had never slept. The classes moved by this spirit were those upon whom more than upon any other the future of England depended, and to whose tastes and feelings the progress of a popular literature must always largely accommodate

---

[1] According to Steevens' conjecture (Malone's *Shakspeare*, ii. 658, *note*) in not more than 250. A proof of the smallness of the issue may be found in the extreme rarity of the First Folio, not known to exist in more than thirty copies. According to Halliwell-Phillips (*Shakesperiana*, p. 43), one copy is in existence bearing the date of 1622.

[2] In 1592, Nashe (in his *Pierce Pennilesse*) spoke of a play as being witnessed by 'ten thousand spectators at least, at several times.' Altogether, it may be assumed that the number of visitors to the theatres increased rapidly till near the close of the century. Cf. *Introduction* to Gosson's *School of Abuse*, p. x.

[3] In 1599 was published *Th' Overthrow of Stage-playes*, by Dr. John Rainoldes, of Queen's College, and afterwards President of Corpus Christi College, Oxford, which was the most important product of the controversy concerning the performance of Latin plays at Oxford between him and Dr. William Gager. See Lowe's *Bibliographical Account, &c.*, pp. 135, 274 ; and Mr. S. Lee's notice of Gager in vol. xx. of the *Dictionary of National Biography* (1889). In the same year King James interfered to protect the English players at Edinburgh, the Session of the Kirk of Scotland having prohibited the faithful from resorting to their performances 'under pain of the church censures' (Collier, i. 332).

itself. In a word, the middle classes of the nation, wherever, as more especially in London, they were brought into contact with the stage, became more and more hostile towards it. The interest in dramatic literature could not but suffer accordingly, and the advance of the appreciation of the merits of our greatest national dramatist be retarded. Puritanism was gradually assuming a far wider and deeper significance than can attach to a mere view of Church government, or to a particular theory of the relations between the system of the State and the forms of religious life. To side with the Puritans, now implied the acceptance of distinct principles in the conduct of life. These principles may perhaps be summarised as an avowed endeavour to regulate the whole of life, in all its aspects and relations, according to fixed laws. The consequent certainty, to which all shrinking back or wavering to the right or to the left was impossible, gave for a time to Puritanism, in peace and in war, a resistless force. But from the same source Puritanism derived the narrowness which remained an unmistakeable feature of the movement. To the Puritan nothing could be a greater abomination than the theatre, with the very conditions of whose existence the laws of his life were in conflict ; nor could any feature of the stage be so great an abomination in his eyes as the boundlessness with which the genius of our Elisabethans, and that of Shakspere above all, had endowed English dramatic literature. Against the theatre, therefore, Puritanism (as has been seen and as will further appear below) directed its assaults with increasing success ; although a transport of zeal may in one instance at least have given rise to a temporary reaction in favour of the stage, which communicated itself to others besides its habitual supporters [1]. Finally, when

Puritanism in Shakspere's later years, and after his death.

---

[1] I refer to Prynne's invective against the Queen on account of her patronage of a dramatic performance at court. Cf. Masson's *Life of Milton*, i. 407–8. Prynne's *Histrio-Mastix* was published in 1632. I shall return to these matters below ; at present I am merely attempting to survey the progress, together with the back-waves occurring in it, of Shakspere's fame.— A passage in *Histrio-Mastix* (cited in *Centurie of Prayse*, p. 195) bitterly reflects on the fact that since the author first undertook his subject, 'some Play-books ... are growne from *Quarto* into *Folio*,' and 'are now printed in farre better paper than most Octavo or Quarto *Bibles*, which hardly finde

the party identified with Puritan opinion, although not as yet with its extreme forms, had become possessed of the control of London before the outbreak of the Civil War in 1642, the closing of the theatres was one of the inevitable incidents of the revolution which this change implied.

His reputation as a dramatist in the time of Charles I.

Under these influences the fame of Shakspere languished, and must have languished even had a careful distinction been drawn in this period between dramatic literature and the literature of the stage. As a matter of course, his genius as a dramatist continued to call forth tributes of praise from those whom it had subjected to its spell. In this choir dramatic writers could not but hold the most conspicuous place; and of the earlier Caroline dramatists a goodly number honoured Shakspere by direct tributes of admiration as well as by less direct testimony to their familiarity

Tributes of Sir John Suckling and others.

with his works. Among them I have already mentioned Shirley and others, whose achievements in part connect them with an earlier and more illustrious chapter of our dramatic history; to their names should be added more especially that of Sir John Suckling, who in verse and in prose, by direct commendation as well as by imitation, honoured himself by proving his regard for the memory of 'my Friend Mr. *William Shakespear* [1],' together with those of Jasper Mayne, Thomas Nabbes, Sir William D'Avenant (of whom more below), and others. Men of letters unconnected with the stage likewise occasionally attested their appreciation of Shakspere's genius. Leaving aside anonymous tributes—although possessed of an intrinsic value of their own—I should regret to leave unnoticed a conversational remark by 'John Hales of Eton,' which at a date probably earlier than 1633 anticipates the free spirit of the best of all 'Shakspere criticism [2].' But apart from such tributes, and

such vent as they.' Marginal notes refer to the folio editions of Jonson, Shakspere, &c., and to the 'best Crowne paper' used for that of Shakspere in especial.

[1] See *Centurie of Prayse*, pp. 209 *seqq.* His gratitude must certainly have derived strength from a consciousness of 'perpetual plagiarism' on his own part. Cf. *Fresh Allusions*, p. 113.

[2] After sitting still for some time during a discussion in which Ben

other incidental illustrations of the popularity of Shakspere's writings[1], it seems undeniable that, in accordance with an ordinary experience, the generation succeeding Shakspere's was not the most ready to acknowledge his claims to pre-eminence. Ben Jonson, indeed, although long the acknowledged chief of living dramatic authors, at no time succeeded in producing, as he had on no occasion attempted to produce, a belief that he outshone the friend whom he so long survived. Still, a second volume of the first collective edition of Jonson's works was published (in a succession of fragments) in the course of his later years and of those following immediately upon the date of his death; and he is repeatedly mentioned by contemporary writers in a way implying that his titles to literary fame were equal to Shakspere's. And, to all appearance, the dramatists who in this particular age called forth the most enduring as well as the most ardent literary enthusiasm, were the two companion-writers who were most nearly allied to it by the bent of their genius and the specialities of their tastes. The fame of Beaumont and Fletcher had come at least to rival that of Shakspere, and at times was treated as surpassing it; while again we not unfrequently find the pair ranked side by side with Shakspere and Jonson as pre-eminent among English

Fluctuations of opinion as to preeminence among the chief dramatists.

Jonson and other literary authorities took part, Mr. Hales observed, 'That if Mr. *Shakespear* had not read the Antients, he had likewise not stollen anything from 'em . . . and that if ⌊Ben⌋ would produce any one Topick finely treated by any one of them, he [Hales] would undertake to show something upon the same Subject at least as well written by *Shakespear.*' (Cited from Rowe's introductory *Account, &c.,* 1709, in *Centurie of Prayse,* p. 198.)

[1] A *curiosum* is the wish expressed by Cowley, when a pupil at Westminster School between 1628 and 1631, that a young lawyer who had offended him might

'Bee by his Father in his study tooke
At Shakspeare's plays, instead of my Lord *Cooke*'—

(something as Dr. Arnold confiscated early numbers of *Pickwick* which Rugby boys had put too near to their Thucydides.) See *Centurie of Prayse,* p. 170 (from *A Politicall Revenge* in *Silva*).—In *The Guardian* (1641) Cowley varied the notion into an injunction to a City maiden (Tabytha) to 'banish *Shakespear* and *Ben Jonson* out of the parlour, and to bring in their rooms *Marprelate,* and *Pryn's* Works.' In *The Cutler of Coleman Street* (1663) he altered the name '*Shakespear*' to '*Fletcher.*' (*Fresh Allusions,* p. 149.)

dramatists[1]. Thirty-six of their plays were published in a collected form in 1647 (they were republished with seventeen others in 1679); of Shakspere's, the First Folio collection, with a corrected reprint in 1632 (the Second Folio), sufficed till after the Restoration. It was reproduced in the Third Folio, published in 1663, and reprinted in 1664 with seven additional plays, all of which (with the exception of *Pericles*) are now usually considered spurious. The Fourth Folio (1685) contained nothing new beyond modernisations of spelling.

The Second, Third, and Fourth Folios (1632, 1663, 1664, and 1685).

It is hardly too much to conclude from the above data, that by the time of the Restoration, when a generation had grown up to which the inside of a playhouse was unknown, and when but few libraries could have contained more than a stray copy or two of Shakspere's plays, his popular fame must have stood in some danger of dwindling into a mere tradition[2]. The danger passed away, when the

His fame after the Restoration revived with the reopening of the theatres.

---

[1] So, for instance, by Owen Feltham (1637) :
          ' Shakespeare, Beaumont, Johnson, these three shall
            Make up the Jem in the point Verticall '
of the crown composed for herself by the Stage. Further quotations are needless; moreover, a mere turn of phrase may at times be mistaken for a deliberate critical intention. But in exemplification of the preference indicated in the text, the lines in honour of Fletcher by William Cartwright prefixed to the First Folio of Beaumont and Fletcher (1647) are notable. (They were quoted by the late Canon Kingsley in his essay *On Plays and Puritans.*) Cartwright (whose own most successful dramatic effort is an obvious imitation of Ben Jonson) places Fletcher's name ' 'twixt Jonson's grave and Shakspeare's lighter sound,' and tells Fletcher that
          ' Shakspeare to thee was dull, whose best wit lies
            I' th' ladies questions, and the fool's replies.
    .   .   .   .
            Whose wit our nice times would obsceneness call—
    .   .   .   .
            Nature was all his art ; thy vein was free
            As his, but without his scurrility'—
a criticism which from the author of *The Ordinary* is nothing short of ludicrous. It may be mentioned that Gifford, in his *Memoirs of Ben Jonson*, quotes from a tract by J. Cooke on Charles I's Trial (1649) the insinuation that 'had King Charles but studied Scripture half so much as he studied Ben Jonson or Shakspeare,'&c. To the anecdote that Charles I described Shirley's *Gamester* (of which he himself was believed to have suggested the plot) as ' the best play he had seen for seven years,' no importance need be attached. In general, justice can hardly be said to have been rendered by English writers to the remarkable literary and artistic intelligence of King Charles I.
[2] Writing about 1653 from Chicksands, where her regular literary nourish-

Restoration was accomplished and when the theatres were reopened. A revival of the popular recognition of Shakspere's greatness as a dramatist inevitably followed. But the hostility of the Puritan Revolution had lasting results, and in so far as the fame of Shakspere is inseparably associated with the most immediate sphere of his activity, the effect of that hostility cannot be said even now to have been completely undone.

Whatever may be thought of the relations between the stage of Charles I's reign and the sentiments and manners of his Court, the theatre of the reigns of the last two Stuart Kings was beyond dispute entirely subject to the influence of the world of court and fashion. No section of the lower orders felt itself, as in the days of Elisabeth, vehemently attracted towards the playhouses. The masses being, for many an age to come, left to themselves in their choice of pleasures, middle-class respectability shunned the theatre, where every effort was made to affront the accepted principles of morality and decency of life. Under the influence of tastes utterly frivolous and vitiated both by the native and by the foreign elements intermingled in them, the whole atmosphere of the theatre in the Restoration age became, in the words of a writer whose knowledge of it is unsurpassed, 'indescribably wicked [1].' Its favourite productions, ushered in by lewd prologues, were either imitations of foreign models, or mere bastards of the Elisabethan drama. Yet to this Restoration stage we owe a revived recognition—in spheres extending widely beyond the section of the public open to the influences of literary criticism—of the genius of Shakspere. The number of Shaksperean characters performed by Betterton, the greatest actor of this period, is indeed small compared with

Shakspere and the Restoration stage.

ment consisted of *Cléopâtre* and *Le Grand Cyrus*, Dorothy Osborne avowed to her lover that 'all the people that I had ever in my life refused were brought again upon the stage, like Richard the Third's ghosts, to reproach me withal.' (*Letters, &c.*, edited by E. A. Parry, edition 1888, p. 115.) This and similar allusions, traceable with more or less probability to direct acquaintance with Shaksperean plays, will hardly be held to contradict the general conclusion in my text.

[1] See Mr. Robert W. Lowe's *Thomas Betterton* (*Eminent Actors* Series), 1891, p. 57. This unpretending little volume is a mine of first-hand information concerning the theatre of the Restoration.

the extraordinarily large number of his other impersonations,
but it amounts to ten (adaptations included), and is not,
I think, equalled by that of the characters from any one
other dramatist performed by him[1]. Of the century and
a half (or thereabouts) of plays which Pepys saw acted in
the course of eight years and a half (1660-9) over which his
Diary extends, about one in fifteen were Shakspere's, while
as many as one in six were by Beaumont and Fletcher, or
by Fletcher alone[2]. Not less than nine of Shakspere's
plays were reserved as the property of the company which
under D'Avenant began its performances in November, 1660;
and when two-and-twenty years later the two theatrical
companies amalgamated, and the great actor Betterton was
virtually placed in command of the chief characters of the
répertoire of the existing English stage, Brutus, Othello,
and Hotspur without delay asserted their claim upon the
sympathies of the theatrical public[3]. These examples
sufficiently illustrate the conclusion that certain of Shakspere's plays found their way back to the stage chiefly
because of the strong characters and of the striking
situations which they contained,—in other words, because
they lent themselves so securely to the requirements of
theatrical effect. Scant reverence was shown by D'Avenant
and Dryden, or by the revivalists who were at work about
the close of this period (the turn of the century), in the
processes to which they subjected the Shaksperean plays
of their choice ; but, quite apart from the important services
rendered to Shakspere's reputation by Dryden, the greatest
of the adapters, in his capacity as a literary critic, he and
his fellow-playwrights unmistakeably advanced the fame of
their great predecessor upon the stage. More and more distinctly Shakspere's genius, isolated in some measure from the
immediate outward conditions and circumstances under
which its dramatic creations had seen the light, asserted
its power in its immediate and proper sphere, even through

---

[1] See the lists *ap.* Genest, vol. ii. pp. 458-462, and Lowe, pp. 188-9.
[2] The calculation is based on the list given in Mr. H. B. Wheatley's
excellent volume *Samuel Pepys and the World he lived in* (1880).
[3] Lowe, *u. s.*, pp. 75, 129.

the veil of versions which at times very much resembled perversions, or when under the infliction of alternating species of
torture,—hacked about by a desperate knife or half-smothered
under frivolous or fatuous additions.   This method of treating
Shakspere left its traces on the English stage long after the
latter had ceased to be the sole or even the principal means
of sustaining and augmenting his fame ; but it is only fair
to remember that some tribute of the kind is exacted by
the theatre from whatever craft enters its sound.   In the
present connexion it will suffice to mention one or two of
the more abnormal of these 'adaptations' of Shakspere[1].
In 1662 *Measure for Measure* and *Much Ado about*
Nothing were unscrupulously blended by D'Avenant into
a single tragi-comedy called *The Law against Lovers*.   It
was he who appears to have conceived the idea, which the
audacity of Dryden afterwards carried into execution, of
heightening the effect of *The Tempest* by a mechanical process of duplication[2].   Dryden's *All for Love, or The World*
well Lost (1678)[3] is an effort of a very different description, which rather places itself in competition (nor ignobly
so) with *Anthony and Cleopatra* than adapts Shakspere's
treatment of the theme ; while the same author's *Troilus*
and Cressida, or Truth found too Late (1678) stands as it
were midway between the two above-mentioned plays, the
modern dramatist having in it, as he says, undertaken to
'correct' what he opined to have been, 'in all Probability,
one of Shakespeare's first Endeavours on the Stage[4].'

Restoration adaptations of Shakspere's plays;

---

[1] An analytical list of *Adaptations and Performances of Shakesperean*
plays from the death of the poet to the death of Garrick was given by Baron
G. Vincke in *Jahrbuch*, &c., vol. ix. (1874), pp. 41–54.
[2] In *The Tempest, or The Enchanted Island* (for the title itself was double-
necked) a youth who had never set eyes on a woman held the balance to
the maiden who had never beheld a man.   Ariel, too, was provided with
a female double (Milcha), and Caliban was supported by Sycorax in the
flesh ; not to mention that Miranda was furnished with a younger sister, and
in some sense a sort of oblique counterpart, called Dorinda.   See the play,
which was acted in 1667 and 1668, in Scott's *Dryden*, vol. iii.
[3] See *ib.*, vol. v.
[4] This, according to his own statement, Dryden effected by 'new-modelling
the plot, throwing out many unnecessary Persons; improving those
characters which were begun and left unfinished, as Hector, Troilus,
Pandarus and Thersites, and adding that of Andromache.' (See Dryden's

Measure for Measure, on which D'Avenant had already tried his hand, was again recast by Gildon, and produced at Lincoln's Inn Fields, in 1700, as a piece 'written by Shakespeare, and now very much alter'd,' with the sub-title of *Beauty the Best Advocate*. D'Urfey, a writer of very low stamp, in 1682 turned *Cymbeline* into something he entitled *The Injured Princess, or The Fatal Wager*, while John Lacy, whose dramatic efforts are of no very different type, in 1667 assimilated *The Taming of the Shrew*, entitling his concoction *Sauny the Scot* in honour of a re-nationalised Grumio[1]. More noticeable is the hash, prepared and announced in a spirit of convinced superiority, for which *The Merchant of Venice* in 1701 supplied 'Granville the Polite' (George Granville, afterwards Lord Lansdowne) with the principal materials. From *The Jew of Venice* the characters of Launcelot Gobbo and his sire are omitted ; in return, a *Masque of Peleus and Thetis* is introduced, during the performance of which Shylock, supping at a separate table, drinks the toast of his lady-love Money[2]. Throughout the whole of this period no species of Shakspere's plays was sacred from these alterations ; histories, tragedies and comedies were alike exposed to them ; by no means only the necessities of the stage, although these must be conceded to have counted for something, but also the dictates of a supposed advance in literary or theatrical insight were accountable for the fashion. John Dennis, of whom as a critic mention will have to be made below, elaborated in 1702 a version of *The Merry Wives* under the title of *The*

Preface ap. Scott, vol. vi. p. 240; and cf., on the whole subject of these efforts of Dryden's, Delius' essay *Dryden und Shakespeare* in *Jahrbuch der deutschen Shakespeare-Gesellschaft*, vol. iv. (1869). Dryden's *Troilus* still held the stage in 1708-9, when Thersites seems to have been the last Shaksperean character assumed by Betterton.

[1] Genest, vol. i. p. 139. The play does not appear to have been printed till 1698.

[2] As to Granville's play, see *ib.* vol. ii. pp. 243 *seqq.* In the Prologue the Ghost of Shakspere apologises not for Granville, but for himself:

> 'The first rude sketches Shakspeare's pencil drew ;
> But all the shining master-strokes are new.
> This play ye Critics shall your fury stand,
> Adorn'd and rescu'd by a faultless hand.'

Comical Gallant, or The Amours of Sir John Falstaff, and in 1720 altered *Coriolanus* into *The Invader of his Country, or The Fatal Resentment.* Colley Cibber in 1700 gave notable proof of his theatrical tact in his version of *Richard III,* which in spite of its impieties holds the stage to this day[1]. John Sheffield Duke of Buckinghamshire's expansion of *Julius Caesar* into two tragedies, for one of which *(Brutus)* Pope wrote a couple of choruses, carries us into the middle of the Augustan age[2]. Among the few Shaksperean plays which appear to have escaped material changes was *Hamlet,* until Garrick essayed the task of revising it for performance—a circumstance probably due to the stage traditions dating from the performance of the chief character by Betterton, who played it at intervals through the whole of the Restoration age, and with signal success as late as 1709, when he was nearly seventy-five years old[3].

---

[1] See Genest, vol. ii. p. 195, and cf. Lowe, *Betterton,* p. 167, where Cibber's version is described as 'full of villainous clap-traps, mixed metaphors, and unmitigated nonsense,' but 'skilfully adapted for stage effect.' Cibber in his process of 'contamination' introduced many lines from other Shaksperean plays, and probably some out of his own head. Genest suggests that the famous line

'Off with his head—so much for Buckingham!'

came 'perhaps from some obscure play, with a slight alteration,' but the 'Off with his head' (Hastings') in Act iv. sc. 4 should not be overlooked.—In Caryl's *The English Princess, or The Death of Richard III* (cf. Pepys' *Diary* under March 7, 1667), there seems to be nothing borrowed from Shakspere (Halliwell-Phillips' *Dictionary,* p. 85).

[2] The construction of Shakspere's tragedy must be allowed to have lent some colour to this procedure.—Betterton's performance of the character of Brutus, Colley Cibber's striking account of which is cited by Lowe, *Betterton,* p. 129, must have been partly accountable for the special popularity of this among Shakspere's tragedies.

[3] Garrick's alteration of *Hamlet* (1772), which was never printed, is described by Genest, vol. v. p. 343, and by Vincke, *u. s.,* pp. 53-4. Steele's notice of Betterton's performance of Hamlet, only a few months before the great actor's death, is well known. (See *The Tatler,* No. 71 (Sept. 22, 1709), and cf. Lowe's *Betterton,* p. 177).—A *List of Plays* altered from Shakspere is given in Malone's edition (by Boswell), vol. ii. pp. 683 *seqq.* However strongly we may feel bound to reprobate tampering with the text of a great national writer, and however much we may now and then be inclined to applaud Pope's sneer (see the *Preface* to his edition of Shakspere) that 'Players are just such judges of what is *right,* as Taylors are of what is *graceful,*' no candid critic will ignore the special exigences of the theatre, or deny that adaptation is

So much as to the treatment of Shakspere on and by the stage, during the half-century or thereabouts which followed upon the re-opening of the theatres. The effects of this treatment have not altogether disappeared to our own day, and, taken as a whole, have rendered the popular admiration of his merits less discriminating, without materially diminishing its warmth. As to Dryden and his fellow-playwrights, they no doubt were at certain times and in certain respects influenced by imperfect or mistaken theories of the dramatic art; but candour compels the conclusion that the license wherewith as a body they treated the master-pieces of a greater past was essentially due to the reckless spirit of their own age, which sought and found in the drama little more than a transitory amusement and a stimulant of sensual passion [1].

a labour in which both reverence and taste have at times most effectively co-operated.

[1] A fair example of the spirit in which the society of the Restoration age regarded the drama may be found in Pepys, who though he had no poetry in his soul was not incapable of higher tastes (witness his love of good music), who had his wits about him and was therefore capable of recognising merit, and who moreover confesses (*Diary*, Dec. 10, 1663) that 'his nature was most earnest in books of pleasure, as plays,' and that he was tempted by copies of Shakspere, Beaumont and Jonson at a book-seller's. He afterwards (July 7, 1664) actually purchased one of the folio editions of Shakspere, and at a later date added the fourth folio (1685), which is now in the Pepysian Library at Magdalene College, Cambridge. (see Wheatley, *u. s.*, p. 88). Pepys, as has been already noted, mentions the performances of not less than eleven Shaksperean plays as having been witnessed by himself; to some he takes exception, of others he approves, though rarely in terms approaching those in which he commends certain of the plays of Ben Jonson. Thus he thought *Macbeth* 'a pretty good play' (Nov. 5, 1664), and 'a most excellent play for variety' (Dec. 28, 1666), and, again (here his criticism is more elaborate than usual), 'a most excellent play in all respects, but especially in diver-tissement, though it be a deep tragedy; which is a strange perfection in a tragedy, it being most proper here. and suitable' (Jan. 7, 1667). With *Hamlet* he was 'mightily pleased' (Aug. 31, 1668). On the other hand, he considered *A Midsummer Night's Dream* 'the most insipid, ridiculous play that ever he saw in his life' (Sept. 25, 1662); and *The Merry Wives* 'did not please him at all, no part of it' (Aug. 15, 1667). *Othello* he had 'ever heretofore' esteemed a mighty good play, but he having so lately read *The Adventures of Five Hours*, it seemed to him in comparison 'a mean thing' (Aug. 20, 1666). This, however, was the impression left upon him, not by seeing *Othello*, but by reading it.—In the *Diary* of Evelyn, a man of genuine iterary taste and training, the only reference to Shakspere as a dramatist

As was indicated above, the general tendency of the literature of the Restoration and next ensuing periods was one of subserviency to foreign influences. Although the force of this tendency has probably been much exaggerated, yet its effects are undeniable. Indeed, it would be difficult to instance any branch of contemporary English literary composition in which the writers of these periods did not in practice largely imitate foreign models, and in theory borrow from foreign dogmatists their conceptions of the rules of their art. The French drama in especial, which in the course of these periods reached the summit of its greatness, was largely, though very far from exclusively, imitated by the writers of English tragedy, and, though by no means to the same degree, by those of comedy also; while not a few of the rules of dramatic art 'read into' the ancients by French literary criticism, as well as of the methods sanctioned by the usage of the chief French dramatists themselves, were commended by English writers and made more or less familiar by English practice. The Elisabethans, and Shakspere above all, did not always fare well at the hands of the English critics of this age; on the other hand, it must not be forgotten that before Dryden literary criticism as applied to the drama was virtually unknown in England, and that, apart from Dryden's noble enthusiasm in favour of genius wherever he recognised it, Shakspere and the Elisabethans could not but gain in reputation far more than they lost, so soon as they began to be criticised at all[1].

Opinion on Shakspere in the Restoration age and in the ensuing period.

is the rather ambiguous notice, under Nov. 26, 1661 : ' I saw *Hamlet, Prince of Denmark* played, but now the old plays began to disgust this refined age since his Majesties being so long abroad.' There is also a mention of a portrait of Shakspere in Evelyn's *Correspondence* (vol. iii. p. 444, ed. 1879).—I may add a reference to two allusions in this period to Falstaff, pointed out to me respectively by Professor Toller and (I think) Mr. Leslie Stephen. In Pepys' *Diary* (Aug. 29, 1666) Sir W. Coventry is mentioned as humorously quoting Falstaff; and in *State Trials*, x. 570, in the curious case of Lady Ivy (1684), Lord Jeffreys says : ' If he should swear as long as Sir John Falstaff fought' (i. e. a long hour by Shrewsbury clock) ' I would never believe him.'

[1] This is excellently brought out by Mr. Ernest Walder in the chapter on Dryden which forms part of his *History of Shaksperian Criticism*, now on the eve of publication. I have freely used what I have seen of this book, and

Milton
(1630–
1671).

For to Dryden, and to no other writer, belongs the credit
of having led the way as a critic of the drama and of its
masterpieces in our literature—a claim impaired but little
by the mistakes into which he may have been led by the
tendencies of his age or by the negligence which was in
a sort a defect of one of the most characteristic qualities
of his genius—its liberality, if I may so apply the word.
Yet it should not be forgotten that in this Restoration age—
more than two years indeed after the first and most important
of Dryden's critical essays was composed [1]—the greatest poet
to whom, after Shakspere himself, England had given
birth, had published his masterpiece, and that no English
writer has ever been better qualified than Milton, both by
training and by inborn powers, for a critical appreciation
of the achievements of his literary predecessors. But the
historic current of his earlier days, and the impetus with
which he had cast himself into it in obedience to the
irresistible dictates of his moral being, were stronger than
the student's aesthetic sympathies with ideals out of the
reach of his actual grasp. In the beautiful twin lyrics,
composed at least four years before the outbreak of the
great conflict whose essential causes he had already divined,
he had referred to the modern stage and its literature,
although in some sense he was in contact with both, in terms
of very restricted approval. 'Gorgeous Tragedy' to his
mind found appropriate representatives in the dramatised
legends of the Attic poets, or in 'what, *though rare,*

Of later age
Ennobled hath the buskin'd stage [2].'

And, albeit that among the writers for 'the well-trod stage'
(a suggestion of disrespect seems to me to lurk in the
epithet [3]) Milton pays a kindly tribute both to Jonson and to

---

of the same writer's Harness Prize Essay on *Shaksperian Criticism, textual
and literary, from Dryden to the end of the Eighteenth Century* (1895), of which
it is an expansion, in revising this section of the present chapter.

[1] Cf. Dr. R. Garnett, *The Age of Dryden* (1895), p. 151.

[2] See *Il Penseroso.*

[3] Such is, however, not the opinion of Mr. F. T. Palgrave, whose perception in such matters is so singularly fine.

Shakspere, yet the latter and more elaborate allusion
suggests that when

—'sweetest Shakespeare, Fancy's child,
Warbled his native wood-notes wild,'—

there was lacking in them something,—shall we say the
perfect discipline of the Muses[1]? The *Epitaph on the
Admirable Dramatic Poet W. Shakespeare* (1630) is considerably earlier in date than *L'Allegro*; its enthusiasm,
which there is no reason for depreciating as the enthusiasm
of youth, is indisputable; but it contains the germ of
the same distinction in the contrast drawn (no doubt
favourably to them) between Shakspere's 'easy numbers'
and 'slow-endeavouring art.' The curious reference in
Eikonoklastes (1649) to Shakspere's *Richard III* as illustrating by a celebrated passage[2], and 'other stuff of this
sort,' which 'may be read throughout the whole tragedy,'
the religious hypocrisy of tyrants, and of King Charles I
in particular, is really beside the mark, except as showing
the writer's familiarity with the source of his illustration[3].

---

[1] See *L'Allegro*. The above, I see, is also the opinion of one of the
most competent of recent editors of Milton, who holds that ' the couplet in
fact is faint praise, and it may be doubted whether Milton had a very keen
sense of Shakespeare's greatness.' See the exhaustive note on the passage
in Mr. A. W. Verity's edition of Milton's *Lycidas and other Poems*, Pitt
Press Series, Cambridge, 1891, pp. 91-2; where it is observed that Milton
was here probably thinking of *A Midsummer Night's Dream* and *The
Tempest*, to which two plays there seem to be ' more allusions in his poems
than to all the rest of Shakespeare's dramas put together.' Mr. Verity adds
that ' the passages in which Milton can be said to have borrowed from
Shakespeare's tragedies are very rare. He tells the story of *King Lear* at
considerable length in his *History of Britain*, but there is no mention of the
play.'—In the *Theatrum Poetarum Anglicanorum*, published in 1675, by
Edward Phillips, Milton's nephew and pupil (edition of 1820, p. 240), we
find a criticism of Shakspere in which we may suspect a reminiscence of the
passage in *L'Allegro*: ' Though some others may perhaps pretend to a more
exact decorum and œconomie, especially in tragedy, never any expressed
a more lofty and tragic height; never any represented nature more purely
to the life, *and where the polishments of art are most wanting, as probably
his learning was not extraordinary, he pleaseth with a certain wild and
native elegance*; and in all his writings hath an unvulgar style, as well in
his *Venus and Adonis*, his *Rape of Lucrece*, and other various poems, as
in his dramatics.'

[2] ' I do not know that Englishmen alive,' &c. (act ii. sc. 1).

[3] Cf. Masson's *Life of Milton*, vol. iv. p. 137 *note*. The sneering assertion

In his old age (1670–1), when himself using the tragic form as a vehicle of his sense of isolation and scorn, Milton would hear of no models of tragedy but the ancients and their Italian followers, and reprobated the 'error of inter-mixing comic stuff with tragic sadness and gravity; or introducing trivial and vulgar persons, which by all judiciers hath been counted absurd, and brought in without discretion corruptly to gratify the people[1].' The author of *Hamlet* must bear his share of the reproach.

Dryden (1667 seqq.).   But Milton, under this as under other aspects, dwelt apart. Dryden not only stood in the midst of the literary activity of the Restoration age, but in his own literary creations, and more especially in those of the dramatic kind, by his own confession too often allowed himself to be carried away by the current which at times no other writer showed himself so capable of directing. While, however, of his own dramatic work it has been said with truth that the style which he was principally instrumental in introducing into English tragedy was but little in consonance with his own natural genius[2], in his dramatic criticism, and more especially in his criticism of Shakspere, the instances are comparatively rare when he failed to think and speak for himself. The general character of this criticism, which will be examined more in detail below, has been frequently misjudged, partly because slight regard has been paid to the order in date of its several phases, and more notably because its minor points have been emphasised rather than its principal issues[3]. Dryden was the first English

that Shakspere 'we well know was the closest companion of these his' (the king's) 'solitudes' is unworthy of Milton, but not intended to depreciate Shakspere.

[1] See the Preface to *Samson Agonistes*. The interesting circumstance that Milton had himself in his earlier years contemplated the dramatic treatment of the theme of *Macbeth* will be noticed below.

[2] Hettner, *Literaturgeschichte des* 18. *Jahrhunderts* (2nd edn. 1865), vol. i. p. 94.

[3] The writings of Dryden noticeable under this head are his magnificent dialogue *On Dramatic Poesy* (originally written in 1665, and published in 1667); the *Defence of an Essay on Dramatic Poesy* (1668); the short Preface to *The Tempest* (1669); the essay *Of Heroic Plays* (1672); the *Defence of the Epilogue to The Conquest of Granada* (1672); the Preface to

critic who gave adequate and ample expression to the
admiration inspired by the greatness and comprehensiveness
of Shakspere's genius, and by his truthful representation of
human nature in its variety and complexity. In view
of this fact, it is of little importance that he could not
wholly free himself from the authority of supposed canons
of dramatic composition—derived not from Aristotle, but
from Corneille's uncanonical interpretation of Aristotle—
recognised as insufficient by Dryden himself; while it is of
still less moment that he for a time upheld a theory as to
dramatic versification at variance with the surer instincts
of Elisabethan practice. And, from this broader point of
view, we may altogether pass by such incidental shortcomings of judgment as appear in criticisms of particular
plays with which Dryden was either imperfectly acquainted,
or which in a way not uncommon with him he rather
negligently remembered, or in the merely fugitive comparison
between Shakspere and Fletcher as having ' writ better,' the
former ' betwixt man and man,' the latter ' betwixt man and
woman[1].' In sum, if an apologetic admixture in Dryden's
criticism of Shakspere may be charged to the account of
influences which he was in too close an accordance with
his times to disown, the secret of Shakspere's greatness was
to him no longer a secret, and was through him first unlocked
for those who could read with understanding.

It was in the nature of the case, that the essence of
Dryden's criticism should only slowly communicate itself to

All for Love (1678), and the essay, interpolated in the Preface to *Troilus and
Cressida*, on *The Grounds of Criticism in Tragedy* (1679); besides the
Prologue to *The Tempest* (1667), described by Sir Walter Scott as ' one of
the most masterly tributes ever paid at the shrine of Shakespeare,' the
Prologue to *Aureng-zebe* (1675), the Prologue to *All for Love* (1678), and
passages in other Prologues. In the Globe edition of Dryden's *Poetical
Works*, p. 399, the late Mr. Christie printed a Prologue to *Julius Caesar*,
without committing himself to the belief that it is by Dryden. The evidence
in favour of the supposition is internal only, and far from strong of its kind.
Its spirit may be gathered from the couplet :
      ' Such artless beauty lies in Shakespeare's wit,
      'Twas well in spite of him, whate'er he writ.'
[1] The sequel of this remark in the essay *On the grounds of Criticism in
Tragedy* should not be overlooked—nor the general comparative estimate
which precedes it.

the literary world of his age. Writers of the older school
still harped upon his 'natural' gifts as contrasted with his
lack of culture. Fuller, when enrolling him among *The*
Worthies of England (published posthumously in 1662),
had been careful to point out that 'his Learning was very
little, so that, as *Cornish diamonds* are not polished by any
Lapidary, but are pointed and smoothed even as they are
taken out of the Earth. so *Nature* itself was all the Art
which was used upon him.' The conceit is quoted with
approval by Langbaine who, in his *Account of the Dramatick*
Poets (1691), 'took the liberty' of testifying to his belief in
Shakspere's superiority to the rivals whom Dryden had
occasionally seemed to place on an equality with him, or extolled at his expense. Langbaine, however, had but a slight
foliage of learning to offer as a personal contribution to the
fame of 'one of the most eminent poets of his time'; and
the revised edition of his compilation by Gildon—Pope's
Gildon, described by his contemporary Boyer as 'a person
of great literature, but mean genius[1]' (1699)—condenses
rather than expands this part of the work.

The nadir of Shakspere-criticism in this, or perhaps in
any, age was reached by Thomas Rymer, the author of
A Short View of Tragedy, its Original, Excellency and
Corruption, with some Reflections on Shakespear, and other
Practitioners for the Stage (1693). The *Short View*,
though it went back upon both Aristotle and St. Augustine,
was, in fact, but the continuation of *The Tragedies of the*
last Age, &c. (1678, republished in 1692), where Beaumont
and Fletcher had been the main victims of the censor's
mauling[2]. This time Shakspere's *Othello* and *Julius*
Caesar were the chosen victims of a critical attempt which,
far from erring wholly on the side of scholastic pedantry,

Fuller
(1661 or
ante.)

Langbaine
and Gildon
(1691 and
1699).

Rymer
(1693)

---

[1] See Mr. Leslie Stephen's article on Gildon in vol. xxi. of *The Dictionary*
of National Biography (1890). I have not seen the *Remarks on the Plays and*
Poems of Shakespeare, by Gildon, included in a volume published by Curll, in
1710, to pass as a seventh volume to Rowe's edition of Shakspere. His
reply to Rymer is referred to below.

[2] Some time before this, in 1673, he had put forth a Preface, in which there
is nothing remarkable, to Rapin's *Reflections* on Aristotle's *Poetics*—itself by
no means a profound piece of criticism.

IV] *SHAKSPERE*

was waged in the much-abused name of 'common-sense [1].'
It is unnecessary to suppose personal motives to have contributed to Rymer's savagery [2]; but while it is difficult,
even in the case of a writer to whom historical students
owe the debt due to the editor of the *Foedera*, to read with
patience his self-sufficient diatribes against great dramatic
poets both modern and (it should be noted) ancient, he
must be allowed to have here and there hit the mark.
Perhaps the method of criticism followed by him can hardly
altogether avoid such incidental success; as a whole, however, it was hopelessly at fault. And this, both because he
insisted on ruthlessly applying rules instead of perceiving,
as even Rapin did, that a valid rule is only nature reduced
to method—and still more because he was incapable of
reverencing genius. Dryden said of Rymer that he blas-
phemed Shakspere [3]; nor can this imputation, though much

---

[1] 'And certainly there is not requir'd much Learning, or that a man must
be some *Aristotle*, and *Doctor* of *Subtilities*, to form a right judgment in this
particular; common sense suffices; and rarely have I known the *Women-
judges* mistake in these points, when they have the patience to think, and
(left to their own heads) they decide with their own sense.' (*The Tragedies
of the last Age*, p. 4.) Curiously enough Rapin blames the French dramatists
for seeking in their choice of themes 'to please the *Women*, who have
made themselves Judges of these divertisements, and usurped the right to
pass sentence.' (*Reflections on Aristotle's Book of Poesy in particular*, sec. xx.)

[2] His tragedy called *Edgar*, which was intended to 'extol monarchical
principles' and at the same time to exemplify fidelity to the third unity
by compressing the entire action into ten hours, was printed in 1678, and
reprinted in 1691 under the title of *The English Monarch*. For an account
of it see Genest, i. 223–5; it does not appear to have been performed.
Addison makes fun of it in *The Spectator* (No. 605), and after him Sir Walter
Scott described it as a proof of the fact 'that a drama may be extremely
regular and at the same time intolerably dull.' Dryden writes to Jonson
(see Scott's *Dryden*, revised by Saintsbury, vol. xviii. p. 112) that he had
received 'an intimation from a friend by letter, that one of the secretaryes,
I suppose Trenchard, had informed the Queen, that he had abused her
government; and that thereupon she had commanded her historiographer
to fall upon his' (Dryden's) 'playes.'—Rymer is thought to be specially
aimed at in Butler's lines *Upon Critics who judge of Modern Plays precisely
by the Rules of the Ancients* (see R. Bell's edition of *The Poems of Samuel
Butler*, vol. iii. p. 104).

[3] 'You see what success this learned critick has found in the world, after
his blaspheming Shakspeare. Almost all the faults which he has discovered
are truly there; yet who will read Mr. Rymer, or not read Shakspeare?
For my own part I reverence Mr. Rymer's learning, but I detest his ill-
nature and his arrogance. I indeed, and such as I, have reason to be

graver than the charge which may be added of his having misinterpreted Aristotle, be held excessive as against a writer who compares the quarrel between Brutus and Cassius to ' a tryal of skill in huffing and swaggering between two drunken Hectors for a two-penny reckoning,' and condemns the story of *Othello* as ' a senseless, trifling tale.'

Replies to Rymer (Gildon and Dennis).

Rymer's criticism was in this sense serviceable to the growth of Shakspere's fame, that it led to a more careful study of writings which had been censured, not without a certain plausibility in some minor points, after so provocative a fashion. Among those who felt it incumbent upon them to take up the implied challenge were Charles Gildon[1], who has already been mentioned, and John Dennis[2], the pair whose ' friendship long confirm'd by age ' Pope's malice afterwards depicted as engaged in fratricidal conflict[3]. In the present instance they were cordially at one in their admiration of the genius of Shakspere; but while Gildon shows himself to all intents and purposes still under the dominion of the restrictions imposed by adherence to the French rules upon a frank acceptance of Shakspere's method, Dennis, who in a later work returned to the general theme, although regretting Shakspere's want of acquaintance with the ancients, vindicated to him an eminence in tragedy unsurpassed in any age.

Jeremy Collier (1698).

The purpose of Jeremy Collier's *Short View of the Immorality and Profaneness of the English Stage* (1698) was an attack upon its actual condition. His remarks on Shakspere and the Elisabethan drama in general are accordingly, of their kind, incidental, and should be judged as illustrations

afraid of him, but Shakspeare has not.' (Dryden to—as it happened—Dennis, Scott's *Dryden*, revised by Saintsbury, vol. xviii. p. 117.) This passage by itself warrants Johnson's declaration (in his ' Life of Dryden,' in the *Lives of the Poets*) that it is more eligible to go wrong with Dryden 'whose criticism has the majesty of a Queen,' than right with Rymer ' whose criticism has the ferocity of a tyrant.' Pope's opinion, according to Spence, that Rymer was ' one of the best critics we ever had,' ' may be accounted for by the relations between him and Dennis.'

[1] *Some Reflections on Mr. Rymer's Short View*, 1693.

[2] *The Impartial Critic*, 1693. *On the Genius and Writings of Shakespeare*, 1712.

[3] See *The Dunciad*, Bk. iii. vv. 173-8. Concerning Gildon and Dennis as critics of Shakspere, see E. Walder, *History of Shaksperian Criticism*, chap. iv.

adduced in furtherance of the author's main object. At the
same time Collier shows a cordial appreciation of the essential merits of the Elisabethan drama, observing that its
main tendency is moral and (*quis negabit?*) that Shakspere
when he misbehaves gains nothing by his misbehaviour [1].

While thus the English stage and its censors—sympa- *Progress*
thetic, supercilious, or hostile—were turning or returning *of the
popularity*
to Shakspere as part and parcel of its fortunes and its fame, *of Shak-*
his own reputation had advanced into the broad light of *spere.*
day. On the stage his ascendency among its older writers,
after being at first disputed by one or two other favourites,
was gradually passing beyond the range of controversy.
Into ordinary libraries a folio edition of his works, or an
unauthorised quarto copy of a popular play bearing his name,
cannot very often have found its way. Some time was
needed for the relations between the supply and what
cannot but have been a growing demand to establish themselves on a more convenient footing [2]. Without the impulse
given by the critical spirit of the Restoration age, and
largely given under the influence of French examples, it
may, however, be doubted whether the notion of editing
Shakspere would have suggested itself so soon as it did to
English men of letters. Of even the beginnings of textual
criticism, a genuine interest in an author, and a belief in
a response to the labour implied in exerting it, as a rule
form indispensable conditions.

The first edition of Shakspere published in octavo, and *Early
editions of*
appealing to the favour of a wider circle of readers, was *Shakspere.*

[1] Jeremy Collier's remarks on the personage of Falstaff may be commended to commentators (including actors of the character) who, in attempting to purge away the grossness, have done injustice to the human
(not to say the moral) significance, of the character.

[2] The late Mr. W. Bodham Donne, when near the close of a literary career
which I regard with sincere admiration he honoured this book with a
notice, took occasion in it to point out how imperfectly Shakspere's works
were known in the early years of the eighteenth century. 'For example,
when passages are cited from them in *The Tatler*, they are either inac-
curately given, or they are copied from the prompter's books. Addison,
who may be said to have introduced Milton's *Paradise Lost* to multitudes of
English readers, seems to have been almost ignorant of Shakspere's existence,
though he is not niggardly of praise to several of the Restoration dramatists.'
See, however, below.

Rowe's edition (1709).

that by Rowe, which bears the date of 1709[1]. Nicholas Rowe, who was poet-laureate, 'sheltered' his edition under the patronage of the Chancellor of the University of Cambridge. Himself a dramatist of more than ordinary merit —of course of the French ' classical ' school—he was able to supply details of a kind which dramaturgic experience is alone fully qualified for furnishing ; he entertained an ardent veneration for the great master of his art, and a love for the man whose biography, with the aid of information gathered at Stratford by the great actor Betterton[2], he was the first to endeavour to construct. But he was neither ambitious of textual criticism nor qualified for it, and unwittingly did ill service to Shakspere by basing the modernised text of his popular edition, which in its turn became the foundation of the text of all subsequent editions before Capell's, upon that of the corruptest of the Folios (the fourth)[3].

Shakspere's literary fame definitively established in the 'Augustan' age.

We are now in the reign of Queen Anne, and in the so-called Augustan age of English literature. It was the age in which the policy of William III had at last borne fruits, gathered through the agency of the great general and statesman to whom he had bequeathed his political inheritance ; the age, too, in which England stood, more decidedly than at any other time in her history, in the van among the states of Europe, as the representative of progress in almost every field of intellectual life. In those days, if our literary men at times aspired to be statesmen, our statesmen desired with at least equal ardour to be accounted literary men, or at all events to stand forth as the sympathetic friends and patrons of literature. In this period Shakspere's literary fame may be said to have been definitively established.

---

[1] The data in the text as to successive editions of Shakspere are mostly taken from the Preface in the *Cambridge Shakespeare*, and F. Thimm's *Shakspeariana from 1564 to 1864* (2nd edn., 1872). See also Halliwell's *Shakesperiana* (1841) and Mr. E. Walder's essay.

[2] R. Lowe, *Thomas Betterton*, p. 178.

[3] Pope used Rowe's text as the basis of his edition, introducing a few readings from the quartos ; Theobald, who went back more diligently to the original prints, Hanmer and Warburton, similarly used Pope ; and Johnson, who restored some readings of the First Folio, Warburton. See Walder, p. 78.

A large number of editions published in succession, and Pope's edition (1725). more or less in rivalry, to one another, attest the growing recognition of his pre-eminent importance and popularity. Of these the first after that of Rowe was Pope's. He had achieved glory and a competence by his translation of Homer; and the booksellers were sure that he would be able to bestow upon the public that perfect edition of Shakspere for which the time had obviously arrived. The work, the result of a labour neither single-minded nor single-handed[1], made its appearance in 1725, in six quarto volumes. As has been well remarked[2], a passage in the Preface to this edition contains a very fair description of what the editor did *not* do in it. For Pope there observes that 'he has discharg'd the dull duty of an editor, to his best judgment, with more labour than he expects thanks, with a religious abhorrence of all innovation, and without any indulgence to his private sense and conjecture.' The keynote to Pope's spirit as an editor is the quality best expressed by a word that has the authority of both Shakspere and Pope himself, viz. the *cocksure*. His canons of spelling, *e.g.*, are so certain and precise that he corrects the loose orthography of the folio followed by Rowe with a schoolmaster's promptitude and rigour; while his confidence in his own power of conjecture is so absolute that he introduces his own emendations into the text with unscrupulous freedom. At the same time Pope's ingenuity and quickness of mind asserted themselves; his emendations are frequently surprisingly able, and often undoubtedly amount to an obvious restoration of the true text. At other times his omissions are mere *corrections*, dictated by that superiority of taste to which all texts must yield. Yet he was not singular in this conception of textual criticism, and, had he been trained a scholar, his name might have stood at no unmeasurable distance from that of the very Bentley whose ' desperate

---

[1] Pope was assisted in it by Fenton, who received ' 30*l.* 14*s.* for his share in Pope's meagre edition of Shakspere. Very little labour was bestowed upon the work, and much of that little was done by Fenton and Gay.' See Elwin's *Pope*, vol. viii. p. 82, *note*.

[2] Preface to *Cambridge Shakspeare*, vol. i. p. xxix.

hook' he ridiculed. The 'awful Aristarch' himself might have done great service to the text of Shakspere, whose text, however, is on the whole to be considered fortunate in having escaped the more than parental supervision which Bentley bestowed on Milton's.

Theobald's (1733).

Upon Pope's Shakspere (which had passed with considerable rapidity through three editions, and afterwards reached a fourth) followed that of Theobald, in 1733. Lewis Theobald had six years previously incurred the wrath of Pope by a too free criticism of the demerits of his edition of Shakspere in a pamphlet devoted to the subject [1]; and Pope's revenge had been to constitute his critic the original hero of the *Dunciad*. Theobald had some knowledge of the ancient as well as of the modern drama [2], and some acquaintance with the books which might have been known to the author whom he criticised [3]. He had for some time made a special study of Shakspere, on passages of whose works he was in the habit of contributing notes to a weekly paper called *Mist's Journal*— 'crucifying Shakspere once a week,' according to a line omitted from the later editions of the *Dunciad*. Theobald's reputation as an editor of Shakspere has, however, survived that of his spiteful predecessor, and justly so. He was, which Pope was not, conscientious, and did his work with care; unlike Pope, again (whose improvements of Rowe were only in a very slight measure due to references to the First Folio and some of the quartos), he

---

[1] *Shakspear Restored, or a Specimen of the many Errors committed as well as unamended by Mr. Pope in his late edition of the Poet* (1726).

[2] Theobald was a Greek scholar of considerable knowledge, which (as Mr. Elwin has sufficiently demonstrated) Pope was not, and published translations of plays of Sophocles and Aristophanes. He adapted *Richard II* for the stage (1720), and published as Shakspere's a play called *The Double Falsehood* (1728), which is founded on the story of Cardenio in *Don Quixote*, and is thought to have been very probably written by Shirley. See Dyce's edition of Shirley's *Works*, vol. i. p. lix; and for an account of the play, Genest, iii. 205. Cf. a note by Professor R. Sachs in *Jahrbuch d. deutschen Shakespeare-Gesellschaft*, vol. xxvii. (1892), p. 195.—The Dyce Library at South Kensington also contains *The Cave of Poverty*, a poem written by Theobald 'in imitation of Shakespeare.'

[3] Warton calls Theobald the first editor of Shakspere who hit upon the rational method of correcting his author by reading such books as the author himself had read. Thimm, *Shakspeariana*, p. 5.

corrected the basis of his text—viz. Pope's own—by means
of a diligent collation of the existing prints ; and he added
many emendations of his own of real ingenuity and acknowledged merit.

Upon the above ensued a series of editions, which it is unne- *Hanmer's*
cessary to seek to characterise individually, more especially (1744).
as some of them are no longer in ordinary use. Sir Thomas
Hanmer's, published in 1774 at the Oxford University
Press, of which the only excellence seems to have been the
beauty of its type, but which called forth a tribute of
recognition from the poet Collins[1], was succeeded by
Warburton's (1747), professing to follow Pope's text, but in *Warbur-*
reality departing very freely from it, and freely intro- *ton's*
ducing the emendations of other editors, and above (1747).
all Warburton's own. According to Mark Pattison[2],
even Johnson's Preface could not open Warburton's eyes
to the fallacy of his belief in himself as a restorer of
Shakspere[3]. Next came Hugh Blair's (1753) ; and Samuel *Blair's*
Johnson's, which was, after a long delay, completed in (1753).
1765. Of this edition the Preface and the brief observa- *Johnson's*
tions on the several plays form by far the most valuable (1765).
portion. For a thorough textual criticism Johnson hardly
possessed the necessary qualifications, besides being hampered by the physical difficulty of a defective eyesight.
His text is based upon Warburton's ; but he had examined
the First Folio, and the dialectical ingenuity and straight-
forwardness of his critical intellect, the robustness of his
memory, and his considerable acquaintance with as much
of our earlier literature as was in his time known to any

---

[1] See Collins' *Epistle addressed to Sir Thomas Hanmer, on his edition of
Shakespeare's Works*. These lines show a warm admiration for Shakspere
on the part of Collins, who speaks of him as ' the perfect boast of time.'
The distinction which he draws between Shakspere and Fletcher is the
same as that attempted by Dryden. While Fletcher was a master in the
depiction of female passion—
    ' Stronger Shakespear felt for man alone :
    Drawn by his pen, our ruder passions stand
    The unrivall'd picture of his early hand.'

[2] *Essays* (1889), vol. ii. p. 124.

[3] Foote's joke (the best, according to his own judgment, he ever made),
about ' Warburton upon Shakspere,' will be remembered.

but a few professed antiquaries[1], frequently helped him to conjectures which have since gained general acceptance. On the other hand, he brought to the study of Shakspere the full power of a large and, in the best sense, liberal intellect. He was indeed still under the influence of the literary tastes of the Augustan age. He could not conceive of a poet greater than Pope. He could think a felicitously-toned description in Congreve's *Morning Bride* superior to any passage to be found in Shakspere. And, moreover, the bent of his mind was not poetical; nor could it be expected that Johnson should exhibit a full appreciation of Shakspere, when even Goldsmith was without it[2]. Thus, the tone of Johnson's Preface is cold when compared with the ardour of Dryden's enthusiasm. But Johnson was wise and broad-minded enough to reject with scorn the 'minute and slender criticisms of Voltaire,' and his perfect reasonableness made it easy for him to see the truth about the 'unities' which Dryden had failed to grasp. 'Whether Shakspeare knew the unities, and rejected them by design, or deviated from them by happy ignorance, it is, I think, impossible to decide, and useless to enquire. We may reasonably suppose that, when he rose to notice, he did not want the counsels and admonitions of scholars and critics, and that he at last deliberately persisted in a practice, which he might have begun by chance. As nothing is essential to the fable but unity of action, and as the unities of time and place arise evidently from false assumptions, and, by circumscribing the extent of the drama, lessen its variety, I cannot think it to be lamented that they were not known to him, or not observed; nor if such another poet should arise, should I very vehemently reproach him that his first act passed at Venice, and his next in Cyprus[3].

Johnson as a critic of Shakspere.

---

[1] In 1753, Johnson wrote a Preface to Mrs. Lennox's *Shakespear Illustrated*, a collection of stories on which his plays are founded.

[2] See, in illustration of this remark, chap. x. (*On the Stage*) of Goldsmith's *Inquiry into the Present State of Polite Learning* (1750).

[3] This cavil had already been advanced with much show of wit in Rymer's *Short View*: 'For the second act, our Poet having dispatcht his affairs at Venice, shews the action next (I know not how many leagues off) in the Island of Cyprus. The audience must be there too ; and yet our Bays had it never in his head, to make any provision of Transport ships for them.'

Such violations of rules merely positive become the comprehensive genius of Shakspeare, and such censures are
suitable to the minute and slender criticisms of Voltaire.'
The passage which I have quoted is written in the true
spirit of criticism ; for it acknowledges, with a distinctness
wanting even to Dryden's protests in the same direction,
the paramount claims of creative genius. As Lessing justly
says[1], the artist of genius contains in himself the test of
all rules, while he understands, retains and follows only those
among them which express his feeling in words. In other
words, as genius varies, so the application of rules must be
varied ; and it is solely by an endeavour to understand
the intellectual life and developement of a great artist (or
indeed of any artist whom it is worth while to criticise
at all) that the critic can vindicate his right to attention in
the capacity of a guide,—for to act as such is the one purpose
of his functions, whatever notions he may entertain of them
himself[2].

In addition to this insight into the nature of true literary
criticism, Johnson was a faithful and acute observer of
human character; and his psychological comments, simple
and to the point notwithstanding their grandiloquence of
diction, will frequently be found to furnish assistance, where
the more ambitious efforts of his successors have a tendency
to darken the author's meaning.

In subsequent editions (from that of 1773 onwards) *Johnson*
Johnson had the advantage of the co-operation of George *and*
Steevens, who had already (in 1766) edited a reprint from *Steevens'*
the Quartos of twenty of Shakspere's plays, and whose *edition*
learning explained, from the literature contemporary with *(1773).*
Shakspere, many passages in him that had previously

---

[1] Cf. Stahr's *G. E. Lessing*, i. 326.

[2] It need not be added that the history of the classical drama in itself
suffices to teach the necessity of keeping in view the relation between rules
and the rights of creative power. Already Ben Jonson very properly says,
after touching on the progressive character of the history of Classical
Comedy : ' We should enjoy the same licence, or free power to illustrate and
heighten our invention as they [the ancients] did ; and not be tied to
those strict and regular forms which the niceness of a few, who are nothing
but form, would thrust upon us.' See *Introduction* to *Every Man out of
his Humour*.

Farmer's essay (1767).

remained obscure.   Johnson also benefited by a variety of information and suggestions furnished by Dr. Farmer, Master of Emmanuel College, Cambridge, who enjoyed a high renown as a Shaksperean scholar.   His essay *On the Learning of Shakspere*, which both Johnson and Warton declared to have permanently settled the question at issue[1], had first appeared in 1767.   Johnson and Steevens' edition had been preceded by that of Capell (1767), of which the Preface was severely commented on by Johnson, but which the Cambridge editors of our own times have not overpraised in describing it as ' by far the most valuable contribution to Shakespearian criticism that had yet appeared[2].' Its distinctive merit lies in the fact that, whereas previous editors had only professed to found their text upon the old copies, Capell had, with infinite labour, really collated them, and critically examined their relative significance and value.   Moreover, he pointed the way which Steevens so successfully took to a thorough study of Shakspere's sources ; and he made a special study of Shaksperean versification. Capell devoted the better part of a life-time to his labour of love, publishing its results under conditions unfavourable to immediate fame, of which like a true scholar he seems to have been careless[3].

Edward Capell's edition (1767).

Malone's (1790).

Johnson and Steevens' edition was republished in 1778, and in 1785 by Isaac Reed, with contributions by Edmund Malone, who in 1780 had brought out a supplementary volume of his own, containing the *Poems*, and in 1790 published his own edition of the *Works*.   In Steevens' own

---

[1] Dr. Johnson's compliment is, however, deprived of its value by his observation in answer to Colman's query on the same subject, ' What says Farmer to this? what says Johnson?' ' Sir, let Farmer answer for himself: *I* never engaged in this controversy.   I always said that Shakspeare had Latin enough to grammaticise his English.'   See Langton's *Collectanea* in Croker's *Boswell*, vii. 365.

[2] *Cambridge Shakespeare*, i. xxxvi.

[3] See Thimm, *Shakspeariana*, p. 7.   The uncouthness of his style interfered with his reputation ; Johnson said that if Capell had come to him, he would have endowed his purposes with words, and Warburton pronounced him an idiot.   (See Howard Furness' Preface to the *New Variorum* edition of *Macbeth*, 1873, pp. vi–vii, where an honourable tribute is paid to him.   Cf. the full and lucid exposition of Capell's merits, *ap.* Walder, pp. 125 *seqq.*

edition, of 1793, he unhappily abandoned safer methods, and while seeking to ridicule Malone forfeited on his own part much of that confidence which was permanently secured by his equally laborious but more faithful rival. The industry of these two rivals supplied the most considerable portion of the learning which fills the great ' *Variorum*' edition of 1821, edited by James Boswell from a corrected copy left by Malone. (For the so-called first and second *Variorums* of 1803 and 1813 Reed had made himself responsible.) The twenty-one volumes of the 'third *Variorum*' remain the fullest storehouse of the English Shakspere-learning of the old school; and it is difficult to believe that they will ever be superseded as the standard edition of ordinary English libraries. Many other editions were published in these years and in those immediately succeeding, which it would serve no purpose to enumerate here [1]. Nor can I touch upon the critical and controversial tracts which some of the chief editions called forth, and among which the pamphlets of Joseph Ritson on the editions of Steevens and Malone (1783, 1788 and 1789), and those of John Monck Mason (1785, 1798 and 1807) were conspicuous [2]. In every size and in every form, in folio and in miniature, illustrated with ponderous splendour and expurgated by timid prudery, Shakspere was now in the hands of the reading public; and it has been calculated that during the eighteenth century alone as many as 30,000 copies of Shakspere's works were dispersed through England [3].

Thus the greatest of English poets had, through the spread of his printed works, at last been popularised among his fellow-countrymen, while the influence of the stage (of

Reed's (1803-13) and Boswell's (1821) Variorum.

Activity of English Shakspere scholarship.

Influence of French taste on the criticism of Shakspere.

---

[1] It is interesting to learn (see *Academy*, April 11, 1874) that an edition of Shakspere was contemplated, and actually commenced, by Sir W. Scott. Three volumes (not including the introductory, to which Scott's own labours were to be chiefly confined) were printed by 1826, and a copy of them is preserved in the Public Library of Boston, U.S.

[2] See *Cambridge Shakespeare*, vol. i. p. xxxix.

[3] Thimm, *Shakspeariana*, p. 8. The most gigantic monument of individual enthusiasm for Shakspere belonging to the eighteenth century is Richard Warner's *Glossary* of his plays, compiled probably some time between 1750 and 1770, which, in seventy-one volumes in quarto and octavo, remains— still in MS.—in the British Museum. *Ib.* p. 6.

which immediately) had with renewed force contributed to
the same result.   Yet it was only gradually that the English
mind, in securing this noble portion of its inheritance, had
freed itself from interference with its enjoyment of the
treasure by tastes and tendencies of alien growth.   Addison[1]
was of service, though but very occasionally, to a closer
study of Shakspere's characteristics as a dramatic poet ; but
it is wonderful that neither he nor any of his literary contemporaries should have given signs that they had freely
opened their natures to his influence in its whole depth
and breadth.   Consciously or unconsciously, the literary
inclinations of Englishmen were still largely swayed by
French taste, with whose models it was difficult to reconcile
the vivid and varied movement of the Elisabethan drama.

*Early
traces of an
acquaint-
ance with
Shakspere
in French
writers
(seven-
teenth
century).*

Its master-spirit Shakspere, cannot, however, have been
wholly unknown in France, even before (in 1726–8) Voltaire
visited England, and, much to the unsettlement of the balance
of his own critical judgments on the subject of the drama,
personally re-discovered Shakspere.   Whether or not an
occasional resemblance to passages in *Hamlet* may be traceable in the *Agrippina* of Cyrano de Bergerac (1654)[2], it is
not easily conceivable that in the course of our Restoration
age some knowledge of the Elisabethan drama, and of
Shakspere's plays in particular, should have failed to find
its way across the Narrow Seas.   St. Evremond, whose
works were published at Paris in 1699, had spent most of
his life in England, and had there attained some knowledge
of the productions of our stage, including to all appearance
at least one play in the Shaksperean canon (*Henry VIII*) ;
and Peter Anthony de Motteux, another refugee, who had
become domiciled in the English world of letters, had interested himself in Rymer's attacks upon Shakspere, and, sympathetically, in Dennis' projected defence of him (1692–3)[3].

---

[1] See *The Spectator*, Nos. 141, 419.   Both passages refer to Shakspere's
treatment of the supernatural.

[2] See Miss Toulmin Smith's note to *Centurie of Prayse*, 2nd edn., in
New Shakspere Society's Publications, 1879, p. 416, correcting a statement
in the first edition of this book for which I must confess myself unable to
furnish a warrant.

[3] See *ib.*, pp. 396 and 415.   Cf. an article on the appreciation of Shakspere

The impulse of Voltaire's wit and fire was however needed *Voltaire and Shakspere.* to stir up the controversial ferment which brought about the spread of a wider interest in Shakspere among French readers, from which the true spirit of critical appreciation— but only very gradually—disengaged itself. Voltaire's claims to the literary leadership of France were sustained by him through a period of unexampled length, and the fact of his predominant share in asserting her intellectual ascendency among civilised nations, and in extending its sphere, has been confirmed rather than weakened by the judgment of generations no longer subject to his dictatorship.   But his temperament was not poetical ; and of the true purposes of the drama a glimpse was only fitfully caught by his restless eye.   With the models of the classical drama his acquaint- ance seems to have been superficial, and the contempt with which he frequently refers to the ancients is by no means the offspring of familiarity[1].   On the other hand, although the lightness with which his mind moved left it constantly open to the reception of new impressions, which his in- comparably clear style never failed to communicate in an effective fashion to his public, they had no permanent abiding with himself, like the old literary habitudes to which the traditions of the great era of the French theatre had inured him.   In his censures of Shakspere there is accordingly both inconsistency and a pertinacity which survives all changes of mood[2].   The impression made upon him by the greatest representative of the Elisabethan drama first became manifest in his *Brutus*, of which the production was deferred to 1730.   In the *Discours sur la Tragédie* addressed to Bolingbroke, prefixed to this play on publication, Voltaire poses as the champion of the methods, including the rimed verse, of French tragedy, but makes no secret of his perception of the force derived by the English tragic stage from the action

in England, France and Germany, by Dr. Riedel in Herrig's *Archiv für das Studium der neueren Sprachen u. Literaturen*, vol. xlviii. p. 25.

[1] See, for illustrations of this, Hettner, *Literaturgeschichte des 18. Jahrhun- derts*, vol. ii. p. 390.

[2] For a full consecutive survey of these, see the essay *Voltaire und Shakespeare*, by W. König, jun., in vol. x. of the *Jahrbuch*, &c. (1875).

which forms its most distinctive feature. Incidental illustrations of Voltaire's insight into Shaksperean workmanship
are noticeable in some of his plays belonging to the ensuing
period of his dramatic authorship [1]. One of his *Lettres sur
les Anglais* (1734)—famous as the first of his productions
condemned to the flames—dealt with Shaksperean tragedy,
in which it acknowledged the presence of powerful genius,
while regretting the absence of a spark of good taste and
of the slightest knowledge of rules [2]. His *Mort de César*,
surreptitiously published in 1735, showed a direct influence
—unprecedented with him—of what may, notwithstanding
all differences of treatment and form, be in this instance
fairly called his Shaksperean model. No such influence
was, however, perceptible in his ensuing dramatic works,
until the revival of the ghost from *Éryphile* in *Sémiramis*
(1748) suggested the criticism of *Hamlet*, and of the
dramatic genius of its author, in the *Dissertation sur la
Tragédie* prefixed by Voltaire to the later play. It is in this
essay that the French public was informed that 'the tragedy
of *Hamlet* is a coarse and barbarous piece, which would not
be tolerated by the lowest mob in France or Italy'; and
that 'seemingly Nature thought fit to unite in the head of
Shakspeare the greatest strength and grandeur imaginable
with the lowest and most detestable characteristics of
coarseness unredeemed by wit.'

*French
versions of
Shakspere
(1746 et
post).*

But, in point of fact, the French public was already being
placed in a position to form for itself, however slowly, an
opinion on the merits of Shakspere. In 1746 had appeared
the first volume of a series of versions (it is stated, ill and
unfaithfully executed) of Shaksperean and other Elisabethan
plays, under the title of *Le Théâtre Anglais*, to which

---

[1] See *Éryphile* (1732) and its ghost ; *Adélaïde du Guesclin* (1634), as
illustrating the effect of the *Histories*; and above all *Zaïre* (1732), one of the
acknowledged dramatic masterpieces of its author, who never confessed
the debt which in it he owed to *Othello*.

[2] This letter contained the counterpart of Hamlet's soliloquy as it *ought
to have been* written :

'Demeure, il faut choisir, et à passer à l'instant
De la vie à la mort, et de l'être au néant,' &c.

Cf. Karl Elze, *Hamlet in Frankreich*, in *Jahrbuch*, &c., vol. i. (1865).

its responsible editor, Laplace, had prefixed a general
dissertation and a biography of Shakspere.   It is true that
after (in 1760) Voltaire had at last published his own
translation of *Julius Caesar*, accompanying it by a commentary depreciatory of the author's taste and breeding in
comparison with those of Corneille[1], the Academy in thank-
ing him regretted that it had been impossible to procure
a copy of the original for purposes of comparison.   The
arrogance with which in his later years Voltaire continued
arbitrarily to mingle praise and blame in his utterances on
Shakspere[2], was, on the face of it, merely the assertion of
a supremacy, of which the days were numbered in relation
to many matters besides those specially affected by these
utterances.   In 1769 J. Ducis brought out his version of
Hamlet, in which, duly mindful of the example set by
supreme authority, he undertook to disengage the northern
light from its concomitant fogs.   This adaptation—which
under different literary conditions might have been termed
audacious[3]—was followed by re-modellings of *Romeo and*

[1] In the observations at the close occurs the assertion that Corneille's
genius stands in the same relation to Shakspere's as that of a man of
birth and breeding to that of a man of the people endowed by nature
with the same intellectual power. The celebrated description of Shakspere as '*le Corneille de Londres, grand fou d'ailleurs et ressemblant plus à
Gilles qu'à Corneille*; *mais il a des morceaux admirables*' seems to belong
to as early a date as 1735. ('*Gille*,' according to the *Dictionnaire de
l'Académie*, is '*un personnage du spectacle de la foire*'). Cf. Hettner, *u. s.*,
vol. ii. p. 232. Voltaire afterwards spoke derisively of 'Gilles Shakespeare,'
and his henchman 'Gilles Letourneur' (König, *u. s.*, pp. 292 and 295).—
His commentary on Corneille, it may be mentioned, was published in 1772.

[2] In the pamphlet published in 1761 under the pseudonym of Jérôme
Curré, and in critical observations published on various occasions in his own
name or contained in his correspondence. See König, *u. s.*, pp. 288–
296. It is impossible to forget that this was the period of Voltaire's career
rendered illustrious by his championship of the cause of Tolerance in connexion with the Calas case ; and it is interesting to note that in the article
Intolérance in the *Dictionnaire Philosophique* he finds a place for Shakspere
among the intellectual élite anathematised, as a matter of course, by the
objects of his scorn. This tribute, as is well observed by Grillparzer in his
aphorisms on Shakspere (*Werke*, 2nd edn., 1874, vol. ix. p. 349), redeems
many of Voltaire's aspersions of Shakspere.

[3] The Ghost (notwithstanding the august Voltairean precedents) is not
admitted on the stage. Ophelia intensifies the plot by becoming the
daughter of Claudius. Hamlet survives the fifth act, ending his theatrical
developement with the *mot* : 'I shall know how to live, which is more than

Juliet, King Lear, Macbeth and *Othello*. The whole series —as at least it seems to me—is commendable in its way, though the way is much that of a modern opera-libretto.

Encouraged by signs favourable to the widening of the literary horizon of his fellow-countrymen, Pierre Letourneur was able in 1776 to commence the publication of his French annotated Shakspere, which, with the co-operation of Counts de Catuelan and Fontaine-Malherbe, was brought to a completion in 1783 [1]. The commencement of this edition —one of those literary feats which vindicate the supreme utility of endowments—provoked Voltaire's *Letters to the Academy* (1776), which, while they exhibit their author as consistent in his inconsistency, also offer illustrations, as humorous as they are lamentable, of the recklessness of subjective criticism *in extremis*. Shakspere is here saluted as a drunken savage, a clumsy rope-dancer, a mountebank in rags—but this 'Thespis' could at times also be a Sophocles, and interpose among the filthy drunkards of his scene heroes in whose features majesty was to be traced [2]. The echoes of anathemas so strangely toned off would probably have died out before very long—more especially as the source of these judgments was no longer regarded as one of literary infallibility—had not the times soon become so prohibitive of an understanding, even in matters of literature, between the French and the English public. As it was, these echoes were audible even in the spacious literary *repetitorium* presided over, with results so admirable on the

Voltaire's final utterances on Shakspere (1776).

to die.'—This revised *Hamlet* had a literary success sufficient to cause it to be translated both into Italian and into Dutch.—The *Othello*, on its production by Talma at the *Théâtre Français* in 1791, was held to have been 'composed by a Moor, not by a Frenchman.' (Cf. Th. Muret, *L'Histoire par le Théâtre* (1789-1851), vol. i. p. 65. See *ib.*, pp. 212 *seqq.*, for a very pleasing account of Ducis.)

[1] It comprised the notes of Steevens and previous English editors, as well as the notes in the German translation by Eschenburg. This publication, which bore the characteristically apologetic motto '*Homo sum, humani nihil*' (as Elze says, not even Shakspere) '*a me alienum puto*,' attracted the sympathetic praises of Diderot.

[2] Hettner, vol. ii. p. 232 ; cf. König, p. 301.—It would be difficult to imagine a more contemptible spectacle than that of Voltaire the courtier laying at the feet of the Princesses of the Blood the stones which Voltaire the critic has been hurling against 'Gilles.'

whole, by the voluminous Laharpe (1799–1805), and in the criticisms of Voltaire's assailant, J. L. Geoffroy (from about 1776 onwards), who vainly sought in Shakspere for 'a trace of the ideas and manner of Sophocles [1].'

At home in England, Voltaire's antithetical mixture of praise and blame to Shakspere's address had not failed either to command attention or to provoke comment. Mrs. Elisabeth Montagu's *Essay on the Writings and Genius of Shakspeare* (1770), designed as an independent criticism, and in point of fact so independent as to attract the dictatorial censures of Johnson, with whose literary principles it was largely in accord, ventured on some direct attacks both upon Voltaire, and, more especially, upon his model tragic poet Corneille [2]. The general merits of Mrs. Montagu's book cannot of course be rated so high now as they were in her own day, when it enjoyed high esteem. Easy in style, and adorned by grace and wit enough to show that our early blue-stockings were also women of the world, it is deficient in depth and originality, and is worthy of enduring remembrance chiefly because of the fearlessness of spirit which is too often the main *desideratum* in criticisms of very masculine pretensions [3]. In 1777 [4] Joseph Baretti, who during his long period of residence in London had secured the esteem of Johnson, published in French his *Discours sur Shakespeare et sur M. de Voltaire*—an essay of noticeably unprejudiced spirit, at least as to the

Replies to Voltaire.

Mrs. Montagu (1770).

Contemporary English criticisms of Shakspere.

---

[1] Cf. Elze, *u. s.*, p. 99.

[2] See E. Walder, *Shaksperian Criticism*, pp. 17–18 ; 55 *seqq.*

[3] Mrs. Montagu's *Essay* received many memorable tributes of praise —among others the expression of what appear to have been Johnson's second—and probably juster—thoughts concerning it—how it was ' *ad hominem,* conclusive against Voltaire,' &c.,—and, as late as 1788, enthusiastic praise from Cowper.—See, for an amusing account of the original reception of the book, Dr. Doran's *A Lady of the Last Century* (1873), pp. 148–156. He relates (p. 207) that in 1776 Mrs. Montagu was present in the Academy during the reading of a furious paper by Voltaire against Shakspere. When the reading came to an end, Suard remarked to her : ' I think, Madam, you must be rather sorry at what you have just heard ! ' The English lady promptly replied : ' I, sir ! Not at all. I am not one of M. de Voltaire's friends.'

[4] This was the year after Baretti's final estrangement from Mrs. Thrale (afterwards Mrs. Piozzi), and two years after their and Johnson's joint visit to Paris.

critical pretensions of the second-named literary magnate [1]. Among English writers who in this period contributed to a larger, if not in all respects adequate, estimate of Shakspere's genius, William Richardson (1774–1797) should find remembrance—one of the Scottish professors of humanity who have vindicated to their chair its opulent title ; for his many and various writings on Shakspere render due honour to the English poet as a classic for all time [2]. He would seem to have been most successful in the branch of criticism essayed in his earliest production, *A Philosophical Analysis of some of Shakespeare's Remarkable Characters* (1774). A very noticeable effort in the same direction was the paradoxical, but singularly able, *Essay on the Dramatic Character of Sir John Falstaff* (1777) by Maurice Morgann, a dilettante of fine type [3].

Shakspere and the English stage in the latter half of the eighteenth century. Thus, then, both in England and, after the fitful fashion described, in France, the fame of Shakspere had in the course of the eighteenth century progressed towards its height in the world of letters. The final impulse towards a full literary recognition of the poet was to come from yet another quarter ; but meanwhile his works had been enabled to make a more powerful appeal than at any previous time to direct popular sympathy in his own land. I have no wish to touch in this place upon the general history of the English stage in the eighteenth century ; but any sketch, however brief, of the growth of the knowledge and appreciation of Shakspere in his native land ought to include at least a reference to the artistic career of Garrick. In the person of this incomparable actor genius of a high order did true service to genius of the very highest.

David Garrick was born in 1716 ; but the birthday of

[1] Cf. König, *u. s.*, pp. 303–4.

[2] See Mr. Thomas Bayne's notice of him in vol. xlviii. of the *Dictionary of National Biography* (1896) ; and cf. E. Walder, *Shaksperian Criticism*, pp. 60–69. Richardson seems at the same time to have shown a singular appreciation of Shakspere's fidelity to nature, although (*more philosophorum*) he entertained doubts as to the sufficiency of such guidance.

[3] Cf. Walder, *u. s.*, p. 18, and Mr. Seccombe's notice in the same volume of *The Dictionary of National Biography*. Morgann's essay was republished in 1825, with a brief notice of the author, who was Under-Secretary of State in Lord Lansdowne's first administration and died in 1802.

his theatrical career was the 19th of October, 1741, when, *Garrick* (1741– 1776). in a small theatre near Goodman's Fields, he made his first appearance in London (*incognito*, for he had adopted the profession of the stage against the wishes of his family), in the character of Richard III. 'That young man,' said Pope, who had been induced to come up from his retirement to witness this performance, 'never had his equal, and never will have a rival.' So far as it is possible to judge in such a case, the history of the English stage seems to have justified Pope's confident prophecy. From the very beginning of his career Garrick occupied an unapproached, though at first not uncontested, pre-eminence in his profession. His unparalleled success seems to have been due, in very unequal proportion, to three causes. First, to his birth, breeding, and natural gifts ;—he had some French blood in his veins ; he was gently born and gently nurtured, and nature had given him an eye, if not a stature, to command, and a mimic power of inexhaustible variety. Secondly, to his education,—both that which he had received at the hands of his teachers (Johnson was one of them), and that which to the last he continued to give to himself. He loved literature, not merely because of its connexion with the profession which he had adopted, but because of an innate and carefully developed taste; he was himself not without literary endowment; and patient study made him a scholar among actors, until he could hold his own as an actor among scholars[1]. Thirdly, and above all, to his genius, which at many points placed him in immediate contact with the genius of Shakspere, and enabled him to perceive intuitively and to reproduce directly the very essence of those characters which the ordinary actor, like the ordinary reader, sees only dimly or in a more or less shadowy outline[2].

---

[1] It was with the view, never realised, of publishing an edition of Shakspere. that Garrick formed the collection of old plays now in the British Museum. Charles Lamb used this collection for his *Specimens*, and afterwards published a special series of *Extracts* from it in Hone's *Table Book* (1827).

[2] 'His' (Shakspere's) 'very spirit,' says Mrs. Montagu in the Introduction to her *Essay*, 'seems to come forth and animate his characters, as often as Mr. Garrick, who acts with the same inspiration with which he wrote,

His services to Shak-spere.   But I must here confine myself to Garrick's direct services to Shakspere. It can hardly be doubted that the *Richard III* in which he first appeared was Colley Cibber's version ; on the other hand, it is certain that *King Lear* and *King John* followed in the same year, and *Macbeth* not long afterwards, in the original text. So unaccustomed had the public and the actors become to this original text, that Garrick's rival, Quin, asked him where he had picked up all the strange words which he had introduced into the play. In 1748, *Romeo and Juliet*, which had not been acted for more than eighty years, was again produced ; and, to sum up, I find from the lists given by a recent biographer of Garrick[1], that he assumed himself seventeen different Shaksperean characters; while during his management of Drury Lane (which lasted from 1747 to 1776) he produced altogether not less than twenty-four of Shakspere's plays. Thus he came very near to realising the plan conceived about this time by Frederick Prince of Wales (who delighted in playing the patron of literature), of producing successively on the stage every one of Shakspere's dramas.

It would at the same time be ill-judged to misstate the nature of the services rendered by this indefatigable interpreter to the poet with whose fame he thus identified his own. Garrick was of course moved to these exertions not solely by his admiration for Shakspere's genius. As an actor, and still more as a manager, he was obliged to consult the taste of his public; nor was his own taste—how could it have been?—on the highest level of pure sympathy with Shakspere's poetic genius. He therefore treated many of the Shaksperean plays which he produced with arbitrary self-will ; he mutilated several of the comedies, and allowed himself alterations and interpolations even in some of the tragedies,—even, as has been already seen[2], in

---

assumes them on the stage.' (So Klopstock wrote in Schröder's *album :* 'Schröder plays no part well; for he is always the man himself.' F. L. Schmidt, *Denkwürdigkeiten*, &c., vol. ii. p. 135). It was therefore a well-merited tribute, and no commonplace compliment, when Churchill, in his *Rosciad*, made Shakspere himself assign the palm to Garrick.

[1] P. Fitzgerald, *Life of Garrick*, 2 vols. (1868).

[2] *Ante*, p. 515 and *note*. The omission of the grave-diggers seems to have

Hamlet, hitherto untouched by English adapters. But
the essence of the service which he rendered was not
only that, surrounded as he was by a brilliant band of
distinguished actors and actresses, he gave a new and
unprecedented impulse to the popular admiration of the
genius of Shakspere, but that he practically corrected the
false view which had pervaded successive generations of
literary criticism, and which Johnson's sedate insight would
not have sufficed to correct, as to the intrinsic rudeness and
imperfection of the gifted pre-Augustan poet.   Garrick
showed, by the quickest and least disputable method of
interpretation, that Shakspere's art is supremely adequate
to its ends ; and thus he vindicated for Shakspere's genius
that which even enthusiastic critics and editors had hitherto
been prone to deny to it.   Remembering this, we may
omit any reference to the excesses and extravagances
into which Garrick was hurried by a vanity anything but
surprising, when not only the general nature but the special
circumstances of his career are taken into consideration.
Thus, we may even pass by the pretentious farce of the
Shakspere Jubilee at Stratford in 1769 (five years after
the Bicentenary of the poet's birthday) which, by the way,
is significant of the subsidiary fact that in helping to make
Shakspere popular Garrick had also succeeded in making
him fashionable. Since Garrick, Shakspere has in good times   *Shakspere
as in evil been held in supreme honour on the English stage ;   *permanently popu-*
it has been impossible either to deny his royalty or to leave   *larised on
him a *roi fainéant* ; and to this day, though the number   *the English
stage.*
of his plays actually holding the boards still falls far short of
the entire canon[1], and though 'all that glisters' in the method
of their performance ' is not gold,'—yet the success which
his works command on the stage is something altogether
different from a mere 'success of esteem' or tribute of
acknowledgment paid to his literary pre-eminence. In other

been due, not to critical prejudice, but to a desire to save the play from
the buffooneries that had become traditional in the scene in question.

[1] If my records serve me, eight of the thirty-seven plays have never been
seen on any English stage since I first became a play-goer, and one or two
more have been only experimentally produced.

words, Shakspere has never lost the popularity which it is the great actor's merit to have definitively and permanently established for his beloved master in their common sphere.

It was thus that the nation which had given birth to Shakspere possessed itself of the readiest key to a just appreciation of its greatest poet, and attained to a perception of the twin truths, that nature and art are not antithetical to one another, and that in Shakspere they are not indeed uniformly and perfectly, but in sum and substance, harmonised. About the same time the same lesson was first impressed upon a kindred nation, with greater force and fulness of theory, though in no sense by the dissociation of theory from practice. The writer who first placed the claims of Shakspere in a clear and indisputable light was the great German Lessing, one of the most original and most powerful critics of all times.

Early knowledge of Shakspere in Germany : ' The English Co-medians.'

Lessing was far from being the first to introduce the plays of Shakspere to the notice of his countrymen. In a previous chapter brief reference has been made to the close connexion which prevailed, in the latter part of the sixteenth century, between the English stage and the theatres of Germany and its borderlands on the North and Baltic seas [1]. A large number of the plays performed in these regions during the period in question consisted of reproductions of well-known English plays—the most popular pieces of Shakspere's predecessors and contemporaries, and not a few of Shakspere's own. Thus, within a few months of the year 1626 the English comedians at Dresden performed, in addition to plays by Kyd, Marlowe and Greene, a *Romeo and Julietta*, a *Julius Caesar*, a *Hamlet Prince in Denmark*, and a *Lear King in England*, all of which may fairly be presumed to have been the Shaksperean plays [2]. Direct

---

[1] See *ante*, pp. 471-3.—As to the performances of the English comedians in the Netherlands (at Gröningen and Utrecht in 1597, at Leyden in 1604 and 1605, &c.), and the literary relations of the seventeenth century to which they helped to give rise, see Lina Schneider, *Shakespeare in den Niederlanden*, in *Jahrbuch*, &c., vol. xxvi. (1891).

[2] See the complete list in A. Cohn, *Shakespeare in Germany*, pp. cxv–cxvi. Cf. *ante*, p. 473 note 3, as to the performance at Graz, in 1608, of a German version of *The Merchant of Venice*.

influences of this description must unmistakeably have operated upon such German dramatists as Duke Henry Julius of Brunswick and Jacob Ayrer in the composition of their dramatic works, whatever may have been the actual relations between particular plays composed by them and their Shaksperean similars[1]; and not many years after the deaths of these two dramatists the plays of the English comedians appeared in print, and were therefore readily accessible to German dramatists. Andreas Gryphius (1616–1664), who survived the Thirty Years' War, confessed to having taken his *Absurda Comica*, or *Herr Peter Squenz*, from Daniel Schwenter (who died in 1636); but the *Midsummer Night's Dream* was undoubtedly its primary if not its immediate source[2]. Christian Weise, whose *Comedy of the angry Catherine* was performed in 1705, must have been acquainted with Shakspere's *Taming of the Shrew*[3]. These examples must suffice to prove the indisputable fact that in Germany some knowledge of Shakspere's plays had survived even the blight which had spread over the intellectual activity of the nation after its seemingly hopeless political collapse.

Early German imitations and adaptations.

But it was as plays of unknown origin, brought over by English actors, that Shaksperean plays had thus become and remained known in Germany; nor can the influence which they and their like exercised upon the literary developement of such a writer as Gryphius be regarded as having

---

[1] Jacob Ayrer's *Comoedia von zweyen Brüdern auss Syracus* was probably imitated from an adaptation of the *Menaechmi* of Plautus earlier than Shakspere's comedy; the relations between his *Sidea* and *The Tempest* form a question of more difficulty and importance, to which I shall return below. Ayrer also wrote a *Comedia vom König Edwarto, dem dritten diss Namens*, &c. See the Introduction to the select plays by Ayrer, printed in Part ii. of J. Tittmann's *Schauspiele aus dem 16. Jahrhundert* (Leipzig, 1868). Of the plays of Duke Henry Julius, as a rule simpler in form, it would be difficult to single out one which shows the direct influence of Shakspere, though this has been thought demonstrable in the case of the *Comoedia von Vincentio Ladislao Satrapo von Mantua*. See the Introduction to Tittmann's edition of select plays by the Duke (Leipzig, 1880).

[2] Cohn, p. cxxx. Cf. as to Gryphius' acquaintance with Shakspere, Goedeke, *Elf Bücher deutscher Dichtung*, i. 374.

[3] Cohn, *u. s.*, seems convincing as against Genée, *Gesch. der Shakespeare'-schen Dramen in Deutschland*, p. 52.

exercised any important effect upon the progress of German literature at large.   Later dramatists, such as Michael Kongehl (1646–1710), treated Shaksperean subjects without betraying the least direct acquaintance with the corresponding Shaksperean plays [1].   German literature, following the classicising direction first given to it by Martin Opitz and, except in certain trivial growths of enduring tenacity, the German stage, which had surrendered itself to the alien rule of the opera, alike ceased to derive any of their inspirations from the English drama.

First German mention of Shakspere personally (1682).

As, from this period onwards, German literature gradually fell into bondage to French taste, the beginnings of a knowledge of Shakspere were extinguished before they had attained to any considerable significance.   His name is first mentioned in a German work in 1682 [2]; but the author of this confesses himself wholly unacquainted with Shakspere's writings.   A second notice occurs in 1704, but only in a secondhand quotation from an English authority [3].   A few other references follow in later years; but Shakspere's name is conspicuous by its absence from the second edition of the *Kritische Dichtkunst*, published in 1737, of Gottsched, the dictator of the German literary world in those days of bondage [4].   It is even more curious that, in 1740 and 1741, Bodmer, who strongly approved of the influence exercised by English literature upon that of his native country, should, although twice adverting to Shakspere, under the disguises, to be sure, of 'Saspar' and 'Sasper,' betray no personal acquaintance with his writings [5].

Bodmer's 'Sasper' (1740-1).

First German translation of a

In the second of these very years (1741) the first attempt at translating Shakspere into German was made by C. W. von

---

[1] Genée, *u. s.*; cf. Cohn, p. cxxxiii.

[2] In Morhoff's *Unterricht von der deutschen Sprache und Poësie.* Cf. Cohn, p. cxxxvi.

[3] Viz. Sir William Temple, in Barthold Feind's *Gedanken von der Opera.* Cf. *ib.* It has recently been discovered that one of the earliest occurrences of Shakspere's name in a French book is in a translation into that tongue of Temple's *Miscellaneous Works* (Utrecht, 1693).

[4] Thimm, *u. s.*, p. 51.

[5] 1 confess, however, that I agree with Elze, *Bodmer's Sasper* in *Jahrbuch*, &c., vol. i. (1865), in perceiving no proof of Bodmer's ignorance of Shakspere as a writer in the mere fact that he mis-spelt (or Germanised) the poet's name.

Borck, who published a version in Alexandrines of *Julius* *Shak-*
Caesar. But although signs now appear of an awakening on *sperean*
play(1741).
the part of literary critics, such as John Elias Schlegel and
even Gottsched himself, to the fact of Shakspere's literary
existence,—the one damns him with faint praise, the other
still treats him with lofty contempt,—twenty years were still
to pass before in 1762 Wieland began the translation of *Wieland*
Shakspere which was first to open a knowledge of the author *and*
Eschen-
to the German literary public[1]. This translation, of which *burg's*
Wieland accomplished twenty-two plays, was completed by *translation*
(1762–
Eschenburg in 1775. It was entirely in prose, with the 1775).
single exception of the *Midsummer Night's Dream*.

In Germany, however, the beginnings of criticism had *Beginnings*
of German
preceded the first sustained attempts at translation; and *Shakspere-*
before Wieland had put forth the first instalment of his *criticism.*
versions[2], and before the stage had begun effectively to
second his endeavours, Lessing had entered the arena.
The vindication of Shakspere's dramatic processes was
but incidental to the great critic's main purpose; yet his
triumphant accomplishment of this vindication formed
a conspicuous as well as an integral part of his victory
over prepossession and prejudice. Lessing's *Literaturbriefe* *Lessing*
(1758 *et*
(1758), which boldly threw down a challenge to Gottsched as *post*).
the champion of French taste and of its predominance over
German literature, asserted in round terms the superiority
of Shakspere to Corneille, and denied the claims of the
French drama to be regarded as truly modelled upon the
example of the ancients, who were indeed more closely
approached by it in the matter of mechanical arrangement,
but to whom Shakspere came nearer in the essentials of his
art. 'The Englishman almost invariably attains to the
end of tragedy, however peculiar and proper to himself
the ways may be which he chooses; while the Frenchman

---

[1] Cf. A. Koberstein's summary of the origin and progress of the knowledge
and love of Shakspere in Germany: *Shakespeare in Deutschland,* in the same
volume of the same Journal.

[2] Wieland's own critical notes appended to his translation by their
supposed coldness and captiousness excited the indignation of Goethe and
other youthful adorers of Shakspere. See *Wahrheit und Dichtung,* Bk. xv.
Cf. Riedel in *Herrig's Archiv,* &c., *u. s.,* vol. xlviii. p. 25.

hardly ever attains to it, although he treads the levelled
paths of the ancients[1].'

*Lessing's
develope-
ment as a
critic of the
drama.* After a few youthful imitations, Lessing had begun his
own original career as a dramatist by a work[2] founded upon
English models. But these models themselves belonged to
a hybrid school, resulting from the union contracted, under
the influence of prose fiction, between domestic tragedy
and sentimental comedy at a time of decadence in our
dramatic literature. Both as a dramatist and as a critic
he was led to a close and careful study of the stage, and to
an examination of the real merits and demerits of those
French plays which then held supreme sway over it—more
especially the plays of Voltaire, whom he had had early
occasion for observing with particular attention. Thus,
from a critical examination of the French school, Lessing
naturally proceeded to a comparison of its products with
those of the Elisabethan, and in particular (although not
exclusively) of the Shaksperean drama, of which Wieland's
translation furnished him with a text for public use. It
will not be overlooked that at the time when Lessing's
writings on the subject of dramatic criticism reached their
height in the *Hamburger Dramaturgie* (1767–9), the victories
of Frederick the Great and their results had infused into
many German minds the beginnings of a national consciousness. About a decade after the rout of Rossbach (1757)
had dispelled the illusion of the invincibility of the French
arms, Lessing's own comedy, *Minna von Barnhelm* (1767),
had testified to the reflexion of this tremendous political
event in the national literature.

*Lessing's
Ham-
burger
Drama-
turgie
(1767–9).* The *Hamburger Dramaturgie*, designed to promote the
success of a theatrical enterprise of which the details
cannot occupy us here, may be said to have first made
clear to modern readers the true principles of dramatic
criticism. The accident that the undertaking which Lessing's
commentary was intended to aid came to a premature

---

[1] *Briefe, die neueste Literatur betreffend*, No. xvii. This letter is a direct
attack upon Gottsched and the French tragic poets ; and contains a specimen
of Lessing's uncompleted *Dr. Faust*, by way of showing how large an English
element is contained in some of the old German plays.

[2] *Miss Sara Sampson*, 1755.

end, enlarged the scope of his arguments, while the jealousies among the actors concerned rendered him unwilling further to concentrate his observations upon their performances. Thus the level of his enquiries, although they were necessarily fragmentary in form, came to be raised to its ultimate height. '*Primus sapientiae gradus,*' according to the maxim which he recalled, '*est falsa intelligere.*' The notion of Voltaire is false, that the object of the drama is to enforce a moral; he has misunderstood the ancients; and out of the flaming pyre of Shaksperean poetry he has but here and there possessed himself of a solitary faggot, of a kind that smokes and sputters rather than diffuses light and warmth. Again, Voltaire's conception is false, that the object of the drama is to teach historical truth; 'the tragic poet makes use of a story not because it has occurred, but because its occurrence took place after such a fashion, that he would find it difficult to invent a better for his actual purpose. If in a real event he accidentally meets with what thus suits him, he bids that real event welcome; but burrowing to that end among history-books is not worth his while. . . . On the stage it is our business to learn, not what any particular man actually did, but what any and every man of a particular character would have done under particular given circumstances. The purpose of tragedy is far more philosophical than is the purpose of history; and the former is degraded from its true dignity when it is converted into a panegyric of famous men, or, which is worse, misused for the purpose of fostering national pride.' Thirdly, the rules set up as the essential rules by Voltaire and the school to which he belongs, are not carried out by them except in mere externals; and in these often coarsely and clumsily. Aristotle's definition of tragedy they have not even comprehended. They have neither understood his meaning in speaking of tragic fear and pity as the motives of tragic effect, nor his proof that the purification of the passions by those emotions is the end of tragedy. It follows, that no true tragedy is to be found among the French and their imitators.

But, '*secundus sapientiae gradus est vera cognoscere.*'

To begin with, so-called perfect characters have no place in tragedy. Secondly, what is evil may find admittance there, as the hideous may in art, in so far as it is terrible. Thirdly, dramatic characters must have an inner unity. Characters are treated after a different fashion in tragedy and in comedy, because in the latter they constitute the main element, whereas the situations are but the means for furnishing them with expression; in tragedy the situations constitute the main element. On this basis Lessing constructed his theory of the drama, and herein he reconciled Shakspere with the Greeks. At the same time he distinctly pointed out that 'a perfect work of art has a claim to emancipate itself even from the rule which keeps asunder the ends of tragedy and comedy; and thus, where the same event in its progress assumes all the various shades of human interest, the one not merely following upon, but springing out of, the other,—where laughter is generated by tears, or sorrow derived from joy,—there criticism demands no separation of the one from the other in the work of art in question, and art contrives to reap an advantage from the very impossibility of such a separation.' This is the justification of the method of the romantic drama—the justification of Shakspere [1].

These fragmentary extracts are merely intended to indicate the general standpoint taken up by Lessing in the campaign of which the *Dramaturgie* forms the final enterprise, and which has a positive as well as a negative side both in its principles and in its results. As for the stage, the Hamburg boards themselves shortly afterwards (1771–1780) became the scene of endeavours which, although indeed successful in permanently establishing a national theatre, almost transformed the existing German stage— more especially by domesticating Shakspere upon it. These results are identified with the name of F. U. L. Schroeder, the greatest German actor and theatrical manager of his century, who deserves to be remembered as having

Schroeder and the German stage (1771–1780).

---

[1] The above quotations are taken from the analysis of the *Dramaturgie* in Stahr's *Lessing* (edn. 1862), vol. i. pp. 328–361. A useful modern edition of Lessing's work is that by F. Schröter and R. Thiele (Halle, 1877).

rendered services to Shakspere's fame comparable only to those which it owes to Garrick [1].

A still more notable influence was exercised upon German literature by the change effected through Lessing's criticism in the national estimate of Shakspere ; but on this I need not here insist at length. Herder, to the width *Herder.* and depth of whose powers of sympathetic insight and appreciation the new era of German literature owed an incalculable debt, passed even beyond Lessing in the liberality of the welcome which he offered to the genius of Shakspere [2]. The young combatants of the *Sturm* *The Sturm* *und Drang*—an army in which everybody was a com- *und Drang.* mander, but not everybody was born to lead—one and all troubled themselves uncommonly little about the problem of harmonising Shakspere with Aristotle, or with any known theory of his art. The successive volumes of Wieland and Eschenburg's translation fell upon all sorts of ground, and the seed they scattered sprang up in all kinds of fruit. Shakspere, it was universally agreed, was the type of a free and independent genius [3]. The worship of him implied emancipation from the dominion of the ancients and the pedants their followers, proclaimed the liberty of life, with the license which it claims as its privilege, and in contrast with the narrow discipline of school [4]. Lenz [5], Klinger, Leisewitz, ' Maler ' Müller and others outvied one another

---

[1] The performance of *Hamlet* at Hamburg on September 20, 1776, is held to have decided the future of Shakspere on the German stage. The tragedy was performed in Hamburg thirteen times within three months, and was speedily produced on other German stages. Schroeder within less than three years brought out seven other Shaksperean plays. See *Allgemeine Deutsche Biographie,* vol. xxxii. (1891), p. 510.

[2] See particularly his essay in the *Blätter für deutsche Art und Kunst* (1773). (Cf. Goethe, *Wahrheit und Dichtung,* Bk. xi.) Herder himself essayed the translation of Shakspere.

[3] The term ' *Genie,*' in its *Sturm und Drang* acceptation, would be inadequately translated by ' genius,' or even by ' original genius.'

[4] Koberstein, in the essay already cited, remarks on the influence exercised in Germany by Young's letter *On Original Composition,* published in 1759, and made known to German readers by two translations. The original was addressed to Richardson. (See Mitford's *Life of Young,* Aldine ed., p. xlii.)

[5] Cf. as to Lenz and his *Anmerkungen übers Theater,* to which was appended a translation of *Love's Labour's Lost,* the passage in *Wahrheit und Dichtung* cited in *note 2, ante.*

in their attempts to follow in the footsteps of their chosen exemplar—with what success need not be here estimated [1]. The vehemence of their idolatry found expression in every form of hyperbole; thus Lenz exults in the Elisabethan drama as having presented Nature to the public as she had come from the hands of God! The entire school of the *Sturm und Drang* had Shakspere—Shakspere as they saw him—on the brain [2].

Goethe.   Of all the young German poets of this age none stood more directly under the influence of Shakspere than the one who was himself destined to achieve greatness. In his Strassburg days Goethe harangued his friends on Shakspere and Nature with all the exuberant rhetoric of youth [3]. And afterwards, in his *Götz von Berlichingen,* and to some extent in *Egmont,* he 'liberated himself' after his well-known fashion from this phase of his literary growth [4], by allowing its impulses to find definitive concrete expression. Many others of his works contain reminiscences of Shakspere. His *Wilhelm Meister* (1795–6) contains the famous criticism of *Hamlet,* with the whole spirit of which the first part of Goethe's romance is in much more than merely incidental contact. Of whatever modifications this criticism itself may stand in need, it stands forth both as a labour of love and as a marvellous product of intellectual sympathy. But it is likewise notable as showing with perfect clearness that Goethe was not prevented by his profound admiration for the poetic genius of Shakspere from taking exceptions to what he regarded as arbitrary or redundant in Shakspere's dramatic form. To this

[1] Cf. C. C. Hense, *Deutsche Dichter in ihrem Verhältniss zu Shakespeare,* (Part i), in *Jahrbuch,* &c., vol. v. (1870).

[2] Very refreshing in contrast with this extravagance is the rude but thoroughly sympathetic enthusiasm of the Swiss autodidact Ulrich Bräker *alias* Näbis Uli, the author of the *Lebensgeschichte des armen Mannes in Toggenburg,* whose *Shakspeare-Büchlein,* composed in 1780, is reprinted by Dr. E. Götzinger in vol. xii. (1877) of the *Jahrbuch,* &c. He had learnt to admire and understand Shakspere from no critic and no teacher; the spirit of his commentary is that of his apostrophe to Hamlet: 'Had not a great artist made thee, thou wouldst not be what thou art—but indeed the doom thou hadst to bear was a heavy one!'

[3] See Lewes' *Life of Goethe.* He read aloud the entire *Hamlet* in one evening to Friederike and her family at Sesenheim. (*Wahrheit und Dichtung,* Bk. xi.)

[4] So he told Eckermann. Cf. Hense, *u. s.,* p. 130.

critical attitude he gave practical expression as director of
the Weimar theatre.   In 1803 he had contented himself
with a few simplifications in the scenic arrangement of
Julius Caesar (together with a single slight addition to the
text); but in 1812 he adapted *Romeo and Juliet* by a series
of important changes, which practically amounted to an
extrusion of the comic element.   To the same period
belongs his essay *Shakespeare und kein Ende*, in which he
described Shakspere as an 'epitomiser' of nature, 'for whose
genius, be it said to his honour, the stage furnished no
adequate space.'   In his later years, in an essay on *Shakespeare als Theaterdichter* (1826), he even ventured on the
assertion that Shakspere was a dramatic poet of the highest
order, but extremely untheatrical [1]—*i. e.* extremely difficult
to put on the stage.   It must, of course, be borne in mind that
Goethe's own views as to what should be produced there, and
as to how it should be produced, had been very deliberately
formed, and were thenceforth very consistently maintained.

Schiller's version of *Macbeth* (1800) is less arbitrary than   *Schiller.*
Goethe's of *Romeo and Juliet*, but dictated by the same
principles.   The most important influence exercised by
Shakspere upon Schiller's own dramatic productivity is not
to be sought in certain 'strong' characters and situations of
his early plays, for which the *Sturm und Drang* tendencies
may no doubt in some measure be held accountable.   It is
above all perceptible in the dramatic treatment of history
which he pursued in his maturest works, and which, although
directed and restricted by laws imposed upon himself by
the poet after much thought and study, is animated by a
formative power such as since Shakspere few, if any, other
dramatists have displayed in the same field.   Schiller's
warm admiration of Shakspere's *Histories* is illustrated
by his design of arranging all the plays concerned with
the Wars of the Roses as a series for representation on the
stage,—a design not actually carried out by him, but realised

---

[1] As to *Shakespeare und kein Ende* and the Weimar version of *Romeo and
Juliet*, see a very interesting account in J. Wahle, *Das Weimarer Hoftheater
unter Goethe's Leitung* (*Schriften der Goethe-Gesellschaft*, vol. viii., 1892),
pp. 243 *seqq.* Cf. K. Heinemann, *Goethe* (Leipzig, 1895), vol. ii. p. 197.

long afterwards on the boards of the theatre with which he had been so intimately associated [1].

It would, however, carry me too far to say more as to the influence of Shakspere upon the literature of the great nation kindred to his own, which had thus rapidly learnt to love and cherish him. No similar instance of the entry by a great writer of one nation into the very heart and mind of another is, I think, to be found in the history of the world; and the phenomenon is the more marvellous, inasmuch as this particular writer was a genuinely national poet. Yet this extraordinary result could only have been accomplished after an imperfect and, so to speak, ambiguous fashion, had it not been for the labours, unfortunately themselves not carried out to the complete extent of their scope, of a writer who merits, in a degree hardly approached even by any of his compatriots, the praise of having been 'a born artist in translation'—and who applied that art to poetic works of the very highest order [2]. Shortly after Goethe had in his *Wilhelm Meister* rekindled the enthusiasm of the German literary public for Shakspere, without himself venturing upon more than a prose version of such fragments of *Hamlet* as were cited by him, August Wilhelm Schlegel published in Schiller's *Horen* (1796) the first specimens of a

Schlegel's translation of Shakspere (1796–1801);

---

[1] In Weimar, at the Tercentenary of Shakspere's birth.—For an estimate of Shakspere's influence on Schiller, and certain of the chief Romantic poets as such, see Part ii. of Hense's essay already quoted, in *Jahrbuch*, &c., vol. vi. (1871).—No definitive judgment as to Schiller's power of dramatically treating historical themes should be formed without taking into account the evidence furnished on this head by his *Dramatischer Nachlass*, recently published with admirable care and completeness by G. Kettner (2 vols., Weimar, 1895). —While abstaining from pursuing the theme of Shakspere's influence upon the progress of German dramatic literature, I should like in this note to direct attention to the special instance of Grillparzer, a poet who narrowly missed (as it seems to me) classical rank in dramatic literature, and who was a specially close student of Shakspere. Cf. W. Bolin, *Grillparzer's Shakespeare-Studien*, in *Jahrbuch*, &c., vol. xvii. (1883).

[2] See M. Bernays, *Der Schlegel-Tieck'sche Shakespeare*, in *Jahrbuch*, &c., vol. i. (1865); and cf. for what follows the same distinguished author's admirable monograph, *Zur Entstehungsgeschichte des Schlegel'schen Shakespeare's* (Leipzig, 1872), which I regret not to have seen before the publication of the first edition of this book.—Within narrower limits, Rückert may perhaps be entitled to a tribute comparable to that which I have cited in the text; but I have no right to criticise translators of Oriental verse or prose, whether German or English.

new translation of Shakspere (portions of *Romeo and Juliet*
and *The Tempest*). In an essay contributed by him to the
same Journal, he clearly stated the principles on which any
translation of Shakspere should proceed which should answer
to the demands to be legitimately placed on such a work [1].
The first of these principles affirmed that a poetic translation which took care to obliterate no characteristic distinction of form, and to preserve the beauties and even the un-
pleasing peculiarities of the original, might in a sense be more
faithful to it than the most faithful prose version. Hitherto
Eschenburg's translation (completing Wieland's) had sufficed,
beneath which, according to Goethe's satire, ' Hercules himself was no longer to be discerned [2].' Schlegel had himself
for some years worked at the translation of Shakspere,
largely under the influence of Bürger, of whose looser
manner of versification the fragments of his early version of
A Midsummer Night's Dream bear the traces; even in
Romeo and Juliet, the first of the plays which he set himself
steadily to complete, Alexandrines repeatedly occur [3]; but
as he proceeded, the influence of Goethe and Schiller's
perfect versification manifestly being upon him, his method
became surer and surer, and his manner more and more
concise, till in the end his verses correspond line by line to
those of the original. And while carrying out, by dint of
unwearying labour, his design of following step by step
'the literal meaning' (*den Buchstaben des Sinnes*) of his
original, he had, thanks to his own rare powers as well
as to the excellence of his method, 'caught part of the
innumerable, indescribable beauties that do not lie in
the letter, but hover above it like an intellectual spirit.'
Thus he proved himself at once master of the language
which his labours enriched, and intellectually akin to the
author whom he reproduced [4].

Between the years 1797 and 1801 seventeen of Shakspere's plays were produced by Schlegel; but it was only

---

[1] *Etwas über William Shakespeare bei Gelegenheit Wilhelm Meisters.*

[2] *Xenien*, 499. See Erich Schmidt and B. Suphan's edition of the *Xenien*,
published by the Goethe-Gesellschaft in 1893, p. 185.

[3] There are hardly any in the original.

[4] These expressions are borrowed from Bernays.

very gradually that the merits of his workmanship, of which self-restraint was not the least, came to be understood by a public to whom, with few exceptions, his original was a closed book. In the end Schlegel's translation came to be justly accounted one of the glories of German literature, but before this he had been diverted from his task by other

completed by Tieck and others (1820–1833).

of his multiplicitous literary interests; so that after an interval of fifteen years its completion was undertaken by Ludwig Tieck (1820), or rather, as it proved, under his supervision, by Count Wolf von Baudissin, and of 'another translator who desires to remain unnamed'—Tieck's daughter Dorothea. These devoted hands brought the work to a conclusion in 1833; but the translations for which Tieck was responsible, although meritorious, were not to be compared to Schlegel's labours, and unfortunately Tieck had seen fit to subject the latter to a revision of his own. The edition of 1867–1871, all questions of detail apart, testified to the enduring esteem in which the work has now for many generations been held as a national classic. Yet it had by no means stood alone; translations by Voss and others preceded its tardy completion, and the extraordinary activity of German Shakspere-scholars has since that time seemed inclined to prefer this to almost any other way —and none deserves to be held more sure—of evincing an intimate understanding of their chosen author [1].

Schlegel, Tieck, and the Romantic School as critics of Shakspere.

But Schlegel and Tieck were critics as well as translators of Shakspere. I have already referred to one of the critical contributions concerning him from the hand of A. W. Schlegel which had found a place in Schiller's *Horen*; but the two brothers Schlegel, as well as Tieck, Novalis, and other members of the Romantic School in their publications frequently discussed the art of Shakspere, and that of the Elisabethan drama generally. Tieck's essay *On Shakspere's Treatment of the Supernatural* was composed as early as 1793; his *Letters on Shakespeare* appeared in 1800, and he returned to the familiar theme

---

[1] Cf. *Jahrbuch*, vol. iii. (1868), p. 403, where not less than three translations of Shakspere in course of publication are noticed in addition to the new edition of the Schlegel-Tieck translation superintended by Ulrici.

in a number of introductions and notes of greater or less
value, though the comprehensive work on Shakspere
which he had so frequently promised somehow never
saw the light. On the other hand, A. W. von Schlegel,
long after the early fermentations of that School had
settled down into conscious and steady effort, while the
greatest poets of the nation had become estranged from its
tendencies, put forth as a mature fruit of his long sojourn
on the heights of letters and learning, those *Lectures
on Dramatic Art and Literature* (1817)[1], which may be
described as the first definite attempt at comprehensive
aesthetical criticism of Shakspere. Both critics, in their
eagerness to combat the prejudices of the past, neglected
the initial part of their task, the discrimination of their
materials; Tieck's views in particular as to the 'doubtful'
plays (for the most part not doubtful to him) frequently
oblige us to hold our breath in respectful amazement;
while Schlegel's inordinate self-esteem led him to place
more reliance upon his own judgment than if he had been
to Shakspere what Warburton persuaded Pope he was to
Pope. Moreover, Schlegel, much as he affected the man
of genius and the man of the world, was, if I may so say,
heart and soul a professor. Everything that he knew or
thought he craved to put at once into the form of demonstration. Thus, he shaded off the whole body of
Shakspere's plays into more or less arbitrary groups,
while justly ridiculing—as Polonius-like—the attempt to
tabulate them in precise classes[2]; his characterisations of
the several dramas are often provokingly concise, and his
statement of the meaning of each play and character is at
times perplexingly oracular. The reputation of his merits
as a Shaksperean critic, however, remains essentially un-
impaired, even after so many of his successors have striven
to surpass him in those efforts of definition on which critics
great and small are at times too apt to pride themselves.
He was endowed with a sure aesthetic tact, with a genuine
power of psychological insight, with a warm receptivity for

---

[1] An English translation by John Black was published in 1818, and reprinted in 1840.   [2] See *Lectures*, vol. ii. Part ii. pp. 91 *seqq.* (Original).

poetic beauty of the most various kinds,—he abandoned
Shakspere in favour of Calderon, — and with a learning
unprecedented, if not unsurpassed, in its width and variety.
Tieck's merits as a critic lay within far narrower limits;
but his sympathy was fed by a more active if not much
stronger creative force of his own.   He rendered, as it were
incidentally, a special kind of service to Shakspere's fame,
by bringing him home in his fulness to cultivated audiences
with signal effect ; for those who were admitted to his
celebrated readings are unanimous in describing them as
unique in their excellence [1].

Later Ger-
man Shak-
spere-
criticism.

No record can here be attempted of the endeavours of
German Shakspere-criticism in more recent times.   Far
from merely following in the footsteps of Schlegel, like
Franz Horn (whom Heine felt sure of meeting in attendance upon his master below), they have pursued and

Gervinus. are pursuing various paths and various methods.   That of
Gervinus is well known to English students, whose debt
to him perhaps exceeds that which they owe to any other
German Shakspere-critic besides Schlegel [2].   His criticism
was, as might have been expected, essentially of the
historical kind, and directs itself to the moral rather than
the aesthetical aspects of his subject [3].   His command
of his materials enabled him to build up out of them
a coherent whole and, lucidly presenting and combining
the successive stages of Shakspere's literary progress, to

Ulrici. construct what long remained the most complete and consistent history extant of the poet's genius.   In Ulrici, now
also gone to his rest, of whose long and unwearying labours
on Shakspere and the Shaksperean drama a small part
only—though that a very important one—is in the hands
of English readers [4], the deductive method is more largely

---

[1] Those of us who have heard Fanny Kemble 'read' Shakspere may, however, be permitted to doubt whether she can at any time have been surpassed
in this collective way of assumption.

[2] The first edition of his *Shakespeare* appeared at Leipzig in 1849–50. Miss
Bunnett's English version was published in 1863, and republished in 1875.

[3] Cf. a few generous words recording the death of Gervinus by his most
eminent fellow-labourer, Ulrici, in the *Jahrbuch*, vol. vi. (1871).

[4] *Shakespeare's Dramatic Art and his relations to Calderon and Goethe*

interwoven with the historical. He was the real chief of a school of German Shakspere-critics which long held the ascendant, the keynote of whose system was an endeavour to evolve the achievements of literary genius out of its own processes, and, in reference to Shakspere in particular, to demonstrate the theory assigning a fundamental idea to each of his works, and grouping them together as a harmonious and self-complementary whole. More congenial to English, *Simrock.* and to later German, methods, were the labours of Simrock in illustration of the sources of Shakspere's plays, although he entered into his researches rather in the comprehensive (at times, all too comprehensive) spirit of a comparative mythologist than in that of a literary historian[1]. Delius, *Other* another indefatigable worker in the field of comment *recently deceased* and research, whose edition long furnished a model of that *German* species of popular and scholarly edition of Shakspere, with *Shakspere-scholars.* brief but sufficient notes, for the production of which in this country publishers are running an interminable race[2];— Elze, whose Life of Shakspere[3] would alone entitle him to a high eminence among Shakspere scholars, and who had studied the Elisabethan theatre as well as its literature;—Alexander Schmidt, whose monumental concordance, or *clavis*, to Shakspere[4] was only the crown of his endeavours,—these and others, who like them have recently passed away, are to be numbered among the true augmenters of our intimacy with the great master's mind and works. The results of their labours—in germ or in completion—are to be found, together with the contributions of a younger generation, in the *Shakespeare Jahrbuch*[5], a treasure-house

(1846).—The *Jahrbuch* is full of this distinguished scholar's contributions. See a brief obituary notice of him, *ib.*, vol. xix. (1889), pp. 319-20.

[1] *Die Quellen des Shakspeare* (2nd edn., Bonn, 1870). The first edition, which appeared nearly forty years previously, was translated into English, with additions by the late Mr. Halliwell-Phillips, for the Old Shakespeare Society (*Publications*, 1850).

[2] *Shakspere's Werke.* Herausgegeben und erklärt von Nicolaus Delius. The third edition, now before me, is dated 1872.

[3] *William Shakespeare* (Halle, 1876). His *Essays on Shakespeare* were published, in an English translation, by Miss L. D. Schmitz, in 1874.

[4] *Shakespeare-Lexicon* (2 vols., Berlin and London, 1874).

[5] The annual publication of this invaluable periodical began in the year of the Tercentenary of Shakspere's birth.

of learning and critical ability, and the fittest memorial
which the piety of German students of Shakspere could
have raised to the object of their devotion. No Englishman
is likely to dispute their right to take an honest pride in
the spirit as well as in the products of their single-minded
labours, or to deny them the gratification of calling
Shakspere their own. He cannot be denationalised by
their love for him [1]; but by its fruits he will be made
more and more what it was his destiny to become,—the
poet above all others of our common Germanic race, and
through that race of Western civilisation at large. There
is no branch of the study of Shakspere in which the
contributions of German learning and scholarship will not
continue to be welcomed by ourselves,—whether in that
of aesthetical criticism, in which they were formerly so
pre-eminently active, or in those of literary and textual,
in which the work of our own students and societies has
more recently received such conspicuous assistance from
their own. A time may even come when a rivalry may
exist between the two national stages—not only in the
production of isolated Shaksperean plays in appropriate
settings, and in the performance of particular Shaksperean
characters by gifted actors, but also in a frequency of representation such as alone can familiarise popular audiences
with the dramatic genius of their author as shown in the
wondrous variety of his creations.

*French
criticisms
and trans-
lations of
Shakspere
in the
present
century.*

Before turning once more to Shakspere's native land,
I may here recall the fact that it was largely due to the
indirect influence of Schlegel that a truer and fuller
appreciation of Shakspere began to form itself in France.
It is true that in Voltaire's later years literary opinion
had begun to emancipate itself from the authority of his
dictatorial utterances on this subject; Diderot, Bayle,
and others had freely declared their unbounded admiration

---

[1] Not even, it may be asserted, with the aid of an attempt to prove
Shakspere's intellectual nationality German and not English, from the
measurements of his skull. See Klein, vol. iv. p. 107, where, fairness
obliges us to state, this theory is advanced on English authority, that of
' James' (*query*, John?) ' Cowles Prichard.'

for a writer whom they were no longer obliged to judge at secondhand. But many years passed before signs of a closer acquaintance with the great English poet became observable in the French world of letters. Charles Nodier's *Pensées de Shakspeare* (1801) was avowedly composed under the inspiration of German studies. And in the very year in which the establishment of the French Empire marked the height of the period of war (1804), Mme. de Staël, a fearless votary of culture for its own sake, in her book *De la Littérature*, written under the manifest influence of Schlegel, brought before French readers broader views of Shakspere's genius, which she further developed in her later work *De l'Allemagne* (1814). In 1821 Guizot, with the aid of Madame Guizot and others, issued a revision of Letourneur's translation; and other translations have since followed—among them one for which Guizot was at least in name responsible (1862). As critics of Shakspere, Guizot himself, whose essays appeared respectively in the earlier and in the later part of his long literary career, Villemain, Philarète Chasles, St. Marc-Girardin and other French writers of the second and third quarters of the present century have earned for themselves the grateful regard of those who study the poet in his own country; nor am I aware that the complaint of one of them is well-founded, according to which French criticism of Shakspere is slighted by his German critics as still a mere echo of Voltaire[1]. There have indeed been occasional instances of reaction, to which it seems unnecessary to refer, and which may perhaps be held redeemed by the excess of enthusiasm in such a rhapsody as that by which in 1864 Victor Hugo inflated the success of his son's translation. The incomparable art of the French theatre may yet, in a less fitful way than has hitherto sufficed for the demands of its public, illustrate in its turn the greatest creations of the romantic drama[2].

[1] See the Preface to A. Mézières' *Shakspeare, ses œuvres, et ses critiques* (1860).

[2] Alfred de Vigny's version of *Hamlet* was produced at the *Théâtre Français* about the year 1829. A *Hamlet* arranged by Alexandre Dumas and Paul Meurice was performed at the *Théâtre Historique* in 1847; and a *Macbeth* revised by E. Deschamps and brought out at the Odéon in 1848, had a run of 100 nights. Of later productions of Shaksperean plays at Paris

The Shak-spere literature of other lands.

No special references are possible in this place to the contributions of other nations towards the reproduction, illustration, or criticism of Shakspere. His works have been translated (I dare say the list is not without *lacunae*), in whole or in part, into Dutch, Frisian, Flemish, Danish, Icelandic, Swedish, Welsh, Italian, Spanish, Portuguese, Wendic, Bohemian, Hungarian, Walachian, Polish, Russian, Finnish, Modern Greek, Bengalee, Chinese, and Japanese [1]. In not a few of the literatures of these several tongues, the insight of critical writers, aided at times by their experience of the efforts of the theatre, has made valuable additions to the Shakspere library of the present age. The most recent of these—at the moment when these lines are written—is the life of Shakspere by the Danish critic Georg Brandes. I much mistake if it will not assert its place in European literature as a book of enduring value—the first Shaksperean biography, so far as I know, which, while resting on foundations of historic solidity, has in its superstructure allowed to the imagination the exercise of its legitimate functions [2].

Popular knowledge of Shak-spere in England about the close of the eighteenth century.

From what was said above, it resulted that the succession of English editions of Shakspere in the course of the eighteenth century had still left much to be done towards a final settlement of the text of his plays, a perfect appreciation of his characteristics as a dramatic poet, and an exhaustive illustration of the historical and literary conditions of his workmanship. It would be easy to mention the names of not a few writers of note who in one or the other of the latter two fields of comment, augmented the annexes already accumulating round Shakspere's special temple of fame. From such a catalogue should be omitted neither the

it need only be said here that they have been few and far between. Probably none have equalled in artistic significance the Shaksperean performances of the two great Italian actors, Rossi and Salvini, and the Lady Macbeth of Madame Ristori.

[1] Cf. Thimm's *Shaksperiana*, and later announcements and reviews in the *Jahrbuch*, from which I will not in this instance attempt to suggest any special selections.

[2] *William Shakespeare* (3 vols., Copenhagen, 1895). A German translation was published in 1896, and a very satisfactory English one, by Mr. W. Archer, in the present year.

philosophically trained essayists of the type of Henry
Mackenzie—ill-remembered as the 'Man of Feeling,'—who
applied to the criticism of Shakspere aesthetic canons derived
from their philosophical training—nor the historical students
of our older literature, to whom Thomas Warton set an
example, which ought to have been set by Gray, of a collective presentment of such researches in an enduring form. On
the English stage, though no equal had occupied the chair
left empty by Garrick, Shakspere's fame was upheld by
a succession of distinguished actors different in many
respects from their illustrious predecessor, but resembling
him in their intentness upon the nobler aims of their art,
and in their love for the greatest master of the modern
drama. In the later years of the century John and Charles
Kemble, and their great sister, Mrs. Siddons, if trained in a
style less flexible than Garrick's, and less able accordingly to
give expression to the variety of Shakspere's genius, made
manifest with a noble dignity[1] proper to themselves the
grandeur of some of his mightiest creations. Yet at how low
a point, notwithstanding the efforts of both literature and
stage, the public knowledge remained of what Shakspere
really was, became manifest at the close of the century
through a most notorious episode in the history of literary
impostures. At the end of the year 1795 an 'unthinking and *The Ireland*
impetuous boy' (to adopt his own subsequent apologetic *forgeries*
description of himself) of the name of William Henry Ireland *(1795-6).*
put forth a succession of legal instruments and miscellaneous
papers which he ascribed to Shakspere, Queen Elisabeth,
the Earl of Southampton, and others. They included
a 'Confession of Faith' from the poet, a letter from him
to Anne Hathaway (accompanied by a lock of her lover's
hair), and—perhaps the most audacious invention of all—
a document showing that an Elisabethan W. H. Ireland
had saved the poet's life. To these were added a *Kynge*

---

[1] It was perhaps in this very direction that Garrick's limits—for all
genius has its limits—were to be found. Mitford, in a note to the *Correspondence of Gray and Mason* (2nd edn., 1855, p. 301), refers to a curious
statement in Monboddo's *Origin of Language,* that Garrick was unable
to pronounce the periods of Milton, and avoided acting in any play written
in that learned and stately style.

Leare and a portion of *Hamblette*, both professing to be printed from a copy in the handwriting of the poet. The age was one of literary forgeries; and the example of his predecessors in this line of activity had not unnaturally fired the brain of the hopeful youth. In his favour there operated the fact that, as Malone observes in his *Inquiry* into the genuineness of these documents, of Shakspere's handwriting there were known not more than eleven letters of the ordinary alphabet, and three capital letters. The spelling of the papers should however have betrayed their authorship; for in chronological accuracy it was on a par with Chatterton's pseudo-archaisms. Ireland however succeeded for a time, as most impostors succeed, by dint of sheer effrontery. A large part at all events of the documents were previously to publication submitted to the inspection of the world of fashion and letters; and many persons testified to their conviction of their genuineness by subscribing a declaration to that effect. Among these were not only Boswell, who fell on his knees in his devout enthusiasm, exclaiming that he 'now kissed the invaluable relics of our bard, and gave thanks to God that he had lived to see them [1],' but also so infallible a scholar as Dr. Parr. Porson, on the other hand, evaded the invitation, declaring that 'he detested subscriptions of all kinds, but more especially to *articles of faith.*'

But the imposture in chief, which finally burst the bubble, was still to come. In 1796 the idea of writing a play 'took possession of' Ireland's mind, and after counting the number of lines in one of Shakspere's, he formed it 'on that standard' (which happened to be an unusually high one). When completed, it was accepted at Drury Lane, then under the management of Sheridan, from whose remark, that 'however high Shakspeare might stand in the estimation of the public in general, he did not for his part regard him as a poet in that exalted light, although he allowed the brilliancy of his ideas, and the penetration of his mind [2],' the author of the newly-found Shaksperean tragedy may have derived con-

[1] The authority for this is Ireland himself, in his *Confessions* (2nd edition), p. 96.   [2] *Ib.*, p. 138.

siderable encouragement.   The production of *Vortigern and Rowena* settled the question of its character and of its author's—as to which the air was already full of doubts, for Malone's *Inquiry* had been announced.   With the judicious aid of Kemble, who with unmistakeable intention emphasised an unfortunate line—

> 'And when this solemn mockery is o'er'—

the play was hopelessly damned.   Malone hereupon published his famous *Inquiry* into the authenticity of the Ireland MSS., and so far as Shakspere was concerned, the matter was at an end.   Ireland, to vindicate his father from the suspicion of partnership in the forgery, published a pamphlet in which he avowed himself the fabricator ; but not all the believers would consent to accept this declaration, and Chalmers, who had been a believer, indulged his spleen against Malone in a lengthy argument, to the effect that 'though the criminal might be guilty, yet the proofs brought by the prosecutor might be defective in their forms, and inconsecutive in their inferences[1].'   The full *Confessions* of Ireland, published with a preface of sublime self-consciousness, and dedicated to the Prince of Wales, ended this melancholy farce, which illustrates glaringly enough the measure of the popular insight into the distinctive qualities of Shakspere.

About the time when Schlegel was lecturing on Shakspere in Germany[2], Coleridge, the most learned as he was the most imaginative of the new Romantic School of English poets, came forward in London as a lecturer on Shakspere and other poets (1810–11), and repeated or continued his lectures at Bristol a few years later (1813).   There was so much in the spirit and manner of his disquisitions resembling those of his German contemporary, and moreover something

The new school of English Shakspere-criticism. Coleridge (1811 et post).

---

[1] *Advertisement to Chalmers' Supplemental Apology for the Believers in the Shakspeare Papers* (1799), p. vii.

[2] Coleridge's own sojourn in Germany belongs to an earlier date (1798–9), when he was chiefly occupied with philosophical and theological studies. His 'translations' of *The Piccolomini* and *The Death of Wallenstein* appeared in 1800.   In 1813 his *Remorse* was performed at Drury Lane ; his *Zapolya*, founded on *The Winter's Tale*, was published in 1817.

so entirely new to English ears in his whole system of
criticism, that it is easy enough to explain how the charge
of plagiarism should have come to be brought against him.
Coleridge spurned this charge with indignant emphasis[1], and
he must be believed on his word.   That the influence of the
tendencies of the German Romantic School, to which Schlegel
gave the first complete and systematic expression, was strong
upon him at this period of his intellectual developement,
it would be at the same time idle to deny.   The appreciation of Shakspere and the dramatic art perceptible in both
the English and the German writer was, as the phrase is,
in the air,—in the air, *i.e.*, breathed by those who stood on
the height of European culture.   Unfortunately, Coleridge's
lectures on Shakspere, having never been regularly committed to writing, could never be printed in a form authenti-
cated by his own approval ; but enough remains, even in
the late Mr. Collier's publication of the transcripts of his
own shorthand notes[2], to show that Coleridge was the first
among Englishmen who gave to the world an adequate
estimate of Shakspere's genius, and who proved his form not
less worthy of admiration than his matter, because the one
is harmoniously adapted to the other.   Herein lies the gist
of Coleridge's Shakspere-criticism, which like Schlegel's
is based upon the principles first proclaimed by Lessing.
Coleridge made it clear[3] 'that the form of Shakspere's

---

[1] See *Notes on Hamlet*, p. 205.

[2] *Seven Lectures on Shakespeare and Milton.*   By the late S. T. Coleridge.
With an Introductory Preface, &c., by J. P. Collier (1856).   Coleridge's
notes on Shakspere in his *Literary Remains* are scattered notes taken by
himself or others from the lectures aforesaid.   His criticisms on the
dramatists have been recently brought together by Mr. T. Ashe in *Lectures
and Notes on Shakespeare and other English Poets* (1885), where Collier's as
well as other contemporary reports are reprinted.

[3] See the late Principal Shairp's Essay on Coleridge, *Studies in Poetry
and Philosophy* (1868), pp. 201 *seqq.*   The last metaphor, in the passage
cited, recalls a beautiful passage in the *Winter's Tale*, where Shakspere as it
were supplies the champions of his genius with the one apology which its
processes require :—

  ' *Perdita.*   Sir, the year growing ancient,
   Not yet on summer's death, nor on the birth
   Of trembling winter, the fairest flowers o' the season
   Are our carnations, and streak'd gillyvors,
   Which some call nature's bastards : of that kind

dramas was suited to their substance, not less than the form
of the Greek dramas had been to their themes. He pointed
out the contrast between mechanical form superinduced
from without, and organic form growing from within; he
showed that if Shakspere or any other modern were to
hold by the Greek writers, he would be imposing on his
creations a dead form copied from without, instead of
letting them shape themselves from within, and clothe
themselves with their own natural and living form, as the
tree clothes itself with its bark. Coleridge's observations on
Shakspere and his fellow-dramatists, moreover, like everything that Coleridge wrote in his better days, abound in
instances of his all but prophetic power of divining deeper
meanings, and of his concomitant gift of revealing them in
a form that seems the language proper to poetic inspiration.

The group of English writers, among whom Coleridge
held so prominent, and might under other conditions have
held a paramount, place, were at one with him in his love of
Shakspere. None of them was so specially qualified for *Charles*
communicating this feeling to his readers as Charles Lamb, *Lamb*
irresistible as a humorist because he could convey unim- *(1807 et*
paired the essence of every humorous or pathetic fancy *post).*
by which he had been congenially attracted.   To the *Tales*

> Our rustic garden's barren ; and I care not
> To get slips of them.
> *Polixenes.*   Wherefore, gentle maiden,
> Do you neglect them?
> *Perdita.*   For I have heard it said
> There is an art, which in their piedness shares
> With great creating nature.
> *Polixenes.*   Say there be ;
> Yet nature is made better by no mean
> But nature makes that mean ; *so, over that art*
> *Which, you say, adds to nature, is an art*
> *That nature makes.* You see, sweet maid, we marry
> A gentler scion to the wildest stock,
> And make conceive a bark of baser kind
> By bud of nobler race : this is an art
> Which doth mend nature, change it rather, but
> The art itself is nature.
> *Perdita.*   So it is.
> *Polixenes.* Then make your garden rich in gillyvors,
> And do not call them bastards.'
>   Act iv. sc. 4.

from Shakespeare (1807), of which he wrote the tragedies and his sister Mary the comedies, many a child—when the literary and artistic tastes of children were still allowed to remain unspoilt—has owed its first guess at the greatness of the dramatist; in his inimitable reminiscences of old actors, and of their identification with Shaksperean characters, even those can take endless delight whose own stage enthusiasms were warmed themselves at much paler fires[1].

Hazlitt (1817 et post).

Hazlitt, although full of vehemences and paradoxes, in his critical work gave proof of a breadth and a candour alike uncommon in any age. As a stage critic he was led to insist from time to time on the disadvantages which counterbalance the advantages of the study of Shakspere in the theatre, where deplorable conventionalities often obliterate the subtler charm of poetical beauties which they were intended to bring into relief. In his *Characters of Shakspeare's Plays* (1817)—dedicated to Charles Lamb notwithstanding differences between him and the author— legitimate opportunities are found for counteracting this perhaps inevitable drawback. His *Lectures on the Dramatic Literature of the Age of Elizabeth* (1820) were probably put together in haste, but contain, like most of his writing, much healthy criticism together with a good deal of crude infallibility. Hazlitt's—and perhaps even Lamb's—most enduring service to the criticism of Shakspere lies in the fact that they were the first to impress upon the English mind the fact that Shakspere did not stand alone, while he remained unequalled, as a representative of the greatest age of English dramatic poetry. Other writers co-operated in keeping alive a wider interest in Shakspere in a period when the English stage still strove to remain in touch with literary criticism; one of these was the poet Campbell, whose moments of inspiration may have been rare, but whose hand was never infelicitous[2].

Thomas Campbell (1833).

[1] The most remarkable evidence of Charles Lamb's power as a critic of dramatic poetry is perhaps to be found in the introductory observations accompanying his *Specimens of English Dramatic Poetry* (1808), and in the selection of those specimens themselves.

[2] *Remarks on the Life and Writings of Shakspere*, in his edition (1833).

Another lettered generation was however growing up in this country, which for the most part, in so far as it directed its energies to the study and elucidation of the greatest of English writers, preferred to occupy itself primarily with the material part of his works.　Herein they not only followed traditions handed down by such commentators as Steevens and Malone, and continued by Drake in his elaborate tomes [1], but showed themselves awake to the demands made upon students of Shakspere by the new era that had opened in the European world of letters for historical and philological criticism.　With certain exceptions therefore—among whom it seems but just to mention the late Mrs. Jameson, a writer of rare artistic cultivation and refinement [2]— English Shakspere-study has during the greater part of the present century been chiefly concerned with the elucidation and restoration of his text, the explanation and illustration of his matter, and the history of all that entered into or surrounded his life and literary career.　I content myself with mentioning the names of J. Payne Collier—himself the worst enemy of his own fair fame—J. O. Halliwell-Phillipps, Alexander Dyce, Joseph Hunter, C. M. Ingleby, and among writers of a popular type Charles Knight, as having by their labours ensured to their names an enduring association with Shakspere's own.　Large stores of illustrative material—documents of interest for the history of the times and of the stage in particular, plays and ballads connecting themselves in subject or otherwise with Shakspere's writings, and antiquities and curiosities of all kinds from Elisabethan and from older English literature—were

Later English editions, criticism and illustrations of Shakspere.

Nothing remains of the edition of Shakspere which was to have been brought out by Sir Walter Scott, aided by Lockhart; three volumes completed by the latter, and printed, are said to have been sold for waste paper after the crash of 1826.　See Andrew Lang, *The Life and Letters of John Gibson Lockhart* (1897), vol. i. pp. 308, 396; but cf. vol. ii. p. 13.—See also *ib.*, p. 167, a very fine tribute to the genius of Shakspere disinterred by Mr. Lang from an article by Lockhart in *Blackwood's Magazine*.

[1] *Shakspeare and his Times* (2 vols., 1817); *Memorials of Shakspeare* (1828).

[2] See in particular her *Shakespeare's Female Characters* (1834).　The foremost English actress of our times, Miss Helen Faucit (Lady Martin), has recently in her retirement composed a work on the same subject (*On some of Shakespeare's Female Characters*, 1885).

accumulated by such societies as the Percy and the Camden, and above all by that which from its foundation in 1840 to its unhappy dissolution was designated by Shakspere's own name.   Lastly, the editions of Singer (1826), Charles Knight (1838 and 1865), Collier (1843–4[1]), Halliwell-Phillips (the folio edition, begun in 1853 and completed in 1865), Dyce (1857 and 1866–7), Staunton (1858), and of Clark and Wright (the 'Cambridge' edition, 1863 and 1891–3), may be said in each case to possess distinctive merits of their own.   In the last-named the results of a complete collation of the texts of previous editions was for the first time placed before the reader.   Of editions still later in date nothing can here be said, although a word of acknowledgment may not be out of place in reference to the enterprise and judgment with which the Oxford University Press[2], followed at a later date by that of Cambridge, has issued a series of annotated editions of Shakspere's plays adequate to the general requirements of students.   I must likewise refrain from dwelling on the labours of living English Shakspere-scholars in the various fields of special research to which they have devoted so much ability and zeal; although of the debts which, in common with other students, I owe to them, I am very fully conscious.   The name of Dr. F. J. Furnivall may at the same time be mentioned without breach of rule, both because as originator and director of the *New Shakspere Society*, founded in 1874, he has sought to bring into one focus the rays of light which are being shed by the efforts of so many fellow-labourers upon the object of their common veneration, and also because his enthusiasm and his unwearying diligence alike typify the spirit of later Victorian Shakspere-study.   The labours of this Society began at the right end, and have done much to settle enduringly the chronological order of his works—the true basis of any valid estimate of the process of his literary growth—largely by means of those tests

----

[1] It was the second edition of 1853 which contained the notorious emendations of the MS. corrector.

[2] Begun by both the editors of the *Cambridge Shakespeare*, the Clarendon Press Series has been carried out by Mr. W. Aldis Wright with a learning, skill, and perseverance unsurpassed in the history of modern scholarship.

of versification which call for ridicule only when they are treated as absolute.

Meanwhile on the other side of the Atlantic both the aesthetic and the philological study of Shakspere in particular, as well as the general criticism and illustration of his writings, have been carried on with indefatigable devotion. The editions of Hudson (1853–6 and 1881) and Grant White (1857–65), of the biographical introduction to which the same author's charming *Life and Genius of Shakespeare* (1865) is virtually a reprint[1], and above all the incomparable *New Variorum* edition of Mr. Howard Furness (of which eleven volumes have been placed in our hands since its commencement in 1873), are enduring monuments of American scholarship and learning. Many lighter, and even incidental, contributions to the literature of Shakspere-criticism, from Washington Irving to Russell Lowell, might be cited to show how deep a root the love of Shakspere has struck in the minds and hearts of our kinsmen, and what choice fruit they have made it bear. In view of these golden gifts we may abstain from looking too closely at a very different sort of contributions to the list of books treating of Shakspere and his works, which is to be placed mainly, though not altogether, to the account of American writers. The honour of having first suggested the 'theory' that Shakspere's plays were written by Bacon is usually ascribed to a gifted lady whose voluminous discussion of her own conception ended in pure paradox ; but it appears that in a shorter treatise published in 1857 an Englishman, Mr. Henry Smith, had anticipated Miss Delia Bacon's discovery, of which English readers at all events remained unaware till six years after it had been made[2]. The notion, which, as has been already mentioned, was elaborated with

American labours in the same field.

The Bacon-Shakspere craze.

---

[1] Hudson's book on *Shakspere, his Life, Art and Characters* (1872), founded, I believe, on an earlier work published in 1848, possesses an acknowledged value as a work of aesthetical criticism. Grant White's delightful *Studies in Shakespeare* (1885) were being prepared for publication by him when seized by a long and fatal illness.

[2] When attention was directed to it by the late Nathaniel Hawthorne in *Our Old Home* (1863). Grant White's *Studies* contain an article on 'the Bacon-Shakespeare craze' which I had not seen when I inserted that expression in my margin.

more speciousness than solidity of argument by Mrs. Henry Pott in her commentary on a previously unpublished commonplace book of Bacon's, became in America the symbol of a rather numerous sect, and was complicated by a further article of belief, that the secret of his authorship was betrayed by Bacon to prominent members of this future sect by means of a 'cryptogram' which he bequeathed to their rare powers of seeing through a brick-wall. Variations of the so-called 'Baconian' doctrine are to be found in the theories that Shakspere's plays were composed by a club of the chief men of genius of his age, and that they were written by the celebrated traveller Sir Anthony Sherley. All these vagaries are at one in the assumption that Shakspere contributed to the plays known under his name nothing but that name itself and more or less of journeyman-workmanship. His poetic individuality—of which some sort of conception is present to the mind of the very humblest among true students of his writings—has not so much as dawned in its merest outlines upon these devotees of idols, forged by their own or (more usually) by other ladies' or gentlemen's brains.

Shakspere and the modern English stage.
To disperse such nonsensical imaginings will be the least important effect of the continued study of Shakspere, who can never again be lost to England, to English-speaking communities, to the Germanic stock of nations, to the civilised world. Literature and the stage, at home and abroad, are certain sooner or later to join hands, in an equal union for the due advancement of his fame. It seemed, indeed, for a time as if the traditions of the English theatre which had descended to a few honourable successors from the Kembles and from that strange and erratic genius the elder Kean, were in danger of dying out. But that fear has passed, or is passing, away. Our nation's love for Shakspere is destined to assert itself more and more abundantly, not only among professed scholars and devoted students of his writings, but in the very face of those dramatic creations themselves,—presented where alone he is known to have desired them to come before the public,— on the stage.

APPENDIX

Page 35, note 3 (*Tropes*).

The liturgical significance of the term *trope*, viz. the insertion of one or more verses of text before or after sung portions of the service, and its employment in England and France, is illustrated in *The Winchester Tropes, from MSS. of the Tenth and Eleventh Centuries*, edited by W. H. Frere for the Henry Bradshaw Society, 1895.

Page 52 (Localities of early dramatic performances in England).

Through the courteous mediation of Mr. I. Gollancz, Canon Hingston-Randolph has kindly permitted me to state that the forthcoming second volume of his edition of *Bishop Grandisson's Registers* will contain a highly remarkable letter addressed, in 1352, by the Bishop to the Archdeacon of Exeter and his officials. Its twofold purpose is to inhibit, as leading to divers evil consequences for both body and soul (riots being evidently indicated under the former head), a contemplated public Sunday performance *in the theatre of the city* of a certain play by handicraftsmen, 'sons of the city'; and to urge upon its traders the duty of adhering to the prices for the sale of their wares fixed by royal statute. Perhaps the most curious point in this episcopal mandate is the implied existence at Exeter, in the middle of the fourteenth century, of a public theatre, apparently under some kind of control or management by the trades and handicrafts of the city. The nature of the intended performance does not appear from the copy of the document kindly communicated to me.

Page 131 (Date of Lyndsay's Satire of the *Three Estates*).

In the *Introduction* to his edition of the *Poetical Works of Sir David Lyndsay*, Edinburgh, 1871, p. xxxiii, Mr. D. Laing maintains, on grounds which are not on the face of them convincing, that the date of the first exhibition of Lyndsay's morality was not 1535, at Cuparfife; but January 6 (Epiphany), 1540, at Linlithgow.

Page 231 (Beginnings of Comedy in Spain).

Ticknor, vol. ii. pp. 256 *seqq.*, when describing the *entremeses*, notes that single scenes of a farcical nature used as *entremeses* (apparently something in the way of the English *drolls* of the Commonwealth period) were called *pasos* or passages. He had previously (pp. 48 and 53) given examples of such comic dialogues, called *pasos*, by Lope de Rueda, who flourished at Seville and elsewhere about the middle of the sixteenth century.

The term *pasos*, of whose various significations it might be a matter of some difficulty to trace the complete history, is applied, as is well known, to the 'painted and graven images' (as they are called in the last edition of Ford's *Handbook for Travellers in Spain*) carried in solemn procession through the streets of Seville in Holy Week by the Confraternities who have long charged themselves with the pious task of preparing and carrying on these exhibitions. My friend Mr. John Finlayson, of Manchester, who has furnished me with a very interesting account of the *Pasos*, as seen by him in 1897, informs me that it is customary for the several Confraternities on the mornings of the processions to issue manifestoes comprising retrospects of their past history. Thus, the Confraternity of the Protection claimed to have already in the earliest years of its existence (about the beginning of the seventeenth century) carried through the streets of Seville the image of our Lord bearing His Cross, which is still preserved in their chapel.

As to the processional element in the beginnings of the modern drama, see pp. 45 and 145.

Page 289 (Date of Lyly's *Endimion*).

In a letter to *The Athenæum*, February, 1894, Mr. J. E. Spingarn, of New York, cites three passages in the play which seem pointedly to allude to his having been waiting *seven years* for the Mastership of the Revels, to which Tylney had been appointed in 1579. This indication certainly tallies with the date of 1587 or 1588 as that of the first performance of the play, suggested by Mr. Fleay. (See p. 292, *note* 2.)   ———————

Page 456 (The Plague in London).

By far the most complete record of the occurrences of Plague in London from the year 1543 to the year 1680, when it ceased to appear in this country, will be found in Appendix No. I of an extremely valuable paper on *The Recent Epidemics of Plague in Bombay*, read by my distinguished friend Dr. H. M. Birdwood, C.S.I., late Member of Council, Bombay, &c., &c., before the Manchester Geographical Society, on May 19 of the present year, and to be printed in the forthcoming volume of the annual *Journal* of the Society. This Appendix consists of notes collected by Mr. Baldwin Latham, M.I.C.E., from various sources, and mainly from the Annual Records of Weddings, Christenings and Burials, kept in pursuance of orders issued by Thomas Cromwell as Lord Privy Seal in September, 1538. The statistics of numbers of burials in London, and of the proportions of plague-burials included in these, are continuous from 1603 onwards. Appendix II to the same paper contains returns of the weekly mortality from all causes, and of the weekly Plague mortality, in London during the years 1592, 1603, 1605–6, 1606–7, 1624–5 and 1664–5 respectively, which include some of the worst Plague years. These have been collected by Mr. Baldwin Latham from the Yearly Bills.

Page 458 (Site of the Newington Butts Theatre).

I have purposely abstained from entering into the history of the early London theatres, or into the question of their respective sites. But it may be worth while to mention that in the single instance where any doubts can be said to have existed as to the locality of a theatre associated with the glories of the Elisabethan drama, these doubts have been successfully removed. The Newington Butts theatre may now be said to have been ascertained to have stood in a position about a quarter of a mile due south from the Elephant and Castle public-house, between Clock (formerly Church) Passage, Newington Butts, Swan-Place (a suggestive name), and Hampton Street. See a very interesting article in *The Daily News* for April 9, 1898, kindly communicated to me by Professor John W. Hales, to whose generous aid this is but one among many debts incurred by me during the preparation of this edition.

Pages 533 *seqq.* (Early references to Shakspere in French literature).

I regret that it should have been impossible for me to revise these pages with the aid of M. Jusserand's papers on *Shakespeare en France sous l'Ancien Régime* (*Cosmopolis*, November, 1896, *et post*), to which I must content myself with referring the reader.

ERRATA

p. 35, note 1, line 3 from top : for *Mary Magdalene* read *Christ's Burial and Resurrection*, printed with *Mary Magdalene*.

p. 84, l. 18 from top : for *Coveniriae* read *Coventriae*.

p. 207: *for* note 3 *read* 2 (both in text and note).

p. 215, note, l. 16 from bottom : *for* Thompson *read* Thomson.

p. 334, l. 14 from top : *for* Hills *read* Hells.

p. 358, note 2, l. 3 from bottom : *for* cavaire *read* caviare.

p. 437, l. 11 from top : *for* David *read* Daniel.

p. 446, l. 11 from top : *dele the words* of a patronage.

p. 458, note 4, line 6 from bottom : *for* Guedertz *read* Gaedertz.

p. 509, note 1, line 3 from bottom : for *Cutler* read *Cutter*.

p. 534, l. 13 from bottom : *for* Cyramo *read* Cyrano.

p. 567, l. 10 from top : *for* bark *read* bark.'